MW01535406

THE TRUMPING OF AMERICA

A WAKE-UP CALL TO THE FREE WORLD

PAMELA HINES

Pamela Hines 2020

◆ FriesenPress

Suite 300 - 990 Fort St
Victoria, BC, V8V 3K2
Canada

www.friesenpress.com

ISBN
978-1-5255-0933-9 (Hardcover)
978-1-5255-0934-6 (Paperback)
978-1-5255-0935-3 (eBook)

1. BPOLITICAL SCIENCE, COMMENTARY & OPINION

Distributed to the trade by The Ingram Book Company

Table of Contents

Dedication

This book would never have been completed without the following people: Dr. Alejandro Ramirez Rios and staff from the Hospital San Javier Marina in Puerto Vallarta, Mexico, who literally saved my life in February 2017. I had a serious case of pneumonia and was intubated for five days and in hospital for almost three weeks. I don't know why I got this second chance, but I did. Not only did I get excellent medical care, I got compassionate care. I have no recollection of the first week and when I did regain full consciousness, I had no mobility. I could not move my arms, hands, feet. I could not roll over. I was dead weight and completely helpless. Whenever I apologized for the extra effort I caused, they said, "No Miss Pamela, that is why we are here. We want you to get better." Special thanks to nurses Mario Alberto Esparza and Jaime Roberto Arvizu Partida who gave extraordinary compassion and uplifted me in my moments of despair. My respirologist at home advised me I was lucky to be alive and that I owed the doctor in Mexico a thank you note!

Dr. Rio, Pam, Dr. Santores, and Frank

Belen, Pam, and Leyla

Belen Hernandez and Leila Vazquez from Adrehab Rehabilitación Avanzada, who exercised my lifeless limbs until I could do it myself and taught me to walk again. The 'devils' were totally committed to my recovery. I never worked so hard in my life.

Luna Mendiola Yahaira, Cesar Rojas, and relief staff from Proviquer Servicios Profesionales, who provided loving twenty-four hour nursing care after I was discharged from the hospital until I had enough mobility to fly home. They took it upon themselves to learn my rehabilitation routine so that I could do it on the days that Belen and Leila were not available.

Cesar, Yahaira, Pam, Belen, and Leyla

When I was finally able to text on my cell phone, I noticed a message from the father of the family we befriended in Mexico. I was able to text enough that he understood I was in the hospital. He came to the hospital the next day to see how I was. That was an hour and a half bus ride on a day that he was working.

I am fully recovered. I cannot even begin to express how grateful I am for the care I received, but also the cheerful disposition with which it was given. Because of them, I was able to dance with my son at his wedding several months later. These people work so hard for so little. No, Donald Trump, you cannot assume just some Mexicans are good people. Most are. I consider them all my extended family in Mexico.

Many thanks to those who edited my work during various stages, providing insights and improving the quality of the manuscript. Special thanks to Maria Diakantoniou, who provided several rounds of copyediting in the final stages. Not only was she meticulous and persistent, but she was patient with me and provided encouragement. Maria persevered in providing assistance even when the project became more than either of us anticipated, despite competing priorities. When she was unable to continue, she did not abandon me, but rather, she referred me to Ryan Paterson to edit the print outlays. This book is much improved because of their editing and feedback.

My family and friends, who have not abandoned me through this journey.

My son Jason and my daughter Tamara, whose love has been a source of joy and inspiration through the years.

Finally, with love and devotion to my husband, Frank, who encouraged me to write the book, reviewed the manuscript several times, provided insightful feedback, and cared for me while I was incapacitated. He believed in me, encouraged me, prepared my meals, and maintained the household while I was writing this book.

trump

To trump is to outrank someone or something, often in a highly public way.[1]

Prologue

America was in the process of choosing the next leader of the free world, and I couldn't vote. I am Canadian. You might ask why I would care. What gives me the right to express an opinion? Everything that happens in the USA affects me, from the air I breathe to the housing bubble burst that affected the growth of my retirement fund, to the threat of terrorism and nuclear war.

Something in the American culture was playing out in the 2016 presidential election. As I conducted my research, my views on some aspects of the election changed significantly, particularly on the perception of American voters having a 'choice between the lesser of two evils.'

I live with my husband in a suburb of Windsor, Ontario—just across the river from Detroit, Michigan. I started following the election process in the United States prior to the primaries. I watched an interview with Bernie Sanders and emailed my cousin in Walnut Creek, California to let her know that I liked this fellow. She and her husband had already donated to his campaign.

As the election process progressed, I became increasingly concerned by the rhetoric of Donald Trump and the possibility of his becoming president. Many American and Canadian friends and acquaintances assured me that it would never happen. Despite that, I was captivated by the underlying dynamics and wanted to understand what was happening. I became convinced that Donald Trump would become the next president of the United States and that he posed a threat to democracy. It seemed that, indeed, truth would be stranger than fiction.

While this book details the election process of how Donald Trump became president of the United States of America, there is a hateful populist movement, based on blame and rooted in fear, sweeping the free world. Although I will use the 2016 US presidential election as the focus for examining the issues, many of my comments apply to all of us in Western civilization. I am not American, so throughout the book, when I refer to "we," I am speaking of all of us in Western society.

Trump alone is not to blame. Candidates like Donald Trump cannot gain the power to threaten our civil liberties unless we elect them. This election was not about policies; it was about individual belief systems. Many of us have taken our civil liberties for granted and failed to accept our responsibilities in exercising them. These responsibilities include not only voting but ensuring that we are informed and taking responsibility for the consequences of our choices. This necessitates self-examination.

Throughout this process, I have performed a personal self-examination which was sometimes most uncomfortable. I have included some of my own experiences and beliefs that have served as the lens through which I examined the issues in this book. The views in this book are my own and are not intended to represent the view of the average Canadian; there is no such thing.

Russian President Vladimir Putin and other dictators in the world are out to destroy democracy by eroding the alliances that have preserved it for so many decades. He has been aided and abetted by voters in Western democracies. Brexit and the Trump victory are but two examples. The erosion of democratic values in Turkey and Venezuela clearly demonstrate what is at stake.

I will share my observations about the election process and explain why, for the first time, I was afraid of the outcome. I will examine my views about the differences among the candidates, the dynamics that frighten me as a Canadian, the role of the media, and my observations about the differences between American and Canadian cultures. Most importantly, I will share my insights and challenge the American electorate to become better informed, engage in dialogue, and consider the responsibilities that come with choosing not just their country's president, but someone for a position which is recognized as 'the leader of the free world.'

This book reflects my reactions during the week-to-week developments of the campaign, the election, and the aftermath. For example, while we all now know that Donald Trump was elected president, I did not know this when writing the first several chapters of the book.

I am not an expert in politics and I have never held a political position. I am a retired, over-sixty-five-year-old Caucasian woman with a Master of Social Work degree. I have worked in child welfare and in government with the Ontario Ministry of Community and Social Services. I retired after almost twenty-five years as the CEO for a community mental health agency. I don't have answers—only some observations, suggestions, and many questions. The result of this election and the coming years of the Trump administration will shape American culture, and perhaps the world, for generations to come.

When I found myself reacting to people who expressed support for Trump, I came to realize I was part of the problem. The more we know, the more we understand—the more we understand, the more we care. I feel a responsibility to challenge prejudice and injustice, but also to encourage open dialogue. Starting with the premise that all behaviour is understandable provides an opportunity for mutual understanding. However, that does not mean that all behaviour is acceptable or tolerable; therefore, my mission has been to become more informed.

This is not intended to be scholarly research. Given the nature of the topic as a current event, I have used widely available media and internet resources. It was often necessary to use several sources to gain a comprehensive view regarding an issue, resulting in more than fifty pages of footnotes and bibliography. Even so, the text remains lengthy, despite my efforts to reduce examples and less relevant material. It has been a struggle for me because it is the details that are most compelling. In the end, rather than further reductions, I decided to leave it to the reader to determine what was or was not compelling.

The reader may want to challenge my sources, my accuracy, or my lack of comprehension in reviewing the issues. While I generally only used one source to make my points, I did go to the extra effort of verifying the information in other publications as well as verifying the credibility of sources used. It is not possible to have all the information all the time. In fact, that is partly my point. How informed was the electorate in making their decision? While the recent election has spurred discussion, the cogent issue is what has happened in American society that has forced people to choose between 'two evils', and what can be done to ensure a successful future that will benefit everyone—not just in the US, but the world.

I implore readers to examine the trends and the implications for democracy in the free world. Have we taken our freedoms and civil rights for granted? Do we appreciate our rights to the extent that we will protect them by being informed and exercising our right to vote? The increasing polarization is not exclusive to the US—it is worldwide. Will you become part of the continuing polarization or part of the healing?

CHAPTER ONE

South Of The Border

No one knows for certain how much impact they have on the lives of other people.
Oftentimes, we have no clue. Yet we push it just the same. [2]
— Jay Asher

The Canadian city of Windsor, where I grew up, is south of Detroit, Michigan, and I currently live in a nearby suburb. American influences and my experiences provide a context for my keen interest in the 2016 presidential election.

Detroit and Windsor are motor cities where automobile manufacturing is the primary industry. Chrysler is still the largest employer in Windsor. This inextricably ties the two cities economically. The auto industry hit its peak in the 1950s and has been in steady decline ever since. We struggle with the bust-boom cycle and the uncertainty of the auto industry. When the auto industry was hurting, Detroit and Windsor suffered together. It was not just those directly employed in the Big Three; the effect on the economy rippled throughout the community, affecting feeder plants, restaurants, and all the other businesses.

There are many other American influences on the Windsor economy. When the Canadian dollar goes up, Windsor restaurants and stores have a significant decline in business. This is particularly true for the casino in Windsor.

There are further cultural connections between Detroit and Windsor. The International Freedom Festival, started in 1959, runs for several days on both sides of the border to celebrate Canada Day on July 1 and Independence Day on July 4. Both Americans and Canadians cross the border to attend activities. The highlight is a spectacular firework display on the Detroit River, one of the largest displays in North America.

Many Windsorites are fans of Detroit teams, such as the Tigers, Pistons, and Lions, rather than Canadian teams. We attend concerts, cultural events, and shopping centres in the US. The drinking age in Michigan is twenty-one, while it is only nineteen in Ontario. That and the strength of the American dollar make it attractive for young Detroiters to flock to Windsor's bars.

Several other partnerships and agreements link the two cities. The Detroit and Windsor Tunnel Corporation is owned and operated jointly by the City of Detroit and the City of Windsor. The Ontario Ministry of Transportation reported that the Windsor-Detroit Gateway is the busiest border crossing between Canada and the United States: "In 2012, the Gateway handled $91.6 billion (or 28.2%) of road trade between Canada and the US with more than $250 million in commodities travelling through the Windsor-Detroit Gateway each day."[3]

The International Joint Commission between Canada and the United States was established in 1909. "The IJC has two main responsibilities: regulating shared water uses and investigating transboundary issues and recommending solutions. The IJC's recommendations and decisions consider the needs of a wide range of water uses, including drinking water, commercial shipping, hydroelectric power generation, agriculture, industry, fishing, recreational boating, and shoreline property."[4]

Windsor's proximity to the border also contributes to Windsor being one of the worst cities in Ontario in terms of air pollution. A report conducted by the Ontario Health Association in 2005 "linked poor air quality to financial and health costs… They estimated that in Essex County (including Windsor), there were 260 premature deaths, 900 hospital admissions, and 2,750 emergency visits associated with poor air quality in 2005."[5] We are limited in our ability to address the problem because 50% of our pollution is from transboundary factors.[6] "Much of the air pollution affecting Windsor comes from upwind sources, such as coal-powered electricity generating stations and industries and cities located in Michigan and the Ohio Valley… Windsor is also highly affected by emissions from transportation corridors. The Windsor-Detroit gateway is the busiest international trade corridor in North America. In 2005, over 16 million cars and trucks crossed the Windsor-Detroit gateway. The third major source of air pollution in Windsor is local transportation."[7]

The North American Free Trade Agreement (NAFTA) has had an impact on the Canadian economy, with American Corporations shifting from Canada to Mexico for manufacturing. This has been particularly true in the auto industry and, hence, for Windsor. *CBC* reported that "Mexico has gone from a bit player in the North American auto sector to the second-largest participant with almost 20 per cent of total production, compared with Canada's 16 per cent."[8] It is also important to note that Canada benefitted in other ways from cross-border investment, agriculture, and trade.[9]

The bursting of the US housing bubble triggered the global financial crisis of 2007-2008. According to Phillip Bergevin on the Parliament of Canada website, "Canadian banks were less active in the sub-prime lending and securitization activities that were at the center of the current financial crisis."[10] While Canadian banks were somewhat insulated, there was nevertheless a considerable impact from the global economic slowdown and reduced exports due to the economic difficulties in other countries.

These are just a few of the many ways in which Windsor and Detroit are connected, and this does not even begin to touch on the many linkages between Canada and the United States. Clearly, a Trump presidency must have a huge impact on Canada's economy, environment, international relations, and financial institutions.

My father worked for the Ford Motor Company most of his working life. My husband retired from the Chrysler Corporation after working there for forty years, and my son is now a Chrysler employee. All have been in union, rather than management, jobs.

I do not have a defined pension plan, but rather a self-directed RRSP (Registered Retirement Savings Plan) that is tied to the market. Because Canadian banks are more closely regulated than American banks, I did not lose my entire savings in the global financial crisis, but the crisis did reduce my balance, and in the following decade, my RRSP did not generate the growth anticipated. While I am comfortable, this has created a challenge in maintaining my standard of living and has posed financial challenges and unexpected expenses.

Though Windsor is a diverse community, I had limited interaction with other cultures during my formative years. According to *Wikipedia*, the demographics reported from Statistics Canada in 2016 advised that Windsor is comprised of only about 4.9% black, 7.4% Arab, and 6.1% Asian people.[11] According to the 2006 Census by Statistics Canada, 783,795 Canadians identified as black, constituting 2.5% of the Canadian population.[12] While Windsor has a higher percentage of black residents than the national average, its proportion of black residents is not among the highest in the country.

Windsor was one of the few communities in Canada that served as the end of the Underground Railroad. Between 1840 and 1860, slaves were assisted to escape to Canada by way of Midnight (Detroit), to cross the river Jordan (the Detroit River) to Dawn (Windsor), the Promised Land, as described by the *Historica-Dominion Institute*.[13]

I had little exposure to the black community in my youth. My first significant relationships with black people occurred when I was a teenager, because I spent most of my social life with Americans in the Detroit metropolitan area. This environment influenced my view on race and the individualistic culture in America.

There were no Jewish people in my neighbourhood, but there were a few in my elementary and high schools. The following was probably my first experience with blatant discrimination, though I did not know what it was at the time. Every morning, the Jewish students had to leave the classrooms as we recited the Lord's Prayer. It set them apart and we knew it. There was also a Jewish man who rode a horse-pulled cart and blew a horn while riding down the street to collect any kind of junk that he could use for resale. The children all loved the horse and so followed the cart down the street. We referred to him as the "Sheeny man" but it was not until years later that I learned it was a derogatory term and an anti-Semitic slur.[14]

As teenagers, we would often go over to Detroit to shop, attend a baseball game (prior to 1967 we could walk across the bridge to Tiger Stadium), attend live theatre, or see a concert.

In 1965, I spent a week with Chuck and Lois, an older couple that I met through church activities. Both were Caucasian and born-again Christians. They lived in the Grand River-Joy Road area of Detroit, in a predominantly black neighbourhood in which Chuck was a lay minister in a local church and professed to be a former member of the Purple Gang.[15] Lois was a registered nurse. One evening, I took a walk. It was early and still very light. I passed an alley and came across several black teenagers. One picked up a bottle and smashed the end off against a building, then started to approach me. I was immobilized. One of the other teenagers knocked the bottle out of his hand and said, "She's at Wharvie's." He then told me to get my "honky ass" back to Wharvie's and not to come out alone after 5 PM.

When I did venture out during the daytime, I realized I was the only Caucasian around. Little children stared at me in open bewilderment. The houses in the area were large and must have been magnificent in their heyday. Some were well maintained with nice lawns and housed only one family. Others were run down and housed numerous families. I later came to realize that this was probably because at that time, suburbs did not welcome black residents, and those who were more prosperous congregated with others less advantaged in the black neighbourhoods. Even at my young age, I noticed that all the stores in their community were owned and staffed by white people. I understood the 5 PM rule. They did not have control of their neighbourhood during the day, but they would have control after the shops closed. I wasn't angry about what happened, but I was sad. This was two years before Black Day in July,[16] the 1967 Detroit Race Riots on 12th Street, mere blocks from where I had been staying.

These collective experiences contributed to my becoming a liberal who believes in collectivism, equal rights, empowering the disadvantaged, human rights, and social justice.

"Prejudice is a vagrant opinion without visible means of support."[17] Have I ever been prejudiced? Yes, and I still have prejudiced thoughts. I am ashamed to admit that I have told racist jokes in the past. One day, I told a joke to a university friend who happened to be black. It was not about black people, but about another ethnic group. Even so, she chastised me soundly, and rightfully so. She made me aware that derogatory humour about any group was hurtful and unacceptable. Later, it was profoundly hurtful to me whenever I heard people, including professionals, talk about people with mental illness in a derogatory manner. I suffer from chronic depression. While many minorities are visible, some are not. Racist comments and jokes can only cause pain.

While I may sometimes have a prejudiced thought, the point is that by acknowledging my prejudice, I can reframe it and respond to the individual rather than assigning these prejudices to everyone in a group. I am a work in progress.

My obsession with the 2016 United States presidential election started in, of all places, Mexico—the other 'south of the border'. My husband and I vacationed there off and on for over thirty years, and now that we are retired, we spend a few months a year wintering there.

The coverage of the American election issues started early in 2015 with the announcements of those running in the primaries. The announcement of the Canadian federal election followed on August 4, 2015. At this juncture, the American media was announcing which nominees would participate in the first Republican debate. I listened to some of the Canadian debates, conducted research, and did my civic duty by voting on October 19, 2015, the day Canada elected Justin Trudeau prime minister. At this point, the US primary debates for both the Republicans and Democrats were still taking place. The Canadian election process was seventy-six days and one of the longest and most costly in Canadian history. My husband and I continued to watch the American primary debates prior to setting out on our trip to Mexico.

The highlight of our vacation was the friendship we developed with a Mexican family. I befriended a security guard at one of our resorts, and he invited us to visit his home and meet his family. Antonio is married with five children. On the trip to his home, I asked him what the average wage for a security guard at the resort was. He told me it was 180 pesos a day, which was $12.80 CAD and $9.87 USD in February 2016. Just for a reality check, a clubhouse sandwich cost 180 pesos at the same resort. He did not express any resentment regarding his lot in life. He was proud of his job and grateful to have it. He spoke warmly and lovingly of his family.

When we arrived, the children greeted their father with enthusiasm and were a bit shy with us, but curious and friendly. Their home was the upper level of a row house. It had a small room that served as the living/kitchen area. It was very clean but sparsely furnished, and the floor was cement. There was only a small wooden table and two wooden chairs. A small bathroom and one bedroom completed the unit. I saw no evidence of a TV, air conditioning, or a computer, though they did have a cell phone and Facebook accounts. Hot water was supplied by the cistern on the roof. The children were delightful and nicely dressed in crisp, clean clothes.

We took the family to dinner and afterwards went to the town square. For years, I had often wondered why the town square was so full of families, including children, especially when they had school the next day. Having been to their home, I understood: the town square was their living room, and there they escaped the heat and the stuffiness of their small quarters.

For our last week in Mexico, we headed for Melaque, nearly five hours south of Puerto Vallarta. Melaque is a small vacation spot for Mexicans, while Barre de Navidad, a few kilometres north, is the tourist area.

While we stayed at the second-highest-rated hotel in Melaque, it was quite rustic, though charming. It was a small studio with a bathroom. Furnishings were older and simple, and there was no hot water in the kitchen or bathroom sinks, but we did have good hot water in the shower from the cistern on the roof. The simplicity did not bother me, but I worried I would feel claustrophobic. Then I thought of the Mexican family and their home that we had visited and felt humbled.

Our unit was a similar size to theirs, but there were seven of them and only two of us. Our unit had flooring, air conditioning, and internet access. We had a TV, but only one English-language station. It was Fox News. I do not get Fox News on my cable line-up back in Canada, so I was not familiar with its history of conservative bias. Of course, I had already heard many of Trump's positions during the debates and was dismayed by almost everything he had said. My dismay escalated while I was in Melaque with only this one channel in English. It was almost exclusively coverage of Trump.

I recall seeing a banner at the bottom of the TV screen that warned of cartel activity at the Texas Border. We would be travelling that way in a few days, and it would be wise to check out what was going on. I never did see any coverage; I had to check it on the computer. While much of the information repeated things that I had heard before, the potent anger and hostility expressed by Trump and Fox News was an assault on my psyche.

I was unfamiliar with this station and felt uneasy and anxious while watching its coverage. The male personalities were of all different shapes, sizes, and ages. This was not the case for the female personalities, who could all qualify as 'beauty queens.'

I think the fact that I was in Mexico heightened my anxiety. I found Trump's characterization of Mexicans and his commitment to building a wall between Mexico and the US offensive. *Salon* reported that Trump pronounced, "'They're sending people that have lots of problems, and they're bringing those problems with [them]. They're bringing drugs. They're bringing crime. They're rapists, and some, I assume, are good people.'"[18] To be fair, he did say that some are good, but his implication is that most are not.

I was not ignoring the reality of the cartels and the crime rates in Mexico. Trump's rhetoric was simply not my experience of Mexicans in my thirty years of travelling there. I had been robbed several times in the United States, but never in Mexico. Our car had not been damaged or broken into in Mexico, but it had been in the United States. In Mexico, items I had misplaced or lost were returned to me. The only time I felt ripped off in Mexico was by a timeshare salesman, who was American.

I always say that everyone is entitled to at least two fantasies a day. One was that Trump would not win the nomination as the presidential candidate for the Republican Party. This fantasy was denied on July 19, 2016, when Trump was proclaimed the nominee.

Even so, America had elected presidents in the past that concerned me, and the world had not ended. I have lived through the Cuban Missile Crisis, the Cold War, and now terrorism, yet I had never been so afraid about the outcome of an American election, not only for America, but for the world.

CHAPTER TWO

The Blue-Collar Billionaire

All that glitters is not gold—
Often have you heard that told.
Many a man his life hath sold
But my outside to behold.
Gilded tombs do worms enfold. [19]
—Shakespeare

While in Mexico, I came to realize that there was a high probability that Trump would win the Republican nomination in the primaries, and he did that on May 26, 2016. I tried to understand what it was about Trump that attracted so many voters, particularly the working class. Describing his father, Donald J. Trump Jr. said, "While he may be the billionaire from New York… he's much more of a blue-collar guy," as reported in *Think Progress*.[20] This chapter will examine Donald Trump as the blue-collar billionaire: his views, experiences, and behaviour as a 'successful' businessman.

Trump supporters would have had the public believe that, despite his gilded lifestyle with his private plane, penthouse in Trump Tower, and Mar-a-Lago club in Palm Beach, through his employment of blue-collar workers, Trump understood them. "I know them better than anybody will ever know them," he said during a recent phone interview. "I grew up on construction sites… I got to know the construction workers, the sheet rockers, and the plumbers, and the electrician, and all of 'em. I worked with them. They were friends of mine."[21] If they were friends of his, one wonders when he last had them for dinner, went to their homes, or played golf with them.

USA Today reported that while Trump said he would protect workers and jobs, hundreds of contractors and vendors claimed that they went unpaid for their work. This included individual workers such as dishwashers, who could ill afford to go without even a week's pay. "Trump's companies have also been cited for twenty-four violations of the Fair Labor Standards Act since 2005 for failing to pay overtime or minimum wage, according to the US Department of Labor data."[22]

According to the *Star*, contractors for the Taj Mahal stopped getting cheques in February 1990, and when they contacted Trump, he advised that he needed to complete audits (does this sound familiar?). When the casino opened in April 1990, it was not long before the truth was revealed. "Over his protests, regulators unsealed a devastating report in August written by Trump's own accountants that showed he had been burning through cash in his personal accounts so fast in the spring that he would have had nothing by end of the year if he didn't take drastic action. The next year, the Trump Taj filed for bankruptcy."[23]

When the casino emerged from Chapter 11 bankruptcy, Trump got a contract to manage it. Others caught up in the Taj turmoil didn't fare as well,[24] most only got thirty-three cents on the dollar, with promises of another fifty cents later. It would take years to collect on the latter, assuming the company survived.

Trump wanted us to believe that he would bring jobs back to America, yet "the US Department of Labor confirmed to *CNN* that between 2013 and the fall of 2015, Trump's Mar-a-Lago club posted 250 seasonal job openings and filled just four of those jobs with American workers. The club requested that the rest of the staff be temporarily imported through the Federal Government's H-2B visa process. Basically, Mar-a-Lago brings in its seasonal staff from overseas."[25] While Trump claimed it is almost impossible to get help, Tom Veenstra, Senior Director of Support Services at the Palm Beach County CareerSource office, said he had "no doubt" that he could fill these positions with American workers.[26]

During the primary debates, Senator Marco Rubio raised the issue of illegal Polish immigrants being employed to build Trump Tower. Trump's contractor hired them, not Trump, and the workers demolished the building to make way for Trump Tower. *PolitiFact* reported that "[t]he Polish employees were off-the-books, working twelve-hour shifts, seven days a week, for $4 to $5 an hour, with no overtime. Some workers were never paid what they were owed."[27] The union sued on the basis that Trump and his contractor cheated the union out of a pension and welfare fund.

While Trump denied knowing that the workers were illegal immigrants, a judge ruled against him on the basis that his representative "knew that the Polish workers were doing demolition work" and that his company participated in a "conspiracy" to cheat the union.[28] Trump appealed the judgment, and the case dragged on for years with Trump finally settling, but the agreement was placed under seal, according to *Reuters*.[29] *NPR* reported that some published reports suggested Trump not only knew about the workers' status, but instigated their hiring. There were also reports that he threatened to turn the workers in to immigration authorities after some complained about work conditions.[30] It seemed that Trump avoided settling lawsuits as a matter of principle, or he simply used this as an evasion tactic. Anyone can build things 'cheaper' if they don't pay for what they get on the backs of the blue-collar workers. By dragging out the process, Trump earned interest on the unpaid money, which offset some of what he lost in the settlement.

Joseph Tanfani provided the following example of Trump's unethical business practices in the *Los Angeles Times*. Mr. Trump, as the owner of three Atlantic City casinos, emerged as a vociferous opponent of the deregulation of gambling, arguing that Native American tribes would be unable to police their casinos as well as he and other established operators did. In 2000, Trump and his associates—without admitting guilt—agreed to pay a $250,000 civil penalty after New York regulators uncovered evidence that he had secretly funded advertisements that attacked a Native American tribe called the St. Regis Mohawks, which was seeking to open a second casino in the state.[31]

Kathy Kiely, reporter for *Common Dreams*, provided a summary of a book entitled *The Making of Donald Trump*, written by Pulitzer-Prize-winning author David Cay Johnston. Johnston wrote that Trump's grandfather ran a "whorehouse" and "[i]n 1927, Fred Trump, Donald Trump's father, was arrested at a Ku Klux Klan meeting in Queens—something his son has tried furiously to deny, but, said Johnston, 'I have the clips.'"[32]

Trump's father allegedly discriminated against African-Americans in the federal housing programme for returning GIs. Donald Trump's efforts to get the racial discrimination charge thrown out were unsuccessful, and the Trumps made a settlement to close the legal case. Their lawyer was "Roy Cohn, former long-time aide to Sen. Joseph McCarthy (R-WI), the disgraced Communist witch-hunt perpetrator."[33] While his father's views do not necessarily make Donald a racist, Donald's own behaviour and comments would lead one to conclude that his grandfather's views about women and his father's views about race were influential.

Johnston gave several examples of Trump's vindictiveness, as reported in *Common Dreams*. Trump once removed an ailing nephew from the family's medical insurance because that family challenged the father's will, though a judge later reinstated it. In another example, a secretary refused to contact a personal banker friend on Trump's behalf for ethical reasons, and she was immediately fired. Trump gloated when she lost her home and her husband left her: "I can't stomach disloyalty… and now I go out of my way to make her life miserable."[34]

During an interview on CNN's *Smerconish*, Johnston spoke to Trump's business behaviour and how it would translate into the type of leader he would be, pointing out that there were still profitable business casinos in Atlantic City. Trump's casinos went bankrupt while he was in charge due to extensive mismanagement. Compared to 496 publicly traded companies, Trump's casinos came in dead last or almost last in every category *Fortune Magazine* measured, including management, use of assets, employee talent, long-term investment value, and social responsibility. Over four thousand lawsuits were filed by people who said they were swindled. He has had lifelong business dealings with Russian mobsters, con artists, violent felons, and swindlers.[35]

According to *Reuters*, Trump maligned companies in an effort to bring jobs back to America, calling for boycotts of companies moving overseas such as Ford, Carrier, Apple, Amazon, and Nabisco. "Some of the companies saw their share prices dip in the wake of Trump's criticism."[36] In many cases the information was simply untrue. For example, rather than challenging Trump, which would be an exercise in futility, Nabisco simply released statements that they would continue to make their cookies in three locations in America.[37]

It is difficult to ignore the hypocrisy when many, if not most, of Trump's goods are made overseas.

Military and Veterans

Trump expressed a deep and abiding commitment to supporting veterans and the military. The following are some examples that contradict his declarations of deep respect and admiration for those who have served their country.

Trump's statements and actions repeatedly contradict proclamations of admiration for veterans or the military. In an NBC forum with both candidates, *Commander in Chief,* Trump said that "the generals have been reduced to rubble" and that "they'll probably be different generals, to be honest with you. I mean, I'm looking at the generals. Today, you probably saw, I have a piece of paper here, I could show it, 88 generals and admirals endorsed me today."[38] On the one hand, Trump was implying that the Obama administration was incompetent and undermined the generals. Contrarily, he was suggesting that the generals were incompetent and that he would fire many of them. He also seemed to be implying that they would be replaced by generals that supported him during the campaign. He further denigrated the generals in a statement claiming, "I know more about ISIS than the generals do. Believe me."[39]

The *New York Times* reported that Trump insulted Republican Senator John McCain, whom, while a prisoner of war in Hanoi during the Vietnam War, refused to be released without his men though he was repeatedly tortured. Trump stated, "He's not a war hero. He's a war hero because he was captured. I like people who weren't captured."[40] This from a man who repeatedly eluded service to his country.

Trump was excused from the draft for four years while he attended university, and somehow continued to evade conscription, even once classified as available for unrestricted military service. There are many discrepancies as to the reasons, and neither he nor his staff has provided an explanation, according to reporter Craig Whitlock from the *Washington Post*.[41]

In Virginia, a wounded veteran gave Trump his purple heart. Trump asked him if it was real, then went on to say, "I always wanted a purple heart," reported the *Washington Post*.[42] Some veterans took exception to this, as no one wants a purple heart; it is awarded to those wounded in combat. Why did Trump not just thank him for his service and tell him he appreciated the gesture? The veteran is the one who sacrificed and earned the medal.

During an interview with George Stephanopoulos on ABC, Trump equated the sacrifice of losing a family member in service to his country to his own 'sacrifice' in working hard and creating jobs. At the DNC Convention, the Khan family spoke out against Trump for his comments about banning Muslims from entering the United States, asserting that Trump's remarks were in opposition to the Constitution. The Khans are a Gold Star family, as their son Humayun Khan gave his life in service of his country. Trump lashed out at the family, first criticizing the mother for not speaking out, implying that, as a woman, she had been restrained from speaking because of her faith, and second saying that the Khans had no right to speak out in front of millions and claim that he had not read the Constitution.[43] Trump never apologized for his criticism.

Other Gold Star families were upset and asked for an apology. Khan asked Trump what he had sacrificed, and Trump responded that he had "made a lot of sacrifices… I work very, very hard. I've created thousands and thousands of jobs, tens of thousands of jobs," *CNBC* reported.[44]

His issues with the military go beyond race and religion. He also commented on the roles of women and gender integration in military sexual assaults. In a tweet, he commented, "26,000 unreported sexual assaults in the military-only 238 convictions. What did these geniuses expect when they put men and women together?"[45] This implied that having men and women work side by side invites rape and sexual assault when, according to Christine Quinn, a Democrat and former Speaker for New York City, "countless countries had women in combat before we did and there is no evidence that as a matter of course causes this to happen."[46] Consistent with Trump's sexist views, he blamed gender integration for the sexual misconduct in the military.

Putin and Russia

Trump said that owning businesses in foreign countries prepared him to be an international leader. While Trump attempted to minimize his interest in Russia, there are many contraindicators.

He appeared to have an obsessive desire to be friends with Putin. Trump struck a $20 million deal to host the 2013 Miss Universe pageant in Moscow, to which he invited Putin, tweeting, "Do you think Putin will be going to The Miss Universe Pageant in November in Moscow — if so, will he become my new best friend?" Putin did not attend.[47]

Trump considered it an honour to be regarded as a great leader by someone with a favourability rating as high as Putin's. Despite Trump's assertions, the *Moscow Times* clarified that Putin did not call Trump "brilliant" and that it was a matter of interpretation. He meant it as in a "colourful personality."[48] While Trump said they met and got on well, to date there is no substantiation regarding his reported contacts.

Trump's desire to gain Putin's approval seemed to supersede his potential relationship with allies who were opposed to the annexation of Crimea. Trump suggested he might accept Putin's seizure of Crimea from Ukraine, *CNN* reported.[49] Would Trump's obsession with Russia put existing alliances at risk?

Trump appeared to have business connections with individuals of dubious character. He had numerous ties to Russia. One was disclosed in David Johnston's book *The Making of Donald Trump*, in which he described ties to a "Russian-born stock fraudster and admitted fellow traveler with the mob," who is now a defendant in a tax fraud case in which Trump and two of his children are named as witnesses.[50]

Trump's business ties in Russia gave rise to speculation about whether his desire for a positive relationship with Russia was in the best interest of America or the Trump Corporation. He was interested in expanding his business dealings into Russia. In 1996, Trump registered the name "Trump Tower," and in later years "Trump International Hotel," "Trump Home," and the Trump crest design. Trump tried several times to build a signature Trump Tower in Moscow. None of these projects have come to fruition, according to *CNN*.[51]

In 2008, Donald Trump Jr. seemed to contradict his father's claims in the following statement: "We see a lot of money pouring in from Russia. There's indeed a lot of money coming for new-builds and resale reflecting a trend in the Russian economy and, of course, the weak dollar versus the ruble," reported *eTurboNews*.[52]

The following background summary was sourced from *Wikipedia*.[53] Many of Trump's colleagues and close advisors have questionable relationships with Russia. Paul Manafort, Trump's former campaign manager, was an advisor to Ukraine's ex-president Viktor Yanukovych, who had a strong affiliation with Russia. Manafort assisted Yanukovych in winning the election in 2010, informed the *Guardian*.[54] Yanukovych tried to bring about closer economic ties with Russia rather than the European Union. The people revolted successfully, and he fled to Russia for asylum, according to *Wikipedia*.[55] The conflicting information and steadfast refusal to criticize Putin, as well as lack of open disclosure, created considerable cynicism.

Trump and Violence

While the following are only a few of Trump's recorded statements that are violent in nature, they provide a context that demonstrates the extremity of this tendency. They speak to the viciousness of his character. When viewed in the context that they are not isolated comments, but rather a pattern, these comments should give us all pause and cause us to question what he would do if his finger were on the button. Most of the comments speak for themselves.

- Trump defended campaign manager Corey Lewandowski and declined to condemn supporters who had attacked protesters at his increasingly chaotic rallies. Trump did not back down from his warning that there would be riots in the streets if the Republican Party denied him the nomination for the November election, despite his being the most popular candidate among Republican voters. "I don't know what's going to happen, but I will say this, you're going to have a lot of unhappy people… I don't want to see riots, I don't want to see problems. But you're talking about millions of people," reported Reuters.[56]

- The *Daily Wire* conveyed that Trump told journalist Timothy L. O'Brien, "My favorite part [of the movie Pulp Fiction] is when Sam has his gun out in the diner and he tells the guy to tell his girlfriend to shut up. Tell that b#tch to be cool. Say: 'B#tch be cool.' I love those lines."[57]

- Trump encouraged the crowd to vent its fury at the protesters. "See, in the good old days, this didn't use to happen, because they used to treat them very rough," he said. "We've become very weak." At least one supporter felt the same way: Videos shot at the event showed a man punching a protester as he was removed. The puncher was charged with assault.[58]

- Donald Trump suggested that the supporters of the Second Amendment do something about Hillary. "If she gets to pick her judges, nothing you can do, folks," Mr. Trump said, as the crowd began to boo. He quickly added, "Although the Second Amendment people — maybe there is, I don't know."[59]

- After hearing the speeches at the DNC Convention, Trump said he wanted to "hit a number of those speakers so hard, their heads would spin. They'd never recover."[60]

- "We have to fight so viciously and violently because we're dealing with violent people," Mr. Trump said. At one point, he asked the crowd, "What do you think about waterboarding?" They cheered as he gave his answer: "I like it a lot. I don't think it's tough enough."[61]

- Trump commented on Saddam Hussein: "Saddam Hussein was a bad guy. Right?" Trump said, "He was a bad guy. Really bad guy. But you know what, he did well? He killed terrorists. He did that so good they didn't read (them) the rights. They didn't talk."[62]

- Trump suggested that Hillary's guards should be disarmed, implying that she did not deserve their protection because she did not support the Second Amendment, which is patently untrue. "She goes around with armed bodyguards like you have never seen before. I think that her bodyguards should drop all weapons… She doesn't want guns… Let's see what happens to her. Take their guns away, okay? It would be very dangerous."[63]

- While the following story told by Trump is a myth, he retells it frequently, seeming to relish the violence of the incident. Donald Trump said that in the Philippines more than a century ago, Gen. John Pershing, after capturing fifty terrorists, "took 50 bullets, and he dipped them in pigs' blood… and they shot 49 Muslim rebels. The 50th person, he said, 'You go back to your people, and you tell them what happened.'"[64]

About Women

While Trump claimed that no one respects women more than he does, the following statements and acts belie that claim. His statements and behaviours have occurred over a period of decades, and most distressing is that they continue to the present day. He has not evolved.

The following are statements and behaviours pertaining to his wives and marriage:

- "I would never buy Ivana any decent jewels or pictures. Why give her negotiable assets?"[65]

- "My wife, Ivana, is a brilliant manager. I will pay her one dollar a year and all the dresses she can buy!"[66]

- Donald managed to get Ivana to sign a prenuptial agreement for $10 million,[67] but she fought it and eventually got about $25 million.[68]

- Marla Maples, his second wife, got $1 million, property, and child support. Trump left her a few months before a requirement in their prenuptial agreement would have resulted in a higher settlement.[69]

- "One thing I have learned: There is high maintenance. There is low maintenance. I want no maintenance."[70]

- In the early 1990s, Ivana Trump alleged rape in a deposition during her divorce from Trump, though she later amended the statement by saying, "not in the criminal sense." Ivana reported feeling "violated" when her then spouse Donald Trump reacted in anger after he underwent a painful scalp reduction surgery to remove a bald spot, blaming Ivana because she recommended the plastic surgeon.[71]

The following are vile remarks that Trump has made about or to women:

- "You know, it doesn't really matter what [the media] writes, as long as you've got a young and beautiful piece of ass."[72]

- "If Hillary can't satisfy her husband… what makes her think she can satisfy America?"[73]

- Trump said of Angelina Jolie, "She's been with so many guys she makes me look like a baby, OK, with the other side, and I just don't even find her attractive."[74]

- "You know, you could see there was blood coming out of her eyes, blood coming out of her wherever," said Trump, speaking about commentator Megyn Kelly.[75]

- "Ariana Huffington is unattractive, both inside and out. I fully understand why her former husband left her for a man—he made a good decision." Trump made this comment about the founder of Huffington Post.[76]

- "You have to treat 'em [women] like s[#]it," Trump said in the article to his friend Philip Johnson.[77]

Trump has limitations regarding his attitude toward women in the workplace:

- "I think that putting a wife to work is a very dangerous thing. If you're in business for yourself, I really think it's a bad idea. I think that was the single greatest cause of what happened to my marriage with Ivana," he said during an interview with ABC News in 1994.[78]

- "When a lawyer facing Trump in 2011 asked for a break to pump breast milk for her infant daughter, The Donald reacted very poorly. 'He got up, his face got red, he shook his finger at me and he screamed, 'You're disgusting, you're disgusting' and he ran out of there.'"[79] Trump's attorney does not dispute that Trump called the lawyer disgusting.

- "I would like to think she would find another career or find another company if that was the case," he said, speaking of his daughter Ivanka, and if she were a victim of sexual abuse in the workplace.[80] Ivanka disagreed.

Trump revealed his arrogant attitude, disdain, and sense of entitlement regarding women in the following statements:

- "Women have one of the great acts of all time. The smart ones act very feminine and needy, but inside they are real killers. The person who came up with the expression 'the weaker sex' was either very naive or had to be kidding. I have seen women manipulate men with just a twitch of their eye—or perhaps another body part."[81]

- Trump made the following statement about himself in the third person: "Love him or hate him, Trump is a man who is certain about what he wants and sets out to get it, no holds barred. Women find his power almost as much of a turn-on as his money."[82]

- "The answer is that there has to be some form of punishment." Trump was referring to punishing women for getting an abortion during an interview with MSNBC in March 2016.[83]

Trump has even sexualized his own daughter: "If Ivanka weren't my daughter, perhaps I'd be dating her," he said during an episode of the *View* in March 2006.[84] *Slate* disclosed that during an interview on Howard Stern's radio program in 2008, Stern described Ivanka as being voluptuous. Trump responded, "She's actually always been very voluptuous."[85] Trump also gave Stern permission to refer to his daughter as "a piece of ass."[86]

Defending men accused of sexual abuse and blaming the victim is a pattern of Donald Trump's. He did the same with Mike Tyson,[87] who endorsed him at the GOP convention, and with Bill Clinton. Roger Ailes was purported to advise Trump on preparation for the debates.[88]

This is not an exhaustive list, but I think there are enough points to show a definite pattern. These comments cannot be construed as anything but misogynistic. Ivanka, his daughter, stated that he was not sexist because he hired her. She excused the behaviour, explaining that he also used strong language with men.[89] That is disingenuous.

Race

Trump has displayed racist tendencies over a number of decades, which have remained unchanged during the campaign and election process. In fact, my obsession with following the election process was first sparked by his comments about undocumented Mexican immigrants.

Trump's generalized depiction of undocumented Mexicans as being mostly criminals is simply wrong. First, it is not just some that are good people; most are. A report released by the American Immigration Council in July 2015 concluded "that undocumented immigrants commit violent crimes at a far lower rate than native-born Americans."[90] Reporter Alan Gomez from *USA Today* pointed out that

> the federal court system handles only a tiny percentage of the nation's violent crimes... Undocumented immigrants (not exclusively Mexican) accounted for 9.2% of federal murder convictions in 2013, but that represents a grand total of eight murder cases. When considering that the FBI estimates there were 14,196 murders in the US in 2013, those few cases handled by the federal court system don't quite register as a reliable sample set.[91]

Donald Trump "vociferously—and repeatedly—defended his claims that a judge overseeing a lawsuit against Trump University was biased because of his Mexican heritage, pushing back against criticism that his objections are racist," Theodore Schleifer from *CNN* claimed.[92] Trump said, "I'm building a wall. I'm trying to keep business out of Mexico. Mexico's fine... He's of Mexican heritage, and he's very proud of it, as I am of where I come from."[93] He believed Judge Gonzalo Curiel, who is of Mexican heritage (though born in the United States), would not be impartial. "Trump again called for Curiel to recuse himself from the case."[94]

Donald Trump repeatedly revealed his disregard for Hispanics. Justin Moyer from the *Washington Post* described the following incident. When asked for comments on two of his supporters who brutally beat and urinated on a Hispanic homeless man while yelling pro-Trump slogans, Trump responded by defending the men as just being "passionate." When asked what motivated the alleged attack, Scott Leader, who was convicted of a hate crime and jailed for a year in the assault of a Moroccan man shortly after the September 11 attacks, stated, "Donald Trump was right, all these illegals need to be deported."[95]

Trump's racist behaviour and comments about black people simply speak for themselves:

- A former Trump's Castle staff member said, "When Donald and Ivana came to the casino, the bosses would order all the blacks off the floor... it was the eighties, I was a teen-ager, but I remember it: they put us all in the back."[96]

- Trump said, "I've got black accountants at Trump Castle and Trump Plaza. Black guys counting my money! I hate it. The only kind of people I want counting my money are short guys that wear yarmulkes every day... I think the guy is lazy. And it's probably not his fault because laziness is a trait in blacks. It really is, I believe that."[97]

- "A well-educated black has a tremendous advantage over a well-educated white in terms of the job market... If I were starting off today, I would love to be a well-educated black, because I believe they do have an actual advantage."[98]

- Trump built a casino in Gary, Indiana, a black majority city, and broke a promise to the mayor about hiring locals. Trump refrained from hiring minorities, except those who would work in service jobs like janitors. The mayor lamented that non-minorities were much more likely to land plum gambling posts such as dealers, managers, or croupiers. "In a 1993 agreement between Trump and Gary city officials, Trump said he would create 1,675 jobs. At issue is his pledge to commit to goals of filling 67% of those jobs with Gary residents and 90% with Lake County residents."[99]

- *Vox* described an event during a rally in which Trump was relaying an incident with protesters and made reference to an African-American supporter who had intervened with the protesters. Trump looked around and pointed out the man with the words, "Look at my African American over here, look at him."[100] At the very least, this comment was highly insensitive.

Ben Shapiro, reporter from the *Daily Wire,* provided the following account of Trump's failure to disavow David Duke. The Anti-Defamation League called on Trump to condemn publicly and unequivocally the racism of former KKK Grand Wizard David Duke. In an interview with Jake Tapper, Trump was asked, "Will you unequivocally condemn David Duke and say you don't want his vote or that of other white supremacists in this election?" Three times Trump refused to disavow, stating he did not know David Duke or what Tapper was even talking about regarding white supremacy. Trump refused to disavow support from the Ku Klux Klan multiple times during the interview, only to change his mind later on Twitter.[101]

According to Shapiro, "While he [Trump] claimed not to know the group, he had disavowed David Duke publicly the week before and previously in August 2015. In 2000, he cited David Duke's involvement in the Reform Party as his rationale for leaving it."[102] In his article, Ben Shapiro questioned if it were possible that Trump wanted to avoid alienating racists and their votes.[103] I had the same reflection.

NPR related an incident in September 2015, when an audience member at an event in New Hampshire expressed concern over Muslims: "We have a problem in this country. It's called Muslims. We know our current president is one. You know he's not even an American. We have training camps growing when they want to kill us."[104] Trump responded by declaring that he was looking into this as well as other things. In both incidents above, Trump made no effort to discourage the supporters' racist views.

NPR elaborated by providing a comparison to an event in 2008, when then–candidate John McCain was put in a similarly awkward position after a woman at an October event stood up and told him she had read that President Obama was an "Arab." She said, "I gotta ask you a question. I can't trust Obama. I have read about him, and he's not, he's not, he's an Arab." McCain vigorously shook his head and said, "No ma'am, no ma'am, he's a decent family man, a citizen that I just happen to have disagreements with on fundamental issues, and that's what this campaign is all about. He's not. Thank you." The audience applauded.[105]

In an article on *MintPress*, Little Bird[106] claimed that 62% of the people Trump retweeted on the week of January 19, 2016 ran white supremacist accounts. Up to 58% of the top fifty white nationalist accounts on Twitter follow Donald Trump.[107] Trump is giving them exposure and endorsing their agenda by providing a platform for them via his Twitter account.

Mother Jones reported that William Johnson, "one of the country's most prominent white nationalists," was on the slate as a delegate in the presidential primary in California.[108] The campaign later claimed the selection was the result of a database error. Johnson told the reporter at *Mother Jones* that "[Trump] is allowing us to talk about things we've not been able to talk about… So even if he is not elected, he has achieved great things."[109] Johnson funded pro-Trump robocalls promoting a white nationalist message, including the following: "The white race is dying out in America and Europe because we are afraid to be called 'racist,'"[110] and "Donald Trump is not racist, but Donald Trump is not afraid. Don't vote for a Cuban. Vote for Donald Trump."[111]

NBC relayed former *Apprentice* contestants' position on Trump's candidacy. Concerned about his divisive rhetoric, six black alumni from the *Apprentice*—Randal Pinkett, Kwame Jackson, Tara Dowdell, Marshawn Evans Daniels, Kevin Allen, and James Sun—teamed up in hopes of "firing" Trump from the campaign trail.[112]

"We stand united as former candidates on the *Apprentice*, not to denounce Donald Trump the man, but to denounce Donald Trump, the presidential candidate's, message." Jackson stated that Trump's rhetoric plays to "the lowest common denominator of fear, racism and divisiveness in our populace."[113] Dowdell said it was her responsibility to speak out as a former *Apprentice* participant, in part because she believed the show had paved the way for Trump's political success.[114] Tara Dowdell added, "the candidate [is] a 'brilliant marketer' who understands what 'triggers emotion in people.'"[115]

Jackson disagreed with Trump's declarations that he is "the least racist person" and concluded, "You don't have to lynch someone, you don't have to burn a cross in someone's yard these days to be a racist… There are very nuanced forms of being racist in 2016."[116]

This illustrated the racist side of Donald Trump that he has attempted to hide or minimize in the media. Here are several more examples:

- Trump kicked the only black Republican official out of an Atlanta Trump event with no explanation.[117]

- According to David Graham, a reporter with The Atlantic, Trump was fined $200,000 in 1992 by the New Jersey Division of Gaming Enforcement for not allowing black people onto his casino floor while a racist Mafia leader was gambling.[118]

- Trump falsely claimed that four out of five white people who were victims of homicide were murdered by black people.[119]

- Trump retweeted a picture of Nazi soldiers in silhouette in an unofficial campaign poster featuring him with an American flag. He later deleted it, and one of his organizers claimed that an "intern accidentally posted" the questionable photo.[120]

Trump's pundits have also been guilty of racist comments. Katrina Pierson referred to Obama as "a negro" who was not a "pure-breed"[121] and later refused to apologize for a tweet in which she referred to President Obama as "head Negro in charge."[122] She "blamed her 'heated' language on liberal Twitter trolls."[123]

High proportions of Trump supporters share racist views:

- 20% of Trump's supporters thought that freeing the slaves was a bad thing.[124]

- 64% of Trump's supporters thought that "Muslims should be subject to more scrutiny."[125]

- 80% of Trump's supporters claimed to have no problem with racist comments.[126]

Trump reaffirmed his base's fear of Muslims. He called for "a total and complete shutdown of Muslims entering the United States until our country's representatives can figure out what is going on."[127]

"Trump argued that anyone belonging to the faith should be considered a potential threat."[128] Ben Rhodes, a Deputy National Security Adviser to President Obama, responded, "We should be making it harder for ISIL to portray 'a war between the United States and Islam, not easier.'" William Banks, a constitutional law scholar at the Syracuse College of Law commented that "[a]side from being outrageous, it [Trump's Muslim ban] would be unconstitutional."[129]

According to Kim LaCapria at *Snopes*, while reports that Trump said Muslims should wear ID badges were false, Trump would not rule out that Muslims should carry special identification, as well as being entered into a database tracking Muslims.[130]

Trump lied about how Muslims celebrated 9/11. The *Washington Post* reported his comments: "Hey, I watched when the World Trade Center came tumbling down. And I watched in Jersey City, New Jersey, where thousands and thousands of people were cheering as that building was coming down. Thousands of people were cheering."[131]

In 1989, Trump signed a full-page ad promoting the execution of the Central Park Five, a group of Latino and Black youths accused of rape. All five were later proven innocent. Trump continued to insist that they were somehow guilty despite DNA evidence proving their innocence, the *Guardian* reported.[132]

According to Noah Bierman from the *Los Angeles Times*, Stephen K. Bannon, the head of conservative website *Breitbart News*, took a temporary leave of absence to take a new position as Chief Executive Officer of Trump's campaign, which effectively demoted Paul Manafort. *Bloomberg Politics* once recognized Bannon as the "most dangerous political operative in America," and he was one of Clinton's harshest critics, having co-written the book *Clinton Cash*. "The Southern Poverty Law Center, which has been critical of Trump's campaign, accused *Breitbart News* in April of shifting to embrace positions on the 'extremist fringe of the conservative right,' including racist, anti-Muslim, and anti-immigrant ideas."[133]

Donald Trump entered the presidential campaign, and his speech centered on his "career and fortune."[134] There is no question that Trump has had success. While he did inherit money from his father and there is some dispute about the amount of his fortune, he is reported to be a billionaire. Trump claimed that his net worth was $10 billion, while *Forbes*, for example, estimated it to be $4.5 billion.[135] Regardless, he is rich and did build on the fortune he inherited.

Jacob Koffler detailed Trump's successes and failures in *Time*. Successes include Trump Tower, 40 Wall Street, Trump Place, the *Apprentice*, and Trump International Tower (Chicago).

Trump renovated Wollman Rink in 1986 after contacting Mayor Ed Koch and offering to complete the renovation for $3 million. He finished the project on time and $750,000 under budget. Wollman Rink remains a Central Park fixture with more than five million annual visitors.

The *Apprentice* gave him an entrée into branding numerous products and projects.[136]

He also had some monumental failures and other projects that fizzled out. Trump did start to experience some serious debt issues that led to "bankruptcy protection, part of a vast and humiliating restructuring of some $900 million of personal debt that Mr. Trump owed to a consortium of banks," reported the *New York Times*.[137]

It is widely reported that he has declared bankruptcy four times, but *Politico* clarified that there were six: The Trump Taj Mahal, 1991; Trump Castle, 1992; Trump Plaza and Casino, 1992; Plaza Hotel, 1992; Trump Hotels and Casinos Resorts, 2004; and Trump Entertainment Resorts, 2009.[138] Trump emphasized that many "great entrepreneurs" have used bankruptcy to restructure debt, free up capital, and improve their businesses.[139]

According to David Segal from the *New York Times*, Trump purchased the Plaza for $407 million. He acknowledged that for "the first time in my life I have knowingly made a deal which was not economic—for I can never justify the price I paid, no matter how successful the Plaza becomes."[140] The Plaza went into bankruptcy in 1990 because Trump was unable to sustain the required $40 million in operating revenue. A few years later, a buyer paid $325 million. In 2004, it was sold again for $625 million, and half the building was turned into condos, which sold for a total of $1.4 billion.[141] Somebody was able to make a profit from it, but it was not Donald Trump.

Trump Airlines never earned a profit, and he defaulted on his loans, forcing the ownership to be turned over to creditors.[142]

The companies that failed because of lack of interest and profitability include Trump Vodka, Trump the Game, *Trump Magazine*, Trump Steaks, and *GoTrump.com*, a travel website that failed despite being powered by *Travelocity*. The Trump Steaks failure may have "had something to do with the Trump Steakhouse in Las Vegas being closed down in 2012 for fifty-one health code violations, including serving five-month old duck."[143]

According to *Time*, Trump University was sued in 2010 when students claimed that the "classes… amounted to extended 'infomercials.'"[144] "In 2013, the New York Attorney General sued Trump and the 'university' for $40 million for allegedly defrauding students."[145]

It seems that spectacular failures counterbalance Trump's financial successes. Does his business ethos represent the values of the American public, and are the skills transferable to the role of president of the United States? His failures suggest a level of risk-taking that is alarming when translated from business to the fate of America and the rest of the world.

Oliver Laughland from the *Guardian* reported that former managers and directors in the Trump Organization described his management style as "prone to micromanagement" and having "little interest in the diversity of executives or the welfare of lower-level employees."[146] He was described as lacking the "temperament to deal with setbacks... impatient with those who do not support or agree with him" and "loyal to those that do."[147] Other characteristics ascribed to Trump include blaming others, taking credit for successes, and being a workaholic.[148]

"He says he's going to get the best people around. But he doesn't do that—he never has," said the source. "Because he doesn't listen to them, and then they leave. And if anybody is ever credited with doing anything good, he gets rid of them because he hates when anybody else gets credit."[149]

When Trump attempted to build the casino in an African-American community in Philadelphia, creating the controversy described earlier in this chapter, "Pinkett, one of the former *Apprentice* contestants, said he was sometimes called upon to be the public face of Trump's business when he needed to engage minority communities."[150] He also claimed that when he expressed reservations about the project, he was told that if he did not support it, there would be ramifications. Pinkett has not been in touch with Trump for years, believing that a call he made to express his offence at Trump's birther campaign in 2008 was perceived as disloyal.

One current employee, who is a part-time server at the Trump Hotel in Las Vegas, revealed that she earns $9.75 an hour with no benefits or health insurance. Even after five years, she has not received a contract. "Her union estimates that Trump pays his hotel workers in Las Vegas, on average, $3.33 less per hour than the average wages on the Las Vegas strip."[151]

It is commendable that these former employees and one current employee spoke out and were so forthright given Trump's propensity to lash out viciously. There are probably many more who would speak out were they not intimidated by the potential reprisal.

Trump is an excellent marketer. The marketer's role is to determine how to sell a product, who the target population is, and what their views and preferences are, and then market the product based on that information.

Just as he denied going bankrupt by reframing his bankruptcies and claiming that he just used the laws to his advantage, he created an excuse if he lost: The election was rigged. Trump doesn't like losers.

CHAPTER THREE

Demon Or Demonized

It's not a lie if you believe it.[152]
— *Seinfeld TV Series*

I was never a great fan of Hillary. This was an impression rather than anything rooted in substance. During an interview on MSNBC's *Morning Joe* program, Hillary admitted that she was not a "natural politician."[153] I didn't dislike her; I was simply unenthused. In the past, it did not matter to me, but the stakes in this election were high. What were the facts about Hillary? Was she a demon, or demonized?

I was initially supportive of Bernie Sanders. He seemed to be genuine and to have integrity. I liked his social justice approach.

About halfway through the primaries, I started to lose enthusiasm. Sanders's speeches were all starting to sound the same, with little information on how he was going to carry out his plans. He began to go on the attack, and when he did, I was surprised to find that I was more in agreement with Hillary's position. She critiqued Sanders's position and voting history on gun laws, and *Mother Jones* reported Hillary's claim that Sanders voted against the Brady Bill, which imposed background checks and a waiting period to purchase guns. Sanders voted in favour of a loophole that required the gun purchase to go forward if the background check was not completed in three days. Sanders reiterated that he had a D-score from the National Rifle Association.[154]

I agreed with Bernie about the Super PACs and the potential for donor influence and pay-for-play. I thought it was fair to challenge Hillary on her involvement with Wall Street and the potential for conflict, but his attack was accusatory, insinuating that she had made decisions influenced by Wall Street. The *Boston Globe* reported that, upon being asked during a debate, Sanders was unable to give one example in which this influenced her decisions or voting.[155] Sanders was beginning to sound inflexible and strident. I was not seeing evidence that he could accomplish his lofty goals.

Hillary won the primary. Despite all odds, Sanders had an incredibly successful campaign, energizing young voters, and prompting a revolution. His support put him in a position to announce the "most progressive platform in the history of the Democratic Party."[156] Sanders was able to negotiate some of his policies in the Democratic platform, including considering amendments to put a price on carbon pollution, taking steps toward legalizing marijuana, creating a public option for healthcare, and raising the minimum wage to $15 an hour.[157] To promote unity, he endorsed Hillary, citing the advancements they made in developing the most progressive Democratic platform, aiming to defeat Donald Trump. It should have been no surprise that Sanders's supporters were protesting at the convention after promises from Bernie that he would take the fight to the convention.

I became more favourable toward Hillary and curious as to why she had such poor ratings. According to *PoliticusUSA*, Hillary had scored a 52% rating for being true or mostly true in statements she made, while Bernie's score was 51%,[158] belying my perception that Sanders's would be higher. Polls from the Pew Research Center reflected that Hillary had high approval ratings while she was Secretary of State, and in August 2014, her approval rating was 58%. By May 2015, it was down to 49%.[159] Bernie had consistently high approval ratings. Given that fact checkers had rated both candidates similarly, why was only Hillary perceived as untrustworthy and why did her approval ratings drop so dramatically?

While I was very supportive of Bernie's platform, I did have concerns about his ability to realize his objectives. I concluded that Hillary seemed to be on a similar progressive path, but with more potential to achieve her objectives. It became Bernie's promises versus Hillary's realities.

If that were the case, why was she portrayed as politically expedient and untrustworthy?

A generally well-informed acquaintance of mine had reservations about Hillary, believing that she was fired from the Watergate Investigation. I found numerous articles online that debunked the myth. *Truth or Fiction*, part of the Library of Congress, disclosed that a viral email was distributed during the 2008 presidential campaign that originated from a column written by Dan Calabrese. In that email, Democrat Jerry Zeifman, a counsel and chief of staff of the House Judiciary Committee, asserted that he had supervised Clinton on the Watergate investigation and that he had fired her for unethical behaviour. Zeifman later admitted that he did not have the power to fire her.[160]

Zeifman wrote a book, *Without Honor,* which was reviewed by Matthew Dallek from the *Washington Post*, who concluded, "The lack of evidence makes it hard to swallow."[161] Despite this refutation, many still believed the myth.

Whitewater

The following background on Whitewater was retrieved from *Wikipedia*. In the 1970s and 1980s, the Clintons lost money in the Whitewater Development Corporation, a real estate business.[162,163] A 1992 *New York Times* article about Whitewater that mentioned the Clintons caught the attention of an investigator from the Resolution Trust.

According to *Wikipedia*, the investigator, L. Jean Lewis, submitted a referral to the FBI naming the Clintons as witnesses. The FBI determined that the referral lacked merit, but Lewis pursued the case. From 1992 to 1994, she resubmitted several referrals against the Clintons and repeatedly called the US Attorney's Office in Little Rock. After the scandal finally became public, the investigator testified before the Senate Judicial Subcommittee in 1995.[164]

David Hale, a former Arkansas banker, worked with Jim McDougal on the $3 million-dollar loan from his lending company and was the source of the charges against the Clintons in

1993. He pled guilty and "was sentenced to two years and four months in prison for fraud unrelated to the Whitewater deal."[165]

As part of this plea, he testified in the Jim and Susan McDougal trial over the failed Savings and Loan, and at no time during that testimony did he ever mention the Clintons being involved with the loan. He did not make the allegations against the Clintons until he faced charges unrelated to Whitewater. It was discovered that a local lawyer, Eugene Fitzhugh, had bribed Hale to give this false testimony. Fitzhugh pled guilty to the charges.[166]

The McDougals and, according to the *Washington Post*, Bill Tucker, Clinton's successor as governor of Arkansas, were convicted of fraud.[167] Susan McDougal received an additional eighteen-month sentence for refusing to answer questions about Whitewater and was later granted a pardon by then president Clinton. After three separate investigations, the Clintons were not indicted. In August 1994, Kenneth Starr was appointed by a three-judge panel to continue the Whitewater investigation.[168]

According to *NPR*, and based on Duquesne law professor Ken Gormley's book *The Death of American Virtue: Clinton vs. Starr,* initial prosecutor Robert Fiske wrapped up his investigation within six months, having found no evidence of the Clintons' involvement in the Whitewater scandal. The Republicans were not satisfied with Fiske's report, even though Republicans had lauded him upon his appointment.[169] The Whitewater investigation turned into several investigations: Travelgate, the Vince Foster Suicide, Filegate, and the Lewinsky Scandal, all investigated by Ken Starr. This suggests a pattern of the Republican Party extending investigations when the outcome does not fit their agenda.

Travelgate

Seven employees of the White House Travel Office were fired following an FBI investigation and a KPMG Peat Marwick review, which found the records to be so sparse that an audit was impossible. The Clinton administration had heard concerns about improprieties, kickbacks, and the media's failure to investigate because of favours accorded to them. "Congress would later discover that in October 1988, a whistleblower within the Travel Office had alleged financial improprieties; the Reagan White House Counsel looked into the claim but took no action."[170]

Meanwhile, Republicans claimed that the Clintons were only trying to bring their own friends into the Travel Office, and Hillary came under scrutiny for playing a central role in the firings. After much controversy, the employees were offered other positions. After seven-and-a-half years, Travelgate concluded with no charges against Hillary Clinton.[171]

I am not sure why this was even an issue when it appears to be within the scope of the president's authority to hire and fire the White House Travel Office staff.

Vince Foster Suicide

Vince Foster, Deputy White House Counsel, was found dead on July 20, 1993 and became part of the investigation into the Whitewater scandal. According to *Wikipedia*, police determined the death to be a suicide, and it was disclosed by the family that he suffered from depression and had sought treatment the day before the incident.[172] Even so, *Newsweek* reported speculation from right-wing newsletters and media that the death was a homicide, which possibly involved the Clintons.[173] Both Robert Fiske and Kenneth Starr investigated the allegations of possible homicide and concluded there was no evidence to support the theory.[174]

What is even more egregious is Donald Trump's continued perpetuation of the myth. During an interview with the *Washington Post*, Trump called the circumstances of Foster's death "very fishy" and stated, "He knew everything that was going on, and then all of a sudden he committed suicide."[175] This is a perfect example of how Trump has created 'fake news' to discredit his opponents.

Lewinsky Scandal

Monica Lewinsky was an intern in the White House whose relationship with President Bill Clinton resulted in a scandal that imperilled his presidency. After fourteen years of Republican attempts to discredit Clinton, this was the only investigation that almost resulted in Bill Clinton's impeachment. It was not the relationship that jeopardized his presidency, but that he lied about it under oath.

My original position had been that this was a witch-hunt and a bogus allegation. It is shameful to engage in extramarital affairs, but what did that have to do with Clinton performing his role as president? The one compelling point raised by Bill Clinton's critics was that some of his relationships, including that with Lewinsky, involved paid government staff. Sexual harassment in the workplace, or sexual involvement with a subordinate, is unacceptable. Lying in a deposition is also unacceptable.

It was fair to hold Bill Clinton accountable for his actions, and he paid the price. According to *Wikipedia*, he was fined by the judge in the Paula Jones case, lost his license to practice law in Arkansas for five years, and later lost his license from the United States Supreme Court, in addition to other sanctions and the impeachment process.[176] Declaring the crimes of obstruction of justice and perjury impeachable offenses, the Republican-controlled House of Representatives voted to issue Articles of Impeachment followed by a twenty-one-day trial in the senate. All the Democrats voted for acquittal. Ten Republicans voted for acquittal on the perjury charges, while five voted for acquittal on the obstruction of justice. President Clinton was therefore acquitted and remained in office.[177]

What was so outrageous, in my mind, was the way the investigation was handled and the self-righteousness and hypocrisy of those hurling the accusations. Dan Rosenheck, writer for the *Harvard Crimson*, related an event in which Larry Flynt, publisher of *Hustler* magazine, offered $1 million for compromising information on Republicans, "seeking to expose Clinton's tormentors as hypocrites."[178] According to Rosenheck, Flynt obtained information that revealed Representative Bob Livingston, "a chief Clinton foe and fervent pro-lifer," had "paid for an ex-wife's abortion."[179] When the *New York Times* phoned to ask for Flynt's response to Livingston calling him a "bottom-feeder," he replied, "Yeah, that's right, but look what I found when I got there."[180]

Despite all this, Bill Clinton was not running for president in 2016; Hillary Clinton was. Unable to leave well enough alone, Hillary's detractors accused her of victimizing her husband's accusers and being a hypocrite regarding her political position on combating sexual harassment and assault.

Breitbart pronounced that "Donald Trump was echoing the words of Bill Clinton's sexual assault accusers when he slammed Hillary Clinton as an 'unbelievably nasty, mean enabler' who 'destroyed' the lives of her husband's mistresses and alleged victims."[181] Again, Trump viciously and without substantiation made allegations to discredit his opponents and put them on the defensive. In doing so, Trump also deflected attention away from his own behaviour.

Filegate

According to *Wikipedia*, in June 1996, there were allegations of unauthorized access to security-clearance documents by the Office of Personnel Management. These documents concerned several hundred individuals, including White House employees from previous Republican administrations.[182] "Allegations were made that senior White House figures, including First Lady Hillary Clinton, may have requested and read the files for political purposes."[183] In 1998, Independent Counsel Kenneth Starr exonerated President Bill Clinton and First Lady Hillary Rodham Clinton of any involvement in the matter.

In 2000, Independent Counsel Robert Ray issued his final report on Filegate, stating that there was no credible evidence of any criminal activity by any individual in the matter and no credible "evidence that senior White House figures or the First Lady had requested the files or had acted improperly or testified improperly regarding Livingstone's hiring."[184]

A separate lawsuit on the matter brought by Judicial Watch, a conservative watchdog group, lingered on for years and was dismissed by a federal judge in 2010.[185]

According to *Parents Advocare*, after fourteen years of depositions and litigations, a judge's ruling found no intentional misconduct: "This Court is left to conclude that with this lawsuit, to quote Gertrude Stein, 'there's no there there.'"[186] "In the legal aftermath, *Swidler & Berlin v. United States* became an important Supreme Court decision. The length, expense, and results of Travelgate and the other investigations grouped under the Whitewater umbrella turned much of the public against the Independent Counsel mechanism. As such, the Independent Counsel law expired in 1999, with critics saying it cost too much with too few results; even Kenneth Starr favored the law's demise."[187]

Finally, the *Boston Globe* noted that in May 2016, Kenneth Starr expressed "regret... that so much of Mr. Clinton's legacy remained viewed through the lens of what Mr. Starr demurely termed 'the unpleasantness.'"[188] He further described Bill Clinton as "the most gifted politician of the baby boom generation… he genuinely cared."[189] Some of Starr's associates expressed regret over the amount of time spent on this, rather than the growing threat of Osama bin Laden.[190]

Shortly after making the above statement, Starr resigned as chancellor of Baylor University on June 22, 2016, amid a sexual assault scandal that involved student athletes, because the administration led by Starr "failed to sufficiently investigate multiple allegations of sexual assaults against students, especially by football players."[191]

It's interesting how personal experience gives us a different perspective on things. I felt at the time that Starr was on an obsessive 'fishing investigation' to find anything to discredit the Clintons. His role became that of a vigilante rather than an investigator. I give him credit for his reconsideration.

Benghazi

PolitiFact reported that "Clinton was secretary of state when Islamic extremists attacked a US diplomatic mission and a CIA compound in Benghazi, Libya, on September 11, 2012. US Ambassador to Libya Chris Stevens and three other Americans died in the barrage."[192] Clinton conducted a review, which she was legally required to do, that found no fault with the State Department. However, it did acknowledge "systematic failures and leadership and management deficiencies" that left the embassy vulnerable, resulting in four resignations within the department. There were seven congressional probes over a period of three years examining the response, intelligence reports, and security of the US facilities, most of which were Republican-led.[193]

In the seventh report, The House Permanent Select Committee on Intelligence released its findings after a two-year investigation in 2014, "exonerating the Obama administration of wrongdoing in its response to the attack. The report found evidence of contradicting intelligence among government officials and concluded officials did not intentionally mislead the public with information in the days following the attack."[194] An eighth investigation by The House Select Committee on Benghazi is ongoing. Democrats have expressed concern about their lack of progress.[195]

Three Republicans, two congressmen and an ex-Benghazi Committee staffer, have admitted that the primary goal of the investigations was to tarnish Hillary Clinton and damage her poll numbers.[196]

There was some credibility fallout for Hillary during the Benghazi investigations. Some of the family members asserted that Hillary lied and told them a video was responsible for the loss of their loved ones. According to Bill Adair and Lauren Carroll from *PolitiFact*, "There was initial confusion, and conflicting intelligence and public statements, about whether the Benghazi attack was part of protests about a video mocking Islam and depicting the prophet Mohammed. The video sparked demonstrations around the Middle East, including one at the

US embassy in Cairo, Egypt, on the same day as Benghazi."[197] Other families did not recollect any mention of the video. Clinton denied talking about the video, though she did mention it days later in a statement not related to Benghazi. This was a highly emotional situation for everyone, and memories could have been fuzzy. Hillary did not make any comments about the families other than to say that she did not mention the video.

Personal Email Server

I have only seen updates and panel discussions on the email server. I have never seen a comprehensive summary with background information and an analysis in the media. After researching several sources, this is my summary and understanding of the issue.

During the 2016 election campaign and the Benghazi investigations, it was discovered that Hillary Clinton was using a private email server for both personal and State Department email correspondence. There was some concern that this practice contravened protocols as well as federal laws governing recordkeeping. Clinton contended that she was in compliance with the laws, and that former Secretaries of State used personal email accounts, but not through their own personal servers.[198]

In July 2015, the government investigators for the Benghazi incident found emails that were designated confidential and referred the matter to the FBI for investigation. Hillary contended that she did not send any emails that were marked confidential. The FBI report did not recommend criminal charges but did convey that her use of a personal email server was "extremely careless."[199] The FBI noted that only a few of the 30,000 emails had confidential markings when they were sent. Over 30,000 emails were released, and approximately 2,000 had since been classified confidential.

Former FBI Director James Comey identified that two emails had a small 'c' marking in their body, designating them as confidential, but he "did not find evidence sufficient to establish that she knew she was sending classified information beyond a reasonable doubt to meet the intent standard."[200] The confidential documents were not properly marked.[201] The problem became compounded when 30,000 emails were deleted on the basis that they were personal, leaving an opening for critics to accuse her of a cover-up. The fact that these emails were missing was covered in the FBI investigation.

While Colin Powell used a personal email as secretary of state, he did not have a personal server, and the rules changed in 2009 and were more detailed during Hillary's time as secretary.[202] Colin Powell also spoke to the problem of having an antiquated system that he modernized during his tenure.[203] In reviewing Powell's emails, the FBI report "concluded that twelve emails [contained] 'national security information classified at the Secret or Confidential levels.' Additionally, it was determined none of the emails contained intelligence information, meaning it was classified for other reasons." Powell disputed these claims.[204]

The *New York Times* reported that during Hillary's deposition with the FBI, she claimed that Colin Powell used a personal email account and recommended that she do the same.[205]

In her article, Chozick related a story from Joe Conason, a journalist writing a book about Bill Clinton, who provided the following account of a dinner at former Secretary of State Madeleine Albright's home: "Toward the end of the evening, over dessert, Albright asked all of the former secretaries to offer one salient bit of counsel to the nation's next top diplomat… Powell told her to use her own email, as he had done, except for classified communications, which he had sent and received via a State Department computer… [s]aying that his use of personal email had been transformative for the department."[206] Powell "thus confirmed a decision [Clinton] had made months earlier — to keep her personal account and use it for most messages."[207]

Colin Powell does not recall the dinner at Albright's home. On September 7, 2016, emails between Colin Powell and Hillary were released that revealed Powell's advice to Hillary.[208]

While the FBI investigation speculated that Hillary's personal email server could have been hacked, there has been no concrete evidence to support that. However, had she used the government's server, she most certainly would have been hacked. According to the *New York Times*, "Russian intruders were thoroughly inside that system for years—since at least 2007—before the State Department shut its system down several times to perform a digital exorcism in late 2014, nearly two years after Mrs. Clinton left office."[209]

Was the GOP accusing Powell of being a threat to national security? No, and it would have been ridiculous to do so. While the GOP claimed that establishing what is confidential should be obvious, it wasn't. The *Huffington Post* provided an excellent article, a contribution by Jeffrey Fields,[210] on confidential information in relation to Hillary's emails and pointed out that even "reasonable people can disagree about the relative sensitivity of particular information."[211] Additionally, how many of these documents were marked confidential after the fact? At the very least, I think we can say that what is confidential is not obvious unless clearly marked in the headers. While some may say it is splitting hairs, Hillary clearly stated she did not send information that was marked confidential in a header. In that case, she was telling the truth to the public, and she did not send material clearly marked confidential. For reporters and the GOP to call it a lie was misleading to the public. Debating it *ad nauseam* did not contribute to the issue beyond the investigation.

Given the information about the dinner party and the correspondence with Powell, it is a fact that Hillary sought his advice. He used a personal email account, whereas she used a personal server. She used an entirely different server for documents and a tent[212] when she was on foreign soil. Hillary's explanation that she used a personal email account on the advice of Colin Powell is understandable and not dishonest. That he would be upset after having been dragged into it because his use of personal email was different (in that Hillary used a personal server) is also understandable. But how did any of this change the issue?

While Hillary had expressed regret about the handling of the email server in the past, in August 2016, she took full accountability. "I have been asked many, many questions in the past year about emails, and what I have learned is that when I try to explain what happened, it can sound like I am trying to excuse what I did," Clinton said. "And there are no excuses. I want people to know that the decision to have a single account was mine. I take responsibility for it. I apologize for it."[213] Hillary sometimes continued to get defensive when questioned about the email server, and this continued to make her appear as if she was trying to excuse it. No one could blame her for feeling frustrated.

Clearly, her transgressions did not warrant charges for breaching national security and the need to "lock her up" that was chanted regularly by Trump supporters. For many Republicans, it was not enough for Hillary Clinton to be defeated at the polls in November; they wanted to see her imprisoned—or worse. Michael Folk, the Republican West Virginia delegate, sent the following tweet to Hillary: "You should be tried for treason, murder and crimes against the U.S. Constitution… then hung on the Mall in Washington, D.C."[214] For months, Republican leaders suggested that Clinton would be indicted, despite legal experts' consensual view that a prosecution was unlikely. According to the *Atlantic*, Republicans were furious when Comey announced that Hillary would not be indicted.[215] The email server may not have been a prudent decision, but suggestions that she threatened national security and that she be locked up were hyperbolic at the least.

This is but one more example that Republicans do not accept results of investigations, even when Republican-led, if the results do not fit their agenda: "Frustrated by the FBI's decision not to indict Hillary Clinton, congressional Republicans were pressing the agency to launch a new investigation into whether the Democratic presidential candidate lied to Congress during her testimony on the deadly attacks in Benghazi, Libya… A group of Republicans [*sic*] senators has introduced legislation to strip Clinton of her security clearance."[216]

House Democratic Leader Nancy Pelosi summed this up nicely, "So let's get this straight: This is going to be an investigation of the decision that is an investigation of the emails that was part of the investigation of Benghazi," she told reporters. "So we had an investigation of the investigation of the investigation. How long can this go on?"[217]

Despite Hillary's apology, the media continued to cover the controversy as an issue of transparency and national security. If this was such an irredeemable act, why did so many lead Republicans and generals publicly support her? These people had expertise, and many of them had worked with her and were staunch Republicans. If they perceived her as a security risk or as untrustworthy, why would they endorse her rather than support Trump?

A review of two websites identified at least eighty Republican leaders who committed their support to Hillary. One was Michael J. Morell, the acting director and deputy director of the Central Intelligence Agency from 2010 to 2013. He said, "Mrs. Clinton is highly qualified to be commander in chief. I trust she will deliver on the most important duty of a president — keeping our nation safe."[218] When asked who is the largest threat to national security, former CIA Director Michael Hayden responded, "Donald Trump."[219] Former Connecticut Rep. Chris Shay said, "Clinton, the Democratic candidate for president, will be getting my vote, not reluctantly, but with a strong conviction that she will be a good president."[220] Ambassador Robert Blackwill, who advised both Bushes on national security, also supported her.[221] A further 110 generals and admirals endorsed her as well.[222] These are individuals who would only ever vote democrat under the direst circumstances.

Hillary admitted she made a mistake. The media used this as leverage to question why she should not be disqualified from the presidency because she shared sensitive material, including information about drone strikes. She provided details regarding how confidential material should be marked and explained how she dealt with classified material. The emails about drone strikes did not include discussions about the covert actions in process. Since these emails were supposedly confidential, I think it is extraordinary that most of them can now be released to the public.

Hillary was accused of being defensive because she explained her actions. During the *Commander-In-Chief Forum,* host Matt Lauer was aggressive in pursuing this issue with Hillary, continually trying to cut her off from giving a complete answer. This level of aggression was not evident in Lauer's interview with Trump, in which Trump provided misinformation, proposed policies that were not legal, or posed a threat to national security.

Was it legitimate to investigate this? Yes. Was it legitimate that she be held accountable? Yes. Did she apologize? Yes. And it is only when one can acknowledge a problem that one can learn from it. Would she do it again? She has said that she would not, and I am confident of that. In a response to some FBI agents saying that she should have been prosecuted, Comey sent out a memo to FBI staff on September 2, 2016, reaffirming his original position and stating that it was "not a cliff-hanger" and that, "despite all the chest beating by people no longer in government, there really wasn't a prosecutable case."[223] He added that "[t]hose suggesting that we are 'political' or part of some 'fix' either don't know us, or they are full of baloney (and maybe some of both)."[224]

The Trump campaign and the media continued to fan the flames on this, magnifying the issue unnecessarily with conspiracy theories about how many devices and emails were missing, which had already been investigated in the FBI report. Further discussion and "leaks" have not added anything of import not already investigated. It was a ruse that unnecessarily heightened public anxiety, misinforming them by not putting it into context, and preventing discussion of the real issues that the media and Trump were avoiding.

Clinton Charitable Foundation

The Clinton Charitable Foundation was established in 2001 by former president Bill Clinton with the goal to "unlock human potential... through the power of creative collaboration... and to transform lives and communities from what they are today to what they can be, tomorrow."[225] Chelsea Clinton, daughter of Bill and Hillary, is the vice chair of the foundation, while Bill Clinton is on the board. The Clintons do not receive a salary or reimbursement for personal expenses from the foundation. Donna E. Shalala is the president of the Clinton Foundation and has an impressive resume, including the Presidential Medal of Freedom, the nation's highest civilian award, presented by President Bush in 2008.[226]

The Clinton Foundation has a four-star rating from Charity Navigator, which is "a leading and respected organization that evaluates and rates charities, so donors can make informed decisions about contributions. The rating itself is a fixed algorithm, described in detail on the watchdog's website. It looks at the financial health of charities and their accountability and transparency. In the Clinton Foundation's case, it scored 94.74 out of 100. It was dinged on two minor issues, its donor privacy policy, and its process for determining the chief executive officer's salary."[227]

There is no question regarding the great work the foundation does. Even Mr. Trump's campaign manager, Kellyanne Conway, admitted that the foundation "does some good work" in an interview with MSNBC's Rachel Maddow. However, she maintained that the foundation was corrupt, and Trump said that it was "the most corrupt enterprise in political history."[228] If that were the case, why did he donate $100,000 to the foundation? Legitimate concerns were raised about the potential for conflict of interest. Emma Roller from the *New York Times* concluded, "The Clinton Foundation revelations — what we know of them so far — hinge on appearances. There is (so far) no smoking gun email, no explicit evidence of pay-to-play or coordination between the State Department and the foundation."[229]

It is common for former presidents to become involved in charity work and foundations. Unfortunately for Bill Clinton, his wife was running for president, and even if there were no pay-for-play, even the mere perception was unacceptable. It is a global charity and therefore fundraises on a worldwide basis. While this is normally not an issue for a charity, it posed questions about the motives of those donating and risks for potential pay-for-play when Hillary was running for president.

The issues most often raised with respect to Hillary's past performance regarding policy include her support of the war in Iraq (to be dealt with in a later chapter), her stance on the Violent Crime Control and Law Enforcement Act of 1994, and her support of the North American Free Trade Agreement.

Violent Crime Control and Law Enforcement Act of 1994

The Violent Crime Control and Law Enforcement Act was signed into law by President Bill Clinton in 1994. It implemented the 'three strikes' mandatory life sentence for repeat offenders, included an expansion of death penalty-eligible offences, and ended funding for college education of prisoners. In addition, "President Clinton championed a 'one strike, you're out' policy for evicting public housing tenants if they or their guests were involved in any criminal activity, causing a jump in evictions, and making it more difficult for former inmates to find housing."[230] While it was intended to produce preventative programmes, the measures were more punitive than rehabilitative.[231]

The legislation has been blamed for the increased prison population and disproportionate sentencing of African-Americans. The *Bureau of Justice Statistics* cited that 37 percent of the 1.5 million men in state and federal prisons in 2013 were black, more than twice the percentage of their share of the population.[232]

Some of the growth had to do with the Violent Crime Control and Law Enforcement Act, but there were other contributing factors. Inmate populations had been increasing since the 1980s. This was a federal bill, and most of the growth had taken place in state systems.

Hillary Clinton, as First Lady, had no official role in voting for or signing the 1994 crime bill, but she did support the policy. The former president [Bill Clinton] seemed to regret the bill's passage: "I signed a bill that made the problem worse."[233]

In a 1996 speech in support of the crime bill, Hillary Clinton used the term 'superpredators' while discussing black youth, and while she was clearly talking about a narrow band of people, the remark was insensitive, particularly considering the fear of crime in those days. That was twenty years ago. On being asked about it recently, she stated, "In that speech, I was talking about the impact violent crime and vicious drug cartels were having on communities across the country and the particular danger they posed to children and families. Looking back, I shouldn't have used those words, and I wouldn't use them today."[234] During the campaign, Clinton committed to making changes in the justice system to avoid creating another "incarceration generation," promising to make the Fair Sentencing Act retroactive and to reduce the mandatory sentences for non-violent drug crimes.[235]

NAFTA

"The North American Free Trade Agreement (NAFTA) sets the rules of trade and investment between Canada, the United States, and Mexico. Since the agreement entered into force on January 1, 1994, NAFTA has systematically eliminated most tariff and non-tariff barriers to free trade and investment between the three NAFTA countries."[236]

NAFTA will be covered more closely in following chapters, but I will discuss it here in relation to Trump's contentions regarding Hillary's position. He said she "supported NAFTA, and she supported China's entrance into the World Trade Organization… She supported the job-killing trade deal with South Korea. She has supported the Trans-Pacific Partnership."[237]

While it is true that Hillary once supported NAFTA and TPP, she had been recommending changes for the NAFTA agreement for over a decade, and she backed away from TPP even though Obama supported it. There are mixed reviews as to the degree to which the South Korea deal impacted jobs.[238]

Donald Trump stated in a news conference, "Yesterday for the first time she said she wants to renegotiate trade agreements. First time, yesterday. Well, because of me."[239] That is clearly not true. As far back as her 2008 campaign, Hillary was calling for a renegotiation of NAFTA.

Another strategy used by Trump to discredit his opponents was name-calling. According to Soopermexican, a blogger and regular contributor to *Political Insider*, "The Donald has shown that he is a master of 'branding' his opponents with visually striking names that stick to them and damage their political standing."[240] The false statements perceived as fact by some voters were further compounded by Trump's name-calling, which reinforced them. These included "crooked,"[241] "evil,"[242] "heartless Hillary,"[243] "marshmallow,"[244] "bigot,"[245] "world class liar,"[246] "mosquito,"[247] "lowlife,"[248] "unfit,"[249] and "the devil."[250]

Jill Abramson, a political columnist for the *Guardian*, made the point that the perception of Hillary as untrustworthy and corrupt was not supported by her (Abramson's) investigations. Admittedly not a fan, she begrudgingly concluded that Hillary was "honest and trustworthy":

> For decades she's been portrayed as a Lady Macbeth involved in nefarious plots, branded as "a congenital liar" and accused of covering up her husband's misconduct, from Arkansas to Monica Lewinsky. Some of this is sexist caricature. Some is stoked by the "Hillary is a liar" videos that flood Facebook feeds. Some of it she brings on herself by insisting on a perimeter or "zone of privacy" that she protects too fiercely... As an editor I've launched investigations into her business dealings, her fundraising, her foundation and her marriage. As a reporter my stories stretch back to Whitewater. I'm not a favorite in Hillaryland. That makes what I want to say next surprising. Hillary Clinton is fundamentally honest and trustworthy.[251]

Abramson's comments articulate my change in attitude as I have researched for this book. It concerns me deeply that, had I relied primarily on television viewing, I would still hold the opinion that Hillary was the "lesser of two evils," as I am sure many of the American voters concluded. I considered myself well informed as a member of the public, but I was greatly mistaken. Even with all the research I had conducted, I had not thoroughly examined every aspect, and I gained new insights every day.

I had already started to suspect that gender bias might be in play. I think it is interesting to note that black males were legally given the right to vote in 1870, while women did not get the vote in the United States until 1920.[252] According to Michelle Cottle from the *Atlantic*, "Just as Barack Obama's election did not herald a shiny post-racial America, Clinton's would not deliver one of gender equality and enlightenment."[253] Barack Obama had been blamed for increased racial tension rather than improving race relations; so too would have Hillary when it came to gender bias. Cottle continued, "Just as Obama's presidency helped bring unresolved issues about race into the mainstream political discussion, a Hillary presidency would likely do the same for issues like equal pay and child care."[254]

However, there has been a major improvement in public acceptance of the idea of having a woman as president. According to the *Star*, "Americans claim, at least, that they are ready for a woman in charge: 92 per cent tell Gallup pollsters they would vote for a female president, up from 78 per cent in 1984 and 52 per cent when Clinton was a young feminist graduating from college in 1969."[255] Even so, "men still dominate the political arena as women hold approximately twenty percent of the seats in the US Congress and only six of the nation's fifty governors are female. There is [a] long way to go until gender parity is achieved in US politics."[256]

As it is with race, there will be pockets of the population that are resistant to a female president. Cottle stated, "There is a latent fear among men that their position in American society will decline further. So, while there are a lot of guys on board for equalizing gender power, there are also quite a few who aren't."[257] There are men who do not want to be perceived as sexist and those who have a view of 'benevolent sexism' in which men support women in traditional roles but not when they seek power or enter male-dominated fields.[258]

Gender might not have been the main contributing factor for how the public voted, but in an election this close, it was important, particularly in the swing states. "Ohio voters have never elected a female governor. They've never put a woman in the Senate. Columbus, the state's largest city… hasn't even elected a female mayor."[259]

Women are held to a different standard than men. In its research on the changing landscape for female candidates, the Barbara Lee Family Foundation reported that the 'likeability' factor is more likely to affect votes between women than between men. If two women were on the ballot, the more likeable candidate won nine out of ten elections. If two men were competing, likeability was not a significant factor.[260] Given that Trump and Hillary had equally unfavourable likability ratings, this could have been a problem for Clinton, particularly in the swing states.

The other dimension in which expectations are higher for women is ethical behaviour. Women are perceived as being more ethical than males, but "when knocked off that pedestal, they suffer disproportionately, according to the Barbara Lee Family Foundation's research. 'Voters expect women to be better.'"[261] This too was a problematic issue for Hillary.

Michelle Cottle concluded, "Sexism is more socially acceptable than racism."[262] A notable example of this is the experience of Julia Eileen Gillard, who served as the twenty-seventh prime minister of Australia from 2010 to 2013. Gillard said,

> In some ways, I think we put a burden on women in the face of gender attacks that doesn't necessarily play out in the face of racist attacks… Take the episode with the anti-tax protesters. I have made the point since that if Australia had an aboriginal Australian prime minister and the opposition leader went and stood in front of signs that said, 'Sack the black,' or inserted any of the dreadful words we have for aboriginal Australians, it would have been a career-ending moment. And if an indigenous Australian prime minister had complained about that, I don't think people would say, 'Oh, he is just playing the victim.' But that is what gets said about women who complain about sexism. There is an added kind of layer that women leaders are just supposed to take it on the chin and not complain about it.[263]

Gillard went on to state that while she thought the worst of the sexism would be experienced in her first few months, it grew worse as her time in office progressed. On one occasion while making a controversial announcement, she was subjected to sexist slurs and signs from the crowd, which the opposition party leader calculatingly used as a backdrop while the media was interviewing him. She later gave a speech taking him on over sexist behaviour and became a global celebrity.[264]

In the previous chapter, I provided an example of how John McCain responded differently than Trump when confronted by someone that referred to President Obama as an "Arab" who could not be trusted. McCain responded with dignity and disavowed the comment. Interestingly, on a different occasion, he did not rebuke a sexist comment. In another rally, John McCain was asked, "'How do we beat the b★★★★?' referring to Hillary Clinton. 'Can I get the translation?' McCain said, laughing. 'But that's an excellent question.'"[265] I found this disappointing.

According to *Jezebel*, one of the nastiest examples of sexism in the media was MSNBC host Chris Matthews's outrageous sexist mudslinging against Hillary in the 2008 campaign. In one interview he pinched her cheek, and he has called her names such as "She Devil," "Nurse Ratched," and "Madame Defarge", and described her as "witchy," "anti-male," and "uppity." He also mocked her laugh by asking, "What do you make of the cackle?"[266] I doubt he would still have a job if he had made similar comments about a person of colour, which would have been equally reprehensible. At least Fox News negotiated the exit of Roger Ailes, while Matthews still enjoys employment with MSNBC.

Sandy Garossino, correspondent from the *National Observer*, reported that Hillary had exceptionally high ratings coming into the presidential campaign. According to a Gallup poll, in 2015 "Americans admired Hillary Clinton more than any other woman in the world. More than Michelle Obama, Malala Yusafzai, or Oprah."[267] What happened? Admittedly, Hillary contributed to this in her handling of the email server issue and the optics of the charitable foundation. But her demise was occurring prior to these becoming major controversial issues. As I watched the media, I observed that Trump was getting far more coverage. Additionally, he received broader coverage of his rallies and other events than Hillary did.

I also noted that the media had been defending itself against Trump's constant accusations of media bias and the Republican refrain that the mainstream media was left-wing. They were not as vociferous in challenging the misrepresentations of Hillary. I noticed a trend. Every day, Trump came up with an outrageous comment, and the hosts got feedback from a Trump pundit who deflected with a derogatory comment about Hillary's emails or charitable foundation. The next day, it would be another issue with Trump and then a follow-up on Hillary's email server or charitable foundation. And so it went.

While not a particular fan of Hillary, I found myself bristling while watching interviews because of the tone of, and insinuations in, the lines of questioning. I was somewhat surprised that my observations were reaffirmed when I started to research information in places other than television coverage. The *Daily Good* reported on a study conducted by the *Harvard Kennedy School's Shorenstein Center on Media, Politics, and Public Policy* based on mainstream media, including CBS, FOX, the *Los Angeles Times*, NBC, the *New York Times*, *USA Today*, the *Wall Street Journal*, and the *Washington Post*. The study determined that Hillary received more negative coverage than other candidates: "Though 28 percent of Clinton's coverage was about issues, 84 percent of those stories were negative in tone. To compare, Trump only notched 12 percent on issues, with 43 percent negative in tone. That's much heavier accountability for the Democratic nominee in a race that received less than half the coverage of the Republican contest."[268] The trend of negativity did not reverse as the Democrats had hoped.

This study did not even mention CNN, but my observations were similar from viewing that station. Could it be that the mainstream media was trying to capture some of the viewership from Fox? Could it be that negative portrayals of Hillary got more viewership for the media? The *New York Times* reported that Trump garnered approximately $2 billion in free coverage while Hillary received less than half that amount.[269]

Then the media baited her by wanting to know why she did not do more interviews. Trump told endless lies about her, undermining her likeability and credibility. Often the media did not challenge these lies. Silence is assent. The media rewarded Trump with $2 billion in media coverage. This is what the media calls reporting, and this same media wants protection under the Constitution. I find this troubling.

While I agree that Hillary was sometimes her own worst enemy, I was also sympathetic to her plight. Donald Trump had the power advantage. Information is power, and withholding it is control. Is it not an imbalance of power if Trump had more information about Hillary and withheld information about himself? Were the concerns about Hillary not derived from information that had been disclosed in investigations, tax returns, and forty years of public service? Hillary was 'guilty' even though she had been found innocent.

What was the incentive for her to voluntarily put forward her speeches and other information? There was no reward for disclosure. Hillary continued to suffer from a public perception of untrustworthiness, sometimes based on allegations that had been proven false but persisted on social media. Her detractors used them, while Trump was rewarded for telling blatant lies and lacking transparency. Is the American public really interested in the truth or only reaffirmation of what they already believe?

There are few people, men or women, who could have withstood the persistent scrutiny and often-unfair allegations and accusations that Hillary was subjected to, yet she refused to give up. To quote Joseph Heller, "Just because you're paranoid doesn't mean they aren't after you."[270] She had good reason to be cautious as developments reconfirmed her concerns.

Hillary does have vulnerabilities, and supporters and detractors had legitimate concerns. She is flawed, and she makes mistakes. However, she is no more flawed than some of the best politicians. She is certainly better than most, especially given the scrutiny—we know more about her than we do most politicians.

According to *Politico*, Hillary had difficulty when asked about her "marquee achievement" in an interview with Diane Sawyer and again during a women's forum. In the latter she responded, "I see my role as secretary—in fact leadership in general in a democracy—as a relay race. You run the best race you can run, you hand off the baton. Some of what hasn't been finished may go on to be finished."[271] She appears to shy away from taking credit for self-promotion. In researching her many accomplishments over the years, including as First Lady, senator, and Secretary of State, I was impressed. The following are a few of the most notable:

- The Clintons have been active in the civil rights movement since the 1960s. When she graduated, Hillary worked for Mrs. Edelman,[272] who sent her to Alabama to help prove that the Nixon administration was not enforcing the legal ban on granting tax-exempt status to so-called segregation academies.[273]

- "Women's rights are human rights" is a phrase often used by the feminist movement. It is from a powerful speech given by Hillary as First Lady of the United States on September 5, 1995 at the United Nations Fourth World Conference on Women in Beijing.[274]

- As First Lady, she helped create and guide through Congress the Children's Health Insurance Program, a key program that brought healthcare coverage to millions of children.[275]

- Hillary sponsored the Lilly Ledbetter Pay Equity Act, which is now law, and changed the statute of limitations for equal pay lawsuits.[276]

- Consistent with her civil rights activism, while in the Senate she introduced the *Count Every Vote Act* of 2007 to combat a "history of intimidation"[277] that served as voter suppression for minorities.

She also worked on the HELP Committee and assisted in writing the *Pediatric Research Equity Act.* This law requires drug companies to study the effect of products in children. The act is responsible for changing the labeling of hundreds of drugs with important information about safety and dosing for children. It has improved the health of millions of children who take medications to treat diseases ranging from HIV to epilepsy to asthma.[278]

Politico reported that Bill Burton[279] defined Hillary's accomplishments as providing leadership of the State Department, during which time the US had a "50% increase in exports to China," doing aggressive work on climate (particularly at Copenhagen)," and "attempt[ing] to create and implement the toughest sanctions ever on Iran—helping to lead us [US] to the Iran agreement."[280] Clinton managed to obtain the cooperation of China, Russia, and the European Union to impose severe sanctions against Iran.[281]

Polls suggested that two-thirds of voters thought she had the experience needed to be president. And, according to Sandy Garossino from the *National Observer*, "despite being widely perceived as a puppet of Wall Street, her Senate voting record is rated mainstream progressive—more progressive than Joe Biden's or Barack Obama's. Nate Silver, a prominent statistician and writer, ranks her record in liberal terms as comparable to Elizabeth Warren, and not all that distant from Bernie Sanders."[282]

With this new information, I came to the following conclusions about Hillary:

- She has the capacity to accept loss and put aside personal grievances to work for the public good and to contribute, as she did after the election of Obama.

- She is willing to negotiate and amend her positions to accommodate inclusiveness, as she did with the Democratic platform by incorporating some of Bernie Sanders's positions.

- Although she tends to be defensive, she takes responsibility for her mistakes and tries to remedy them.

- She has been consistent in policy and action regarding her pillar values and policies on healthcare, children and education, racial justices, women's rights, gun violence protection, immigration reform, and criminal justice reform.

- While she is consistent on many of her basic beliefs and principles, she also demonstrated that she could evolve. Even though, as a senator, she opposed a Constitutional amendment banning gay marriage in 2004, she made a contradictory statement on the Senate floor: "I believe that marriage is not just a bond but a sacred bond between a man and a woman."[283] In a video in 2013 she announced her support for same-sex marriage.[284]

- Though she regrets her vote and expressed concerns on the floor of the Senate, her support of the Iraq War under Bush[285] demonstrated that she would be bipartisan when she believed it to be in the best interest of the country.

- She performs and produces. While she suffered from an image problem, her approval ratings as a senator and as Secretary of State were very strong.

The Republicans demonized Hillary for decades, and Trump reinforced these insinuations and allegations as facts. I finally came to the realization that my previous perception was based on years of misinformation. Hillary is no saint—but she is no demon either.

CHAPTER FOUR

In God We Trust: The Separation Of Church And State

Believe, or I detest thee; believe, or I will do thee all the harm I can. Monster, thou sharest not my religion, and therefore hast no religion; thou shalt be a thing of horror to thy neighbours, thy city, and thy province... The supposed right of intolerance is absurd and barbaric. It is the right of the tiger; nay, it is far worse, for tigers do but tear in order to have food, while we rend each other for paragraphs.[286]
—*Voltaire*

Religion became a central issue in the presidential campaign and was a factor in its outcome. Meghan Murphy-Gill, reporter for *US Catholic*, provided an example of the rhetoric used to influence voters. According to Murphy-Gill, Franklin Graham, son of evangelist Billy Graham, told evangelicals, "Hillary Clinton and her followers live in a non-Christian world, and her pro-abortion stance and the effect she'd have on the Supreme Court are more important than Trump's moral lapses."[287] Murphy-Gill added that Graham recommended evangelicals "view a vote for Trump as a vote against Hillary Clinton and matters such as Roe v. Wade."[288] The blurring of the line between church and state contributed to the civil unrest and the divide in American society, which were exacerbated during this last election.

There is a difference between 'freedom of religion' and the state favouring the tenets of a religious sect. Is there democracy if there is no separation of church and state?

Christian Today advised that in May 2016, both candidates had highly unfavourable ratings with evangelicals. Trump's was slightly more favourable than Hillary's.[289] Trump needed to engage these voters and claimed that he was religious. Evangelicals struggled with their choices. Other religious leaders came out against him, including Russell Moore, president of the Southern Baptist Convention's Ethics & Religious Liberty Commission. A professor of biblical studies at Boyce College, Denny Burk, blogged in March 2016 that Trump did not seem to understand the pro-life position and that his statements supporting torture presented a "real threat to our constitutional order." He also wrote, "I am not joking or being hyperbolic when I say that he is a Mussolini-in-waiting."[290] Erick Erickson, the conservative blogger behind the *Resurgent,* told Katie Couric, "If the Republican Party wants to go in [Trump's] direction, I guess I'm not a Republican anymore."[291]

Religious Rights

Trump stepped up the pro-Christian rhetoric and proclaimed, "I'm going to protect Christians, who are losing their power in American society."[292] One of his key proposals was to repeal the Johnson Amendment, which "absolutely prohibits" 501(c)(3) tax-exempt groups from "directly or indirectly participating in, or intervening in, any political campaign on behalf of (or in opposition to) any candidate for elective public office" or making "contributions to political campaign funds or public statements of position."[293]

Deacon Keith Fournier wrote an article supporting repeal of the legislation. He argued that the IRS contributed to secularism, an anti-religious approach. The IRS was the sole arbiter and presumed the assumption of guilt, censuring the church and restricting participation. Fournier articulated his position in the following statement:

> Using the Johnson Amendment, the IRS often seeks to censor Christian claims that the right to life, as well as natural marriage between one man and one woman, are both written in the "laws of nature and of nature's God," and so should be recognized in the civil law. They exclude such positions as "religious." They rule them out as unfit for public display and try to silence their advocates when they can.[294]

There is a difference between a non-sectarian state, which welcomes all religious expressions or none, and Secularism, an anti-religious approach. We are on a slippery slope when state laws and policies reflect the religious beliefs of specific groups. The First Amendment to the United States Constitution states that "Congress shall make no law respecting an establishment of religion, or prohibiting the free exercise thereof."[295] If the state cannot prescribe a religion or prohibit free exercise of religion, surely the state cannot protect the rights of Christians in preference to other religious beliefs.

Not all Christians subscribe to the tenets of pro-life and natural marriage between a man and a woman. According to *Gallup*, "Half of Americans consider themselves pro-choice on abortion, surpassing the 44% who identify as pro-life. This is the first time since 2008 that the pro-choice position has had a statistically significant lead in Americans' abortion views."[296]

The First Amendment prevents the government from establishing a religion, which means it cannot prescribe a religious belief. That includes Christianity and the evangelical right. There is nothing stopping Christians from holding and practicing these beliefs, but they should not be encoded in legislation, and thus deprive other religious or non-religious groups from practicing their beliefs.

What did Trump mean by "protecting religious values"? He proposed revoking the law that prohibits organizations receiving tax exemptions from political participation. This law does not prevent individual church members from participating. It does not prevent its leaders from preaching about abortion and other church beliefs or their members from practicing them.

The First Amendment does not provide for tax exemptions. Churches are not being deprived of their right to participate in the political process, and if it is that important to them, they can forgo their tax exemption. I am not sure why churches get a tax exemption instead of a deduction based on their charitable works. Not all revenue in the church is used for charitable purposes.

Although Trump questioned Hillary's religious background, she has acknowledged its importance to her throughout her public life. While Trump claimed that his church was Marble Collegiate Church, the "church [said] he [was] not an active member."[297] He was a friend of Norman Vincent Peale, former pastor of that church and a well-renowned "prosperity gospel preacher."[298] Trump's statements about his faith could have raised speculation about his sincerity. According to *CNN*, he does not ask God for forgiveness, he mistakenly referred to putting money in the "communion plate" rather than the collection plate, he referred to the communion sacraments as "my little wine" and "my little cracker," and he cited his favourite bible verse as "an eye for an eye."[299] There are many examples that challenge Trump's religious sincerity and whether his professions were genuine or for political expedience.

Catholicism dominated the beginning of John F. Kennedy's campaign. Americans were concerned that the pope would influence a Catholic president. Kennedy emphasized the necessity for separation of church and state, declaring that nothing would take precedence over the Constitution. This enraged Catholics, who accused him of "placing ambition over faith." This "spurred many non-Catholics to accuse of [*sic*] him of acquiescing to bigotry."[300] It's interesting that the GOP did not seem to have the same compunction as Kennedy.

Religious Terrorism

Trump and many Republicans criticized Obama for not using the term "Islamic terrorism," alleging that he did not recognize the problem for what it was.[301] I have examined religious terrorism and will provide an analysis in my subsequent comments. I will explain why I reject the notion that ISIS or similar groups are Islamist terrorists and how they have striking similarities to domestic terrorism, sometimes driven by extreme religious beliefs.

According to *Wikipedia*, Protestants, Confederates, and Democrats founded the Ku Klux Klan (when did the Republicans and Democrats switch sides?) after the Civil War to "re-establish Protestant Christian values in America by any means possible."[302] The Klan targeted black people, Jews, and Catholics. It was known for its white sheets, lynching, and tar and feathering. The modern Klan is also responsible for numerous 'terrorist acts,' including but not limited to the following:

- The murder of Michael Donald on March 21, 1981—the last recorded lynching by the KKK in the United States. His body was "hanged from a tree in the pattern of mob lynchings."[303] One attacker, Henry Hays, was convicted and put to death, while the other, James Knowles, was sentenced to life in prison. This was the first execution in Alabama since 1913 for a "white-on-black crime."[304] Hays was the only known KKK member to be executed "during the twentieth century for the murder of an African American."[305]

- While it is categorized as right-wing antigovernment extremism, Timothy McVeigh had deep ties to the Klan[306] and was responsible for the death of 168 people in the Oklahoma

City bombing in 1995 in retaliation for the government's raid in Waco involving a religious group, the Branch Davidians.[307]

- More recently, Frazier Glenn Cross, a former grand dragon of the Klan, was found guilty of shooting and killing three people near Kansas City at a Jewish community center and retirement home in 2014.[308]

The KKK has clearly perpetrated terrorist acts in the name of Christianity as evidenced above. Similarly, The Army of God promotes the use of violence against abortion clinics and the homosexual community and uses biblical justification to be critical of the US government for not upholding what it views as Christian values. "Most famously it was associated with bombings [sic] at the 1996 Atlanta Olympics, which killed one person and injured over a hundred others… In 1998, a member of the Army of God (James Kopp) shot and killed Dr. Barnett Slepian [a doctor who performed abortions]."[309]

Wikipedia provides a list of anti-abortion violence, and I counted no less than thirty-four incidents covering the period from 1982-2015.[310] It is impossible to know if any of these events were linked to the Army of God because "it is believed the group operates a basic terrorist cell system."[311] It is sometimes difficult to assign acts of violence to specific groups that are shrouded in secrecy. They limit interaction with one another; their bond lies in ideology. The next example cannot be attributed to a specific group, but it certainly fits the ideology.

According to the *Colorado Independent*, in November 2015, the Republican Study Committee of Colorado held a daylong hearing on Planned Parenthood, which included an analysis of a video released by the anti-abortion Center for Medical Progress. This video accused Planned Parenthood of trafficking in aborted fetus body parts.[312] *Click2Houston* advised that a grand jury cleared Planned Parenthood of breaking the law against selling fetal body parts and instead handed down indictments against two people accused of making the video and the related allegations, which were subsequently dismissed by a different grand jury.[313]

On November 27, 2015, following three weeks of committee hearings and wide publicity of the video, Robert Lewis Dear killed three people and injured nine others in the same Colorado Springs Planned Parenthood clinic featured in the abovementioned video. After a five-hour siege on the clinic, Dear was arrested and "told investigators 'no more baby parts'—an apparent reference to the video."[314]

On January 22, 1973, the Supreme Court in Roe v. Wade decided that "a woman's right to an abortion fell within the right to privacy (recognized in Griswold v. Connecticut) protected by the Fourteenth Amendment."[315] *Pew Research* reported that fifty-six percent of US adults said it should be legal in all or most cases, compared with 41% who said it should be illegal.[316]

How would Christians react if we were to refer to the Ku Klux Klan and other white supremacists as Christian terrorists? Most Christians would not describe Timothy McVeigh's actions as Christian terrorism. Similarly, calling ISIS Islamic terrorism is a misrepresentation of the religion. Trump claimed calling it ISIS instead of 'Islamic terrorism' was a failure to recognize the problem. This was a red herring. He also refused to acknowledge domestic terrorism, itself a great threat to American citizens.

I would not propose that the KKK, the Army of God, or others be called Christian terrorists for the same reason that I do not accept that ISIS is Islamist terrorism; each is a gross manipulation of the religion. To do so emboldens hate and retribution. We must stop stereotyping and start treating people as individuals.

The most chilling part of the story, in my view, was the reaction of some Republicans to the Robert Dear case after the Republican hearings made public, and gave credibility to a misleading and inaccurate video. Most were silent on the subject, while a small minority said, "there is no difference between the Planned Parenthood shooter and the organization."[317] The Douglas County GOP tweeted, "Abortionists and Planned Parenthood are Just Two Sides of the Same Coin."[318]

Abortion is a highly sensitive subject that goes to the core values of every individual. Notwithstanding the right to abortion, most Americans support it, and it is legal. That gives pro-life supporters the right to try to persuade others to their point of view. It does not give them the right to kill those who disagree, or to endorse such killings, which is what some Republicans did.

I am pro-choice, not pro-abortion. It is not my right to tell someone else what is right for them, especially in cases where the woman's life is at risk, the fetus has died (some religious hospitals will not conduct an abortion in these situations even if the woman's life is in danger), the woman was raped, or for whatever reason. It seems to me that some Republicans and religious groups agree to respect the voters' preferences, the Constitution, and the laws only when they support their agenda. How is Robert Dear any different from an ISIS member who uses religion to justify killing?

Islam

Muslims submit to the deity Allah (Arabic for God)—the same one that Christians worship. Islam is a faith; it is not a race. According to *Wikipedia*, Arabic countries have only 20% of the world's Muslims. Muslims are diverse, and the largest population is in Indonesia, followed by Pakistan and India. A 2010 Pew Research Center study "found more Muslims in the United Kingdom than in Lebanon and more in China than in Syria."[319]

According to *Al Islam*, it is frequently misquoted that the Koran says, 'Kill the infidel.' This is a manipulation of Islam. The verse actually reads, "And when the forbidden months have passed, kill the idolaters wherever you find them and take them prisoners, and beleaguer them, and lie in wait for them at every place of ambush. But if they repent and observe Prayer and pay the Zakat, then leave their way free. Surely, Allah is Most Forgiving, Merciful."[320] The word is idolaters, not infidels. The last part of the verse is usually omitted in the reference, and the historical context is missing. This relates to those tribes who continued hostilities against the Muslims even after they migrated. There is a comparable passage in the Holy Bible espousing violence: "But as for these enemies of mine, who did not want me to reign over them, bring them here and slaughter them before me."[321]

CNN aired a programme called *Why They Hate Us*, hosted by Fareed Zakaria, that I thought was particularly enlightening. The following is my summary of the most salient points. Radicals twist Islamic ideology; most are not devout believers and are relatively ignorant about the religion. They take sections of the Koran out of context and some of them will get a surprise, as they believe they will go to heaven with a promise of seventy-seven virgins for their martyrdom. This is a mistranslation; the literal translation is raisins, as in a lush harvest. Jihadist followers are frequently petty criminals, dropouts, unemployed, and drug users. Most never had anything to do with religious training and "latch onto radicalization to act out their alienation. It's easier to brainwash recruits who have no religious background."[322]

FactCheck reported that "Trump wrongly claimed that a Pew Research Center survey found that among the world's Muslims, '27 percent, could be 35 percent, would go to war' against the US." That would be 250–300 million Muslims.[323] In fact, there are, at most, 100,000 people fighting for jihadist causes in all Islamic terrorist groups worldwide. In 2014, ISIS killed 30,000 people worldwide, and the majority of victims were Muslims. ISIS hates the modern world, and they hate Muslims who embrace it even more. "ISIS is the product of broken politics and the stagnant economy of Muslim countries."[324] ISIS is the enemy of modern Islam, and we should embrace the followers of Islam as allies.

Trump promotes profiling. If Muslims are a heterogeneous group, then profiling is not helpful. Let me use an analogy. I was CEO of a mental health organization during the 1980s when AIDS and HIV became a public health problem. People were unaware of how HIV was contracted and discriminated against people because of it. Some of the nurses and support staff who worked for the organization were concerned about treating people diagnosed with AIDS or HIV. My response was that it was the undiagnosed that they had to be concerned about. At least with diagnosed individuals, the staff knew to take precautions. My point to them was that precautions should be taken at all times. Targeting and discriminating against people made them go underground. They did not want to disclose their health status for fear of discrimination. This indeed happened with some AIDS and HIV patients who did not want to present at clinics.

It appears that attraction to ISIS is more a community matter than a religious one. The *Guardian* reported that a July 2014 ICM poll suggested that more than one in four French youth between the ages of eighteen and twenty-four had a favourable or very favourable opinion of ISIS, although only 7–8% of France is Muslim. It's communal. More than three of every four who join ISIS from abroad do so with friends and family. Most are young and in transitional stages in life, like immigrants, students, those between jobs, and mates that have just left their native families. They join a "band of brothers (and sisters)" ready to sacrifice for significance.[325]

If we discriminate against the Muslims and promote hate and fear, will the Muslim community be supportive when we need their help to identify those among them who may pose a threat?

Considerable controversy followed a bombing in New York on September 19, 2016 when the mayor delayed calling it a terror attack until he had more details. Is terrorism being associated primarily with jihadist terrorism? If that incident was terrorism, then why was it called a hate crime when Dylan Storm Roof walked into a South Carolina church and fatally shot nine people as they attended Bible study class?[326] We must use the same language for the same kinds of incidents; otherwise, we are discriminating based on religion or race.

Trump insisted on referring to jihadist terrorism as 'Islamic extremism,' but the crimes of the KKK and those cited above were 'hate crimes.' Why not terrorism? As Chengu aptly stated, "The US government allows the Klan, unlike ISIS, to freely hold rallies in America, fundraise, and even appear on TV to promote their ideology. Recently Frank Ancona, a KKK leader, appeared on national television and threatened 'lethal force' against black protestors."[327] While I was unable to find any reaction from Trump on this statement, it is interesting to note that when asked by the *New York Times* as to the most dangerous places he had ever been, Trump cited Oakland and Ferguson. The article provided a list of the fifty most dangerous cities in the United States; neither Oakland nor Ferguson was on that list.[328] Was Trump implying that protesting systemic racism was the sole criterion for designating these cities as dangerous?

One of the concerns often expressed about Muslim countries is their treatment of women. Following the interview with the Khans, which I discussed previously, Trump made a comment about Mrs. Khan not speaking at the convention, suggesting that perhaps she was not allowed to because of her religion. She later explained that her silence was because she was too emotional about her son's death.

Let's examine the implication. Like Christianity, Islam has many sects, and while some may not respect women's rights, many do. Do not some Christians hold gender biases? Women cannot become priests in the Roman Catholic or Mormon churches. Some apostolic sects do not accept women in leadership roles.

According to *Egyptian Streets*, nine Islamic states have had women as leaders. They include Tansu Çiller, Prime Minister of Turkey from 1993-1996; Megawati Sukarnoputri, President of Indonesia from 2001-2004; Mame Madior Boye, Prime Minister of Senegal from 2001-2002; Atifete Jahjaga, President of Kosovo from 2011-present; Roza Otunbayeva, President of Kyrgyzstan from 2010-2011; Sheikh Hasina, Prime Minister of Bangladesh from 1996-2001 and 2009-present; Benazir Bhutto, Prime Minister of Pakistan from 1988-1990 and 1993-1996; Khaleda Zia, Prime Minister of Bangladesh from 1991-1996 and 2001-2006; and Ameenah Fakim, President of Mauritius from 2015-present.[329]

The United States has yet to elect a female president.

Islam 101 explains that Muslims also respect Jesus: "Allah took Jesus to heaven, where he awaits until the Day of Judgment when he will return to earth (3,55). Muslim traditions teach that Muhammad died not knowing if he would be judged worthy to enter paradise – where God has already placed Jesus. Muhammad is dead and buried in Saudi Arabia. Jesus is alive both with God in heaven (paradise) and in spirit with his followers on Earth."[330]

Groups such as the KKK are outlawed in Canada by the Criminal Code, which makes hate crimes an indictable offence. This includes anyone who advocates or promotes genocide, anyone who "by communicating statements in any public place, incites hatred against any identifiable group where such incitement is likely to lead to a breach of the peace… [and]

anyone who wilfully promotes hatred against an identifiable group other than in private conversation." Hate propaganda can also be seized.[331]

There have been several prosecutions in Canada for hate crimes. The following, detailed on *Stop Racism and Hate Canada*, are but a few examples: James Keegstra was convicted in 1984 for teaching anti-Semitism to his students. In 1985, Don Andrews, the leader of a white supremacist organization, was sentenced for producing a newsletter that "decried 'race-mixing' and denied the Holocaust."[332] Robert Reitmeier, a neo-Nazi skinhead, was sentenced to thirteen years for an unprovoked murder in 2011 and had his bid for a reduced sentence dismissed in 2016.[333]

Ernst Christof Friedrich Zündel lived in Canada for forty years but was never approved for Canadian citizenship. He was charged for publishing material that denied the Holocaust, and while found guilty by two juries, the Supreme Court determined that the section of the criminal code was unconstitutional.[334] Further attempts to charge Zündel for continuing hate crimes through the internet were foiled because the internet site was based in the United States and was not covered as a hate crime under US law, and the site was in the name of a US citizen.[335] The hate crime legislation in the United States is limited to bodily injury and does not recognize verbal or written communication of or distribution of hate propaganda.[336] In 2005, a Canadian federal court determined that Zündel was a threat to national security, and he was deported to Germany. He was tried and sentenced to five years in prison.[337]

Some of the rhetoric in the 2016 presidential campaign might well have been indictable in Canada and in the British Isles. In fact, *CNN* reported that Suzanne Kelly from Aberdeen, Scotland, who previously campaigned against the development of the Trump International Golf Links, "petitioned the government to ban Trump from entry to the British Isles on hate speech grounds."[338] She gathered over 5,740,000 signatures and it was debated in Parliament. While no decision was made, concerns were expressed about Trump's proposed travel ban on Muslims entering the United States and his comment that "parts of London were so radicalized that British police feared for their lives."[339] There is precedent for banning the entry of those holding views that are considered 'hate crimes.' "People who have been barred previously include Quran-burning US pastor Terry Jones, a Hamas lawmaker, and a former Ku Klux Klan leader."[340] As a result of Trump's offensive, hateful rhetoric, Trump was stripped of an honorary degree conferred on him five years ago by Scotland's Robert Gordon University due to "a number of statements that are wholly incompatible with the ethos and values of the university."[341] There are more severe consequences for this type of behaviour in other democratic countries.

"In God We Trust" has appeared on American currency since the late 1800s "because of the increased religious sentiment existing during the Civil War,"[342] and it was designated the national motto on July 30, 1956.[343] It replaced the former motto which was "E pluribus unum," Latin for "Out of many, one."[344] The current motto is not inclusive or respectful of religious freedom: people of certain ideologies such as Hinduism, Buddhism, and atheism, do not believe in a god, and spiritualists reject theism. Are these people not Americans? Some Christian sects consider abortion and homosexuality a sin, while other Christian sects do not hold these views. Laws prohibiting the free practice of religion to those who do not hold Christian beliefs are unconstitutional.

Islam is not our problem; terrorists are. They include members of the Ku Klux Klan, the Army of God, radicals, mass murderers, and yes, ISIS. They all have some common characteristics: they are disenfranchised, sometimes from discrimination and bullying; they feel hopeless and economically deprived; and they are angry with the status quo. Some are drug addicts, and some have a mental illness. They are distraught and feel they have nothing to lose, including their lives or the lives of others.

People have ways of exacting revenge for oppression, even when the persecutor of the oppression is completely unaware. I once heard a story that goes something like this: There was a cook on a cattle drive and the cowboys teased him mercilessly. One night around the campfire after a nice meal, they told him he had been a good sport and they were going to stop tormenting him. He responded, "Good, now I won't have to pee in the coffee anymore." If we persist in oppressing the disenfranchised, we may become our own victims, even without being aware of it.

In 2008, my husband planned a Mediterranean cruise followed by a week in Italy to celebrate our twenty-fifth anniversary. One of our stops on the cruise was Ephesus, Turkey. We docked in Kuşadasi, and I made my way to the market to buy pashminas for my mother and myself.

We had been informed that shopkeepers would negotiate the prices. It was suggested that when we agreed to a price, we not show that we were pleased, lest it appear to a shopkeeper's peers that he had made a poor deal, and thus embarrass him. Instead, it was common to offer them a trinket or gift. I offered a Canadian souvenir and the shopkeeper accepted, but only if I would join him and share some Turkish apple tea. We sat and chatted for about a half-hour and it was the most delightful shopping experience I have ever had.

I returned to work and was sharing my experience in Turkey with a psychology student whom I was supervising in my role as CEO of a mental health agency. He was Turkish, and I mentioned that I had no discomfort while I was in Turkey. He explained that unlike many other Muslim countries, Turkey had separation of church and state. David Boyajian of the *Dissident Voice* explains that "[s]ome Turks feel that their country is secular because the Diyanet's hegemony moderates Islam against extremist tendencies. There may be some truth to that."[345]

Yet, according to Boyajian, others have characterized Turkey's secularism as a myth because the government funds Sunni Islam, Sunni clergy are salaried civil servants, the Diyanet (the government body that represents and directs all Sunni Islam in Turkey) writes or controls the content for all the sermons for its clergy, the government funds the building of mosques, and there is persecution of persons of other religions. While secularism in Turkey may be a myth, Turks are concerned that the proposed secularism-free constitution will introduce Sharia law into their republic. Sadly, there is no doubt that Turkey is drifting away from any semblance of secularism.[346] I am not alone in the view that democracy is eroding in Turkey. As conveyed by reporter Harry Sterling in the *Vancouver Sun*, Turkey elected a dictator, Recep Tayyip Erdoğan, who revised their constitution. This gave Erdoğan additional power, which is dangerous in this now divided society, and "could further undermine the very democratic system and rule of law established by Kemal Ataturk a century ago."[347]

The relationship between religion and the erosion of democracy has been most clearly articulated by Thanassis Cambanis, a reporter with the *Boston Globe*: "Erdogan has shifted the balance of Turkey's republic away from secular nationalist pluralism toward majoritarian Islamism. The once-oppressed rural and religious have acquired new rights and in the process, have taken away some rights from the secular and urban."[348] There is a similar shift in America toward the religious right.

It occurs to me that Christian sects and members of the Jewish faith all worship the God of Abraham, and that Allah in the Islam faith is also the God of Abraham. In that case, why are we not celebrating what we have in common? Because each religion has its own tenets, which are often contradictory; some of these religions consider divorce, homosexuality, birth control, and abortion sins, while others do not. In some, women are religious leaders; in others it is not allowed. Some prohibit the consumption of alcohol, tea and coffee, pork and shellfish, and mixing dairy and meat; others prohibit blood transfusions and vaccinations. If you do not share a religion's distinct beliefs, followers may say that you are headed for Hell and damnation.

I was raised in a Christian sect that tended more to the grace perception of God, with a figurative interpretation of the Holy Bible rather than a vengeful, punitive perception that holds to literal interpretation of its teachings. Having read the Holy Bible at least twice, albeit many years ago, I am aware of its many contradictions and incongruities. One apparent contradiction is particularly relevant in today's political environment. In 2 John, Christians are told to reject those who do not share their beliefs: "If there come any unto you, and bring not this doctrine, receive him not into your house, neither bid him God speed. For he that biddeth him God speed is partaker of his evil deeds." On the other hand, in Matthew, Christians are instructed as follows: "Ye have heard that it hath been said, [t]hou shalt love thy neighbour, and hate thine enemy. But I say unto you, [l]ove your enemies, bless them that curse you, do good to them that hate you, and pray for them which despitefully use you, and persecute you." The Trump administration seems to ascribe only to the former while I accept the latter, believing only in this way can we achieve peace.

I confess that in more recent years, I have become disillusioned with the institution of formalized religion. I am not negating the genuine devotion of millions of followers in each religion, but as I have already stated, they cannot all be right. I do believe that there were benevolent reasons for many of the rules to protect the citizens based on the period and the environment in which they were established. For example, to mix dairy and meat prior to refrigeration could be deadly. Rules such as do not kill, steal, or lie were for the public good and not limited to Christianity. Is it any wonder that snakes are prominent in the Australian aboriginal faith when Australia has the eight most poisonous snakes in the world?

On the other hand, religious institutions have had insidious aspects: controlling the masses; promoting male supremacy; preying on the vulnerable, both financially and sexually; using the church for personal gain, covering up corruption and abuses; rationalizing wars, and seeking power and wealth. Atheists can have a spiritual and moral fibre. There are many who ascribe to not; lying, killing, committing adultery, and stealing. Is it not commendable when they make choices to do the right thing in absence of a belief that they will have the benefit of everlasting life, or the threat of going to hell? Both are very powerful motivators.

Having had an editor for this manuscript, I am acutely aware that the misplacement of a period or comma, or the wrong connotation of a word, can radically change the intended meaning of the written word. How many times has the Holy Bible been translated, and by whom? Who made the decision as to what writings became part of the scriptures and which did not? That did not mean that it was not a book of inspiration and moral guidance, but how could I take it literally?

While I am pro-choice, I highly regard those who are pro-life, especially when they are faced with circumstances where they must make a choice and choose to live by their values. Men will never have to make those choices, but it is men, often of the church, who have made these rules. Trump promised to restore Christian religious rights, reaffirming the view that the religious right has been suppressed. Separation of church and state did not prevent Christians from practicing their beliefs. In fact, Christians enjoy a public expression unlike any other religion, especially during holidays such as Christmas and Easter. Religious displays are only prohibited in government buildings. There was nothing to stop Christians from saying Merry Christmas, expressing their faith, choosing not to have an abortion, or not practicing homosexuality.

It appears to me that the real agenda of the religious right is to encode their beliefs into legislation to make abortion, homosexuality and transgender identity illegal, imposing their beliefs on the rest of America. They do this, even though other Christian sects, religions and atheists do not share these same views. Some fundamentalists use the scripture, not only to justify their position and legalize their beliefs, but also to discriminate and even persecute those not conforming to their beliefs. I conform to Jesus' challenge to citizens who were about to stone an adulterer, "Let him who is without sin cast the first stone."[349] I respect a person's right to believe what they want to believe and to practice it, until it infringes on my right to do the same.

It occurs to me that for thousands of years, though many considered adultery and prostitution sins, the acts themselves involve both men and women, and yet only the women were punished. I cannot reconcile this as God's command. Nor can I reconcile that God would want a woman to stay in an abusive marriage, or if her life was at risk, though many consider divorce a sin.

Evidence of the intention to encode the religious right's views into law is Trump and the GOP's efforts to fill an unprecedented number of vacated judge positions in the Federal courts and Supreme Court with conservative judges who support prolife, are anti-gay, and anti-transgender. It was not only the vacant Supreme Court position that Republicans obstructed during Obama's last year in office, there are well over 100 vacant federal court positions. *Reuters* reported that one of Trump's candidates was disqualified because he posted a blog in support of the KKK and failed to disclose that his "wife works in the White House Counsel's office, which oversees judicial nominations."[350] According to CNN, another candidate was disqualified because he referred to transgender children as being part of "Satan's plans."[351] Even though they were not confirmed, can there be any doubt as to Trump's agenda? These are lifetime appointments and will shape the judiciary for generations to come.

The conflict between religions stems from fear of the enforcement of contrary religious tenets, thus threatening the practice of one's own religious beliefs. While I am averse to living under Sharia law, I am equally averse to living under the law of the Christian right. I want freedom of religion. If prolife is such a major principle for these fundamentalist Christians, why is Alabama one of the few states that still has corporal punishment? How do Christians reconcile that, especially when so many have been wrongfully executed?

The forefathers were brilliant in writing the First Amendment. They understood that to have peace, freedom of religion, and separation of church and state were paramount. There is no guarantee that conservative judges will overturn the Supreme Court decisions. How is the Republican agenda consistent with the constitution?

The evangelical right has enjoyed considerable influence in this presidential campaign. Initially, I was surprised at the overwhelming support for Trump in the Christian community, particularly from evangelicals. While his position against abortion and promise to "protect Christian rights" may have been incentives, it is astonishing that Christians could ignore other behaviours and beliefs that were so contradictory to Christian values. Franklin Graham claimed that Hillary's stance on abortion was far more dangerous than Trump's hypocrisy. I disagree.

Paul Prather, a religious columnist, illuminated this in an article about the research findings of Matthew MacWilliams, a Ph.D. candidate in political science at the University of Massachusetts. MacWilliams asserted that there had always been a "split within our faith [Christianity] between disciples who focus on authority and those who focus on freedom; between those driven by fear, and those propelled by hope and joy."[352]

MacWilliams described those tending toward authority (Law people) as driven by fear, claiming that they thrive on order and "God's authority, the Bible's authority, church leaders' authority, men's authority, [and] civil authority."[353] In contrast, "Grace people serve a God who is unimaginably merciful, infinitely liberating, and surprisingly understanding of every kind of birdbrain."[354]

Prather contended that everything works best in balance; Law people need Grace people and vice versa. In their fear, voters sought an illusion of security and chose authoritarianism, which superseded all other values.

While a man of deep religious beliefs, Thomas Jefferson was a staunch believer in separation of church and state and wrote a letter to that effect now referred to as the 'Wall of Separation Letter.'[355] Just as in Turkey, where the government supports Islam at the expense of other religions, the United States supports evangelicals at the expense of other religions. It is interesting that "In God We Trust" was included on coinage "because of the increased religious sentiment existing during the Civil War," as noted earlier in this chapter.[356] Religion is being used to polarize America and to control the agenda, not to respect 'freedom of religion' and unify its people.

CHAPTER FIVE

Pride & Prejudice

Prejudice is a burden that confuses the past, threatens the future and renders the present inaccessible.[357]
—*Maya Angelou*

Patriotism was exploited for its emotional influence during the presidential campaign, particularly as it relates to the Constitution. Race became a primary issue, played out through each candidate's position regarding terrorist and violent incidents in the United States. I will examine patriotism as it relates to democracy and a troubling connection with racism.

Wikipedia defines the 'Ugly American' as "a pejorative term used to refer to perceptions of loud, arrogant, demeaning, thoughtless, ignorant, and ethnocentric behavior of American citizens mainly abroad, but also at home."[358] The 'ugly American' was particularly evident in the Trump rallies. I have sometimes admired and envied American patriotism and wished Canadians expressed more national pride. However, the patriotism that I witnessed while viewing the coverage of Trump rallies was insidious and not to be envied. Trump surrounded himself with American flags, and he criticized the Democrats for not having more at their convention, insinuating a lack of national pride. Patriotism at Trump rallies was used to engender an emotional connection while making promises to "lock her up" and "build that wall," which became a common refrain chanted by his supporters. The crowd chanted "USA" with fists in the air, while Lee Greenwood's *Proud to Be an American* streamed into the venue. Trump played to the crowd and nurtured the populist angst while assuring voters that he and he alone could "Make America Great Again." Trump committed to protecting the Constitution while he made statements and exhibited behaviours that flew in the face of the Constitution.

Indeed, the Second Amendment, which supports the right to bear arms, may be the only section of the Constitution that Trump genuinely endorses, while falsely claiming that Hillary would eradicate it. The First Amendment allows for freedom of the press, but Donald Trump has a complete disdain for the media, constantly accusing it of bias and lying about him, often threatening to sue. His supporters were abusive toward reporters at rallies, who were regularly harassed. In at least one case, a woman attacked a reporter, hitting him with her Trump sign.

Katy Tur, from MSNBC, became a preferred target of Trump's. Unhappy with her coverage of him, Trump demanded an apology. When she did not apologize, he started tweeting, "@KatyTurNBC & @DebSopan should be fired for dishonest reporting."[359] He called her out at rallies, making the crowd turn on her. During a rally, a Trump supporter yelled, "Katy Tur is a whore!"[360] He pledged that when he became president, he would change the libel laws to make it easier to sue the media.[361]

While Trump believes in and exercises his right to free speech—in my view, to the point of defamation—he oppresses the free speech of others whenever he perceives that they have been negative toward him. He then threatens them with lawsuits or tries to destroy them. The *Washington Post* advised that Trump threatened to sue Ted Cruz after Cruz aired a commercial that included interview footage of Trump supporting abortion.[362] A former Miss USA contestant was sued by Trump for having criticized him and the USA pageant on her Facebook page. Trump won a $5 million judgment because her lawyer failed to appear for the arbitration. She eventually sued the lawyer and never had to pay Trump out of her own pocket, but the case tied up her life in a legal battle for three years.[363] He sued author Timothy L. O'Brien, who wrote *Trump Nation: The Art of Being the Donald*, for $5 million because O'Brien questioned his net worth, asserting it was less than Trump claimed. The case was dismissed.[364] The number of lawsuits is legion because Trump is vindictive and sues anyone who criticizes him.

When Trump was asked about the Constitution regarding his proposal to close off the internet to stop ISIS, Trump scorned, "Somebody will say, 'Oh freedom of speech, freedom of speech.' These are foolish people. We have a lot of foolish people."[365] It appears only Trump is allowed freedom of speech.

While he claimed that he would defend religious rights as protected in the First Amendment under freedom of religion, Trump proposed to ban all Muslims from entering the US and at one point advocated for a religious test to enter the country. In Chapter 4, I cited reasons for questioning his "protection of religious rights" with respect to his proposal to repeal the Johnson Amendment and Roe v. Wade.

According to Ben Shapiro from *Daily Wire*, Trump's proposals regarding Muslims, while morally questionable, were constitutional, as the proposals would apply to non-US citizens.[366] The Constitution protects American citizens. Nevertheless, his statements were not in the spirit of the Constitution. His proposal to close mosques, however, was unconstitutional. According to *CNN*, Trump made the following statement during an interview with MSNBC: "Well, I would hate to do it but it's something you're going to have to strongly consider… Some of the absolute hatred is coming from these areas… The hatred is incredible. It's embedded. The hatred is beyond belief. The hatred is greater than anybody understands."[367]

Trump exhibited disdain for the Eighth Amendment, which states, "Excessive bail shall not be required, nor excessive fines imposed, nor cruel and unusual punishments inflicted."[368] The late Justice Scalia argued that to garner information was not punishment and therefore waterboarding and other such tortures were constitutional. Obama signed an executive order prohibiting interrogation methods beyond those permitted by the US military, which included waterboarding. Trump proposed to rescind all of Obama's executive orders. Trump also proposed punishing the families of terrorists, and this would be against international law.

Article III, Section 1 of the Constitution allows for the separation of powers of the judiciary, particularly the Supreme Court. Each of the branches of the government has separate or limited powers and serves as a check and balance. In June 2016, Trump declared that District Judge Gonzalo Curiel was unfit to preside over lawsuits against Trump University because of the judge's Mexican heritage. Trump complained, "I'm telling you, this court system… ought to look into Judge Curiel. Because what Judge Curiel is doing is a total disgrace, okay? But we'll come back in November. Wouldn't that be wild if I'm president and I come back to do a civil case?"[369] His threat to have Curiel removed showed complete disregard for the independence of the judiciary. As explained by Corey Brettschneider, a writer for *Politico*, "The judicial branch is not supposed to be beholden to personal interests of the president. In fact, the founders designed the judiciary to counter the power of the presidency."[370] Trump also alluded to packing the Supreme Court with judges who would do his bidding with respect to Roe v. Wade and other positions on the Constitution.

The American Civil Liberties Union (ACLU) is nonpartisan and regularly reports on politicians by outlining their policies in relation to civil liberties. "If implemented, Donald Trump's policies will spark a constitutional and legal challenge that will require all hands on deck at the ACLU," said Executive Director Anthony Romero.[371] The ACLU identifies several constitutional issues with Trump's policies, including the Muslim ban, mass deportation, the no catch and release policy, the wall, surveillance of Muslims, the creation of a Muslim database, the proposed use of torture, and his positions on libel and abortion. The ACLU position on changing Roe v. Wade is that it would be unconstitutional and violate the Fifth Amendment of due process. "The right to obtain an abortion is longstanding and has withstood challenges in the Supreme Court, in Congress, and with voters."[372] The Trump presidency could be a threat not only to civil liberties, but to democracy itself.

Racial tension was a lightning rod in this election campaign. While Trump and his campaign denied racism, his statements, and proposed policies, as well as the behaviour of some of his supporters, were racist. Rather than renouncing the behaviour, he inspired it. It seemed as if it was the continuation of the Civil War. I can't help but reflect that it was only in July 2015 that as a sign of goodwill and healing, South Carolina passed a bill to remove the Confederate flag on statehouse grounds. While many associated the flag with racism and hate and some neo-Nazi groups adopted it, others saw it as an emblem of their heritage. Evidently, for some, the Civil War is not over. Trump has tapped into that.

Race

Trump declared himself the 'law and order candidate.' He vowed to increase the number of officers and end "the anti-police atmosphere."[373] Trump proposed the use of stop and frisk[374] and, according to the *New York Times*, promised to expand a federal program which would enable local police to enforce federal immigration law.[375] Trump added that Hillary and those "peddling the narrative of cops as a racist force in our society" shared "the responsibility for the unrest" in the country. "She is against the police, believe me."[376]

The *Washington Post* reported, "A federal judge ruled that the way New York police practiced the tactic equated to a 'policy of indirect racial profiling.'"[377] Research demonstrates that stop and frisk is not effective in reducing crime.

Hillary's proposals included "ending the era of mass incarceration," addressing the systemic racism in the criminal justice system,[378] and strengthening "bonds of trust between communities and police."[379]

The following are a few relevant statistics regarding the criminal justice system that demonstrate the difficulties in obtaining accurate information on deaths of officers in the line of duty and the systemic racism in the justice system.

According to the Officer Down Memorial Page, there were 129 deaths in the line of duty in 2015, 133 in 2014, and 114 in 2013.[380] During the ten years from 2006 to 2015, the average annual number of police deaths was 49.6. There are 250,000 more police officers than there were thirty years ago.[381] The numbers in the *BBC* article from the Criminal Justice statistics do not match those from the Officer Down Memorial Page, which is higher. Former FBI Director James Comey said in the House of Representatives in October, "We can't have an informed discussion, because we don't have data."[382]

According to *Statista*, "as of April 19, 2016, the United States had the second highest prisoner rate, with 693 prisoners per 100,000 of the national population."[383]

The following statistics from the *NAACP* substantiate the racial disparities in the criminal justice system:[384]

- "African-Americans now constitute nearly 1 million of the total 2.3 million incarcerated population."

- "African-Americans are incarcerated at nearly six times the rate of whites."

- "Together, African-American and Hispanics comprised 58% of all prisoners in 2008, even though African-Americans and Hispanics make up approximately one-quarter of the US population."

- "According to Unlocking America, if African-American[s] and Hispanics were incarcerated at the same rates as whites, today's prison and jail populations would decline by approximately 50%."

- "One in six black men had been incarcerated as of 2001. If current trends continue, one in three black males born today can expect to spend time in prison during his lifetime."

- "One in one hundred African-American women are in prison."

- "Nationwide, African-Americans represent 26% of juvenile arrests, 44% of youth who are detained, 46% of the youth who are judicially waived to criminal court, and 58% of the youth admitted to state prisons (Center on Juvenile and Criminal Justice)."

The *Mapping Police Violence* website reported the following key findings:[385]

- "Police killed at least 104 unarmed black people in 2015, nearly twice each week."

- "Nearly one in three black people killed by police in 2015 was identified as unarmed, though the actual number is likely higher due to underreporting."

- "37% of unarmed people killed by police were black in 2015 despite black people being only 13% of the US population."

- "Unarmed black people were killed at five times the rate of unarmed whites in 2015."

- "Only ten of the 102 cases in 2015 where an unarmed black person was killed by police resulted in officer(s) being charged with a crime, and only two of these deaths (Matthew Ajibade and Eric Harris) resulted in convictions of officers involved. Only one of two officers convicted for his involvement in Matthew Ajibade's death received jail time. He was sentenced to one year in jail and allowed to serve this time exclusively on weekends."

Deputy Bates, who killed Eric Harris, was convicted of second-degree manslaughter.[386]

The public is becoming increasingly privy to videos of police shootings and related protests. The following are a few examples:

On September 16, 2016, Terence Crutcher was unarmed and held his hands in the air when a police officer fatally shot him. The police claimed that the victim was not following commands. Video footage from the police cam showed Crutcher with his arms in the air. Police claimed he was going for a gun through the window of his car and had a vial of PCP in the car. Before the shooting, a police officer in a helicopter said, "That looks like a bad dude."[387] The police officer involved was charged with murder.

Regarding the protesters, Rep. Robert Pittenger (R-NC) had this to say on BBC's *Newsnight* as reported by *CNN*: "The grievance in their mind is that the animus, the anger—they hate white people, because white people are successful and they're not. I mean, yes, it is, it is a welfare state. We have spent trillions of dollars on welfare, where we put people in bondage so that they cannot be all that they're capable of being." He apologized, explaining that those were the comments he heard protesters making.[388]

In June 2015, Patrolman Michael Slager was indicted on a charge of murder after fatally shooting Walter Scott.[389] In an unrelated case, Keith Scott, a black man, was fatally shot in an incident in which he failed to follow police commands and was thought to have a gun. Following the shooting and resulting protests, the Mahoning County chair for Donald Trump's campaign, Kathy Miller, resigned her volunteer position and apologized for making the following comments: "I don't think there was any racism until Obama got elected... If you're black and you haven't been successful in the last fifty years, it's your own fault. You've had every opportunity; it was given to you... You've had the same schools everybody else went to. You had benefits to go to college that white kids didn't have. You had all the advantages and didn't take advantage of it. It's not our fault, certainly."[390]

On July 8, 2016 in Falcon Heights, outside Minneapolis, the police pulled over a car purported to have a broken taillight. The driver, Philando Castile, was in the car with his girlfriend, Diamond Reynolds. Her four-year-old daughter was in the back seat. According to Reynolds, her boyfriend advised the police that he had a gun and permit. The police asked for his identification, and as he reached for his wallet in his pocket, the police shot him four times. Reynolds live-streamed the aftermath with her cell phone while her boyfriend was dying. Police Officer Jeronimo Yanez was charged with second-degree manslaughter. The police videocam showed that Castile was polite and non-threatening. He volunteered that he had a gun and permit.[391] The car did not have a broken taillight. Dispatch audio discloses that the incident was racial profiling. The officer said, "The two occupants just look like people that were involved in a robbery." The man in the audio added, "The driver looks more like one of our suspects, just 'cause of the wide set nose."[392] This is insidious racial profiling.

Fox News' Bill O'Reilly said, "Racial persecution really isn't the problem in Baltimore, it's personal behavior."[393] He went on to try to make the case that the cause of the riots could not possibly be persecution since Baltimore has a population that is largely black, and the city and police are controlled by black people. This shows complete obliviousness toward the injustices black people face in this society. According to Chauncey Degage, as reported by *Salon*, "the American people are robbed of any meaningful social or historical context for the police abuse in Baltimore, Ferguson, and the many other locales where police thuggery and state violence are routinely visited upon black and brown Americans, as well as the poor and the mentally ill, with relative impunity."[394]

The Justice Department investigated, and their report found reasonable cause to believe that the Baltimore City Police Department (BPD)

> engages in a pattern or practice of conduct that violates the First and Fourth Amendments of the Constitution as well as federal anti-discrimination laws. BPD makes stops, searches, and arrests without the required justification; uses enforcement strategies that unlawfully subject African Americans to disproportionate rates of stops, searches, and arrests; uses excessive force; and retaliates against individuals for their constitutionally protected expression. The pattern or practice results from systemic deficiencies that have persisted within BPD for many years and has exacerbated community distrust of the police, particularly in the African-American community.[395]

These are a few of the examples of abuse from a summary provided by *CNN*:[396]

- "About 44% of police stops occurred in two small predominantly African-American neighborhoods that contain only 11% of the city's population."

- "Hundreds of individuals were stopped at least ten times during this period, and seven were stopped more than thirty times."

- "Only 3.7% of those stops resulted in citations or arrests."

- "BPD stops African-American drivers and pedestrians at disproportionate rates, subjecting them to greater rates of searches than whites… creating racial disparities at every stage of law enforcement actions, from stop to arrest."

- "BPD officers found contraband twice as often when searching white individuals compared to African-Americans during vehicle stops and 50% more often during pedestrian stops."

- BPD used "overly aggressive tactics that escalated encounters and increased tensions" and failed "to de-escalate encounters when appropriate to do so."

- BPD "frequently resort[s] to physical force when a person does not immediately respond to verbal commands, even if the subject poses no imminent threat to the officer or others."

Another troubling element in the justice system is the number of wrongly convicted felons, especially those on death row. Even more troubling, the *Innocence Project* reported that "the majority (63%) of those exonerated through DNA evidence are African American."[397] *NBC* reported on the unfair practices of police abuse and harassment of black Americans, especially in poor neighbourhoods, which, when coupled with the overwhelming percentage of African-Americans found innocent from DNA evidence, raised questions of a presumption of innocence for African-Americans in the justice system. National Registry of Exonerations, a project at the University of Michigan Law School, reported that in 2015, 149 convicted felons were exonerated from a variety of offences such as "47 drug crimes, to major felonies, including 54 murder convictions that were overturned... five of the latter convicts were awaiting execution... more than two-thirds were minorities, including half who were African American."[398] The following are a few examples that demonstrate the insidious nature of the implications.

According to the CBS News program *60 Minutes*, Glenn Ford was exonerated on March 10, 2014 after having served almost thirty years in solitary confinement on death row. The maximum-security prison has a reputation for harsh penalties and conditions.[399] Ford had been convicted of robbing and killing Isadore Rozeman, a Shreveport, Louisiana jeweler. The original prosecutor who put him there, Marty Stroud III, has been apologetic and admitted that Ford should never have been arrested because the main evidence was a witness who eventually recanted.[400]

Dale Cox was the prosecutor that got Ford released upon receiving the informant's information. One would think that would make him a hero, but in his view, not only did Stroud do nothing wrong, but he should not have apologized.

When asked if Glenn Ford had gotten justice, Cox's response was, "I think he has gotten delayed justice... it's better than dying there and it's better than being executed."[401] It was even more chilling watching Dale Cox in the interview, as the article did not convey his total lack of remorse and uncompromising diction. "I'm not in the compassion business... We're in the legal business. So to suggest that somehow what has happened to Glenn Ford is abhorrent, yes, it's unfair. But it's not illegal. And it's not even immoral. It just doesn't fit your perception of fairness."[402]

According to Louisiana law, Ford was entitled to compensation of $11,000 a year for a total of $330,000, which he was also denied. Cox and the Louisiana justice system continued to question his innocence, made additional accusations that were never proven, and claimed he must prove his innocence to be entitled to the compensation.[403]

The state of Louisiana gave him $20 for a bus ride home from prison. Ford was diagnosed with stage-four cancer a few months after his release. He died on June 12, 2015, penniless, and was buried with charitable donations. This crosses the boundaries of inhumanity—it was evil.

These cases reaffirmed my growing supposition that Trump alone was not the problem. He did not create the prejudice; he emboldened it. The next case has a direct connection with Trump.

The Central Park Five was another horrific case. The crime itself was awful. A twenty-eight-year-old woman was attacked in Central Park on April 19, 1989. After being chased and knocked down, she "was stabbed five times, raped, sodomized, and beaten almost to death. She was found naked, gagged, and tied up, covered in mud and blood, about four hours later."[404]

Five juveniles were convicted, four black and one Hispanic, and sentenced from six to fifteen years. They "spent between six and thirteen years in prison."[405]

In 2002, another Hispanic male confessed to the crime, which was confirmed by DNA, but he could not be charged as it was past the statute of limitations. The five who were convicted sued for malicious prosecution, but Mayor Bloomberg refused to settle the case. In 2014, new Mayor Bill de Blasio supported the settlement, and the city settled the case for $41 million.[406]

Donald Trump has a direct connection to this case. In May of 1989, an outraged Trump took out a full-page ad in the *Daily News* with the headline "BRING BACK THE DEATH PENALTY. BRING BACK OUR POLICE!" He wrote, "How can our great society tolerate the continued brutalization of its citizens by crazed misfits? Criminals must be told that their CIVIL LIBERTIES END WHEN AN ATTACK ON OUR SAFETY BEGINS!"[407]

Even more disturbing, in October 2016, "He described the men as guilty, and then demonstrated, once again, that he is a master at the dark art of using long-standing racial fears, stereotypes, and anxieties to advance his personal and political goals."[408] Korey Wise, one of the wrongfully convicted, went on to say, "Donald Trump told the world that my life had no value, no quality. And he's still saying pretty much the same thing today."[409]

According to *History*, "After the US Civil War (1861-65), the 15th Amendment, ratified in 1870, prohibited states from denying a male citizen the right to vote based on race, color or previous condition of servitude." Even though it was prohibited by legislation, blacks were prevented from exercising their right to vote. During a peaceful voting rights protest in Selma, Alabama, on May 7, 1965, the protesters were attacked by state troopers and many were severely beaten. This was captured on national television and the public was outraged.[410]

History added that "[in] a speech to a joint session of Congress on March 15, 1965, the president outlined the devious ways in which election officials denied African American citizens the vote. Election officials often told blacks attempting to vote that they had gotten the date, time, or polling place wrong, that they possessed insufficient literacy skills, or that they had filled out an application incorrectly. The population, which suffered a high rate of illiteracy due to centuries of oppression and poverty, would often be forced to take literacy tests, which they inevitably failed. Johnson also told Congress that voting officials, primarily in Southern states, had been known to force black voters to 'recite the entire Constitution or explain the most complex provisions of state laws,' a task most voters, including whites, would have been hard-pressed to accomplish. In some cases, even blacks with college degrees were turned away from the polls."[411] To overcome the legal barriers at both state and local levels, Johnson signed the Voting Rights Act on August 6, 1965.[412]

Throughout the general election campaign, however, Trump claimed the system was rigged and alleged voter fraud. He tweeted, "Of course there is large scale voter fraud happening on and before election day. Why do Republican leaders deny what is going on? So naive!"[413] Yet numerous studies indicate that voter fraud in US elections is rare. Commenting on Trump's assertions, Republican campaign lawyer Chris Ashby said there was no evidence and that the charges were "unfounded" and "dangerous."[414]

On the other hand, voter suppression, despite the Voting Rights Act, is still practiced, primarily by the Republicans. Tactics of voter suppression include requiring photo ID, which disproportionately affects minorities, the handicapped, and the elderly; purging voter rolls; citizens losing their rights due to felony convictions;[415] misinformation about voting procedures; underfunded election areas that create long lines, discouraging voters; and voter caging.[416]

In August 2016, *Rolling Stone* printed an article about twenty-eight states that subscribed to the Interstate Voter Registration Crosscheck Program, promoted by a powerful Republican operative paid to identify duplicate voters. But according to reporter Greg Palast, "the Crosscheck list disproportionately threatens solid Democratic constituencies: young, black, Hispanic and Asian-American voters—with some of the biggest possible purges underway in Ohio and North Carolina, two crucial swing states with tight Senate races."[417] Oregon opted out because they found the information unreliable. Voters were being identified as duplicate if middle names, addresses, or other identifying information did not match. Once identified, a plain postcard was sent out and those who did not respond were purged from the list. The problem is that it had a built-in racial bias. White voters were more likely to respond than black people or Hispanics, homeowners were more likely to respond than renters, and young people were more likely to respond than the elderly. Greg Palast from *Rolling Stone* reported that "[t]hose on the move—students and the poor, who often shift apartments while hunting for work—will likely not get the mail in the first place… So far, Crosscheck has tagged an astonishing 7.2 million suspects, yet we [*Rolling Stone*] found no more than four perpetrators who have been charged with double voting or deliberate double registration."[418] Only four perpetrators—but how many were purged from the voting lists?

In July 2016, the US Court of Appeals for the Fourth Circuit ruled that the voter ID laws in North Carolina "target[ed] African Americans with almost surgical precision."[419] *Reuters* reported, based on evidence from emails, that North Carolina Republicans conspired to limit the operating hours of early voting polling places to suppress minority turnout. In October 2016, a federal court judge ordered three counties not to purge their voter rolls. By the time the judge ruled, over four thousand voters had already been challenged in three counties.[420] The GOP in North Carolina celebrated their voter suppression efforts in a statement called "North Carolina Obama Coalition Crumbling." The statement read, "As a share of Early Voters, African Americans are down 6.0%, (2012: 28.9%, 2016: 22.9%) and Caucasians are up 4.2% (2012: 65.8%, 2016: 70.0%)."[421]

I did find two cases of Democratic voter suppression. Voting regulations require that individuals are not to solicit, promote, or oppose a candidate or party within 150 feet of a polling station. Bill Clinton visited two polling stations in Massachusetts and is reported to have had his picture taken on the request of one person, and on one occasion said, "Pull the lever for Hillary."[422] In 2005, in Milwaukee, five Democrats were charged for slashing the tires of twenty-five Republican-rented vans that were for driving voters to polling stations. This did not prevent anyone from voting. Four were found guilty and sentenced from four to six months in jail.[423] While unacceptable, these are the only two circumstances of Democrat voter suppression that I could find. There are numerous examples and allegations of Republican voter suppression, many in which elections were carried out regardless. This is the party that claims to uphold the Constitution.

On the September 9, 2016 episode of *CNN Tonight with Don Lemon*, there was a panel discussion with commentators about Hillary's remarks at a fundraiser, which were as follows: "You could put half of Trump supporters in what I'd call a basket of deplorables… They're racist, sexist, homophobic, xenophobic, Islamophobic. You name it." She then went on to say that the other 50% of Trump supporters feel that the government let them down, the economy let them down, and nobody cares. The GOP political strategists and Trump supporters solidly slammed Hillary for depicting Trump voters in such a demeaning manner.[424] While the first part of her comment was widely reported, the second half was not.

Van Jones, a political commentator and Hillary supporter, expressed disappointment with her choice of words, but also made a case that she was trying to make a good point.

Paris Dennard, a political strategist and Trump supporter, demanded to know if Hillary should apologize. This followed a lengthy discussion on the Obama birthing issue, in which he and Boris Epshteyn, another political strategist and Trump supporter, vociferously argued that Trump did not owe an apology. Their position was that Hillary's insult was directed at the voters and Trump supporters. I fail to understand how Paris Dennard, an African-American, could harangue Hillary for her 'superpredator' comment of twenty years ago and her 'basket of deplorables' comment during the campaign while ignoring and defending Trump's racist comments and actions, especially his harassment of the Central Park Five and handling of the birther issue.

Bob Beckel, a CNN commentator and Hillary supporter, raised an excellent point. Both he and Van Jones acknowledged when their candidate made a mistake; Trump surrogates seldom, if ever, acknowledged that Trump made a mistake, lied, or owed an apology, no matter the evidence.

According to CNN, the same night that Hillary made the controversial statement, Trump said that "[s]he is so protected right now. She could walk into this arena right now and shoot somebody with 20,000 people watching—right smack in the middle of the heart—and she wouldn't be prosecuted."[425] Trump continued to claim that the rules did not apply to Hillary and that she was above the law, when it was Trump that had this sense of entitlement.

The next day, Hillary did apologize for the generalization. She apologized for saying half the supporters, but not that some had deplorable behaviours.[426]

Trump has yet to apologize for referring to undocumented Mexican immigrants as "racists and murderers." Nor has Trump apologized to the Khans for implying that Muslim women are oppressed. Trump insulted voters with his vile comments about Mexicans, Muslims, women, and Obama's birther controversy.

I do agree that Hillary's decision to characterize half of Trump's supporters as "a basket of deplorables" was unfortunate. While she expressed herself poorly, I think Hillary was making a valid point. There are Trump supporters who exhibit deplorable behaviours and express racist views.

Public Policy Polling results for Trump supporters during the campaign in February 2016 revealed racist attitudes:[427]

- 80% supported banning Muslims from entering the United States.

- 70% supported the Confederate flag hanging on the capital grounds.

- 40% supported shutting down all mosques in the United States.

- 38% wished the South won the Civil War and 38% weren't sure.

- 44% believed Islam should be illegal in the United States and 22% weren't sure.

- 32% supported the policy of Japanese Internment.

- 31% supported banning homosexuals from entering the United States.

Apparently, these opinions are in line with what some consider 'patriotism,' though these views violate the spirit of the Constitution. Those who understand the true spirit of the Constitution value true liberty for all. There simply is no equivalence between Hillary's singular poor choice of words and Trump's constant insults, including racist and sexist remarks.

Milwaukee County Sheriff, David Clarke Jr., spoke at the Republican National Convention and declared, "Blue lives matter" to wild applause. He also wrote an op-ed in the *Hill*, arguing that "Black Lives Matter is the enemy."[428] Trump said, "I think they're trouble, I think they're looking for trouble," about Black Lives Matter on Bill O'Reilly's Fox programme.[429] To respond with "All lives matter" or "Blue lives matter" does not acknowledge the issue, which is the systemic racism that makes African-Americans feel their lives have been devalued. The best analogy that I've heard is as follows: If someone goes to the hospital with a broken leg, the doctor does not then say, "All body parts matter. Let's not just focus on the leg." The sad fact is that numerous reports have validated the perception of systemic racism. Of course all lives matter; police lives matter, but the system is broken with respect to racism, not all lives.

According to the Officer Down Memorial Page, 133 police officers were killed in 2015. The race of the shooters was not provided in the statistics. In that same year, police killed 102 unarmed black people. Both need to be addressed. The point that Black Lives Matter is trying to make is that one is not being addressed: systemic racism. Trump has not acknowledged the issue, never mind proposing solutions.

Innumerable reports have been written to identify the problem and recommend corrective action. The Kerner Report's recommendations addressed the issues of economic opportunity, failed housing, education, and social services as well as the bias in mainstream media. I am confident that some gains have been made, but obviously, more are necessary.

Even though the statistics are not reliable for some calculations, there is enough information to confirm that systemic racism is prevalent in the criminal justice system and must be acknowledged and addressed. Besides the human rights issues, which in my view should be reason enough, one must consider the financial implications. The average inmate cost in the US in 2010 was $31,286 per year, money far better spent on education, healthcare, and job development. If the US has the second highest rate of incarceration in the world, surely there are people in prison who do not belong there.

Trump's law and order approach and proposed solutions like 'stop and frisk' are only going to escalate the problem. Americans who hold these prejudiced beliefs are inciting the very thing they fear. As long as there is racism in police departments, there will be distrust, even in those situations in which the police are legitimate in their actions.

How does supporting *Black Lives Matter* mean that person is against the police? "The Mothers of the Movement are named in reference to the Black Lives Matter movement that has emerged to raise awareness about the deaths of their children and other minorities at the hands of police."[430] The membership includes several mothers "whose unarmed African-American children have been killed by law enforcement or due to gun violence."[431] Their mission is to create cooperation between police and communities of colour. They could have chosen to lash out in their pain with hate, rhetoric, blame, and inciting the supporters and protesters. They did not. Instead, they are trying to bring about understanding, wanting to work together with the police and their communities.

There is a lesson we can take from history. Society has shifted who is to blame. In the 1800s, there were strong anti-Catholic sentiments and at least six riots, including the tarring and feathering of a Catholic priest, Father John Bapst, in 1854. There was a strong anti-immigration sentiment, particularly against Irish Catholics. There was also an anti-German sentiment. The New York City Draft Riots in 1863 were provoked by the draft to fight in the Civil War, and while some could pay to avoid the draft, the Irish working class could not. The Irish attacked the free black people that they thought were competing with them for jobs.[432] In 1956, the Lumbee Indians of Robeson County, North Carolina achieved official recognition, and this infuriated a local Ku Klux Klan leader, James Cole. Within a year, Cole, who also fancied himself a preacher, was denouncing the Lumbee Indians as half-breeds with African origins.[433]

The FBI statistics on hate crimes are not reliable because a lot of police departments do not report, but they do show trends. "According to the data, 47% of these 2014 hate crimes were motivated by racial prejudice. Crimes motivated by religious and sexual orientation were next, at 18.6% each. These were followed by crimes motivated by ethnicity (11.9%), gender identity (1.8%), disability (1.5%) and gender (0.6%)." Sixty percent of the reported religious hate crimes were against Jews.[434]

Now the targets for hatred are undocumented Mexicans and Muslims. Abdication makes us part of the problem. When will members of the white community who may not be guilty of racism understand that even though they are not racists, racism does exist? If we do not reject injustices because they do not affect us personally, eventually they will. This is so aptly phrased in the following poem, written by Martin Niemöller, a German Lutheran pastor, after the Holocaust. In not speaking out, Niemöller believed that the Germans "had been complicit through their silence in the Nazi imprisonment, persecution, and murder of millions of people."[435]

First they came for the Communists, and I did not speak out—
Because I was not a Communist.
Then they came for the Socialists, and I did not speak out—
Because I was not a Socialist.
Then they came for the Trade Unionists, and I did not speak out—
Because I was not a Trade Unionist.
Then they came for the Jews, and I did not speak out—
Because I was not a Jew.
Then they came for me—and there was no one left to speak for me.[436,437]

The summer Olympic games were broadcast alongside the ongoing coverage of the election campaign during the month of August 2016. This provided an interesting backdrop, particularly in relation to American democratic values and patriotism. The spirit and values inherent in the ancient games have been compromised, and the political and social values expressed in the Constitution have been similarly at risk in this election campaign.

The ancient Olympic Games started in 776 BC and continued to AD 393—a span of 1,169 years. They ended with the advent of Christianity because the games were associated with the Greek gods and ancient worship, which had been banned. This was thought provoking to me since religion played such an influential role in the campaign. The Olympic Games are credited with having been instrumental in the development of ancient Greek civilization and the birth of democracy, the foundation for today's Western society. According to Triant and Valavanis, "The Greek mentality cultivated both mind and body and athletes of the games were taught the principles of fair play, qualities of humility… as well as respect for their opponents and the adjudicators… the contest was only justified when it helped improve the moral fiber of men, athletes, and spectators."[438]

The modern games could serve this same purpose of uniting countries and ethnic groups, but they do not because they have lost the values and mission of the ancient games. National pride and winning have become the valued attributes. The games (including the Olympic Committee) are rife with scandals of corruption, racism, politics, human rights issues, doping, and biased judging. National pride has become so dominant that host countries have taken extreme measures to avoid embarrassment. Protesters of the games were killed in Mexico 1968,[439] and the marginalized and homeless were displaced in Beijing 2008.[440] Nations are burdened with Olympic debt that threatens the economy and social network, as in Brazil 2016.[441]

In addition to those problems Brazil created themselves, such as the corruption scandal, there were many challenges that were visited upon them, such as a fluctuation in oil prices, which caused an economic slowdown; the Zika virus; and the press being extremely negative coming into the games. Despite it all, Brazil put on a spectacular opening while struggling to create a positive impression to garner economic benefits following the Olympics. That positive image was shattered when members of the American swim team claimed to have been robbed at gunpoint, deeply embarrassing Rio de Janeiro.

The American swimmers gave several versions, but it was finally disclosed that they were at a gas station and caused some damage to a sign and a washroom. They had been out partying, were quite drunk, and were trying to get into the wrong cab. When they finally got the right cab, the security guards asked them to step out because of the damage they caused, and a gun was pulled out to prevent them from leaving. They were given a choice to pay for the damage or face the police. Contrary to their original allegation, there was no robbery.[442] Ryan Lochte was one of the swimmers involved. Lochte and his mother became a focus in the incident because of the mother's reporting to the press, but he came home ahead of some of his teammates. One of Lochte's teammates paid an almost $11,000 fine as a donation to a Brazilian charity,[443] but I found no evidence that Lochte has offered to do the same. Numerous tabloids dubbed Lochte the "ugly American." Despite his infamy, he went on to become one of the dancers on the 2016 season of *Dancing with the Stars* in an effort to redeem his reputation. Apparently, for some Americans—Trump included—an international scandal is less damaging than justifiable expressions of protest or a perceived offence to national patriotism.

Contrast Lochte's experience with the controversy over Colin Kaepernick, the San Francisco 49ers quarterback who refused to stand for the national anthem. "I am not going to stand up to show pride in a flag for a country that oppresses blacks and people of color," he said.[444] He came under a barrage of criticism and backlash, with fans burning his jersey in protest, telling him to go to Canada. According to the *Guardian*, Trump's comments were as follows: "I think it is a terrible thing. Maybe he should try and find a country that works better for him. Let him try. It won't happen."[445] A former player whose brother is a marine said that Kaepernick's refusal to stand for the national anthem was disrespectful and shameful.[446] Yes, the marines fighting for America deserve respect, but are Kaepernick's actions any more disrespectful than what is happening to people of colour in the United States?

I am not opposed to Lochte having been given an opportunity to redeem himself. I am dismayed that Kaepernick has been subjected to greater revile than Lochte, under the guise of patriotism. Kaepernick has done nothing illegal and has not created an international incident; he has simply exercised his constitutional rights. Yet it is Kaepernick whom people have suggested should leave the US and go to another country.

Years ago, I saw an interview with a black celebrity who shared that despite his fame and wealth, he had difficulty hailing cabs in New York.[447] I remember because I thought it was so profound. Is this the American dream? As recently as August 2015, a taxi driver was fined $25,000 because he refused to pick up a black woman and her two children.[448] How often does this happen, but the victim does not want to be bothered with a lawsuit, or the cab driver claims to be off duty and then picks up someone else once out of sight? Colin Kaepernick has become successful, but can he get a cab in New York?

It is absurd to suggest that because some people of colour have achieved financial success, anyone can achieve the American dream (thereby proving the system is not rigged). First, it negates the fact that despite their wealth and achievements, there are times when even 'successful' members of minority groups face discrimination. It also negates the fact that there are injustices and inequities in the criminal justice system, housing, access to jobs, and quality of education for the poor, and disproportionately for black people. According to the *Legal Information Institute*, the Supreme Court rendered a decision regarding coerced patriotism and ruled that the expression of patriotism must be voluntary, not prescribed. The following is a quotation from their decision.

> To believe that patriotism will not flourish if patriotic ceremonies are voluntary and spontaneous, instead of a compulsory routine, is to make an unflattering estimate of the appeal of our institutions to free minds. We can have intellectual individualism and the rich cultural diversities that we owe to exceptional minds only at the price of occasional eccentricity and abnormal attitudes… If there is any fixed star in our constitutional constellation, it is that no official, high or petty, can prescribe what shall be orthodox in politics, nationalism, religion, or other matters of opinion, or force citizens to confess by word or act their faith therein. If there are any circumstances which permit an exception, they do not now occur to us.[449]

While Trump's campaign was built on preserving the Constitution, he and many of his nationalist, patriotic supporters would deny Colin Kaepernick his constitutional right to protest peacefully.

According to many in white America, protests like Black Lives Matter's are not acceptable, Beyoncé's protest at the Super Bowl was not acceptable, and sitting down or kneeling for the national anthem is not acceptable. Yet a large proportion of white America fails to acknowledge the real issues. Is it going to take riots like those in the 1960s for these concerns to be acknowledged in a meaningful way? Yes, black people and other non-whites need to be part of the solution, but that cannot happen until white America stops blaming them for systemic racism. I think these two stories are sad commentaries on national pride in the United States, the lack of compliance with the Constitution, and the erosion of civil rights.

The children are our future. Education, being informed and open to other perspectives, and seeking to understand others will change attitudes. *Frontline* reported that "[t]eaching the subject of the Holocaust and the Nazi era is mandatory in German schools and in addition to the classroom curriculum, almost all students have either visited a concentration camp or a Holocaust memorial or museum."[450] *Wikipedia* noted that the purpose of the German educational curriculum is to learn from mistakes and not to hide from history.[451] Perhaps school systems in the US and other countries need to incorporate education about slavery and gender bias and, particularly, the history and benefits of immigration. I once mentioned to an acquaintance that Canada ended slavery a hundred years before the US. He said, "There was slavery in Canada?" Oops. Canada's educational system has obviously been remiss!

Personal interaction can have a profound impact and make real change. In 1987, one of the first episodes of *Oprah* featured skinheads as guests, hoping to expose the ignorance of racism. She later regretted it, "I realized in that moment that I was doing more to empower them than I was to expose them, and since that moment, I've never done a show like that again." Twenty-five years later, on May 13, 2011, two of the former skinheads apologized to her.[452] One shared that he changed when he went to jail for assault. Everyone on his crew was black, and despite his Nazi tattoos, they treated him as an equal. "Everyone is a human being; we can't just hate people," he said. He referred to himself as being "lost" as a young man. The other recruited a group in Oregon that ended up killing an Ethiopian student, and that was his wake-up call. He realized there are "consequences to ideas."[453]

The Mothers of the Movement are role models for how we can rise above pain and work to bring about cooperative solutions. Being resentful and bitter is like drinking poison and waiting for the other person to die.[454,455] We forgive others not because they deserve forgiveness, but because we deserve peace.[456,457]

There are so many things that I admire about America and the leadership it provides to the free world. I admire their patriotism, but it is a double-edged sword. I have often wondered at the intensity of the patriotism, and it has occurred to me that it was used to heal and unite the country after the Civil War. It has not worked. National pride is admirable. I love my country too, but I do not think that Canadians are superior to Americans or any other nationality.

CHAPTER SIX

Fear Factor

Fear is the main source of superstition, and one of the main sources of cruelty.
To conquer fear is the beginning of wisdom.[458]
—Bertrand Russell

Trump employed fear as a tool in his campaign, particularly in relation to national security, the economy, and free trade. Terrorism and inadequate international security are complex and global issues threatening us all. They are serious concerns that are complicated by the need to have an approach that includes and involves international allies. The following are some examples of Trump's fear mongering and inability to lead.

Terrorism and National Security

In an interview with Howard Stern on September 11, 2002, Trump expressed support for the war in Iraq, though he blamed President Bush for it.[459] He said that "George W. Bush's Iraq invasion 'may have been the worst decision' in presidential history."[460] In the debates, Trump claimed, "They lied. They said there were weapons of mass destruction, there were none. And they knew there were none. There were no weapons of mass destruction."[461]

Then Trump blamed Hillary for Iraq. Referring to her actions regarding Iraq, Libya, and Syria, Trump exclaimed, "Hillary Clinton invented ISIS with her stupid policies. She is responsible for ISIS."[462]

Trump then said he never supported the war, despite evidence that he had. He claimed that he was against the war in Iraq the whole time and predicted that it would create instability in the region.[463] There is no evidence to support that he was against the Iraq war from the beginning.

Hillary did support President Bush's policy to authorize the use of force against Saddam Hussein's regime in Iraq, as did most senators (from both parties) and the House of Representatives, including Trump's running mate, Mike Pence. Hillary later said she regretted that vote.

According to the *Washington Post*, Hillary expressed that she had struggled with her decision and made the following speech on the floor when casting her vote:

> This is a difficult vote. This is probably the hardest decision I have ever had to make. Any vote that may lead to war should be hard, but I cast it with conviction. I take the president at his word that he will try hard to pass a United Nations resolution and seek to avoid war, if possible… Because bipartisan support for this resolution makes success in the United Nations more likely and war less likely — and because a good-faith effort by

the United States, even if it fails, will bring more allies and legitimacy to our cause — I have concluded, after careful and serious consideration, that a vote for the resolution best serves the security of our nation.[464]

In contrast, Mike Pence stated that even "if he had known in 2002 that Saddam did not have weapons of mass destruction, he would have voted for the war. 'Absolutely. No regrets.'"[465] Trump excused Pence's vote as a mistake, but accused Hillary of creating ISIS.

Trump later claimed to have a foolproof plan to deal with ISIS but refused to share it. "I do know what to do, and I would know how to bring ISIS to the table or, beyond that, defeat ISIS very quickly, and I'm not [going to] tell you what it is tonight," he said. "I don't want the enemy to know what I'm doing."[466] While he claimed to have a plan, if he would not share it, how could voters determine that it was foolproof and compare it to Hillary's?

Trump released ten foreign policy proposals on September 7, 2016. One said, "Immediately after taking office, I will ask my generals to present to me a plan within 30 days to defeat and destroy ISIS." There were also seven proposals to increase military spending, "enforce all laws relating to the handling of classified information... conduct a thorough review of United States cyber defenses, and identify all vulnerabilities in our power grid, our communications systems, and all vital infrastructure."[467]

The USA has the strongest armed forces in the history of the world. The country spends 39% ($600 billion) of the global distribution on military expenditures, more than the next ten countries combined.[468] What would expansion of the military achieve? Would Trump get enough support to accomplish it, even from a Republican Congress?

There are about 100,000 ISIS armed insurgents, and the USA could defeat them, but according to Fareed Zakaria, the problem is, what does the victor do then? Who is going to manage that truce and run the country?[469] Lt. Gen. Mark Hertling differed in his opinion about USA troops eliminating the threat of ISIS in two months. They had this same situation in Afghanistan with fewer insurgents, and they faded away. "Unless you have an indigenous force that is actually fighting and knows where they are, it becomes counterproductive. It is best to have the indigenous force do it and support the indigenous force afterwards. We have tried to do too much," Hertling said.[470]

Trump said he would take the oil from Iraq; however, pillaging is prohibited by The Hague Regulations (1899 and 1907), Geneva Convention V, International Criminal Court, US Field Manual (1956), US Rules of Engagement for Desert Storm (1991), The US Naval Handbook (2007), and the US Manual for Military Commissions (2010).[471]

According to *PolitiFact,* Republicans blamed Obama for not keeping 10,000 troops in place in Iraq, which they said could have deterred the opening for ISIS. However, Obama inherited from Bush a timeline to exit Iraq, and that did not include an agreement to leave a large force behind.[472]

In contrast to Trump's strategy, Hillary said that the American people had to have "resolve, not fear" because the threat of terrorism is "real, urgent, and borderless... ISIS and terrorist groups like them are constantly adapting and operating across multiple spaces, so our response needs to be just as nimble and far-reaching."[473]

In August 2015, Trump spoke in Michigan. *PolitiFact* reported that Trump said, "Iran, the world's top state sponsor of terrorism, has been put on the path to nuclear weapons, was given $400 million in ransom payment cash, where they just yesterday caught Obama in yet another lie."[474] The United States owed this money to Iran. In 1979, the then Shah of Iran paid the US $400 million to purchase military parts, which were never delivered because of the revolution that toppled the government. The Iran-U.S. Claims Tribunal adjudicated this dispute, among many others, and the US was to pay the $400 million plus $1.3 billion in interest.[475] While the negotiations regarding this payment and release of prisoners were conducted separately, "[n]egotiators took advantage of the convergence in order to ensure that Iran returned the prisoners by withholding the payment until the American detainees were in the air and headed out of Iran."[476]

Following a review of the ransom policy, in a statement on June 24, 2015, President Obama reaffirmed "that the United States government will not make concessions, such as paying ransom, to terrorist groups holding American hostages."[477] He said this to discourage incentives for hostage taking and prevent such money from being used to fund terrorist activities. In falsely portraying the payment to Iran as a ransom payment, Trump put Americans at risk by giving terrorists the impression that ransom with the US was a possibility.

Unlike Trump's vacillation regarding the war in Iraq and Hillary's regretful support, Canada's position was consistent. On March 17, 2003, Prime Minister Jean Chrétien stated in the House of Commons, "If military action proceeds without a new resolution of the [United Nations] Security Council, Canada will not participate."[478]

There have been successes and failures in the war on terrorism. It is a war unlike anything the world has ever encountered. It is not against a country or isolated to any specific areas, and the enemy is not wearing a uniform. Wiping out Syria would not eliminate the enemy because ISIS is everywhere. However, experts and many Republicans expressed support for Hillary and recognized her competence for the role of commander-in-chief while expressing considerable concern about Donald Trump for that role.

Michael J. Morell was the acting director and deputy director of the Central Intelligence Agency from 2010 to 2013. He is neither Republican nor Democrat, and has never supported a candidate in his thirty-three years of service. He made it clear that he would support Hillary Clinton because he considered her qualified to be commander-in-chief and that "Donald J. Trump is not only unqualified for the job, but he may well pose a threat to our national security."[479]

Robert Gates, who led the Defense Department under Presidents George W. Bush and Barack Obama, said of Trump, "At least on national security, I believe Mr. Trump is beyond repair. He is stubbornly uninformed about the world and how to lead our country and government, and temperamentally unsuited to lead our men and women in uniform… He is unqualified and unfit to be commander in chief."[480]

Fifty of the nation's most senior Republican national security officials, many of them former top aides or cabinet members for President George W. Bush, signed a letter declaring that

Donald J. Trump "lacks the character, values, and experience" to be president and "would put at risk our country's national security and well-being."[481]

I subscribe to the theory put forward in a *Newsweek* article written by Kurt Eichenwald. He contended that ISIS tried to inflame the West by showing beheadings on TV to provoke a reaction, resulting in an attack that killed a lot of Muslims, thereby inflaming hatred of the US, and deflecting it away from ISIS.[482]

In that case, Trump's plan will simply inflame hostilities and abet the jihadist cause.

Domestic Terrorism

ISIS and undocumented Mexican immigration dominated the national security agenda, almost to the exclusion of homeland terrorism and violence, which I think pose a much greater threat to American society. In the former segment on religion, I posited that the terrorists are not Islamic, but rather all those disenfranchised individuals that act out their aggressions by committing terrorist acts.

How would profiling have made a difference in the case of Ahmad Khan Rahami? He lived in the US for over twenty years and was radicalized as an American citizen.[483] The question is, why was he vulnerable to radicalization? What is the difference between this case and Timothy McVeigh, for example? Both are acts of terror. In other words, if they did not have ISIS as an excuse for their aggression, they would find another.

Right after the bomb went off, Trump made an announcement before authorities in New York released the official details. "We better get very, very tough. It's a terrible thing that's going on in our world, in our country, and we are going to get tough and smart and vigilant."[484] Clinton was more cautious, stating, "We need to do everything we can to support our first responders—also to pray for the victims. We have to let this investigation unfold." She added, "I think it's always wiser to wait until you have information before making conclusions, because we are just in the beginning stages of trying to determine what happened."[485]

This was a perfect example of the difference between the two candidates. Trump escalated fear without having conclusive information, while Hillary reserved specific details until the information was provided. Trump engendered fear to garner support for his law and order approach and his draconian proposals to deal with terrorism.

Wikipedia reported that in 2004, the FBI gave congressional testimony stating that the Jewish Defense League was "a proscribed terrorist group" that committed fifteen of eighteen known terrorist attacks between 1980 and 1985. The most recent charges were in 2001 when Irv Rubin, JDL Chairman, and Earl Krugel perpetrated "bomb attacks against the King Fahd Mosque in Culver City, California, and on the office of US Representative Darrell Issa, who is of Lebanese and Czech descent."[486] Rubin committed suicide in jail. At that time, the FBI claimed they had thwarted at least one other terrorist attack related to this group.[487]

There are several other identified terrorist groups in the United States that are not known to have committed terrorist attacks in recent years. However, the public is not always made aware that the FBI or other law enforcement have prevented an event. These groups include the Animal Liberation Front, Alpha 66 and Omega 7, Aryan Nations, Black Liberation Army, the Covenant, the Sword, the Arm of the Lord, Earth Liberation Front, May 19th Communist Organization, the Order, Phineas Priesthood, Symbionese Liberation Army, United Freedom Front, and the Weathermen.[488]

While Trump engendered fear of Muslims and Islamic terrorism, he ignored domestic terrorist acts and shootings that were a far greater threat to American citizens.

The *Washington Post* published an interesting article on mass shootings. The data they provided covered from August 1, 1966 to 2016 and included 127 events that did not include gang killings, other crimes, or those instances involving only the shooter's family. There was a total of 874 victims, including 144 children. Semi-automatic 9mm weapons were used in two of the deadliest mass shootings. An AK-47 and a semiautomatic handgun were used in a 1989 school shooting in which five children were killed and thirty students and teachers were injured. "Twenty-seven percent of the mass shootings occurred in workplaces, and 1 in 8 took place at schools. Others took place in religious, military, retail and restaurant, or other locations."[489]

It is very difficult to accurately assess the scope of shootings in the US, as pointed out in in an article entitled "Behind the Bloodshed": "Poor reporting by police agencies to the FBI also means some mass killings were left out, while others that don't meet the standard were included. Erroneous and excluded cases leave FBI data with a 57% accuracy rate."[490]

The following is a summary of one case described by *USA Today* that took place in Samson, AL in 2009 and was not included in the FBI data. "Michael K. McLendon abruptly quit his job at a sausage plant and the next week shot his mother and set her body aflame. McLendon drove twelve miles to his uncle's house, where he shot and killed five people on the front porch, then killed four other family members and strangers." A letter was found in which the shooter said that "he was depressed and frustrated that he would never become a police officer or a Marine."[491]

On September 23, 2016, a Caucasian male entered the Macy's at the Cascade Mall in North Seattle, Washington and fatally shot five people. The police had video of the individual and were seeking help from the public in identifying and finding the suspect.[492]

Wikipedia provides a list of school shootings by year. From February 5, 2010 to September 9, 2016, there were 121 incidents that resulted in 123 deaths and 181 injuries. The following were the two deadliest.

On December 14, 2012, Adam Lanza entered Sandy Hook Elementary School, where he shot and killed twenty-six people (including twenty first-grade children), and then himself. Two others were injured. Prior to that, he had killed his mother and taken her guns. Lanza drove to the school, bringing four guns with him. In a follow-up report conducted by Child Advocate, they disclosed that he had had years of mental health issues that had gone untreated. The report writers acknowledged "the 'significant role' that assault weapons and high capacity ammunition magazines played and said Lanza's easy access to them 'cannot be ignored as a critical factor in this tragedy.' The ready availability of assault weapons in the US is a critical public health issue."[493]

On October 1, 2015, Christopher Harper-Mercer opened fire in a hall on the Umpqua Community College campus, killing eight students and one teacher and injuring nine others. He then committed suicide.[494] Mercer was discharged from the army halfway through his ten weeks of basic training in 2008. He was described as "a deeply troubled, anti-religion, anti-government recluse obsessed with guns."[495]

Following the shootings at Umpqua Community College, President Barack Obama had this to say:

> We are the only advanced country on Earth that sees these kinds of mass shootings every few months. Earlier this year, I answered a question in an interview by saying, "The United States of America is the one advanced nation on Earth in which we do not have sufficient common-sense gun-safety laws — even in the face of repeated mass killings."... Tally up the number of Americans who've been killed through terrorist attacks over the last decade and the number of Americans who've been killed by gun violence, and post those side-by-side.[496]

Obama was correct. *Trace* collated some data on gun violence. Here is a sample of their results:[497]

- "As of December 23, a total of 12,942 people had been killed in the United States in 2015 in a gun homicide, unintentional shooting, or murder/suicide."

- "From 2005 – 2015, 71 Americans were killed in terrorist attacks on US soil. 301,797 were killed by gun violence in the same period."

- "Unsecured guns have turned dozens of toddlers into killers — and many more into victims. In 2015, on average, a toddler in America shoots someone once a week."

- "Guns are now ending as many American lives as cars... at a rate of 10.3 deaths per 100,000 people."

The firearm-related death rate per 100,000 people is 10.94 in the United States, 7.64 in Mexico, and 1.97 in Canada.[498] Trump blamed Muslims for terrorism and undocumented Mexicans for crime in the US while ignoring evidence of the role of domestic violence, except in Chicago's inner city neighbourhoods.

Trump engendered fear when he claimed that Hillary "wants to essentially abolish the Second Amendment." He did not believe in more gun control or expansion of background checks. He said, "The government has no business dictating what types of firearms good, honest people are allowed to own."[499] Voters were led to believe that Hillary would deny them of their right to protect their homes and families.

Trump's allegations were disputed by the fact-checkers at *PolitiFact*: "She has repeatedly said she wants to protect the right to bear arms while enacting measures to prevent gun violence."[500] Clinton's plan included expanding background checks on more gun sales, removing the industry's sweeping legal protection for illegal and irresponsible actions, revoking licenses from dealers who break the law, and keeping guns out of the hands of domestic abusers, other violent criminals, and the severely mentally ill.[501]

The research demonstrated that a large portion of the public, even gun owners, were in favour of stricter gun policies. There were numerous studies about the American public's views on gun control. I used the Pew Research Center data for the purposes of this book, though others revealed similar findings. While there were some disparities between Democrats and Republicans on specific issues, most were also in favour of background checks for gun shows and private sales, as well as laws preventing the mentally ill from buying guns. While most Americans favoured a federal database and a ban on assault weapons, Republicans were less inclined.[502]

The Second Amendment of the United States Constitution reads, "A well-regulated militia, being necessary to the security of a free state, the right of the people to keep and bear arms, shall not be infringed."[503] If the right to bear arms is related to having a militia to secure a free state, why does someone need to own an AK-47 and walk around with it in public, as is permitted in open-carry states?

Fifty-four percent of Americans believe that gun ownership protects people from crime. I would like to see a study on how many gun incidents prevented a crime versus how many unwarranted or accidental gunshot deaths occurred.

The international community is also concerned about some dynamics in the United States, so much so that these concerns are starting to appear in travel advisories. Canada warns that "the possession of firearms and the frequency of violent crime [in the US] are generally more prevalent than in Canada,"[504] China warns about road rage, Mexico warns its citizens that they might be harassed, and Australia warns about exorbitant medical expenses. Canada "warns travelers of the legality of civil asset forfeiture—a widespread practice where US police officers confiscate cash during traffic stops."[505]

The US embassy of Bahrain, a tiny Middle Eastern island nation, urged citizens via Twitter to "be cautious of protests or crowded areas occurring around the US."[506] The Bahamas, a Caribbean nation where most people identify as being of African heritage, warned its people to be careful when visiting US cities rocked by "shootings of young black males by police officers."[507] "The United Arab Emirates also urged its students and other citizens in the United States to be careful, using similar language… the US State Department employs when warning Americans about countries that have fallen victim to attacks by extremists."[508] New Zealand and Germany's warnings focus on gun violence and terrorism in the US.[509]

According to the *New York Times*, Trump's proposed plan for military expansion could cost an additional $90 billion a year.[510] Estimates vary, but even taking into account improving economies, the cost is staggering. Apparently, Americans would pay an additional $90 billion a year to destroy 100,000 terrorists but would not invest in universal healthcare, improved mental health services, education, job creation, or an equitable justice system. These could reduce the conditions that contribute to incidents of violence in the US.

ISIS has become synonymous with terrorism, or as Trump calls it, Islamic extremism. I daresay that may be the reason the mayor of New York was hesitant to refer to the bombing as terrorism until he had more information, because he did not want to inflame the community. I think it is interesting that there was such controversy in calling this incident terrorism, but when a Caucasian male entered the Macy's at Cascade Mall in North Seattle and fatally shot five people, terrorism was not even mentioned.

Blaming a race or group only increases the threat to society by cultivating a sense of isolation and resentment by those who are targeted. In fact, we need to do the opposite. Embracing the Muslim community within our own will reduce the hostility that results in aggressive acts. Thus, that community will be an ally in identifying those who threaten security.

Economy

Trump has preyed on the fears of those Americans who feel economically 'left behind,' reaffirming their angst and fear by misrepresenting the economic environment nearing the end of the Obama administration. The *Economist* pronounced, "Mr. Trump paints a picture of the economy that is irreconcilable with the facts. He says jobs are scarce, poverty is rising, and incomes are stagnant. But, America's economy is the strongest in the rich world."[511]

Those who felt 'left behind' before are going to be even further left behind. Just as it was with those who lost their jobs at Carrier after expecting their jobs would be saved, so will it be for the coal miners and many others.

By late 2016, the economy had added more than nine million jobs,[512] and the unemployment rate was only 4.9%, while the historical median is 5.6%.[513] The number of long-term unemployed Americans had dropped by 614,000 under Obama, but it was still 761,000 higher than at the start of the Great Recession. Corporate profits were up 166%; weekly wages were up 3.4%.[514] "The official poverty rate in 2015 was 13.5 percent, down 1.2 percentage points from 14.8 percent in 2014."[515]

Trump's plan included cutting taxes, deregulating, and cutting/changing trade deals. His former proposal was to cut taxes to 25%, but instead he proposed cutting them at the top level from 39.6% to 33%. Trump wanted to cut taxes for everyone and reduce the number of tax brackets from seven to three.[516]

The *New York Times* reported that Trump promised to "take on 'the hedge fund guys' and their carried interest loophole. He thinks it's 'outrageous' how little tax some multimillionaires pay. But his plan called for major tax cuts not just for the middle class but also for the richest Americans—even the hedge fund managers."[517]

Mr. Trump proposed eliminating the estate tax or inheritance tax completely, which only "applies when a family member passes on more than $5.45m worth of assets to an individual or $10.9m to a married couple."[518]

Trump would reduce the US corporate tax rate to 15% from the previous rate of 35%. He proposed an increase in manufacturing jobs, but this could be problematic, as the job loss was not necessarily from outsourcing but rather technology.[519] To boost growth, Trump promised to free the economy from "onerous" government regulations and cut corporate taxes in half.[520]

The *Economist* reported that "Mrs. Clinton on the other hand, want[ed] to raise taxes on the wealthy, increase spending on job training and lower taxes on companies that hire more

Americans."[521] Taxes would stay the same for most Americans, but she would add a new category and a 4% tax on those earning $5 million or more. This new revenue would be used to pay for such programmes as free university for low- and middle-income earners.[522] She did not propose raising taxes on the middle class, as Trump frequently asserted.

The *Economist* described Hillary's policy for job growth as being more specific and included increasing job training, paid for by tax revenue from wealthier Americans, infrastructure spending, and investment in new energy to lift the number of jobs in those sectors.[523]

Clinton promoted her plan, saying, "The economy always does better when there's a Democrat in the White House."[524] *PolitiFact* investigated this claim with several economists, all of whom agreed that, using the Gross Domestic Product (GDP) as a measurement, this statement is true. However, they pointed out that there are other factors such as oil prices and international conditions. "Christian Weller, a public policy professor at the University of Massachusetts Boston, studied GDP data since 1947. He found that the economy, through the last quarter of 2015 and after inflation, grew 3.8 percent under Democrats and 2.4 percent under Republicans."[525] While Obama's growth rate was only 2% (prior the end of his 2016 term), it was still higher than Bush's when he left office in 2008.[526]

Politics That Work is an independent website with no external source of funding and no political affiliation. It aims to gather research studies and information not readily available to the public for making informed decisions, particularly political decisions. Several reputable papers including the New York Times and Huffington Post have published its works.[527] *Politics That Work* summarized several research papers regarding opinions of economists (each of the research studies or papers is linked to its summary for further study by the reader). Their findings were as follows:[528]

- "71% of economists favor using government to redistribute wealth and only 8% strongly oppose it. In fact, the concept of the diminishing marginal utility of wealth is a very well established and non-controversial economic principle. Even Adam Smith[529] expressed the view that the government should redistribute wealth."

- "Only 12% of economists take the view that the costs of the [economic] stimulus outweighed the benefits—a view passionately held by nearly all Republicans."

- "75% of economists favor government tuning the economy with monetary policy—an idea often vehemently rejected by the Republican Party while only 4% of economists strongly oppose it."

- "Zero percent—not a single economist in the entire sample—of economists agree with the central tenet of Republican fiscal policy that cutting tax rates would boost the economy enough to cause revenues to increase."

- "94% of economists support taking action to address climate change."

These policies obviously support the Democratic platform. *Politics That Work* stated that Democrat economists outnumber Republican economists 2.5 to 1. In the one opinion study that I reviewed, one thousand economists were selected randomly from the American Economic Association.

Briton Ryle from *Wealth Daily* disclosed that "[s]ince the mid-seventies, wages as a percentage of GDP have fallen 7%, while corporate profits have risen 7%. That's a pretty compelling relationship."[530]

Chris Matthews of *Fortune* concluded that "[i]f you are born poor in America, you have a much greater chance of staying poor than if you were born into the same class in places like Canada or Denmark."[531] It is clear that the taxation policies Trump espoused would do nothing to alleviate the problems of those 'left behind.' The data from *Politico* and *Politics That Work* is also supported by Chris Matthews's article in *Fortune Magazine*. He writes, "Wealth inequality is even more extreme, with a recent study estimating that in America, the wealthiest 160,000 families have as much as the poorest 145 million families."[532]

Deregulation and reduction of corporate taxes, as proposed by Trump, will not trickle down to the blue-collar workers. The following are corporate examples to substantiate that the American public will not benefit with Trump's policies—corporations will.

"On February 6, 2014, General Motors (GM) recalled about 800,000 of its small cars due to faulty ignition switches, which could shut off the engine during driving and thereby prevent the airbags from inflating."[533] Eventually, over thirty million cars worldwide were recalled, and GM had been aware of the defect for over a decade. While compensation was paid out on 124 deaths, more than 90% of claims were rejected for the compensation package, and this number did not include claims that were part of the ongoing multidistrict litigation. GM decided that replacement would be too costly and payouts for any lawsuits would be more economical.[534] While there have been fines and financial compensation to families, no one is in jail. This is premeditated mass murder.

Warren Buffett owns Berkshire Hathaway and is regarded as an ethical businessman who is very philanthropic. Buffett has a net worth of $67.7 billion[535] and recently donated another $2.86 billion of his holdings in the company's stock to the Bill & Melinda Gates Foundation and four family charities as part of his plan to give away nearly his entire fortune. While that is a sizable donation, it is only 4.22% of his wealth.

According to *CBC*, in 2013, Berkshire Hathaway purchased the Heinz Company and fourteen months later announced the closure of the plant in Leamington, Ontario, which was the first Canadian plant and had been opened in 1909. "It's really a question of having an unprofitable plant and concentrating production in a more profitable plant,"[536] said Buffett. More profitable? That sounds as if the plant could have been profitable already, but they just wanted more. "Last fall, Buffett vowed 'very generous severance' for the displaced workers."[537] Even the union felt the agreed-upon severance was fair.

A new consortium called Highbury Canco signed a contract to package some products, including tomato juice, for Heinz and hired 250 employees, though the new workers would make less.[538] The only reason that Heinz was contracting this company for tomato juice is a regulation in Ontario that requires tomato juice be made from fresh tomatoes, not tomato paste with water.[539] Ontario regulations did not hurt workers; they preserved jobs.

Business Insider reported that Buffett pledged to donate up to 99% of his wealth during his lifetime or at the time of his death.[540] Note that he is now eighty-six years old and has only started doing this in recent years.

I don't begrudge billionaires their profit. If they worked hard and took the risks, then they should reap the rewards. However, when there is no trickle-down to workers in receiving fair compensation and increases for their hard work in helping the company achieve those profits, this is corporate greed. Workers making a fair wage spend money, which improves the economy.

Why should billionaires not have to pay their fair share of corporate and personal taxes? According to *CNN*, "Warren Buffett says even though he and other top earners are paying higher taxes this year, he thinks he's still paying a lower rate than his secretary."[541]

When billionaires like Buffett donate to charities, they are controlling where that money goes and determining the priorities based on their interests. I reviewed all the Gates Foundation's donations, and they are laudable causes. If they are using the money after they have paid their fair share of taxes, that is great. How much is donated globally versus in the United States? The wealthy are not paying their fair share, and that limits the government's ability to address the priorities and needs of the American public, such as healthcare. In general, I concede that Buffett is trying to be an ethical businessman who is concerned about people, but why should billionaires get to choose where their money goes for 'charity' while the rest of America pays taxes to fund services the American public requires?

In *Wealth, Income, and Power*, William Domhoff makes the argument that progressive taxation does not make much difference in addressing income inequality.[542] Citizens for Tax Justice is a research group that studies tax issues. They found that when you consider all taxes (not just income) for the year 2009, "taxes are progressive for the bottom 80%" of the population, but they slow down for the top 20% of earners and actually go down further for the top 1%. For example, the bottom 20%, with an average income of $12,400 per year, paid 16% of their income in taxes; the next 20%, making $25,000 a year, paid 20.5% in taxes; the middle 20%, making $33,400 a year, paid 25.3% in taxes; the next 20%, making $66,000 a year, paid 28.5% in taxes; the next 10%, making $100,000 a year, paid 30.2% in taxes; the next 5%, making $141,000 a year, paid 31.2% in taxes; and the next 4%, making $245,000 a year, paid 31.6% in taxes. The top 1%, which made $1.3 million per year on average, paid 30.8% in taxes.[543]

Additionally, the top 0.05% can avoid taxes by holding their wealth in off-shore tax havens, and there are many other loopholes that allow them to "hide their money and delay on paying taxes, and then invest for a profit what normally would be paid in taxes."[544] Transfer payment programmes such as social security and food stamps do not have much of an impact on improving redistribution and creating income equality. There is a global scale for comparing income equality between countries based on the GINI coefficient, a mathematical scale to rank countries. Sweden is first for distribution of wealth, Canada ranks thirty-fifth, and South Africa is ranked last. "The United States ends up ninety-fifth out of 134 countries that have been studied—that is, only 39 of the 134 countries have worse income equality."[545]

The cost of healthcare was a lightning rod during the election. The problems with the Affordable Health Care Act are discussed elsewhere in the book. There is another healthcare cost that creates a considerable, and I think unnecessary, burden on the average American: "Americans pay anywhere from two to six times more than the rest of the world for brand name prescription drugs."[546] The reason is twofold: First, the United States does not benefit from purchasing power that can lower costs due to the inordinate number of organizations buying drugs; secondly, by law, Medicare cannot negotiate drug prices. Hillary asserted that this needed to be changed.[547]

According to *Wikipedia*, the health system in Canada is less complex "[t]he Patented Medicine Prices Review Board determines a maximum price for all drugs. Government drug purchasing is similar to the way the United States purchases medications for military personnel, but on a much wider scale."[548] While drug companies argue that the reason the prices are so high is research and development, critics say this is not the case and that they charge so much because they can.[549] Because of the price differential between the US and Canada, Americans spend more than $1 billion USD on brand-name drugs from Canadian pharmacies each year as of 2004, simply to save money.[550]

There are two recent examples of price gouging by drug companies. The CEO for Turing Pharmaceuticals purchased the drug Daraprim, which had been on the market for sixty-two years. Surely, the research and development cost were long expired. Turing raised the price from $13.50 to $750 per pill overnight. This is an important medication for HIV/AIDS patients because it is standard care for individuals having a parasite, which can cause serious problems for those with a compromised immune system.[551]

Mylan has a virtual monopoly on epinephrine injectors, which are used for severe allergies. "Roughly 40 million Americans have severe allergies to spider bites, bee stings, and foods like nuts, eggs, and shellfish." Mylan raised the price from $93.88 to $600 for two syringes.[552]

The most critical factor contributing to the economic plight of the middle class and those 'left behind' is corporate greed. Large corporations making huge profits without meaningful increases in wages are essentially committing murder and extortion for required lifesaving drugs, yet Trump wanted to deregulate for businesses to prosper with the promise of a trickle-down economy.

These are some hourly salaries of individuals who would benefit from Trump's tax reductions. In 2013, Julia Roche of *Insider Magazine* provided the following CEO salaries:[553]

- "Warren Buffett: He made $12.7 billion… or $37 million per day; $1.54 million per hour; or $25,694 per minute."

- "Bill Gates: He earned $11.5 billion… which works out to be $33.3 million per day; $1.38 million per hour; or $23,148 per minute."

- "Mark Zuckerberg: The Facebook founder made $10.5 billion… $30.4 million per day; $1.27 million per hour; or $21,135 per minute."

In 2010, ABC reported that "Walmart CEO Michael Duke's $35 million salary, when converted to an hourly wage, worked out to $16,826.92. By comparison, at a Walmart store planned for the Windy City's Pullman neighborhood, new employees being paid $8.75 an hour would gross $13,650 a year."[554]

Bernie Sanders impassioned the youth. He started a revolution, and he wanted those youths who were not as impassioned by Hillary to join the cause. Hillary may not have been as charismatic, but Bernie had the sense to know that the cause was more important. To take the opportunity to keep it alive, he negotiated the Democratic platform. He didn't betray them; he was saving their dream! He understood that while he and Hillary had their differences, she made things happen; she was willing to listen and compromise, and she was basically on the same page, just with different time frames. He didn't give up.

Corporations cannot be trusted to make ethical decisions when there are competing values between profit margins and the public good, even in the case of loss of life. Taxes and regulations do not seem to be hindering them from garnering huge profits. Nevertheless, wages are depressed while the corporations prioritize short-term profit over improving wages in the labour force and investing in the future.

Trump's proposed tax cuts would benefit the wealthy. He claimed that eliminating the inheritance tax would benefit farmers, but in truth, that would affect very few farms. According to Glenn Kessler from the *Washington Post*, there are exemptions for farms, and the "US Department of Agriculture estimates that with the exemptions, only 0.6 percent of farms would have to pay an estate tax. [Another 2.1 percent would file returns but would owe no taxes.] The nonpartisan Tax Policy Center estimates that only 120 farms and small business, where at least half the assets are in farm or business assets, had to pay the estate tax in 2013."[555] But the estate tax would benefit Trump and his family, as would the reduction in corporate taxes.

Removing the inheritance tax would reduce government revenues in the hundreds of billions, but 91.9% of Americans do not pay inheritance tax.[556] "Only 1.6% of Americans receive $100,000 or more in inheritance."[557] Another 1.1% receives $50,000 to $100,000. Elimination of the inheritance tax would only benefit 0.06% of the wealthiest heirs.[558]

The wealthiest are able to circumvent the inheritance tax, as many states eliminated the "rules against perpetuities" that made "it impossible for a 'trust' to skip a generation before paying inheritance taxes." Trust funds in those states can be set up in perpetuity, allowing the descendants of the wealthy "to own new businesses, houses, and much else... and even to allow the beneficiaries to avoid payments to creditors when in personal debt or sued for causing accidents and injuries."[559]

The term 'the rich get richer and the poor get poorer' is not just a catchphrase. An anonymous contributor wrote an article for the University of Southern California at Santa Cruz's website *Who Rules America,* a site about how power is distributed and wielded in the United States.[560] The investment manager wrote the article "An Investment Manager's View on the Top 1%" anonymously, as he did not want to jeopardize his relationship with wealthy clients. He made the point that it is not the top 1% ruling America, but rather the top 0.01%. He clarified that there are two tiers in the top 1%, with the entry point being approximately $1.8 million. For the top 0.01%, it is $24 million. "Wealth distribution is highly skewed towards the top 0.01%, increasing the overall average for this group."[561]

Within the top 1%, 0.99% is largely comprised of doctors, lawyers, small business owners, and professionals who work for their money. While they are well off compared to the rest of society, "they generally don't participate in the benefits big money enjoys."[562] Members of the elite 0.01% are generally bankers, employees in financial services, real estate developers involved with those industries, and general contractors. The anonymous investment manager concluded, "I think it's important to emphasize one of the dangers of wealth concentration: irresponsibility about the wider economic consequences of their actions by those at the top. Wall Street created the investment products that produced gross economic imbalances and the 2008 credit crisis. It wasn't the hard-working 99.5%."[563] They made huge profits in the build-up to the crisis, but when things collapsed, they were bailed out. While the rest of America is still dealing with the economic damage, they continue to benefit from it.[564] Recall Trump's comment in 2006: "If there is a bubble burst, as they call it, you know you can make a lot of money."[565]

Trump was proposing tax reductions for the wealthy while Hillary proposed an increase. Why shouldn't the wealthy pay their fair share? According to David Cay Johnston, "The government relies far more on the bottom 99 percent than the top 1 percent for federal income taxes."[566]

Free Trade

Trump preyed on his voters' fears regarding economic uncertainty by attacking the North American Free Trade Agreement (NAFTA). He would have Americans believe that trade agreements favour every country except America and that NAFTA is responsible for job loss and unemployment. He insisted that he, and he alone, could fix this. To be fair, there is a case for renegotiating the trade agreements. Canadians have concerns about the agreement and want changes as well.

All three countries in NAFTA have had benefits as well as negative consequences. NAFTA was not the only factor affecting job loss. The intention behind NAFTA was to remove barriers to the exchange of goods and services and avoid disputes regarding each other's taxes, or tariffs, on the goods imported from abroad and on issues when the market is flooded with large quantities; hence, this would depress prices driving those domestic producers out of business. I think the expectation was that, if businesses prospered, there would be a trickle-down effect by creating employment and an improvement in the middle class.

While the companies did well, as did the 1%, the average workers did not. The middle class in Mexico did not fare well. Companies made larger profits but did not increase the salaries of the Mexican workers to a level for enjoyment of a middle-class lifestyle. According to Gordon Laxer of the *Globe and Mail,* "The big losers have been the lower-income and middle classes in the rich countries. That underlies the populist revolts of Brexit and the presidential candidacies of Donald Trump and Bernie Sanders."[567] *Reuters* reported that the hourly wage for Mexicans has not increased substantially. "Low wages are a huge incentive for both Mexican and foreign firms. One in seven Mexican workers earns the average minimum wage of 65.58 pesos ($5.10) a day or less, national statistics office INEGI says. Manufacturing workers fare better with wages averaging about $2.70 an hour but they make up only 16 percent of the labor force and their pay is way below the $19.50 per hour in the United States."[568] According to Ranking America, Mexico ranked highest for working hard, with the average Mexican working 2225.7 hours in 2012, while the US ranked 11th, with the average American working 1789.9 hours.[569] The low pay results in weak spending and productivity. Wouldn't we all benefit if Mexican families had more spending power to buy the things Americans are making in their country? How many Mexican families can afford a car?

Instead of focusing on job loss from trade agreements (because that is not the only factor for unemployment), focus should be on issues that would create a fairer playing field with respect to regulations for quality, environmental protection, and requirements for corporations to improve wages as profits increase.

Most economists have said that free trade was not the major factor in job loss, that technology had a great deal to do with it, and that getting tough on free trade and applying new tariffs would only make it difficult for the US to compete on a global stage. As an example of the impact of technology on jobs, the Changying Precision Technology Company factory in Dongguan, China, replaced 590 workers with sixty robots.[570]

Many of my extended family members were farmers. When I was very young, most of my uncle's cows were milked by hand, and he had numerous farmhands. In later years, machines did all the milking, and there were fewer farmhands around. Trump's proposal was akin to saying that buggy whip manufacturing used to be successful, so why don't we start making them again? Because the world has changed. Every country is struggling with this reality. It takes fewer workers to produce more goods.

Trump blamed Canada for free trade problems. Canadians may view this very differently. Canada has been sued thirty-five times by foreign investors and has paid out more than $200 million dollars on cases because companies have the right to sue if government laws hurt their profits. More than two-thirds of the cases related to Canada's environmental protection laws.[571] The following are three examples provided by Maude Barlow in an article posted in *Common Dreams*.

"Ethyl, a US chemical corporation, successfully challenged a Canadian ban on imports of its gasoline that contained MMT, an additive that is a suspected neurotoxin. The Canadian government repealed the ban and paid the company $13 million for its loss of revenue."[572]

"New Jersey-based Bilcon Construction is demanding $300,000 in damages from the Canadian government after winning a NAFTA challenge when its plan to build a massive quarry and marine terminal in an environmentally sensitive area of Nova Scotia and ship basalt aggregate through the Bay of Fundy, site of the highest tides in the world, was rejected by an environmental assessment panel."[573]

"Eli Lilly, a US pharmaceutical giant, is suing Canada for $500 million (approximately €337 million) after three levels of courts in Canada denied it a patent extension on one of its products. This case is particularly disturbing because it challenges Canadian laws as interpreted by Canadian courts and represents a new frontier for ISDS [Investor–State Dispute Settlement] challenges."[574]

While he regularly inflamed the voters and his base by saying the US got a raw deal and that NAFTA was biased in favour of Mexico and Canada, Trump failed to tell them that the United States has a trade surplus with Canada.[575]

American laws, it would appear, are more concerned with corporate profit than eliminating neurotoxins that are poisonous or destructive to nerve tissue and preserving an environmentally sensitive area. The corporate profit of a drug company is more important than making sure that people receive the lifesaving medications they need.

Though there have been twenty claims against the United States, the US government has "won eleven of its cases and never lost a NAFTA investor-state case or paid any compensation to Canadian or Mexican companies."[576] According to Gordon Laxer from the *Globe and Mail*, "Canada sought free trade in the 1980s to overcome unfair US trade laws, such as those that then limited (and still limit) Canadian softwood lumber exports."[577] He went on to point out that instead of changing poor US laws, NAFTA has tribunals run by corporate lawyers to decide which Canadian companies hurt US profits in Canada.[578]

NAFTA's energy proportionality rule requires that member countries continue to make available for export the same proportion of total energy supply that they have over the previous three years. Since Canada had seemingly unlimited resources, it made sense to give unlimited access to the United States.

President Barack Obama broke the key understanding underlying NAFTA when he stopped TransCanada's Keystone XL oil pipeline in January 2012, ending Canada's unrestricted access to the US energy market.[579] I personally have mixed feelings about the pipeline, but the fact is that this breach has never been acknowledged.

Mexico has an exemption to the proportionality rule, and Canada should seek the same exemption. "According to Environment Canada, the oil and gas sector was responsible for 25 per cent of Canadian emissions in 2013."[580] If we do not reduce these emissions, we will not meet our international environmental commitments in the Paris Agreement. A revised trade agreement needs to have mutual benefits for all parties.

According to the *Economist*, "Protection would threaten high-value manufacturing jobs. It would disrupt the global supply chains, which see routine work done overseas."[581] Manufacturing's share of employment has fallen mostly because of technology, so imposing tariffs on Chinese and Mexican imports would not bring back jobs. "Those few jobs that did return would cater only to domestic demand: high-cost American workers would not be able to sell to the world as they did."[582]

Trump did not just prey on the fears of Americans; he created them. He used the mob mentality to reinforce those fears and then made promises that he would set things straight. However, nothing in his past behaviour as a businessman should make Americans believe that he genuinely cares about the common worker. His economic policies may give some breadcrumbs to common workers to entice them to provide support, but they benefit the super wealthy—including Trump—most.

Trump claimed that he understood the common workers' plight because he was one of them. Why did this rationale not apply to Hillary in working with Wall Street to understand the issues and to develop a remedy that would deal with the inequity while striking a balance in addressing it? No agreement is going to work if it is one-sided. Hillary's proposal was going to deal with the Super PACs and the tax inequities for the wealthy. Her job creation was based on training and infrastructure development.

Did the media provide information that was helpful to the voting public in understanding the pros, cons, and implications on the policies for national security and economy for each candidate?

In the Prologue, I acknowledged that I was part of the problem, but it was not until much later that I recognized the dynamics. My behaviour was being driven by my fears of the Trump supporters' fears!

How could I not understand that fear blinded their decision-making and behaviour when I was subject to the same dynamics? Fear is a powerful motivator. If fear motivates both sides, how do we get past the polarization? It affects personal relationships, organizations, the political establishment, countries, and inter-global relations.

The following is an apt quote from the *Anatomy of Peace*, published by the Arbinger Institute: "The more sure I am that I'm right, the more likely I will actually be mistaken. My need to be right makes it more likely that I will be wrong! Likewise, the more sure I am that I am mistreated, the more likely I am to miss ways that I am mistreating others myself. My need for justification obscures the truth."[583]

Even if I was justified in my concerns and correct in my assessments, I was not coming from the right place, as eloquently stated in another quote from *Anatomy of Peace*: "The same action can be done from a heart at peace or a heart at war."[584] This book may have taken a very different direction had I had this revelation earlier. I am leaving it as is, in the hope that my evolution may inspire transformation.

I will continue to work on conquering my fear. It isn't easy.

CHAPTER SEVEN

The Establishment: The Good, The Bad, and The Ugly

Any intelligent fool can make things bigger, more complex, and more violent. It takes a touch of genius, and a lot of courage to move in the opposite direction.[585]
— *E. F. Schumacher*

I cannot claim to fully understand how those Americans who were fed up with the establishment felt because I was not dealing with it. I can appreciate being fed up with lies, corruption, and gridlock in the government. I can understand that if the economy were improving while I was left behind, I too would want change. A candidate with a successful business career and fresh ideas would be attractive and might make an excellent president. In this case, I simply did not view Donald Trump as a suitable candidate. Though I lean toward the left, this was not about Democrat versus Republican for me. Had any other Republican candidate won the nomination, I would not be writing this book.

I did, however, learn a great deal about the Republican and Democratic parties. While I initially perceived Trump's tactics as characteristic of him rather than the Republican Party in general, I started to become aware of disturbing patterns that challenged this assumption.

The history of the evolution of the Democratic and Republican parties is far more complex than I expected. The following is a brief summary on the origins of the Democratic Party from *Wikipedia*. While the Republican Party is nicknamed the Grand Old Party (GOP), the "Democratic Party of the United States is the oldest voter-based political party in the world, tracing its heritage back to the 1820s,"[586] prior to the establishment of the Republican Party in 1854.

The Democratic-Republican Party, established in 1792, was the precursor to the present Democratic Party and organized to oppose the elite, wealthy, aristocratic Federalist Party, which wanted to establish a national bank and emphasize national over state government. The Democratic-Republican Party supported states' rights, literal interpretation of the Constitution, and family-based agriculture. The popularity of the party increased because of fear of a government too similar to the monarchy, and thus Thomas Jefferson was voted into office in the 1800 election. The Federalist Party disbanded after the War of 1812 (Canada won this war when the United States tried to overtake it). This left the Democratic-Republican Party without opposition. It was the only party existing between 1816 and the early 1830s, when the Whig Party was formed.[587]

In 1828, the Democratic-Republican Party split and became known as the Democratic Party. "They viewed the central government as the enemy of individual liberty... feared the concentration of economic and political power… [and] believed that government intervention in the economy benefited special-interest groups and created corporate monopolies that favored the rich."[588] The party was split regionally in the 1840s and 1850s between the North and the South. The South wanted to protect slavery, while the North resisted. The party split in 1860 at the presidential convention when the South nominated John C. Breckinridge as their candidate and adopted a pro-slavery platform, while the Northern Democrats nominated Stephen Douglas.

In 1854, the Whigs met and formed a new party, which became the founding of the modern Republican Party. Abraham Lincoln won the election in November 1860, and this was quickly followed by South Carolina's secession from the union. Within six weeks, five other southern states also seceded.[589] Eventually, there were eleven states involved in the Confederacy. The Civil War raged from 1861 to 1865.[590] Abraham Lincoln issued the preliminary Emancipation Proclamation on September 22, 1862, stipulating that if the southern states did not cease their rebellion, the proclamation would go into effect. On January 1, 1863, Lincoln issued the second proclamation, changing the course of the war. Prior to that, the purpose of the war had been to preserve the union. Now it was also about freeing the slaves.[591] On May 10, 1865, the war ended. On February 1, 1865, Abraham Lincoln had submitted the proposal of the Thirteenth Amendment, abolishing slavery in the state legislatures.[592]

While Lincoln was the president who abolished slavery, his position and motives were far more complex. According to Paul Escott from *Salon*, "As a young politician, Lincoln engaged in the race-baiting and racist rhetoric that was common among Illinois politicians."[593] Indeed, he accused a presidential nominee of "love for free negroes."[594] The divide between Republicans and Democrats on the issue of slavery was not as clear-cut as it seemed. In 1846, David Wilmot, a Pennsylvania Democrat, "declared that slavery should not be allowed into any lands gained through the war with Mexico."[595]

Lincoln's empathy regarding slavery did not emerge until the 1850s, though he had expressed anti-slavery sentiments prior to that, having stated in 1837, "Slavery is founded on both injustice and bad policy."[596] While Lincoln was anti-slavery in principle, he was not necessarily supportive of racial equality. He supported freeing the slaves, but Paul Escott provided the following quote from Lincoln: "it was impossible to 'free them, and make them socially and politically our equals. My own feelings will not admit of this,' nor would the feelings of 'the great mass of white people.'"[597]

Another issue that Lincoln raised in making new territories slave states was the disadvantage to free states for representation according to the Constitution. Five slaves counted as the same as three white men, and therefore states like South Carolina, with half as many whites as Maine, had the same representation in the number of voters, though of course the slaves could not vote. Lincoln did not want the new territories to have this same advantage.

While researching the histories of both parties, I came across an article on *Fox News* that included excerpts from Dinesh D'Souza's book *Hillary's America: The Secret History of the Democratic Party*. D'Souza is a neoconservative; not surprisingly, his book describes the Republicans as the historical heroes and the Democrats as having "a virtually uninterrupted history of thievery, corruption, and bigotry."[598] In my reading of the excerpt, D'Souza was selective in what he included or excluded for each party, and he was biased in favour of the Republican Party. The fact is that both parties have corruption and bigotry in their history.

There is a dark past in the Democratic Party as it relates to slavery and discrimination, which the party acknowledges; most notable are the Jim Crow laws. According to *Wikipedia*, those laws essentially constituted state laws to provide for 'separate but equal' policies. In the South, this was manifested in "segregation of public schools, public places, public transportation, and... restrooms, restaurants, and drinking fountains for whites and blacks." There was also a high rate of lynching in the South. In the North, segregation was in "patterns of housing segregation enforced by private covenants, bank lending practices, and job discrimination, including discriminatory labor union practices." Segregation was also extended to the military and federal workplaces.[599]

According to the *National Archives*, the first ten seats on public buses in Montgomery, Alabama used to be reserved for white people. On December 1, 1955, a bus became crowded and Rosa Parks, a black woman who was sitting in the first row of seats behind the reserved white seats, was asked to move to the back. She refused, was arrested, and is now regarded as the mother of the civil rights movement. Her actions set off a community-wide protest, which involved a young preacher named Martin Luther King Jr. In a decision on another case, the court ruled that segregation on public transportation was unconstitutional, and this ruling started to unravel the Jim Crow laws.[600] It was, however, the Democratic Party under Lyndon Johnson who signed the Civil Rights Act of 1964 that made the most progress in ending segregation and the Jim Crow laws.[601]

During the 1860s, Republicans dominated the northern states and were expanding federal power with the transcontinental railroad, the state university system, the settlement of the West, a national currency, and a protective tariff. The Democrats, strong in the South, opposed these measures. When Roosevelt, a Democrat, won the election in 1936, he did so on a platform that aimed to address the Depression by regulating financial institutions, reforming welfare, and developing infrastructure. The party formerly against big government was now promoting it. This had to do with wooing Western voters, who had not benefitted from the Republican federal expansions that served to benefit big businesses. Natalie Wolchover from *Live Science* reported that Eric Rauchway, professor of American History at the University of California, Davis, argued, "Although the rhetoric and to a degree the policies of the parties do switch places, their core supporters don't — which is to say, the Republicans remain, throughout, the party of bigger businesses; it's just that in the earlier era bigger businesses wanted bigger government and in the later era they don't."[602]

Wolchover answered my previous question as to when the parties switched sides with respect to positions on race. She explained that after emancipation, the black community voted Republican, but since 1932, most of the black community has been voting Democrat. This is when Franklin D. Roosevelt introduced the New Deal. This would help the black community, who had fared worse than most during the Depression. Blacks did not start thinking of themselves as Democrats until 1948, when Truman ended segregation in the military and set up regulations against racial bias in federal employment.[603]

Both parties have good and bad points in their history. What is more relevant is where the parties have positioned themselves in the past thirty years. I became interested in the parties and their history because of something I came across while researching the scandals that plagued Bill Clinton's presidency. I learned about the Arkansas project, which was one of the key factors in shifting my view of Hillary as the 'lesser of two evils' to a candidate that I admired for her accomplishments, her policies, and yes, her character. The Whitewater investigations and all those that followed during the Clinton administration were the precursors for Hillary's demonization.

The Arkansas Project

There have been herculean efforts to discredit the Democrats in general, and the Clintons in particular, over the years. According to John Ponder in the *Pensito Review*, the Arkansas Project was launched in the early 1990s, spearheaded by the *American Spectator* and its editor-in-chief, Emmett Tyrell Jr. Pittsburgh billionaire Richard Mellon Scaife funded the project with the sole purpose to "dig up dirt on Bill and Hillary Clinton in their home state" by "spreading lies, half-truths, and rumors."[604] Hanna Rosin from the *Atlantic* reported that with approximately $2.4 million, the project hired investigators to dig up anything they could, which led to Whitewater and all the subsequent investigations.[605] Ponder disclosed that the administrator of the project, Ted Olson, was a long-time friend of Kenneth Starr, the independent counsel for the Whitewater and subsequent investigations.[606]

Rosin explained that the motive for the eleven individuals closely involved in the project, according to Tyrell, was "Clinton disdain."[607] The parochial conservatives saw in the Clintons what they hated in the 1960s revolution: hippies, pot smokers, draft dodgers, and vehement feminists. Tyrell described them as "brats" and went on to say that they were "the most self-congratulatory generation in the American republic… and it was all based on balderdash! They are weak! The weakest generation in American history."[608]

According to Rosin, the legacy of the Arkansas Project endured in the 2016 election in the form "of opposition-research shops, media outlets, and grass-roots activist groups. A couple of these shops [had] stationed staff in Little Rock to rifle through files in search of something new—or even something old that can be framed in a newly relevant way."[609]

Rosin added that America Rising is a conservative PAC, founded in 2013 by Mitt Romney's 2012 presidential campaign manager, Matt Rhoades, with a mission to provide opposition research. Unlike some of the other 'oppo researchers,' this new firm recognized that "nasty tidbits" and wild theories would hurt their credibility. Hanna Rosin, reporter for the *Atlantic*, explained that "[t]he best dirt has become the kind that can help build a consistent and unappealing image of a candidate, or even a party."[610] This group does research and conducts focus groups to determine what segments of the population like or do not like, then go after material to reinforce that aversion.

Christopher Ruddy worked for Richard Scaife to write articles and books to discredit the Clintons and is now the CEO of the conservative website *Newsmax*. He regrets that they went too far. Of Scaife, he said, "Both of us have had a rethinking." While he expressed that he would vote for the GOP candidate, he stated, "Clinton 'will be a good president. She's going to surprise a lot of people.'"[611]

Rosin advised that in his book *Blinded by the Right*, David Brock "describes how he worked as a 'hitman,' writing deliberately false news stories about the Clintons' personal lives at the behest" of Emmet Tyrell Jr.[612] He has regrets and in 2004 founded Media Matters, whose goal is to monitor misinformation that comes out of the right to ensure that it is corrected immediately.[613]

According to the *Huffington Post*, in his book *Do Not Ask What Good We Do: Inside the US House of Representatives*, Draper reported that on the night of Obama's inauguration, there was a meeting with fifteen high-powered Republicans including Kevin McCarthy (Calif.), Paul Ryan (Wis.), Bob Corker (Tenn.), and Newt Gingrich (R–GA). Senate Minority Leader, Mitch McConnell (R-Ky.), and House Minority Leader, John Boehner (R-Ohio), were not present. McCarthy was quoted as saying, "If you act like you're the minority, you're going to stay in the minority… We've gotta challenge them on every single bill and challenge them on every single campaign."[614]

This Republican agenda to gain a majority in Congress by an all-out campaign to "attack vulnerable Democrats" and to discredit Obama by showing "united and unyielding opposition to the president's economic policies" was not in the best interest of the American people.[615]

In October 2010, McConnell told the *National Journal*, "The single most important thing we want to achieve is for President Obama to be a one-term president."[616] The remark drew criticism even from some Republicans, who accused McConnell and the GOP of sabotaging Congress to make it appear dysfunctional in the eyes of voters. Before he retired, Mike Lofgren, a GOP aide to the House and Senate Budget committees, wrote, "Evidently Senator McConnell hates Obama more than he loves his country."[617]

According to comments and a video posted by contributor keepemhonest on *Daily Kos*, "On June 12, 2012, Newt Gingrich admitted he and Paul Ryan, and eleven other GOP Congressmen did, indeed, have a meeting to ensure that Obama did not win the 2012 election."[618] I listened to and transcribed the relevant parts of the interview. Gingrich said, "It was an important meeting; I was glad and honoured to be part of it. As we left the inaugural ball, I said, 'If he [Obama] sticks to the kind of moderations and bipartisanship that he is talking, he will split the Republican Party, he'll govern like Eisenhower, and he will get re-elected.'" After the meeting, when they had a strategy, Gingrich stated, "You will remember this day; the seeds of 2012 were sown."[619]

The Republicans carried out their promise to obstruct the Obama administration. During roll call on November 11, 2013, Pete Sessions stated, "Everything we do in this body should be about messaging to win back the Senate." This took precedence over anything that might help the American people.[620] The Democratic Whip's document on the House Republicans' Record on Obstruction lists multiple occasions in which the Republicans sabotaged the Obama administration, and this document does not include the period of September 2014 to November 2016. I am going to highlight only a few occasions that were recorded in the media.

Gingrich excused the behaviour of the group of fifteen by stating that it is only reasonable to assume a party will strategize to win the next election. That is true. But to deliberately strategize to prevent a president from being successful by blocking him on everything he puts forward is immoral. I am outraged for the Americans that put Obama in office. They elected him based on their support for his proposals. The GOP had no respect for the office of the presidency or what the voters wanted, until they used 'what the voters wanted' as a rationale to support Donald Trump as their nominee.

On the one hand, Gingrich said that if Obama had been more compromising and involved them in the economic stimulus, he would have had more cooperation. However, Gingrich then said that the GOP would never have cooperated on Obamacare and the economic stimulus.[621] The GOP had already made up their minds not to cooperate. This was simply providing a rationale, after the fact, for what they had already decided. Even if their decision regarding the economic stimulus had been righteous, their motive was not.

Dana Milbank from the *Washington Post* reported, "The chairmen of the House and Senate budget committees announced, for the first time since their panels were created more than forty years ago, that they would not have hearings on the president's budget or allow administration officials to testify. They decided this before President Obama released his budget, refusing to contemplate any budget from Obama — sight unseen."[622] Other incidents identified by Milbank include the following:

- A refusal to consider or even meet with any Supreme Court nominee

- The Senate Banking Committee's refusal to act on any Obama nominee for fourteen months

- A delay of eleven months in approving the head of the Treasury Department's terrorism section

- Postponing action on a budget to provide funds to deal with the Zika virus, opioid addiction, and the water in Flint, Michigan

There were 298 House-passed bills awaiting action by the GOP-controlled Senate. "The day Obama asked Congress to take action on closing the Guantanamo Bay prison, Sen. Pat Roberts (R-Kan.) released a video of him throwing a printout of Obama's plan in the trash."[623]

Most Americans thought that the economy was the single most important issue; that there was support for increasing the minimum wage and addressing the male-female income disparity, and that there was a need for comprehensive immigration reform. Despite the interests of Americans, the Republicans obstructed the Obama administration's bills to address these issues, refusing even to negotiate.

CNN reported that the US Congress did not pass a law to appropriate any funds past September 30, 2013. This resulted in a shutdown of the government for sixteen days with a cost of $24 billion to the American economy.[624] Why? According to Ian McCullough, a reporter for *Forbes*, the Republicans failed to block Obamacare from being passed in 2010, lost several appeals and a Supreme Court decision in 2012 to have it repealed, and lost the election in 2012. They refused to pass the appropriation of funds without "a provision to a spending bill that required eliminating funding for the implementation of the PPACA [The Patient Protection and Affordable Care Act] in order to fund the rest of the U.S. Federal Government."[625]

EducationVotes reported that Congress refused to pass a temporary funding bill in September 2013 because House Democrats were insisting that they include aid to Flint, Michigan to deal with the toxic water situation. The Democrats yielded "after a last-minute agreement was reached among House leaders to include help for the beleaguered city in a water infrastructure bill that was expected to pass Congress when it returned in mid-November."[626] The Republicans demonstrated that they would go to any lengths to achieve their political agenda to obstruct Obama, even to the detriment of the American people.

According to *Reuters*, "The Constitution says that it is the president who 'shall receive ambassadors and other public ministers' from foreign governments."[627] Yet former House Speaker John Boehner secretly invited Netanyahu to speak to Congress regarding the Iran nuclear negotiations. This occurred while Netanyahu had an impending election in Israel.

The *Washington Post* disclosed that Rep. Kevin McCarthy (R-Calif.) was slated to be the next Speaker of the House but later dropped out of the race because of the following indiscretion, in which he told Fox News' Sean Hannity, "Everybody thought Hillary Clinton was unbeatable, right? But we put together a Benghazi special committee, a select committee, and what are her numbers today? Her numbers are dropping, why? Because she's untrustable. But no one would have known any of that had happened, had we not fought."[628]

Research confirms that women politicians are most vulnerable to factors of trust and ethics. Donald Trump had a relentless campaign intended to discredit Hillary specifically on these two factors. He made gross misrepresentations of her policies and the state of the nation under Obama's leadership and continues to repeat them.

An army of funded investigators has tried to bring down the Clintons since the 1990s, and they did not care if the information contained truth, half-truth, or rumours. The spreading of rumours is bullying. It does not matter if you are the originator.

I did not take exception to Bill Clinton being held accountable and facing consequences. However, I take great exception to the methods, motives, and hypocrisy involved in the investigations. The lengths and the expense that the Republicans went to in order to find something on the Clintons was reprehensible and held no benefit whatsoever for the American people. It was a vicious vendetta that cost millions in taxpayer dollars. What made it even more offensive was that when the Republicans did find something, those who were going after Bill Clinton were engaged in similar, if not even more inexcusable, behaviour.

The following indiscretions were disclosed in *Wikipedia*. The quotes are from *Wikipedia*, and the footnotes are the original sources identified by *Wikipedia*.[629]

"Dan Burton, Republican Representative from Indiana, had stated, 'No one, regardless of what party they serve, no one, regardless of what branch of government they serve, should be allowed to get away with these alleged sexual improprieties.'"[630] The hypocrisy is astounding as he later admitted to having an affair in 1983, which produced a child.[631]

If it was inappropriate for Bill Clinton to be involved with a government staffer, why did this not apply to Newt Gingrich? *SFGate* disclosed that "Speaker of the House Newt Gingrich, Representative from Georgia and leader of the Republican Revolution of 1994, admitted in 1998 to having had an affair with a House intern while he was married to his second wife, at the same time as he was leading the impeachment of Bill Clinton for perjury regarding an affair with intern Monica Lewinsky."[632]

"Republican Helen Chenoweth-Hage from Idaho aggressively called for the resignation of President Clinton but later admitted to her own six-year affair with a married rancher during the 1980s."[633]

Representative Bob Barr, a chief Clinton detractor and ardent pro-lifer, paid for an ex-wife's abortion, and infidelity allegations caused him to resign as the next Speaker of the House.[634] I did not see any equivalent attempts on the part of the Clintons or the Democrats to have these individuals under investigation for years on end, nor did I find that any of them had been charged.

These relentless investigations and accusations continued into the 2016 election campaign. I had other areas of concern with the Republican Party, including the ultra-right media, voter suppression, and gerrymandering. I obviously developed a bias while writing this book; conscious of that bias, I made an effort to include the positives and negatives on both sides. I went as far as to try to find information about similar behaviour from the left.

For example, in the discussions on systemic racism, I found numerous examples of voter suppression on the part of Republicans. I did a specific search for similar incidents conducted by Democrats and found two, which I cited in detail. There is no equivalency.

There is a view that the mainstream media favours the left. This may be true in some cases, and I express my concerns about the media in Chapter 8. I think the major issue with the mainstream media, however, is sensationalism. They misrepresent issues by using misleading sound bites. I found examples of this on both sides. I did not find deliberate attempts by the media to provide false information. The mainstream media also does not give an exclusive voice to the left. There are conservative media outlets such as Fox News, *Breitbart*, and *Drudge*, as well as many other radio hosts such as Rush Limbaugh and Glenn Beck, who provide an almost exclusively right-wing perspective, some without any regard for the truth. Others, like *Breitbart*, give a platform to white supremacists.

The following are only a few of the prolific and damaging lies perpetrated by the right-wing media, and in many cases repeated by Trump and his campaign staffers.

Truthfeed was described by *Media Bias/Fact Check* as extreme right and a questionable source. Amy Moreno from *Truthfeed* said, "You'll recall recently Hillary referred to Trump supporters as a 'basket of deplorables,' and now we've found out via leaked audio that Hillary refers to Bernie supporters as #BasementDwellers. How can such a divisive and mean-spirited person think she can unite a divided country?"[635] This message went viral on social media and was tweeted by Donald Trump and Kellyanne Conway. One tweet had a poster with a picture of

Hillary and the comments: "F[##]ing Jew Bastards, That GD N word, Stupid Kikes, Bring them to heel!" (I redacted the vilest comments.) This had Hillary's name below as if she had made these comments. The problem is, Hillary never called Bernie's supporters basement dwellers.[636] She was empathizing with their plight. "Some are new to politics completely. They're children of the Great Recession. And they are living in their parents' basement," she said. "They feel they got their education and the jobs that are available to them are not at all what they envisioned for themselves. And they don't see much of a future."[637]

The *Washington Post* reported that fake ads using Hillary's logo and font were circulated to Hillary supporters, advising them that they could text in their vote, along with instructions. How many thought this was real and that they had voted?[638]

In early November, before the election, *BuzzFeed* reported that a group of young people in Macedonia (formerly Yugoslavia) created more than a hundred pro-Trump websites, which ran plagiarized information from right-wing sites in the US. *Worldoliticus* claimed that Clinton would be indicted for her email scandal. The page got 145,000 shares on Facebook. According to *BuzzFeed*, the young people running these sites did not care about Trump. They cared about money. Apparently, each click on Facebook generated money, and according to them, "the best way to generate shares on Facebook is to publish sensationalist and often false content that caters to Trump supporters."[639]

BuzzFeed was able to interview some of the youth running these sites, which have hundreds of thousands of 'likes' on Facebook. The Macedonians reported that they tried a pro-Bernie site, but it did not generate enough traffic. The pro-Trump sites were the most lucrative, and "research also found that the most successful stories from these sites were nearly all false or misleading."[640]

One of the most successful stories was from a fake news website called *Conservative State*, which posted the headline "Hillary Clinton In 2013: 'I Would Like to See People Like Donald Trump Run for Office; They're Honest and Can't Be Bought.'"[641] This generated 480,000 shares on Facebook. *BuzzFeed* pointed out that in comparison, a story in the *New York Times* about Trump's $916 million loss generated only 175,000 Facebook interactions.[642] The claims that the Pope endorsed Trump and that Mike Pence said the Michelle Obama was the most vulgar First Lady ever were among the most popular posts and generated over one million Facebook interactions.[643]

Vox reported that there were paid trolls in Russia pretending to be Americans on multiple social media accounts making pro-Trump comments on traditional publications like the *New York Times* as well as on Facebook and Twitter. "The lies and false information often gets [sic] parroted by both conservative news outlets like Fox News and Trump himself… Are Russian trolls to blame for that?" a female troll asked comedian Samantha Bee. "Maybe people are to blame too. They're lazy and believe everything they read."[644]

Brian Stelter on CNN reported that a 'dubious' site called *Your News Wire* claimed that "Michelle Obama has scrubbed all references to Hillary Clinton from both of her Twitter accounts," implying that this action was the result of FBI investigations into Clinton.[645] The story went viral. A contributor to *ForexLive* posted an item asking, "Is the First Lady distancing the Obamas from the Clintons?" Jack Posobiec, host of a website called *Citizens for Trump* (not endorsed by the candidate), said, "Elizabeth Warren just unfollowed Hillary, and Michelle Obama deleted all her tweets about Hillary," later adding President Obama's name to the list.[646] Sean Hannity reported this on the *Sean Hannity Show* (radio), asking his producer if it was true. On later being told that Barack Obama and Elizabeth Warren unfollowed Hillary, Hannity exclaimed, "Wow, that means they know it's huge. You know why? Because Obama's implicated! He's implicated here, and he's pissed. You know what his legacy might be? Jail."[647] Hannity later apologized, but his followers had already shared it on social media. Again, too little, too late. The damage was already done. How many people who read the information heard the apology? I could not find an article or reference to this on Fox News when I Googled it.

Trump and his campaign cannot be blamed for the lies generated on social media, but they can be held accountable for retweeting and repeating them. If Fox News and Hannity want to be considered legitimate news media, then they need to verify information before airing it and causing irreparable damage.

Having said that, I am rethinking Trump's responsibility. Where did the Macedonians and other pro-Trump media get some of their misinformation from in the first place? Including statements from 2008 to November 2016, I counted twenty-nine false statements by Hillary on *PolitiFact* and seven Pants on Fire statements. For the much shorter period of the years 2011 to November 2016, *PolitiFact* recorded 113 false statements made by Trump and during the same period, it reported fifty-seven Pants on Fire statements.

The following are some of the twenty-two outrageous false statements and fourteen Pants on Fire statements attributed to Hillary by Trump and his campaign, cited by *PolitiFact*.[648,649]

- Hillary pledged to create open borders for the United States.

- It was Hillary Clinton's agenda to release violent criminals from jail.

- "Hillary Clinton says she wants to, 'raise taxes on the middle class.'"

- "Hillary Clinton and her campaign of 2008 started the birther controversy."

- "Just look at what the FBI director said about her (Hillary Clinton) — her misconduct is a disgrace and embarrassment to our country."

- The Benghazi victims were "left helpless to die as Hillary Clinton soundly slept in her bed."

- Clinton's energy agenda would "cost the U.S. economy over $5 trillion."

- Clinton wanted "to raise taxes on African-American owned businesses to as much as nearly 50 percent more than they're paying now."

- Clinton was "let off the hook" for her email scandal, while Gen. David Petraeus had his life "destroyed for doing far, far less."

- She helped a man accused of raping a twelve-year-old; "she's seen laughing on two separate occasions, laughing at the girl who was raped."

- "In her campaign for president, Hillary Clinton has received $100 million in contributions from Wall Street and hedge funds."

In addition, there was the health conspiracy. Throughout the campaign, Trump continually raised concerns about Hillary's health, claiming that "mental and physical stamina" were essential to be president.[650] In late 2012, Hillary fell and had a concussion and was later treated for a blood clot. Her doctor stated, "It should not interfere with her career."[651] Right-wing social media and some Trump supporters made assertions that she had brain damage.[652] A near fainting spell from a case of pneumonia in September 2016 further fuelled Trump and the media's speculations about her health. Her doctor provided a medical report that cleared her medically after this incident.[653]

There were only three combined False and Pants on Fire statements attributed to Hillary and her campaign about Trump and his policies, cited on *PolitiFact*.[654,655] That comprises more than four times less than the number of Trump's Pants on Fire statements alone.

- Donald Trump "doesn't make a thing in America."

- ISIS was "going to people showing videos of Donald Trump insulting Islam and Muslims in order to recruit more radical jihadists."

- "Back in the Great Recession, when millions of jobs across America hung in the balance, Donald Trump said rescuing the auto industry didn't really matter very much. He said, and I quote again, 'Let it go.'"

However, I only listed many, not all, the lies Trump made about Hillary and her policies. In Hillary's first lie, she said that Trump made nothing in America. While most of Trump's items are made overseas, his campaign paraphernalia and some apparel items were made in the US.[656] If she had said that Donald's insults regarding Islam and Muslims could be used for recruitment of jihadists, the statement would have been truthful. While her statement was not truthful at the time it was made, two weeks later, *PolitiFact* reported that Al Shabaab had released a recruitment video featuring Trump and his proposal for "total and complete shutdown of Muslims entering the U.S."[657] Hillary's comments about Trump not supporting the rescue of the auto industry were false. While he sometimes varied his position on the bailout, suggesting bankruptcy as an alternative, he was unwavering about saving the Big Three.[658]

In contrast, Trump's statements were a character assassination of Hillary to support his claims that she was 'crooked.' He used misrepresentation of her policies to generate fear and deflect questions about his own behaviour in order to escape scrutiny. The strategy was sinister in its persistence and prevalence on social media. A lie is a lie. I do not excuse Hillary's misrepresentation, but there is no equivalence.

In contrast, I found just one left-wing hoax identified by *Snopes* that claimed the Pope had endorsed Bernie Sanders.[659]

A website called *Your News Wire* claims to provide unfiltered truth but is described by *Snopes* as being satire[660] and included by *Fort Liberty* in a list of websites that mix legitimate news and hoaxes.[661] *Your News Wire* featured an article in August 2016 claiming that *Snopes* was lying for Hillary. They acknowledge that *Snopes* is "the definitive 'Urban Legends' web source to identify false stories on the internet, email hoaxes, and other pollution of public information," but *Your News Wire* claimed that once *Snopes* got into the political fact-checking arena, they had a decided Hillary bias.[662] They cited four examples, which I reviewed and found no merit in. Just to provide one example, *Your News Wire* claimed that Hillary laughed when the accused perpetrator of a rape was not found guilty. Hillary did laugh inappropriately (as she sometimes does when she is uncomfortable) but not about the outcome of the case.

I found four cases of 'unethical' practices by Democrats during the election. The *Guardian* reported that following a Russian hack of the DNC emails, the chair of the DNC, Debbie Wasserman Schultz, was asked to resign after emails were revealed showing active favouritism for Hillary against Bernie.[663] Bernie Sanders was an independent and made a choice to run on the Democratic ticket to take advantage of the Democratic machine. It should be no surprise to Bernie that Democrats would prefer their own candidate. Even so, the Democratic Party accepted him as a contender in the primaries, and Wasserman Schulz's practice was unethical, and showed a lack of respect for the Democratic voters supporting Bernie.

Donna Brazile stepped in as acting chair of the DNC on a temporary basis. Russian-hacked emails from John Podesta, chair of Hillary's presidential campaign, were leaked by *WikiLeaks*. Despite her initial denials, emails purportedly revealed that Brazile claimed to have questions for the upcoming town hall debate, and had shared them with the Clinton campaign. She had been suspended as a CNN commentator when she took the interim position as chair of the DNC, but after the email leaks, she did not return to the network.[664] I was profoundly disappointed by this apparent lapse of integrity, because I have often appreciated her perspective and balance in her contribution to discussions.

The *Washington Post* quoted Trump's claim that "[i]f you look at what came out today, on the clips, where I was wondering what happened with my rally in Chicago and other rallies where we had such violence. She's the one, and Obama, that caused the violence. They hired people — they paid them $1,500, and they're on tape saying be violent, cause fights, do bad things."[665] This issue was more complex. There was a video produced by a group called Project Veritas Action, a conservative group founded by activist James O'Keefe, that featured clips of a man named Scott Foval describing how he (Foval) sent in individuals to create conflict and incite supporters outside of Trump rallies. The video was edited, and Project Veritas is known for "purposefully editing footage to advance their agenda."[666] The *Washington Post* reported that Trump donated $10,000 to Project Veritas the previous year.[667]

The *Washington Post* explained that Scott Foval was not an employee of the DNC. He was a subcontractor working for Democracy Partners, a consulting firm that was working for the DNC. The interviewers made leading statements that sometimes suggested things were said that were not. Even so, there was some evidence on the video that individuals attended the rallies to engage Trump supporters with intent to incite them. The DNC denounced this behaviour, and there was no direct evidence of DNC involvement. There was no evidence of Obama's involvement. There was one payment of $1,500 to one individual, not multiple people, and it is still not clear what that payment was for. The person receiving the payment was not on the video, and the video did not identify her as a trainee of Foval's.[668]

A large group of anti-Trump protesters mobilized to shut down the Chicago rally, comprised mostly of university students and Bernie supporters. The evidence on the tape did not support the claim that individuals had engaged in physical confrontation, but rather that they had baited the Trump supporters. The incidents had not occurred inside the rally but outside.[669]

The *Washington Post* and *PolitiFact* did not come to any firm conclusion. Trump's statements were exaggerated. There is no evidence that the DNC was directly involved. It appears that the disruption from Foval's group was confined to the Chicago rally, and people were not being paid. There does seem to be substantiation that some people may have attended solely to incite Trump supporters, but they certainly were not the majority of the individuals at the protest in Chicago. This does not excuse Trump for the way he incited his crowds at rallies, which in some cases emboldened his supporters to engage in physical altercations.

According to the *Atlantic*, the right-wing media accused Correct the Record, a Hillary Super PAC, of paying trolls to intimidate Trump supporters online. Correct the Record funded a digital task force as part of their Breaking Barriers Project to push back against the overwhelming number of negative and false stories maligning Hillary. They provided online messaging in response to negative comments made by Trump supporters by responding with a positive message about Hillary. The *Atlantic* provided the following example: "Proud Donald J Trump supporter" tweeted out the following: "Hillary is scum." The next day, a Correct the Record account replied with the hashtag #ImWithHer and a graphic that read, "Hillary's platform is LOVE & KINDNESS."[670]

I understand the frustration and the desire to push back and correct the record. While it may have been more ethical if they had identified themselves as Correct the Record, I am not sure how effective these unsolicited emails were. They seem to have served the purpose of just giving the diehard Trump supporters more fodder for condemning Hillary. Other allegations from right-wing social media said that individuals were posing as different people and responding to Trump supporters' comments. If this were the case, it would have been unethical in my view, but if it did occur, there does not seem to be evidence that it was tied to Correct the Record.

In searching for unethical practices for both Democratic and Republican parties, gerrymandering came to my attention. This is a nefarious practice in which states manipulate voting boundaries for congressional seats to provide an advantage on a partisan basis. The *Guardian* described two methods of gerrymandering: first, drawing the boundaries so that most of a party is in one district, which they will win, while diluting their presence in other districts of the state. The other is dividing the supporters of a party among multiple districts so that the party falls short in each district.[671]

I had difficulty finding examples of gerrymandering in Democratic states, but I did. Both parties practice it, although it is far more prolific in Republican states, which dramatically skews the representation in Congress. According to *Daily Kos*, Maryland is a Democratic state in which gerrymandering is evident. Stephen Wolf contended that Democrats in Maryland did not try to maximize partisan advantage but rather "sought particular turf to aid their own personal political ambitions. In contrast, Republicans tried to maximize their seat count in nearly every state they drew, such as a twelve-to-four edge in the swing state of Ohio."[672]

In an article in the *Washington Post*, Christopher Ingraham listed the ten most gerrymandered districts. The districts were in the following states: Maryland, Florida, Pennsylvania, North Carolina, Texas, Illinois, and Louisiana. He added that three of the most gerrymandered districts are in North Carolina and that "Republicans drew Congressional boundaries in six of the ten most-gerrymandered states... Republicans picked up about eleven more seats than you'd expect from simply looking at the parties' vote shares."[673]

According to the Princeton Election Consortium, Sam Wang's research estimated that "Republican-controlled redistricting led to a swing in margin of at least twenty-six seats, almost as large as the thirty-one-seat majority of the new Congress" for the 2012 election.[674] Wow. I did not view anything about this in the mainstream television coverage of the election.

The media and Trump surrogates frequently questioned why Hillary did not have more of a lead, given her support from President Obama, Michelle Obama, Bernie Sanders, Elizabeth Warren, and Bill Clinton. I can provide several reasons.

- Donald Trump and his surrogates had at least twelve months until September 2016 in which they had almost continual media coverage to present their agenda and misrepresent Hillary's character and policy positions without being challenged or corrected, even on patently false information.

- Hillary was held to a different standard than Trump by many in the public and the media throughout the campaign.

- The media portrayed both candidates as if they were equal in dishonesty and trustworthiness (false equivalence).

- The media and a portion of the general population exhibited gender bias, and Hillary's competitor perpetuated misogyny, reinforcing that gender bias.

- Russian interference including 'fake news,' Russian hacking of DNC emails, and WikiLeaks and related fallout

- FBI intervention in the election

- Hillary and Bill Clinton contributed to the issues: her judgement regarding the email server, her fierce privacy, Bill Clinton's near impeachment during his presidency, and his indiscretion in meeting with Lynch during the email investigation with Hillary.

- 2016 was a change year because it would be the third term for the Democratic Party.

- Dynasty fatigue, Bushes and Clintons

- Voter suppression

- Gerrymandering. While this practice was not a factor in the outcome for Hillary, it was a factor in the Democrats being under-represented in the House.

- The electoral versus popular vote favouring Republicans

- Social media promulgating false news stories and conspiracies

- Republican viciousness and legal attacks

His supporters described him "as the 'embodiment of strong', and where necessary, ruthless enforcement of 'law and order,' the representative of 'popular justice,' the voice of the 'healthy sentiment of the people,' putting the nation first before any particularistic cause and wholly detached from any personal, material, or selfish motives, and regarded as a God-fearing and deeply religious man."[675]

Though these words sound as though they are describing Donald Trump, these are in fact direct quotes describing Hitler. It is the 'Hitler Myth,' the image he created as part of his propaganda strategy. I know this is controversial. Some would say I am foolhardy to deal with this subject. Trump inspires me to include this, for he, his son, and his surrogate Jeffrey Lord frequently invoked images, references, and comparisons to Nazism with far less cause. There have been many comparisons of Trump to Hitler or Nazism that have been highly criticized. In one case, a teacher was suspended for discussing the parallels in his history class, and some wanted that teacher fired. He was not saying that Trump was Hitler, but he was drawing the comparison.

This teacher was Frank Navarro, who is described as a Holocaust scholar, teaching his high school history class to demonstrate how "history repeats itself." He drew comparisons between Hitler's promises to get rid of foreigners and make Germany "great again" and Trump's proposals to build the wall to keep immigrants out and "make America great again." A petition was circulated to revoke the suspension, which collected over 17,000 signatures.[676] I sourced this from *Breitbart* because I was curious about how they would cover it. Interestingly, they did not condemn the comparison.

When asked why he felt he had to discuss the Hitler comparisons in his high school class, Navarro stated, "I feel strongly about this. To stand quiet in the face of bigotry and to turn your eyes away from it is to back up the bigotry, and that's not what I, or any history teacher, should be doing in our work."[677]

I was going to leave this out because it occurred to me that it could be offensive, until I read the following in a 1990 *Vanity Fair* article: "Ivana Trump told her lawyer Michael Kennedy that from time to time, her husband reads a book of Hitler's collected speeches, *My New Order*, which he keeps in a cabinet by his bed."[678] Bruce Loebs, a history professor at Idaho State University, described Hitler as a "charismatic speaker, and people, for whatever reason, became enamored with him… People were most willing to follow him, because he seemed to have the right answers in a time of enormous economic upheaval."[679] Trump also gave permission by example, as he has referred to the CIA as Nazi Germany and often invoked references or images of Nazism.

The following is Hitler's propaganda strategy, as described by Ian Kershaw in the *'Hitler Myth'*, and my comments regarding a striking similarity to Trump's strategy.

- "The gross underestimation of Hitler again paved the way for at first reluctant or condescending, and then wholehearted, enthusiasm for the way he apparently mastered within such a short time the internal political situation which had seemed beyond the capabilities of an upstart rabble-rouser."[680]

- Trump was underestimated and surprised the Republicans in defeating all his competitors in the primaries, even though he had no political experience.
- "He polarized feelings between bitter hatred and ecstatic devotion."[681]
  - Trump stated that his supporters were so loyal that "[he] could stand in the middle of 5th Avenue and shoot somebody and [he] wouldn't lose voters."[682] Democrats and many Republicans were outraged by this rhetoric.
- Hitler held deep hostility toward the failed democratic system and a belief that strong, authoritarian leadership was necessary for any recovery.[683]
  - Trump regularly described the system as rigged and corrupt. He admires Putin's leadership.
- Bourgeois circles continued to see in Hitler the social upstart and vulgar demagogue, mouthpiece of the hysterical masses, and head of a party containing some wild and threatening elements.[684]
  - Trump's rhetoric created divisiveness among the American people. He incited his supporters at rallies. He is their voice and says what they believe.
- Those taking a less-than-favourable view of Hitler's qualities were incarcerated or silenced by fear and repression.[685]
  - Trump regularly threatened people with lawsuits when they spoke out against him. He threatened to have Hillary put in jail. He was going to change the libel laws to sue the media.
- Even church leaders with a reputation for hostility to Nazism were persuaded of Hitler's sincerity, belief in God, and acceptance of the role of Christianity and the churches.[686]
  - Trump garnered the support of the evangelical right and promised to protect Christian rights.
- While he remained fanatical to exclude Jews from German society, Hitler began to distance himself from public association with "the generally unpopular pogrom-type anti-Semitic outrages."[687]
  - Trump modified his position from banning all Muslims to those entering from terrorist regions.
- "Without at least the prospect of an improved living standard, the extent of the effective integration produced by the 'Hitler Myth' would have been difficult to achieve."[688]
  - Trump promised that he would bring jobs back to America and that the 'left behind' would no longer be forgotten.

There are more unsettling comparisons. Trump is obsessed with genetics. In an interview with Oprah in 1998 about his book, *The Art of the Deal,* he ascribed his success to having the right genes.[689] "I'm a gene believer... Hey, when you connect two race horses you... usually end up with a fast horse."[690]

There was a subliminal picture of Nazi soldiers in an unofficial poster that Trump retweeted,[691] as well as the Jewish Star of David in a flyer about Hillary that her campaign perceived as anti-Semitic.[692] Then there were his statements that he "would consider requiring Muslim-Americans to register with a government database, or worse, mandating that they carry special identification cards that note their faith."[693] Donald Trump Jr. tweeted, "The media has been her [Hillary's] number one surrogate in this. Without the media, this would not even be a contest, but the media has built her up. They've let her slide on every discrepancy, on every lie, on every DNC game trying to get Bernie Sanders out of this thing. If Republicans were doing that they would be warming up the gas chamber right now."[694] While Don Jr. insisted it was a reference to capital punishment, others believed it recalled the mass killings during the Holocaust.

While Donald Trump's supporters said that he was to be taken seriously, not literally, what were individuals to take from his statement, "I would bomb the S#IT out of 'em! I would blow up every inch, there would be nothing left."[695] What is this if not annihilation? Even if he did not mean it literally, he has expressed admiration of Putin, who was bombing Aleppo and has reportedly killed two thousand civilians in six months.[696]

Trump prevaricated on denouncing David Duke and retweeted messages from white supremacists. David Duke said, "the reason a lot of Klan members like Donald Trump is because a lot of what he believes in, we believe in."[697] Trump also hired Stephen Bannon as his campaign manager, who, as CEO of *Breitbart*, gave a platform to white supremacy.

I don't know if he is a fascist or not. At the very least, it appears that Trump copied not only Reagan's campaign slogan, but also Hitler's propaganda strategy.

I have friends and family who are Trump supporters. I do not believe that Trump supporters are all racists and misogynists. Some are die-hard Republicans believing in less government, some are religious right who want Roe v. Wade overturned, some are fervent Second Amendment supporters, some are afraid of immigration because of terrorism, and some have been left behind economically. Others truly are racists and misogynists. Some just wanted change.

The campaign was so divisive, though, that many avoided discussions for fear of confrontation. Some friends of mine who are of mixed race have said that they do not listen to the news or discuss politics because it is so toxic and upsetting. They feel there is nothing they can do about it, so they would rather focus on enjoying their lives. I think many people feel that way.

There are sometimes personal risks to ethical behaviour. I remember an experience that I had while doing my practicum for my graduate degree in social work. We were required to work two days a week in a social agency, without pay, for experience under supervision, for which we were graded. I requested that I be placed in an agency in Detroit to avoid conflict of interest. I worked for the Ministry of Community and Social Services with the government of Ontario and funded many of the local social agencies. My placement was at the Jewish Welfare Federation in Detroit, and I developed the Jewish Information Service, which included public and Jewish services. One of the components was to provide crisis intervention for those who lived through the Holocaust as well as their children. Not knowing a great deal about it, I visited the Holocaust Memorial Center in Michigan. I spent the whole day viewing films, talking to survivors, and reading materials. Some of the exhibits were interactive, and one had several vignettes in which visitors could select a course of action as to what they would do in each of the circumstances. I selected choices I thought were the morally correct actions. I died in each scenario.

When I returned home, my husband asked what was wrong and I said nothing. A week later, my supervisor asked me about my visit to the memorial and I started to cry. I did not realize how traumatized I had been. While the horrific scenes were upsetting, I think what bothered me even more was that I could not be sure if I would have taken the morally correct course of action.

Both the Republican and Democratic parties have ethical issues, but I have concluded that, in this campaign, there was no equivalence. Contrary to being an aberration in the Republican Party, Trump is a reflection of the party. Many Republican leaders have normalized Trump and attempted to justify the indefensible.

I don't countenance deception or corruption in either party. However, the Republicans do not seem to care that most Americans are pro-choice and that the Supreme Court has upheld this ideology. While some Republicans are self-righteous about pro-life, some seem to have no problem with abortion when it affects their personal lives. They do not care that most Republicans favour some kind of gun regulations, nor do they seem to care about what is in the best interest of the American people. I have seen no evidence that trickle-down economics has ever benefitted the working class. The Republicans obstructed any bills that may have benefitted the American people, including the Affordable Care Act.

Of course, there are some ethical Republican politicians. Republican legislators and leaders who have demonstrated they are willing to risk standing for principles rather than partisan politics include John Kasich, Susan Collins, John McCain, Michael J. Rogers, and CNN contributor Anna Navarro, to mention a few. I was impressed when Marco Rubio refused to give credence to the information from *WikiLeaks*, pointing out it could happen to Republicans as well. Too many Republican leaders are not as willing to stand for principles.

Are we going to take lessons from history? I believe Donald Trump did.

CHAPTER EIGHT

Is The Media Contributing To Public Enlightenment?

Democracy cannot succeed unless those who express their choice are prepared to choose wisely. The real safeguard of democracy, therefore, is education.[698]
—*Franklin D. Roosevelt*

The *Society of Professional Journalists* proclaims that the role of journalism is "public enlightenment," which "is the forerunner of justice and the foundation of democracy."[699] The *American Press Institute* defines the elements of good journalism, whose "first loyalty is to" the citizenry and includes having an obligation to the truth and a responsibility of providing reliable information through the "discipline of verification."[700]

The First Amendment to the Constitution protects the freedom of the press: "Congress shall make no law… abridging the freedom of speech, or of the press… the Supreme Court has held that speakers are protected against all government agencies and officials: federal, state, and local, and legislative, executive, or judicial… the government cannot be trusted to decide what ideas or information 'the people' should be allowed to hear."[701]

In 2016, the United States' press freedom ranking in the Reporters Without Borders[702] report was forty-one out of 180. Canada ranked eighteenth. While Canada's ranking improved from twenty-first in 2010, the United States' ranking dropped from twentieth, a difference of twenty-one points. In other words, freedom of the press in the United States is perceived as having been compromised. South Africa, Chile, Samoa, and Ghana are just a few of the countries ranking better than the United States. Reporters Without Borders contends that "[f]reedom ends where national security begins. US media freedom, enshrined in the First Amendment to the 1787 Constitution, has encountered a major obstacle – the government's war on whistleblowers who leak information about its surveillance activities, spying and foreign operations, especially those linked to counter-terrorism. Furthermore, US journalists are still not protected by a federal 'shield law' guaranteeing their right not to reveal their sources and other confidential work-related information."[703]

Has the media honoured that sacred trust, or have they betrayed the public confidence? There was a time when I believed that anything I saw in print or on the news was truth. According to Alison McKenzie from *Al Jazeera*, "While American journalists have long been hailed as flag bearers of the profession … we have seen a number of cases of fabrication by journalists who have shamed the profession at large and undermined public trust. The more journalism loses popular support, the greater the leverage the public and government officials have to restrict press freedom."[704] Public enlightenment and public trust in the media have been compromised.

The following are just some of the incidents of plagiarism and fabrication by journalists in the United States.

Stripes reported that "NBC Nightly News anchor Brian Williams admitted… he was not aboard a helicopter hit and forced down by RPG fire during the invasion of Iraq in 2003, a false claim that has been repeated by the network for years."[705]

While Bill O'Reilly lamented the distortions of the leftist media regarding Williams's disgrace, according to *Mother Jones*, O'Reilly refused to respond to multiple requests questioning similar misrepresentations of his own experiences as a war correspondent, including a claim of being in the conflict in the Falklands when the British media and US media emphasized that access was very restricted. O'Reilly was a representative for his own network at the time. CBS News producer Susan Zirinsky discredited O'Reilly's claim in the following statement reported by *Mother Jones*: "Nobody got to the war zone during the Falklands war… You weren't allowed on by the Argentinians. No CBS person got there."[706]

Poynter revealed that "Juan Thompson, who until November [2015] was a reporter for the *Intercept*, has been fired from the national security site after editors unspooled 'a pattern of deception' that revealed he fabricated quotes and misled colleagues in order to cover his tracks."[707]

In a separate article, *Poynter* disclosed that Joseph Mayton, a freelance writer for the *Guardian*, had thirteen items removed from its website based on allegations of fabrication for which he was unable or unwilling to provide sources.[708]

Plagiarism Today reported that Jonah Lehrer, a science and technology reporter for the *New Yorker*; Fareed Zakaria, a CNN correspondent and editor of *Time Magazine*; Jayson Blair, a journalist for the *New York Times*; Lloyd Brown, an editor for the *Florida Times-Union*; and Nada Behziz, a reporter at the *Bakersfield Californian* either admitted to, or were found guilty of, plagiarism or fabrication.[709]

Trump repeatedly accused the media of exhibiting bias and misrepresenting him throughout the campaign process. The media took great exception and vociferously defended their position in each case. Most of Trump's claims were ridiculous, but perhaps he sometimes had a point.

Mollie Hemingway of the *Federalist* accused the media of "hyper-literalism," and Pascal-Emmanuel Gobry, a columnist at the *Week*, agreed. In an interview on August 11, 2016, Hugh Hewitt, a conservative radio host with the Salem Radio Network, tried to get Trump to explain his statement that Obama was the founder of ISIS. He gave Trump several opportunities to revise his position. Finally, at the end of the interview, Trump commented, "If he would have done things properly, you wouldn't have had ISIS." Hewitt replied, "I'd just use different language to communicate it." Trump had the final say: "But they wouldn't talk about your language, and they do talk about my language, right?" Both Hemingway and Gobry made the argument that reporters should have listened to the interview with Hewitt until the end. Gobry concluded, "I hate Trump, and I hope he loses. But I fear one consequence of his candidacy will be an even more biased press in the future."[710]

Instead of focusing on the semantics of Obama's founding of ISIS and the literal definition of 'founding,' the media could have focused on the consequences of a conspiracy theory and its implications. These comments were made in the context of Trump continuing to question Obama's birthplace and referring to him as Barack Hussein Obama. The implication was that Obama was linked to Islam, and Trump was connecting him with ISIS. Russian propagandists exploited Trump's words to spread misinformation. At a rally in Lebanon, Hezbollah leader Hassan Nasrallah cited Trump's statement that Obama "founded ISIS" as proof of its truth, adding, "This is an American presidential candidate who is saying this."[711]

My week in Melaque, Mexico, with only Fox News available in English, was the impetus for my obsession with this election. I was troubled with the nature of the coverage. It was not until I arrived home and started doing research that the reason for my intense agitation while viewing that station crystalized. While the Fox Network claimed to be impartial, other news outlets, politicians, and various groups alleged that it had a right-wing bias to promote the Republican Party. Indeed, in January 2010, Rupert Murdoch's son-in-law stated that "members of the media mogul's family are 'ashamed and sickened' by the right leaning tendencies of Fox News in the opening salvo in a bid to displace Roger Ailes, the founder and CEO of Fox News."[712]

Rupert Murdoch, the owner, and CEO of Fox News, was criticized for the "dumbing down" of news and for introducing "mindless vulgarity" in place of genuine journalism. In addition, he was said to have his own outlets produce news that served his political and financial agendas.[713]

PunditFact produced a scorecard on fact-checks conducted on selected news coverage. About "60 percent of the [Fox News] claims checked have been rated Mostly False or worse" by *PunditFact,* and "[a]t MSNBC and NBC, 44 percent of claims have received a rating of Mostly False or worse."[714] The ratings of false claims for both Fox News and NBC are significantly higher than the rating for Hillary on *PolitiFact*'s scorecard for 'Mostly False' or worse at 26%.[715] In their study, *PunditFact* claimed that CNN "had the best record among the cable networks, as 80 percent" of their reporting was 'Mostly True.'[716]

Following an allegation of sexual harassment that ferreted out additional complaints in a follow-up investigation, Roger Ailes, Chairman, and CEO of Fox News, resigned on July 21, 2016 after twenty years. According to Brian Stelter and Dylan Byers from *CNN,* "[a]nother option for Ailes, once a feared Republican political consultant, is a return to the political arena. He has had a friendly relationship with the GOP nominee Donald Trump for decades."[717]

Brendan James of *Vice* reported on Trump's undaunted support of Ailes and quoted Trump as saying, "'I can tell you that some of the women that are complaining, I know how much he's helped them… It's very sad, because he's a very good person. I've always found him to be just a very, very good person.'"[718]

Mnar Muhawesh and *MintPress News* provided the following warning from political advocate and comedian Jon Stewart: "It's recommended you only watch Fox through a tiny pinhole poked in a piece of cardboard… You can't look directly at Fox. It will indelibly burn your soul!"[719]

Well, that explains it. I was not using the peephole cardboard in Melaque! It also explains the visceral reaction I had when watching Fox News. While I am uncomfortable referring to my earlier impression of female correspondents as 'beauty queens,' I would be remiss if I did not put it in the context of recent revelations. I was reacting not only to the misinformation and rhetoric of Fox News, but also to the subliminal gender bias. I am confident that Roger Ailes held similar views to Donald Trump, who declared to a reporter, "you wouldn't have your job if you were not beautiful."[720]

This Fox phenomenon is of concern when one considers its potential to influence elections. Fox News was introduced in 1996 and is a conservative media outlet. A study was published in the *National Bureau of Economics* that reported results of Fox's impact on voting between 1996 and November 2000.[721] The study conducted by Stefano DellaVigna and Ethan Kaplan concluded "We find a significant effect of the introduction of Fox News on the vote share in presidential elections between 1996 and 2000. Republicans gained 0.4 to 0.7 percentage points in the towns that broadcast Fox News."[722]

This report went on to say that Fox News also affected voter turnout and "convinced 3 to 28 percent of its viewers to vote Republican."[723] In a campaign as close as this one, it could have been a deciding factor in the outcome. This is scary indeed when one considers the 60% false reporting for Fox. I had not been watching Fox News, but if I was frustrated by the coverage on CNN, I shudder to think what the coverage was like on Fox and how it may have impacted viewers' decisions.

It has been reported by the *New York Times* that Fox News paid out over $13 million to settle workplace sexual assault/abuse charges against Bill O'Reilly.[724] Trump supported him, asserting that O'Reilly "did nothing wrong."[725] Advertisers withdrew support, but viewership increased.[726] Something is amiss with the values of some people in America when an individual who admitted to sexual assault becomes president and the TV viewership increases for another. O'Reilly was finally let go by Fox News following an investigation, but O'Reilly will probably get a settlement of around $25 million.[727]

There is nothing "just" about it when the perpetrators receive buyouts much larger than the settlements for victims and when the victims are the ones who lose their jobs. If Fox News were seriously interested in improving the workplace for female employees, why did the company renew O'Reilly's contract when it was known for years that there had been several complaints? Moreover, why did Fox News make buyouts to cover up sexual harassment by O'Reilly over many years?

Fox News has other problems. This culture has existed at Fox since its inception with Roger Ailes. Other personalities at Fox News appear to embrace this sexist culture. Jesse Watters is known to make vile sexist and racist remarks.[728]

While the right constantly charges the mainstream media of leaning left, the right-wing media blatantly supports the Republicans and regularly derides the left, often providing false information. I have no problem with the concept of right-leaning media. I do have an issue when that right-leaning media creates its own facts. On-air personalities like Sean Hannity and Jesse Watters erode Fox's credibility. Like O'Reilly, they are smug, behave rudely to any guest that has a leftist view, and have a vague acquaintance with the truth.

While interviewing Sean Hannity on *CBS Sunday Morning*, Ted Koppel reaffirmed the negative influence of Fox News when he told Sean Hannity he was "bad for America." According to *USA Today*, the "segment examined the polarization of the country and the phenomenon of 'fake news' and how conservative pundits like Hannity may be contributing to broad societal confusion and the inability to distinguish between ideology and fact."[729] I agree. This kind of 'bad' journalism created the environment needed for the success of a Trump election.

However, I did make a concerted effort to watch Fox News during my last two visits to Mexico with the goal of gaining a better insight on the conservative perspective and developed a growing appreciation for Howard Kurtz and Chris Wallace in particular. There is no drama, sensationalism, innuendo, or derisiveness; they present credible facts and allow generally respectful discussion of liberal and conservative views. This is what I consider journalism. It is like my experience in viewing CBC News (Canadian Broadcasting), although some perceive it to have a liberal bias. I am becoming more convinced that the nature of the US 24-hour cable news stations, with their sensationalism and speculation, contribute to the polarization, not the education of the American people. While I think there is a place for opinion and discussion, not when it overtakes the factual news and the lines are so blurred that the public is unable to distinguish them.

The coverage of the election was fragmented, and the overwhelming amount of information contributed to "information overload" by the media, making it difficult to understand an issue. This resulted in poor decision-making.[730]

I was a regular viewer of CNN for American news. My experience while following this election campaign was frustrating and profoundly disappointing, mostly because I expected better. CNN hired Corey Lewandowski as a paid political commentator immediately after he was fired as Trump's campaign manager. CNN defended their decision on the basis that Lewandowski could be a valuable asset because there were few people who knew more about Trump's campaign. This seems a bit disingenuous, since Lewandowski acknowledged that "he signed a nondisclosure agreement with Trump that prevents him from disparaging the candidate or revealing proprietary information about the campaign."[731] His glowing comments about Trump and his defense of anything Trump said or did would seem to confirm the assessment that the non-disclosure agreement was in full force—though that trait seemed to be shared by all Trump supporters.

Jeffrey Lord was also a paid pundit who supported and, in his moderated way, interpreted Trump. He sometimes even made sense of Trump's actions and comments. While his interpretations occasionally seemed reasonable, they were often not accurate portrayals of what Trump said or did. Kayleigh McEnany was a Trump pundit with CNN, and she was the most strident. Not only did she unfailingly defend him, but she interrupted and talked over other commentators, often with a disdainful demeanour. She was adept at deflecting the question toward criticism about Hillary. CNN hired some commentators, most of them being Trump surrogates, that had no capacity for open dialogue or critical analysis.

I have the capacity to appreciate the contribution of right-wing commentators. They can provoke me into examining things from a different perspective. Trump's pundits had no credibility, however, because they would not provide critical analysis, and they defended the indefensible. Unlike Trump surrogates, the Hillary surrogates that I saw on TV seemed to have the capacity to question her and Bernie's behaviour, as well as to acknowledge positives from the other side.

I was disappointed in general with the hosts of various programmes on CNN. I had the impression that, in reaction to Trump's unrelenting attacks on the media, the media was on the defensive and pandering to him to prove that he was mistaken regarding bias. There were times that I railed at the television, begging the speakers to challenge the blatant lies, provide some background information, or put something in context.

One example of misleading reporting regarded Hillary's position on the coal industry. The media emphasized the sound bite, "We're going to put a lot of coal miners and coal companies out of business."[732] Trump repeatedly used this to say that Hillary would take their jobs.

Missing from the media were the following statements: "We're going to make it clear that we don't want to forget those people," Clinton said. "Those people labored in those mines for generations, losing their health, often losing their lives to turn on our lights and power our factories. Now we've got to move away from coal and all the other fossil fuels, but I don't want to move away from the people who did the best they could to produce the energy that we relied on."[733] By the time this was clarified in the media, the damage had been done.

Another example of misinformation was the Associated Press tweet that was covered in all the media. It read, "BREAKING: AP analysis: More than half those who met Clinton as Cabinet secretary gave money to Clinton Foundation." It was a misleading tweet, and in response to complaints, the AP agreed it was "sloppy" but initially refused to take it down. "The decision to delete the tweet comes after 'near unanimous agreement' among journalists that the AP's tweet was inaccurate and false, and widespread criticism of the underlying AP report, which provided no evidence of wrongdoing and scandalized Clinton's effort to aid a Nobel Peace Prize winner. House Republicans… used this botched report to call for an investigation into the Clinton Foundation."[734] This announcement to take it down was made on September 8, 2016, and the AP stated that the controversy made them reflect and that they would change their practices.[735]

Hillary's image was damaged. I saw the coverage of the original tweet numerous times, but I never saw the retraction in the television coverage. My perception that Hillary was being held to a different standard was confirmed when Dana Bash from CNN said, "I think the stakes are much higher in this debate and all the debates for Hillary Clinton because the expectations are higher for her because she's a seasoned politician. She's a seasoned debater. You know, yes, we saw Donald Trump in the primaries debate for the first time, but he is a first-time politician. So, um, for lots of reasons. Maybe it's not fair, but that's the way it is. The onus is on her."[736]

I had an impression that the media was more interested in appearing to be impartial than being so. I made a concerted effort to become informed and felt overwhelmed by information and confusion as to what was fact.

I did not understand the issue about the personal email server. While there were numerous updates on the issue and days of discussion panels, I did not see a comprehensive summary of the issue and the related facts to provide context for the updates and discussions. Had I not done exhaustive research, I would have believed that Hillary sent emails marked confidential, that she personally deleted or directed the deletion of the emails in contravention of a subpoena, and that she misrepresented having received detailed advice from Colin Powell. I have never seen a discussion of the email from Colin Powell, released in September 2016. I did not hear anyone challenge statements that Hillary deleted the emails. Those were important distinctions.

Hillary was held to a different standard than Trump. If he did not make an outrageous comment in a debate for forty minutes, he was praised, even though much of what he said was misinformation. A frequent comment was made that if he would just stay on point with his economic platform, he would do well. Why? Most economists said that he would not create jobs, but he would add considerably to the deficit, and he did not address dealing with inequities for the wealthy, but rather enhanced their advantages. Donald Trump was given a pass by the media based on his not being a politician. He was running for the most powerful position in the world. He and his surrogates stated that he had the qualifications and skills just because he was the CEO of a giant corporation.

Throughout the campaign, the media and commentators continually suggested that neither candidate was considered trustworthy. The following is just one example, but there were countless other incidents. On November 4, 2016, on *CNN Newsroom* with Carol Costello, she commented, "There are so many lies on both sides," as if there were an equivalence between the two candidates. On *PolitiFact*, Hillary had a much better record with respect to telling the truth; Donald had the worst ever score for false statements. The fact checking after debates showed that Donald Trump made far more false statements. In addition to the difference in the frequency of the false statements, there was also a difference in their nature. Hillary's were generally innocuous, while Trump's were misrepresentations intended to engender a strong emotional response. Yes, hold both sides accountable for false statements, but it was a disservice to the American voters to portray this as equivalent.

Another imbalance in the media concerned the transparency of both candidates. In fact, there was an emphasis on Hillary's lack of transparency, particularly relating to the email server, her health issue when she had pneumonia, and her accessibility to the media. Trump was only accessible to the media if he controlled the process and was able to put forth his own agenda without accountability. That is not transparency. He did not disclose his taxes, he did not provide a medical record (and to date I have seen no follow-up on this once he released it on the *Dr. Oz Show*), and he did not provide information about his charitable donations and foundations. He did not provide information about potential conflicts of interest with his business affiliations, particularly foreign relationships. While Hillary was protective of her privacy, she provided a significant amount of personal information, plus details of numerous investigations, most of her emails as Secretary of State, leaked emails from Russian hacks of the DNC and her staff, and private confidences to a friend from diaries archived at a university. There was no equivalence.

There were frequent comparisons in which both candidates were said to be running negative campaigns. Trump defeated fifteen opponents to win the primaries and did so by lying and demeaning his competitors. Trump began the general campaign by calling his opponent "crooked Hillary." He implied that the Clintons were involved in the Vince Foster suicide. He invited the Russians to hack her emails and made veiled suggestions that Second Amendment supporters should 'take care of it' if she were to become president. He accused her of creating ISIS. That is just to mention but a few of his vicious attacks. Hillary's campaign was negative because she used Trump's own words in commercials and called him out on racism and misogyny.

Trump and his supporters regularly referred to Hillary as corrupt. Whenever they were asked about Trump's taxes, charitable donations, or behaviour, they invariably pivoted to condemning Hillary and were allowed to do this without interruption until about September 2016. After that, some attempts were made to bring the Trump surrogates back to the original question, but those attempts were often ignored. Trump and his surrogates most often controlled the interviews and panel discussion.

Twenty-four-hour news stations could make one minor adjustment that would reduce the blurring of news versus opinion. Provide a designated half-hour of the news at least three times a day that is reporting. Just the facts, with opposing viewpoints, and their rationales, if appropriate. No speculation, no panel discussions. Updates could be provided on the successive segments when available.

Other coverage that I would have found immensely helpful during the 2016 campaign includes the following:

- A comprehensive comparison of both candidates' positions on the significant policies and issues, including trade agreements, economic policy and job development, and Obamacare. This could have been posted on the *CNN* website and updated as information changed. Some Americans did not even think that Hillary had a plan, though it was far more detailed than Trump's.

- A comprehensive report on major issues during the campaign. In this election, the topics would have been Russian interference in the election, racism as a factor in the campaign, a comparison of potential conflicts of interest for each candidate, and the FBI investigation on Hillary's email server.

- While there was much coverage that Hillary made history as the first female presidential nominee of a major party and potentially the first female president, I did not see a full discussion regarding the gender aspect of the election and how it may have been influencing voters. For example, Ohio is a swing state. How many female governors and mayors have been elected there? The race was close, and while gender bias may not have been a major factor, it could have decided the outcome, especially coupled with the issue of trade agreements.

The following are the major concerns that I had with the election coverage

- It was particularly vexing to me that the media consistently allowed statements that Hillary deleted the emails to stand. This should have been clarified each and every time detractors used this as an argument that Hillary was "crooked" and should be "locked up." Hillary did request that her computer technicians delete her personal emails before the investigation ensued. However, Hillary and her lawyer then advised her computer technicians that the investigators had directed that no emails be deleted, in accordance with the subpoena. One of the computer technicians deleted the personal emails following this edict. I conjecture it was because he realized he had forgotten to do so when Hillary first made the request. This was a critical distinction that the media consistently failed to illuminate.

- In general, I do not think the media took the Russian interference as seriously as it should have during the campaign. The scandalous news and Trump's tweets overtook the media in lieu of covering the real issues. It should have been the other way around. When the Democrats raised the warning during the campaign that this was a serious issue, the media treated them as if they were whining.

- The media knew about the 'fake news' stories coming out of Russia and could have exposed the major hoaxes throughout the campaign.

- While Trump was not transparent about his potential conflict of interest, there was significant information available that could have been disclosed regarding his business practices and potential conflicts of interest during the campaign. Just as one example, the lease agreement of the Washington property was a clear conflict of interest. I am unable to find a disposition on that matter. I have not seen a recent update of his many lawsuits.

While there was some excellent coverage, I found it difficult to integrate. Nothing gave me a complete report on an issue with the facts and updates. Coupled with the media bias and the lack of credibility, this created a lack of public confidence.

I was disappointed and did not feel well-informed watching CNN. It used stream-of-consciousness reporting and editorialized talk shows—a lazy alternative to real reporting. I was not alone in this assessment. Pew Research Center's American Trends Panel claimed, "None of the source types asked about in the survey was deemed most helpful by more than a quarter of US adults." The most popular source for election updates was cable news at 24%, followed by social media at 14% and TV at 14%. News websites were a source for 13% and, surprisingly, nightly news came in at only 10%.[737]

That viewers did not find news sources to be particularly helpful is not surprising. There was no one programme that simply reported the events of the day. The issues discussed in the various programmes and panels on Trump changed from day to day because there was a new outrageous comment every day. Issues pertaining to Hillary focused almost exclusively on the email server and the potential conflict of interest relating to the Clinton Charitable Foundation. Instead of reporting on any developments, every programme had a panel covering the same subject for days on end, twenty-four hours a day. Did this not give an unwarranted sense of gravity in comparison? How was this not biased?

Fox News topped the ratings for the fifty-third-consecutive quarter with 1.72 million primetime viewers. CNN came in second with 535,000 total primetime viewers, and MSNBC was third with 316,000. Fox News had 869,000 more viewers than CNN and MSNBC combined! A recent *Gallup* poll reported that trust in the media is at an all-time low and that 60% of Americans do not trust the media.[738]

Trump tapped into the fact that some of his supporters didn't care about the truth; they simply wanted to hear their own opinions affirmed. If the truth was not their priority, what was the hidden agenda? Was it a fear of loss of control or loss of privilege over other groups? Perhaps a more pertinent question is why was it being permitted? Is the right to free speech in America more sacred than the truth, even if the lies ruin people's lives or incite hatred?

Chris Cillizza from the *Washington Post* made the following point: "If there is no agreed-upon neutral arbiter, there are no facts, and as I have written before, what is happening in the Republican race is that most of the candidates — save Trump, and at times, Ben Carson — are playing by an established set of rules around what you can say and do. Trump is not only not playing by those rules but there are also no referees to enforce his blatant flouting of them."[739]

Hillary Clinton was not the only one having to deal with trust issues. Her rating for trustworthiness was more favourable than most of the media's. MSNBC had a significant drop in ratings, and Rush Limbaugh took credit for it, claiming that the network had much higher ratings until he stopped using its news bites and banned them.[740]

Whether that is valid or not, given the viewership of Fox News, it is irrefutable that the right-wing media had a powerful influence on this election. It seemed that the mainstream media was pandering to the right and Trump as a defense against the constant accusations of media bias. It also appeared that the media was trying to increase viewership with sensationalism and entertainment to cater to what the public wanted to hear instead of providing true journalism.

The *Daily Wire* disclosed that Les Moonves, the CEO of CBS News, acknowledged the impact of Trump coverage on the station's bottom line when he declared that "Trump's rise 'may not be good for America, but it's damn good for CBS… Man, who would have expected the ride we're all having right now? The money's rolling in and this is fun. I've never seen anything like this, and this going to be a very good year for us. Sorry. It's a terrible thing to say. But, bring it on, Donald. Keep going.'"[741] These statements would seem to confirm that sensationalism, viewership, and profits were driving the coverage. That is sad for America and a sad commentary on journalistic mores. I always understood that good journalism was an accurate and concise account of the who, what, why, where, when, and how. I experienced little if any of this in the reporting.

It was a struggle to do the research as I wrote this book, and I came to realize that I was unable to analyze any aspect or issue while relying solely on television. I decided to inform myself on the issues. I was surprised at how many external sources I needed to access to gain a comprehensive perspective on each issue. Hence the number of sources in the bibliography and footnotes. I may have missed some critical information, and that is the point. How is the American voter supposed to make an informed decision? I am retired, so my time is flexible, but most American voters are tired after work and raising a family or caring for elderly parents, so they do not have the time to research as I did. Since I was viewing regularly, I should not have had to work so hard to be informed.

This is not about partisan politics or defending candidates. This is about the media's role in keeping them honest and informing the public to make an educated decision. This election was more perilous than any other. It is my opinion that the media failed miserably in public enlightenment during this electoral process.

The issues in this election were complex, and CNN did not synthesize the information with the facts and keep people honest by consistently exposing misinformation. By September, when the media started to provide more information about Trump and fact-check his surrogates, most of the public was already convinced that it was a choice between two evils and that Hillary was corrupt. The media aided and abetted Trump's propaganda and agenda. Even when CNN was being more assertive, it was not consistent.

For example, the Smerconish interview with David Cay Johnston[742] and Betsy McCaughey[743] was informative, and Smerconish made a valiant effort to get McCaughey to respond to the questions and stop "giving soundbites." When Johnston waited patiently and asked to make a comment, Smerconish said he would get back to him and never did.[744] McCaughey took over the interview, and I was frustrated that Smerconish did not get back to Johnston. This was a very short interview. Johnston was providing substantive information that was generally ignored during the campaign. Why was this interview not a matter of discussion on the innumerable panels on CNN? This is just one of many examples as to how Trump and his surrogates were treated differently than Hillary and her surrogates.

Perhaps members of the media ought to put themselves under the same scrutiny they apply to politicians and provide fact-checks on their reporting for the public. If the media wants the respect and protection of the First Amendment, then it needs to revisit its mission and values to re-establish public trust. The first step would be to clearly distinguish fact-based news and reporting from editorials, talk show opinion formats, and entertainment. That the president of the United States cannot distinguish between 'fake news,' opinions, and fact-based news should have been a warning sign that many in the general public may have the same difficulty. If a station or programme is billed as news, then fact-based news should comprise most of the programming. Editorials and opinion-based forums should supplement the real news, not overtake it.

There is a difference between free speech for all citizens to express their opinions and the purpose of journalism. Since the free press is protected by the Constitution, why not ensure standards of practice and accountability? The Society of Professional Journalism has a comprehensive code of ethics, but it has no mandate for oversight and accountability.[745] Perhaps it should.

If a journalist does not meet those criteria, then he or she should not be protected by the Constitution. A record of 80% in telling the truth is not good enough. That is their job. Some of these programmes are like watching the *Jerry Springer Show*. That may be an unfair indictment of the *Jerry Springer Show* because it does not purport to be the news; people know exactly what they are watching.

CNN's *New Day* addressed the issue of media bias,[746] which I had identified as an oversight in the coverage. The subject was raised in the context of Trump's campaign manager responding to queries about the plagiarism in Melania's speech at the convention. The campaign manager called the question badgering and then asked, "Are you saying we're lying?"[747] It was patently obvious that her words were plagiarized.

Brian Stelter stated, "People who are on Trump's side or Clinton's side don't want to believe what the press is saying about their candidate, but I think viewers at home, they should see through the obvious tactics that the campaigns use. When they are beating up on us it is because they don't want to hear what we're saying and don't want to acknowledge the truth of what we are reporting."[748]

Kellyanne Conway complained that their campaign was being badgered. In this discussion, the media panelists pivoted to Hillary's campaign. They noted that Hillary's campaign had its own version of this and pointed to Obama's comments on the campaign trail the day before that he was "concerned about the way in which this campaign is covered."[749] Really? It wasn't bad enough that Trump's campaign constantly pivoted? Rutenberg went on to say that sometimes there was a false equivalency. "How can we treat Clinton and Trump the same when Trump makes more misstatements, for example?"[750] The media had a choice to provide balance in the coverage.

Trump did not have to pay for advertisements because he had free media. Surely this was abetting his agenda. Other candidates such as John Kasich were virtually ignored during the primary. Could it be that Trump was just more sensational and improved viewer ratings?

For the print media, this may be a challenge, but for the television, I think reporting on the misstatement and then moving on to coverage about other relevant issues like how each candidate will deal with the economy or terrorism would be more useful. One programme that resembles journalism and provides reporting is *Fareed Zakaria GPS*. He does the research, presents the facts, and augments them by having interviews, and then sums it up. He sometimes has panel discussions (that do not turn into a circus) to provide different viewpoints on a topic. He is clear when he states his opinion. He is also respectful when asking questions and does not do it with a derisive tone full of innuendo. It is one of the rare programmes on CNN for which the topic is clear because a description of the subject is often in the TV guide.

I am not ignoring Zakaria's suspension from CNN and *Time* in 2012 for plagiarism, which he described as a mistake. Since then, there have been twelve other allegations of plagiarism from critics, but other journalists dismissed them as referring to well-known facts,[751] while others criticized him of 'patch writing,' using others' ideas but rewording them to disguise them without giving credit.[752] I am not forgiving plagiarism, should that have occurred. I am commending the format used by Zakaria in his reporting.

I did not have a horse in this race; I could not vote in the US. I went into this project with a negative perception of Hillary, and yet, I found myself bristling at how she was being treated in the media coverage. Why is that? I agree that the media should have challenged Hillary to be more transparent and to be accountable for issues like the email server and the Clinton Charitable Foundation, but I did not observe a similar examination of Trump.

The journalist Jason Easley from *PoliticusUSA* said, "There is a fundamental element of dishonesty in the media's approach that has set up a corporate press created narrative that is designed to make the election closer… Instead of objectively reporting the facts of the election, some in the press have decided that Trump must be graded on a curve… The sort of journalistic malpractice that some members of the media are engaging is not only a threat to journalism, but it is how a completely unfit and unqualified candidate could become the next president."[753]

Technology has radically changed how the world receives information, including that from governments. There is a thin line between national security and whistleblowing. The media needs to ensure that the government is held accountable to prevent abuses while not posing a risk to national security. The new age of technology poses new challenges in disseminating information and ensuring accountability.

Another element has impacted how people consume their information and is being used to insidious effect by political campaigns: social media. One advantage of social media is that it reaches out to the masses, and quickly. The disadvantage of social media is that it spreads rumours, lies, and misinformation just as quickly.

Social media had a profound impact on the election. Donald Trump and his son Donald Jr. were and are very active on Twitter. While Trump made much use of the mainstream media during the primary, that dwindled considerably when he started to get questions on issues that were covered in a manner to which he took exception. He began to circumvent the media and started to use social media almost exclusively.

In Chapter 7, I described the websites in Macedonia that were circulating false news about the election. *BuzzFeed* compared the top twenty stories in mainstream media to the top twenty false stories using the number of engagements on Facebook. While mainstream media was higher in the earlier months of the election, the fake stories had more traction in the last three months. "The research turned up only one viral false election story from a hyperpartisan left-wing site. The story from *Winning Democrats* claimed Ireland was accepting anti-Trump 'refugees' from the US." The rest were right-wing stories.[754]

Ending the Fed, a website registered in March 2016, was responsible for four of the ten most viral stories, including "Pope Francis endorsing Donald Trump," "Hilary Clinton selling weapons to ISIS," "Hillary Clinton being disqualified from holding federal office," and "FBI director receiving millions from the Clinton Foundation."[755]

My husband and I hosted a visitor in August 2016 who was a relative of a friend from Utah. The visitor, a former Canadian, was a supporter of Trump. Curious, I asked why. She started giving her reasons against Hillary, and knowing some of these were myths, I asked where she was getting her information. She was getting it in emails from friends who were forwarding information from social media sites. When she returned home, she started forwarding them to me. She was excited when she sent one of the emails that were critical of Hillary, pointing out that it was from a left-wing magazine, the *New Yorker*.

I questioned the authenticity of the article. I clicked on the link to it and it did not connect. I then went to the *New Yorker* and reviewed every article on the election. The article was not there. I forwarded the information to her. This was my first wakeup call that people were relying on social media for news, regardless of its veracity.

This frightened me even more. While mainstream media was dependent on the pollsters, social media was taking off and having a significant influence. I continued to be concerned about the possibility of a Trump presidency.

While the *Gateway Pundit* is an ultra-conservative website, Jim Hoft made a convincing argument based on social media statistics that Trump would have a decided win in the election. Hoft compared the statistics for Trump and Hillary on various social media sites. On Facebook, Trump had 10,174,358 likes, and Clinton had 5,385,959. Trump's live stream posts had 18,167 shares, while Hillary's had none. Trump had 10.6 million followers, while Hillary had 8.1 million. Trump's YouTube livestream received an average of 30,000 viewers per stream, while Hillary's got five hundred. Trump had 2.2 million followers on Instagram, while Hillary had 1.8 million. Trump had 197,696 subscribers on Reddit, while Hillary had only 24,429, and there were 52,228 subscribers to "Hillary for Prison." Social media may not only have been a predictor of the outcome of the election, but a deciding factor in influencing people's voting decisions.[756]

I was almost misled into using a hoax for this book. Someone sent me a link to an article entitled "Trump Claims America Should Never Have Given Canada Its Independence."[757] When I tried to verify this on other publications, I could not find it. I examined the *Burrard Street Journal* website of the article, and in the About Us and Disclaimer sections, the website advised that it was satire and fabrication. Personally, I think this should have been more visible and that the disclaimer should have been right under the name of the website on the homepage.

These hoaxes and false news reports are damaging and a threat to democracy. They are often divisive and sometimes promote racism, sexism, and xenophobia, using blame and hatred as the vehicles. While there are many advantages to social media, it is also a source that is contributing to serious social issues, including bullying, sex crimes, child prostitution, and terrorism, and it also influences elections. I was amazed by the number of people who relied solely on social media for information about the election.

Social media is a global issue. Ashton Kutcher, in partnership with Demi Moore, established an organization called Thorn to fight sex slavery and child pornography. Since most of this is done online, they have collaborated with several technology companies like Facebook and Google.[758] Perhaps Facebook and Google could team up with a news fact site such as *PolitiFact* or *Snopes* to verify stories that are trending on social media. But, as consumers of social media, we also have a responsibility to report and demand action from the technology companies when we identify deliberately false information. We should demand that the technology company respond, up to and including closing the account of the perpetrator. It is profoundly disappointing to me that mainstream media did not aggressively debunk these viral hoaxes during the campaign.

Going into this project, it was not my expectation to conduct an indictment of the media, but rather to examine the American cultural dynamics that resulted in the widespread support of Trump's movement. I had a naïve intrinsic faith in the mainstream media, particularly CNN, as a source for my research—and found myself profoundly disappointed.

I am empathetic to the mainstream media, as this was a highly unusual election campaign with an incendiary candidate who presented unusual challenges, especially when the media was put on the defensive due to constant allegations of bias. However, informing the public, in my view, should have been made a greater priority than the challenges and the need to defend themselves against Trump's allegations. In fact, the overcorrection confirmed his allegations, for different reasons. Their overcorrection created the same effect for which they were criticized, but now the bias was against Hillary.

My greatest fear for Americans is that many made this monumental voting decision in absence of adequate information and without understanding the implications, only to be disappointed when the American dream is not realized: namely, the coal miners who will not get their jobs back and the people who will lose their healthcare. The wealthy and corporations are making huge profits, while the average American wages are stagnant. I am even skeptical as to what Trump will accomplish in terms of real job creation and the economy. Trump is too chaotic, and the market does not like uncertainty.

The media need to stop congratulating themselves. They seem to feel that because both sides complained about media bias, this meant they were doing their jobs. If education is the 'safeguard of democracy,' it was not well served by the media in this election coverage. While some of the coverage provided information in the last two months prior to the election, it was too little, too late.

CHAPTER NINE

The Final Countdown

I'm just thinking to myself right now,
we should just cancel the election and just give it to Trump, right?[759]
—*Donald Trump*

Americans were about to make a monumental decision, one that would affect not only America, but the entire world. As so aptly stated by J.E.B. Spredemannthe, "Choices made, whether bad or good, follow you forever and affect everyone in their path one way or another."[760] The election was fast approaching. One of the most critical factors in this campaign was the fear that both candidates were equally flawed. The media perpetuated this perception.

"A Choice Between the Lesser of Two Evils"

Hillary and Trump are described as the least popular candidates of all time. Trump had a 58% unfavourable rating, and Hillary was not far behind with 56%. According to *Morning Consult*, "23 percent of American voters we polled have an unfavorable view of both Clinton and Trump."[761]

The media characterized this election as choosing the "lesser of two evils." If so, that is a sad pronouncement on the state of democracy in America. But was it truly the case?

At the GOP Convention, Trump declared, "But here, at our convention, there will be no lies. We will honor the American people with the truth, and nothing else."[762] While he often made this claim, his behaviour belied his declarations. His penchant for lying was revealed in an article written by Marie Brenner in *Vanity Fair*: "'Donald is a believer in the big-lie theory,' his lawyer told me. 'If you say something again and again, people will believe you.'" When asked about it, Trump exclaimed, "One of my lawyers said that? I think if one of my lawyers said that, I'd like to know who it is, because I'd fire his ass. I'd like to find out who the scumbag is!"[763] It is interesting that the following quote is often attributed to Adolf Hitler: "If you tell a big enough lie and tell it frequently enough, it will be believed."[764] In fact, "Trump's statements were awarded *PolitiFact's* 2015 Lie of the Year."[765] While Trump tried to discredit the rating, it is interesting to note that *PolitiFact* won a Pulitzer Prize for its fact-checking in the 2008 presidential campaign.[766] In contrast, despite being portrayed as untrustworthy, Hillary had a high rating on *PolitiFact* for telling the truth.[767]

Hillary was far more transparent than Trump. Two glaring examples are the release of tax forms and medical records. Hillary released thirty-eight years of personal taxes, seventeen audited statements, and IRS 990 forms on the Clinton Foundation.[768] Trump promised to submit his taxes numerous times. He promised that if Obama made his birth certificate public, he would make his tax returns public. Even though he refused to submit tax returns for more recent years because he claimed he was being audited, he refused to submit tax returns for years that were not being audited. CNN disclosed a copy of a letter from Trump Enterprise tax lawyers, which seemed to indicate the tax returns were complete up to and including 2008.[769]

It was widely reported that Hillary submitted health records that met the same standards of those submitted by Mitt Romney and Barack Obama. She did not disclose her condition of pneumonia until it interfered with her ability to remain at a public appearance and a videotape was released showing her stumbling while getting into a car. The media speculated that they never would have known had a bystander not released the video. Her doctor gave a status report two hours after the incident, and she committed to providing a follow-up medical report. The media was critical that this took several hours.

Numerous media outlets disclosed that Trump submitted a letter from his doctor that stated, "If elected, Mr. Trump, I can state unequivocally, will be the healthiest individual ever elected to the presidency." Immediately following Hillary's pneumonia controversy, Trump appeared on the *Dr. Oz Show* and released a one-page medical report from his physician. According to *CNN*, Hillary's doctor provided an updated report on her health status on September 17, 2016, saying that it was not part of a larger issue.[770]

Trump continued to assert that he was more accessible and transparent with the media than Hillary. When he did get an interview or press conference, he controlled it and presented his agenda.

He blacklisted reporters from his rallies if they printed anything he perceived as critical. Since June 2016, he refused interviews at CNN, using Fox News as his primary outlet. He did not provide information about his taxes, charities, and foreign businesses. Again, he is a master at creating a certain image. Disclosure veiled in lies is not transparency.

Vitriolic criticisms and allegations of corruption have been hurled at the Clintons spanning four decades, chronicled in earlier chapters, but despite the efforts to find wrongdoing, Hillary has never been charged. In comparison, there was considerable evidence of corruption and conflict of interest on the part of Donald Trump, and this would follow him into the presidency. Contrary to his assertions that Hillary would be tied up in legal battles, it was he that would be subjected to this burden.

Trump's charities are not rated by any charity evaluator. The *Washington Post* disclosed that Trump was charged $2,500 by the IRS for making an "improper donation, a $25,000 gift from the Donald J. Trump Foundation, in 2013 to Pam Bondi's election campaign. At the time, Attorney General Pam Bondi was considering whether to investigate fraud allegations against Trump University. She decided not to pursue the case." In that year's tax filings, the *Washington Post* reported that the Trump Foundation did not notify the IRS of this political donation.[771]

The *Washington Post* investigated Trump's charities and donations. Reporter David Fahrenthold found several irregularities that pointed toward 'self-dealing' in the use of charitable funds. Since Trump did not contribute to his own foundation, its money was from other people. Trump allegedly used those funds for personal benefit rather than charitable causes. Examples of payments from Trump's charitable foundation include settling a business lawsuit with a cheque to a charity, paying for two portraits of himself at charity auctions, settling a lawsuit to pay a charity in the amount of $158,000, purchasing a football helmet at a charity auction, and donating in exchange for sponsorship of a charity (the sponsorship was advertising Trump's business).[772]

One of the settlements involved a lawsuit by an individual who won a prize of $1 million in a charity event at a Trump golf course for a hole in one. He was later told he did not win the prize because the rules required that the shot had to go 150 yards. Trump's course had made the hole too short. The individual sued and signed off on an agreement for Trump to donate to the individual's charity of choice. Trump paid with a cheque from his foundation.[773]

Mike Pence claimed that Trump made donations of "tens of millions"[774] to charities, though Trump had not made a personal donation to the foundation since 2008, Fahrenthold disclosed.[775] Trump would not release details about his donations. There was no substantiation for this claim. Evidence to date would suggest this claim about large donations is false.

There is now evidence that Trump may have used a consulting firm, under the guise of charity travel, to try to conduct business in Cuba in 1998. If this were true, he would have been in contravention of the Cuban embargo.[776] I have been unable to find any evidence that this was under investigation, never mind the possibility of related charges. This is just another example showing that Trump is concerned only about himself, not America.

The *New York Times* reported that Melania Trump gave a speech at the GOP convention that incorporated segments almost word-for-word from Michelle Obama's 2008 speech. At first, Trump's campaign denied that it was plagiarism. On her website, Melania falsely claimed that she received a degree in architecture, which she did not. When this was disclosed, she removed the claim from her website. She explained that it was removed "because it does not accurately reflect my current business and professional interests."[777]

According to the *Hill,* Trump proclaimed that he and his wife would hold a news conference to address questions about Melania's entry to the United States as an immigrant.[778] For months, the Trump campaign refused to provide information. The news conference never happened, but the *National Post* reported that Melania provided a letter from a lawyer on September 14, 2016 stating her entrance was legal, but she provided no documentation to verify it.[779] Why would the Trumps not provide the documents to the public? Trump demanded the long form of Obama's birth certificate! On November 5, 2016, the *Guardian* released an Associated Press (AP) story that Melania Trump earned $20,526 as a model and that the modeling company paid her rent, loaned her money, and paid for her pager between July 18, 1996 and September 26, 1997, prior to her obtaining a work visa on October 18, 1996.[780]

The modeling firm was dissolved in the 1990s and the records put in storage. The AP asked for a response from Melania's lawyer and Trump's campaign. The lawyer responded that the documents had not been verified and did not reflect their records of her passport stamps. The AP verified the documents through a former employee, as it was the former employee's signature on the document. The documents were also consistent with those filed in a New York court regarding a legal dispute on the dissolution of the modeling firm.[781]

All of this could have been clarified if the Trumps had released her immigration and passport information to the public. The AP conveyed that, technically, the government could revoke her US citizenship based on the concealment of facts or misrepresentation, but that is very unlikely, as this is most often done in cases of terrorism or war crimes.[782] I am certainly not proposing that her citizenship be revoked. The outrageous part of this is its conflict with Trump's position on illegal immigration, a pillar in his campaign. He hires illegal immigrants, is married to someone who may have received her citizenship under circumstances compromising her visa, wants to deport eleven million illegal immigrants, and promulgated the birther issue with Obama. That, combined with Melania denying plagiarism in her speech, lying about having a degree, defending her husband's statements about inappropriately forcing himself on women, and announcing that cyber bullying would be her cause were she to be the First Lady (when her husband is the champion of cyber bullying), is just too ironic.

Some of the commentators on CNN gave her a pass because she was not used to politics. I disagree. That is highly disingenuous, especially given her history of misrepresentation. Not being used to politics does not excuse her from telling the truth or being responsible for her actions.

Hillary came under considerable criticism by Bernie Sanders, Trump, and others for using Super PACs and for her relationship with Wall Street, and she was criticized for fundraising during the campaign. Again, despite considerable scrutiny, there was no evidence of pay-for-play.

According to the *Washington Post*, the Make America Great Again PAC, established by Mike Ciletti to raise money for Trump, decided to close the PAC following questions regarding connections to the Trump campaign. While Ciletti denied receiving donor information from the campaign and denied that the work he did for Trump was done before the electoral campaign, he nevertheless shut it down.[783] The Super PAC would not have shut down if they had not been concerned about further scrutiny.

Trump did not provide a remedy for the issue of fundraising and undue influence regarding election campaigns. Hillary did.

According to *USA Today*, Hillary reiterated her campaign promise from 2015 to "call for a constitutional amendment to overturn the Supreme Court's Citizens United decision in her first thirty days as president."[784] Fredreka Schouten explained in *USA Today* that the Supreme Court ruling of 2010 allowed unlimited corporate and union spending in elections. Her plan was to "challenge the stranglehold that wealthy interests have over our political system." She promised to sign "an executive order requiring companies with federal contracts to disclose their political spending."[785] It is interesting that the AP noted that Donald Trump hired Citizens United President David Bossie to serve as his deputy campaign manager.[786]

On *Breitbart News Radio*, Lewandowski said on November 11, 2015, "Mr. Trump is funding his campaign on his own, he's not taking donor money. He isn't beholden to those people and can't be accountable to those people who want special interests out of the government. He's gonna do what's right for the country."[787]

Surely, he was just as beholden to his major donors, funding both his campaign and charities, as Hillary was. We are unable to determine to whom he may or may not be beholden regarding his businesses. What foreign investments or debts owing might pose a conflict of interest?

Trump repeatedly lied about his opponents to discredit them. An example was his allegation that Ted Cruz's father was involved in JFK's assassination.[788]

The *Huffington Post* reported that "racial slurs, nasty rhetoric, and violence" at Trump's events had "become commonplace against protesters, bystanders, and reporters." The article explained that "rather than denounce these incidents, Trump is making them part of his brand and uses them to rev up crowds."[789]

The *Star* reported the following quote from Marty Rosenberg, former vice president of Atlantic Plate Glass, one of the contractors swindled out of payment in the Taj Mahal bankruptcy: "If ethics or morality has nothing to do with business, he's a very good businessman."

With respect to character, Trump accused Hillary of 'victimizing the victims' in relation to her husband's scandals. He tried to smear Hillary with the Clinton scandal from the 1990s, saying that she was a hypocrite on her policy to support women's rights because she destroyed victims' lives. I was only able to find one reference to Hillary having disparaged Lewinsky. It was reported that she called Lewinsky a "narcissistic loony toon," which is a statement from a friend's diary[790] that was found by an opposition research investigator. It was not a public statement. Can she not be forgiven for making a private statement to a friend during a period of humiliation?

When questioned by Anderson Cooper in the second debate, Trump denied ever having behaved inappropriately toward a woman. He claimed it was just locker room talk.[791] Following that, several women, so offended that he had denied behaviour that they, too, had been subjected to, came forward with similar accusations. Trump claimed Hillary was responsible for bringing the women forward and said the allegations were false; the women were not attractive enough for him to have sexually assaulted,[792] and he was going to sue them after the nomination.[793] Not only did Melania Trump excuse her husband's behaviour in the video, but she blamed Billy Bush for encouraging him.[794]

Hillary was held to a higher standard; while Trump's predatory behaviour was normalized, she was expected to be perfect. Disagree about her policies, be disappointed that she made a mistake about the email server, be frustrated that she is so fiercely private and blurs the lines sometimes, but make no mistake—there was no equivalency in trustworthiness, transparency, ethical behaviour, or corruption in this election. This was not "a choice between the lesser of two evils." What have you got to lose, America? Democracy.

Just when you thought there could no more surprises and that this election campaign had already exceeded the most outrageous dynamics imaginable, the drama escalated. I will summarize what I thought were the significant events during the last several weeks of the campaign, including Powell's advice to Hillary regarding personal email; *WikiLeaks*; voter suppression; the final debate; Comey's announcement to reopen the investigation regarding Hillary's emails; and the results.

In September 2016, Colin Powell's email to Hillary regarding personal emails was released and received little media attention. I will provide background leading up to the release of Colin Powell's emails to establish context for some startling events that occurred just prior to the election. On March 15, 2015, it became public that Hillary Clinton was using her private email server for communication rather than the government server. After questions were raised regarding confidentiality, the FBI initiated an investigation. This is detailed in Chapter 3. On July 2, 2016, Bill Clinton had a private, unplanned meeting with Attorney General Loretta E. Lynch on her plane at the Phoenix airport, just as the FBI was concluding the investigation on Hillary and the personal email server.[795]

Dan Balz from the *Washington Post* explained that, while Loretta Lynch stated that it was a personal discussion between friends, the decision to meet was an inexcusable error of judgment on both of their parts when the Justice Department, for which Lynch was responsible, was about to come to a decision regarding the FBI investigation on Hillary's email server. I tend to believe it was an innocent meeting, as they made no effort to hide it. However, given the circumstances, as well as the rhetoric from Trump that the 'rules do not apply' to the Clintons, the meeting between Lynch and Bill Clinton was untenable.

The *Washington Post* reported that though she did not recuse herself fully, Loretta Lynch stated, "I will be accepting their recommendations," regarding any conclusion from the FBI. She added that her decision "would mean I wouldn't even be briefed on what the findings were."[796]

On July 5, 2016, FBI Director James B. Comey released a statement to the public on the outcome of the FBI's investigation on Hillary Clinton's email server. He advised that the Justice Department did not have any knowledge about what he was going to say. In his public announcement, he stated, "Although there is evidence of potential violations of the statutes regarding the handling of classified information, our judgment is that no reasonable prosecutor would bring such a case. Prosecutors necessarily weigh a number of factors before bringing charges. There are obvious considerations, like the strength of the evidence, especially regarding intent. Responsible decisions also consider the context of a person's actions, and how similar situations have been handled in the past."[797]

The *Washington Post* advised that on July 7, 2016, Comey testified before the House Oversight and Government Reform Committee about the recommendation that Hillary Clinton not be prosecuted for her handling of government emails on a private server. Comey stated that Clinton was "extremely careless; I think she was negligent," but that they found no evidence to bring a criminal case.[798]

On September 7, 2016, Rep. Elijah E. Cummings, Ranking Member of the House Committee on Oversight and Government Reform, released a series of emails between Hillary Clinton and Colin Powell regarding the use of personal email. In 2014, the State Office requested copies of Colin Powell's emails, and on March 8, 2015, in an interview with George Stephanopoulos, Powell advised that he no longer had emails from his personal account. Another request was made on October 15, 2015 for Colin Powell to ask his provider, AOL, if any of his emails were on that system. Colin Powell did not respond. On February 3, 2016, information was released that Secretary Powell and the immediate staff of former Secretary Condoleezza Rice received classified national security information on their personal email accounts. Cummings obtained the emails "through a unique statutory provision known as the Seven Member Rule, in which any seven members of the Oversight Committee may obtain federal records from federal agencies."[799]

As reported by Josh Gerstein in *Politico*, the emails revealed that, contrary to Colin Powell's previous assertions, his advice was given not a year after she started using the personal server, but rather two days after she became Secretary of State. His response was detailed. He advised her that he had had a personal computer hooked up to a phone and had used it to communicate with friends and conduct business with foreign leaders without going through the State Department servers. This does not seem very different in function from a personal email server. Powell advised that he had also used it when travelling. While he did not have a Blackberry, he did have a personal digital assistant (PDA). He expressed frustration with the various security agencies, stating, "They never satisfied me and the NSA/CIA would not back off. So we just went about our business and stopped asking."[800]

He warned her to be careful in using a Blackberry or personal email because it could become an official record and said, "I got around it all by not saying much and not using systems that captured the data."[801] In an interview on *60 Minutes*, Hillary said she got advice from someone that it would be convenient to have a personal email system but refused to provide a name. In the FBI interviews, she named Colin Powell, but she said his advice did not affect her decision to have a private account.[802]

In October 2016, *WikiLeaks* dumped thousands of hacked emails from John Podesta's account, as well as sixty Hillary Clinton speeches. There was consensus in the intelligence community that the Russians hacked the emails. It is curious to me that it was the DNC email and John Podesta's emails that were hacked, not Hillary's. Even more provocative is the fact that though seventeen intelligence agencies confirmed that it was the Russians who hacked the emails, Trump and his campaign continued to claim that they had no idea who did it.

Many countries, including the United States, do not pay ransom because they do not want to incentivize hostage taking. Even though the information was in the public domain, if the media, Trump's campaign, and the GOP had ignored it, would this not have given a signal that the United States was not going to allow a foreign country to interfere in the American election process? And really, what was discerned from these email leaks? It is my view that the media, the GOP, Trump's campaign, and the public provided an incentive and an invitation for future foreign interference.

I did not review the thousands of emails on *WikiLeaks*, but I read several articles summarizing the revelations from them, including coverage on right-wing websites. They are not flattering. For the most part, they are strategic discussions within the campaign, reflecting uncensored thoughts and frustrations. The right focused on the emails from Donna Brazile leaking debate questions to Hillary's campaign staff, a speech that indicated, contrary to her public position, that Hillary favoured open borders, that the King of Morocco bribed her, and that she hated Americans. I have already addressed the Donna Brazile issue in Chapter 7. There was no evidence in the emails that Hillary has been personally provided with the questions.

According to Kenneth Vogel from *Politico*, "When it comes to Morocco, there's no evidence that Clinton provided special treatment to the royal family or companies in which it's invested because of their donations to her family's foundation."[803] The emails of the campaign staff did reflect an ethical dilemma with respect to donations from foreign countries, especially those countries with ongoing human rights issues. Hillary had been entertaining the notion of attending a Clinton Foundation Conference in Morocco in relation to a donation, but declined.

Right-wing news portrayed an email from John Podesta as saying that Hillary hated everyday Americans. The phrase from the email, reported by *Business Insider,* read, "I know she has begun to hate [the phrase] everyday Americans, but I think we should use it… [when] she says I'm running for president because you and everyday Americans need a champion."[804] Podesta was not saying that she hated everyday Americans—only that she hated using the phrase 'everyday Americans'!

In another email referring to the Iran deal, *Town Hall* reported Republican Mark Kirk's statement: "This agreement condemns the next generation to cleaning up a nuclear war in the Persian Gulf. This is the greatest appeasement since Chamberlain gave Czechoslovakia to Hitler."[805] John Podesta agreed. So there was controversy about the Iran deal. There is nothing new about that. The point is that the deal allows oversight and prevents Iran from developing nuclear weapons for ten years. While the deal did not solve the problem for the long term, it provided time to explore a long-term solution.

Other emails exposed relationships and strategies. For example, on one occasion, Podesta said that "[Hillary's] instincts can be terrible." Podesta referred to Bernie Sanders as a "doofus." The Clinton campaign was floating Bill Gates as a possible vice president, and a former personal aid of Bill Clinton's referred to Chelsea as a brat.[806] Imagine if we were privy to all of the emails between Trump's campaign staff.

Yousef Saba reported in *Politico* that Jennifer Palmieri, one of Hillary's staffers, purportedly wrote in an email that "people of means find conservatism more palatable from Catholics than evangelicals."[807] Palmeri said she did not "recognize the emails from Wikileaks and added, 'I'm a Catholic.'"[808] Hillary and her views were not mentioned in the string of emails on this subject. Even so, at a Catholic charity event where presidential candidate traditionally "give speeches with a few self-deprecating jokes and a couple of jabs at their opponent," Trump stated, "Here she is tonight, in public, pretending not to hate Catholics."[809] Given the circumstances, this was a low blow and misrepresentation. Some in the crowd booed when he made this statement.

Most of the emails were between staffers and about Hillary rather than from her. There are some exceptions. An ironic *Huffington Post* article entitled "These Wikileaks Emails Prove Just What a Monster Hillary Clinton Is"[810] summarized several emails from Hillary. She expressed concern about a ten-year-old Yemeni girl, asking if there was any way they could help her. She tried to get medical supplies to doctors in Haiti, as well as food and water. She expressed concerns about raising awareness regarding child trafficking in Haiti, and she expressed sadness about the closing of an Illinois group home that helped abused and neglected young boys.[811] What a demon!

According to *PolitiFact*, there were tens of thousands of emails, as well as Hillary's speeches to Wall Street, that were leaked. Hillary's campaign refused to acknowledge them because they were hacked by the Russians and sent by *WikiLeaks* with a view to interfere in the election. There was also the concern that some had been doctored. Evidence was found that there were doctored documents produced in relation to the DNC hacking. While experts were able to verify the signatures for some of the Podesta emails, they were unsuccessful with others. Hackers often included a few doctored documents among many authentic ones.[812]

I assume that the most salacious emails were summarized in the various articles that I reviewed. I fail to see what, if anything, we really learned from them that we did not already know. With all this information, this is the most scandalous that they could dig up? While they were embarrassing, they were hardly 'lock her up' material. But the major point was being overlooked by many Democrats, Republicans, and reporters. The story should have been about the attempts by Russians to interfere with, not just the presidential election in the US, but democracy around the globe! As reported by *NBC News*, Marco Rubio was the only Republican who got it. "I will not discuss any issue that has become public solely on the basis of Wikileaks. As our intelligence agencies have said, these leaks are an effort by a foreign government to interfere with our electoral process and I will not indulge it... I want to warn my fellow Republicans who may want to capitalize politically on these leaks," he said. "Today it is the Democrats. Tomorrow it could be us."[813] The media was almost dismissive when Hillary's campaign staff raised the issue of their concerns about the Russian hacking and hardly expressed alarm that this was occurring. The media focused on the details of the hacked emails.

The *Hill* reported that throughout the campaign, Donald Trump said the system was rigged and that illegal immigrants were voting. He encouraged his supporters to be vigilant and said, "I hear too many stories, and we can't lose an election because — you know what I'm talking about. Go and vote and go check out areas, because a lot of bad things happen and we don't want to lose for that reason."[814]

Reuters stated that Trump filed a lawsuit in Nevada alleging that early voting stations stayed open beyond closing time, requesting that the early votes be kept separate. This was given as an example of an attempt by Trump and his campaign to rig the system. While polls closed at 7 PM, they remained open until everyone in line prior to 7 PM could vote. On November 8, 2016, the judge denied the request.[815] On the other hand, the *Hill* reported that a Republican woman was arrested in Iowa on the suspicion that she voted twice.[816]

According to reporters Green and Issenberg from *Bloomberg*, Trump's campaign knew that he had a narrow path to win the election, and instead of using a strategy to increase votes for him, a senior official in the Trump campaign disclosed to *Bloomberg* that they focused on "three major voter suppression operations... They're aimed at three groups Clinton needs to win overwhelmingly: idealistic white liberals, young women, and African Americans. Trump's invocation at the debate of Clinton's WikiLeaks e-mails and support for the Trans-Pacific

Partnership was designed to turn off Sanders supporters."[817] Trump's campaign bought ads on several African-American radio stations using Hillary's 'superpredator' comment and paraded out women who said they were sexually assaulted by Bill Clinton to discourage the female vote. To discourage the Miami vote, they blasted the media with controversial information about the Clinton Foundation and Haiti.[818]

The third and final debate was held on October 19, 2016. The following are some of its misrepresentations and highlights.

Throughout the campaign, Trump repeatedly claimed that Hillary would "take your guns away" and reinforced this in the debate by stating that if Hillary won, "we will have a second amendment which will be a very, very small replica of what it is right now." He described Chicago as having "the toughest laws and… tremendous gun violence." What Trump failed to acknowledge was that guns were being brought in from other states with less strict gun control laws, as *NPR* reported.[819]

Trump proclaimed that Hillary's position on abortion meant "you can take the baby and rip the baby out of the womb on the ninth month on the final day." *NPR* claimed that this was a misrepresentation intended to invoke revulsion. *NPR* clarified that most abortions are performed between twenty and twenty-four weeks, and only 0.2% use the dilation and extraction method. It is used only when the mother's life is at risk and/or the fetus shows signs of severe abnormalities.[820]

During the debate, Trump stated, "We need the wall. The border patrol, ICE, they all want the wall." In *NPR*'s fact check, John Burnett clarified that while the unions of the National Border Patrol Council and the National Immigration and Customs Enforcement Council endorsed Trump, the federal bureau of Immigration and Customs Enforcement did not. Burnett added that, "neither union publicly agrees with his plan to build 'an impenetrable and beautiful wall' separating the U.S. and Mexico."[821]

Linda Qiu from *PolitiFact* advised that *WikiLeaks* released portions of Hillary's speeches to Wall Street. Hillary was quoted saying, "My dream is a hemispheric common market with open trade and open borders." This statement, according to Hillary, was taken out of context and used by Trump and the GOP to imply that she said one thing to Wall Street and another to the voting public. Hillary said that reading further reveals that she was talking about energy, not global international trade. Her full statement was, "My dream is a hemispheric common market, with open trade and open borders, sometime in the future, with energy that is as green and sustainable as we can get it, powering growth and opportunity for every person in the hemisphere."[822]

The debate also covered the issue of Russia. Trump declared, "I don't know Putin." *PolitiFact* cites four occasions in which Trump identified ties with Putin. In November 2013, Thomas Roberts of MSNBC asked Trump, "Do you have a relationship with Vladimir Putin?" Trump responded, "I do have a relationship, and I can tell you that he's very interested in what we're doing here today. He's probably very interested in what you and I am [sic] saying today, and I'm sure he's going to be seeing it in some form."[823] In March 2014, Trump said Putin sent him a present when he was in Moscow for the Miss Universe contest. In May 2014, while addressing the National Press Club, he stated, "I was in Russia, I was in Moscow recently and I spoke, indirectly and directly, with President Putin, who could not have been nicer, and we had a tremendous success."[824] Finally, in a Fox News debate in November 2015, he said, "As far as the Ukraine is concerned… if Putin wants to go in—and I got to know him very well because we were both on *60 Minutes*. We were stable mates, and we did very well that night."[825] They were on different continents for the filming.[826]

In response to concerns expressed by Hillary about Russian interference in the election, Donald Trump responded, "She has no idea whether it's Russia, China, or anybody else. She has no idea."[827] *NPR* advised that the intelligence community was in full agreement that the cyber-attacks were related to the Russian government.

The following details of the debates were provided in the transcripts on the *NPR* website. With respect to American bases in Japan, South Korea, and Saudi Arabia, Trump exclaimed, "We are being ripped off by everybody—we're defending other countries. We are spending a fortune doing it. They have the bargain of the century."[828] The American bases protect the US as much as the other countries. For example, the US has a base in South Korea to deter North Korea from ramping up their nuclear programme, to be close to China, and to provide "stability" in East Asia. During the past year, this has escalated, and North Korea is close to having an ICBM (intercontinental ballistic missile) that can reach the US. *NPR* reported that "Japan pays about $2 billion a year in maintenance and utilities for American bases… South Korea paid about $866.6 million in 2014 for the U.S. military presence there."[829]

As for the economy, Trump claimed, "Look, our country is stagnant. We've lost our jobs." Again, he did not acknowledge the growth during the Obama administration. In reality, according to *NPR*, "There are 10.7 million more people working today than when President Obama took office. Employers have added 15 million jobs since the trough of the recession in 2010… Unemployment, which peaked at 10% in October 2009, has fallen to 5%."[830]

Hillary stated, "One of the biggest problems that we have [with] China is the illegal dumping of steel and aluminum into our markets."[831] The Commerce Department confirmed that imports of stainless steel from China were being sold at less than fair value. Hillary went on to point out that while Trump decried the plight of the steel workers in the US, he bought Chinese steel for some of his projects, giving "jobs to Chinese steelworkers, not American steelworkers."[832]

Trump accused Hillary of losing $6 billion. "You ran the State Department. Six billion dollars was either stolen—they don't know. It's gone. Six billion dollars." The money itself was not missing, though the "inspector general of the State Department found that contract files were incomplete."[833]

Trump said of Clinton, "She gave us ISIS because her and Obama created this huge vacuum." This was a continuing refrain of Trump's during the campaign. While it may be true that US troops prevented ISIS from gaining so much ground in Iraq, Trump failed to acknowledge that the troops were removed because of an agreement signed by Bush at the request of the Iraqi government.[834]

During the debate, moderator Chris Wallace questioned Trump about the women who had come forward and accused him of groping or kissing them without consent, when at the last debate, he said his boasting about grabbing women was just talk. Trump said, "First of all, the stories have been largely debunked." He then went on to accuse Hillary of being responsible for these women coming forward. The accusations had not been debunked, and the women said that they came forward after being outraged when Donald Trump said he never engaged in that kind of behaviour.[835]

Then the most startling exchange in the debate occurred. Chris Wallace asked, "Mr. Trump, I want to ask about one [more] question in this topic. You have been warning at rallies recently that this election is rigged, and that Hillary Clinton is in the process of trying to steal it from you. I want to ask you here on the stage tonight, do you make the same commitment that you will absolutely, sir, that you will absolutely accept the result of the election?"[836]

Trump responded by saying the media was corrupt and "poisoning the minds of voters" and that Hillary should not be allowed to run because she is guilty of a serious crime.[837]

Chris Wallace replied, pursuing the question, "But sir, there is a tradition in this country, in fact one of the prides of this country, is the peaceful transition of power and that no matter how hard fought a campaign is, that at the end of the campaign, that the loser concedes to the winner, not saying that you are necessarily going to be the you [sic] loser or the winner, but that the loser concedes to the winner and that the country comes together in part for the good of the country, are you saying that you are not prepared now to commit to that principle?" Donald Trump replied, "What I'm saying now is I will tell you at the time. I will keep you in suspense, okay?"[838]

These are just some of the significant misrepresentations and outrageous comments during the debate. While there were fact-checking reports and commentary after the fact, how many voters reviewed them? It would have been impossible for Hillary to respond in detail to every lie, as her time in the debate would have been devoted only to that. These are the same refrains that Trump repeated throughout the campaign, often without being challenged, so that many accepted them as fact. I am confident that many Trump voters believed that Hillary was going to take away their guns and have open borders for immigration, that she lost $6 billion while she was Secretary of State, that she told something different to Wall Street in her speeches than she told the voters, and that she should be locked up because she was not charged in the email investigations. Trump used inflammatory language to appeal to emotion, not reason.

The intrigue intensified. According to the *Washington Post*, following the last debate on October 19, 2016, Hillary's polls increased considerably, and she had more than a six-point lead on Trump. Indeed, there was speculation about the possibility that the Democrats could gain control of the House.[839]

Newsweek reported that on October 29, less than two weeks before the election, Comey advised Congress that the FBI was investigating new emails that may be linked to Hillary Clinton that were discovered in devices being examined in connection with the former Democratic Representative Anthony Weiner's sexting scandal. Huma Abedin, recently separated from Weiner, was Hillary's vice chair of the campaign and close confidant. Comey felt obliged to advise Congress because he was concerned that the information might be leaked from within his agency.[840]

According to *NBC News*, Bret Baier, an anchor at Fox News, falsely reported that five foreign intelligence agencies had hacked Hillary's email server and "that a separate FBI investigation of the charitable Clinton Foundation was likely to lead to an indictment of Clinton after Tuesday's election."[841] He later apologized, but not before "Trump told a Florida crowd that… 'The FBI is conducting a criminal investigation into Hillary Clinton's pay-for-play corruption during her tenure as secretary of state.'"[842]

According to Wayne Barrett from the *Daily Beast*, two days before, Rudy Giuliani, former mayor of New York and Trump surrogate, was on Fox News and said, "I think [Donald Trump's] got a surprise or two that you're going to hear about in the next few days. I mean, I'm talking about some pretty big surprises."[843] He boasted about being in contact with FBI agents who shared how disgruntled they were about the decision not to charge Hillary Clinton and about his knowledge of the investigation. He later tried backtracking by stating it was former agents that he talked to. Giuliani's legal firm is general counsel to the FBI Agents Association (FBIAA). He obviously knew something in advance.

Even though a decision wasn't expected until well after the election, Comey surprised everyone on November 6, 2017 by announcing that there was nothing in the newfound emails that would change the decision made by the FBI in July. In the meantime, Hillary had fallen in the polls. Many had already voted in early polls. I don't think Comey had nefarious intentions, but he did influence the election process. Initially, he was placed in an awkward position when Lynch was in a conflict of interest and determined that she would accept whatever the FBI recommended. While Lynch said she would accept the findings of the FBI investigation, she did not give permission for unprecedented actions such as giving an opinion about the findings and making a presentation to Congress. Comey compounded that by making a public statement days before the election that they were investigating new emails without even knowing what they had. I think Comey said what he did about the investigation in July because he knew he had disgruntled internal FBI employees and was trying to prevent them from potentially undermining the findings of the report. In the second case, he expressed concern that the reopening of the investigation might be leaked. These are internal security breaches and disciplinary issues within the FBI, not excuses for influencing the outcome of an election!

Even though the lead narrowed in many cases to within the margins of error, the media, the Democrats, and even some Republicans predicted a Hillary Clinton victory. I had no such confidence. Watching the polls on the night of the election was a nail-biting experience. Shortly after 2 AM, John Podesta, Chairman of the Hillary Clinton Presidential Campaign, announced, "Some states are too close to call. We're not going to have anything more to say tonight." At 2:30 AM, Hillary called Donald Trump and conceded, congratulating him as the president-elect. In a stunning upset, Donald Trump became the president-elect of the United States of America.

Hillary Clinton won the popular vote, but Trump won the Electoral College and a Republican majority in the House and Senate. He has a clear, unfettered mandate unless the Republicans take issue with any of his proposals.

Donald Trump gave a gracious victory speech in which he expressed gratitude for Hillary Clinton's service to the country and pledged to be a president for all Americans.

In the true spirit of a peaceful transfer of power, *USA Today* reported that Obama called Trump to congratulate him and invited him to a meeting at the White House that Thursday to discuss "the smooth transition of power."[844]

The *New York Times* quoted Hillary's concession speech the following morning in which she expressed hope that Trump would be "a successful president for all Americans" and stated that she respected and cherished the peaceful transition of power. She told her supporters that they must accept that Mr. Trump would be president and added, "We owe him an open mind and a chance to lead."[845]

In the spirit of true grit, Democrats as well as Republicans began calling on the American people to respect the office of the presidency and to join together as Americans in support of their new president. This was necessary to begin to repair the growing schism in American society.

The rest has been left up to Donald Trump. I cannot help but wonder what he would have done if he had lost the election. He had said the election was rigged and refused to commit to a concession and peaceful transition if he did not win the election.

America voted. America now has the Trump brand and will be enfolded as part of the Trump Corporation.

CHAPTER TEN

Transitioning: Rhetoric To Reality

It's funny how humans can wrap their mind around things and fit them into their version of reality.[846]
— *Rick Riordan*

The transition period leading to the inauguration was no less dramatic than the campaign. In fact, it became more intriguing. Donald Trump sent no less than 365 tweets from the date of the election to the inauguration date. Many of them were just as, if not more, controversial than those he tweeted in campaign mode. This chapter will include a few of the highlights during the transition, which clearly demonstrate that expectation of a shift to 'presidential' behaviour was a fallacy.

Following his speech on the night of the election in which he spoke about unifying the country and representing all Americans, Donald Trump tweeted, "Just had a very open and successful presidential election. Now professional protesters, incited by the media, are protesting. Very unfair!"[847] This is the real Donald Trump. The next day he tweeted, "Love the fact that the small groups of protesters last night have passion for our great country. We will all come together and be proud!"[848] This is the managed Trump. It is unfortunate that this was not his first and only tweet on the subject, suggesting he was not genuine about unifying the country.

Many of those who did not vote for Trump were and are frightened: they fear the deportation and separation of families, the loss of healthcare, the impact of loss of trade agreements, the damage to the environment, the threat to alliances such as NATO and the UN, and the potential impact on national security. Many women are concerned about their rights being trampled upon. *Reuters* reported that hate crimes increased by 20% in the period following the campaign.[849]

If Trump wants to unify the country, he needs to acknowledge these fears and give fearful citizens reason not to be afraid. His first tweet incorrectly stated that the protesters were professional and incited by the media. Again, he had to blame someone because he simply would not accept accountability for escalating divisiveness and fear.

We had come full circle. My husband and I were back in Puerto Vallarta, Mexico for the winter. A few weeks before we arrived, the father of the family we met last year contacted me to verify we were coming to Mexico and invited us to a party. When we arrived at our resort, Connie, the agent for members of the resort, ran over and greeted us with a hug. Thankfully, Fox News was not the only English-language channel at this location. When we visited Blake's, one of our favourite restaurants, Carlos came running over to welcome us and give us a hug. It felt good to feel we belonged. Our friends from home, who also winter in Puerto Vallarta, would be arriving soon. It is our home away from home. It made me realize how painful it must be to feel unwelcome in your own country. Many Americans now are made to feel they do not belong. That is a sad commentary on the 'land of the free.'

While Trump had innumerable opportunities to demonstrate that he will represent all Americans, he has failed to do so. He tweeted, "For many years our country has been divided, angry, and untrusting. Many say it will never change, the hatred is too deep. IT WILL CHANGE!!!!"[850] However, he cannot coerce, threaten, or order unity. He has displayed no interest in providing leadership to bring about healing.

While he can say outrageous things, he does not recognize anyone else's right to free speech or protesting. He tweeted, "Nobody should be allowed to burn the American flag - if they do, there must be consequences - perhaps loss of citizenship or year in jail!"[851] He does not respect the Constitution.

How are Muslims supposed to feel inclusiveness when Trump tweets, "ISIS is taking credit for the terrible stabbing attack at Ohio State University by a Somali refugee who should not have been in our country"?[852]

Trump did a 'thank you' tour to states that were instrumental in getting him elected. Originally billed as a 'victory tour,' which describes the exercise more accurately, this tour was a continuation of his campaign rhetoric, focused on self-aggrandizement while demonizing Hillary and the media. He continued to speak to his supporters, not the rest of America.

Discrediting the Media

Trump's war against the media continued throughout the transition, as he sent numerous tweets attempting to discredit the media for a variety of reasons. Trump claimed in a tweet, "The @nytimes states today that DJT believes 'more countries should acquire nuclear weapons.' How dishonest are they. I never said this!"[853] Yes, he did. On November 11, 2016, *New York Times* reporter Max Fisher wrote, "Trump has suggested that more countries should acquire nuclear weapons, to protect themselves without Washington's help."[854] According to several other news outlets, he did just that. In an interview with Maggie Haberman and David E. Sanger from the *New York Times,* when asked if he would object to Japan or South Korea having nuclear weapons, Trump stated, "Pakistan has them. You have, probably, North Korea has them. I mean, they don't have delivery yet, but you know, probably, I mean to me, that's a big problem. And, would I rather have North Korea have them with Japan sitting there having them also?"[855]

Politico reported that Trump had a protracted issue regarding a meeting with the *New York Times*.[856] Just prior to Trump's cancellation of the scheduled meeting, the *New York Times* printed three stories questioning Trump's potential conflicts of interest: the first revealed that foreign dignitaries purchased services from the Trump Corporation; another story detailed unprecedented conflicts of interest posed by his wide international business holdings; and according to *CNN*, in yet another, he asked Nigel Farage to oppose wind farms that would damage the views at his golf course.[857]

While Trump shunned most of the mainstream media, he continued to participate in interviews on Fox News. "I will be interviewed today on Fox News Sunday with Chris Wallace at 10:00 (Eastern) Network. ENJOY!"[858]

According to the *Hill*, Trump tweeted, "Has anyone looked at the really poor numbers of @ VanityFair Magazine. Way down, big trouble, dead! Graydon Carter, no talent, will be out!"[859] Trump tweeted this after *Vanity Fair* printed a review of Trump Grill in Trump Tower, stating, "Trump Grill — a steakhouse in the lobby of Trump Tower — could be the worst restaurant in America... The allure of Trump's restaurant, like the candidate, is that it seems like a cheap version of rich... [It] reveals everything you need to know about our next president."[860] He was using the exalted position of president-elect for his personal business, entangling the two.

A stream of tweets addressed a story released by *CNN* regarding allegations that the Russians had compromising information on Donald Trump. *CNN* reported that anti-Trump Republicans hired a private investigator, who used to work for the British MI6, as an opposition researcher and that Democrats later joined the anti-Trump Republican group. Intelligence claimed they were sharing the information to inform Trump what information was circulating about him.[861]

Trump reacted swiftly and vigorously sent a string of tweets. "FAKE NEWS - A TOTAL POLITICAL WITCH HUNT!"[862] "Russia has never tried to use leverage over me. I HAVE NOTHING TO DO WITH RUSSIA - NO DEALS, NO LOANS, NO NOTHING!"[863]

CNN broke the story in the media and came under considerable criticism from the Trump administration. *CNN* vociferously defended their position, claiming that the Trump administration was failing to differentiate between what *CNN* reported and what *BuzzFeed* later did. In an interview with Anderson Cooper, Kellyanne Conway claimed that *CNN* posted a link to the thirty-five-page report.[864] *BuzzFeed* did; *CNN* did not. In the video interview provided with the *CNN* article, Kellyanne Conway claimed that the headline for *CNN* was, "Intel chiefs presented Trump with information that Russia had information to compromise him."[865] The *CNN* headline said, "claims of Russian efforts."[866] This is a major distinction: Kellyanne's version suggested a conclusion, while the *CNN* headline did not. Kellyanne Conway stated that Trump did not receive a two-page summary of the report. While *NBC* and *Fox News* reported that Trump did not get a two-page summary, it was later verified that not only did he get it as an attachment to his intelligence briefing, but FBI Director James Comey personally briefed the president-elect.[867]

It is unfortunate that CNN was not as vociferous in exposing the blatant lies perpetuated by Kellyanne Conway about Hillary and her policies, Trump, and his surrogates throughout the campaign. I do not agree with *BuzzFeed*'s posting a link to the report. It was salacious and unverified information. This kind of information takes on a life of its own and perception becomes some people's reality. But isn't that what Trump and his surrogates did to Hillary throughout the campaign? Isn't this what the Republicans have done with their 'oppo' research for years against the Clintons? This dossier was from an investigator that was hired to do 'oppo' research by anti-Trump Republicans—the Democrats did not initiate it!

Technically, *CNN* did not provide fake news. Even though the media may be accurate when they report alleged information, perhaps there should be more discretion about reporting such information until there is substantiation because of the potential damaging consequences that cannot be undone.

Trump demanded an apology from the CIA for sharing the dossier. Trump did not apologize to John McCain, Ted Cruz, Hillary, the Khan family, or any of the others. Trump accused the CIA of leaking the information: "Intelligence agencies should never have allowed this fake news to 'leak' into the public. One last shot at me. Are we living in Nazi Germany?"[868] Does Trump owe the intelligence community an apology? While Trump and his supporters take great exception to any Hitler or Nazi comparisons, they freely invoke them on a regular basis.

Donald Trump and his transition team made his disdain for the media clear. Trump relies on Twitter to speak directly to the people and to avoid media interpretation and 'fake news.' That would have been laudable were his tweets honest and free from bullying and harassment. That is Trump's *modus operandi*: to discredit the 'enemy,' in this case the 'lying' media, to justify his actions and avoid accountability. As frustrated as I have been with the media, Trump's attacks on the media, accusing them of 'fake news,' are frightening. I am not alone in that view. *CNN* reported the following quote from John McCain, that dictatorships "get started by suppressing free press."[869] Though it was well past the campaign phase, Trump continued to tweet misinformation. Unlike the media in a press conference, Twitter does not ask difficult questions or hold Trump accountable.

Election Results

There was a flurry of tweets about the election results. I think this was the subject Trump tweeted most about during the transition. He wrote, "If the election were based on total popular vote I would have campaigned in N.Y. Florida and California and won even bigger and more easily."[870] This was followed by, "The Electoral College is actually genius in that it brings all states, including the smaller ones, into play. Campaigning is much different!"[871] This was Trump's response to the news that Hillary won the popular vote by a large margin. Apparently, it annoyed him that Hillary had, according to *CNN*, 65,844,954 (48.2%) votes to his 62,979,879 (46.1%) in the final count.[872] This was a lead for Hillary of approximately 2.9 million votes with a 2.1% margin. Hillary surpassed the number of votes for Barack Obama in the 2012 election by 389,944 votes.[873] Despite this, Trump and his supporters claimed a "massive landslide victory."[874] *CNN* claimed it was one of the narrowest victories—the eleventh-closest margin—in the last fifty-four elections.[875]

Victories in states like Wisconsin, Michigan, Ohio, Pennsylvania, and Florida gave Trump the electoral vote. Donald J. Trump won the Electoral College with 304 votes compared to 227 votes for Hillary Clinton. According to the *New York Times*, "Seven electors voted for someone other than their party's candidate."[876] Trump tumbled the 'blue wall,' including Wisconsin, Michigan, and Pennsylvania, states that had voted Democrat for decades.[877] In

Wisconsin, Trump had 47.2% with 1,405,284 votes, and Hillary had 46.5% with 1,382,536 votes.[878] Michigan had Trump at 47.3% with 2,279,543 and Hillary at 47.0% with 2,268,839 votes.[879] In Pennsylvania, Trump had 48.2% with 2,970,733 votes, and Hillary had 47.5% with 2,926,441 votes.[880] The total variance was only 77,744 votes. Essentially, Hillary lost the electoral vote by less than 80,000 votes. She lost Wisconsin and Pennsylvania by only 0.7% and Michigan by 0.3%.

Over 200 million people were registered to vote in the 2017 election, a record high. This means at least 70 million did not vote—more than those who voted for either Hillary or Trump! Those 70 million people did not support Trump enough to vote for him, nor did those who voted for Hillary, so Trump did not have the support of 135 million voters—more than 67% of registered voters! While the abstentions can be applied to either candidate, my point is that most Americans did not endorse Trump. Though he did win, he has not demonstrated that he will represent that majority.

Trump then went on to say, "In addition to winning the Electoral College in a landslide, I won the popular vote if you deduct the millions of people who voted illegally."[881] He continued to assert this throughout the transition and following the inauguration. There was absolutely no substantiation for his assertions. According to *Wired*, Jesse Richman, the author of the research most often quoted by Trump and his team, said that they were misinterpreting and exaggerating the results.[882]

John Walcott from *Reuters* reported that "U.S. intelligence analysts have concluded that Russia intervened in the 2016 election to help President-elect Donald Trump win the White House, and not just to undermine confidence in the U.S. electoral system."[883] Trump negated the reports and stated, "These are the same people that said Saddam Hussein has weapons of mass destruction… The election ended a long time ago in one of the biggest Electoral College victories in history. It's now time to move on and 'Make America Great Again.'"[884]

Obama ordered the intelligence community to review cyber-attacks and foreign intervention in the 2016 election and deliver a report before he left office. The following are some of Trump's tweets on the subject:

- "Serious voter fraud in Virginia, New Hampshire and California - so why isn't the media reporting on this? Serious bias - big problem!"[885]

- "@Filibuster: @jeffzeleny Pathetic - you have no sufficient evidence that Donald Trump did not suffer from voter fraud, shame! Bad reporter."[886]

- "Unless you catch 'hackers' in the act, it is very hard to determine who was doing the hacking. Why wasn't this brought up before election?"[887]

The fact is that Russia hacked emails with intent to affect the election for the President of the United States. This should concern everyone, not just Democrats or Republicans. The Russians meddled in the election of the leader of the free world! Just as disconcerting was Trump's continued denial of the facts. However, this should be no surprise. It was consistent with Trump's behaviour throughout the campaign. If he does not agree with information, he denies it. This behaviour was not isolated to the campaign; it is his *modus operandi*. This is of particular concern regarding how he will deal with issues of national security.

Some criticized Obama for not releasing more information about the Russian hacking before the election. However, everyone already knew the Russians hacked the DNC and John Podesta's emails. The media did not treat the story with proper urgency, the Republicans wanted to win, and if Hillary supporters raised the issue, they were told they were trying to find excuses or were cut off as if they were just whining. The hacking issue was not taken seriously in the moment, and the drama created by Trump took precedence.

Trump tweeted, "Can you imagine if the election results were the opposite and WE tried to play the Russia/CIA card. It would be called conspiracy theory!"[888] While Trump continually stated that he had not been communicating with Russia, *Reuters* disclosed that Russian Deputy Foreign Minister Sergei Ryabkov stated, "There were contacts… We are doing this and have been doing this during the election campaign… Obviously, we know most of the people from [Trump's] entourage. Those people have always been in the limelight in the United States and have occupied high-ranking positions."[889]

Many in Trump's administration, as well as Donald Jr., failed to disclose meetings with Russians during the campaign. Trump and his administration steadfastly refused to admit that Russia tried to interfere with the election.

Contrary to Trump's claims of rigging and voter fraud, the Democrats do have legitimate concerns about the extent to which the election might have been influenced by Russian hacking, as well as by Comey's intrusion into the election process due to his unorthodox handling of the email investigation. Despite that, Hillary Clinton and President Obama facilitated a peaceful transition of power.

According to *Reuters*, Trump was avoiding intelligence briefings. On January 9, 2017, he finally acknowledged that Russia was involved in the hacking but did not acknowledge that Putin was involved.[890] The intelligence report concluded the following, as reported by the *Washington Post*: "We assess Russian President Vladimir Putin ordered an influence campaign in 2016 aimed at the US presidential election. Russia's goals were to undermine public faith in the US democratic process, denigrate Secretary Clinton, and harm her electability and potential presidency. We further assess Putin and the Russian Government developed a clear preference for President-elect Trump. We have high confidence in these judgments."[891] Trump continued to push back, not accepting the intelligence report. This cannot be a matter of ego; Putin's agenda is to discredit democracy and make Russia a world power. This must become a nonpartisan issue. The report added, "Russia collected on some Republican-affiliated targets but did not conduct a comparable disclosure campaign."[892]

According to *CNN*, in response to the Russian interference in the election, the Obama administration ousted thirty-five diplomats.[893] Russia did not retaliate by doing the same and instead invited the children of US diplomats to a Christmas party. Russia continues to deny involvement in the hacking and interference in the election, reported the *New York Times*.[894] Trump's response on Twitter was, "Great move on delay (by V. Putin) – I always knew he was very smart!"[895]

There were numerous other tweets from Trump about the hacking, blaming the Democrats for being careless in security of emails, rebuffing the notion that Russia was involved, and defending his interest in working closely with Russia. "Having a good relationship with Russia is a good thing, not a bad thing. Only 'stupid' people, or fools, would think that it is bad! We... have enough problems around the world without yet another one. When I am President, Russia will respect us far more than they do now and... both countries will, perhaps, work together to solve some of the many great and pressing problems and issues of the WORLD!"[896,897,898,899]

It is ironic to me that CNN commentators were so intent on Hillary falling on her own petard and confessing her contribution to her loss while consistently failing to acknowledge their own culpability. There is plenty of blame to go around, and I have provided several contributing factors that affected the outcome of the election, including the media. Since the election was so close, any one of those factors could have tipped the scales. But the media had a higher mission, and therefore a higher accountability, because they are responsible for public enlightenment.

Economy, Free Trade, and Bringing Jobs Back to America

Trump's quotes during the transition conveyed his desperation to demonstrate some kind of win. While he promised a resurgence in manufacturing, the steel industry, and the coal industry, if those promises were realistic, why did Trump need to create a false impression of his contribution?

I am genuinely pleased for the Carrier workers whose jobs were saved in Indiana, but let's be clear: this was a political win, not an economic win. It appears that United Technology may have been concerned about the loss of federal contracts, which amounted to $6.7 billion, according to *Politico*.[900] It is not a sustainable strategy for dealing with companies that may take their manufacturing outside the US. A short-term win is not a long-term victory. The workers are facing either concessions or job loss in the future.

Chuck Jones, the president of the union at the Carrier plant in Indianapolis, told CNN's Chris Cuomo that while they were grateful that President-elect Trump saved some jobs, "He didn't tell the truth. He inflated the number, and I called him out on that."[901] Trump consistently stated that 1,100 jobs were being saved at the Carrier plant. In fact, three hundred of those jobs were never going to Mexico. Only eight hundred jobs were saved.

After Trump's announcement, people thought that their jobs had been saved and learned later that 550 were not.[902] Jones had to deal with the despair and anger of those individuals whose hopes had once again been dashed. The company will also be investing $16 million to automate the plant, thereby eliminating more jobs.

Chuck Jones was very circumspect in his comments about Trump. I believe that Trump knew the number of saved jobs that he cited was inflated. This was about his image, not results. To make matters worse, Trump tweeted a criticism of Jones: "Chuck Jones, who is President of United Steelworkers 1999, has done a terrible job representing workers. No wonder companies flee country!"[903] He followed up with another tweet: "If United Steelworkers 1999 was any good, they would have kept those jobs in Indiana. Spend more time working-less time talking. Reduce dues."[904] The union had no control over the company's proposed move to Mexico. Even Trump, with the leverage of government contracts and reduced taxes, was not able to save all the jobs. I hope those in the Rust Belt who voted for Trump took note, because I believe this will be looked back on as only the first of many such disappointments. Jones offered to work with Trump on keeping jobs in America. If Trump were genuine, he would have accepted this offer.

I have another opinion regarding Trump's strategy for bringing jobs back to America. Many companies are moving to Mexico not because they are unprofitable in the US, but because they could be even more profitable in Mexico. Carrier was profitable, according to the *New York Times*.[905] Corporate greed is the issue, not necessarily free trade. If Trump is going to renegotiate the free-trade agreements, maybe fair wages, as Hillary proposed, need to be a key part of the discussion. I doubt Trump will consider this, as he is opposed to having a minimum wage or overtime pay. It would not be in the best interest of the Trump Corporation.

When the most powerful man in the world criticizes companies on Twitter, whether the information is fact or 'alternative fact,' their stocks are at risk of going down. This is unfair bullying. Even if companies complied during the Trump presidency, this autocratic style of negotiation will not be sustainable.

I will credit Trump's election for the amazing rise in the stock market. *Fortune* advised that "Since Election Day, the Dow Jones Industrial Average is up 8.7 %, the S&P 500 is up 5.8% and Nasdaq is up 5.2%—all of which fall short of Trump's 10% claim."[906] Was there any surprise when Trump promised to eliminate 75% of regulations and reduce corporate taxes by 20%? While surely there were some regulations that could be eliminated because they were cumbersome, and their merit was questionable, many protected the consumer from unethical practices. Where is the evidence that these measures have benefitted the average worker?

How many of the 'left behind' have savings to benefit from this market upswing? How many of them might have benefitted from Obama's mortgage fee cuts that Trump rescinded in an executive order? What company was largely responsible for the upswing? "Goldman Sachs stock is responsible for a whopping 29% of the Dow's overall bump since the election."[907]

I don't want the market to fall. My retirement income is directly tied to the market. But when consumer confidence has "gotten too high in the past, recessions have followed," according to *CNN*.[908] However, if Trump keeps his promises about imposing tariffs, this could result in trade wars, triggering a negative impact on the market.

Conflict of Interest

During the campaign, both Trump and his daughter Ivanka stated that the businesses would be put into a blind trust, as had been done by other presidents, including Bill Clinton and George W. Bush. The Trumps also mentioned that the children would run the businesses. These are very different scenarios.

Forbes explained that a blind trust would involve liquidating assets and having the financial portfolio managed by someone unknown to Trump. Trump would not know what was bought and sold with his money but would receive a report on how much the portfolio generated. If the children managed it, it would not be a blind trust.[909]

Trump tweeted, "Prior to the election, it was well known that I have interests in properties all over the world. Only the crooked media makes this a big deal!"[910] Trump claimed that the people did not care whether he retained his businesses because they knew all along he had a large company that spanned the world, but the people also believed that he would put his businesses in a blind trust.

Since Trump had dealings with Russia, and he obviously wanted to do business there because he had registered several trademarks in the country, Americans had no sure way of knowing that his decisions involving Russia were not motivated by personal gain. If he had debt with a country, how was America to know that his decisions regarding that country were not pay-for-play? Jennifer Wang of *Forbes* wrote, "There's a deep-seated principle about not using public office for private gains."[911] How could we trust that his children would not share information? He had already requested security clearance for his son-in-law. It was difficult for Americans to simply accept "trust me." He did not make equal allowances for Hillary and her charity.

Trump announced in a series of tweets that he would "be holding a major news conference in New York City with my children on December 15 to discuss the fact that I will be leaving my... great business in total in order to fully focus on running the country in order to MAKE AMERICA GREAT AGAIN! While I am not mandated to... do this under the law, I feel it is visually important, as President, to in no way have a conflict of interest with my various businesses... Hence, legal documents are being crafted which take me completely out of business operations. The Presidency is a far more important task!"[912,913,914,915]

It is no surprise that the news conference did not take place on December 15. He announced his plan on January 11, 2017. This was not what he promised during the election, but then he found out the president is exempt from the regulations regarding conflict of interest, to which other government positions are bound.

Before he was inaugurated, there was coverage about the government lease of the property in Washington, which was the site of a new Trump hotel. According to Venook, a reporter for the *Atlantic*, the law stated, "No... elected official of the Government of the United States... shall be admitted to any share or part of this Lease, or to any benefit that may arise therefrom."[916] What is the status on this? Secondly, his sons were intimately involved in the transition, privy to information like the technology meeting that no doubt gave them an advantage. Their relationships are primarily about business, and Trump is known to be a very hands-on CEO. Are we to believe that behind closed doors they will not discuss the business and he will not seek their advice on national matters?

This is a Trump family presidency.

On another point, he tweeted, "I settled the Trump University lawsuit for a small fraction of the potential award because as President I have to focus on our country."[917] This was an easy out for Trump. The court would not have pressured for a settlement if it did not think there was merit to the lawsuit. Trump tried to postpone the trial regarding fraud in the Trump University case, which had already been deferred until after the election. The case had been pending for over six years, according to *Politico*.[918] The judge refused further delays. Trump does not believe that any rules apply to him. I have not seen any updates about the status of the other seventy-four pending lawsuits.

Trump lamented that his son Eric's charity would no longer be raising funds for a children's charity because of his presidency. Eric's motives may not have been so righteous.

Trump's sons were subjected to critical scrutiny regarding the charity. The two brothers sponsored an online auction to have coffee with Ivanka Trump, as well as a new charitable foundation offering a hunting trip with either of the brothers. This is the same behaviour that Trump accused Hillary of during the campaign. While he claimed that charity events were held at Trump properties at little to no cost, Brandy Zadrozny from the *Daily Beast* reported that the "ETF [Eric Trump Foundation] spent $881,779 on its annual Golf Invitational at Trump-owned clubs, a portion of which—$100,000 in 2013 and $88,000 in 2014—was reported as paid directly 'to a company of a family member of the Board of Directors.' In other words, Donald Trump himself."[919] There were other questionable expenses and donations cited in this article, but enough said. If Trump would disclose his tax returns, perhaps those documents would have information to support his claims regarding charitable donations.

Trump Bullying

Hypocrisy and selfishness are unattractive traits. Combined with bullying by the most powerful person in the world, they become dangerous to democracy. The following are just a few examples of Trump's bullying tactics, particularly on Twitter.

CNN reported that the crowd booed Paul Ryan during Trump's thank-you rally in Wisconsin on December 13, 2016. Trump stopped them, saying, "He's like a fine wine. Every day that goes by I get to appreciate his genius more and more."[920] Paul Ryan is a native of Wisconsin and was critical of Trump during the campaign. While the media widely covered the comparison to fine wine, most, if not all, omitted Trump's following comment, which was, "Now if he ever goes against me, I'm not going to say that, okay?"[921] The latter quote is only in the video coverage, not the article. This is intimidation and a threat. Like so many others, Paul Ryan was silenced from expressing dissent; otherwise, he risked being ostracized or maligned.

Freedom of speech is not reserved exclusively for Donald J. Trump and those who subscribe to his agenda.

Trump tweets misinformation and nastiness about others, yet never apologizes or accepts the consequences. Billy Bush lost his job over the Access Hollywood videos exposing Trump's comments, but Trump became president. Reagan was described as the 'Teflon President' because nothing stuck to him. In this regard, there is a legitimate comparison between them.

In an NBC interview, "Rep. John Lewis, D-Ga., said he does not believe Donald Trump is a 'legitimate president.'" He continued by explaining, "I think the Russians participated in helping this man get elected. And they helped destroy the candidacy of Hillary Clinton."[922]

In response, Trump tweeted, "Congressman John Lewis should spend more time on fixing and helping his district, which is in horrible shape and falling apart (not to... mention crime infested) rather than falsely complaining about the election results. All talk, talk, talk - no action or results. Sad!"[923,924]

PolitiFact disputed Trump's characterization of Lewis's district and stated, "While it has higher unemployment and poverty rates than the national average, it still has a thriving economic hub in Atlanta and higher educational attainment."[925] *PolitiFact* also reported that the crime rate in Atlanta was on the decline.[926] Perhaps if Trump had made an effort to reach out to Lewis, there would not have been a groundswell of approximately seventy Democratic politicians boycotting his inauguration. Instead, he increased divisiveness.

What concerns me most is that Trump's tweets generate death threats against those who criticize him. These tweets are dangerous. Chuck Jones received death threats. Megyn Kelly received death threats. *Boston* reported that a nineteen-year-old student received death threats after Trump tweeted, "The arrogant young woman who questioned me in such a nasty fashion at No Labels yesterday was a Jeb staffer! HOW CAN HE BEAT RUSSIA & CHINA?"[927] She was not on staff with Jeb Bush during the primaries; she was a Hillary supporter. She simply said she did not think Trump was a friend to women and questioned whether she would be paid the same as a man and if she would have control of her body. Who knows how many more people have endured harassment after a tweet from Trump because he perceived criticism. The difference between democracy and dictatorship is the ability of the people to challenge and criticize the government and leaders. Trump does not embrace this democratic principle.

Cabinet and Senior Positions

Many of the people Trump has appointed demonstrate dubious competence, reflecting the concerns expressed by former employees and *Apprentice* contestants regarding his ability to select and retain 'the best' in managerial leadership.

Trump appointed Stephen Bannon, former executive chairman of Breitbart News, to serve as his chief White House strategist, a position that does not require vetting. Many Trump supporters and Republicans contend that Bannon is not a bigot, but the *Globe and Mail* reported that Breitbart provided a platform for the 'alt-right' (white supremacists, misogynists, xenophobes, anti–Semites, and those with hatred toward other vulnerable groups) to enrage the grassroots against Hillary Clinton.[928]

Retired Lt. Gen. Michael Flynn was named national security adviser, a position not requiring Senate approval. This appointment was no less concerning than Bannon's. He was fired by the Obama administration in 2014 as the lead of the Defense Intelligence Agency because of concerns about his management style.[929] *Reuters* reported that he told so many falsehoods that his colleagues referred to them as "Flynn facts."[930] Flynn portrayed his firing as the result of his approach to Islamic extremism.[931]

Flynn is known for his extreme Islamophobia. Flynn tweeted, "Fear of Muslims is RATIONAL."[932] He referred to Islam as an ideology and stated, "This is Islamism, it is a vicious cancer inside the body of 1.7 billion people on this planet and it has to be excised."[933] *CNN* reported that fifty-three organizations signed a letter asking for Flynn's removal, claiming that he said "[Islam] 'hides behind being a religion' and continuously peddles the nonsensical fear of 'Sharia law' spreading in the United States."[934]

According to the *New York Times*, while working as an advisor for the Trump campaign, Flynn spoke at a forum for the state broadcaster Russia Today, which promotes Putin's propaganda, and lobbied for a company having ties with Erdoğan. Additionally, Flynn wrote an "article urging the extradition of a Turkish cleric whom the Turkish government said was the mastermind of the attempted coup in July."[935]

During the Republican Convention, Flynn joined the crowd in chants of "Lock her up" in reference to Hillary. The *Hill* reported that Flynn bragged about breaking rules in an interview with the *New Yorker*, including the following: "He would sneak out of the CIA station in Iraq when he was assigned there without the 'insane' required approval from headquarters," and "he gave classified information to NATO allies without approval, which resulted in an investigation and a warning from superiors."[936] "In addition, Flynn openly admitted to the *New York Times* that he had technicians illegally install an internet connection into his office at the Pentagon, so he could give 'classified information to NATO allies without approval' of those above him."[937]

His worldview sets up a conflict between Christians and his perceived enemy, Islam. This is the person that President Trump selected as his chief adviser on national security and foreign policy issues and as the person responsible for providing updates and advice in a crisis.

Although Nikki Haley was very critical of Trump during the campaign, describing him as "one of America's angriest voices," she was Donald Trump's nomination for US Ambassador to the UN, *CNN* reported.[938] While she would bring some diversity to the Cabinet, being a female and Indian, she has little experience in foreign affairs.[939] Trump questioned the US commitment to the UN during the campaign, so perhaps he did not consider this an influential position. As governor of South Carolina, Haley was instrumental in the removal of the Confederate flag from the state grounds following the shooting of several people in a church by a white supremacist.[940] *Vox* reported that Haley did express variance from some of Trump's positions during the hearings in which she confirmed her belief that "Russia committed war crimes in Syria" and "violated the international order when it annexed Crimea and invaded Ukraine."[941]

Trump considered Gen. David Petraeus as Secretary of State. By all accounts, *Business Insider* reported, Petraeus was highly regarded as a commander and director of the CIA until his affair with his biographer became public. In 2012, Petraeus resigned his position at the CIA and was later charged with mishandling classified information in 2015. He pled guilty, and his penalty was a $100,000 fine and two years of probation.[942] "Petraeus gave Broadwell eight notebooks that he kept while he was the commander of coalition forces in Afghanistan, containing everything from his daily schedule to classified information about identities of covert officers, war strategy, intelligence capabilities, diplomatic discussions, quotations from high-level National Security Council meetings, and discussions with the president, according to court documents. He also lied to FBI investigators about giving Broadwell classified information, according to court documents."[943] He spent no time in jail.

What I find so reprehensible is the hypocrisy of Trump and the Republicans in maligning Hillary and convincing supporters that she should be locked up when Trump made Flynn National Security Advisor and praised Petraeus, both of whom were found guilty of the crime Trump accused Hillary of having committed.

Trump's ultimate nomination for Secretary of State was Rex Tillerson, the ExxonMobil chief executive. Though Rex Tillerson is arguably competent to serve as Secretary of State, he is not necessarily qualified. I think Tillerson has several positive qualities and that he will be tough without being a bully. I am concerned that he does not have any diplomatic experience and that many of the career diplomats that could have advised him were removed by Trump prior to Tillerson's having assumed the position.

Michael Tomsky from the *Daily Beast* pointed out that the interests of Exxon and the United Sates are not necessarily the same. He asked, "Is the vantage point of a fossil-fuel extractor really the vantage point that we want to privilege in the role of the world's most important diplomat?"[944] The *Daily Beast* also noted that "Exxon spent years spearheading a public campaign denying a human role in climate change."[945]

The *Washington Post* reported that Trump's nomination for Attorney General was Jeff Sessions III, who was the junior senator from Alabama, the first senator to support Trump publicly. Sessions was not confirmed in 1996 when Reagan nominated him to serve as a federal judge due to allegations that he made racially insensitive statements. His former deputy, Thomas Figures, now deceased, accused Sessions of having warned him to be careful of what he said to "white folks" following an intense argument Figures had with a white colleague. Figures was black. Figures also claimed that Sessions called him "boy" on multiple occasions and said, "Sessions had joked about the Ku Klux Klan, saying he thought its members were okay, until he learned that they smoked marijuana… Sessions acknowledged at the hearing that he once 'may have said something about the N.A.A.C.P. being un-American or Communist, but I meant no harm by it.'"[946] To this day, Sessions denies this racist characterization, citing his efforts in school integration, his prosecution of members of the KKK, and his efforts to shut down gerrymandering.[947]

According to the *New York Times*, one of the most controversial cases for Sessions as a state attorney in west Alabama was a case charging three African-American activists with voter fraud. Bolstered by the Voting Rights Act of 1965, Albert Turner and his wife started an effort to support registration of black voters, trying to convince them that the new legislation made it safe for them to vote. While there was a considerable backlash of voter suppression, Sessions charged the Turners and a friend with voter fraud and accused them of filling out absentee ballots and mailing them in. The judge dismissed many of the charges, and the jury acquitted them of the rest.[948]

For the current hearings, Sen. Dianne Feinstein (D-Calif.) "read a letter from more than 1,000 legal scholars at law schools across the country who questioned whether Sessions had changed since the Senate committee rejected his nomination for a federal judgeship."[949] Sessions' detractors cited his voting record, and he was described as "one of the Senate's most hardline anti-immigration lawmakers, and he has opposed the Voting Rights Act."[950]

It does not matter whether he is racist. Why select someone so divisive and controversial for the chief law enforcement position in the land when you are supposedly trying to unify the country and represent all Americans? Because Trump was beholden to Sessions.

Trump tweeted, "General James 'Mad Dog' Mattis, who was confirmed as Secretary of Defense, was very impressive during his hearings."[951] Mattis appears to be an anomaly. During the hearings, he impressed me as being competent and qualified.

According to *Heavy*, during an interview in 2013, Mattis raised concerns about a perception of US bias toward Israel. He said, "I paid a military security price every day as the commander of CentCom because the Americans were seen as biased in support of Israel, and that moderates all the moderate Arabs who want to be with us, because they can't come out publicly in support of people who don't show respect for the Arab Palestinians."[952]

Politico reported that while Mattis was hesitant to recommend pulling out of the deal with Iran, he was also critical of the Obama administration, believing that the US needed to be more aggressive. He believes that Russia is a major threat to national security[953] and opposes waterboarding. "I've never found it to be useful," he said. "I've always found, give me a pack of cigarettes and a couple of beers and I do better with that than I do with torture," *CNN* reported.[954]

Another serious concern over the appointment of individuals who have shown themselves to be less than qualified and less than competent is the fact that Trump's new cabinet, as it stands now, lacks diversity. Thirteen of the sixteen are white males, many have no government or diplomatic experience, and many are billionaires. His defense for the billionaires is that their experience with Wall Street and their understanding of how it works will benefit the cabinet. Why did that rationale not apply when Hillary was working with some people on Wall Street? At least she had proposals that were going to deal with the inequity. Trump still has not provided a clear policy in this regard. It remains to be seen if this expertise will benefit all Americans or just the super-rich.

"All of my Cabinet nominee[s] are looking good and doing a great job. I want them to be themselves and express their own thoughts, not mine!"[955] While Trump said he would respect the advice of his cabinet, he does not have to. He may go through the motions of consultation with his administration, while taking advice from others.

Other Issues During Transition

On November 21, 2016, a Wisconsin court determined that "state assembly voting districts drawn up by Republicans five years ago are unconstitutional and violate the rights of Democrats," the *Guardian* disclosed.[956] While this ruling did not affect the presidential election, it could affect future seats in the House of Representatives. My concern is whether the Supreme Court, with Trump's new nomination, will uphold this.

Gerrymandering was also responsible for an imbalance of Republicans in the House of Representatives and Congress in Michigan. For the state representative for Congress, 2,244,765 (48.351%) voted for the Republican candidate, and 2,164,893 (46.630%) voted for the Democratic candidate, yet fourteen representatives are Republicans and only five are Democrats. "In other words, even though fewer than 50% of Michigan voters chose the Republican candidate for Congress, Republicans will make up 64.29% of Michigan's congressional delegation," according to *Fix the Mitten*.[957] For the House of Representatives, even though there was only 0.1% difference in votes, "Republicans will hold 57.27% of the seats and Democrats will hold only 42.73% of the seats."[958]

Trump recommended that Britain make the Brexit leader Nigel Farage ambassador to the US: "Many people would like to see @Nigel_Farage represent Great Britain as their Ambassador to the United States. He would do a great job!"[959] According to the *New York Times*, when Trump proposed this, "the first minister of Wales, Carwyn Jones, said it would be like 'giving a child a chain saw.'"[960] The Prime Minister's office provided a diplomatic response: "There is no vacancy. We have an excellent ambassador to the U.S. in Kim Darroch, a former national security adviser."[961] Is this the kind of diplomacy we can expect from the Trump presidency?

After reports that his approval rating dropped to "40%, according to a new *CNN/ORC* Poll, the lowest of any recent president and forty-four points below that of President Barack Obama," Trump rejected polls, tweeting, "The same people who did the phony election polls, and were so wrong, are now doing approval rating polls. They are rigged just like before."[962] His behaviour has not been more presidential since his win. He will not change. He has shown us who he is.

CHAPTER ELEVEN

Inauguration To Governance

In questions of power, let no more be heard of confidence in man,
but bind him down from mischief by the chains of the constitution.[963]
— Thomas Jefferson

As I expected, his behaviour did not change. The events during the transition and Trump's inauguration speech did not provide hope that he would heal the divisiveness.

Inauguration

One of Trump's preoccupations with the upcoming inauguration was the number of celebrities who were not interested in performing. He reframed the lack of celebrity participation in the following tweet: "The so-called 'A' list celebrities are all wanting tixs [tickets] to the inauguration, but look what they did for Hillary, NOTHING. I want the PEOPLE!"[964] According to the *Daily Beast*, numerous celebrities declined invitations to perform.[965]

If Trump was going to offend millions of people without apologizing and treat people with disrespect, then he should have expected consequences. Too bad Aretha didn't attend and perform "Respect!" Trump and his team needed to recognize and acknowledge that he would also represent the 67% of registered voters who did not vote for him.

Trump insulted many celebrities in truly vile ways. He objected to their using their platforms to express political views, although he used his position as a presidential nominee and president-elect to promote his business interests. At least the celebrities weren't using their platforms for personal gain.

Trump's questionable associations continued to promote divisiveness into the events of the inauguration. *Heavy* provided background on the traditional private service at St. John's Episcopal Church across the street from the White House, presided over by a Dallas pastor, Dr. Robert Jeffress, who was selected by Trump's inauguration committee. Jessica McBride reported that Jeffress made the following controversial remarks: "The deep, dark, dirty secret of Islam: It is a religion that promotes pedophilia – sex with children. This so-called prophet Muhammad raped a 9-year-old girl – had sex with her."[966] He described Islam as "evil," "oppressive," and "violent."[967] He also referred to Mormonism as a "cult" and said the Catholic Church "cannot be trusted."[968]

McBride added, "Jeffress has said that gays live a 'miserable lifestyle' predisposed to 'depression, or suicide, or alcoholism'; that gay rights will lead to the 'inevitable implosion of our country'; and that gays are brainwashing the public."[969]

While Trump defenders deny that he is a racist and a misogynist, he continually surrounds himself with people who espouse those views. This is one of the many reasons Trump detractors have difficulty accepting his commitment for unification. The inauguration took place on January 20, 2017. Donald J. Trump officially became the forty-fifth president of the United States.

While his supporters found his speech hopeful, others thought it was dark and negative. His administration supported his speech, and they continued to say it was what his voters expected.

Trump's inauguration speech appeared to be more self-serving than it was concerned with unifying the country. The *NPR* transcript quoted Trump as saying, "The establishment protected itself but not the citizens of our country. Their victories have not been your victories."[970] They were Trump's victories. Trump benefitted from the 2008 financial crisis. One cannot deny that there is corruption in government and that government is sluggish. His scathing remarks about the establishment were directed at both Democrats and Republicans. Yet Trump failed to address the degree to which the Republican Party obstructed the Obama administration.

"What truly matters is not which party controls our government but whether our government is controlled by the people. January 20th, 2017 will be remembered as the day the people became the rulers of this nation again."[971] Trump focused only on those actions that his voters supported and did nothing to engage the rest of the country.

Trump continued to portray America in stark terms without acknowledging the truth: crime has decreased, and the economy has improved. While problems in places like Chicago do exist and there is a need to continue improving the employment rate by developing jobs and dealing with the inner-city issues, this portrayal was not America. Since many of these issues are controlled by the state, it will be interesting to see what influence, if any, Trump will have on Republican states to change these conditions.

Trump claimed, "The forgotten men and women of our country will be forgotten no longer."[972] Immediately following the inauguration, President Trump signed an executive order reversing Obama's mortgage fee cuts. *Time* reported that Warren Mayor Doug Franklin provides leadership in a rust belt community that flipped from Democrat to Republican this election. In an article in *Time*, he warned about the impact of Trump's policies for his community which include loss of the following: housing programs, "infrastructure programs in low- to moderate-income areas," "education programs that help low-income families," and senior services. He concluded, "[T]hey'll all go away."[973] This raises the concern that vindictiveness motivates the destruction of Obama's legacy rather than a moral belief that these changes will be good for the American people. For Trump, there is no differentiation between Obama's executive orders that are not consistent with the Trump platform and those that may have benefitted the people. It seems he will eradicate them all.

"We will seek friendship and goodwill with the nations of the world. But we do so with the understanding that it is the right of all nations to put their own interests first. We do not seek to impose our way of life on anyone but rather to let it shine as an example. We will shine for everyone to follow."[974] His tweets do not reflect the sentiment of seeking friendship and goodwill with nations of the world, including allies.

His actions to date belie the words in his speech. He spoke of unifying a divided America. The previous divisions in America do not compare to the polarization that has occurred following his campaign and election. He humiliated the President of Mexico, threatened to dissolve NAFTA, threatened to pull out of NATO and the Paris agreement, proposed a ban on refugees and immigrants from specific Muslim countries, and participated in a Twitter war with China.

The *Globe and Mail* reported that there were numerous protests the day of the inauguration, most of them peaceful. The day after the inauguration, the Women's March in Washington attracted over 500,000 people with marches in cities across the US and the world. There were thirty marches in Canada with a crowd of 60,000 in Toronto alone. These marches were peaceful.[975]

On January 20, 2017, the day after the inauguration, the *New York Times* reported that the crowds at Trump's inauguration were smaller than those at Obama's first inauguration. This apparently upset Trump because the next day he visited the CIA to mend relationships following several instances in which he trashed the intelligence community. There were mixed reactions as to his success. Former CIA Director John Brennan stated that he was "deeply saddened and angered at Donald Trump's despicable display of self-aggrandizement in front of CIA's Memorial Wall of agency heroes," reported *CNN*.[976]

According to *PolitiFact*, during his address to the CIA, Trump said that most of the CIA voted for him, which was offensive to many operatives, as they are non-political. Trump spent considerable time denigrating the media: "I have a running war with the media," he said. "They are among the most dishonest human beings on Earth. And they sort of made it sound like I had a feud with the intelligence community."[977] Trump was obsessive about the crowd at the inauguration. This is not the way to mend fences. There were not a million people in the mall.

Sean Spicer, then the White House Press Secretary, lambasted the media and said, "This was the largest audience to ever witness an inauguration – period," the *Atlantic* reported.[978] He later explained that he was not speaking solely of those in the mall, but rather the total audience, including those watching on TV. That clearly is not what Trump was referring to. Spicer went on to say that Trump was being "demoralized" by the press and that these were efforts to delegitimize the presidency.[979]

Let's flash back to Obama's inaugurations. The following are tweets from Donald Trump following Obama's election in 2012: "The electoral college is a disaster... This election is a total sham and a travesty. We are not a democracy... Our country is now in serious and unprecedented trouble... Like never before... We can't let this happen. We should march on Washington and stop this travesty. Our nation is totally divided... Lets fight like hell and stop this great and disgusting injustice! The world is laughing at us."[980,981,982,983]

Many of the protesters after Obama's 2008 election seemed to be motivated by racism. Much of the rhetoric from the Tea Party and Republicans was racially charged. Consider just a few examples:

A member of John McCain's Virginia Leadership Team, Bobby May, was fired "for writing a newspaper column that said that if Obama were elected he'd hire rapper Ludacris to paint the White House black and change the national anthem to the 'Negro National Anthem.'"[984]

The president "of a Republican women's club in San Bernardino County, Calif., resigned… after she sent out a newsletter with a drawing of Obama on a bogus food-stamp coupon surrounded by ribs, watermelon and fried chicken."[985]

"South Carolina Republican activist Rusty DePass compared an escaped gorilla from a Columbia zoo to First Lady Michelle Obama's ancestors."[986]

International leaders expressed a willingness to work with the Trump administration and sent congratulations. On November 9, 2016, Prime Minister of Canada Justin Trudeau released a statement congratulating Donald Trump on his election win.

> Canada has no closer friend, partner, and ally than the United States. We look forward to working very closely with President-elect Trump, his administration, and with the United States Congress in the years ahead, including on issues such as trade, investment, and international peace and security. The relationship between our two countries serves as a model for the world. Our shared values, deep cultural ties, and strong integrated economies will continue to provide the basis for advancing our strong and prosperous partnership.[987]

Trudeau was reminding Trump of the importance of the countries' commonality in values while extending an invitation to work cooperatively. The relationship between Canada and the US did serve as a model of cooperation, and I fervently hope that this will continue.

The Travel Ban

Trump has been busy signing executive orders, but what will the implications be once they are enacted? The ban on specific Muslim countries is but one example. His cabinet was not even in place. Trump demonstrated that he does not value the advice of the intelligence community or seasoned civil servants.

Trump promised an extreme vetting process for refugees and immigrants during the campaign, and it was obviously a priority. Contrary to the impression Trump conveyed to voters, the US already had an intense vetting process that took eighteen to twenty-four months. Trump never did explain what he thought was weak or missing from the previous vetting process.

Had the Trump administration spent the two months prior to inauguration improving the vetting process before implementing it, the revisions may have received wide approval. Nobody would object to a process that will ensure national security. However, the vetting process should be applied to all refugees and immigrants and not discriminate against any nationality or religion. Terrorists could enter from any country. Targeting specific groups makes no one safer. The vetting process is not the true agenda; banning Muslims is.

Trump signed an executive order that was not clear, nor was it widely consulted. Apparently, Steve Bannon was heavily involved in its development and even Rudy Giuliani was consulted. The implementation was a debacle. Joanne Walters from the *Guardian* reported the following experiences. People with green cards were being denied entry. Hundreds were being held at airports. People were being denied access to lawyers, and some were put on return flights. One seventy-eight-year-old grandmother came to visit her children and was held for twenty-seven hours. She had diabetes, high blood pressure, and kidney problems. She fell ill during her detention. She refused to sign a paper agreeing to withdraw her application for admission to the US with her valid visa. Her cell phone was confiscated at one point.[988]

The *Huffington Post* described the story of a five-year-old American boy travelling with a family member who was detained for hours, by himself, at Dulles airport, despite Maryland Sen. Van Hollen having informed authorities of the child's impending arrival. The boy was not allowed to see his waiting mother.[989]

As reported by Sara Elizabeth Williams in the *Telegraph*, the ramifications of a travel ban may have a far greater impact on national security than any potential risks from refugees. After two years, an Iraqi former US Army interpreter was in the last stages of the resettlement process, but the ban prevented him and his family from escaping the danger they faced because he aided the Americans. His two brothers were killed by terrorists because of his job. His brother already had a green card, but he could not go to Iraq, so they were separated. He stated, "I trusted the Americans, I gave everything for them, and they let me down. The US Army has this thing they say, 'we don't leave anyone behind' – but they left us."[990] There were several similar stories in the same article. Who knows how many more? Surely Iraqis will feel they cannot trust America and may be reluctant to provide interpretive services.

According to *CNN*, experts contended that this was what ISIS wanted and that it would be used in their propaganda as a recruitment tool. "On social media right now there's a lot of people quoting Anwar al-Awlaki [the late spokesperson for al Qaeda in the Arabian Peninsula] and his last speech when he said that America will turn on the Muslims."[991]

The United States has troops and contractors in some of those countries. What is the risk to them now that they are in hostile territory?

According to the *Nation*, the ban may negatively impact the US relationship with Iran. There were those who were hopeful of an improved relationship that would generate new opportunities for American investors and manufacturing that might help to lessen the tension between the two countries. It is possible that these opportunities will go to Russia, China, and Europe.[992]

It was widely reported in the media that opposition to the ban and its implementation was swift and widespread. Thousands protested at airports, not just in the US, but around the world. British Prime Minister Theresa May expressed disapproval and threatened to challenge the US if it had adverse effects on British nationals.[993] The Labour leader "called for Trump to be banned from visiting Britain until the temporary travel restrictions are rescinded."[994]

There was a petition posted on the British Parliament's website that garnered hundreds of thousands of signatures to rescind an invitation for President Trump to meet Queen Elizabeth II.[995]

According to the *Independent*, German Chancellor Angela Merkel expressed regret about the ban and in a telephone call with Trump cited the 1951 Geneva Refugee Convention that calls on signatories to take in people fleeing war.[996]

While several nationalist parties in Europe lauded the move, "Italy's Interior Minister Marco Minniti, who had held top security roles in recent governments, warned against 'equating immigration and terrorism.'"[997]

The Prime Minister of Canada tweeted, "To those fleeing persecution, terror & war, Canadians will welcome you, regardless of your faith. Diversity is our strength #WelcomeToCanada."[998]

The *Atlantic* reported on companies against the ban. Ford, Tesla, Google, Apple, Starbucks, Amazon, General Electric, and other companies spoke against Trump's travel ban. "Netflix CEO Reed Hastings said the ban is hurting his employees around the world, and that 'these actions will make America less safe.'"[999] More than two thousand Google staff walked off the job and staged protests. Airbnb offered to host people impacted by the ban free of charge, and Lyft pledged $1 million to the American Civil Liberties Union. Many of the CEOs of these companies were involved in Trump's Strategic Policy Forum in December and agreed to counsel him in the coming years but said, "the president failed to realize the U.S. economy is not just reliant upon immigrants, but that immigrants are its foundation."[1000]

According to *Fortune*, at least twenty Republicans have spoken out publicly against the ban and its implementation. Senators John McCain and Lindsay Graham issued a joint statement that ended with, "Ultimately, we fear this executive order will become a self-inflicted wound in the fight against terrorism."[1001] Rep. Justin Amash (R-Mich.) tweeted, "It's not lawful to ban immigrants on basis of nationality. If the president wants to change immigration law, he must work with Congress." Sen. Ben Sasse (R-Neb.) stated, "If we send a signal to the Middle East that the U.S. sees all Muslims as jihadis, the terrorist recruiters win by telling kids that America is banning Muslims and that this is America versus one religion. Our generational fight against jihadism requires wisdom."[1002]

Even Dick Cheney, former Vice President in the George W. Bush administration, weighed in, stating, "I think this whole notion that somehow we can just say no more Muslims, just ban a whole religion, goes against everything we stand for and believe in… I mean, religious freedom has been a very important part of our history and where we came from. A lot of people, my ancestors got here, because they were Puritans."[1003]

Here are some of the facts reported by *Salon*: "Of the approximately 15,000 Syrian refugees living in the U.S., exactly none of them have been implicated in terrorist plots… of the 784,000 refugees now in the U.S., 'a total of three have been charged with plotting terrorist attacks,' according to the Migration Policy Institute… only '0.02 percent of Muslims in the world are terrorists, based on State Department statistics.'"[1004] The human suffering and potential consequences of the ban are legion, and for what? Political grandstanding.

While Trump and his administration have continually asserted that the ban was not driven by religious discrimination and was intended to protect Americans, there are several indicators that lead one to question this executive order's motives. The incompetent implementation was not the only issue. The communication from Trump and his administration was as, if not more, unsettling. They have provided no evidence or support to rationalize their claims and the potential benefits and risks of the ban. Trump and his administration cited the fact that it is not a Muslim ban because numerous Muslim countries are not on the list.

Trump referred to the attacks on New York on September 11, 2001 in the executive order banning refugees and immigrants from specific countries, mostly Muslim, that pose a threat to America. Not one of these countries was involved in 9/11. This reference was made to engender fear and an emotional connection. The allies depend on the cooperation of these countries in fighting terrorism. The 9/11 Memorial & Museum advised that fifteen of the nineteen terrorists involved in 9/11 were from Saudi Arabia, two were from the United Arab Emirates, one was from Lebanon, and one was from Egypt.[1005] These countries were not included in the ban.

We do not have Trump's income tax returns to be certain, but there is reason to believe that he has business interests in those countries. He does not appear to have business affiliations in the countries listed in the ban.

While Trump and his administration deny that it is a Muslim ban, Trump declared that he would prioritize Christian refugees from these countries. Daniel Burke from *CNN* quoted Trump speaking about his rationale: "'If you were a Muslim you could come in, but if you were a Christian, it was almost impossible and… that was so unfair.'"[1006] This is not true. Pew reported that in 2016, the numbers of Christians and Muslims admitted into the US were almost equal.[1007] Prior to this, the US did not consider religion. Was Trump implying that the Obama administration was giving preference to Muslims and blocking Christians? The *Hill* reported that in an interview with Fox News, Giuliani explained, "When [Trump] first announced it, he said 'Muslim ban.' He called me up, he said, 'Put a commission together, show me the right way to do it legally.'"[1008] In 2015, Mike Pence tweeted, "Calls to ban Muslims from entering the U.S. are offensive and unconstitutional."[1009]

Though Trump frequently referred to the executive order as a ban, his administration refers to it as a 'pause,' saying it is temporary. The ban on Syrian refugees is indefinite, not temporary. Trump will pay attention only to those tweets and leaders who support his view, and his administration will support him unquestioningly, including Vice President Mike Pence.

Several of his senior advisors urged him not to use the term "radical Islamic terrorism" because the phrase is counterproductive. According to *Business Insider,* the most recent senior advisor to discourage the use of this phrase was Trump's new national security adviser, Lt. Gen. H.R. McMaster.[1010] Despite that, Trump used it in his State of the Union address, enunciating each word separately and distinctly, like a defiant adolescent. While Trump has denounced the violence and hate crimes against the Jewish community, I have not once heard him denounce the ever-increasing hate crimes against the Muslim community.

While he has not proposed internment camps, let's review history. During WWII in Canada and the United States, a registration was made for all Japanese-Canadian and Japanese-American citizens. Then a curfew was imposed; then their bank accounts were frozen; then they were carted off to internment camps. This is one of the greatest assaults to democracy in the histories of these two countries, and was based on fear that had no substantiation in fact. So far, Trump has proposed a registry and ban of Muslim immigrants. It is a slippery slope.

Jeffrey Lord and Trump supporters tried to portray Trump as Reaganesque, and Trump used Reagan's former campaign slogan, "Let's Make America Great Again." Reagan's most brilliant skill was that he could take the most complex issue and describe it in terms that the public could understand. My favourite moment was his speech in Germany on June 12, 1987.

> Mr. Gorbachev, tear down this wall! I understand the fear of war and the pain of division that afflict this continent-- and I pledge to you my country's efforts to help overcome these burdens. To be sure, we in the West must resist Soviet expansion. So, we must maintain defenses of unassailable strength. Yet we seek peace; so we must strive to reduce arms on both sides.[1011]

Reagan wanted to tear down a wall; Trump wants to build one. The wall was a cornerstone of Trump's campaign and one that his base still expects him to fulfill. Members of the Reagan family said they felt insulted by the comparison. Michael Reagan, a conservative strategist and Ronald Reagan's son, said that he did not vote for Trump and that his father would not have voted for him. He added, "Donald Trump is no Ronald Reagan."[1012]

Not only did Reagan beseech Gorbachev to tear down the wall, but he apologized to the Japanese who were interred and made reparation. Who is going to end up apologizing to the Muslims?

Trump's mistakes may have longstanding and dire consequences, not just for America, but for the world.

Firing of Acting Attorney General Sally Yates

CNN reported that acting Attorney General Sally Yates wrote the following (now public) statement regarding the travel ban executive order: "At present, I am not convinced that the defense of the executive order is consistent with these responsibilities nor am I convinced that the executive order is lawful."[1013] The *Guardian* reported that she instructed lawyers in the Justice Department not to defend the order.[1014]

The Trump administration reacted immediately by sending a hand-delivered letter stating that she had been removed from the position, as reported by the *New York Times*. The White House quickly followed up to justify their position by criticizing Yates. "Ms. Yates is an Obama administration appointee who is weak on borders and very weak on illegal immigration."[1015] *CNN* reported that she was fired for "refusing to enforce a legal order designed to protect the citizens of the United States" and "betray[ing] the Department of Justice."[1016]

There is no contention that Trump had the legal right to fire Yates. The question is, did Yates have the responsibility to express her objections? Much of the media reporting did not include the distinction and detail provided by Yates. Noah Feldman, reporter for *Bloomberg*, provided clarification. It coincided with my view, expressed earlier, that the motive of the ban is pivotal, not just the text.

According to *Bloomberg*, the Office of Legal Counsel found the executive order to be constitutional. Their decision was based solely on the text of the order. Yates contrasted the role of the Office of Legal Counsel to her duty as acting Attorney General, which went beyond the consideration of the actual text of the order to include the context. In this circumstance, the issues of Trump's statement about Christian preference and Giuliani's statements about a 'Muslim ban' were considered in her decision. "She said that her job, unlike the OLC's, included considering 'whether any policy choice embodied in an Executive Order is wise or just.' That's completely appropriate for someone in a position of responsibility, who is required to consider the morality of government enactments, not merely their legality."[1017]

One might give credence to Trump's rationale for his actions but for one very critical, ironic event. *Business Insider* disclosed that during her confirmation hearings in 2015 for Deputy Attorney General, Sally Yates was asked a question by none other than Jeff Sessions, Trump's nominee for Attorney General. Sessions asked, "Do you think the attorney general has a responsibility to say no to the president if he asks for something that's improper?" Yates responded, "Senator, I believe that the attorney general or the deputy attorney general has an obligation to follow the law and the Constitution, and to give their independent legal advice to the president."[1018] She made this clear, and Sessions agreed that her role was not to follow the bidding of the president, but rather to give independent legal advice.[1019]

Yates was not alone in her legal assessment questioning the executive order. The United States District Court for the Eastern District of New York issued an emergency stay on Trump's executive order, according to the *Daily Dot*,[1020] as did a Boston Federal Court.[1021] Other legal challenges are being mounted, *WBUR News* reported.

Could Yates have used a less public option? Perhaps, but I surmise that she expected that whether she did it privately or publicly, she would be dismissed, and like Trump, determined that she wanted to personally deliver her own message to America instead of the White House spin.

More concerning is the communication from the White House. *MSN* explained that during the Vietnam War, a mechanism called the 'dissent channel' was created for career diplomats to express their dissent to the Secretary of State, which included recommended solutions. Several were sent last year about the policy on Syria. "State Department rules are supposed to protect dissenters from being retaliated against."[1022] The dissent channel on the executive order restricting immigration in some countries had over a thousand signatures, with more expected. That is "far more than any dissent cable in recent years."[1023] *Politico* provided White House Press Secretary Sean Spicer's response: "These career bureaucrats have a problem with it? I think they should either get with the program or they can go."[1024]

Spicer's statement should be taken in context. The Trump administration asked for details and names of people in the EPA. Jeffrey Lord expressed that Trump may want to purge civil service positions to make sure that the people in place will support his policies. There was a heightened criticism of the central intelligence community by Trump and his administration. Bannon considered the media the opposition party, and according to *Occupy Democrats*,

Kellyanne Conway suggested that the media that had not been supportive of Trump should be fired, adding, "We know their names."[1025] Does this sound like democracy?

The Mosque Killings in Quebec

On January 29, 2017, a day after Trudeau's Welcome to Canada tweet, a horrific act of violence was committed in a Quebec City mosque during evening prayers. A twenty-seven-year-old man entered the mosque and opened fire, killing six and injuring nineteen others. *CBC* reported that the tragedy, described as a hate crime, resulted in six dead and eight injured. Two possible suspects were detained until further investigation, in which they determined that one was the shooter while the other was a witness.[1026]

Justin Trudeau immediately reached out to the Muslim community and Canadians with the following message: "We condemn this terrorist attack on Muslims in a center of worship and refuge… It is heart-wrenching to see such senseless violence. Diversity is our strength, and religious tolerance is a value that we, as Canadians, hold dear."[1027]

Fox News inaccurately claimed that the shooter was Moroccan. Actually, the shooter was Alexandre Bissonnette, "a twenty-seven-year-old man of French-Canadian origin," the *Star* disclosed.[1028] It took intervention from the office of the Prime Minister of Canada to have the inaccurate information removed. Fox News complied at that point, with apologies.[1029]

Kate Purchase, Director of Communications in the Prime Minister's Office, conveyed the sentiments of that office: "These tweets by Fox News dishonour the memory of the six victims and their families by spreading misinformation, playing identity politics, and perpetuating fear and division within our communities." She added, "We need to remain focused on keeping our communities safe and united instead of trying to build walls and scapegoat communities."[1030]

The *Star* reported that even though Sean Spicer clearly stated that Prime Minister Justin Trudeau was "cautious to draw conclusions of the motives at this stage of the investigation,"[1031] Spicer was quick to use the situation to support Trump's executive order by adding, "We condemn this attack in the strongest possible terms. It's a terrible reminder of why we must remain vigilant, and why the president is taking steps to be proactive, rather than reactive, when it comes to our nation's safety and security."[1032] This was an unabashed use of misinformation of a tragic situation for political gain.

The shooter was not Muslim, a refugee, or an immigrant. This situation had no relationship whatsoever to Trump's executive order. According to the *Globe and Mail*, Alexandre Bissonnette was described by acquaintances as "a right-wing troll inspired by the French extreme right who supported U.S. President Donald Trump."[1033] He was also reported to have been inspired by France's populist leader, Marine Le Pen.[1034]

Supreme Court Announcement

Trump announced the nomination of Neil Gorsuch as a lifetime member of the Supreme Court. He is only forty-nine years old, and this would provide a conservative majority that could influence Supreme Court rulings on gun control, abortion, the death penalty, and religious rights. This nomination was particularly contentious given the Republicans' refusal to provide even a hearing for President Barack Obama's nominee following the death of Judge Scalia in February 2016. During the Nixon administration, there was a lengthy vacancy before the Senate finally approved the president's third nomination. *Reuters* identified that "[a]side from that one, no other Supreme Court vacancy since the U.S. Civil War years of the 1860s has been as long as the current one."[1035] Mitch McConnell and the Republicans were shamefully disrespectful of the office of the presidency in not allowing the customary hearings.

It is a sad irony that the Republicans are now being rewarded, when they were, in my view, most responsible for a dysfunctional government with their gridlock to block any advancement of Obama's agenda, including job creation. Under the Obama administration, the infrastructure bill was intended to improve highways, bridges, and other projects in the amount of $478 billion in new spending over six years without increasing the deficit, and that would create new jobs. The *Fiscal Times* reported that the Republicans vetoed the bill in March 2015.[1036] In July 2015, the Republicans blocked a bill that would have created one million jobs for youth, to be funded by closing a tax loophole for billionaires, *PoliticusUSA* reported.[1037] In his victory speech, Trump committed to improving the infrastructure and creating millions of jobs. One can only hope that this will be an agenda on which both sides will find agreement.

The question is, which of Trump's election promises were genuine, and which were politically-motivated falsehoods used to garner support? In an interview on CNN's *New Day* with Chris Cuomo on November 10, 2016, Rudy Giuliani was asked if he would entertain being the attorney general. Giuliani replied that he has the energy and is the most qualified. When asked about Trump's commitment to hire a special prosecutor to indict Hillary Clinton, Giuliani implied that if there was enough evidence to go forward, this was highly possible, but if there was 'no there, there,' it may not be pursued.[1038] During the election campaign, Trump and his supporters continually hammered away that the system was rigged and that Hillary was guilty of corruption. On numerous occasions, Giuliani and Chris Christie asserted that there was evidence to indict her. This prevarication appears to belie their previous assertions that Hillary's guilt was definitive.

I agree with Hillary's comments in her concession speech, detailed in the *New York Times*:

> Donald Trump is going to be our president. We owe him an open mind, and the chance to lead. Our constitutional democracy enshrines the peaceful transfer of power. And we don't just respect that, we cherish it. It also enshrines other things: The rule of law, the principle that we are all equal in rights and dignity, freedom of worship and expression. We respect and cherish these values too, and we must defend them.[1039]

Unlike the Republicans who obstructed the Obama administration, I hope that Democrats will commit to supporting and working with the Trump administration on endeavours such as the proposed infrastructure projects, which will benefit the American people, while resisting proposals that threaten democracy.

CHAPTER TWELVE

Promises, Promises, Promises

Words can be twisted into any shape. Promises can be made to lull the heart and seduce the soul. In the final analysis, words mean nothing. They are labels we give things in an effort to wrap our puny little brains around their underlying natures, when ninety-nine percent of the time the totality of the reality is an entirely different beast. The wisest man is the silent one. Examine his actions. Judge him by them.[1040]
— *Karen Marie Moning*

Trump made a contract with the American people for the first hundred days of his presidency.[1041] The following is summarized from a piece on *CNBC,* as of April 11, 2017.[1042]

The Trump administration has completed slightly over 50% of the objectives and none of the legislative measures they set out for the first one hundred days. Some of the more significant completions include creating a requirement that for every new federal regulation, two existing regulations must be eliminated; enforcing a five-year ban on White House and Congressional officials becoming lobbyists after they leave government; announcing to renegotiate NAFTA or withdraw from the deal; announcing withdrawal from the Trans-Pacific Partnership; and selecting a replacement for Justice Scalia.[1043]

Some of the key objectives not completed were imposing term limits on all members of Congress, labeling China a currency manipulator, cancelling all federal funding to sanctuary cities, beginning to remove the more than two million 'criminal' illegal immigrants from the country and cancel visas to foreign countries that won't take them back, and cancelling every unconstitutional executive action, memorandum, and order issued by President Obama.[1044]

The following are observations regarding a few of the objectives for the first hundred days.

Selecting a replacement for Justice Scalia:[1045] There were two major issues during the campaign that had import for the Supreme Court appointment: preservation of the Second Amendment and re-establishment of Christian values, particularly pro-life values.

Trump and the GOP will ensure that the Second Amendment will not undergo any changes and that there will not be any new gun regulations. Americans will continue to be able to buy AK-47s and carry them in public in open-carry states. Police will continue to have to be wary about their safety every time they stop a car, encounter a suspect, and discern who are the good guys carrying guns in a crowd as opposed to who are the shooters.

A conservative judge might well support Trump's anti-abortion agenda. However, Trump said that the Supreme Court's decision on same-sex marriage is settled law. The question would be, after all the challenges to Row v. Wade, why is this not also settled law? It is doubtful that the Supreme Court, even with another conservative judge, will overturn it. While improbable, if it is overturned, then America will join six countries in the world in which abortion is illegal: Holy See, Malta, Dominican Republic, El Salvador, Nicaragua, and Chile, as reported by the *Independent*.[1046] In another thirteen countries, the laws are so restrictive that it is almost impossible to be approved for abortion. The *Independent* provided an example of a ten-year-old who was raped by her stepfather being denied a legal abortion in Paraguay.[1047]

I remember relatives who had two healthy children. Their third was born with multiple life-threatening issues. They named the child and loved her for her few short days in this world. They, and we, mourned their loss. They wanted another child and refused amniocentesis to determine if the fetus was healthy because they do not believe in abortion. The fourth child was healthy, but they had the moral fibre to accept the potential consequences of their convictions, whatever they might've been. They had four children, not three. I am not sure that I would have had such moral conviction if my life were in danger due to a pregnancy.

Would Trump or the male pro-life legislators have the moral fibre to support their convictions if they had a ten-year-old daughter that was raped, or whose life was in danger due to a pregnancy? Pro-lifers have the ability to make that choice for themselves. Do they have the right to force those beliefs on others, or should they leave that judgement to their Almighty?

Only twenty-four states and the District of Columbia require sex education in US schools, and thirty-three states and the District of Columbia require parental permission.[1048] The Republican healthcare insurance is unlikely to subsidize birth control, though it will probably cover Viagra. With these attitudes, it is no surprise that the teen pregnancy rate in the US is three times higher than it is in other developed countries, despite a dramatic decline in teen pregnancies in recent years.[1049]

If contraception is not covered under the health plan, there will be an increase in abortions. If abortion becomes illegal, women will seek unsafe abortions, which have a mortality rate of 13% and result in long-term health issues.[1050] Teen mothers are more likely to live in poverty and "their children are more likely to suffer health and cognitive disadvantages, come in contact with the child welfare and correctional systems… drop out of high school, and become teen parents themselves."[1051]

More likely, Trump and the Republicans will be successful in defunding abortion providers. Unless this is accompanied by a reduction in teen pregnancies and rapes, and there is not a rise in deaths from illegal abortions, such a policy could not be deemed a success. It may well end up costing the taxpayer more in social programs.

Just as there is white privilege for retention of superiority of whites, there is male privilege. The fact that there were thirteen men and no women on the committee to write the new healthcare bill while women's issues were on the agenda for elimination attests to this. Some of the basic services at risk include maternity coverage, childbirth for those on Medicaid, mammograms, contraception, and cervical cancer screening. If men were the ones affected, would there be such strong objection to pro-choice?

Legislative Measures

Trump pledged to work with Congress to introduce the following broader legislative measures and to fight for their passage or in some cases, elimination of the act, within the first hundred days of his administration.[1052] To date, none of these have been completed. These include the Middle Class Tax Relief and Simplification Act, Offshoring Act, American Energy and Infrastructure Act, School Choice and Education Opportunity Act, American Energy and Infrastructure Act, Affordable Childcare and Eldercare Act, End Illegal Immigration Act, Restoring Community Safety Act, Restoring National Security Act, and Clean up Corruption in Washington Act, as well as Repeal and Replace Obamacare.[1053]

The following are observations regarding a couple of the identified goals for some of the legislative objectives.

Grow the economy 4% per year:[1054] During the campaign, Trump claimed, "our country is stagnant,"[1055] which was a false portrayal of the US economy. During the Obama administration, the economic growth rose each year after 2009 and was on a steady upswing when he left office with a 2.6% increase in 2015, *FactCheck* reported.[1056] Economists are doubtful that Trump can reach his target of 4%, according to *Business Economy*. If he did, then one might well make a rationale that his policies were responsible for this remarkable achievement.

Trump inherited a healthier economy than his predecessor. If the economic gains are only marginal during the Trump administration, this would constitute a gain that might have occurred under any administration. How could that be considered a Trump victory measured against the loss of revenue from the proposed reductions in corporate taxes and the consequences to deregulation? Undoubtedly, the market has benefitted, and corporations will benefit, but unless there is a significant increase in higher-paid full-time jobs and a substantial increase in wages, this will not be a success for those 'left behind.'

Create at least 25 million new jobs through massive tax reduction and simplification:[1057] In March of 2017, *NBC* did a fact-check on Trump's job claims. The details clearly verified that Trump takes credit for creation of jobs that are not related to his policies or intervention and exaggerates those that are. In mid-March 2017, Trump announced, "Just today, breaking news, General Motors announced that they're adding or keeping 900 jobs right here in Michigan and that's going to be over the next 12 months," but nine days before, the company had announced a layoff of 1,100 employees, for a net loss of two hundred, *NBC News* disclosed.[1058]

NPR reported that Trump took credit for Exxon's announcement of 47,000 new jobs, but this investment started in 2013 and is expected to continue until 2022.[1059]

Trump claimed to have saved a Ford plant from being moved to Mexico. The company did abandon plans to build a new plant there, but it made no difference in jobs because they are continuing production at the existing Mexican plant. To be fair, the company announced an investment in the US, creating seven hundred new jobs. While they denied that it was a result of a deal with Trump, his pro-business policies were an influencing factor.[1060] In fact, five Ford plants were temporarily closed, including one in Flat Rock, Michigan, due to stagnant sales.[1061] This may well be a foreboding of what is yet to come. There are numerous other examples, which involved GM,[1062] Sprint/OneWeb/SoftBank,[1063] Intel, and Alibaba.[1064]

If Trump is such an effective negotiator and so confident he will succeed, why does he have to lie?

Executive Orders

While Trump decried the number of executive orders signed by Obama, he signed more executive orders in his first hundred days than Obama did. This is even though the Republicans have the White House, the Congress, the Senate, and a newly appointed conservative judge on the Supreme Court. In fact, Trump has signed more executive orders in the first hundred days than any president since WWII. According to *Wikipedia*, Trump signed thirty-three executive orders (many of them repealing some of President Obama's signature executive orders), twenty-five presidential memoranda, and thirty-five presidential proclamations.[1065]

Given the volume of Trump's executive orders as retrieved from *Wikipedia*, only those for which there is additional information or comments on the issues have been included.

1. April 29, Trade Agreement Violations and Abuses[1066]

   Trump backed off his intention to sign an executive order to withdraw from NAFTA and has agreed to renegotiate but will pursue withdrawal if the negotiations are not satisfactory. With all the trade deficits experienced by the US, there is a trade surplus with Canada. Yet Trump has chosen to attack Canada first, particularly regarding dairy and soft lumber.

   CBC reported the conclusion of Sarah Lloyd, a Wisconsin dairy farmer, who stated, "Blaming Canada for restricting market access to ultra-filtered milk is missing the real issue facing Wisconsin farmers... Small farms are getting squeezed out, and no one's doing anything about it... We have overproduction here in Wisconsin, and we really need to address that here at home."[1067]

   According to the *Globe and Mail*, Trudeau countered, "The U.S. has a $400-million dairy surplus with Canada so it's not Canada that's the challenge here. Let's not pretend we're in a global free market when it comes to agriculture."[1068]

   Perhaps Americans should examine the "$77 billion in subsidies" received by the corn industry over the past fifteen years, as reported by the website *Mercola, Take Control of Your Health*.[1069] The website points out that most corn is genetically modified with a pesticide that "kills bugs by making their stomachs explode... which is then consumed by you... Studies now show that, contrary to industry assurances, this built-in Bt toxin survives the journey through your digestive system, and can make you allergic to a wide range of substances."[1070] They cite research that high-fructose corn syrup is hidden in food and consumed daily, contributing significantly to obesity in the US, "so the US government is, in essence, subsidizing obesity and chronic disease."[1071] The *Star* ran an article written by Caitlin Dewey, a reporter from the *Washington Post*, which stated,

   > The peer-reviewed study, published in the Canadian Medical Association Journal, found that as tariffs on high-fructose corn syrup dropped over a four-year period, consumption grew: from 21.2 calories of corn syrup per day in 1994, to 62.9 calories per day by 1998. NAFTA may thus have contributed to growing obesity and diabetes rates over that time, its authors say.[1072]

While Statistics Canada reported an increase in obesity for both countries, the *Star* provided the following comparison, "In 2007 to 2009, the prevalence of obesity in Canada was 24.1%, over 10 percentage points lower than in the United States (34.4%)."[1073]

The US lumber industry accused Canada of having an unfair advantage, claiming the Canadian industry is subsidized because the companies are on government land, resulting in lower prices. These allegations are recurring, and decades old, in addition to being unfounded. In 2002, the US demanded that Canada use timber auctions, and Canada has been complying with this to set the prices of lumber, the *Globe and Mail* clarified.[1074] "It's led to a cycle of American punitive action, followed by trade cases mostly won by Canada, and then a compromise settlement."[1075]

According to *Forbes*, "The National Association of Homebuilders [in the US] estimated last year that a 15% tariff would cause a 4.2% rise in home prices and cost 4,666 workers their jobs. You have to wonder whether this is worth making an example of."[1076] Trump is proposing a tariff of up to 24%. This does not help American homebuyers.

Canadians are becoming angry over what appears to be trade harassment, especially on the timber issue. Except for a brief segment on an episode of Fareed Zakaria's programme, I have seen very little in the American media acknowledging the Canadian perspective on this issue. Blaming Canada for the dairy and lumber issues will not result in a satisfactory solution for the US because it addresses the wrong issues. Until the US examines how they are contributing to their problems, a solution will be elusive.

2. April 28, America-First Offshore Energy Strategy[1077]

Again, Trump is blaming environmental rules for the downturn in oil when it was really caused by a "an epic glut of crude, causing prices to crash so low that dozens of companies filed for bankruptcy and some 200,000 workers were laid off," according to *CNN*.[1078] A solution addressing the wrong problem cannot be successful.

Matt Egan from *CNN* explained, "Coal's biggest problem is the abundance of cheap natural gas, thanks to the shale revolution. That market force is responsible for 49% of the decline in domestic US coal consumption since 2011."[1079] Therefore, Trump's deregulation is unlikely to rejuvenate significant jobs in the coal industry but will probably increase corporate profits in that industry.

3. April 25, Agriculture and Rural Prosperity in America[1080]

According to Dan Merica of *CNN*, this executive order establishes a task force "to produce a report for the president in 180 days on the impediments to farming in the United States."[1081] The order "also sunsets the White House Rural Council, an Obama-era project that was meant to focus federal programs serving rural areas."[1082] The farming community is particularly concerned about access to a reliable workforce, especially as Trump increases his efforts to deport undocumented immigrants.

4. April 18, Buy American and Hire American[1083]

While Trump bullies and threatens corporations in an effort to bring manufacturing back to the US, and to buy and hire American, the Trump Organization is not subject to the same expectations. There has been no announcement that the Trump family has or will bring the manufacturing of their goods back to America. They hire foreign workers for seasonal help at Mar-a-Lago and on construction sites.

While buying American and hiring American sound appealing, there may be negative consequences to Americans. If, for example, a country is importing a significant number of cars from the US, will they not want some of the manufacturing done in that country? If the manufacturing is returned to the US, will that country buy elsewhere or impose tariffs and cause a trade war?

This executive order is directly related to Trump's campaign promise to bring jobs back to America.

Even a 20% reduction in the corporate tax rate does not make up for the cheaper labour in other countries. A policy is required. The issue has been corporate greed, not corporate taxes. Free-trade agreements need to require minimum wages, occupational health and safety requirements, and environmental protections to be fair and competitive. These issues were addressed to some degree in the TPP (Trans-Pacific Partnership).

Trump is removing disincentives to the coal industry. This means coal miners will have the right to work and contract black lung disease, perhaps with a diminished and more expensive healthcare plan, or no healthcare plan, instead of job retraining in the clean air energy industry (as proposed by Hillary). I will still have to stay indoors on humid summer days to avoid the air pollution from the Ohio Valley.

Some union members have become supportive of Trump because of deals like the one with Ford to build in Michigan instead of Mexico. Unions and the labour force need to be vigilant in monitoring the credibility of the information, the nature of the jobs, the sustainability, and the level of the wages. These jobs may dwindle in the next few years because of robotic technology.

Trump is not a friend of unions. Andrew Puzder, his new Secretary of Labor, is the former CEO of fast food chains. He is against having a minimum wage. He told *Business Insider* that he would prefer automation and robots in the food industry because they are "always polite, they always upsell, they never take a vacation, they never show up late, there's never a slip-and-fall or an age, sex, or race discrimination case."[1084]

5. March 29, President's Commission on Combating Drug Addiction, and the Opioid Crisis[1085]

An implementation plan would be far more beneficial than striking a commission. The crisis is now. There are already new painkillers being developed that do not result in "highs" and are therefore not addictive. Adequate resources must be made available for addiction treatment, and there must be strict penalties for doctors who over-prescribe.

The opioid crisis is directly related to bringing jobs back to America. While Trump and many Americans blame NAFTA and undocumented immigrants for the unemployment of Americans, drug tests are a significant contributor. According to Nelson Schwartz from the *New York Times*, employers are falling back on production because of difficulties in filling positions, largely because of failed drug tests which range from 25% to 50%.[1086]

When Obama left office, the unemployment rate was already at levels close to what is considered full employment. There is little point in bringing jobs back to America if employers do not have access to a workforce that is being compromised not only by the drug testing, but also by broken trade deals and the deportation millions of immigrants and 'dreamers' who contribute to the economy. Providing healthcare and treatment for the drug crisis would be a progressive first step in making some of those 'left behind' employable.

Drug treatment could be funded by reducing the prison rate. According to *FiveThirtyEight*, a polling and aggregation website and blog, "The US has roughly 5 percent of the world's population, but a quarter of its prison population."[1087] In the federal prisons, roughly half are incarcerated for drug offences, and in the state prisons this drops to about 16%.[1088] Surely the dollars spent on imprisonment would be better spent on drug rehabilitation for those who do not pose a threat to the community.

6. March 27, Revocation of Federal Contracting Executive Orders[1089]

Trump repealed President Obama's executive order that required federal contractors to follow labour laws. Employers guilty of violating wage and safety laws are now eligible to obtain federal contracts. Examine Trump's actions, not his words. This plan will increase corporate profits on the backs of the workers.

In January 2017, Trump signed an administrative order to halt Obama's order to lower monthly fees for those with a down payment of less than 20%. According to *Fox News*, "The order will make home loans more costly for a large group of buyers — about 40% of millennial buyers use the program targeted by the Trump order. That, in turn, can make life harder on older owners looking to sell their homes and trade up."[1090] This is from *Fox News*, Trump's media champion. I fail to understand how Trump voters perceive this as being a demonstration of Trump's commitment to be a champion for the workers.

7. February 28, Reviewing the 'Waters of the United States' Rule[1091]

Trump revoked the Waters of the United States Rule. I have a one-word response: Flint.

8. February 9, Protecting Law Enforcement[1092]

The killing of police is tragic and unacceptable and must be addressed. Equally unfortunate is the failure to address the connection between police killings of black people and endemic, systemic racism. In fact, neither has been acknowledged by Trump. Dealing with the protection of law enforcement in isolation of these other two issues is doomed to fail.

9. January 28, Drain the Swamp[1093]

This order bans people in the administration from lobbying for five years after they leave office. One of the challenges will be the legislation that requires disclosure and the legions that are able to avoid registering. Many in Trump's administration made herculean efforts to avoid reporting waivers in order to get around the rules, but the Office of Government Ethics persisted.[1094] More problematic is the swamp Trump has created with his unprecedented conflicts of interest; nepotism; lack of transparency, accountability, and credibility; and a Wall Street cabinet. These issues could significantly affect decision making, especially with foreign countries.

10. January 25, Cutting Funding for Sanctuary Cities[1095]

CNN advised that a US court halted this executive order on the basis that it could be unconstitutional, and the cities made the case that it would cause "immediate irreparable harm."[1096] Trump's administration has vowed to take it to the Supreme Court.

Presidential Memoranda

While there were twenty-five presidential memoranda, only two have been highlighted because of their significance.

1. January 23, Barring International Non-Governmental Organizations that Perform or Promote Abortions from Receiving US Government Funding[1097]

This policy was first enacted by Ronald Reagan and was supported by successive Republican, but not Democrat, governments.[1098] Not only do Republicans insist on imposing their views regarding abortion on American citizens, even when not supported by most Americans or the Constitution, but they also impose their views on other countries.

Amnesty International advised that "[t]he World Health Organization has found that laws that totally ban abortion do not, in fact, decrease abortion rates. Rather, they drive women and girls to seek unsafe, clandestine abortions."[1099] High rates of unwanted teen pregnancy are related to lack of education and contraception and "failure to protect women and girls from violence, including rape and other forms of coercion."[1100] The American funding to international organizations is presumably for charitable purposes to address social issues in underprivileged countries. It is an aberration to impose a condition that would exacerbate some of those social problems.

2. January 23, Withdrawal from the Trans-Pacific Partnership Negotiations and Agreement[1101]

Trump signed an executive order withdrawing from the TPP, upsetting the agreement's eleven remaining participants. There were trade opportunities for the US with Asia in this agreement. This may well give China a decided economic advantage in Asia. The eleven countries could consider the possibility of an agreement with China in lieu of the US. Trump is promising special consideration to countries like the United Kingdom because he supports Brexit, not the alliance of the European Union. He is playing divide and conquer with the allies and using trade as leverage. It is my fervent hope that the rest of the world does not accept Trump's bullying, or his strategy of dividing and conquering.

Victory Speech Pledge to the International Community

In addition to promises articulated in his contract to the American people for the first one hundred days, Trump made a pledge to the international community during his victory speech. "I want to tell the world community that while we will always put America's interests first, we will deal fairly with everyone, with everyone. All people and all other nations. We will seek common ground, not hostility; partnership, not conflict."[1102] Trump's behaviour in international relations during the first hundred days is diametrically opposed to this pledge.

ABC reported that, not even a hundred days into his presidency, Trump managed to insult several allies, including the president of Mexico, by insisting that Mexico pay for the wall and threatening to send US troops into Mexico to deal with the "bad hombres."[1103] He also offended the Prime Minister of Australia by bragging about his election victory, remonstrating about a deal made with the Obama administration for the US to accept a small number of refugees from Australia, and abruptly hanging up after telling the Australian leader that "this was the worst call by far" that he'd had with a foreign leader, *Vox* reported.[1104]

During the campaign, Trump continually criticized German Chancellor Angela Merkel for making what he considered a catastrophic mistake regarding her open-door policy to refugees. He compounded that criticism by ignoring her outstretched hand when she came to the White House and then making a joke that they had something in common: "As far as wiretapping, I guess, by this past administration, at least we have something in common perhaps," reported *CNN*.[1105] According to the *Los Angeles Times*, the Snowden leaks revealed wiretapping on Merkel by the Americans, and Trump recently accused Obama of wiretapping him. "How low has President Obama gone to tapp [*sic*] my phones during the very sacred election process. This is Nixon/Watergate. Bad (or sick) guy!"[1106]

CNN disclosed that Trump insulted the British by accusing the British GCHQ, an intelligence agency, of having assisted President Obama by spying on Trump when he was running for president. This made it awkward for British Prime Minister Theresa May, who had recently met with and supported Trump.[1107]

Throughout the campaign and after, Trump accused China of manipulating currency and product dumping. Then, immediately after the election, he defied the One China policy by accepting a call from Taiwan's president, Tsai Ing-wen. Trump provocatively proclaimed that he did not have to be bound by the One China policy. China has been clear that the policy is non-negotiable, and Trump has since told President Xi Jinping that he will respect it.

Below, Trump's rhetoric and behaviour toward several countries are examined, clearly demonstrating a failure to seek common ground and partnership and to avoid conflict and hostility.

North Korea: North Korea withdrew from the United Nations Nuclear Non-Proliferation Treaty and, in defiance, developed a nuclear and missile programme. Since 2006, sanctions have been imposed and extended by the UN, but China continues to be North Korea's major supplier. The UN last strengthened sanctions on November 30, 2016.[1108] According to Reuters, Trump indicated that if China did not help, the US was prepared to go it alone, and warned that he would not let everyone know ahead of time what his actions would be. US President Donald Trump and his Chinese counterpart Xi Jinping met on the weekend of April 7, 2017. While there were no confrontations, there were also no resolutions. Trump urged China to do more to help end North Korea's nuclear programme, "and the two agreed to a hundred-day plan for trade talks aimed at boosting US exports and reducing the gaping U.S. trade deficit with Beijing."[1109] There were no definitive results.

The Obama administration had set up mechanisms to deal with economic issues, which did not result in any substantive outcomes. Contrary to his promise to designate China a currency manipulator on his first day as president, Trump later declared the opposite.

In response to North Korea's missile testing, Trump announced that he was sending an "armada", including a battleship, to the Korean Peninsula as a show of force against North Korea's nuclear threat. It was later discovered that the "armada" was not headed north but rather south to meet with the Australian navy to conduct exercises, and only afterward would it head to the Korean Peninsula.[1110]

Reuters reported that Vice President Pence visited South Korea and provoked North Korea further by proclaiming, "Those who would challenge our resolve or readiness should know we will defeat any attack and meet any use of conventional or nuclear weapons with an overwhelming and effective American response."[1111] North Korea responded by threatening to sink a US aircraft carrier.[1112]

After Trump accused China of 'raping the US,'[1113] he sought support from China in dealing with North Korea. Upon meeting with President Xi Jinping, Trump acknowledged that while he originally thought China had much power over North Korea, he now realizes it is more complicated.[1114]

Israel: In response to Netanyahu's announcements for unprecedented proliferation of settlement housing, according to the Jerusalem Post, Spicer said, "The American desire for peace between the Israelis and the Palestinians has remained unchanged for fifty years. While we don't believe the existence of settlements is an impediment to peace, the construction of new settlements or the expansion of existing settlements beyond their current borders may not be helpful in achieving that goal."[1115] This statement by Spicer indicates a shift in Trump's original position. Common international wisdom is that the settlements are an impediment to peace. Trump and the Republicans threatened to reduce funding to the United Nations over the UN resolution condemning Israel's escalation of building settlements. If new settlements are a threat to peace, surely the existing settlements are an equal threat for the same reasons. Trump has said that he would like to mediate peace between Israel and Palestine, yet his policies indicate a demonstrated bias toward Israel, and positions such as this simply reinforce it.

Iran: While the State Department certified that Iran is living up to the nuclear agreement, in the same week, Trump said Iran was not living up to the spirit of the agreement, announcing that the National Security Council would evaluate whether Iran complies. While he railed about the Iran agreement during the campaign, threatening to shred it and stating that it was "the worst deal ever negotiated," he has not revoked it. Perhaps President Trump realized that it is the best option at the present time and that the situation is more complicated than he first thought.

Turkey: International observers to the election in Turkey noted, "Fundamental freedoms essential to a genuinely democratic process were curtailed," the Guardian reported.[1116] Despite that, Trump called Recep Tayyip Erdoğan to congratulate him on his narrow win and was the only leader of a democratic country to do so.[1117] *Mother Jones* advised that "[o]n Bannon's radio show, Breitbart News Daily, Trump said on December 1, 2015, 'I have a little conflict of interest 'cause I have a major, major building in Istanbul. It's a tremendously successful job. It's called Trump Towers—two towers, instead of one, not the usual one, it's two.'"[1118] Trump acknowledged that his business interests influence his international relations.

Syria: Defeating ISIS is a priority of the Trump administration. Trump declared that he is the president of the US, not the world. According to the Washington Post, Haley said, "We don't see a peaceful Syria with Assad in there."[1119] Tillerson asserted that it is up to the people of Syria to decide Assad's fate and that regime change was not the objective.[1120] It's difficult to be clear regarding the policy of this administration. The war on ISIS was making progress during Obama's administration. The result of Trump's change in strategy is not discernible.

The *Guardian* provided the following details. Russia, Iran, and Hezbollah have been supporting and propping up Assad in Syria. Under the guise of fighting ISIS, they have, on a few occasions, actually been fighting the Syrian rebels and have slaughtered thousands more citizens than terrorists. On April 4, 2017, Assad attacked northern Syria with the chemical weapon sarin. At least seventy-two died, many of them children.[1121] "Donald Trump denounced the carnage as a 'heinous' act that 'cannot be ignored by the civilized world.' But he also laid some of the responsibility on Barack Obama, saying in a statement that the attack was 'a consequence of the past administration's weakness and irresolution.'"[1122]

New York Magazine reported an incident Trump described, in which, while eating the "most beautiful piece of chocolate cake," he advised Chinese President Xi Jinping of an attack he ordered of fifty-nine missiles on Iraq. Xi Jinping corrected him, saying that he meant Syria.[1123] It is difficult to accept that Trump understood the ramifications of his order when he casually referenced eating chocolate cake while conveying it to another leader, named the wrong country, and had to be corrected.

Trump's errors in referring to Iraq instead of Syria and making misleading statements regarding the location of the super carrier as a show of force to North Korea were not necessarily critical, but this lack of precision could be deadly in different circumstances.

Brooke Baldwin, CNN host, asked Democratic Congresswoman Barbara Lee, California representative, "do you… give President Trump any credit for having the guts to do something that President Obama couldn't quite bring himself to do?"[1124] The veiled implications of this comment were layered and profoundly misleading. I daresay Obama made plenty of mistakes, and I am not sure that his response to the use of chemical weapons by Assad had the best outcome, but to imply that he did not have the "guts" and "couldn't quite bring himself to do" something after establishing the red line is simply obfuscation. Obama garnered international support and requested support for a military strike, which was denied by the Republican-controlled Congress.

According to the *Atlantic*, on August 13, 2013, 1,400 Syrians were killed with sarin gas on the outskirts of Damascus. Soon after, there was a surprise deal between Putin and Obama. Assad was forced to admit to having chemical weapons, which he had denied in the past. Inspectors were allowed to inventory and remove all the chemical weapons that Assad declared and that the inspectors could find. The Chemical Weapons Agreement of 2013 put the responsibility on Russia to secure and destroy chemical weapons and to monitor that situation.[1125]

The following is just one of eight tweets Trump posted in 2013 regarding Syria's use of chemical weapons: "What will we get for bombing Syria besides more debt and a possible long-term conflict? Obama needs Congressional approval."[1126] Trump was typical Trump. During his own presidency, he went ahead autocratically without seeking Congressional approval.

While Trump blamed Obama for Assad's chemical weapon attack on April 4, 2017, wasn't Putin really to blame? Either Russia was incompetent, or they were complicit in Assad's activities. Because Trump saw pictures of children dying from the sarin gas, he bombed the airfield in Syria to send a warning that chemical weapons were unacceptable and would not go without a challenge from the US. Trump's administration called Russia one hour before the attack so that Russians would not be caught in the fallout.

Only history will reveal whether Obama's strategy or Trump's actions were most effective in dealing with Assad. The motivation for Trump's actions, whether successful or not, is questionable in the absence of a clear strategy. The 2013 attack with chemical weapons by Assad was much worse, and there are hundreds of pictures and videos on the internet of this atrocity. Why didn't Trump feel this same outrage about that attack and those pictures when he was posting all those tweets to Obama? *Politico* reported that Trump stated, "No child of God should ever suffer such horror."[1127] They are Muslim. Does he realize that he is banning these same children whose parents are trying to escape the oppression and terrorism in Syria? I did not hear that he had cooperated or worked with NATO on this mission. It was an action based on Trump's feelings. It was reactionary. While this is of grave concern, I comforted myself with the notion that the preferred options were vetted by US Secretary of Defense James Mattis and National Security Adviser HR McMaster.

I was 12 years old and in grade six during the Cuban Missile Crisis and I recall the fear every time a plane flew overhead or we held exercises going into the hallway with our arms over our heads. On reflection, we laud President Kennedy for averting a nuclear incident and he did so having the trust of the allies, consulting widely and allowing Khrushchev to save face. None of these are attributes of President Trump. Yet today Obama is being condemned because he did not have the "guts" to bomb Syria. We will never know the ramifications had he done so.

Russia: Only significant updates since the campaign are included in this section. CNN reported that Nikki Haley, US Ambassador to the United Nations, declared, "The United States continues to condemn and call for an immediate end to the Russian occupation of Crimea... Crimea is a part of Ukraine. Our Crimea-related sanctions will remain in place until Russia returns control over the peninsula to Ukraine."[1128]

Haley also said that there is no question Russia was involved in the US presidential election and insisted that President Donald Trump would fully support strong action against the Kremlin once investigations were complete. She contended that there was no contradiction between her tough stance and Trump's repeated public statements seeking to minimize Russia's role. She said Trump "has not once" told her to stop "beating up on Russia," according to the *National Post*.[1129] The *Hill* reported that Haley "tore into Russia... over Syrian President Bashar Assad's suspected use of chemical weapons against the Syrian people the day before, as the U.N. Security Council took up a resolution condemning the attack."[1130]

During an emergency of the U.N. Security Council, Haley declared, "Russia has shielded Assad from U.N. sanctions. If Russia has the influence in Syria that it claims it has, we need to see them use it... We need to see them put an end to these horrific acts. How many more children have to die before Russia cares?"[1131]

Russia and Iran threatened to respond with force if there were any more attacks on Syria. Putin said relations with Russia were worse since Trump took office, and according to the *Guardian*, Trump admitted that relations with Russia "may be at an all-time low."[1132]

BBC provided background on Marine Le Pen. Like other populist candidates (including Donald Trump), France's Marine Le Pen admires Putin. There are allegations that Putin was interfering in the French election as he did in the US election, making nasty allegations against Le Pen's main opponent, Emmanuel Macron. Le Pen accepted money from a Russian bank to fund her campaign. Similar to many of Trump's positions during the campaign, she was critical of NATO and recommended that France pull out. She considered globalization, migration, and the economic ties to the EU to be threats. She was highly critical of the EU's immigration policy, especially in regard to Syrian refugees.

An anti-racism group filed a complaint, which led to a judicial inquiry being launched in 2012. Ms. Le Pen was eventually stripped of her immunity from prosecution by the European Parliament in 2013.

Le Pen was accused of incitement to discrimination, violence, or hatred towards a group of people because of their religious affiliation and if found guilty could face up to a year in jail and a fine of €45,000 (£33,000; $51,000). The French Council of the Muslim Faith said her remarks had fed a climate of Islamophobia.[1133]

Is it despite all of the above or because of it that Trump made the following prediction about Marine Le Pen? The *Telegraph* reported that Trump stated, "She's the strongest on borders and she's the strongest on what's been going on in France… Whoever is the toughest on radical Islamic terrorism, and whoever is the toughest at the borders, will do well in the election."[1134] It is significant that there are striking similarities between the leaders of this populist movement around the globe. Why is it that Trump is not held accountable for inciting Islamophobia in the US as Le Pen was in France?

CNN provided an interesting posting of the timeline of events during the Trump campaign and his administration team's contact with Russia.[1135] Trump's associates have not been transparent about their involvement with Russia. In addition to those already detailed elsewhere, Jarred Kushner met with a Russian banker who has ties to Putin. There are many more. The lack of transparency and failure to tell the truth about meetings and what transpired only adds to the skepticism regarding their involvement and possible collusion with Russia.

Devin Nunes was the chair of the congressional committee investigating the president's connections to Russia. According to the *Guardian*, Nunes conveyed information to Trump which he claimed reaffirmed Trump's assertions that he has been the victim of improper leaks. Nunes was untruthful when he denied that the White House had been responsible for giving him the information for these allegations.[1136]

If 'there is no there, there,' as Spicer asserted, why the lack of transparency?[1137]

Make America Great Again

Trump made another promise to Americans: to make America great again. It is not clear what this really means, but according to an article in *ThinkProgress*, "Let's make America great again" was Reagan's campaign slogan.[1138] One of the major differences is that Reagan's slogan invited all Americans to participate. Trump's did not, and thus far he has shown no interest in doing so. Part of Reagan's platform was a war on the poor, not poverty. While Reagan lowered taxes in the beginning, in response to a huge growing government debt, he raised taxes eleven times. Even so, he nearly tripled the federal debt. Unemployment and income inequality increased.[1139] Fred Kaplan from *Slate* explained the Reagan connection with Osama Bin Laden. The Reagan administration illegally sold arms to Iran, and Reagan "also played a major role in bringing on the terrorist war that followed—specifically, in abetting the rise of Osama Bin Laden."[1140] Republicans hold him in such high esteem because the rich got richer and the corporations thrived.

Will we never learn from history? As Gore Vidal eloquently said, "We live here in the United States of Amnesia. No one remembers anything before Monday morning. Everything is a blank. They have no history."[1141] The evolving dynamics of the Trump presidency, and the resultant public sentiment, bring to mind three significant historical events: the French Revolution, the Treaty of Versailles after WWI, and the race riots in the US in the 1960s.

Even though the expression "Let them eat cake" floated around for years before it was attributed to Marie Antoinette, the point remains valid. In the late 1780s, France was experiencing a serious national debt from overspending. Taxes grew, and the burden was placed mostly on the poor. Crops were failing and there was massive unemployment.[1142] *Wikipedia* cites Antonia Fraser's biography of Marie Antoinette and clarifies that, contrary to being insensitive to the plight of the peasants, Marie Antoinette "was a generous patroness of charity and moved by the plight of the poor when it was brought to her attention."[1143] While many of the charges for which she was found guilty of treason were fabricated, there was no doubt that she continued to spend extravagantly and lived a lavish life while the rest of France was starving, sparking outrage, anger, and the bloody revolution.[1144]

If we persist in living lavishly while disregarding the unfortunate circumstances of others living under conditions for which we are sometimes responsible, we invite civil retaliation, not only in our own countries, but abroad. The security of the castle did not protect the French monarchy, nor will gated communities protect us from this kind of revolution. Groups such as ISIS revile Western civilization and what it represents. Nuclear weapons will not protect us from acts of violence within our own communities.

We could learn a lesson from the oppressive conditions imposed on Germany following WWI and the devastating consequences later experienced by the winning allies.

After World War I, Germany was in a state of economic crisis. The Treaty of Versailles required the country pay exceptionally high reparations to France and Britain, while also forcing Germany to give up at least 13% of its land. Most agree that the treaty was too harsh, and this crippled Germany's already devastated economy, leaving the people in despair.[1145]

The allies compounded these problems when they placed protective tariffs on German goods. Germany could not sell their goods in foreign countries. The United States made loans to Germany, but when the Great Depression hit in 1929, the US demanded payment on the loans. According to Daniel Castillo on the University of California, Santa Barbara website, "This, in addition to all of Germany's other problems, practically caused the German economy to collapse."[1146] Hitler was a charismatic orator and persuaded the people that there were "easy solutions to the complex problems the German people faced." He "blamed Germany's problems on its weak government… blamed outsiders for causing problems in the nation," and promised to return Germany to greatness.[1147]

Erik Moshe on the *History News Network* website concluded that without the promise of ending unemployment and reviving the economy, Hitler would have encountered difficulty in his rise to power. "The working class remained the social grouping least impressed by the 'economic miracle' and relatively immune to the image of Hitler as the creator of Germany's striking new prosperity… Through repression and intimidation, low wages, and longer hours, the 'economic miracle,' as most realized, was being carried out on their own backs."[1148] Hitler used the prosperity to fund his army. The allies from WWI created the impetus for the angst that led to the rise of Hitler and WWII. The allies wanted to bring Germany to its knees, but the allies ultimately paid a high price for this in WWII.

A wave of race riots swept the United States in the 1960s. "From 1964 to 1971, there were more than 750 riots, killing 228 people and injuring 12,741 others," according to the *New York Times*.[1149] In July 1967 during the riots in Detroit, Lyndon B. Johnson set up a commission to examine why the riots were happening and what could be done to prevent them. This became known as the Kerner Commission, and the report was released in 1968. "Its finding was that the riots resulted from black frustration at lack of economic opportunity. Martin Luther King Jr. pronounced the report a 'physician's warning of approaching death, with a prescription for life.'"[1150]

The report berated federal and state governments for failed housing, education, and social-service policies. The report also aimed some of its sharpest criticism at the mainstream media. "The press has too long basked in a white world looking out of it, if at all, with white men's eyes and white perspective."[1151] The report's most famous passage warned, "Our nation is moving toward two societies, one black, one white—separate and unequal."[1152] *Wikipedia* summarized the report as follows:

> Its results indicated that one main cause of urban violence was white racism and suggested that white America bore much of the responsibility for black rioting and rebellion. It called to create new jobs, construct new housing, and put a stop to de facto segregation in order to wipe out the destructive ghetto environment. In order to do so, the report recommended for government programs to provide needed services, to hire more diverse and sensitive police forces, and most notably, to invest billions in housing programs aimed at breaking up residential segregation.[1153]

Meanwhile, the pundits on the right assigned the blame to the black community.

Following the death of Freddie Gray in April 2015, there were protests and riots. Referring to the rioters in Baltimore as "thugs and thieves," Rand Paul went on to say that the root cause was "the breakdown of the family structure, the lack of fathers, the lack of a moral code in our society… The police have to do what they have to do, and I am very sympathetic to the plight of the police in this."[1154]

Republicans want to shift from a social paradigm to an opportunity paradigm. The system is rigged. We cannot claim self-righteously that there is equal opportunity when the conditions for most prevent that opportunity. As so aptly stated by Anatole France, "The law, in its majestic equality, forbids the rich, as well as the poor, to sleep under the bridges, to beg in the streets, and to steal bread."[1155] Does everyone in America have an equal opportunity to achieve the American Dream? Consider the following examples:

- The contractors who worked hard building Trump's casinos: While Trump made money despite having declared bankruptcy, "[h]e put a number of contractors and suppliers out of business when he did not pay them," said Stephen P. Perskie, who was New Jersey's top casino regulator in the early 1990s.[1156]

- The disabled whose conditions render them unable to work, limit their work options, or cause them to be discriminated against by employers not willing to accommodate their disability

- The individuals at Walmart, and those in similar circumstances, who work hard, making minimum wage, while the corporation prospers

- The middle-class family who goes bankrupt because of medical bills

- The innocent and their families who have been wrongfully incarcerated

- The families whose homes have been severely damaged by earthquakes caused by wastewater disposal wells in the oil industry in Oklahoma,[1157] and cannot afford to repair them[1158]

- The families displaced by hurricanes and other natural disasters

- The unemployed and uneducated that are unable to find work

- The families in Flint, Michigan who, through no fault of their own, are suffering long-term health problems as a result of heavy metal poisoning from the Flint River after the state stopped sourcing their water from the Detroit River for economic reasons: children are experiencing hair loss, aching muscles, seizures, anemia, memory loss, and fatigue, and more symptoms could develop.[1159]

America is great and provides opportunities for some people to become successful with hard work. For others, not so much. Surely it is possible to continue to provide those opportunities while acknowledging a responsibility to correct inequities.

It will be a monumental challenge to evaluate the Trump administration over the next four years. Many say that he is 'result-oriented' rather than concerned with ideology. The evidence demonstrates that he is more successful at the creation of an image of success rather than results. He takes credit for the success of others, exaggerates accomplishments, and creates chaos and unproductive busywork to divert attention from his lack of accomplishments. Trump presented an overstated, negative portrayal of the economy and jobs during the Obama administration to exaggerate any improvements or gains during his administration, whether or not they are related to his policies and decisions.

While many Americans would wish for a successful presidency, most do not agree with many of Trump's policies and therefore do not hope for success in implementation. For those who did vote for Trump, there is no consensus of support for his policies. For example, not everyone who voted for him based on his economic and employment platforms agreed with his pro-life stance. Many voters took him 'seriously' and not 'literally.'

At the end of the first one hundred days, while there was the appearance of action, no legislation had been passed, some executive orders were held up by the courts, and there was no consensus in the Republican Congress and Senate. Trump is governing by executive order.

CHAPTER THIRTEEN

Choosing The Leader Of The Free World

We live in a globalising world. That means that all of us, consciously or not, depend on each other. Whatever we do or refrain from doing affects the lives of people who live in places we'll never visit.[1160]
—*Zygmunt Bauman*

The primary concern in choosing a president is what is best for America. At the same time, the international reaction to the decision will impact Americans. It is not just that our decisions affect others. It is the negative consequences of those decisions that merit consideration. Are the potential global consequences of America's choice going to benefit Americans?

Americans take pride in the assertion that their president is the 'leader of the free world.' The outcome of this election had serious implications across the globe. The moniker 'leader of the free world' was assigned to the president of the United States following World War II as the US established itself as the most powerful nation in the world, both militarily and economically. Harry S. Truman described America as "the greatest nation that the sun ever shone upon."[1161] For him, American exceptionalism placed a responsibility on the United States to ensure "peace and freedom in the post-war world."[1162] In providing leadership to the free world, Truman did not seek dominion but assured Congress, "I believe that we must assist free peoples to work out their own destinies in their own way… The free peoples of the world look to us for support in maintaining their freedoms. If we falter in our leadership, we may endanger the peace of the world—and we shall surely endanger the welfare of our own nation."[1163]

I focused on America in this book because Canada was not electing the leader of the free world. How much do Americans know about their Canadian neighbours, who are greatly affected by their choices? Not much, nor do they care to according to Bill Mann, a humour columnist for *USA Today*. As a new American immigrant to Canada, Mann wrote a satirical book entitled *The Retarded Giant: Introducing the Canadian Definitive Joke*. It was intended to be humorous but was described by Andy Nullman, President of *Just for Laughs*, as "one of the most dangerous books ever released about my beloved homeland of Canada."[1164]

Mann makes snarky jokes such as, "Why does a haircut cost $4 in Toronto? Answer: A buck for each corner." Another reads, "Q. How do you spot a Canadian? A. When he walks in a room, it's like someone just left."[1165] Mann goes on to say that he knows better now and that he has "developed a deep and continuing respect for Canada's decent society and evolved political system and laws."[1166] He shared an experience visiting a Rotary Club in Washington, right near the Canadian border. He asked them what the capital of Canada is, and about half knew the answer. Fewer than half knew the prime minister, and only a handful knew the provinces. We only have ten provinces and three territories! Mann said Americans just are not interested. "Sadly, many—most—Americans don't just have their heads up their butts. They also seem to enjoy the view."[1167]

While I have met Americans who were knowledgeable about Canada, I must confess that I have also met many who were not. I have given up telling Americans where I live. When asked, I just say Canada. That is enough for most Americans. People from Wisconsin or Minnesota often comment that it must be cold up there. We are south of both of those states and on the same latitude as Northern California. If they ask what city, I have to provide an American reference and advise them we are across the river from Detroit, Michigan.

In an interview with CBS after being elected prime minister, Justin Trudeau said, "I think we sometimes like to think that, you know, Americans will pay attention to us from time to time too." In a *60 Minutes* interview, he was asked what Canadians do not like about Americans. He did not answer that question but rather said his country "wishes Americans paid more attention to what's happening around the world, including with their neighbors to the north."[1168]

Only then will Americans begin to appreciate the import of their choices and the possible consequences, not only for other countries, but for America.

There are many similarities and differences between Canada and the United States. As a country, Canada's land mass is second only to Russia, but our population is only 10% of the United States'—Canada with about 35 million and the United States with about 324 million. The United States ranks fourth in world populations, while Canada ranks thirty-ninth.[1169] To put that in perspective, the number of Americans who voted for Trump is almost double Canada's whole population!

This poses a challenge to Canadians, as expressed most aptly by former Prime Minister Pierre Trudeau in 1969, while addressing the National Press Club in Washington.

> Americans should never underestimate the constant pressure on Canada which the mere presence of the United States has produced. We're different people from you and we're different people because of you. Living next to you is in some ways like sleeping with an elephant. No matter how friendly and even-tempered is the beast, if I can call it that, one is effected [sic] by every twitch and grunt. It should not therefore be expected that this kind of nation, this Canada, should project itself as a mirror image of the United States.[1170]

Canada and the United States share the longest international border in the world.[1171] The border has no military defense, and while it has been peaceful in recent decades, this has not always been the case. According to *Mental Floss*, there have been a few attempts by Americans to invade Canada. While several were skirmishes, the most notable conflicts are the attempts to annex Canada during the American Revolution in 1775 and then again during the War of 1812.[1172]

The War of 1812 lasted until 1814 and was between Great Britain and the United States, sparking when *Chesapeake*, an American frigate carrying British deserters, refused to be boarded by the British *HMS Leopard*, which fired on them and boarded. Canada only became involved by default when President Madison, interested in General Dearborn's assertion that

Canada would be easy to overtake, declared war on June 1, 1812. The battles raged until a peace treaty was negotiated by the Russian Czar on Christmas Eve, 1814.[1173] Isn't that ironic considering the current international relations?

Both Canada and the United States started out as British colonies. The United States gained its independence after the American Revolution in 1776. Canada did not gain independence until 1867, when the Dominion of Canada was officially established as a self-governing entity within the British Empire. Canada remains a member of the Commonwealth, and the Queen of England is Canada's monarch. While the monarch is head of Canada's parliament and the commander-in-chief of the Canadian armed forces, this authority is delegated to politicians on behalf of the monarchy.

The Canadian system of government is a parliamentary democracy: Canadians vote for a representative in their electoral district, and the party that wins the most districts is the party in power. Their leader becomes the prime minister. A simple majority vote is required to pass a law. If the party in power has fewer than half of the seats, it is a minority government, and they are forced to negotiate with another party to get legislation passed. Gridlock is not an option in the Canadian government. If the government loses confidence or loses a vote regarding the Speech to the Throne and budget-related bills, the prime minister either resigns or calls a new election.

There are pros and cons to each system of government. Unlike Canadians, Americans vote for their president separately from their state representatives. While the United States regularly votes on proposed state and federal laws, Canada has had only three national referendums—on prohibition, conscription, and the Charlottetown Accord—regarding the Canadian Constitution. The referendum addressing the separation of Quebec was provincial.[1174]

In Canada, the 2016 election date was announced, and we had a new prime minister within three months! Workplaces are required to allow employees fifteen paid minutes off to vote. Most often, that is how long it takes. I know the election process in the US is more complex and this timeline may not be reasonable, but Sheryl Crow's petition to have a shorter election season may have considerable merit.

Canada had a peaceful process of independence from Britain, while the United States did not. Similarly, Canada ended African slavery, which existed in Canada for almost two hundred years, through a relatively peaceful process. "Canada was the first British colony to implement legislation to move towards abolition in 1793."[1175] It took a bloody Civil War to abolish slavery in the United States on December 18, 1865, almost a hundred years later.[1176] The conditions were different and far more complex, particularly in the latter, but the facts reveal the two countries' cultural differences, and cast light on how historical events shaped the distinct values of the American and Canadian societies.

American society is based on individualism, whereas in Canada it is more of a collectivist society. Individualism stresses individual freedom and rights in the United States, especially to achieve the American Dream. Collectivism is concerned about the welfare of the group.

Canada is more of a hybrid because individualism is valued, but not at the expense of what is best for the collective society. Former Prime Minister Pierre Elliott Trudeau expressed the value of individualism in the Canadian culture most aptly:

> Uniformity is neither desirable nor possible in a country the size of Canada. We should not even be able to agree upon the kind of Canadian to choose as a model, let alone persuade most people to emulate it. There are few policies potentially more disastrous for Canada than to tell all Canadians that they must be alike. There is no such thing as a model or ideal Canadian. What could be more absurd than the concept of an "all-Canadian" boy or girl? A society which emphasizes uniformity is one which creates intolerance and hate. A society which eulogizes the average citizen is one which breeds mediocrity. What the world should be seeking, and what in Canada we must continue to cherish, are not concepts of uniformity but human values: compassion, love, and understanding.[1177]

Canadians believe that by taking care of the collective society, we benefit as individuals. This is apparent in our priorities relative to the US, and the resultant outcomes. In 2012, the US ranked second for income per capita out of sixteen peer countries, while Canada ranked eighth.[1178] On the other hand, Canada ranked thirty-fifth on the global scale for comparing income equality, while the United States ranked ninety-fifth.[1179] For health outcomes, Canada ranked tenth out of seventeen peer countries, while the US ranked seventeenth.[1180] Canada's healthcare spending was only 10.9% of the GDP, while the United States' was 16.9%. Life expectancy in Canada was 81.5 years, while it was 78.7 years in the US.[1181] The Peter G. Peterson Foundation reported that the per capita healthcare cost in the US was $9,024 while it was only $4,506 in Canada.[1182] According to *Ranking America*, the United States ranks twenty-fourth in literacy; Canada ranks ninth.[1183] The United States ranks ninth in retirement security; Canada ranks sixth.[1184]

Some Canadians would have supported a Trump presidency, but a poll in August 2016 reflected that 79% of Canadians were very, or moderately, concerned about a Trump presidency. The Prime Minister of Canada, Justin Trudeau, wisely refused to directly criticize Trump, "saying he [Trudeau] has confidence Americans will make the right decision and that he rejects the politics of fear," the *Huffington Post* reported.[1185] Several conservative leaders, on the other hand, were highly critical of Trump, and 62% of conservative voters in Canada would not have supported Trump. The United States could be promoting unity among Canadians with the common interest of concern about Trump! 48% of Canadians watched this election more closely than past US elections, myself included.[1186]

I am not opposed to America wanting to revisit trade agreements or questioning the financial commitments of NATO members, including Canada. What troubles me is the delegation of blame based on misinformation: the perception that other countries, including Canada, benefit from the US while contributing little in return. Of greatest concern are the threats made when a country has not complied with the Trump administration's demands, supported by many Americans as a sign of strength, regardless of their validity. Some Americans have embraced Trump's allegations that the American taxpayer is being ripped off by those NATO partners not contributing the 2% GDP. The *National Interest* explained that the 2% is a guideline agreed upon in 2014 with an objective to implement over the next decade.[1187] It is not a requirement; the money is not due to the US or NATO. It is an expectation of what each country will spend on its own military. If all the partners in NATO paid the 2% GDP guideline, would that reduce the US spending on military? I seriously doubt it. Trump vowed, "I'm going to make our military so big, so powerful, so strong, that nobody — absolutely nobody — is gonna... mess with us."[1188] According to the *Guardian*, only five of the twenty-eight countries in NATO pay the full 2%, and this number has not changed since Trump's speech in March 2017, though he has claimed credit anyway.[1189]

Donald Trump threatened that, under his leadership, America would not necessarily come to the aid of a NATO ally under attack, saying he would first consider how much they have contributed to the alliance.[1190]

In Chapter 6, I explained some of the disadvantages for Canada in the free-trade agreement regarding foreign investors suing because Canada's environmental protection laws limit their profits and the proportionality rule. During the campaign, Trump promised to go forward with the Keystone XL Pipeline, but according to the *Globe and Mail*, he vowed, "I want it built, but I want a piece of the profits... That's how we're going to make our country rich again."[1191]

The lumber agreement between the two countries expired in 2015 and is a longstanding, contentious issue. The Republicans are challenging Canada's GST (Goods and Services tax) as an unfair practice. Canada simply does not benefit from economies of scale the way the United States does. Consider that we have a larger country with one-tenth the population to sustain our infrastructure. I do not have confidence that a Trump administration will consider those issues that are a disadvantage to Canada.

Trump thinks the NAFTA agreement favours Canada and Mexico. The *US Census Bureau* reported that Canada is the United States' top trade partner and the top importer of US goods. China is the top country for imports to the US.[1192] The Office of the United States Trade Representative advised that the US has a trade surplus with Canada. "Exports were $337.3 billion; imports were $325.4 billion. The US goods and services trade surplus with Canada was $11.9 billion in 2015."[1193] The AP reported that in 2015, Fiat Chrysler sold 1.898 million new vehicles in Canada, a new record for the third year in a row.[1194] I have bought only Chrysler vehicles for over thirty years. If Fiat Chrysler pulled out of Windsor, I would not buy another. I have no doubt that many other Canadians would have the same reaction.

If American protectionism cripples the Canadian economy, I am not sure what the implications will be, but I fear that Trump is not either. Most assuredly, many Americans are unaware. The impact could reach far beyond economic issues and have nasty, unanticipated consequences not just for Canadians, but Americans as well.

It is concerning that an American perception that they are being 'ripped off' and taken advantage of by Canada could result in punitive retaliation in trade and national security.

Canada has been a good neighbour to the US and has contributed, at least proportionately, given our much smaller population and economic base. The following are just a few of the numerous contributions made by Canada.

The *CBC* reported that in 1979, Iranian students, angry at the US for accepting deposed Shah Mohammed Reza Pahlavi into America for cancer treatment, stormed the US embassy.

They wanted Pahlavi returned to face justice. Six of the more than seventy embassy staff escaped and hid in the Canadian embassy for three months until they were smuggled aboard a plane disguised as a film crew and flown to Frankfurt, Germany.[1195]

On September 11, 2001, American airspace was closed, and thirty-eight planes were diverted to the little town of Gander, Newfoundland, which had a population of about 10,000. This little Canadian community opened their homes, sheltered, and fed almost 6,600 passengers for several days until American airspace was reopened, according to the *Telegram*.[1196]

Canadians were among the first to arrive and help in New Orleans after Katrina. Canadians donated over $1 million, and Canada sent supplies and volunteer teams to assist the community.[1197]

After the attack on Pearl Harbor, Canada declared war on Japan before the US did.[1198] While I could give innumerable examples, these are just a few that some Americans may not know.

Canada will not always do the bidding of the US, as in the case of the Iraq War. Americans should challenge Canadians and persuade them that a policy or action is also in their best interest. But threats and punitive action without an appreciation of Canada's contribution, in absence of the facts and the Canadian perspective, may put the 'good neighbour' relationship at risk.

These concerns of threats, blame based on misinformation, and insinuations of countries' lack of contributions extend to other countries as well. For example, while allies and partners had agreements with the US to place military bases in strategic world locations, this was mutually beneficial to both parties, as it was also in the interest of US national security. Contrary to what Trump conveyed, most of these countries (all but Israel) do make financial contributions. The following are further examples as to the danger of supporting a radical policy that threatens another country, without knowledge of the implications not only for the other country, but also for America.

China

Trump was baiting the Chinese throughout his campaign and as president-elect, and he even challenged their government. "Angry over what he views as US kowtowing to the Chinese, Donald Trump declared… that China 'is our enemy' and 'wouldn't exist' without America as the biggest market for its products," *Newsmax* reported.[1199]

According to *Vox*, the Communists assumed control of the mainland in 1949, during the Chinese Civil War, while the defeated Nationalists took refuge on the island of Taiwan. China considers Taiwan part of China, not a separate country. This is the One China Policy. Most countries, including the US, do not have diplomatic relations with Taiwan. After winning the election, Trump accepted a call expressing congratulations from President Tsai Ing-wen of Taiwan. This breached a policy of forty years. The transition team made a public announcement referring to Tsai Ing-wen as president, which contravened the One China Policy, and then Trump tweeted about the call.[1200]

At first, it was thought that Trump accepted the call spontaneously and that he might be unaware of the protocol. However, a spokesperson for Tsai Ing-wen advised that both sides agreed before making the call. Sources told the *Washington Post* that the call was planned months in advance.[1201]

Bloomberg disclosed that China issued a warning to Trump. Wang Tao, head of China economic research at UBS AG in Hong Kong, said, "Taiwan is considered the utmost core interest of China, not for bargaining."[1202]

Why the change in position? This is explained by Pedro Nicolaci da Costa, a correspondent for *Business Insider*, in the following statement: "It's worth noting that a few days after that phone call, something else happened: China granted Trump's business a valuable 10-year trademark. The trademark was considered a surprise win for Trump."[1203]

Bloomberg reported that on December 16, 2016, the Pentagon disclosed that the Chinese would return an American underwater drone that they removed from the China Sea. The Chinese have been building and arming reefs in the China Sea on the pretext of protecting their interests. Americans have been conducting navigation exercises to "underscore the right to free passage in international waters"[1204] because this waterway is a thriving fishing zone and a major trade passageway.

While Americans claimed that the drone "is an unclassified 'ocean glider' system used around [the] world to gather data on salinity,"[1205] water temperature, and sound speed, the Chinese claimed that they took it for security reasons, suspecting the drone's mission was to detect submarines.

Trump escalated the incident by tweeting, "China steals United States Navy research drone in international waters—rips it out of water and takes it to China in unprecedented act." In a follow-up tweet, he added, "We should tell China that we don't want the drone they stole back—let them keep it!"[1206]

America's desire to renegotiate some elements of their arrangements with China may have some merit. It is Trump's approach and its potential consequences that I am challenging. Trump is a demagogue provoking international demagogues who, like himself, do not appreciate being ridiculed in public and like having things their own way. They are used to operating on the international political stage, but Trump is not. They may not have the same domestic constraints for retaliation.

As the authors of an article in *Bloomberg* explained, "Options [for the Chinese] include recalling the ambassador, stopping international cooperation, fighting a trade war—even severing diplomatic ties."[1207] Additionally, China has trade relations with North Korea that could be instrumental in dealing with North Korea's nuclear advancement. If Trump antagonizes China beyond its tolerance, he may lose China's support regarding North Korea.

North Korea

Trump continued to provoke North Korea and China. On January 2, 2016, he tweeted, "North Korea just stated that it is in the final stages of developing a nuclear weapon capable of reaching parts of the U.S. It won't happen!"[1208] Another from the same day read, "China has been taking out massive amounts of money & wealth from the U.S. in totally one-sided trade, but won't help with North Korea. Nice!"[1209]

North Korea withdrew from the Non-Proliferation Treaty to develop nuclear weapons as a defense against a perceived threat from the US. While I abhor the idea that North Korea has nuclear weapons, there is some justification for Kim Jong-un's concern. He has only to think of the fate of Muammar Gaddafi, the deposed leader of Libya. *CNN* explained that after agreeing to give up pursuing nuclear weapons, Gaddafi was captured with the help of NATO, who bombed his entourage while he was trying to escape, and he suffered a gruesome death.[1210] Reinforcing Kim Jong-un's fear will only make him more resolute.

There have been many Americans who have expressed concern about Trump having access to the nuclear code, yet America would be outraged should the United Nations or another country demand that the US not be allowed to have nuclear weapons. Even though he has declared that he does not want to be the 'world leader,' Trump is trying to control other countries by bullying and threatening them.

Trans-Pacific Partnership (TPP)

During the campaign, Trump promised to withdraw from the Trans-Pacific Partnership negotiated by President Barack Obama. He accomplished this by signing his first executive order on January 23, 2017.

BBC explained that China and the United States are the two largest economies in the world. Many countries in Asia are growing in size and wealth, creating a demand for more high-quality products. They can obtain them from America or China. The TPP was a strategy to strengthen the US as the primary economic resource for Asia in lieu of China. The countries participating include the US, Japan, Malaysia, Vietnam, Singapore, Brunei, Australia, New Zealand, Canada, Mexico, Chile, and Peru. China was excluded. The deal eliminates tariffs on US products imported from other countries. In the wake of the United States' withdrawal, New Zealand suggested that the countries go forward without the US, while Japan considered an agreement without the US to be meaningless.[1211] According to the Peterson Institute for International Economics, the TPP includes some of the most ambitious labour provisions to protect jobs in America, and it includes working condition requirements for countries that have weaker labour laws than the US. There are provisions on workers' rights, minimum wage, working hours, and health and safety, according to the Peterson Institute for International Economics.[1212] There is concern that there is no room for negotiation with Trump. China is likely to be the winner in this event.

This could have significant consequences for Canada. According to Adrian Morrow, reporter with the *Globe and Mail*, "It is unlikely that, without the United States' massive economic weight, Canada could ever achieve a deal that eliminates as many trade barriers as the TPP with Japan, Australia and other Pacific Rim countries."[1213]

America may not care how it affects Canada, but these actions have potential implications to the US as well. In a *Forbes* article, journalist John Brinkley put forward the argument that Trump's withdrawal from the TPP is "a gift to China." Brinkley pointed out that the main reason that Asian countries were interested in a trade agreement with the US was to avoid complete economic dependency on China. China is America's primary economic competitor and has expressed willingness to "take over the leadership role in global trade," which the US no longer holds.[1214] Brinkley further elaborated that trade agreements with China cut tariffs, but without any rules or standards, "and [leave] every man to himself to ensure he doesn't get cheated."[1215]

Brinkley concluded that the TPP "had the highest standards ever included in a free trade agreement," which required an overhaul by governments in terms of employees' rights and environmental conservation, in turn reducing "the incentive for American companies to off-shore jobs to those countries."[1216] Brinkley also asserted that the standards were enforceable and the US would have had the ability to hold accountable those countries that did not live up to the agreement.[1217]

The time is long past when protectionism could have been a strategy to halt globalization. Western countries would be wise to embrace the agreement and find solutions to make it work. The TPP had standards that would have created a more even playing field.

Israel

On December 22, 2016, Donald Trump tweeted, "The resolution being considered at the United Nations Security Council regarding Israel should be vetoed."[1218]

While Trump has ranted about NATO, complaining that it provides military support for member countries not paying their fair share, and has even suggested other countries develop nuclear weapons, he has not criticized Israel in this regard. However, America's largest contribution to a foreign country's national security is given to Israel with no reimbursement. Why is that not problematic to Trump?

Trump reaffirmed America's choice to be the nuclear power of the world, tweeting, "The United States must greatly strengthen and expand its nuclear capability until such a time as the world comes to its senses regarding nukes."[1219]

Prime Minister of Israel, Benjamin Netanyahu, expressed a willingness to consider a two-state solution. Fifteen countries on the United Nations National Security Board, as well as many of the Jewish population in Israel and the United States, also support it. Trump is persistent in supporting Israel's settlement of occupied territory when it is clearly a barrier to a two-state solution.

It is untenable that the Palestinians will not accept Israel as an independent state and that they will inflict constant violence on Israel. It is equally untenable that Israel has ruled over the Palestinians for decades while denying them their rights and encroaching on occupied territory by building new settlements, which is against international law and destroys the hope for any two-state solution.

NPR provided background on Trump's nomination of David Friedman, his bankruptcy lawyer, as ambassador to Israel. Friedman, having no diplomatic experience, considers "the two-state solution an 'illusion,' and compared liberal American Jews to 'kapos,' Jews who aided Nazis during the Holocaust."[1220] While some Jewish-American groups welcomed the nomination, others did not. *NPR* reported that the New Israel Fund, which supports progressive social programmes in Israel, said, "[Friedman] represents extreme fringe views that are appalling to most American Jews" and that the Rabbi Rick Jacobs, president of the Union for Reform Judaism, the largest Jewish denomination in the US, also expressed concerns.[1221]

Trump pledged to move the US embassy to Jerusalem, a move that had been deferred by previous administrations since 1995. According to Aaron David Miller, a former Middle East negotiator and adviser in Republican and Democratic administrations, while it has claim to the west side of the city, "Israel has extended its law over the entire city—east and west—and since 1967 expanded the municipal boundaries of what it calls its 'eternal capital,'" as reported by the *New York Times*.[1222] Miller explained that the Arab world claims the east side of Jerusalem for a Palestinian capital. To move the US embassy to Jerusalem would signal tacit approval of Israel's encroachment. Miller asserted that to do so would also eliminate any possibility of the US being a mediator in the peace process, and this decision not only affects Palestinians, but the whole Arab world.[1223]

Trump's position is contrary to international wisdom, and I have to assume that the US embassy's relocation to Jerusalem, and support for Israeli settlements, will further destabilize the region. This may inflame the hatred toward Israel and the United States while also providing additional ammunition to terrorist groups.

Trump, abetted by the media, portrayed the American vote on the UN resolution during the previous administration as an attempt by Obama to spite Netanyahu. According to reporter Rebecca Kheel from the *Hill*, Netanyahu claimed that he had evidence of US involvement in the crafting and approval of the resolution put before the UN Security Council but would only give that evidence to the president-elect, stating that the US "not only failed to protect Israel against this gang-up at the U.N., it has colluded with it behind the scenes."[1224]

In March 2015, just weeks before the election in Israel, Netanyahu defiantly disregarded Obama and accepted an invitation from then Speaker of the House John Boehner to speak before Congress against the proposed Iran nuclear deal. President Obama refused to meet with Netanyahu, "citing a precedent that U.S. officials have a longstanding practice of not meeting with foreign leaders so close to their elections," reported Rebecca Kaplan from *CBS News*.[1225]

Tim Diaiss from *Forbes* explained that while Netanyahu described the deal as an "historic mistake," Shemuel Meir, a former Israeli Defense Forces (IDF) analyst and associate researcher at the Jaffee Center for Strategic Studies at Tel Aviv University, supported the Iran deal, stating that "it is beneficial to Israeli security, and thus must be safeguarded... [The deal] removed the existential threat hovering above Israel... blocked Iran's path to a nuclear weapon, and prevented the emergence of an arms race in the Middle East."[1226] He added, "The deal also closed off the chapter of pre-emption strikes scenarios on Iran's military targets and reduced the risks for a new and long regional war. A possibility that could become relevant should Iran deal be ripped up."[1227] After the election, the *Times of Israel* wrote an article expressing concerns that rolling back the deal could alienate international allies and isolate the US.[1228] As an example, Britain's prime minister publicly warned Trump that the Iran nuclear deal was "vital."[1229]

During the campaign, Trump regularly criticized the deal, promising to tear it up, and Republicans in Congress expressed similar opposition, according to the *Huffington Post*.[1230] *CNN* reported that while about 60% of American voters were pro-Israel, 80% of Republicans were pro-Israel. Sen. Lindsey Graham has vowed "to propose a measure to pull US funding for the United Nations unless the UN Security Council repeals the resolution it passed condemning Israeli settlements."[1231]

Reporter Tracy Wilkinson from the *Los Angeles Times* claimed that contrary to Trump's criticism of the deal, there is now widespread opinion, including in Israel, that the Iran deal negotiated by the Obama administration has been instrumental in eliminating an imminent nuclear threat. To rip up or renegotiate the treaty would erode any credibility of the US with Iran as well as other countries who were involved in the negotiations, including England, France, China, Russia, and Germany. It could also allow Iran to renege on their commitments and renew their nuclear programme.[1232]

Despite attempts by the Republicans, Trump, and Netanyahu to humiliate Obama about the Iran deal, the Obama administration approved the largest deal ever to provide Israel with $3.8 billion annually over the next ten years for its national security and defense, according to the *New York Times*.[1233] The United States did not make this contribution for humanitarian reasons

What then are the American interests in the Middle East, and how does the United States benefit by contributing billions of dollars to Israel? Emma Green from the *Atlantic* clarified that even though the imminent threat of nuclear proliferation is sidelined in Iran, the United States shares similar concerns to Israel regarding Iran's destabilizing activities. The new money was to pacify Israel regarding continuing threats from Iran. There is a provision in the agreement requiring "that money will go toward purchases benefitting the defense industry in the United States."[1234]

According to the *Washington Post*, the UN resolution was passed by fourteen countries, and the United States abstained rather than vetoing the resolution, which allowed it to pass. "The resolution declared that settlements built on land Israel has occupied since the 1967 Arab-Israeli war have 'no legal validity' and are a threat to the possibility of creating two states — one for Israelis and one for Palestinians."[1235]

I do not understand how anyone can posit that Obama did this as a parting payback to Netanyahu. The permanent members on the UN Security Council include China, France, the Russian Federation, the United Kingdom, and the United States. A veto from any one of these countries would have defeated the resolution. Term members include Bolivia (2018), Egypt (2017), Ethiopia (2018), Italy (2018), Japan (2017), Kazakhstan (2018), Senegal (2017), Sweden (2018), Ukraine (2017), and Uruguay (2017).[1236] Many Jewish-Americans support the two-state solution, as do most Israelis.[1237] Nir Hasson from *Haaretz—Israel News* claimed that the resolution was consistent with past administrations, both Democrat and Republican. The main contention was the abstention at the Security Council, which allowed the resolution to pass.

While Trump is entitled to shift policies from the previous administration, I did object to his efforts to malign Obama and the Iran deal, when there is wide consensus as to its success. While Obama made an effort to execute a smooth transition because of his respect for the office of the presidency, Trump and the Republicans have had no such compunction. Having Netanyahu speak in front of Congress, thereby supporting a foreign leader over the president of the United States, was not respectful to that office. This provided an opportunity for Netanyahu to publicly criticize Obama and the administration.

There has been a shift in Netanyahu's attitude toward candidate Trump and President Trump. During the campaign, according to Tom LoBianco from *CNN*, Trump said he cancelled a trip to Israel to meet with Prime Minister Netanyahu. In fact, the prime minister cancelled it because he objected to Trump's remarks about Muslims. "The state of Israel respects all religions and strictly guarantees the rights of all its citizens."[1238] It is interesting how this has shifted since Trump won the election.

As with the case of China, Trump's conflicts of interest implore one to consider whether his motives are for America or personal gain. While Trump has made efforts to expand into Israel, Jared Kushner's (Trump's son-in-law and key White House advisor who was charged with coming up with a peace settlement in the Middle East) business ties in Israel are of far greater concern, according to an article in the *Center for American Progress*. They disclosed that Kushner has numerous significant loans and lines of credit with Israeli banks and that the Kushner Companies "continue to profit from the deal through the collection of tenants' rent payments."[1239] The article went on to point out that, while Kushner resigned from more than two hundred positions in the company, he "will continue to benefit from the family business."[1240]

Cuba

There is one notable exception to Trump's expression of admiration for tyrants — Fidel Castro.

Fidel Castro was a brutal dictator who committed atrocious crimes against humanity. Castro violated basic human rights, committed mass murders, and oppressed those who spoke out against his regime. Thousands of citizens, including children, were killed by firing squad under his order. Cubans did not have freedom to leave the country, and it is estimated that approximately one million people tried to escape on rafts or boats. In March 1994, seventy-two Cubans, including women and children, tried to illegally escape in a state-owned tugboat. A

Cuban coast guard boat rammed the tugboat, and forty-one people died in the water that day. Jehovah's Witnesses, gays, and vagrants were sent to labour camps. Even though 90% of the country was Catholic, Castro deemed Catholics 'social scum,' closing all churches and curtailing religious celebrations. In 1996, 166 people were drained of their blood prior to being executed, resulting in cerebral anemia, which causes paralysis and unconsciousness. The blood was sold to the Vietcong.[1241]

In December 2014, President Obama announced a change of policy with respect to Cuba, stating that the fifty-year-old policy of isolation and sanctions did not bring about the desired "objective of empowering Cubans to build an open and democratic country… We cannot keep doing the same thing and expect a different result. It does not serve America's interests, or the Cuban people, to try to push Cuba toward collapse. We know from hard-learned experience that it is better to encourage and support reform than to impose policies that will render a country a failed state. We should not allow U.S. sanctions to add to the burden of Cuban citizens we seek to help."[1242]

In 2006, because of failing health, Fidel Castro appointed his brother Raúl Castro as president. Fidel Castro died on November 26, 2016. Here is part of Obama's message on Fidel Castro's death: "At this time of Fidel Castro's passing, we extend a hand of friendship to the Cuban people. We know that this moment fills Cubans—in Cuba and in the United States—with powerful emotions, recalling the countless ways in which Fidel Castro altered the course of individual lives, families, and of the Cuban nation. History will record and judge the enormous impact of this singular figure on the people and world around him… Today, we offer condolences to Fidel Castro's family, and our thoughts and prayers are with the Cuban people. In the days ahead, they will recall the past and also look to the future. As they do, the Cuban people must know that they have a friend and partner in the United States of America."[1243]

In contrast, Trump said, "Fidel Castro's legacy is one of firing squads, theft, unimaginable suffering, poverty, and the denial of fundamental human rights… While Cuba remains a totalitarian island, it is my hope that today marks a move away from the horrors endured for too long, and toward a future in which the wonderful Cuban people finally live in the freedom they so richly deserve."[1244]

Without praising Castro, Obama expressed condolences to the people, recognizing that many of them had a great love for their leader. He also acknowledged that there would be mixed emotions and that history would pass judgement. I cannot fault Trump's feeling, but given the fact that Raúl is stepping down in two years, this period may provide an opportunity to influence the direction of Cuban leadership, shifting toward more democratic governance, and instilling human rights. It is the people of Cuba who will have to accomplish this.

Prime Minister Trudeau's response was perplexing. While he acknowledged that Castro was controversial, he gave high praise and acknowledged that his father considered him a friend. His father was Pierre Elliot Trudeau, former prime minister of Canada. I cannot fathom how or why Trudeau considered him a friend. Robert Wright, a professor of history at Trent University in Peterborough, Ontario and author of *Three Nights in Havana: Pierre Trudeau,*

Fidel Castro, and the Cold War World, offered an explanation. Pierre Trudeau believed that one must see the "humanity of the enemy" in order to lessen tensions to enable dialogue with the enemy.[1245] Justin's position is a bit more complex. He has acknowledged that Castro was a dictator but did not think it appropriate to underscore this upon his death. Trudeau did not go to Cuba for the memorial. He also emphasized that he discussed human rights issues with Raúl on his visit two weeks prior to Fidel's death.[1246]

Trump tweeted, "If Cuba is unwilling to make a better deal for the Cuban people, the Cuban/American people and the U.S. as a whole, I will terminate deal."[1247] I am not sure as to what would be the most effective policy with Cuba. Canada had an open relationship with Cuba and made efforts to influence Castro on human rights issues. I personally am unaware of any meaningful changes that resulted. The US strategy of isolation and sanctions did not produce positive results. Trump's strategy may have some merit, but even if it does, I doubt his motives. I suspect he did it to gain votes from the Cuban expatriates in Miami and to further erode Obama's legacy. If this is the case, then even if the policy is sound, the execution will be a failure.

Russia

There has been nothing more baffling or more troubling than Donald Trump's rhetoric about Russia and Putin. Most would not argue that the United States would like to build a relationship to work more cooperatively with Russia. That is the rationale provided by Trump to justify his position with respect to Russia. Accepting this rationale, in my view, would be gullible. Throughout his adult life, Trump has had a fascination with fascist tyrants such as Hitler, Mussolini, and Putin. I fear that he not only admires them, but wants to emulate them.

A summary of some of Putin's more heinous behaviour includes the following. Putin is described as a petty thief and a thug. New England Patriots owner Robert Kraft claimed that when he showed him his 124-diamond Super Bowl ring, Putin pocketed it and then surrounded himself with KGB, who walked him out. Russian journalist Masha Gessen told a similar story about Putin's guards. At his nod, they took a souvenir glass replica of a Kalashnikov automatic weapon filled with vodka, which was shown to him at New York's Guggenheim Museum, and walked out with it.[1248]

He is known to be a philanderer and wife beater.[1249]

It is reported that when he was deputy mayor of St. Petersburg, Putin "allegedly organized a number of scams involving meat imports into the poor, starving city," which is the source of his current wealth.[1250]

Putin has a disdain for the media that exceeds even that of Donald Trump. Russia ranks 148th out of 180 countries for freedom of the press.[1251] This has gotten worse since Putin's rise to power in 2000, and his regime has been overtaking the media. In 2000, authorities raided NTV, a major television network, arresting the owner for fraud and releasing him only when he signed over the network to the state. As stated by *PolitiFact*, "More often, the Kremlin makes it difficult for independent outlets to operate in roundabout ways, including denying broadcast licenses, coordinating providers to dump channels, banning advertising on cable, limiting foreign ownership of media, and firing journalists for 'extremism.'"[1252] Thirty-four journalists have been murdered since 2000, and this number does not include those killed on assignments, in war, or where motives were unclear. "Of the thirty-four killings in Russia, many of the suspected perpetrators are military officials, government officials, or political groups."[1253] While there is no direct evidence of Putin's having directed or been involved in the killings, "according to Katrina vanden Heuvel, editor of the liberal magazine the *Nation*," he certainly "'created the climate' in which the murders [were] possible."[1254]

Mikhail Khodorkovsky, owner of the energy giant Yukos, was once Russia's richest man. Following a presentation he made to Putin and other officials about corruption, Khodorkovsky was jailed for tax evasion. While the company was able to settle the tax issues, it was thought that this was Putin's bid to take over the energy company.[1255] Putin issued a pardon for Khodorkovsky, who was released in December 2013. His assets were unfrozen, and he now lives in Switzerland, where he is considered the Russian government's strongest critic in exile.[1256]

Devastating bombings of apartment buildings in Russia that killed over 293 people and injured approximately a thousand were blamed on terrorists, but there is a "somewhat credible… rumor that the FSB [the successor agency to the KGB] engineered the bombings as a 'false flag' to garner support for Putin and a new war in Chechnya."[1257]

In September 2016, an international investigative team led by the Dutch and based on forensic evidence concluded that the Russians smuggled a surface-to-air missile into Ukraine and brought down Malaysia Airlines Flight 17 in 2014, killing all 298 aboard.[1258]

Putin occupied and seized the Crimean Peninsula in the Ukraine. In an interview with George Stephanopoulos, Trump insisted, "He's not going into Ukraine, all right? You can mark it down. You can put it down." When Stephanopoulos pointed out he was there already, Trump responded, "Okay, well, he's there in a certain way."[1259] How could a presidential nominee be ignorant of this fact? Even generally informed people who watch the news would be aware of this. Meanwhile, "The Russians [were] already in Ukraine, waiting for the right moment to send their tanks toward the capital of Kiev, perhaps after the November election."[1260]

USA Today reported that Putin carpet-bombed Aleppo, killing thousands of non-combatant Syrians trapped in the city. Russia proclaimed that "the airstrikes [were] focused on ammunition depots, groups of terrorists and their training centers, and facilities being used to manufacture weapons of mass destruction."[1261] According to *Mother Jones*, Russia's indiscriminate bombing has killed nearly four thousand civilians and almost three thousand non-Islamic rebel groups in comparison to only 2,746 ISIS members in the past year.[1262] From what I can understand, the rebels are fighting Assad's ruthless regime, with thousands killed in a civil war, producing millions of refugees. *CNN* reported that Assad's forces marched on Aleppo to destroy ISIS. Putin supports the Assad regime. Former Secretary of State John Kerry beseeched the Russians to stop the bombing and allow the rebels to leave safely for humanitarian reasons, as there were 100,000 people trapped in Aleppo.[1263]

CNN disclosed that the Syrian regime took control of Aleppo in December 2016, which virtually ended a six-year civil war that has resulted in 400,000 deaths. Turkey and Russia drafted a ceasefire agreement.[1264] It is my conviction that Trump so undermined the Obama administration that it made negotiations with the Russians impossible and created the environment that resulted in the Russian and Syrian alliance, excluding the US.

In early 2016, according to *Bloomberg*, a story went viral about an alleged rape of a thirteen-year-old Russian girl, Lisa, by immigrants in Germany, inciting protests about Chancellor Angela Merkel's open-door policy. The problem is that it never happened. Rather, German officials claimed it was the dishonest creation of Putin's regime to undermine the April 2016 regional elections in Germany, which resulted in major losses for Merkel's party. Russian-German voters joined the German Alternative für Deutschl (AfD), a right-wing populist party reported to have received funding from Russia, which they deny. Even so, there is no question from German leadership of Putin's intent to undermine the party in power in Germany. In France, Marine Le Pen's far-right National Front received funding from a Russian lender. Nigel Farage, the force of the Brexit movement, is a Putin admirer.

The intelligence community has forensic evidence that suggests Russians perpetrated the cyber-attacks on the DNC and John Podesta with Putin's knowledge, and with the goal to undermine Hillary Clinton's campaign. In December 2016, *CNN* disclosed that a Burlington Electric Company laptop had malware that had indicators matching the same code of the Russians who attacked the DNC. While the electric grid was not breached, it does raise the question of the potential damage that could be generated.[1265]

Putin enjoys exercising his power and superiority by being late for meetings with foreign dignitaries, keeping John Kerry waiting for three hours on one occasion in 2013.[1266] *Business Insider* claimed that Russian intelligence and security services were harassing and intimidating US diplomats and their families. While this has been longstanding, it has escalated since the sanctions in response to Russia's intervention in Ukraine. While it is most prevalent in Moscow, it has spread to US diplomats posted in other European countries. The harassment includes following diplomats and their families, breaking into their houses, tossing things around and leaving televisions on to let the family know they had been there. In one case, the pet dog was killed, and in another, they defecated on the carpet. The Russians claimed that the harassment was in response to the mistreatment of their diplomats in the US, but Evelyn Farkas, who served as Deputy Assistant Secretary of Defense for Russia, claimed there was no equivalency between restrictions on Russian diplomats in the US and the harassment of American diplomats. Josh Rogin from the *Washington Post* concluded, "The fact that the Russian government stands accused of murdering prominent diplomats and defectors in European countries adds a level of fear for Russia's targets."[1267]

This is the man Trump purportedly admires while disparaging President Obama. I must assume that with his security briefing, Trump had even more information about Putin and the Russians available to him. Maybe he did not attend this briefing, or maybe he simply does not care.

The following is a summary of some of Trump's connections in Russia.

While he has five patent brands in Russia and yearns to have a Trump Tower in Moscow, Trump denies having any business dealings there. When denied loans by American banks following his bankruptcies, Trump sought unorthodox funding, including investors who had ties to Putin. Many of his senior advisors have business ties to Russia.

Jeff Nesbitt from *Time* explained that Paul Manafort, Trump's former campaign manager, was a consultant to Viktor Yanukovych, the president of Ukraine with Russian support, who was overthrown in 2014. "Manafort did multimillion-dollar business deals with Russian oligarchs. Trump's foreign policy advisor, Carter Page, has his own business ties to the state-controlled Russian oil giant Gazprom... Another Trump foreign policy advisor, retired Army Lt. Gen. Michael Flynn, flew to Moscow last year to attend a gala banquet celebrating Russia Today, the Kremlin's propaganda channel, and was seated at the head table near Putin."[1268]

The *New York Times* reported that "secret ledgers in Ukraine contained references to $12.7 million in payments earmarked for him [Manafort]." These payments were supposedly set aside by Viktor Yanukovych for illegal, undisclosed payments. Manafort denied this, stating that the payments directed to him were for his entire team, including operatives and researchers.[1269]

Manafort's business associates "included Russian oligarch Oleg Deripaska, who was a close ally of Russian President Vladimir Putin," *Roll Call* disclosed.[1270] Rick Gates formerly worked for Manafort's consulting firm and was involved in a lawsuit with Manafort for racketeering. Gates worked briefly on Trump's campaign and is now working behind the scenes on inauguration activities. He is a lobbyist who arranged meetings between Ukrainian officials and members of Congress.[1271]

Carter Page is an investment banker and had been a policy advisor to the Trump campaign, but Trump's team distanced themselves from him after he was scrutinized by the FBI following a reported meeting with a former Russian security advisor just before the Republican Convention.[1272]

Rex Tillerson, CEO of ExxonMobil and Trump's Secretary of State, has ties to Russia and is considered a friend of Putin, having been awarded the Order of Friendship, Russia's highest honour for foreigners, *USA Today* reported.[1273]

Roger Stone is a Trump confidant and long-time GOP operative. While he denied collusion with WikiLeaks over the hacked emails of the DNC and John Podesta, he bragged about being in regular contact with WikiLeaks founder Julian Assange through mutual friends. The following tweet suggests that Stone knew that Podesta's emails would be leaked in October, which raises questions as to the extent of his involvement. Months before, "Stone predicted an October surprise that would disrupt Clinton's campaign and his recent Twitter posts suggested Podesta would soon be facing scandal, including an August update stating, 'Trust me, it will soon [be] the Podesta's time in the barrel.'"[1274] Stone is known for regularly posting false information. A false email from Stone reported "that Clinton secretly met with a Broward County, FL, election official in order to rig the election." Trump regularly relied on Stone's information during the campaign.[1275]

Media Matters disclosed that there was a lawsuit over Trump SoHo, which alleged that Bayrock, the company supporting the Trump transaction, was supported by criminal Russian financial dealings. While the court absolved Trump of knowledge of that activity, he later hired a principal partner in Bayrock to a position in the Trump organization. After the *Times* article was published, they added a response from Bayrock: "The allegations made by Jody Kriss in the lawsuit are completely baseless and unsubstantiated. The allegations of tax fraud, as well as other allegations from his original complaint that are quoted in this article, were not included by Kriss when he filed a second amended complaint in the lawsuit."[1276] Why then did they make a settlement? Bayrock is involved in many of Trump's projects around the world, including some in the US. Bayrock brokered an investment deal worth $50 million with billionaire Alexander Mashkevich, who settled a corruption lawsuit. Trump bragged about meeting with Russian oligarchs to discuss business projects around the world.[1277]

The following are additional facts that invite speculation regarding Trump, his family, his campaign, and potential involvement with Russia.

While President Trump says he has nothing to do with Russia, his son contradicted that assertion; according to Donald Trump Jr., "Russians make up a pretty disproportionate cross-section of a lot of our assets. We see a lot of money pouring in from Russia."[1278] Russian Deputy Foreign Minister, Sergei Ryabkov, claimed that the Russians were in regular contact with Trump's entourage during the campaign.[1279]

Trump repeatedly expressed both admiration of Putin's leadership and an interest in working more closely with him. On November 14, 2016, Putin called Trump to congratulate him, and the two discussed "a range of issues including the threats and challenges facing the United States and Russia, strategic economic issues, and the historical U.S.-Russia relationship that dates back over two hundred years," according to Trump's transition team.[1280] The Kremlin reported that they agreed on "uniting efforts in the fight with the common enemy No. 1 – international terrorism and extremism," according to *USA Today*.[1281] The next day, after a month-long hiatus on bombing, Russia began massive airstrikes on Aleppo. Is it possible that Trump gave his approval for this Russian action? Trump did say he would "bomb the hell out of them."[1282] It would be convenient if Russia did the deed since Trump may have had difficulty executing what he really wanted to do. Indiscriminate bombing violates international rules of war, according to *CNN*.[1283]

Not only was there potential for conflicts of interest for Trump regarding Russia, but also with several of his top advisors. While Trump wants a "friendly" relationship with Russia, many Republicans want even stricter sanctions than those imposed by Obama, including Lindsey Graham, Paul Ryan, and John McCain. Trump's position regarding Russia is out of step with other US allies.

During the transition and first few months of his presidency, Trump was only attending one national security briefing per week instead of daily. Given his lack of experience in foreign affairs and government, as well as his cabinet's lack of experience in foreign affairs, one would assume that this would be a priority, especially given the escalation of Russian involvement in Syria and the escalation of nuclear development in North Korea. Trump is not seeking advice from the State Department. As a member of the free world, this concerns me. While he does not have to follow the advice, I think he has the responsibility, at the very least, to consider it.

After the election, most world leaders called Trump with congratulations and expressed a willingness to work together on common issues. Even so, one cannot demand respect; it is earned, and it is not accorded when it is not mutual.

Throughout this election process, Trump and his popularity with the voters have changed the image of America on the world stage. America has been an icon of democracy and has led by example. The world is starting to question America's 'exceptionalism' and America's self-appointed right to be an umpire and enforcer of democracy, human rights, and freedom. The international community is justifiably concerned that America will use its power to accommodate American interests without regard for those of the rest of the world.

Obama said, "The only way Russia can affect the U.S. is if we lose track of who we are" and "abandon our values… Mr. Putin can weaken us just like he's trying to weaken Europe if we start buying into notions that it's okay to intimidate the press, or lock up dissidents, or discriminate against people," reported *CNBC*.[1284] Russia is winning. Democracy is at risk, not only in the United States, but across the globe. Trump seems determined not just to renegotiate agreements with allies, but to disrupt and destroy them. This includes NATO, the United Nations, NAFTA, the Trans-Pacific Partnership, the One China policy, the Russian alliance, and a two-state solution in Israel. Trump tweeted the following: "The United Nations has such great potential but right now it is just a club for people to get together, talk and have a good time. So sad!"[1285]

I think it is incumbent on allies to make honest efforts to negotiate with Trump, but without a willingness on Trump's part to seek "win-win" solutions that have benefits for all parties, the US is at risk of isolation. I do not think this benefits the US or the international community. If that is the case, the partners for trade or security will have to create new alliances in exclusion of the US. Sadly, Trump is already using a 'divide and conquer' approach; *CBC* reported that he promised the Brexit government in Britain a free-trade deal within weeks of his inauguration.[1286] Trump is predicting that other European countries will follow. Is this what we can expect for the future? Will countries voting in populist governments that admire Putin get preference from the US? *Time* magazine announced German Chancellor Angela Merkel as its Person of the Year for 2015. Trump tried to undermine Merkel by describing her as "ruining Germany… What she's done in Germany is insane. It's insane" (referring to the influx of Syrian refugees in Germany).[1287] Trump is predicting a populist sweep in Europe with other countries leaving the EU. Of course, that is what Putin wants.

If we value democracy, all citizens in the free world have a responsibility to protect it. We must not succumb to "fake news" designed to create fear and blame. We must not become agents of Putin by electing the populist governments that Putin supports and that will undermine our allies and the media. It will be the responsibility of our governments to remain united and prevent divisiveness of the type encouraged by Putin or Trump. It is also the responsibility of our leadership to address the people's concerns with their governments and the establishment. None of us is immune. I am already seeing the populist sentiment expressed by some Canadians.

Even if satisfactory arrangements are negotiated with Trump, the international community is now on notice that this is not the America that reflected Truman's vision of the free world and that we could count on as a partner. The accepted vision could change at a moment's notice. Must countries start making contingency plans for national security and economic trade apart from the US? Many countries agreed not to develop nuclear weapons. Those countries may now have to reconsider their involvement in the Non-Proliferation Treaty for self-defence, but it is unlikely that this would increase US security, nor would it reduce costs for the US. The TPP was supposed to keep China at bay and benefit the US. The US may be squandering an opportunity to arrest China's growing economic power and influence. The US took on the role of the leader of the free world to protect its own national security. With the current arrangement, the US and its allies receive support, financially and practically. The US military is in zones that currently protect US interests. That will not change, but the support from allies could if the US becomes isolated. The point is, while the US may be the most powerful nation, it relies heavily on the relationships it holds with other countries.

CHAPTER FOURTEEN

Chaos And Crises

The battlefield is a scene of constant chaos. The winner will be the one who controls that chaos, both his own and the enemies.[1288]
—*Napoleon Bonaparte*

This book was written primarily as events unfolded, and it covered the period from January 2016 to the first hundred days of the Trump presidency. Prior to publication, several events took place that I felt compelled to discuss. Keeping the book current and comprehensive was an elusive goal. The constant crises and outrageous incidents have been unprecedented.

FBI Director Fired

Trump's firing of FBI Director James Comey on May 9, 2017 is an example of his disregard for the checks and balances meant to hold him accountable. While Democrats and Republicans alike had issues with Comey, firing him while he was investigating potential Russian interference, the role of the Trump campaign, and administration, was highly suspect.

At the very least, it was bad optics. At the most insidious, it was an obstruction of the investigation. It would have been more credible if the Trump administration had not claimed that the cause of his firing was Comey's unfair treatment of Hillary during the email investigation, as reported by *Reuters*.[1289] That is not believable after Trump's constant refrains during the campaign and afterward, praising Comey for this same behaviour. There was a personal vindictiveness in this firing, as demonstrated by how it was delivered. According to *Reuters*, Comey was out of town in a meeting with FBI employees when he saw it on a TV monitor. That the action was not related to the Russian investigation was belied by the short letter firing Comey. In it, Trump wrote, "I greatly appreciate you informing me, on three separate occasions, that I am not under investigation."[1290] This suggests the Russia investigation was the cause.

Republicans were outraged when Bill Clinton spoke with Attorney General Lynch before the conclusion of the investigation regarding Hillary's emails, yet many defended Trump's behaviour. He tweeted that Mr. Comey had "better hope there are no tapes of our conversations," suggesting that such recordings, if they existed, might contradict him.[1291]

According to the *Huffington Post*, Trump claimed that he acted on the recommendation of Deputy Attorney General Rod Rosenstein. While Rosenstein denies this, it is safe to say that he was not happy with this spin on the firing of Comey. In a later interview, Trump said that he had wanted to fire Comey from the beginning and that it was his decision. "I was going to fire Comey, knowing there was no good time to do it…[a]nd in fact, when I decided to just do it, I said to myself, I said, 'You know, this Russia thing with Trump and Russia is a made-up story, it's an excuse by the Democrats for having lost an election.'"[1292]

The *Washington Post* reported that Comey kept contemporaneous notes, as is the custom of most lawyers. Associates of Comey advised that the notes conveyed a request from Trump "to close the investigation into Trump's former national security adviser, Michael Flynn."[1293] Trump said, "I hope you can see your way clear to letting this go, to letting Flynn go… He is a good guy."[1294] This was a private meeting with Comey after other advisers had been dismissed, including Attorney General Jeff Sessions and Vice President Mike Pence. Just prior to this incident, the *New York Times* printed a story claiming, "Trump sought a loyalty pledge from Comey at a dinner shortly after Trump's inauguration."[1295]

CNN reported that James Comey made the extraordinary decision to circumvent the attorney general in the public announcement he made on the disposition of the investigation regarding Hillary's emails. Comey did so based on a memo that he knew was false and created by Russian intelligence. The memo conveyed that Loretta Lynch, former attorney general, had provided assurances to Hillary that "the Justice Department wouldn't take the email probe too far."[1296] While Lynch recused herself from participating in the investigation and the disposition, she did not abdicate the role of the Justice Department or the normal protocols for announcing such a decision. When Comey told Congress on October 28, 2017 that he was reopening the case about Hillary Clinton's email server, she had a 5-7% lead in the national popular vote. Following his notification of the reopening, it dropped 3%, making it within the margin of error.[1297] There can be no question that this was a deciding factor in the outcome of the election.

While Republicans continued to argue against this, Attorney General Rod Rosenstein appointed former FBI chief Robert Mueller as special counsel to investigate alleged Russian interference in the 2016 US election and possible collusion between President Donald Trump's campaign and Moscow. Trump's response came by tweet: "This is the single greatest witch hunt of a politician in American history!"[1298]

Sharing of Confidential Information

On May 10, 2017, President Trump met with Russian officials in the oval office. While the US media was banned from the meeting, the Russian media was present. It was later reported by the *Washington Post* that Trump had shared highly confidential information with the Russian officials. While Trump did not reveal the source of the information, it could be traceable by the Russians, placing the source in potential jeopardy. The information was considered so sensitive that it was not shared with allies, but Trump shared it with the Russians.[1299] While it is true that Trump can declassify information at a moment's notice at his own discretion, what was the national security rationale for taking this risk? While Israel claims the relationship with the US is solid, other countries have reservations.

The *Guardian* reported that, following the horrific Manchester terrorist suicide bombing, Prime Minister Teresa May confronted Trump about reports in the US media that included confidential information about the Manchester investigation. The UK temporarily curtailed sharing information until Trump promised to plug the leaks.[1300]

Trump's First Visit Abroad

On May 20, 2017, Trump embarked on a nine-day tour, visiting five countries, attending the NATO summit, and going to the annual summit meeting of the Group of Seven. His tour was described as a success by his administration and the media. He was scripted and had his most valued advisors at his side; everything was planned well in advance. Despite that, Trump exposed his narcissism, obliviousness to how other world leaders view him, and ignorance of world events. How many presidents have rudely shoved another NATO leader out of the way to make their way to the front for a group photo op? Trump did.[1301]

At the NATO summit, Trump soundly scolded NATO members who, according to him, were not paying their fair share on defense spending.[1302] To those Americans who praised Trump's aggressiveness and strength on this matter, I have the following comments.

Some of the media expressed that a few countries may not be able to meet that target because they are still in an austerity program. Is that a euphemism for the global financial crisis of 2008, created by Wall Street because there were no safeguards to prevent it? This is the same banking system that Trump intends to deregulate. Some countries were decimated by this financial crisis. Lives were ruined, and people are still experiencing hardship through no fault of their own. When will the US apologize to the world for this catastrophe?

In Chapter 6, I explained how Trump misrepresented the 2% GDP issue. Even though many NATO countries are not meeting the target, this did not prevent them from coming to the aid of the US after 9/11 and supporting the US in Afghanistan. According to the *Star*, this was the only time in a sixty-eight-year history that the NATO countries invoked Article 5, the mutual defense agreement. Simply put, if one NATO ally is attacked, the other countries will come to their aid. Trump failed to explicitly reaffirm the US's commitment to come to the aid of a NATO ally under attack,[1303] especially when, during his campaign, he suggested that under his leadership this aid would be measured by the ally's contribution to the alliance. While his administration provided assurances, the omission was deliberate. There is no confidence in assurances when Trump delivers mercurial promises motivated only by ego.

Trump has the right to encourage NATO countries to meet the guideline. Yet as Trump has acknowledged, healthcare and the Chinese relationship with North Korea are more complicated than he thought. Perhaps NATO is as well. Instead of taking up this issue with NATO countries in a meeting, he chose to lecture and rebuke America's allies at an event commemorating the fall of the Berlin Wall and the September 11, 2001 terrorist attacks. Considering NATO's support after 9/11, this was offensive.

CNN disclosed a report from NATO in June 2017, which identified that "Europe and Canada will increase defense spending by 4.3% in 2017."[1304] Trump immediately "claimed credit for some of the defense increases… 'because of our actions, money is starting to pour into NATO.'"[1305] The fact is that, according to NATO Secretary General Jens Stoltenberg, since 2014, the "European Allies and Canada spent almost $46 billion more on defense."[1306] They were pledging increases well before Trump was even a candidate. *CNN* advised that "[e]xperts see concerns about Russia as the principle driving factor behind increasing defense budgets."[1307] While NATO officials "also credited Trump with drawing attention to the issue," Stoltenberg added, "At the same time, it's important to understand that this is implementation of a decision we all made together."[1308] Public humiliation and castigation were not necessary, as the NATO members were already moving in this direction. Discussing this in meetings with US allies would have had the same outcome without generating rancour with allies who came to the aid of the US.

At the G7 talks, according to *BBC*, "[s]ix world leaders reaffirmed their commitment to the Paris Accord, the world's first comprehensive deal aimed at reducing greenhouse emissions… The US has refused to recommit to the agreement, saying it will make a decision next week."[1309] Regarding the Paris Accord, the *Globe and Mail* reported that "Mr. Trudeau had privately urged the president to stay in the accord, arguing that advances in green technology would create millions of new jobs in America."[1310] Merkel was disappointed with discussions at the NAFTA summit and the G7 discussions with Trump, and made the following statement upon her return to Germany, as reported by the *Guardian*: "Europe can no longer completely rely on its longstanding British and US allies… the EU must now be prepared to 'take its fate into its own hands.'"[1311] This was one of my greatest fears with Brexit and a Trump presidency. He created polarization not only within the US, but globally. Putin is winning. There is a lack of trust and credibility. There is division in the EU and the G7, and Trump has not confirmed the US position on Article 5. The world would be less safe without these alliances.

Repeal and Replace Obamacare

Repealing Obamacare was a signature platform for Trump and the Republicans during the campaign. The *New York Times* reported that Trump asserted that the replacement for Obamacare would include coverage for pre-existing conditions and children would remain on their parents' plan until the age of twenty-six.[1312] Trump signed an executive order soon after the inauguration to keep good on his promise to roll back Obamacare.

The Republicans refused to approve improvements to the legislation during the Obama administration; they decried Obamacare for at least six years and yet have not agreed to a replacement plan. There have been three failed attempts by the Republicans to pass a bill to repeal and replace.[1313]

After the first proposed healthcare bill failed to garner enough Republican support, Trump commented, "Nobody knew healthcare could be so complicated."[1314] Yes, we did. Almost everybody did.

On July 28, 2017, Senator John McCain gave a thumbs-down to the Republican plan to repeal Obamacare and was the one vote that ensured it would not pass the Senate. McCain later tweeted, "Skinny repeal fell short because it fell short of our promise to repeal & replace Obamacare w/ meaningful reform."[1315]

Many Republican senators voted for the bill with the promise from Paul Ryan that it would not be implemented by the House as is. Senator Lindsey Graham proclaimed, "I'm not going to vote for a bill that is terrible policy and horrible politics just because we have to get something done." But he did. He also called the bill a "disaster" and a "fraud."[1316]

In response to these developments, Trump tweeted: "3 Republicans and 48 Democrats let the American people down. As I said from the beginning, let Obamacare implode, then deal. Watch!"[1317] Trump is not only hoping that Obamacare implodes, he is sabotaging it, regardless of how it will negatively affect millions of people.

On October 12, 2017, *Politico* reported that President Trump signed an executive order that will eliminate the subsidy payments for Obamacare.[1318] Only 17% of Americans supported the first healthcare proposal crafted by the Republicans, while 68% of Americans wanted to fix Obamacare rather than 'repeal and replace.'[1319]

In each failed effort to repeal and replace, there have been two common barriers: the lack of support from health organizations and the assessments of the Congressional Budget Office (CBO). This administration has not demonstrated that they sought advice from experts in the development of a policy direction, and their implementation is chaotic. *CNBC* reported that in response to the Graham-Cassidy bill, the American Medical Association, the AARP (American Association of Retired Persons), and sixteen other organizations opposed it.[1320] The CBO estimated that 24 million people would lose their healthcare by 2026 with the revised Republican healthcare plan, while reducing the federal deficit by $337 billion. The report advised that the number of people receiving Medicaid would be reduced by 25%. The elderly would experience increased costs. Many Republican voters expressed concerns about the party's plan, according to the *New York Times*.[1321] These issues remain consistent for each successive plan, including Trump's executive order.

Insurers expressed concern that there would be no incentives to obtain coverage, "a situation that… would leave them with a pool of sicker, costlier customers."[1322]

At least eighteen states refused federal funding under the Affordable Care Act on the basis that they could not afford the additional costs. All but two had Republican governors, and for those who had Democrat governors, Republicans controlled the Senate.[1323] This is flawed thinking. *CNBC* provided an example in which Louisiana claimed they would save $1 billion and expand Medicare services to more individuals by accepting the federal funding.[1324]

In absence of coverage, the healthcare for the poor is emergency care, one of the costliest options. Furthermore, lack of access to housing and nutritious food negatively impacts their health. It is costing the American taxpayer more by denying these basic services. Health problems and lack of housing are barriers to gaining employment and financial independence. The refusal of those states to expand Medicare was not justified on a fiscal basis. It was simply obstruction of Obamacare.

The free market approach has not resulted in competitive healthcare prices in the US. More concerning, it has not resulted in better health outcomes. For example, *NPR* reported that the "U.S. has the worst rate of maternal deaths in the developed world" and that it is rising in the US as it declines elsewhere.[1325] How is that acceptable to the American people?

Trump continued to bait the Democrats to come to the table and develop a bipartisan plan. *Business Insider* reported that on August 31, 2017, a bipartisan plan to 'fix' Obamacare was announced by Governors John Kasich of Ohio (R) and Brian Sandoval of Nevada (D) with the following statement: "As Congress considers reforms to strengthen our nation's health insurance system, we ask you to take immediate steps to make coverage more stable and affordable. The current state of our individual market is unsustainable, and we can all agree this is a problem that needs to be fixed."[1326] Five Democrats and three Republicans were involved in developing the plan. Why is this option not at least being explored?

None of the plans proposed by Republicans or Trump provide for more affordable and better healthcare, because contrary to what they say, that is not their agenda. The Republicans want the savings from healthcare to offset the tax reforms. Trump and many Republicans have demonstrated that they are willing to sacrifice the healthcare of millions of Americans to achieve that goal. Trump has affirmed that he cares more about destroying Obama's legacy than he does about the American people.

Staff Resignations and Firings

The chaos continued. Even though 85% of top roles in the White House remained unfilled,[1327] Trump was considering a shake-up in the communications department because of the confusion following the firing of James Comey.[1328] Instead of blaming others for all the missteps and crises, he should examine his own responsibility in the creation of these issues.

The following is my summary of the significant departures in the Trump administration during the first seven months of his presidency, based on an article in the *Los Angeles Times*. Sally Yates, Acting Attorney General, was fired after eleven days; Michael Flynn, National Security Adviser, 'resigned' within twenty-three days; Craig Deare, National Security Council Senior Director for Western Hemisphere Affairs, was fired after twenty-seven days; Katie Walsh, Deputy White House Chief of Staff, resigned within seventy days; Angella Reid, White House Chief Usher, was fired after 106 days; James B. Comey Jr., FBI Director, was fired after 110 days; K. T. McFarland, Deputy National Security Advisor, resigned within 118 days; Elon Musk, advisory council, resigned within 133 days; Robert Iger, advisory council, resigned within 134 days; Walter Shaub, Director of the Office of Government Ethics, resigned within 181 days; Sean Spicer, White House Press Secretary and White House Director of Communications, resigned within 183 days; Michael Short, Assistant Press Secretary, resigned within 187 days;

Derek Harvey, National Security Council Middle East Advisor, resigned within 187 days; and Reince Priebus, White House Chief of Staff, resigned within 189 days.[1329]

Walter Shaub resigned as ethics office director on July 6, 2017 and provided a warning as to what can be anticipated as Trump's presidency progresses. As stated in Shaub's letter of resignation, "The principle that public service is a public trust, requiring employees to place loyalty to the Constitution, the laws and ethical principles [should be] above private gain."[1330] NPR reported that Shaub made the following statement: "The current situation has made it clear that the ethics program needs to be stronger than it is."[1331] Shaub was critical of Trump's lack of ethics compliance, including Trump's failure to move his assets into a blind trust, initial refusals to make public the waivers given to Trump appointees to "get around ethics rules,"[1332] and failure to discipline Kellyanne Conway "after she made an on-air endorsement of the clothing line of Ivanka Trump."[1333] Shaub also warned the president to "stop going to your properties or announce that White House officials won't go to those properties... Those visits amount to free promotion."[1334]

Sean Spicer resigned as White House press secretary on July 21, 2017, following the appointment of Anthony Scaramucci as White House communications director.[1335] Trump may have known that Spicer would resign under these circumstances, a result Trump intended, rather than incur criticism for yet another firing in his administration. Trump has only himself to blame for the tumultuous period with the press during Spicer's tenure because, according to CNN, Trump "repeatedly undermined [him] in his role as the White House's public-facing spokesman by the President's own public statements and tweets."[1336] Soon after, on July 29, 2017, Reince Priebus resigned as chief of staff, and Trump appointed General John Kelly to replace him.

On July 31, 2017, Kelly fired Scaramucci. In his first week on the job, Scaramucci proved to be crude and vicious. The *New Yorker* reported that Scaramucci accused Reince Priebus of having leaked information about his income, which the reporter later denied. This was probably the catalyst for Priebus's resignation. Scaramucci said of Priebus, "Reince is a f[##]king paranoid schizophrenic, a paranoiac."[1337] As a former mental health provider, I am dismayed by his negative reference to a serious mental illness. There are already enough stigmas surrounding mental illness, and for a high-ranking official of the government to make such a crude reference is inexcusable.

On August 19, 2017, Kelly fired Steve Bannon. Voters elected Trump on the premise that he was a stellar businessman who would hire only the best. Did he? Even Trump didn't think so. Absolute loyalty to Trump is the primary criterion for being hired, taking precedence over competence and qualifications. He fired them or had someone else do it. In some cases, he simply created conditions in which he knew they would resign. Although he is famous for the phrase "You're fired," Trump does not seem to have the fortitude for this and often leaves the unpleasant task for others.

North Korea

On July 28, 2017, North Korea tested an intercontinental ballistic missile capable of striking the US mainland.[1338] As Jeffrey Lewis[1339] pointed out in an opinion editorial in the *New York Times*, Trump tweeted, "It won't happen!" but it has, twice. Lewis made an interesting argument as to why Americans did not see the warning signs and drew the following conclusion:

> The reality is that the United States is now vulnerable to North Korea's nuclear-armed missiles — and has no choice but to live with that reality. Trying to disarm a nuclear-armed North Korea would be madness, even if some politicians find that fact too emasculating to acknowledge. Since admitting our vulnerability is a humiliation, we simply close our eyes and pretend it isn't real.[1340]

On August 22, 2017, *Reuters* reported that tensions were already high in North Korea during the annual military exercises conducted jointly by South Korea and the US. North Korea perceived "the war games as a preparation for invasion."[1341] During these games, North Korea launched a missile over Japan, further escalating the tensions. On behalf of North Korea, Rodong Sinmun made the following statement: "The U.S. should know that it can neither browbeat the DPRK with any economic sanctions and military threats and blackmail nor make the DPRK flinch from the road chosen by itself."[1342] While "Pentagon spokesman Colonel Robert Manning said diplomacy was still Washington's preferred option," Trump stated, "Threatening and destabilizing actions only increase the North Korean regime's isolation in the region and among all nations of the world. All options are on the table."[1343]

NPR reported that while Nikki Haley failed to convince China and Russia to implement stricter sanctions, including a "total oil embargo," "an asset freeze," and a "global travel ban," she did make progress in gaining a unanimous vote from the UN National Security Council to impose new sanctions against North Korea.[1344]

In a speech to the UN on September 19, 2017, President Trump made the following statements about North Korea and Kim Jong-un, as reported in *Reuters*: "The United States has great strength and patience, but if it is forced to defend itself or its allies, we will have no choice but to destroy North Korea… Rocket Man is on a suicide mission for himself."[1345] Kim Jong-un's response was that "he will make Trump 'pay dearly for his rude nonsense calling for destroying the DPRK.'"[1346] North Korea's foreign minister hinted at one such measure: an aboveground thermonuclear explosion over the Pacific.

On September 30, 2017, Rex Tillerson acknowledged that there are open lines of communication between the administration and North Korea but, according to the *New York Times*, "gave no indication of what the administration might be willing to give up in any negotiations, and Mr. Trump has made clear he would make no concessions."[1347] Certainly China and others in the region desire to defuse the "threats being exchanged" by both leaders.[1348]

This has become a battle of egos between Trump and Kim Jong-un, which could set off a catastrophe and potentially result in nuclear war, if only by mishap of a nuclear test. President Trump is sabotaging the efforts of his administration to seek a non-military solution and risking the confidence of his country's allies, just as he had with his continual threats to withdraw from the Iran agreement. Is it possible that enemies of democracy, such as Russia, China, and North Korea, could collaborate in opposition to our allies?

Since North Korea perceives a threat from the US, the only way to deescalate the situation with Kim Jong-un and mitigate the threat is to reduce the fear of annihilation from the US and to persuade Kim Jong-un to come to the table and negotiate. Trump is escalating the fear and reducing the possibility of cooperation from China and the United Nations. Trump is alienating those he needs to settle this issue with North Korea diplomatically. The other options are catastrophic.

Trump has proposed that other allies or partners such as Japan develop nuclear weapons. It used to make me feel more comfortable if an ally was armed. The Trump presidency is a warning that there is no guarantee of rationality and a commitment to democratic values, even in the leadership of a democratic country like the US.

Immigration

In a speech to lawmakers and the relatives of crime victims in Brentwood, Long Island on July 28, 2017, while discussing his immigration plan, Trump talked about the treatment of criminals by the police. The *Guardian* reported Trump's statement: "I said, 'Please don't be too nice.' Like when you guys put somebody in the car and you're protecting the head… 'You can take the hand away,' OK?"[1349] The *New York Times* advised that many police organizations and officials were highly critical of the remarks. As stated by Michael Harrison, Chief of the New Orleans Police Department, the comments "stand in stark contrast to [their] department's commitment to constitutional policing and community engagement."[1350] This kind of bombast, encouraging violence, was not confined to the campaign and has continued into Trump's presidency.

On August 22, 2017, *CNN* reported that Trump pardoned former Arizona Sheriff Joe Arpaio. Arpaio was found guilty of racial profiling of Latinos and was ordered to stop. US District Judge Susan Bolton stated, "Not only did [Arpaio] abdicate responsibility, he announced to the world and to his subordinates that he was going to continue business as usual no matter who said otherwise."[1351] Arpaio defied the Constitution, and Trump's rationale for the pardon was, "So was Sheriff Joe… convicted for doing his job?"[1352] He was not doing his job. He was racially profiling and conducting illegal policing. Trump, too, defied the Constitution.

On August 2, 2017, Trump announced a proposed bill for merit-based immigration like that in Canada and Australia.[1353] The proposed plan would end "the preference for uniting family members in the current immigration system."[1354] According to Alexander Panetta, reporter with the *Globe and Mail*, there are significant variances between Trump's proposal and the Canadian immigration system.

The number of immigrants coming to Canada is already proportionately greater than those going to the US. Trump's proposal will "cut net immigration in half."[1355] Panetta reported that Stephen Miller, a presidential adviser, claimed that they took the Canadian plan and added to it. Panetta responded, "More precisely, they subtracted things: People."[1356] Some of the proposed key points in the Trump administration plan are as follows: that residents could only sponsor spouses and minor children, not other relatives; that immigrants must be proficient in English; that children must be under eighteen rather than the current age of twenty-one; and that points of skilled workers be deducted if their spouse is less skilled.[1357]

Panetta stated, "The point of commonality is a points-based system in which applicants with high skills are favoured in Canada and Australia."[1358] Canada accepts several categories of immigrants for permanent residence. In addition to economic class immigrants, it admits specified family members and adopted children under the family class category, refugees, and others not falling into these specific categories who qualify for entry on humanitarian or compassionate grounds or for public policy reasons.[1359] Repeatedly, Republicans promote their plan comparing it to Canada's as a merit based system. At no time have I heard the media clarify the difference in the two plans, which I think are significant.

When the Supreme Court ruled on Trump's travel ban in June 2017, it excluded those with "a credible claim of a bona fide relationship" with an American relative. The ban that was to be imposed by the Trump administration excluded grandparents and other extended relatives. Matt Zapotosky from the *Washington Post* reported, "U.S. District Judge Derrick K. Watson wrote that the government's 'narrowly defined list' of who might be exempt was not supported by either the Supreme Court decision partially unfreezing the ban or by the law."[1360] Attorney General Jeff Sessions is taking this to the Supreme Court. The Trump administration appears to be intent on pushing the envelope of even Supreme Court decisions. How can a grandparent not be considered a 'bona fide relationship'?

In February of 2017, President Trump promised, "We are gonna deal with DACA with heart."[1361] According to *Vox*, DACA (Deferred Action for Childhood Arrivals) has protected nearly "800,000 young adult unauthorized immigrants from deportation and allowed them to work legally since 2012."[1362] On September 5, 2017, Jeff Sessions announced President Trump's decision regarding DACA. As reported by Stephen Collinson, correspondent at *CNN*, Trump has set a deadline of March 5, 2018 for "Congress to act to preserve the program's protections before the program's beneficiaries begin losing their status."[1363] Dreamers trusted the American government and were encouraged to identify themselves, putting them at risk of being easily targeted for deportation. Even Trump acknowledged that they committed no crime; their parents brought them over. It is unlikely that Congress will be able to resolve this issue when they have been unable to do so in the past eight years. Even if they did, the uncertainty for these young people is cruel and unnecessary. If they are deported, America will be deprived of the contributions that these individuals make to the country they embrace as theirs, including military service. He did not keep his promise to deal with DACA with heart.

In early August 2017, the Canadian media reported that thousands from the US were seeking asylum in Canada, primarily through Quebec. The *Globe and Mail* identified that at least 90% were Haitians.[1364] After the devastating earthquake in 2010, both Canada and the US provided temporary status to Haitians "until Haiti was able [to] rebuild enough for them to return home," the *Toronto Sun* reported.[1365]

Candice Malcolm from the *Toronto Sun* reported that the wave of Haitians into Canada was prompted by a "WhatsApp hoax" advising Haitians in the US that Canada would automatically accept them and pay the bill.[1366] In fact, the Trudeau government ended this program in 2016 when "Haiti was stable and safe enough to suspend the program."[1367] While those who met Canada's "health and national security standards could apply for permanent residency,"[1368] only 38% received permanent residency. The Trump administration is recommending ending the program in the US with a six-month extension in which residents should prepare "for their return to Haiti in the event Haiti's designation is not extended again."[1369]

The Trump administration is attempting to end the program, similar to what Canada has done. The problem is the lens, the motives, and the implementation. It is being conducted in the context of Trump having stated that his administration would focus on violent offenders and those committing illegal acts when dealing with immigration reform. It is being proposed while many in the US are outraged at the treatment of the 'dreamers.'

July 2017 Employment Report

On August 4, 2017, *Reuters* indicated that a strong employment report in July resulted in 183,000 new jobs. Trump inherited a healthy economy from the Obama administration. While there are new jobs, wages remain sluggish: Lucia Mutikani, a reporter from *Reuters,* stated, "Lack of strong wage growth is surprising given that the economy is near full employment."[1370] It's not surprising to me. While the market and economy remain strong, corporate greed rules the day and many employers put profit over fair treatment of employees.

Eugene Kiely from *FactCheck* questioned statements made by Scott Pruitt, administrator of the Environmental Protection Agency, who advised that the coal industry had added almost 50,000 jobs since the fourth quarter of last year.[1371] However, the Bureau of Labor statistics reflected that only 1,300 of those jobs were coal mining. "The rest of the mining jobs were created in gas, oil, metal ores, and non-metallic mineral mining and quarrying, as well as support jobs in the mining sector."[1372] Kiely also pointed out that the figures were not from the last quarter but rather from October 2016. The Trump administration is influencing how government agencies report information to suit their own agenda.

Robert Murray, founder and chief executive of Murray Energy, was pleased to have Trump create a more positive political climate for coal mining, especially since Trump repealed Obama's Stream Protection Rule, which prevented mining companies from "dumping mining debris in streams."[1373] Murray also wants the legislation designating carbon dioxide as a pollutant repealed. Even Murray acknowledged that the coal mining jobs "were lost to technology rather than regulation and to competition from natural gas and renewables, which makes it unlikely that he [Trump] can do much to significantly grow the number of jobs in the industry."[1374] While Murray said that new plants using "clean coal" technologies could soon be built, he doesn't expect that coal's share of the market will rise significantly in the future, the *Guardian* disclosed.[1375] Even Robert Murray, "the largest privately held coalminer in the US," concedes that coal-mining jobs were lost due to technology, not NAFTA, and that coalmining is unlikely to have a great comeback![1376]

Be clear about this. Murray is pleased that he can increase corporate profit because the Trump administration will allow him to pollute drinking water and pollute the air, even though it is unlikely to create a substantial number of new jobs. They care about corporate profit; they are not concerned about the fate of the employees or the health of the American people.

During the campaign, Trump declared that he would increase the GDP growth to 4%. However, Dominic Rushe, editor for the *Guardian*, noted, "Meaningfully increasing GDP will take time, but it does seem like Trump is already scaling back his growth goal of 4% or more. Treasury Secretary Mnuchin talked about sustained 3% growth when he introduced Trump's tax plan on Wednesday."[1377]

I heartily agree with another of Rushe's comments that training for growing sectors is needed in the job market rather than "trying to revive declining industries."[1378] In 2008, Obama inherited the worst economic downturn since the Great Depression.[1379] Yet despite Trump's advantage in inheriting a heathier economy than Obama, according to economic analyst Kimberly Amadeo, "If the World Bank's latest forecast—released this week—is right about global GDP growth, Trump will wish he had Obama's numbers."[1380] Trump promised a healthier GDP and job growth than the Obama administration. So far, there is no evidence that the "left behind" are going to benefit any more with Trump's policies than Obama's—probably less.

Charlottesville

On August 12, 2017, a Unite the Right march was organized by white nationalists in opposition to the removal of Confederate General Robert E. Lee's statue from Emancipation Park in Charlottesville, Virginia. Counter-protesters also gathered to express their disapproval of the white nationalist march. Despite police efforts to keep the two parties on different sides of the street, there were bloody riots and a tragic death.[1381] James Alex Fields Jr. of Ohio, known by many to have racist views,[1382] slammed a car into a crowd of the counter-protesters, wounding thirty-four people and killing thirty-two-year-old Heather D. Heyer of Charlottesville, reported the *New York Times*.[1383]

According to Blake Montgomery of *BuzzFeed*, most of the white supremacists were well armed: "Yes, lots of guns, utilizing Virginia's loose firearm laws… They used militarized defensive maneuvers."[1384] Counter-protesters came armed with sticks, spraying chemicals and "balloons filled with paint or ink."[1385]

The *New York Times* reported the following incident:

> Ézé Amos, a photographer from Nigeria who lives in Charlottesville, alleged that a man punched his camera which hit him in the face. He claimed that it happened in front of the police, who denied seeing the incident and only took his name. His reaction was profound as he observed, "I am a black man photographing this. I kept telling myself, 'If it gets out

of hand, the cops will jump in and save me'… I saw a white woman get hit, and they did not do anything. That's when I actually got really scared of the whole thing."[1386]

These are only a few of the numerous eyewitness accounts of this nature reported by various media outlets.

The *New York Times* reported that it took two days before President Trump made a statement condemning the violence, saying, "Those who cause violence… are criminals and thugs, including the K.K.K., neo-Nazis, white supremacists and other hate groups that are repugnant to everything we hold dear as Americans."[1387] While belated, it was an appropriate and measured response. But that was the scripted Trump, and in typical style, the real Trump emerged but a few days later, saying, "You had a group on one side that was bad. You had a group on the other side that was also very violent. Nobody wants to say that. I'll say it right now."[1388]

The *Washington Post* disclosed that counter-protesters did come armed with clubs and other instruments and did initiate some of the attacks. This does not compare to the behaviour of the white supremacists armed with guns and chanting, "Jews will not replace us" and "Jews are Satan's children."[1389]

While I admire American purism with respect to freedom of speech, I marvel at the protection of hate speech that is so vitriolic and dangerous. *CNN* reported that white nationalist groups like the KKK and neo-Nazis hold "the belief that white people are superior to all other races and should therefore dominate society."[1390] They share the goal of "a white ethno-state where each race lives in a separate nation."[1391] These beliefs are not consistent with the Constitution.

Trump's response was an assurance to the alt-right that he had not abandoned them. There were consequences to his rhetoric. Trump terminated the Strategy & Policy Forum and the Manufacturing Council after numerous corporate leaders resigned, objecting to his comments after Charlottesville. Denise Morrison, CEO of Campbell Soup Company, stated it most eloquently: "Racism and murder are unequivocally reprehensible and are not morally equivalent to anything else that happened in Charlottesville."[1392] I regret that more Americans, especially those who had previously voted for Obama, did not express this sentiment in the voting booth.

Military leaders, who seldom become involved in politics, also censured Trump's comments. As W.J. Hennigan reported in the *Los Angeles Times*, "The members of the Joint Chiefs of Staff—the senior uniformed brass of the Navy, Marine Corps, Army, and Air Force—all posted messages on their official Twitter accounts to denounce the far-right extremists behind Saturday's violence in Charlottesville, Va."[1393]

Sarah Pulliam Bailey from the *Washington Post* advised that while many evangelicals have remained supportive, one pastor, A.R. Bernard, resigned from the evangelical advisory council. Bernard was the pastor for the "Christian Cultural Center, which claims 37,000 in membership [and] has been described by the New York Times as the largest evangelical church in New York City."[1394] He sent out a public statement on Twitter saying, "It became obvious that there was a deepening conflict in values between myself and the administration."[1395] It troubles me that more evangelicals have not reached the same conclusion. Not only has Trump ignored those who did not vote for him, he has ignored some of those who did and has pandered to the alt-right base.

While things usually slow down in the summer, that has not been the case with this administration. In fact, the crises and chaos have intensified. The following is a chronological list of additional significant events, each with a brief description.

Russia Investigation

On May 17, 2017, *Mother Jones* revealed that Michael Flynn, former national security adviser who was fired by Trump, had advised the Trump administration team weeks before the inauguration that he was under FBI investigation "for his undisclosed lobbying work on behalf of Turkish interests."[1396] Furthermore, he attended a meeting with Susan Rice, President Barack Obama's national security adviser, asking her to delay a military operation that Turkey would not have supported. He lied about his discussions with the Russian ambassador regarding Obama's sanctions. On "August 9, 2016, Flynn, and his company, the Flynn Intel Group, ink[ed] a $600,000 contract with Inovo BV, a company owned by Ekim Alptekin, a Turkish businessman and ally of President Recep Tayyip Erdogan."[1397]

If Ivanka Trump and Jared Kushner play a role in moderating the president, as perceived by the public, and are so concerned about social issues, why did they express support of Flynn's interest in the national security position in a meeting on November 9, 2016, as reported by *Mother Jones*?[1398] They were aware of his radical ideas and Islamophobia. They were aware of his past behaviours in bucking authority regarding his email server and sharing confidential information. They were aware of the FBI investigation and his lobbying.

Trump's son-in-law, Jared Kushner, was under investigation in the Russian probe. The *Washington Post* reported, "Jared Kushner and Russia's ambassador to Washington discussed the possibility of setting up a secret and secure communications channel between Trump's transition team and the Kremlin, using Russian diplomatic facilities in an apparent move to shield their pre-inauguration discussions from monitoring, according to U.S. officials briefed on intelligence reports."[1399] While it was not necessarily illegal, it certainly raised speculation about the nature of the communication and expressed a decided interest on the part of Trump's team in working with the Russians to defeat Hillary. Trump and his administration have only themselves to blame for the scrutiny and suspicions regarding involvement with Russia because of their lack of transparency and unprecedented actions and views regarding Russia.

Politico advised that Democratic Sen. Richard Blumenthal, a member of the Senate Judiciary Committee, said that "Michael Flynn and Paul Manafort are almost sure to be indicted as a result of Special Counsel Robert Mueller's probe into Russian interference in the 2016 election."[1400] *Politico* also reported that Manafort had been under investigation since 2014 by the FBI for his political consulting with Ukraine, but this investigation "has since been folded into Mueller's investigation and includes a review into Manafort's lobbying work with a variety of pro-Russian clients."[1401] They also reported that Manafort's home was raided by federal agents.

The *New York Times* reported that Roger Stone, longtime confidant to President Trump, confirmed the possible indictment, advising that his lawyers were told this by Manafort's lawyers.[1402]

According to *Newsweek*, "Mueller reportedly asked for the name of the person who represented two Russians with connections to Trump's Miss Universe pageant in Moscow in 2013 during a 2016 meeting attended by Donald Trump Jr."[1403] The *Washington Post* reported that an eighth person was identified who attended the meeting with Donald Trump Jr., Paul Manafort, and Jared Kushner. The meeting was arranged "on the promise that he [Donald Trump Jr.] would be provided damaging information about Democratic candidate Hillary Clinton as part of a Russian government effort to help his father's presidential campaign, according to emails released by Trump Jr. last week."[1404] The eighth person was Ike Kaveladze, who "attended the meeting as a representative of Aras and Emin Agalarov, the father-and-son Russian developers who hosted the Trump-owned Miss Universe pageant in Moscow in 2013."[1405]

Additional disclosures about the Russian investigation in the *Newsweek* article included the following: the establishment of a grand jury, "a search warrant for Facebook accounts linked to Russian operatives that aimed to influence the 2016 presidential election," and investigation into Ivanka's and Jarred Kushner's emails, as well as those from other senior White House aides.[1406]

To date, there is nothing tying President Trump directly to any wrongdoing, but two questions remain. Is Trump guilty of obstruction of justice in the firing of FBI Director James Comey, and was the Trump campaign colluding with the Russians? The false denials from the Trump administration and Trump that there was no contact with Russia during the campaign; the web of relationships with Russians by Trump, his family, and members of his senior team; and Trump's extraordinary admiration of Putin give rise to considerable speculation.

The *Independent* reported that Facebook finally admitted "that thousands of advertisements had been bought by Russia-linked pages… At least 3,000 politically divisive ads were bought by Russia at the time of the presidential campaigns and elections… Facebook believes the entire Russian propaganda effort was seen by 10 million people, and cost just $100,000 (£76,000)."[1407] The *Independent* reported that Sheryl Sandberg, chief operating officer of Facebook, made the following statements: "Things happened on our platform that shouldn't have happened… the company owed the American people an apology over foreign meddling."[1408]

The Pew Research Center reported that "[t]wo-thirds of Facebook users (66%) get news on the site, which amounts to 44% of the general population."[1409] This might have potentially influenced voters in swing states. *CNN* reported that some Russian-linked ads specifically targeted Michigan and Wisconsin, which Trump won by less than one percent.[1410]

Perhaps Trump's obsession with the outcome of the election, even if he was not involved in collusion with the Russians, was because there may have been just cause to question the legitimacy of the election.

Even though the Russians did not manipulate the actual votes, can there be any doubt that some, if not many, voters were influenced by fake news? For example, I saw numerous interviews with former Democrats who voted for Trump based on their conviction that Hillary was going to take away their Second Amendment rights. If Americans had observed this in another country's election, along with voter suppression, gerrymandering, and a winning candidate who made blatantly false statements throughout the campaign, would they view it as legitimate? There is a distinction between the validity of varying perspectives and flagrant lies.

In the meantime, the *Hill* reported that "[t]he Senate Judiciary Committee has launched a probe into a Russian nuclear bribery case, demanding several federal agencies disclose whether they knew the FBI had uncovered the corruption before the Obama administration in 2010 approved a controversial uranium deal with Moscow."[1411] This may be worthy of investigation, but I cannot help but wonder if the Republicans will be as vociferous in their investigation of Niger as they were with the investigation of Benghazi. Will Mueller's special investigation be as vociferous as the fourteen-year Whitewater investigation? Will the Republican investigation on Jarred Kushner's use of personal email be as vociferous as the one on Hillary's personal email server? I doubt it. Some Republicans set very different standards for similar behaviours when the transgressors are Democrats. They seem to be more politically motivated than focused on the truth to address issues and seek preventative measures to improve.

If there were evidence that Trump was guilty of obstructing justice or colluding with the Russians, would the Republicans support impeachment? If the Trump campaign were guilty of collusion with the Russians, would that be cause for nullifying the election? If not, what did Vice President Mike Pence know, and how would that play out if Trump were impeached?

CNN reported that "White House lawyers have begun researching impeachment procedures in an effort to prepare for what officials still believe is a distant possibility."[1412] If Trump and his administration are so confident that the Russian connection is baseless, why the frequent lies and denials regarding meetings and connections with Russians during the campaign? Unlike some Republicans who were plotting Hillary's impeachment if she won, *CNN* reported that Democrats have tried to "calm impeachment talk out of concern it is premature."[1413]

On the other hand, *Business Insider* reported that Bannon warned President Trump of the possibility that he could be removed from office under the 25th Amendment, which "allows the vice president and a majority of the Cabinet to vote the president out of office."[1414] *Vanity Fair* added that, "according to a source, Bannon has told people he thinks Trump has only a 30 percent chance of making it the full term."[1415]

Were that to be the case, Mike Pence would become president. While not bombastic and more disciplined, he has supported and defended the indefensible. I doubt that his policies and positions on trade and international security would be all that different from Trump's. What credibility would Pence have with the international community? How could Pence be trusted any more than Trump? The other consideration is how Trump's base would respond to his removal from office for any reason. During his campaign, Trump warned that if he did not receive the nomination as the Republican candidate that there would be "riots," an invitation to his supporters to riot should he not gain the nomination. During the presidential campaign, Trump and his supporters escalated concern over the election process being "rigged" to make a case that should he lose, the election would be compromised. The *Washington Post* quoted

Roger Stone, confidant to Donald Trump, as stating, "if there's voter fraud, this election will be illegitimate… we will have a constitutional crisis, widespread civil disobedience, and the government will no longer be the government."[1416] Stone added that Trump has "gotta put them on notice that their inauguration will be a rhetorical… bloodbath."[1417] Bannon has declared war on not just the GOP, but the establishment and institutions. I am concerned that should Trump be removed for any reason, his supporters have been indoctrinated to incite violent civil unrest at the very least, with potential for all-out civil war. The argument often used to support the Second Amendment is so that people can defend themselves against a tyrannical government. If Trump were to be removed from office, would his supporters not make this case?

Leaks

Transcripts of Trump's calls with Mexico and Australia were leaked to the *Washington Post* that revealed that Trump's public versions of the calls were misleading. The *Washington Post* reporters disclosed the following points: "Trump seems to acknowledge that his threats to make Mexico pay had left him cornered politically,"[1418] and he asked Peña Nieto to stop saying publicly he would never pay for the wall. Trump said to Peña Nieto, "But you cannot say that to the press. The press is going to go with that and I cannot live with that."[1419]

Similarly, the transcripts of Trump's call to Prime Minister Turnbull of Australia revealed that the call did not demonstrate as positive a relationship between the two nations as his administration portrayed.[1420] Turnbull requested that the US keep its pledge to accept the Syrian refugees and clarified that it was 1,250 refugees, not 2,000 as Trump conveyed. Trump responded, "This is going to kill me. I am the world's greatest person that does not want to let people into the country."[1421] The call lasted twenty-four minutes and, contrary to Trump's denial, near the end of the call he stated, "I have had it. I have been making these calls all day and this is the most unpleasant call all day. Putin was a pleasant call. This is ridiculous."[1422]

After being publicly belittled by Trump on numerous occasions about being weak on pursuing leak investigations, Attorney General Jeff Sessions announced that the administration would intensify these investigations and that they would devote significant "resources to hunt down disclosures that have plagued the Trump administration."[1423] Sessions added, "We respect the important role that the press plays and will give them respect, but it is not unlimited. They cannot place lives at risk with impunity." In rebuttal, the deputy managing editor of the *New York Times*, Matt Purdy, said, "There's a distinction between revelations that make the government uncomfortable and revelations that put lives at risk. We have not published information that endangers lives."[1424]

Afghanistan

On August 21, 2017, Trump announced a major shift from his campaign rhetoric, stating that he would pull out of Afghanistan and calling it a "total disaster."[1425] The *Washington Post* reported that Trump acknowledged the change in direction by agreeing to add troops and stated, "I heard that decisions are much different when you sit behind the desk of the Oval Office."[1426] Republicans generally expressed support, while Democrats were concerned about the lack of specifics. House Minority Leader Nancy Pelosi said, "When President Trump says there will be no ceiling on the number of troops and no timeline for withdrawal, he is declaring an open-ended commitment of American lives with no accountability to the American people."[1427] This may be one of those rare moments when President Trump admits his limitations and listens to the expertise of his advisors. The problem is, he often changes his mind and conveys his thoughts on Twitter.

Newsweek reported the following statement from Trump: "But Kim Jong Un, I respect the fact that I believe he is starting to respect us. I respect that fact very much. Respect that fact."[1428] Trump fantasized that Kim Jong-un was starting to respect him. He has no awareness as to how others perceive him. Kim Jong-un responded by announcing that the North Koreans had conducted the test of a hydrogen bomb on September 3, 2017. I hope that Trump understood Kim Jong-un's message.

Natural Disasters and the Environment

Oliver Milman from the *Guardian* reported that emails had been uncovered from the Trump administration to staff at the US Department of Agriculture requesting to use the phrase "extreme weather" in lieu of "climate change adaption."[1429] This followed the release of a report in March 2017 "by the Medical Society Consortium on Climate and Health, that mapped how climate change threatens the health of people across the United States and how those threats vary by region."[1430] This report, which acknowledged that "most climate scientists agree that humans are causing the planet to warm," also warned that it poses a risk to human health.[1431] The east coast has experienced extreme weather and there has been increased rainfall and flooding across the US, especially in the summer, which "has resulted in the spread of bacterial infections."[1432] The west coast has experienced extreme heat and drought, causing wildfires that pollute the air.[1433] These are but a few of the many threats to our planet and health directly related to the government's refusal to acknowledge the facts.

According to the *Union of Concerned Scientists*, the United States is second only to China in 2011 per capita carbon dioxide emissions from the consumption of energy and contributes 17% of the world's CO_2 emissions.[1434] Even so, the head of the Environmental Protection Agency, Scott Pruitt, announced that he would provide a proposal to rescind the Clean Power Plan, "a regulation on power plants that would have reduced domestic demand for coal and curbed the country's planet-warming emissions."[1435] While the Trump administration purports that this will bring back coal mining jobs, this is unlikely. However, according to the

New York Times, "the country would save $33 billion by not complying with the regulation and rejected the health benefits the Obama administration had calculated from the original rule."[1436] The resultant savings could facilitate the implementation of Trump's proposed tax cuts for corporations and the wealthy.

Trump referred to climate change as a hoax on numerous occasions, as demonstrated in a 2014 tweet: "NBC News just called it the great freeze - coldest weather in years. Is our country still spending money on the GLOBAL WARMING HOAX?"[1437] His actions to date would appear to affirm that he is still of the same view. As reported by Mark Abad in *Business Insider*, when asked if the recent hurricanes "made him rethink his views on climate change,"[1438] Trump responded, "We've had bigger storms than this."[1439]

In the meantime, the US is being ravaged by record-breaking hurricanes on the southeast coast and record-breaking, devastating wildfires on the west coast. On August 25, 2017, Texas and Gulf States braced for "extreme weather" with the landfall of Hurricane Harvey, a Category 4 storm that reached 130 miles per hour, *CNN* reported.[1440] Houston and Louisiana experienced extreme flooding, resulting in a death toll of at least eighty-two people.[1441] Hurricane Irma quickly followed, hitting the Florida coastline on September 10, devastating the Florida Keys and moving north to Naples, Florida, resulting in a death toll of at least sixty-one people.[1442] Hurricane Maria made landfall in Puerto Rico on September 16, 2017 as a Category 4 hurricane, the "strongest storm to hit Puerto Rico in 85 years," with a death toll of at least sixty-four people.[1443]

CNN reported general approval for Trump's handling of Harvey and Irma: "A broad 64% of Americans say they approve of how Trump's government reacted to the recent storms."[1444] The polls for Trump's handling of the aftermath of Maria provide a stark comparison, as reported in the *Washington Post*: "Just 36 percent say the federal government has done enough, while 55 percent say it hasn't."[1445]

Business Insider disclosed that Trump and his administration claimed that Puerto Rico was getting the same level of support but was hampered by the fact that it is an island, as proclaimed by Trump: "The response and recovery effort probably has never been seen for something like this... This is an island surrounded by water, big water, ocean water."[1446]

Some of the differences in the handling of the three hurricanes are as follows.

CNN indicated that the Jones Act was immediately waived after Harvey and Irma but initially was not waived for Puerto Rico on the pretext that "there were enough American ships to do the job."[1447] It took eight days before President Trump waived the Jones Act for Puerto Rico; The act limits shipping by foreign vessels to protect US shipbuilders but also makes "it twice as expensive to ship things from the US mainland to Puerto Rico as it is to ship from any other foreign port in the world."[1448] Lifting the act not only expedited distribution of supplies, but also reduced costs in shipping the supplies. Is there any question that the Jones Act (and perhaps even the financial crisis created by Wall Street) was a contributing factor to the debt load in Puerto Rico?

Trump visited Texas and Florida four days after landfall, but according to an article in the *New York Times*, "six days elapsed after Maria struck Puerto Rico before he had even promised to go there."[1449] He did not visit Puerto Rico until October 3, almost two weeks after the event, according to the *New York Times*.[1450] *NPR* reported that Trump delayed visiting the devastated area because he did not want to create a distraction, saying, "The focus must be life and safety."[1451] Just a reminder that he was highly critical of Obama's response to Hurricane Sandy in 2017, including Obama's delayed visit to the area. He also could not resist the opportunity to comment about the crowds who came out for his visit: "What a crowd, what a turnout."[1452] *Esquire* reported that Trump stated, "But you've thrown our budget a little out of whack. Because we've spent a lot of money on Puerto Rico, but that's fine. We've saved a lot of lives."[1453]

According to Eric Levenson from *CNN*, 31,000 people were dispatched almost immediately to provide relief after hurricane Harvey, and more than 40,000 were provided after Irma, while only 10,000 personnel were provided in Puerto Rico.[1454] Corporate and private donations for Harvey totalled approximately $125 million; for Irma, $222 million; and for Puerto Rico, $8.1 million.[1455]

The *New York Times* posted tweets from FEMA that provided information regarding relief measures dispatched after each hurricane.[1456] It is difficult to provide a comparison of the FEMA tweets because they do not provide comparable information for each hurricane, especially about Maria.

The following is my summary and comparison of the three, based on information provided in the FEMA posts. After Harvey, 11 million meals were distributed; after Irma, 8.1 million (combining North Carolina, Florida, and Alabama); and after Maria, 1.4 million (combining Puerto Rico and the US Virgin Islands). Water distribution for Harvey was 16.8 million; for Irma, 5.5 million; and for Maria, water distribution was not identified.[1457]

The posts for Maria simply identified that two US Navy and nine coast guard ships provided "water, lift, search and rescue and commodities delivery capabilities" and that six commercial barges provided "meals, water, generators, cots and other commodities."[1458]

Several days following Hurricane Maria, Trump expressed his views, not in a public statement, but rather in three successive tweets, as reported by *CNBC*: "Texas & Florida are doing great but Puerto Rico, which was already suffering from broken infrastructure & massive debt, is in deep trouble… It's [*sic*] old electrical grid, which was in terrible shape, was devastated. Much of the Island was destroyed, with billions of dollars… owed to Wall Street and the banks which, sadly, must be dealt with. Food, water and medical are top priorities – and doing well. #FEMA."[1459] He blamed the victims.

CNN reported that the response from acting Homeland Security Secretary Elaine Duke did not reflect the perils facing the people of Puerto Rico. She told reporters, "I am very satisfied… it is really a good news story in terms of our ability to reach people and the limited number of deaths that have taken place in such a devastating hurricane."[1460] It is no wonder that the Puerto Ricans feel it necessary to remind the Trump administration that they are Americans and that they and their relatives on the mainland feel they have been abandoned. Within days, the media was able to access remote areas to report on the devastation; why not the search and rescue teams and FEMA staff?

As of October 13, 2017, *CBS* advised, "Roughly 36 percent of the population still lacks clean drinking water, and almost half have no communication. Three weeks later, 91 percent of the island is still without electricity. And four deaths on the island this week from contaminated water has spread fear."[1461] Paul Ryan visited the island and promised more aid. President Trump changed his tone and stated, "I love the people of Puerto Rico, and we're going to help them."[1462] How is that believable when on October 12, 2017 he tweeted, "We cannot keep FEMA, the Military & the First Responders, who have been amazing (under the most difficult circumstances) in P.R. forever!"[1463]

Mayor Maria Carmen Yulín Cruz told *CBS News*, "Two people died yesterday because there was no diesel in the place where they were… In San Juan, a hospital."[1464] How many more will be found as they reach into the more remote areas? It confounds me that helicopters were not immediately dispatched to the remote regions to provide supplies, FEMA staff, and evacuation for individuals who were at risk.

The people of Puerto Rico were abandoned. In context of Trump's many aspersions on Hispanic people, can there be any doubt that this was operative in his attitude toward Puerto Rico and the relief efforts? Trump has revealed his priorities. Whether athletes stood for the national anthem took precedence over the humanitarian crisis in Puerto Rico.

Wildfires ravaged through the western states, including Oregon, Idaho, Montana, and California, causing devastation and threatening the homes and communities in their paths.[1465] According the AP, and reported by *CNBC*, the California fires in wine country "have killed at least 40 people and destroyed at least 5,700 homes and other structures… roughly 75,000 people were under evacuation orders, down from nearly 100,000 the day before."[1466] Acknowledging the fact that human behaviour is contributing to climate change would require us to change our behaviour rather than have immediate gratification. Unfortunately, it would also negatively impact corporate profit margins.

Las Vegas Massacre

NBC provided details of the Las Vegas Massacre. At the end of a concert on October 1, 2017 in Las Vegas, Stephen Paddock started raining bullets on the dense and unsuspecting crowd from the 32nd floor of the Mandalay Bay Resort and Casino. This resulted in the worst shooting massacre in the history of the US. As of this writing, there were fifty-eight dead and over five hundred wounded. When the police finally gained entrance to the hotel room, they found the shooter dead. Paddock's motive is enigmatic, but the shooting appears to have been meticulously planned.[1467] What is this, if not domestic terrorism? The heroic actions of many Americans in the crossfire as well as first responders were a testament of extraordinary bravery and compassion. Where there is compassion, there is hope.

According to the *Hill*, Bill O'Reilly said of the massacre, "This is the price of freedom… Violent nuts are allowed to roam free until they do damage, no matter how threatening they are."[1468] What an obtuse statement from someone who allegedly fabricated experiences as a war correspondent during the conflict in the Falklands. Many democratic countries have the right to gun ownership but do not pay the same human costs that the US does. A ban on Muslims is not going to keep Americans safe, nor is a wall. How does gun ownership, in absence of controls, keep Americans safe?

In a meeting with military leaders on October 5, 2017, Trump remonstrated the group by stating, "Moving forward, I also expect you to provide me with a broad range of military options, when needed, at a much faster pace. I know that government bureaucracy is slow, but I am depending on you to overcome the obstacles of bureaucracy," as reported by Jeff Mason of *Reuters*. In that same meeting, Trump reiterated that the goal for North Korea is denuclearization, and that this "lived up to the spirit of an agreement."[1469] Trump ended the photo op with a mysterious statement: "You guys know what this represents?... Maybe it's the calm before the storm, "[1470] refusing to provide an explanation.

With Trump, there has been no calm. He creates chaos that serves as a screen to create confusion and anxiety, deflecting the media and the public from the real issues and what he is doing. Nothing matters except what Trump wants. Trump controls the chaos.

CHAPTER FIFTEEN

Trump's Legacy: A Democracy Governed By The People?

The receptivity of the masses is very limited, their intelligence is small, but their power of forgetting is enormous. In consequence of these facts, all effective propaganda must be limited to a very few points and must harp on these in slogans until the last member of the public understands what you want him to understand by your slogan.[1471]
— *Adolf Hitler*

The Trumping of America throughout the 2016 election created conditions that have serious long-term implications for the world. Brexit and Trump's victory in the United States were like canaries in a mine; they were wakeup calls showing that this populist movement could threaten any democracy. We are all vulnerable unless we take measures to address the conditions that create discontent.

Awareness, particularly for the free world, may be the positive outcome of these two significant and historical events. The American people chose change over any other priority. The advantage for those democracies that have not yet been subject to a populist uprising is the ability to assess the impact of Brexit and a Trump presidency, as well as international events, including Russian intervention.

In Canada, Kevin O'Leary contemplated running for prime minister with a platform similar to Trump's. He is a conservative Canadian entrepreneur best known as one of the investors on the reality television show *Shark Tank*. On January 18, 2017, Kevin O'Leary announced his bid to run for the leadership of the Conservative Party in Canada, *CBC* reported.[1472] According to the *Star*, O'Leary praised "King Trump" and would have voted for him. He also recognized that a Trump-style campaign that was unfavourable to multiculturalism would not fly in Canada. O'Leary's focus would be on jobs. O'Leary also conveyed that he would make a better negotiator to protect Canada's interests in dealing with Trump. These may appear to be alluring tenets to many Canadians, but let us not forget what his values and attitudes really are. He attempted to downplay former controversial statements by stating, "I wasn't making policy, I wasn't running as a candidate to govern the country. There's a difference. People aren't stupid in Canada, they get it."[1473]

On the November 18, 2011 episode of the *Lang and O'Leary Exchange*, O'Leary said, "Here's the right thing to do: Elect me as prime minister for fifteen minutes. I will make unions illegal. Anybody who remains a union member will be thrown in jail."[1474] He described unions as 'evil' and suggested that without them, workers would get market salaries higher than what the union negotiates. This has not proven to be the case, as salaries remained flat while corporations were making record profits in the past several years. Unions are not perfect, but they are a buffer for working people.

Time reported O'Leary's comment that the world's eighty-five richest people are equal to the wealth of the 3.5 billion poorest. He said, "Of course I applaud it. What could be wrong with this?"[1475] He went on to explain that this condition is a great motivator for people "to pull themselves up by their bootstraps and make something of their lives."[1476] He was also against raising taxes on the wealthy.[1477]

Arlene Dickinson is the Canadian CEO of Venture Communications, a self-made millionaire who appeared with Kevin O'Leary on *Dragon's Den*, the Canadian version of *Shark Tank*. Unlike Donald Trump, who now realizes the presidency "involves heart, whereas in business most things don't involve heart,"[1478] Dickinson has a conviction that heart is needed in both politics and business. She commented, "After thirty years of being an entrepreneur, I've learned that business is about people… Business is personal."[1479]

Of O'Leary, she stated, "Kevin's total lack of empathy toward these Canadians who put their heart and soul on the line, I can assure you, was genuine… Kevin is … intelligent and a savvy self-promoter. But at his core, he's an opportunist. He doesn't do anything that doesn't offer a path to power, fame, or fortune — and that should have us all afraid… he represents capitalism in its very worst form — a soulless system that bases decisions solely on dollars and cents, profit, and margin."[1480] Thankfully, due to his lack of support, and a movement to prevent his nomination, O'Leary withdrew his candidacy for leadership of the Conservative Party in late April 2017. Hopefully this is a rejection of a Trump-style leadership in Canada. I include this information to demonstrate the similarities in the thinking of these nationalistic, populist leaders and the seduction of their strategies based on personal success. The electorate in democratic countries around the world will face choices of this nature during the next few years as populist leaders gain increasing approval.

Dickinson's comments about corporate culture are also noteworthy. Trump supporters expressed that they wanted a strong leader, with successful business experience, that would take on the world and negotiate for America first. It appears that it does not matter if this is based on false information, bullying, and threats. Trump's business practices were well known prior to the election. Often, the media and supporters excused his behaviour because he was from the corporate world and new to politics. Why are these practices even acceptable in the corporate culture?

What is great about America is the Declaration of Independence, which proclaims "that all men are created equal, that they are endowed by their Creator with certain unalienable Rights, that among these are Life, Liberty and the pursuit of Happiness."[1481]

What is great about America is the Constitution, free exercise of religion, freedom of speech, freedom of the press, the right to peaceful assembly, and the right to petition for a governmental redress of grievances.[1482]

What is great about America is the sentiment encrypted on the Statue of Liberty: "Give me your tired, your poor, your huddled masses yearning to breathe free, the wretched refuse of your teeming shore. Send these, the homeless, tempest-tost to me, I lift my lamp beside the golden door!"[1483]

Most Americans subscribe to these values and beliefs. However, what the world has witnessed in the past year demonstrates that many Americans do not. Trump's victory is viewed as a reflection of the American people.

The Trump campaign and presidency have been rife with bullying, hostility, and anger. This is being ignored or endorsed by some Americans, many of whom are parents. As so eloquently stated in the title of a poem by Dorothy Law Nolte, "Children learn what they live."[1484] I am frightened for our future and our children. Research from National Voices for Quality Education and Enlightenment (NVEE) demonstrates that many children are already struggling with pain from neglect or abuse as well as the wounds of poverty: "3.3 million children [in the US] witness domestic violence in their homes each year."[1485] UNICEF found that in the US, the richest country in the world, "30 percent of children reportedly live in poverty, significantly above the 20 percent global average."[1486]

According to the NVEE website, in 2016, "86% of students said, 'other kids picking on them, making fun of them or bullying them' causes teenagers to turn to lethal violence in schools."[1487]

Children are committing suicide over being bullied. Disenfranchised and confused youth are joining cults like ISIS because they don't feel as if they belong anywhere. Trump's behaviour permits this bullying, physical violence, and hate.

CNN reported that hate crimes have soared since the election. Children are baiting Hispanic children, yelling, "build that wall";[1488] *BuzzFeed* added that young people are taunting them with "white power";[1489] graffiti promoting white supremacist intimidation is being written in public places; and people are being threatened and even physically attacked. The *Washington Post* disclosed that in one case, according to his family, a boy of mixed race was hung by a rope.[1490] These are simply a few examples of incidents reported in numerous articles. What is happening that is unreported?

I am concerned for the children who are perpetrating hate crimes, for they may be even more damaged than the victims of their hate. There have also been isolated attacks on Trump supporters, and this is equally reprehensible.

I agree with Melania Trump in her statement at the UN luncheon on September 20, 2017, reported by *Politico*: "We must teach each child the values of empathy and communication that are at the core of the kindness, mindfulness, integrity and leadership which can only be taught by example… By our own example, we must teach children to be good stewards of the world they will inherit."[1491] It is unfortunate that her husband, the president of the United States, the most powerful person in the world, fails to provide this example.

Sexual Harassment Cases

Misogyny was a recurrent issue throughout the campaign, yet Trump was elected to the most powerful position in the world amid allegations of sexual harassment and demonstrated predatory and lewd behaviour. Similar allegations levied against celebrities, two of whom were cohorts of Trump's, have occurred following Trump's election and resulted in very different outcomes.

Two reporters from the *New York Times*, Jodi Kantor and Megan Twohey, broke a story on October 5, 2017 with the headline, "Harvey Weinstein Paid Off Sexual Harassment Accusers for Decades."[1492] Since then, numerous women have come forward with additional allegations.[1493] Weinstein was a major donor to the Democratic Party, and several Democrats pledged to donate Weinstein's contributions to women's charities. According to Sophie Tatum of *CNN*, "In the wake of the report, the Republican National Committee released a statement calling on Democrats and the DNC to return his [Weinstein's] donations."[1494] Perhaps the fact that some Democrats had already done so inspired this call from the Republicans. The media and Republicans levied substantial criticism because it took five days for Hillary and Obama to disavow Weinstein, who had been a steadfast supporter of both.[1495] Each made a public statement five days after the first media report.

Compare this to the reaction the year before when Roger Ailes resigned on July 21, 2016 following an investigation on sexual abuse. This was quickly followed by the firing of Bill O'Reilly under similar circumstances. Trump supported both, and not only did he refuse to criticize their behaviour, he said they did 'nothing wrong.' He expressed sadness about what happened to Ailes and O'Reilly, not the victims. I could find no evidence of an outcry from Republicans denouncing their behaviour. Fox News renewed O'Reilly's contract, knowing there had been settlements for sexual harassment. Rogers Ailes, former CEO of Fox News, died on May 18, 2017 at the age of seventy-seven. He had built a media empire that was successful in influencing the views of the right and increasing support for Republicans in elections, sometimes based on 'fake news.' Since Ailes's resignation, there have been more revelations regarding the culture at Fox News and the proliferation of 'fake news.' I suspect that the Murdochs, Fox Network, Roger Ailes, and Bill O'Reilly made significant donations to Republicans and the GOP. Are Republicans going to disavow Ailes and O'Reilly? It has been fifteen months, not five days. Are they going to return any political contributions?

The sexual harassment issues followed Trump into the White House. Jessica Garrison broke the story to *BuzzFeed* that Summer Zervos, a former contestant of the *Apprentice* and one of the women who alleged sexual harassment by Donald Trump during the campaign, is suing for defamation.[1496] Several women came forward after the release of the *Access Hollywood* tape, outraged that Trump had dismissed it as locker room talk and told Anderson Cooper during a debate that he never behaved that way. The suit is based on Trump's response to the allegations, which characterized them as lies. Zervos's lawyer, Gloria Allred, filed a subpoena for files from the Trump campaign.[1497] What, if anything, will come of this lawsuit is unknown.

These cases are often hard to prove; yet there are nineteen women who have made allegations consistent with Trump's words in the *Access Hollywood* video.

During the same period, a group called Ultraviolet arranged a demonstration of the *Access Hollywood* videotape on a screen "10-by-16 feet to air the footage — which includes sound and subtitles — in front of the Washington Monument."[1498] The tape demonstrated very lewd behaviour on the part of Donald Trump and included an acknowledgement on his part of sexual assault in the following quote: "I've gotta use some Tic Tacs, just in case I start kissing her […] You know I'm automatically attracted to beautiful — I just start kissing them. It's like a magnet. Just kiss. I don't even wait […] And when you're a star they let you do it. You can do anything. Grab them by the pussy. You can do anything."[1499] His denials in the face of evidence incited the women to come forward.

In 1998, while Bill Clinton was testifying about his relationship with Lewinsky, Trump contemplated how his relationships with women would transpire were he to be president. "Can you imagine how controversial I'd be? You think about him with the women — how about me with the women? Can you imagine."[1500] Is that not also an admission of inappropriate behaviour?

Presidents are not exempt from legal actions that pre-date their taking office. It is interesting to note that the Paula Jones lawsuit with Bill Clinton resulted in the Supreme Court providing the case law that a president is not exempt from legal actions that occurred before taking office and that they can go forward while the president is in office. The irony continues. Kellyanne Conway's husband, George Conway III, wrote the Supreme Court brief for the Paula Jones case.[1501] It would be karma should a case come forward with irrefutable proof of sexual harassment in which Trump were found guilty because of a Supreme Court decision written by Kellyanne's husband.

Sexual harassment and abuse are endemic. I would be surprised if there is a single woman who has not been subjected to this kind of behaviour at some point in her life. I was the victim of sexual harassment. My job required considerable travel, and I remember waiting for a full elevator to ensure that I would not encounter solicitation while alone at a hotel. I also ate in my room to avoid being accosted because of assumptions about unaccompanied women. There were few women in management roles in the late 1970s and early 1980s. I often had to meet with CEOs and managers, usually men, in out-of-town meetings at hotel conference rooms and restaurants. I also received numerous calls from men. One time, a hotel receptionist asked me what it was that I did. She then reminded me that this was a family hotel! There are many more examples, but I, fortunately, was never in a position that I could not rebuff the inappropriate behaviour.

Women and men who excuse this kind of behaviour give permission to those who engage in it, perpetuating it. Women like Gretchen Carlson, who have been brave enough to speak out publicly, are changing the dynamics. The *Huffington Post* reported that Carlson made the following comment: "What we're seeing happening now with the Harvey Weinstein revelations, to me this is the watershed moment… This is the tipping point I've been working so hard for over the last 15 months. People are finally saying 'enough.'"[1502] I hope that she is right, but I have doubts. Trump was elected president despite all the public information regarding his own statements about women and his behaviour. *CNN* reported on a poll conducted by Monmouth University, which found that "72% of female Trump approvers say they will never strip their support, vs. only 54% of male Trump approvers."[1503] This is condoning the behaviour at the very least. What lesson does this provide to their children, male and female? The cycle is being perpetuated.

Constitutional Issues

Colin Kaepernick started a ritual of refusing to stand during the national anthem at the start of NFL games to protest the "oppression of blacks and people of color."[1504] He changed from sitting to kneeling because the former was being perceived by some as disrespectful to the men who serve their country. Kneeling is a sign of reverence, used when greeting royalty, proposing marriage, and attending church. In February of 2017, Kaepernick donated $100,000 to black veterans.[1505] Disrespect of the troops was clearly not his intention.

More NFL players started this practice in reaction to Trump's comments following Charlottesville and his defense of white supremacists. *CNN* reported that in a rally in Alabama on September 23, 2017, Trump told the owners, "Get that son of a b[#]tch off the field right now, he's fired. He's fired!"[1506] The NFL responded with more players and even owners joining the protest. Trump was preoccupied with the issue, shooting off tweets at a rapid pace. The gist of the tweets is captured in the following quote: "If NFL fans refuse to go to games until players stop disrespecting our Flag & Country, you will see change take place fast. Fire or suspend."[1507] Trump shamelessly preyed on the emotions of the American people, invoking national pride in an attempt to reframe the players' protest against systemic racism as an expression of disrespect for the troops. He tried bullying the owners by beseeching spectators to refuse to attend games, and according to *Business Insider*, it worked; attendance was down.[1508]

Fans have the right to express their displeasure and to refuse to attend games if they perceive the protest as disrespect. However, kneeling and exercising civil rights is an homage to those who have served to protect those freedoms, not a denial of them. Owners and the NFL have the right to establish what is acceptable behaviour for players during games. They chose not to, and instead, some owners joined in the protest. The NFL and the players are working on a plan to move from protests to action to address the issues of racial inequity, but according to the NFL, it "has no plans to mandate players stand for the national anthem."[1509] Trump does not accept the right of the NFL to choose and responded, "The NFL has decided that it will not force players to stand for the playing of our National Anthem. Total disrespect for our great country!"[1510]

As a private citizen, Trump would be free to express his views. As President of the United States, the head of the government, he was defying the Constitution and the Supreme Court. In Chapter 6, I detailed the decision of the Supreme Court regarding coerced patriotism. In summary, they determined that "patriotic ceremonies… must be 'voluntary.'"[1511] Furthermore, they determined that "coerced patriotism" was dangerous.[1512] As president, Trump had a responsibility to uphold the Constitution and leave it to the people. Instead, he engendered the anti-protest movement and financially injured a private business, a clear abuse of power. Which is more disrespectful to the nation, defying the Constitution and threatening democracy or kneeling for the national anthem?

This is a core issue that strikes at the deepest emotions for each side. I cannot possibly fully understand either because I am not a person of colour, I have only one immediate family member in the military, and I have never suffered the loss of a family member serving their country. However, I do think it is unfortunate that those who denounce the practice of kneeling are unable to appreciate that this act of protest still accords reverence to the troops. That is what America is all about.

It is relevant to highlight that Trump's preoccupation with the NFL took place immediately following Hurricane Maria, deflecting attention away from the devastation and plight of the people of Puerto Rico who were struggling with a humanitarian crisis, which persisted a month after the hurricane.

On October 11, 2017, Trump tweeted, "With all of the Fake News coming out of NBC and the Networks, at what point is it appropriate to challenge their License? Bad for country!"[1513] This was, according to Matthew Yglesias from *Vox,* in response to two reports from *NBC* that Trump objected to. NBC reported that Tillerson called Trump a "f[##]ing moron," purportedly because of Trump's request to "increase the size of the US nuclear arsenal tenfold."[1514] Yglesias concluded, "Such an increase would be financially costly, break international law, surely lead to more nuclear proliferation, and accomplish nothing, since the US already has plenty of nukes to deter anyone. It was, in short, pretty moronic."[1515] While many considered this an empty threat, I wonder if the Russian media had the same reaction when Putin started to convince the people that the media was corrupt and then slowly took over the media. The many examples of Trump's attempts to discredit the media are evidence that he does not respect, and openly defies, the freedom of the press, a constitutional protection for democracy.

Conflicts of Interest and Personal Gain

In April 2017, *BBC* provided a detailed list of conflicts of interest for the Trump presidency, including holdings in several countries such as Argentina, Brazil, Israel, Japan, the Philippines, and Taiwan, to mention a few.[1516] The following are some examples of the conflicts of interest reported by *BBC*.

"Eric Trump told *Forbes* in March he may share quarterly reports with his father, despite a statement that they would not discuss business or government with each other. Shortly after, *ProPublica* reported Mr. Trump could draw money from the trust at any time, without external disclosure."[1517] I have previously questioned whether it was reasonable to believe that the family would not discuss business. It isn't.

In Chapter 6, I raised the issue of the lease agreement in Trump's Washington hotel and the lack of a disposition in the media. The *BBC* article advised that the Trumps were compliant with the lease agreement of the Old Post Office building because "the hotel had been placed in a revocable trust, which he would see no personal benefit from during his term in office."[1518] The problem is that he will benefit when he leaves office. "Meanwhile, the hotel has already been pitched to foreign diplomats as a place to stay while in Washington, raising concerns that foreign governments could see booking expensive rooms at the Trump International as a way to gain favour with the Trump administration."[1519]

BBC reported, "On 3 November, the National Labor Relations Board (NLRB) ruled that Trump International Hotel Las Vegas – which Trump co-owns – broke the law by refusing to negotiate with a hotel workers' union."[1520] According to the article, Trump is responsible for appointments on the NLRB, has already named the acting chair, and will be able to make appointments for two vacant positions on the board.[1521]

The Trump transition team reported that the president sold all his stocks in June 2016; however, *BBC* advised that "the campaign did not furnish proof nor provide an updated list of Mr Trump's investments."[1522] Similar to my previously-stated concerns, *BBC* raised the issue of Trump's interference with companies and the effect on their stocks, pointing out that if he still owns stocks in those companies, he can make money buying and selling after sending tweets that cause swings in the market.[1523]

Further evidence of conflicts of interest and Trump's proclivity for profiting from the presidency includes the rent dispute between Trump Tower and the Secret Service. According to Ed Mazza, reporter with the *Huffington Post*, the Trump administration released the following statement: "After much consideration, it was mutually determined that it would be more cost effective and logistically practical for the Secret Service to lease space elsewhere."[1524] According to the *Huffington Post*, Trump's lavish lifestyle poses a challenge to the Secret Service's budget. For example, the military lease space in Trump Tower cost $130,000 a month. The rent for the Secret Service must have been at least comparable. It has also been reported that the Secret Service spent $35,000 just on golf cart rentals at Trump's Mar-a-Lago resort in Florida during the first three months of his administration.[1525] This is direct revenue for the Trump Corporation.

The *Palm Beach Post* reported that Trump lost an appeal to have his taxes reduced at his golf club in Jupiter, Florida.[1526] Once again, Trump displayed his greed and steadfast resolution not to pay his fair share of taxes. What was most egregious was that the hard-earned tax dollars paid by Americans were being frivolously wasted on this litigation.

CNN reported that the Trump re-election campaign is spending one out of every ten dollars donated to the campaign on legal fees, including Donald Jr.'s.[1527] Reporter Jeremy Diamond hypothesized that the unprecedented early fundraising for the 2020 campaign may be related to the need for legal fees and questioned whether there is full disclosure to donors as to how the money is being used.[1528]

Leadership

The qualifications of Trump's appointments, firings, and resignations confirm concerns expressed during the campaign by former staff and *Apprentice* candidates regarding his leadership style.

On October 17, 2017, *CNN* disclosed that ten nominees had withdrawn from administration jobs offered by Trump. While this does not initially appear unusual when compared to other presidents, it is when considering the number of confirmed positions: "Trump has 174 confirmed nominees; Obama, former President George W. Bush, and former President Bill Clinton all had well over 300 at this point in their first term."[1529] Trump provided the rationale that he will not be filling many of the positions because they are not needed. According to *FactCheck*, the Trump Corporation has approximately 22,500 employees,[1530] and *Forbes* estimated Trump's net worth at 3.1 billion in 2017.[1531] According to *Inside Gov*, the total projected spending budget for the federal government is approximately $3.65 trillion.[1532] I don't think Trump understands the complexity or the breadth, depth, and scope of government.

In addition to the limitations in Trump's leadership, he does not know how to delegate. While he says he has all the answers and knows how to fix problems, evidence is to the contrary. Trump has failed to provide effective leadership. There is a lack of clarity in expectations and a lack of cogent knowledge on the issues. Instead of meaningful involvement to support efforts to advance his agenda, Trump abdicates responsibility by transferring it to Congress or his administration for resolution. He sabotages their efforts, changes his mind, and then threatens, bullies, and blames others when there is no resolution.

The 'repeal and replace' plan for Obamacare is an example. After three failed Republican attempts endorsed by Trump, which did not include his promises for retention of pre-existing conditions and protected benefits, nor were they going to be cheaper for the most vulnerable, he demanded a bipartisan plan. Two have been put forward, and the last one he endorsed and then backed off of the next day, according to the *Washington Post*.[1533]

He is mercurial and does not comprehend the issues. There is no continuity with the changeover of staff. They spend an enormous amount of time on damage control, thanks to the president. They are beleaguered and have no confidence that he will have their backs, though he demands total loyalty. This is a dangerous condition for an administration that is involved in such critical decision-making.

Character

Four green beret soldiers lost their lives in a surprise attack in Niger on October 4, 2017: Sgt. La David T. Johnson, Staff Sgt. Bryan Black, Staff Sgt. Jeremiah W. Johnson, and Staff Sgt. Dustin Wright.[1534] The sacrifice of life in service of one's county is one of the most solemn events for families, yet somehow, Trump was able to make it all about him.

The *Star* reported that during a press conference on October 16, 2017, a reporter asked why they had heard nothing from the president about the Niger attack, as it had been twelve days.[1535] Trump responded, "I felt very, very badly about that. I always feel badly. It's the toughest -- the toughest calls I have to make are the calls where this happens. Soldiers are killed. It's a very difficult thing. Now, it gets to a point where, you know, you make four or five of them in one day."[1536] He did not start out by expressing his condolences to the family for their loss and his appreciation for their sacrifice; his address was about how he felt. How can making condolence calls be compared to the lifetime a wife and children will spend without their spouse and father? He did not answer the question about why it took twelve days before he mentioned the incident in Niger.

While his defenders accused the media and Congresswoman Frederica Wilson of politicizing the issue, it was Trump who did this. Trump responded that he had written letters that would be sent out and that he would make phone calls to the families. But then he said, "So the traditional way -- if you look at President Obama and other presidents, most of them didn't make calls. A lot of them didn't make calls. I like to call when it's appropriate, when I think I am able to do it."[1537] In a follow-up question he stated, "All I can do -- all I can do is ask my generals. Other -- other presidents did not call, they'd write letters. And some presidents didn't do anything."[1538] The reference to generals was later clarified when in an interview with Fox, Trump remarked, "'you could ask Gen. Kelly, did he get a call from Obama?'"[1539]

The *Hill* confirmed that Kelly did not get a call, but "Obama hosted Kelly at a breakfast for Gold Star families about six months after his son died."[1540] My question was, would it be Gen. Kelly or his son's wife, if he had one, who would have received such a call? After searching, I could only find two references in the media that begged this question. Amy Davidson Sorkin from the *New Yorker* advised that Kelly's son did have a wife, Heather.[1541] But that is hardly the point. Again, Trump is responsible for politicizing the issue and taking the focus away from the families who lost loved ones. According to *CNN*, he also brought General Kelly, who is known for keeping his personal loss a private matter, into the discussion.[1542] Compounding this awkward situation for Kelly, according to the *CNN* transcript, Sarah Huckabee Sanders proclaimed in a press conference, "I think General Kelly is disgusted by the way that this has been politicized, and that the focus has become on the process and not the fact that American lives were lost. I think he's disgusted and frustrated by that."[1543]

PolitiFact reported that "presidential dealings with soldiers' families are traditionally kept private out of respect."[1544] In other words, past presidents did not make spectacles of these dealings or politicize them. And while past presidents did not necessarily call a family member in every case, Trump misrepresented the facts when he implied that he did more than other presidents or that Obama did not make calls to families.[1545]

Trump did follow up, at least with some, in making condolence calls. Congresswoman Frederica Wilson was in the car with her friend Myeshia Johnson, the widow of Sgt. La David Johnson, when the latter received a call from Trump on speakerphone. *Business Insider* reported that, according to the congresswoman, Trump said, "He knew what he signed up for, but when it happens, it hurts anyway."[1546] The *New York Times* reported that Congresswoman Wilson claimed that this upset Myeshia Johnson. Wilson said of the incident, "When she got off the phone, she said, 'He didn't even know his name. He kept calling him, "Your guy"'… And that was devastating to her."[1547] Trump denied the report of the congresswoman and claimed that he had evidence to the contrary, while the congresswoman stood by her account.[1548] Sgt. Johnson's mother verified the congresswoman's account. The press secretary for the White House acknowledged that there was no tape of the call but that "Ms. Wilson had willfully mischaracterized the spirit of the conversation."[1549] If that is how the family experienced it, then it was not mischaracterized.

Another woman widowed as a result of the Niger attack, Whitney Hunter, related her experience in an interview on CNN and conveyed that although she had been advised she would receive a call from the president, she did not. While she did receive a certificate, she did not receive a personalized letter. Her comments were as follows:

> I don't like that I was told that I would receive the phone call, but then I never did... my husband died for our country. He died for our nation in defense of our nation. And I don't want that to have been in vain or to have been -- I don't want it to be taken for granted. And I don't have anything negative to say about our president, but I do know the difference between right and wrong. And whenever you say you're going to do something, you're supposed to do it.[1550]

In response to a question about Trump's alleged comments during the condolence call to Myeshia Johnson, Hunter responded, "You spend every day knowing what you signed up for. But whenever you are dealing with the tremendous amount of grief that me and any other fellow widow is [sic] experiencing right now, that's not something I think anyone, whether a family member or anybody has – it's not their position to say that."[1551]

Following continuing media coverage on the matter, General Kelly made a rare public statement. In the video accompanying a *New York Times* article, Kelly made a powerful and moving speech about the processes when they lose a soldier. He said, "Typically, the only phone calls a family receives are the most important phone calls they could imagine, and that is from their buddies."[1552] In the transcript provided in the *New York Times*, Kelly reported that he recommended the president not make the calls. He advised the president that Obama did not call his family, that some presidents call, and that all send letters. In response to President Trump's question as to what to say, Kelly advised the following:

> Let me tell you what my best friend, Joe Dunford, told me — because he was my casualty officer. He said, Kel, he was doing exactly what he wanted to do when he was killed. He knew what he was getting into by joining that 1 percent. He knew what the possibilities were because we're at war. And when he died, in the four cases we're talking about, Niger, and my son's case in Afghanistan — when he died, he was surrounded by the best men on this Earth: his friends. That's what the President tried to say to four families the other day.[1553]

Kelly added, "And he was where he wanted to be, exactly where he wanted to be, with exactly the people he wanted to be with when his life was taken."[1554] Even if that were true, is there any widow who, in the grief of her loss, wants to hear that her husband would rather be with his comrades than his wife and children?

Kelly then soundly criticized Congresswoman Wilson with the following statements: "It stuns me that a member of Congress would have listened in on that conversation. Absolutely stuns me. And I thought at least that was sacred."[1555] In fact, Kelly was further politicizing the issue by assigning presumptive motives to the congresswoman and casting aspersions on her. The fact is, had Trump simply made a statement that he regretted that his words of condolence had not been received in the way he intended, adding that he and the country appreciated the sacrifice and service of her husband, using his name, the controversy would have been over.

I agree with everything Kelly said but for his criticism of the congresswoman and his reference to her as "this woman." He said that Trump "tried" to convey the words that Kelly shared, but was that a quote from Trump, or had Trump adapted it? That may be consoling to someone in the military, but as affirmed by Whitney Hunter, this is not necessarily consoling to some grieving widows. I don't doubt that Trump was well-intentioned, but if this is a message commonly used, then Trump and those who give condolences need to be made aware of how they may be received by those who have suffered a loss and consult Gold Star families in an effort to understand what is and is not helpful in these circumstances. Hopefully, this will bring about changes to avoid future misunderstandings, and perhaps the public will be more educated on the process and the experiences of Gold Star families.

Whether or not there is validity to the insinuation that the congresswoman hates Trump and used this for political expedience is conjecture. The congresswoman is a friend of the family and was reacting as such. Her having heard the phone call was not nefarious. According to the *New York Times*, she was in the limousine with the slain soldier's family, waiting for the plane bringing back the remains of Sgt. Johnson, when the call was taken on speakerphone.[1556] I daresay Sgt. Johnson's mother was interested in hearing the call. It was Donald Trump that politicized the situation, not Congresswoman Wilson.

I empathize with Kelly, because whether he did this of his own volition or was urged to by Trump, it was Trump who had thrust him into the fray in the first place. But Kelly did not acknowledge Trump's transgressions in politicizing the situation, nor did his statement consider Trump's reprehensible statements about John McCain and the Khans. Had this latest issue been the only insensitive moment, it would not have had traction.

There have been numerous occasions in which members of Trump's administration have made public statements in praise of Trump and reaffirmed that they are either not being fired or are not quitting following a controversy. *Business Insider* reported that following continuing reports that "the chief of staff has repeatedly clashed with President Donald Trump and was only staying in his job out of a sense of duty," General Kelly had a press conference in which he said he was not "quitting" or being "fired."[1557] Yet according to *Reuters*, "reports of both Kelly's and the president's frustrations have persisted, sparking continued speculation of pending shakeups."[1558] *Reuters* added that sources familiar with the White House have said that "Trump has confided to friends that he has felt constrained by some of Kelly's moves to limit access to him and some administration officials have privately chafed at the restrictions as well."[1559]

Regarding the ongoing criticism of the congresswoman, I have the following comments. In his speech, Kelly called her an "empty barrel" and castigated her for taking credit for raising $20 million for the new FBI building.[1560] She said nothing in her speech regarding raising money; she was not a congresswoman when the money was raised. She acknowledged the bipartisan efforts in obtaining approval to name the building after the fallen FBI agents before its opening, a process that usually takes one year. She recognized the families and mentioned the names of the two FBI agents, and she recognized the Director of the FBI, James Comey. She did discuss her role in expediting approval in order to name the building in time for the scheduled opening, but she acknowledged those who accomplished it. Afterwards, she requested that all people who work in law enforcement and first responders "stand up so that we can applaud you for what you do — we are proud of you — for your courage. Thank you."[1561] She then provided a lengthy and detailed tribute to the two slain agents, discussing the events of their tragic deaths, her appreciation of their sacrifice, and the courage and bravery of the FBI.[1562]

Having watched the entire video, I am unclear as to why General Kelly and his colleagues would have felt "stunned" and "appalled."[1563] But there is no right or wrong when it comes to feelings. His portrayal of the incident, however, was inaccurate. I admired General Kelly, and the first half of his speech was eloquent and impactful. The second half sounded like a page from Trump's playbook. Clearly, the Trump administration continues to escalate the controversy, politicize it by casting unwarranted aspersions based on false information, and take the focus away from the Gold Star families. I expected better from Gen. Kelly, and contrary to my previous belief that he was a buffer, I now have grave reservations.

Lastly, Wilson tried to put an end to the matter. On October 18, 2017, she posted a public statement which included the following sentiment: "The loved ones Sgt. Johnson leaves behind are my constituents and my job now is to do all that I can to help them heal. I'll save the bully pulpit for the necessary task of uncovering the circumstances surrounding the ambush and working to help ensure that our soldiers have all the resources and support that they need while putting their lives on the line to keep others safe."[1564] She felt it necessary to respond and correct the misrepresentation of her in Kelly's press conference.

Following reports that he was frustrated and considering quitting, Tillerson had a press conference. In the transcript posted on *Politico*, he too declared that he was not considering leaving his post, and in the question period refused to confirm or deny the "moron" reference. Tom Price and Jeff Sessions had similar press conferences declaring their intention to stay in their positions following controversy with Trump.[1565,1566] These reaffirmations seem to be unprecedented, as I do not recall anything similar in another administration. This may be related to Trump's narcissism and his need to spin a positive image, despite the facts.

Even if Trump was well-intentioned, his condolences were upsetting to the family. He is the president of the United States and sends Americans into war. He needs to understand the implications of that when making those decisions. He cannot distance himself from the ramifications or deny his responsibility to express appreciation for that sacrifice on behalf of the American people. It doesn't matter how he felt or what other presidents did. His focus should have been on the sacrifice made by the families—that and nothing more.

This one incident revealed much about Trump's character: in particular, his extreme narcissism, tendency to blame others, capacity for lying, incapacity to empathize, ignorance, lack of comprehension, unwillingness to accept responsibility, habit of using people for political gain, and deflection.

This whole debacle deflected not only from the families who suffered an unimaginable loss, but also the pertinent issue about the lengthy silence over the attack in Niger. Many questions are outstanding. According to *CNN,* "The Defense Department is conducting an initial review of the mission in Niger and the ambush by 50 ISIS-affiliated fighters that left four US soldiers dead and two wounded."[1567] The *Hill* provided Congresswoman Wilson's proclamation: "This is [Trump's] Benghazi, and that is the reason why it took him so long to acknowledge it had happened."[1568] According to *Newsmax,* it was two days before Johnson's body was found;[1569] yet *CNN* reported that he was separated from the others and there may have been a beacon activated at his location.[1570] If so, why did it take so long to find him?

Will the investigation turn into a seven-year process with multiple committees as it did with Benghazi? In Chapter 3, the details were provided on eight committees that were struck on Benghazi, most Republican led. Not satisfied with the results, the Republicans pursued further investigations in search of evidence to discredit Hillary and bring her down in the polls. The House Select Committee on Benghazi was incomplete at the time. On June 28, 2016, the *Guardian* reported the following findings: "House Benghazi report faults military response, not Clinton, for deaths."[1571] The chair, Trey Gowdy, is Republican. It took almost four years from the date of the actual incident to conclude the investigations. Despite these investigations, the Republicans continued to politicize the Benghazi investigation to find fault with Hillary.

During the campaign Trump and his supporters called for Hillary to be 'locked up' for her use of a personal email server. However, the *New York Times* reported that at least six members of Trump's administration, including his son-in-law Jared Kushner, Steve Bannon, and Reince Priebus, had used personal email to conduct government business.[1572] This is after the controversy with Hillary, and as reported in the *New York Times*, Sarah Huckabee Sanders confirmed that "[a]ll White House personnel have been instructed to use official email to conduct all government related work."[1573] *Politico* reported that "the White House has launched an internal probe of private email use" following its story revealing the practice.[1574]

Meghan McCain, cohost on the *View* and daughter of Senator John McCain, made an excellent point on the politicization of this issue, saying, "We are missing the main point; we have soldiers who are dying waiting for health care, at the VA in line, PTSD is a raging problem… I would like to talk about what our veterans need in this country… let's use this platform; if people in DC are not going to talk about it then we might as well take the reins and do it here."[1575] Whoopi responded, "We also have to hold this gentleman to his supposed job."[1576]

International Security

World Nuclear News disclosed President Trump's announcement on October 16, 2017 that he refused to certify the Iranian deal as required in the agreement every ninety days, claiming that Iran had not met the spirit of the agreement.[1577] Contrary to his campaign promise and threats to cancel the agreement, Trump has shifted the responsibility to Congress to reach a solution. He added, "in the event we are not able to reach a solution working with Congress and our allies, then the agreement will be terminated. It is under continuous review, and our participation can be cancelled by me, as President, at any time."[1578]

The Joint Comprehensive Plan of Action (JCPOA), also known as the Iran Nuclear Deal, was signed by China, France, Germany, Russia, the UK, the USA, and the European Union and implemented in January 2016.[1579] *Forbes* reported that "[t]he Deal itself was only to stop Iran from getting a nuclear weapon, and to help bring it back into the global community so Iran wouldn't want to produce one in the future. It wasn't supposed to deal with other non-nuclear issues."[1580] *Forbes* added that "Mogherini [EU Vice-President] has already stated that the EU wants to be Iran's largest trading partner."[1581] It was the hope of those countries in the agreement that, absent of the threat of nuclear weapons, trade could be used to develop a relationship with Iran during the ten-year period.

Mogherini claimed that there had been no violations of the agreement and stated that "[t]he plan of action [of the JCPOA] is an annex to a United Nations Security Council Resolution, not a bilateral agreement, and cannot be terminated by a single country… It is clearly not in the hands of any president of any country in the world to terminate an agreement of this sort."[1582] She added, "The EU encourages the US to maintain its commitment to the JCPOA and to consider the implications for the security of the US, its partners and the region before taking further steps."[1583]

Yukiya Amano, Director General of the International Atomic Energy Agency (IAEA), declared, "the nuclear related commitments undertaken by Iran under the JCPOA are being implemented… At present, Iran is subject to the world's most robust nuclear verification regime."[1584]

According to *Forbes*, "since the Deal was codified through a United Nations Security Council resolution, re-imposing sanctions by the United States, or withdrawal from the agreement, would contravene international law and place the United States in legal jeopardy."[1585] However, the US is on the National Security Council, so the US "can veto anything and just stop the grievance process from going forward. This would give Iran tacit approval to restart its nuclear weapons program."[1586]

James Conca, reporter for *Forbes*, concluded, "Worse yet, Trump's action plays into the hands of Iran's hardliners, who have been telling the world, and their own people, that the United States cannot be trusted."[1587] And the moderates have staked their survival on the success of this nuclear deal.[1588]

Conca added, "The only thing that our withdrawal from the Deal would accomplish is to further isolate the United States and really damage our credibility to negotiate future agreements in good faith."[1589]

President Hassan Rouhani of Iran has chosen not to escalate the situation and said that "the country [Iran] would continue to cooperate with the IAEA and the JCPOA… as long as our interests require and, as long as we enjoy its benefits, we will respect the JCPOA."[1590]

This deal was put into place to prevent a situation like the current challenges being faced with North Korea.

The *Independent* reported that "North Korea has said they are not interested in diplomatic solutions to its tensions with the US until it develops a missile capable of reaching the east coast of America."[1591] On October 10, 2017, the *New York Times* revealed that North Korea hacked the computer network of the South Korean military, obtaining "classified wartime contingency plans jointly drawn by the United States and South Korea," which included the "South Korean military's plan to remove the North Korean leader, Kim Jong-un, referred to as a 'decapitation' plan, should war break out on the Korean Peninsula."[1592]

Trump has eroded his credibility and trust with allies and the international community by pulling out of the Paris Accord on climate change and the TPP, refusing to certify the Iran nuclear deal, threatening not to support NATO's Article 5 to come to the aid of an ally under attack for those not meeting the 2% GDP guideline, and threatening to pull out of NAFTA.

With the revelation of the "decapitation plan," Kim Jong-un has justifiable reason to distrust the US in any agreement. While the concern regarding North Korea's nuclear proliferation was well underway prior to his administration, Trump has exacerbated the situation, intensifying Kim Jong-un's resolve and prompting an escalation in the program and testing.

According to *CNN*, "US-backed militias on Friday declared the 'total liberation' of the Syrian city of Raqqa, which for more than three years was the de facto capital of ISIS."[1593] *CNN* reported on an interview with the *Chris Plante Show* in which Trump took credit for the achievement; he said, "I totally changed rules of engagement. I totally changed our military, I totally changed the attitudes of the military and they have done a fantastic job."[1594] Trump later added that he changed the rules about a month ago, which would have been September 2017.[1595]

This raises questions as to how much Trump's changes contributed to the success. The local insurgents, the Syrian Kurds and Arabs, and the American forces backing them up, deserve the credit. I have been unable to discern much difference in strategy since Obama's administration, during which much progress had already been made. While Trump did defer to the authority of his generals for expedited decision-making, I was unable to find any other information on changes in the rules of engagement. This delegation of authority also has a hidden benefit for Trump in absolving him of responsibility should anything untoward happen. He took credit while failing to acknowledge that most of Mosul had been taken under Obama's administration. Additionally, Trump did not acknowledge the fact that local insurgents were responsible for the victory on the ground, or the contribution made by the allies.

There are other outstanding questions. What role, if any, will the US have in stabilizing the region? The Kurds, who have been a longstanding ally of the US in the fight against ISIS, felt let down by the US, as reported in the *Wall Street Journal*: "Several hundred Kurdish demonstrators protested outside the U.S. consulate here on Friday, accusing one of their closest allies of standing by as Iraqi forces dislodged them from a contested territory in the north of the country."[1596] Niger has been a wakeup call to the public that ISIS has a stronghold in other regions, and as reported by *CNN*, ISIS is reaching into Africa.[1597] Social media is a key recruitment tool for ISIS, and I think radicalization is a greater threat on US soil. I have heard nothing in the media about progress or efforts in this regard. It is a bit early for President Trump to be claiming victory.

Forbes pointed out that "two-thirds of Americans feel that President Trump will get us into another major war, and half of Americans think he will use nukes when he gets the chance. Neither of these is good for America."[1598] This was reaffirmed by Senator Bob Corker, the Republican chairman of the Senate Foreign Relations Committee, in an interview with the *New York Times*: "President Trump was treating his office like 'a reality show,' with reckless threats toward other countries that could set the nation 'on the path to World War III.'"[1599] Corker was a Trump supporter during the campaign and, according to the *New York Times* interview, withdrew from consideration for Secretary of State "in part because he said he found it frustrating to discuss foreign policy with [Trump]."[1600] Corker went on to add that his "concerns about Mr. Trump were shared by nearly every Senate Republican."[1601]

This was my concern in Melaque, when I witnessed Trump descend the escalator to announce his candidacy on Fox News. These issues are so complex that it is difficult for the public to have an informed opinion, myself included. We all depend on our military to have expertise and our leaders and legislators to make informed decisions that keep us all safe. In the case of the United States at this time, I do not have this confidence or trust. Neither do most Americans, as reflected in Trump's continuing low approval ratings.

Trump Support

Trump's approval rating has dropped to 37%, yet his supporters, largely older, white, blue-collar workers, continue to approve of his behaviour.[1602] In my calculations, that represents 76 million registered voters.

CNN also reported that "(61%) [of people who approve of Trump] say they can't think of anything Trump could do that would make them disapprove of his job as President, according to a Monmouth University poll."[1603] This indicates that he has a solid base no matter what he does.

According to *CNN*, 63% of Republicans trust Trump more to handle major issues, while only 29% trust the Republicans in Congress.[1604] A real dilemma for the Republican Party will be the potential impact of Steve Bannon's "war on the GOP."[1605] During the Alabama primary, Trump backed establishment candidate Luther Strange to fill the seat vacated by Jeff Sessions. Strange went on to lose to Steve Bannon's candidate, Roy Moore, as reported by *CNN*.[1606] That had to sting for Trump, and no doubt he is distrustful of those who encouraged his endorsement of Strange. Following the victory of his candidate, Bannon declared, "Right now it's a season of war against the GOP establishment," according to the *New York Post*.[1607] *Slate* reported that Bannon has two criteria for supporting candidates to challenge incumbents: they must remove Mitch McConnell as Senate majority leader, and they must "support killing the filibuster, which has evolved into a de facto requirement that the party in power maintain a supermajority to enact its legislative agenda."[1608] Is this not a path to absolute power?

Throughout the campaign, election, and presidency, Donald Trump has only shown interest in preserving his base, not expanding it. If he were to start a new party or run as an independent, as other authoritarian leaders have done in the past, he could win a second term and decimate the Republican Party. Third-party candidates took 11% of the vote; if the Democrat and Republican votes were split for 51% of the vote, Trump could win an election with a solid 37% approval rating of his base.

CNN polls reflected that, "Going forward, 74% of Democrats say the party should mainly work with Republicans to try to get some of the party's ideas into law."[1609] This is very unlike the Republicans, whose sole effort for two terms had been to stop the Obama agenda. The Democrats have already demonstrated willingness to cooperate on issues that will benefit the American people. Democrats have been involved in two bipartisan healthcare proposals and have discussed a plan for saving the dreamers with Trump, just to mention a few. Republicans, on the other hand, created gridlock for eight years with the Obama administration, and this has occurred while they had control of the House, the Senate, and the White House.

How does it reflect on North American societal values when wealth trumps humanity, selfish individualism trumps compassion, the need to be entertained and to win trumps truth, and racism and misogyny are rewarded with the most powerful position in the world?

This will be Trump's legacy. Much of the damage he has perpetrated cannot be remedied. The following is an example. An undocumented immigrant, a husband and father, was deported to Mexico when he presented to US Immigration and Customs Enforcement in compliance with his status. He was not a criminal, but in 2000, the family took the wrong exit while travelling on vacation and ended up in Canada. It was incorrectly classified as a voluntary departure. This was the rationale used to deport him. Even though there was a legal motion to stay his removal, ICE suddenly deported him prior to the judge's ruling.[1610] Even if this is rectified, the damage to his children and family cannot be undone. He owned a restaurant and employed many people. He had been in the US for twenty years. This man was well regarded in his community, which is largely Trump country. Some Trump supporters, including the man's wife, feel betrayed.

While Trump assured the American people that deportation efforts would focus on violent criminals, the *Washington Post* reported that by April 16 2016, "Immigration arrests rose 32.6% in the first weeks of the Trump administration, with newly empowered federal agents intensifying their pursuit of not just undocumented immigrants with criminal records, but also thousands of illegal immigrants who have been otherwise law-abiding... Arrests of immigrants without criminal records more than doubled to 5,441."[1611] How does this improve national security? The pain and disruption to the families involved is unconscionable. Some are young people, who through no fault of their own, and sometimes without their awareness, are undocumented. Thousands who have been adopted by American parents are learning, to their shock, that they are undocumented and at risk.[1612]

I think this is only the beginning of the disappointments in store for Trump supporters. While Obama had an 82% approval rating with Canadians in a 2009 poll, Canadians did not agree with all of Obama's policies, and he had concerns about Canadian positions and policies too.[1613]

In an historic address to the Canadian Parliament on June 29, 2016, Obama asserted the US position that Canada was not meeting its NATO obligations regarding troops on the ground in the Baltics (Canada was planning to send troops to Latvia). Over the years, Canadians were concerned about Obama's protectionist position on trade (the 'buy American' in the stimulus package). Trade barriers, border issues, Arctic sovereignty, and stopping TransCanada's Keystone XL oil pipeline were also issues on which the two countries disagreed.[1614]

Why has there been such peace at the Canada-US border despite our policy differences? There is something of greater importance that binds us: we value democracy and humanity. As Obama said in his speech, we agree on "values such as equality, tolerance, openness, fairness, compassion, justice, [and] freedom under the rule of law."[1615] Those commonalities provided the environment to enable dialogue and to work out differences and come to mutual understanding.

This could change. Canadians tend to be more passive than Americans when it comes to politics and become almost apologetic regarding disagreements. Canadians could be galvanized if they experience a dissonance in the common values. The free world cannot vote for the president of the United States, but it can reject the notion that the president of the US is its leader. If the free world perceives that America no longer espouses these values and that it experiences protectionism akin to bullying, the US may well lose its influence over its allies, resulting in the creation of new alliances; as the saying goes, "The enemy of my enemy is my friend." This is not what the world wants; we need America. Isolation did not work during World War II, and it will not work today. While America is the most powerful country in the world, America needs the free world as much as the free world needs America.

There is no democracy where there is no truth. There is no democracy where there is no transparency and accountability. There is no democracy without freedom of the press. There is no democracy without checks and balances. There is no democracy when elections are compromised, not just by foreign interference but also by voter suppression, gerrymandering, and false representation. There is no democracy when systemic racism and gender bias are being ignored and there is no social equity or justice. Democracy is compromised if there is not separation of church and state. Democracy in the US is at risk.

It is my conviction that the seeds for the Trump presidency were sown over a long period with the radical right-wing media such as Rush Limbaugh, Fox News, *Breitbart*, and others who have been breeding discontent with their fake news for years. The Republicans have been trying to destroy the Clintons since the Arkansas project in the 1990s. The 2016 presidential election provides a blueprint for how a country can incrementally shift toward authoritarian leadership without its people being aware of this threat. I am not convinced that American voters made an informed decision.

Democracy is at risk in the US, but Trump alone cannot be held responsible. Democracy is a system in which the power is vested in the people. The people should hold Trump accountable before he has eroded all checks and balances and it is too late.

Following fifteen years of economic erosion, despite having some of the planet's largest oil reserves, Venezuela's people are protesting because they want free elections. With the promise of democracy, Cubans supported Castro, who became a dictator. Turkey made great strides toward democracy, which is now eroding at the hands of its current leader, Erdoğan. Hitler won the election in Germany with the promise to bring back German nationalism and jobs.

Trump is disdainful of any peaceful efforts on the part of the black community to address its concerns, particularly the systemic racism in the justice system. These include marches, Mothers of the Movement, and refusal to stand during the national anthem. The Kerner Commission cautioned that the US was moving toward two separate societies. I fear that we are in that place. Trump and his administration fail to acknowledge the issue. How, then, can it be addressed?

It should be no surprise that Jeff Sessions has no intention of addressing the issues in the justice system. According to the *Huffington Post*, "He's going to roll back recent police reforms, reopen the private prison system, stop investigating and monitoring local police departments and eliminate the National Commission on Forensic Science."[1616] What options does that leave for the black community? As stated so eloquently by Desmond Tutu, "Differences are not intended to separate, to alienate. We are different precisely in order to realize our need of one another."[1617]

Change and disruption that lead to positive outcomes would be beneficial to the country. I fail to see any evidence, thus far, that there have been, or that there will be, constructive changes from Trump's administration. Unlike his career in real estate, Trump's presidency will be branded for demolition, not construction. His administration and this nationalistic movement threaten not only democracy, but also international security. I think history will be very favourable toward the preservation of President Obama's legacy. Unfortunately, the American people were deprived from enjoying most of the benefits of his policies because Trump destroyed them. Trump has clearly communicated that his administration is not a democracy 'controlled by the people,' nor is it for the people, and this will be his legacy. It will also reflect the perception of America on the world stage.

Epilogue

Trump alone is not the problem; he is a symptom of the problem, as are Nigel Farage, Marine Le Pen, and the other international leaders of this nationalist, populist movement that admire Putin. Even so, many American voters continue to support Trump. According to Tony DiTommaso Jr., the secretary-treasurer of the Western Reserve Building Trades, "Our members, flat-out, voted for him… They wanted a change. They didn't care what it was."[1618] This is not unique to the US; there are people in other democratic countries, including Canada, that view Trump positively.

Robert Ferris of *CNBC* shared the results of a study conducted by Hemant Kakkar and Niro Sivanathan entitled "When the Appeal of a Dominant Leader is Greater than a Prestige Leader." They found that "threat of economic uncertainty leads people to prefer leaders whom they see as decisive, authoritative and dominant" and that there was "a similar correlation between fear of terrorism and preference for dominant types."[1619] The researchers also reviewed a three-decade-long study and concluded that there was not only a preference for a strong leader, "but someone who is also willing to ignore constitutional procedures."[1620]

This makes the votes for Trump more understandable and not necessarily predicated on racism, misogyny, and xenophobia. Nevertheless, there is evidence to suggest that these prejudices were a motivational factor for some of those in Trump's base. Voting for a populist, authoritarian leader may be understandable, but is it justifiable to ignore and normalize behaviour and attitudes that are diametrically opposed to beliefs that one purports to value? More ominous is the researchers' conclusion that "the leaders voted into power in turn set economic policies that shape the next generation's well-being and preferences."[1621]

The judicial appointments will impact policies for generations to come, as will the tax bill passed by Republicans on December 2, 2017. The corporate tax reductions are permanent — the individual tax cuts are time-limited. While it has been lauded as a legislative win for Trump, it is not a win for middle-class Americans, despite Trump marketing the tax bill as such in order to garner support. Trump declared that "[t]he beating heart of our plan is a tax cut for working families."[1622] The GOP and Trump claimed that he would take on the hedge fund managers, that he and the wealthy would not benefit, and that the tax plan would pay for itself.

While middle-class workers will experience an immediate increase in their take-home pay, corporations and the super wealthy are the major winners, including Trump and his family. The *Financial Times* reported the Tax Policy Center's conclusion that the wealthiest 1% will experience an overall savings of 2.2%, nearly half the total benefit of the savings, while the middle class will save only 0.4%.[1623] According to the *Washington Post*, the repeal of the estate tax, which is scheduled for 2024, could save Trump's family a billion dollars or more. Trump and the family business would benefit by gaining special provisions for tax breaks in the real estate industry that are not applicable to other industries.

The *Washington Post* also disclosed that Trump has admitted he consulted with his accountants to determine how the tax bill would affect him personally.[1624] How can we not conclude that this legislation is about personal gain? The more you earn and have, the more you gain.

There is a consensus that the GOP tax plan will increase the deficit by $1.5 trillion dollars.[1625] The Republicans argue that the debt will be offset by GDP growth of 4%, but there is no evidence to support this.[1626] According to the *Washington Post*, the "Senate rules require the Tax Cuts and Jobs Act not to add to the federal deficit after 10 years."[1627] Given that the corporate tax cuts are permanent, this only leaves taxes on individuals as a target for increased tax revenue. If the GOP really believes that the tax plan will pay for itself, why are they already considering measures to reduce the debt, including cuts to entitlements such as social security, Medicaid, and Medicare, despite Trump's assurances to the contrary?

According to the *Atlantic*, most economists dispute the GOP assertion that the tax bill will pay for itself. While the Tax Policy Center estimated that perhaps 20% of the corporate tax savings may be applied to wage increases, they cautioned that "of the money going to workers, much of it would flow to managers and executives, not minimum-wage or average employees."[1628] While Trump promised to ensure that middle-class Americans would keep more of their hard-earned money, to the contrary, the *Atlantic* concluded that "families in the middle of the income distribution would on average see no benefit from the plan as of 2027, whereas families at the top would be paying far less in taxes and many families at the bottom would actually be paying more."[1629] Consequences such as these will not be realized until after the 2018 mid-term elections and the 2020 presidential election. Americans are accepting short-term gain without considering the long-term costs.

The GOP argues that the corporate tax cuts will benefit the working class by increasing both job opportunities and wages. *Vox* reported that at a meeting of the *Wall Street Journal* CEO Council, when asked if the tax savings would be used to increase investment, which would include job growth and investment in their employees, most CEOs did not raise their hands.[1630] The GOP's implication that wages will increase is simply not supported by any facts. *Vox* reported on the experience in Britain, where they cut corporate taxes from 30% to 19% and the median wages decreased. *Vox* explained that "as UK corporate tax rates fell, so did real (inflation-adjusted) median wages. That is, wages moved in the opposite direction from that predicted by the CEA."[1631] Taxes in the US remained at 35% and there was a slight increase in median salaries.[1632] Who will benefit from the tax cuts? According to corporate CEOs, "they would use a tax reform windfall to buy back shares, retire debt and other shareholder-friendly moves."[1633] While companies such as Walmart have finally come forward and increased wages, most are offering one-time bonuses. Let's face it. These increases are long overdue and were not implemented while corporations were already making huge profits. They are making a token effort now, not in the workers' best interest, but their own. They recognize that, if they do not do something to support the GOP promises of increased wages, there could be voter backlash. While Apple is bringing business back to America, they have been using offshore accounts to avoid paying taxes for years. But, even if wages do increase, at what cost will it be? What happens when there is a market correction, or when inflation rises? Will wages experience the same decline as in Britain? Trade has become a major worldwide issue. Will this result in tariffs and increased prices, or trade wars?

Since this writing, the market experienced a correction and plunged over 10% in one week in February 2018. That essentially eliminated any benefit from the Trump bump and it is expected to remain volatile after a nine-year bull market. It is believed that fear of inflation and increased interest rates were the driving forces behind this volatility. Increased cost of living will certainly erode the modest increases some of the middle class experienced in their paychecks with the tax cuts. That is prior to any consequences from cuts to entitlement programs the GOP may implement to reduce the increasing deficit, which has become a flash point for many Republicans, especially after the bipartisan budget approved by the House and the Senate.

Voters would be wise not to prematurely celebrate the modest increase in wages or one-time bonuses. What will be the social costs, and the financial costs of the debt incurred to give this additional gift to corporations? Who will pay for this $1.5 trillion debt? Not the corporations or the wealthy.

The most egregious aspect of this legislation is the increasing divide between the wealthiest Americans and the rest of the population. It will be interesting to see where the US ranks on income equality with the Gini scale in the upcoming years.

Trump has been credited with the booming economy and high employment rate. The global economy was strong prior to his presidency and remains so. Any president would have benefitted from these circumstances. In Davos, Trump declared that "When the United States grows, so does the world," The European economy grew faster than the US economy in 2017. Perhaps it should be that when the world economy does well, so does the US.

Trump boasted that he was responsible for the stock market doing so well. The world market was doing well. I will accord Trump credit for a bump in the market, but how much variance can be attributed to Trump alone? Of more concern are the reasons that Wall Street has such confidence: deregulation and the corporate tax cuts, which most assuredly will have long-term implications for Americans.

Employment rates were on the upswing when Trump took office. Which policies implemented by the Trump administration support the claim that he was responsible for this achievement? Since the US has almost full employment, and some companies are already having difficulty filling positions, what is the benefit of creating more jobs? If drug testing is a major barrier for many Americans to gain employment, this tax bill is not a solution. A robust apprentice program, training, and access to drug treatment programs would be more productive solutions. Had the employment increase been related to job creation, perhaps some credit could be attributed to Trump, but the *Washington Post* reported that job creation lagged slightly behind its level during the first year of the Obama administration.[1634]

Those who abstain from participating, being informed, and voting are the greatest risk to democracy in this environment. Some choose to do so because they are frustrated and angry with the establishment, some because they believe all politicians are the same and it makes no difference which individual leads, some because they believe fake news, and some because they are just weary. I fear that many are so stressed in this environment that they are immobilized. I am concerned that the movements like Me Too and Never Again will lose energy because of all the other competing crises and chaos, with relatively minimal, if any sustainable gains. This administration sucks the energy out of everybody. Indeed, I think it is a strategy: wear everyone down until they become so beleaguered that they no longer have the energy to fight back.

This phenomenon is taking place worldwide. In the case of the US, the Trump presidency is so toxic that I am of the conviction that it is negatively affecting the mental health status of many Americans, as well as people like myself around the globe. I am troubled by the potential consequences of this tension. The Trump administration causes near-daily crises, chaos, and uncertainty, with no checks and balances from the Republican congress. This administration's permissive attitude toward hate and blame has extended to other countries, including Canada. In its "Best Countries" rankings, *The US News* divulged that Statistics Canada reported a 3% increase in hate crimes since Trump's presidency.[1635] This is alarming.

Islam is not our enemy. Terrorism, including ISIS and domestic terrorism, is our enemy. Bigotry, hate, and blame are our enemies. Poverty is our enemy. Ignorance is our enemy. Pollution that is destroying our earth is our enemy. Corporate greed is our enemy.

The super-rich are connected and organized on a worldwide basis. The Bilderberg Conference is an annual private meeting of a small group of the super-rich and powerful. According to Adam Lusher, correspondent for the *Independent*, consistent with the group's practice in prior years, at the upcoming meeting, "[n]o minutes will be taken. No reporters will be allowed in. There will be no opening press conference, no closing statement, and participants will be asked not to quote each other."[1636] According to Lusher, group members deny "that they are a global ruling class that can start wars and decide who becomes the next US President" and claim that the group is a "forum for informal discussions about the world's 'megatrends' and a chance for participants to 'reflect and gather insights.'"[1637] Whether well intentioned or not, they have managed to maintain the status quo. A 2016 *Reuters* article provided information from an Oxfam report that stated,

> Just 62 people, 53 of them men, own as much wealth as the poorest half of the entire world population… The wealth of those 62 people has risen 44 percent, or more than half a trillion dollars, over the past five years, while the wealth of the bottom half has fallen by over a trillion…. Far from trickling down, income and wealth are instead being sucked upwards at an alarming rate.[1638]

The citizens of the free world are not connected and organized. It may be surprising coming from a retired CEO, but one effective mechanism for organizing the masses on a worldwide basis could be unionization. Perhaps, like the super-rich, representatives from across the world could meet annually to share and gather insights. I do not understand American workers' apparent aversion to unionization. *Norma Rae* was a popular movie, championed by Americans, about unfair labour practices and health issues in the workplace. Those issues are as salient today as they were in the 1970s, during which the real-life situation that inspired the movie took place. Canada has healthcare today because of unions.

I experienced that if you have a responsible bargaining unit, the process keeps you honest as an employer. The organization for which I worked became unionized when the healthcare system was undergoing an integration process and the unionized workers from the hospitals were claiming that they would be entitled to the jobs in non-union community organizations. Communication and empathy for the worker's perspective made for better decisions. The union was not always right, nor was the employer. My biggest mistake was creating a position of director of human resources as the organization grew and allowing the individual in that position to become the main contact with the union, cutting me out of the communication loop. The CEO needs to keep a direct line of communication with the union. Otherwise, there is the risk of bias and filtering of information to the CEO. That did occur in my case, much to my detriment, and not from the union. Notwithstanding that, my experience with the bargaining unit, for the most part, was that they were reasonable if you were honest and fair, even when taking an unfavourable position.

I am aware that some union members are apathetic or disenchanted with unions that are corrupt or more interested in building their own empire than serving their original purpose to provide effective representation to protect workers' rights. Unions can be a key resource in educating and advocating for the necessary change, but this requires trust on the part of membership.

During the campaign and following the election, I was confused when I heard commentators and the media speak about issues of elitism within the Democratic Party. I think I have a better understanding now by relating it to a personal experience. When my husband and I were dating, several of his acquaintances tried to discourage him from dating me because I was a 'professional.' One of my acquaintances tried to dissuade me as well, saying that dating a factory worker was 'beneath' me. I never felt that way and they were wrong. We have been married now for over thirty years and have learned from each other, appreciating and valuing our differences. This is but one illustration that people with radically different world-views can not only co-exist, but benefit from one another's perspective.

Collaboration between labour and management makes the environment better for everyone. That cannot be achieved as long as the working class and liberal elites view each other with mutual prejudice. Communication must be reestablished in order to move forward. Trump is not only narrowing the opportunity for diplomatic strategies on an international basis, but he has heightened polarization within America, between not only politicians but the people as well, preventing the meaningful dialogue that is necessary for achieving solutions.

The populist movement gaining support across the globe has tapped into the dissatisfaction with the establishment. There is legitimacy to this discontent. But while this populist movement promotes blame and hate, and creates divisiveness, we are deflected from the real issues of establishing social and income equality. This maintains the status quo and threatens our civil rights.

The disenfranchised need a champion. Much of the support for this populist movement is based on misinformation, often perpetrated by the Russians. Now more than ever, politicians, unions, and the media need to reach out to those who feel left behind, communicate a genuine concern, and provide an alternative to this hateful movement.

Trust will not be reestablished if the establishment does not purge the corruption in their own ranks. There will be no trust if politicians are perceived as acting for personal gain, unions are perceived as building empires no different than the corporations, and the media is perceived as being driven by profit and viewership. The voters and members of these organizations have a responsibility to hold them accountable and put an end to corruption. Unions have contributed immensely to addressing issues of social injustice. The media's role is public enlightenment. If both unions and the media took a nonpartisan approach and demonstrated a sincere interest in the well-being of the people, they would be powerful forces in establishing a dialogue between the disenfranchised and the establishment to further the values of democracy.

There are actions being taken around the world to combat injustice, inequality, and tyranny. Brazil's President, Dilma Rousseff, was removed from office following an impeachment vote in the Senate.[1639] Ai Weiwei is a world-renowned artist in China who speaks out against human rights abuses and advocates for political change.[1640] Sanctuary cities are refusing to arrest undocumented immigrants based solely on their immigration status in the US, and places of worship are providing refuge for undocumented immigrants. We do not have to be victims; in democratic countries, we have choices.

Other advocacy options include contacting elected representatives, attending public forums and protest marches, keeping informed from a variety of sources, learning how to identify fake news, donating to causes that we support, signing petitions, running for office or volunteering for a candidate, and most importantly, voting. I want to amend this. Most important of all is compassion.

Pamela Taylor from Brownsville, Texas wants border security, but she shows compassion by leaving bottled water for both the border patrol and illegal immigrants. The skinheads from the Oprah show became repentant for their racist views after having been treated with compassion by those whom they had oppressed. The Mothers of the Movement, though dealing with the unfathomable loss of their children, often simply because of the colour of their skin, are not seeking hateful and indiscriminate vengeance, but rather a cooperative understanding between the police and communities to prevent similar incidents. Peter Tefft's father abhors his son's behaviour but still allows an open door should his son renounce his hateful beliefs. James Franklin McGraw apologized to Rakeem Jones for punching him in the face at a Trump rally, and Jones forgave him with a hug.

Former Presidents Jimmy Carter, George H.W. Bush, Bill Clinton, George W. Bush, and Barack Obama appeared in a video and asked Americans to respond to the devastation wrought by the hurricanes.[1641] According to *CNN*, the Presidents Club conducted similar efforts in the past, which included the sitting president, but while Trump did provide a gracious videotape, he was not invited to the event because of his uneasy relationship with the past presidents.[1642]

There was another major effort to combat injustice and tyranny following the Weinstein sexual abuse allegations. Innumerable courageous women and a few men came forward with sexual harassment complaints in Hollywood, the media, corporations, and the political realm. Samantha Cooney, correspondent for *Time,* identified ninety-nine men who have been accused of sexual misconduct since the Weinstein incident.[1643] Some of the more notable, identified by Cooney, who were fired or resigned include actor Kevin Spacey, fired from *House of Cards* by Netflix; Matt Lauer, host of NBC's the *Today Show*; Charlie Rose, journalist for CBS and PBS; and Andy Dick; fired from the independent film *Raising Buchanan.* The list is growing.[1644]

Many on the list were reporters from mainstream media outlets. I wonder how much subliminal gender bias we have been exposed to over the years. I thought it was particularly evident while Matt Lauer hosted the *Commander-in-Chief Forum*.

The response from the political arena regarding allegations of sexual misconduct was not as swift as those in Hollywood, the media, and corporations. In the wake of numerous allegations, Al Franken, Democrat senator representing Minnesota and former comedian, announced his resignation, and John Conyers, top Democrat on the House Judiciary Committee, reluctantly announced his retirement.

Trent Franks, Arizona Republican representative, also announced his resignation while Texas Republican Representative Blake Farenthold, steadfastly denounced the allegations levied against him, though there are professed witnesses to some of the incidents.

The response from the Republican Party has been profoundly disappointing. Republicans in Alabama selected Roy Moore as their candidate for the Senate seat vacated by Jeff Sessions. According to *Quartz*, nine women came forward during the campaign with sexual misconduct allegations against Moore.[1645] The most disturbing story is from a woman who was fourteen at the time. The detailed account of the reported interaction with Moore constitutes sexual assault of a minor.

Prior to these disclosures, there were other controversial issues regarding Moore's nomination. Moore stepped down from the bench twice after being suspended for advising lower court judges not to obey the Supreme Court ruling legalizing same-sex marriage. He was removed from office for ethics violations including refusal to remove a statue of the ten commandments from the judicial building and opening court with a prayer, as both had been deemed unconstitutional under the First Amendment. Goggin reported that Moore called homosexual behaviour "an inherent evil, and an act so heinous that it defies one's ability to describe it" and declared that it should still be illegal.[1646] Goggin reported that Moore claimed 9/11 was a punishment by God because Americans legalized sodomy and abortion. In 2016, Moore announced that he did not believe Obama was born in the US.[1647]

According to *Metro*, Moore expressed that if the US got rid of everything in the Constitution after the Tenth Amendment, which includes ending slavery and granting women the right to vote, many problems would be eliminated. Moore specifically referenced the 17th Amendment, which requires election of the Senate by voters rather than state legislatures. *Metro* added that Moore does not believe Muslims should serve in Congress. When asked by a black member of the audience at a rally when he last thought America was great, Moore responded, "I think it was great at the time when families were united — even though we had slavery — they cared for one another. Our families were strong, our country had a direction."[1648] This is what I fear many Trump supporters really believe would make America great again.

This is a man who, according to the *Washington Post*, many Alabama voters "consider… a stalwart Christian willing to stand up for their values."[1649]

Trump decided to back Moore and the GOP followed, even to the extent of funding Moore's campaign. They were willing to sacrifice principles for power. They did not want to lose a Republican seat in the Senate. It was expected that Moore would win in this ruby red state, despite his character flaws, because of his opponent's pro-choice stance.

The Republicans lost the seat to Democrat Doug Jones, who pledged to represent all the people of Alabama. On the *View*, Meghan McCain did not consider Moore's supporters to be complicit in the promotion of his racist agenda, as they had been attracted to his anti-abortion position.[1650]

I disagree. They are complicit. It plagues me to this day that I cannot state with absolute conviction what I would have done had I been in Germany during the rise of Hitler; it may have been understandable had I been silent and looked the other way, but even so, I would have been complicit. For the same reason, those who voted for Moore were complicit, as their votes normalized his racist, misogynistic, and hateful views. If Moore's anti-abortion position was truly the primary concern, there had been another viable Republican candidate for the nomination: Luther Strange, a strong conservative and supporter of Trump's policies. However, the Republican voters selected Moore. While I admire the conviction, and support the use of persuasion and conversion to the anti-abortion view, I take exception to the coercion, especially in light of the undeniable fact that some lawmakers that want to encode anti-abortion have demonstrated a lack of moral conviction when it was convenient to them. These are the same lawmakers who refuse to support gun control even though, according to *Slate,* 150,00 students have experienced a shooting since Columbine in 1999.[1651] That does not include those who were witnesses to, or impacted by, the shootings, the children who must cope with survivor's guilt and the horrific images which will forever remain memories. How do the voters reconcile this dichotomy?

The parallels between the political environment and the Olympics extended to the sexual misconduct movement. The most shocking revelations of sexual abuse in which the victims were not taken seriously were the accusations of sexual abuse Olympic gymnasts made against USA Gymnastics team doctor Larry Nassar. Nassar pled guilty to first-degree criminal sexual conduct with children under the age of 16 and was sentenced to 175 years in jail, following almost 160 powerful and disturbing victim statements. What is equally, if not more troubling is that, had the Olympic Committee, USA Gymnastics and Michigan State University taken the first allegation seriously, the subsequent abuses could have been prevented.

Standing up for one's values sometimes results in unpleasant consequences, as those who have done so, like Colin Kaepernick, are keenly aware. Failure to stand up for one's values will result in loss of self-respect, and the long-term consequences could be even greater in the loss of civil liberties, or even democracy. I do not say that in a cavalier way because I once had to make such a decision. I was informed by my director that I could lose my job after having refused a directive from the Minister of Community and Social Services because I thought it was unethical. It was a frightening prospect because I was a single parent at the time with two young dependents. Eventually, that same minister publicly commended me for demonstrating professional ethics, but I did not know that would be the outcome when I made the decision.

Compassion does not mean ignoring unacceptable behaviour with impunity. It precludes the use of unnecessarily excessive, punitive, and retaliatory actions in favour of reducing the threat and achieving the goals with less intrusive measures. Consequences can be imposed in a compassionate way. We do not have to lose our humanity. We will if we promote hatred and blame, and indiscriminately punish the innocent. This only breeds more hate.

Fox News reported that on December 5, 2017 at the Economic Club of Chicago, Obama stated, "We have to tend to th[i]s garden of democracy or else things could fall apart quickly. That's what happened in Germany in the 1930s, which despite the democracy of the Weimar Republic and centuries of high-level cultural and scientific achievements, Adolf Hitler rose to dominate. Sixty million people died. So you've got to pay attention and vote."[1652] The headline was "Gutfeld: Obama compares Trump to Hitler."[1653] No, Obama did not compare Trump to Hitler, but he did invoke a comparison to the conditions in Germany at the time.

On Jake Tapper's program, *State of the Union*, Tapper described Obama's characterization as "stark," asking CNN political commentator Amanda Carpenter for her thoughts. She responded, "I think history is rich with examples of disgraceful leadership. And this is a form [of] intellectual laziness that I don't expect from President Obama… If you want to draw historical analogy, I would probably stick to Watergate."[1654]

I vehemently disagree. As a member of the free world, during the Watergate scandal, I was not concerned about an administration that appeared intent on provoking unnecessary global conflict, threatening allies while admiring tyrannical regimes, terminating international agreements which could threaten international security and our planet, and eroding democratic values. The Republican party demonstrated its commitment to America by holding its leader accountable. Not so in this administration.

Trump's approach to international trade is not only protectionist, but it is a win-lose strategy. Canada has not eliminated the possibility of a free-trade deal with China. While the Trump administration's protectionist policy will likely have a negative impact on Canada and other countries, there will also be consequences for America. If the Trump administration were truly interested in free, fair, open reciprocal trade, then they would have made progress on negotiations for NAFTA. After all, the US has a trade surplus with Canada, right? The negotiations are not looking hopeful because, contrary to claims that the Trump administration wants a level playing field, it is making impossible demands that defy agreement.

Canada and the ten other countries in the former TPP have agreed to move forward without the US.[1655] Canada and Mexico have agreements with the European Union. If NAFTA fails, perhaps Canada and Mexico will develop their own agreement without the US. Trump is not the great dealmaker. He is just a bully. As nations develop new alliances, how will this affect the US economy?

Adam Sacks, the president of Tourism Economics told the *New York Times*, "It's not a reach to say the rhetoric and policies of this administration are affecting sentiment around the world, creating antipathy toward the U.S. and affecting travel behavior."[1656] It is already affecting tourism in the US. As a direct result, the *Hill* reported that tourism spending was down $4.6 billion dollars in 2017, and 40,000 jobs in that industry were lost as a result.[1657] This same antipathy will surely be operative in how American tourists are treated around the world.

I suspect that Trump's strategy was to create the perception of immediate gains for the middle class, while the costs and diminishing returns are delayed until after the 2018 mid-term elections and 2020 presidential election. The type of jobs that Trump is repatriating will become obsolete with robotics. A friend visiting family in Kuala Lumpur posted a picture of a restaurant where they were served by robots. Autonomous vehicles are already being produced. Drones are being examined as a possible delivery system. Technology is the major challenge to job creation in the future.

I am personally concerned that the Trump administration's policies regarding the environment threaten the preservation of the Great Lakes and air quality along the border. If politicians don't care about destroying American rivers like Flint, why would they care about the Great Lakes? Deregulation exposes the international community to banking risks, which were responsible for creating the 2008 financial crisis, and to the corporations' propensity to prioritize profit, rather than the health and safety of the public.

It is my contention that Trump has created a firestorm that poses a threat of nuclear war. Some of the strategies implemented by his administration have been effective, including sanctions, but Trump continues to undermine their efforts, reducing opportunities to seek diplomatic solutions. The following message tweeted by Trump illustrates his recklessness: "North Korean Leader Kim Jong Un just stated that the 'Nuclear Button is on his desk at all times.' Will someone from his depleted and food starved regime please inform him that I too have a Nuclear Button, but it is a much bigger & more powerful one than his, and my Button works!"[1658]

North Korea made contact with South Korea after two years of silence. Trump took credit for this and probably deserves it. Rather than crowing about it, Trump should be concerned about Kim Jong-un's motives, which appear to be to circumvent the US. More importantly, South Korea is engaging in dialogue with North Korea, perhaps because the US was not engaging them. There is no doubt that North Korea is initiating this dialogue to circumvent the US and to advance Kim Jong-un's agenda. Perhaps South Korea is open to the dialogue because they feel they can no longer trust the US.

South Korea has negotiated a meeting between President Trump and Kim Jong-un to discuss denuclearization. Trump expressed a willingness to meet, and following several weeks of discussion in preparation for the meeting, Trump announced the release of three hostages from North Korea, a gesture of good faith prior to the meetings. Trump, his administration, and newly-appointed Secretary of State Mike Pompeo are to be commended for this accomplishment. They are to be commended for achieving the agreement of a meeting with Kim Jong-un with the expressed objective to denuclearize North Korea. Trump and his supporters believe that his tough talk and style of communication are responsible for this transformation. I do credit the Trump administration for their tough stance and sanctions, which I do believe put pressure on Kim Jong-un, creating a scarcity of resources for him to maintain his people's loyalty.

The ongoing taunts were unnecessary and escalated risk of a conflict. If Trump and his supporters believe it was this rhetoric that was responsible for the turnaround, I am concerned about future conflicts in which the response may be unpredictable.

In a situation of extreme crisis, autocratic decision-making may be necessary and effective, but not as the leadership style of a democratic leader, especially in absence of listening to advisors, articulating clear rules, demonstrating reliability, and recognizing the contributions of others. We can hope that Trump will be successful in these negotiations, but it is premature to celebrate this as a success. North Korea has not upheld international agreements in the past. Similarly, Trump has demonstrated that he cannot be trusted to uphold international agreements. If these negotiations fail, what then? Will we be in an even more precarious situation? China seems to have been sidelined; how will this manifest in the long term?

The Trump administration has not articulated a clear foreign policy. How could Trump possibly know how Kim Jong-un will react to his taunts? Trump is a risk-taker. One has only to recall his purchase of the Taj Mahal. Trump did not pay the price, but the contractors and workers did, and he didn't care. Contrary to his assertions that he, and only he, has the answers, someone else was able to make the Taj Mahal profitable when he could not. When nuclear war is a possible outcome, is this kind of risk-taking acceptable?

The fact that the Olympics were about to take place in South Korea should have provided further reason to deescalate tensions with North Korea. The international community was already anxious about the escalating tensions in the region; France even considered pulling out.

The American media and Americans appear focused almost exclusively on how the Russians influenced the presidential election. The efforts of the Trump administration and the GOP to discredit the Mueller investigation have given rise to concerns that the GOP would rather preserve its power than find out the truth regarding Russian involvement. While some make the argument that it should be a nonpartisan issue, it has been politicized along party lines. It is not just a nonpartisan issue, and it is not just about what the Russians did to discredit Hillary; it is a threat to the free world and democracy.

What is happening in Europe should be alarming to any democratic country. The Brexit vote and the election of Trump have emboldened Putin, who has developed an alliance with Turkey.[1659] While Emmanuel Macron won the election in France, Marine Le Pen, the French nationalist candidate supported by Putin and Trump, gained significant popularity. The *Independent* reported that the Freedom Party, the far-right nationalist party founded by ex-Nazis in Austria, has formed a coalition with the conservative People's Party to form a government.[1660] According to the *EUObserver*, the year before, the Freedom Party signed a five-year pact with Russia, which included "mutual non-interference, the promotion of dialogue and economic development and 'the raising of younger generations in the spirit of patriotism and work enjoyment.'"[1661] The last objective is a particularly frightening prospect.

In September 2017, German Chancellor Angela Merkel was re-elected, but by a narrow margin, having faced an aggressive challenge from "the far-right, explicitly xenophobic Alternative for Germany (AfD)."[1662] Though Merkel won the election, she required a coalition to form a government, and this has been elusive. Failure to form a coalition would have necessitated a new election. According to *USA Today*, the AfD had 12.6% of the German vote and "won enough votes… to enter Germany's national parliament for the first time."[1663]

While many puzzled over the seeming lack of interference from Russia in the German election, Maria Snegovaya from the *American Interest*[1664] reported that their techniques had become more sophisticated, targeting the Russian-speaking Germans on social media. She concluded that "there is a correlation between the presence of a Lisa protest in early 2016 and a 2017 vote share for AfD exceeding the regional average of 12.7 percent. What's more, the highest AfD results were achieved only in the towns where Lisa protests occurred."[1665] The Lisa situation was described in Chapter 13 and is a reference to the fake news story perpetuated by the Russians about Muslim immigrants allegedly raping a young girl in Berlin. German authorities have debunked this story.

Of equal concern is the American alt-right's interference in the German Election, as reported by Kim Hjelmgaard in *USA Today*. This is not surprising given President Trump's repeated efforts to discredit Merkel and her immigration policy. Hjelmgaard reported that Simon Hegelich, a professor of political science data at the Technical University of Munich, conducted an analysis of 300 million tweets which "show[ed that] Germany is a hotspot for posts that use the hashtag '#AltRight.'"[1666] Hegelich concluded, "A lot of the stuff we are seeing in Germany can be linked to, or is at least inspired by, the 'alt-right' movement in the U.S."[1667] The *Independent* reported that the four-year coalition between Merkel's conservative Union bloc (CDU) and the Social Democrats was coming to an end as the Social Democrats, discouraged by the election results, made a decision to go into opposition. Following two failed attempts by Merkel's party to develop a coalition, the Social Democrats have agreed to reconsider.

Germany did have some advantages. Hjelmgaard reported that Joerg Forbrig, a Berlin-based political affairs expert at the German Marshall Fund of the United States, advised that German voters observed what happened in the US and France during their elections, so there was a heightened awareness. He added that "Germany's media is… generally more 'balanced and calm' and lacks 'shrill voices' compared to its counterparts elsewhere… [and] its media is still viewed as a trusted source of information — not always the case in President Trump's Washington."[1668]

Hjelmgaard reported that Merkel established the "Network Enforcement Act, a law that… will fine social media companies up to $57 million if they do not remove hate speech, defamation and incitements to violence within 24 hours."[1669] German politicians also agreed not to use social bots during the election, and organizations were established to monitor the media to discourage and debunk false information.[1670]

Merkel is poised to be the leader of the free world with Trump's abdication of the role. She has been a steadfast champion of democracy, the European Union, and its allies. I hope she is successful, but I do believe that these events have hampered her influence. Merkel's influence and integrity are much needed on the world stage.

Putin is intent on destroying democracy and the alliances that have protected it for decades. Daily, more information is being revealed as to his involvement: namely, interfering in democratic elections around the globe, particularly with 'fake news,' to support candidates that he perceives will be more favourable to his agenda and discredit those who are not. The Russians are using social media to promote divisiveness in American society. *Fox News* reported that Russians sent out hashtags to promote kneeling and boycott the NFL.[1671] This is but one example of the Russian strategy to create divisiveness around the globe, and they are making considerable progress. This assault on democracy can be defeated only if the citizens of the free world do not allow the Russians and Trump to divide us.

There are commonalities between the leaders of this insidious populist movement and authoritarian leaders. Many of them admire Putin, undermine freedom of the press, discredit the establishment, and promote a protectionist, nationalistic sovereignty. They are anti-immigration and divisive, and they blame others for their plight. They gain power and popularity by claiming to be the 'voice of the people' by arousing the emotions, passions, and prejudices of the people. They lead by issuing threats and evoking fear.

Citizens of America and 'the free world' must make choices while they still have that option available. The choice is between people and nations isolating themselves and living in fear, or lifting each other up with compassion so that everyone benefits. History has borne out that authoritarian politics do not result in improved economic conditions for average citizens, nor has it made them safer. The people of Turkey and Venezuela elected authoritarians, and choice is no longer an option. While many in those countries are now protesting, it would have been much easier had they made an earlier choice that would not have threatened their civil liberties. Surely, dictatorships such as Russia, North Korea, China, Cuba, etc. are not to be envied by citizens of the free word.

For those who felt that the Democrats did not take care of them during the Obama administration, what responsibility will they accept for electing a Republican House and Senate that obstructed the Obama administration from accomplishing their goals? Then they rewarded the obstructionists. While the Democratic Party is in need of self-reflection, perhaps the registered voters would benefit from it as well. Unlike the Republicans, the Democrats have at least demonstrated a willingness to cooperate on bipartisan issues when they are able to support them, such as the proposals on health care and DACA.

The media appears not to have accepted any responsibility and has failed to reflect on its contribution to the election outcome. While there has been some excellent investigative reporting, the continuing coverage of the presidency has been convoluted and fails to provide concise, factual reporting to articulate the consequences of the polices of this administration, focusing instead on the day to day sensations. For example, the Trump administration regularly implies that they are emulating the Canadian merit immigration system. This is misleading, and I have seen little clarification by the media. Trump regularly misrepresents chain migration, which is very seldom corrected by the media. Many perceive that ISIS has been defeated which is far from accurate. The economy and increase in wages is often attributed to Trump yet the fact that some European countries are actually performing better is often overlooked. There has been little acknowledgement that these bonuses are temporary and that wage increases will not be distributed equally.

America is not the greatest, but it could be. Jeff Daniels played the fictional character Will McAvoy in the HBO political drama series *Newsroom*. Excerpts from the dialogue are as follows:

> We stood up for what was right. We fought for moral reasons, we passed laws, struck down laws for moral reasons, we waged wars on poverty, not poor people… we cared about our neighbors… we never beat our chest. We aspired to intelligence, we didn't belittle it, it didn't make us feel inferior… we didn't scare so easy… We were able to be all these things, and to do all these things, because we were informed. By great men, men who were revered. First step in solving any problem is recognizing there is one.[1672]

Blaming globalization, trade agreements, and immigration for job loss may feel good, but that does not lead to effective solutions because doing so is addressing the wrong issues. While I could find no evidence that authoritarian leadership has positive effects on economic conditions for the average citizen or for security and safety, there is substantiation for positive outcomes in democratic societies.

According to *Ranking of America*, Singapore, Hong Kong, and Italy are the top three countries in achieving healthcare efficiency, while the US ranks forty-fourth.[1673] The Gini Index identifies the top three countries in equality of income distribution as Finland, the Faroe Islands (part of Denmark), and Slovakia, while the US ranks fortieth.[1674] The United Nations Office on Drugs and Crime 2012 statistics identified Singapore, Iceland, and Japan as having the lowest homicide rates, with Sweden, Spain, and the Netherlands close behind.[1675,1676] According to *Ranking America*, the US ranks forty-third in homicide rates.[1677] The *World Prison Brief* from the Institute for Criminal Policy Research ranked countries according to prison populations. While the countries having the lowest rates are not necessarily comparable to larger countries, examples of countries with low prison populations include the United Kingdom, Denmark, and Sweden. The US has the highest prison population.[1678] *Ranking of America* reported that the United Nations Economic and Social Commission ranks Norway as having the highest ranking for human security,[1679] and the report identifies Canada and Australia with high scores for this indicator. The US ranks sixty-fourth.[1680] As reported by Leyland Cecco in the *Globe and Mail*, Iceland, Canada, and Australia have the highest rankings for tolerance and inclusion, while the US ranks ninth.[1681]

There seems to be a correlation between success in the above-mentioned indicators and happiness. According to *Ranking of America,* the top three countries in reported happiness are Denmark, Norway, and Switzerland. Canada ranks a close sixth. The US ranks seventeenth.[1682] There is much that can be learned by examining these successes and how they might be adapted to work for those countries that desire improved outcomes. The current priorities and values of America are reflected in the country's rankings.

Economic prosperity, successful corporations, and the 'American Dream' do not have to be sacrificed to achieve better outcomes.

It may come as a surprise that I agree with some of Trump and the GOP's stated policy intentions. I agree with the need for secure immigration policies, more affordable healthcare, job creation, improvement in the infrastructure, healthy corporations, solutions regarding growing financial debt, and a review of NAFTA, just to mention a few. If I believed everything they said, I would vote for Trump and the Republicans! I just heard a representative of the Trump administration in Davos blaming the individual tax cuts' impermanence on the Democrats, because the Democrats did not vote for the tax bill. Hogwash! Remember, the Republicans were constrained from making them permanent because they cannot create a debt load that exceeds ten years. The GOP chose to make corporate tax cuts permanent instead. What I object to are the motives for, and implementation of, these proposed solutions, which are often inconsistent with the promises made when promoting them to the public.

The raging debate on Trump's mental health status is irrelevant, as is mental health status' relevance in the gun control debate. People having a mental illness have much to contribute to society and many famous, accomplished people have or had mental illnesses, including: Abraham Lincoln, his wife Mary Todd Lincoln, Winston Churchill, John Nash, Martin Luther King, and Isaac Newton, just to mention a few. It is not a diagnosis of mental illness that is important, but rather the level of dangerousness and predisposition to violence that should be at issue. A person may have a history of physical abuse and violence without having been diagnosed with a mental illness. Should they have a gun, or their finger on the button?

The problem is the polarization, in part facilitated by the Russians to promote discord. After Democrat Conor Lamb won in the Republican state of Pennsylvania, he declared that it is Congress' job "to attack the problems, not each other." This I believe is the only viable solution.

At the same time, I do think it is imperative that voters understand and accept responsibility for the consequences of their decisions. In the case of Trump supporters, even though their desire for change and economic prosperity is understandable, they are complicit because they are able to ignore or endorse the fallout from his agenda and rhetoric.

Just prior to the final print outlay for this book, several critical issues came to light in mid-March 2018 which pertain to the dangerousness of Donald Trump and the potential consequences of this administration. The following information is not sourced but has been widely reported by numerous media outlets and is easily verifiable.

I do not fault Trump for wanting people around him that will support his agenda. He had the right to fire Secretary of State Rex Tillerson and there appears to be some merit to the firing of FBI Deputy Director Andrew McCabe by Attorney General Jeff Sessions. While McCabe's allegations that he was publicly attacked by Trump on an ongoing basis have considerable merit, it does not explain away the findings of the FBI Office of Professional Responsibility that he lacked candor while providing testimony under oath during an investigation as to how the FBI and Justice Department handled themselves during the 2016 presidential election. Unfortunately, this may provide justification for further investigation into the Clinton email server. That and the report from the Republican member of the House Intel Committee that there was no collusion with Russia by the Trump campaign. Both of these incidents provided ammunition for Trump to challenge the validity of the Mueller investigation.

Trump went on a twitter rant for several days, and contrary to his administration's assertions that there is no discussion about firing Mueller, it is evident that Trump would like to do so but is being restrained. While Democrats and some Republicans are urging that the special council be allowed to conclude his report, warning not to do so would create a constitutional crisis, some Republicans support Trump's call to shut down the investigation because it has gone on too long. The Republican-led Travelgate investigation, only one of the many in the Whitewater investigation during the Bill Clinton administration took seven years. There are clearly different standards applied to Democrats and Republicans by Republicans when it concerns accountability. And to that point, if McCabe did break the rules, I think there needs to be accountability. However, are we to believe that there have not been similar FBI breaches perpetrated by Republicans? I mentioned an issue regarding Rudy Giuliani disclosing information that was purportedly leaked to him by the FBI regarding Hillary Clinton's email investigation. Is this being examined? I also held the belief that Comey took the extraordinary measure of commenting on the report to shut down agitation from FBI agents that were upset that Hillary was not charged. Trump does not hold the belief that he should be held accountable.

The dangerousness of Donald Trump lies not in his desire to have people surrounding him of a like ideology, it is his unwavering conviction that he, and he alone, has all the answers. While he portends to consult, and creates a perception that he wants bipartisan solutions, the resulting actions belie those declarations. He has rejected bipartisan plans for health care and DACA. After consultation with students and families following the Parkland school shooting, his proposal for gun control did not include increasing the age limit for access to automatic weapons as promised and did include arming trained teachers to have weapons in schools, which was not supported by most teachers and the group that met with him.

In firing Rex Tillerson, he noted that one of the reasons was their variance on the issue of Iran. It appears that Trump is determined to escalate conflict with Iran, despite considerable pushback from advisors and world leaders.

Indeed, on May 8, 2018, Trump cancelled the Iran deal, contrary to the advice of international partners to the agreement and many in his administration, including Secretary of Defense James Mattis. There were other options to address Trump's concerns regarding Iran, including one proposed by French president Emmanuel Macron to develop an additional deal with Iran, while keeping the original in place. Is Trump's motive to keep America safe or is he more interested in destroying Obama's legacy? I am convinced it is the latter. How will this impact negotiations with North Korea? Even if an agreement is reached, who will breach it first?

His lies to world leaders, his viciousness, his conflicts of interest, lack of accountability and divisiveness on the world stage are dangerous. In March 2018 he bragged about lying to the Prime Minister of Canada that the US had a trade deficit with Canada. At first, he claimed he did so without knowing (how can that be?) but once knowing, he doubled down later in a tweet repeating that the US had a trade deficit with Canada. He is eroding the trust of allies and those, like North Korea, with whom he intends to negotiate denuclearization. His viciousness was once again displayed in his firing of Rex Tillerson, who found out about it in a tweet which was intended to humiliate him. If Trump will do this to someone who was working for him, what is he capable of when dealing with a nuclear crisis?

His lack of empathy makes him dangerous. How can he casually reference eating the most beautiful piece of cake while informing Chinese president Xi Jinping that he just launched missile strikes on Iraq, was corrected by Xi Jinping that he meant Syria, without any understanding of the solemnity that he just ordered strikes that could result in deaths of civilians (at least 9 civilians, including 4 children were killed in the strike), even if the strike was self-righteous? Contrary to his assertions that he would deal with DACA with heart, he created an untenable position for them, has turned down bipartisan proposals and used them as a political pawn.

Trump's potential conflicts of interest are of concern because there is no candor, and motives regarding any international negotiations are suspect, particularly as it relates to Russia. Several members of Trump's administration were denied security clearance, including Trump's personal aid and son-in-law Jared Kushner. His personal aid was escorted from the building but later hired with the Trump campaign. Consideration is being given to providing Kushner with another role in the White House. Security concerns were related to high stake gambling, which is not illegal. While Kushner has denied all wrongdoing, he has failed consistently to pass a security clearance after having had a temporary top security clearance for over a year. Why? Trump's interest in Russia has already been detailed in other chapters.

Although bipartisan legislation was passed in the summer of 2017 for additional sanctions on Russia, Trump refused to impose them until he was forced to act when Britain announced that they had evidence that Russia was responsible for the poisoning of a former double agent Russian/British spy and his daughter with a military-grade nerve agent (chemical weapon) known to be made by Russia. Trump's response was delayed and fell short of the sanctions in legislation passed in the previous summer. The US is blaming Russia for attacks on American electrical grids, water, transportation and nuclear grids. The tensions with Russia are escalating. Even though the intelligence community has determined that Russia is a cyber threat attempting to undermine American institutions, National Security Director and head of US Cyber Command Mike Rogers informed a Senate panel that he has not been given direction by the President and he does not have the authority to counter these attacks. This is dangerous, not only for the US but the world. The world's tensions with Russia are quickly escalating in an environment fraught with global crises. What are the motives for this reluctance to take on Putin? It is difficult to believe that it is in the best interest of America, as opposed to personal gain.

Trump congratulated Putin on winning yet another 6-year term in office as President. John McCain tweeted, "An American president does not lead the Free World by congratulating dictators on winning sham elections. And by doing so with Vladimir Putin, President Trump insulted every Russian citizen who was denied the right to vote in a free and fair election."[1683] I could not have said it better myself. Trump is a threat to democracy.

The Trump administration is moving forward to address opioid addiction, designating it as a national public health emergency instead of the promised national emergency designation, limiting access to federal funds. The plan includes law enforcement and prohibition, prevention and education, and treatment. The $6 billion allocated to address the epidemic falls short of the funding required, especially considering that President's Council of Economic Advisers estimated that in 2015 the cost of the opioid drug epidemic was $504 billion. Fifty per cent of opioid addiction is from prescribed drugs. It was not clear what efforts would be made to curtail over-prescription or, more insidious, the selling of opioids by doctors for personal gain, and the dumping of opioids by pharmaceutical companies for corporate profits in communities with the full knowledge that they are not for legal use.

The problem is that, as access to prescriptions is curtailed, there is an increase in use of illegal synthetic opioids primarily coming from China through the mail, but also coming through Mexican and Canadian border crossings. The Wall is not going to stop this trafficking and if Trump were truly interested in addressing this epidemic, the money would be better spent on the opioid crisis.

The greatest danger of Trump's plan is the proposal to apply the death penalty to drug dealers. There is no definitive research that this would provide an effective deterrent. While I am empathetic to the rationale in that thousands die as a result of the drug dealers' illegal behaviour, it is a draconian measure more characteristic of a tyrannical dictatorship like that in the Philippines, Cuba, China, and North Korea, than a democracy. Would this measure also apply to pharmaceutical companies that have essentially been trafficking opioids for corporate gain?

A whistleblower exposed that Facebook allegedly breached the privacy of 50 million Facebook users whose information may have been harvested by Cambridge Analytica, a UK firm contracted by the Trump campaign to target voters with their profiles and behaviours for the 2016 election. The question is whether this information was harvested without the knowledge of Facebook users, and if so, were these people targeted to promote Trump's campaign, or were they bombarded with fake news to manipulate the voters? On the March 20, 2018 episode of the *View*, Meghan McCain said that Obama did the same thing. This is a false comparison. I think it is legitimate to do surveys with users' knowledge as to how it is being used, so that people and organizations are able to educate and promote services and products. As a mental health provider, I regularly did this to dispel the myths regarding mental illness. I believe this is what Obama did, using social media as a way to communicate. However, the allegations regarding the methods used by Cambridge Analytica for the Trump campaign take this to a new level. It is interesting to note that this whistleblower worked for the Canadian federal Liberal party in 2009 and his contract was not renewed because he put forward a similar proposal to the one used by Cambridge Analytica and the party felt it was too invasive and were uncomfortable with the concept.

Hopefully this will be investigated on a worldwide basis, resulting in more stringent regulations to prevent this invasion and misuse of private information. Yes, regulations are paramount to protect users from nefarious corporate practices. While I do think Facebook needs to be held accountable, it does continue to astound me that Trump dispenses fake news daily, and does so with impunity, as do Fox News and other ultra-right sites.

Meghan McCain obviously has the capacity to admire and respect those with whom she disagrees politically, Joe Biden being but one example. In the case of Hillary Clinton and Obama, I detect a personal animosity. Like her father, she has expressed the view that Hillary should stop talking and should not have written a book. After losing the 2008 election to Obama, John McCain was not threatened with investigations, jail, and maligned on an almost daily basis. There have been several occasions on which McCain's criticism of Obama and Clinton was unwarranted. Given Putin's efforts to discredit Hillary and other world leaders in an effort to influence elections, I think we have much to learn from their experiences.

It has occurred to me that Meghan McCain has informed viewers several times that she did not vote for Trump based on personal reasons, primarily the way that Trump has treated her father, particularly during his illness. I have the impression that, had it not been for that, she, like many of her friends, may have voted for Trump. It has also occurred to me that Obama defeated her father's bid for the presidency.

I think it is fair to make comparisons if based on factual information, but without proper context, or complete information, is Meghan McCain contributing to the divisiveness? I do not agree with her father's politics, but I do admire him as a person with integrity. I also value her contribution to the *View*, providing the conservative perspective. I agree with her point that the demonization has to stop. I agree with some of her examples of the left exceeding boundaries. Hillary has apologized on those occasions as did Joy Behar regarding her comments about Pence's religious beliefs. Jim Carrey's pictures depicting Republicans in vile ways do not have any redeeming value and only serve to incite divisiveness. Yet Hillary's apologies are rejected by the right. On the other hand, this administration's continued bullying has been directed at politicians, organizations, segments of American society, as well as individuals. Yet I do not see any apologies, nor have I seen accountability. Republicans do not seem to recognize that their expressions have been not only offensive, but have caused considerable damage to those targeted. There is a difference between holding someone accountable and demonizing them.

Trump is dangerous, and just as alarming are those who continue to defend him, normalize him, and give him a chance, either because they do not recognize the danger or because they do not care. The level of danger was evident prior to his election. Whether the result of ignorance or any other reason, those who support him have sanctioned his behaviour. The leaders of the GOP are guilty of having endorsed his hateful speech and bullying. In contrast, consider a recent incident in Canada. *CBC* disclosed that Senator Lynn Beyak was kicked out of the Conservative caucus for making racist comments. The Senator holds a view that the establishment of residential schools for indigenous children was a well-intentioned policy. The government and most Canadians consider this policy reprehensible, and the government is negotiating reparations for the extensive damages experienced by people who, as children, were separated from their families and communities, and were subjected to physical and sexual abuse. The Senator posted a letter online that was considered racist, and she refused to be educated on the subject and to remove the offending passages. She was censured by the Conservative party, and removed from the Conservative caucus, not for holding a view contrary to government policy, but rather for making racist comments.[1684]

For those supporters who regularly bemoan that Trump has not been given a chance and that the constant barrage of criticism is unfair, I would argue that Trump and his supporters are responsible. Who, more than Justin Trudeau, has given President Trump a chance and made ongoing efforts to engage him, absent of criticism? Yet Trump bragged about lying to him in discussions regarding NAFTA. Leaders like Theresa May and Angela Merkel were willing to reach out and give him a chance, but they were embarrassed on the world stage by Trump. Trump did not give those who did not support him a chance. He speaks to his base at the exclusion the rest of the country. Those like Chuck Jones, who correct him and hold him accountable, become victims of Trump's vitriolic missives on twitter, resulting in harassment and death threats from his supporters. Trump has had numerous opportunities to demonstrate that he would represent the people, but has chosen to abandon them. While Republican leaders have refused to hold Trump accountable, it appears the courts are. A New York court has denied Trump's request that Summer Zervos's defamation case be dismissed. The court supported the decision using the Paula Jones Supreme court decision discussed earlier in this book. You may recall the brief to this decision was written by Kellyanne Conway's husband.

President Trump expressed ongoing frustration that the Department of Justice had not pursued further investigation of his opponent, Hillary, regarding potential pay-for-play in relation to the Clinton Foundation while she was Secretary of State. These allegations were not substantiated in previous investigations. Is it just coincidence that according to *BBC*, the Department of Justice is now investigating the Clinton Foundation in relation to donations and possible pay-for-play? Journalists have investigated this for years with no substantiation.[1685] Will the GOP investigate Trump for possible pay-for-play for reversing his positions on China after his family business received a valuable ten-year trademark from its government? If the current investigation finds no reason to indict Hillary, will the GOP accept the results, or will they find a reason to open another investigation? If a Democrat president had done any one of the things that Donald Trump has done, the Republicans would be up in arms.

Will actions be taken to prevent the threat of Donald Trump initiating a nuclear incident, or will this only occur once it is already too late?

He has eroded the trust of the international community, its leaders, and allies. How can this make the world a safer place? Trump cannot be trusted even when he makes an agreement because he frequently changes his mind. He made a media spectacle out of a meeting in which he committed to accepting a bipartisan plan that included a solution for 'the dreamers,' as long as the plan included border security measures and funding for the wall. He clarified that only portions of the border needed a wall. Trump said that if that group came forward with a bipartisan plan, "I'm signing it. I mean, I will be signing it. I'm not going to say, 'Oh, gee, I want this or I want that.' I'll be signing it, because I have a lot of confidence in the people in this room that they're going to come up with something really good." They did and he didn't.

Three Republicans and three Democrats worked together to craft the Graham-Durban plan. Both sides made concessions and fully expected the President's endorsement but were blindsided in a heated meeting in which Trump made some inflammatory comments. The news cycles for the next several days became a debate as to whether Trump said "sh#thole" or "sh#thouse" while referring to several countries with primarily black populations, and referred to Norway as a desirable source of immigrants to the US. While the White House insists that race did not play a role in the development of the merit-based plan, Trump's intent is clear: a preference for immigration from white countries.

Trump's failure to keep his word is not an aberration, but part of a pattern. If he cannot keep his word with members of his own party, there is no reason to believe that he will keep his word with allies or other countries. There is no reason to trust him. It is one thing for domestic issues; it is another on the world stage, especially when it involves nuclear weapons.

I am grateful that my friends and family, who do not agree with my views, have not abandoned me. I will not reject them for supporting Trump. I did however declare that I will not accept racist expressions on my Facebook and I will unfriend anybody who does so. I will not be silent when confronted by information designed to generate hate and divisiveness. Perhaps shows such as the new *Roseanne* and the *View* will provide an opportunity for us to seek understanding and dialogue about what we have in common.

Responding with hate to the racism of Donald Trump is not the answer. As so eloquently said by Martin Luther King Jr. "Let no man pull you low enough to hate him."[1686] That does not preclude identifying the issue for what it is – racism. This is a long-time pattern with Trump and many people have let him know it is unacceptable behaviour. At this time he is unwilling to change so it is imperative that it is repudiated.

The choices that the citizens of the free world make during this reign of chaos will reveal the beliefs, values, and desires of those citizens, which will determine the outcome on the world stage.

The leader of a nation, elected by the people, represents the values of the people. The 2016 US presidential election was not about policies; it was about belief systems. It would appear that Americans value wealth and power above social equality, income equality, health care, risk to the environment, civil rights, the constitution, the increased threat to nuclear war, and democracy. It would appear that Americans will accept bullying, lying, blaming, corruption, racism, and misogyny in exchange for a modest, temporary increase in their pay checks and encoding the tenets of the religious right. These priorities are reflected not only in *Ranking of America* data, but also in the *US News* 2018 Best Country rankings, which measures global performance in numerous categories.[1687] Not surprisingly, the US ranked first in economic and military power. However, the US ranked only eighth overall, with Switzerland, Canada and Germany ranked as the top three for best country.[1688]

Confidence in US leadership has taken a sharp decline around the world except for Russia and Israel. America as a beacon of light has dimmed. This perception is supported, not only in the *Ranking of America* data, but also a Gallup poll conducted in January 2018 which reported an 18% drop in the approval of US leadership during the first year of Trump's presidency.[1689] *US News* 2018 Best Country elaborated on America's fall in rank as "fueled by the world's perceptions of the country becoming less progressive and trustworthy, more politically unstable and a president who after just a year in office is far more unpopular than any other head of state or company CEO."[1690] Trump had the lowest approval rating from citizens around the world, lower than that of Vladimir Putin and Rodrigo Duterte. The world did not abandon America. America abandoned the world. Could the flame on the Statue of Liberty be extinguished?

It matters not that many Americans do not share Trump's values; he was elected by the people of the US and speaks for America. Americans will have an opportunity in the midterm elections and the 2020 US presidential election to change that perception. Citizens of the free world will also have opportunities in upcoming elections. The outcome of those elections will reveal the values of the people. The power is in the hands of the people. We as citizens of the free world can make a difference if we make informed decisions and understand and are willing to accept the consequences.

We, as voters, need to remember that whoever runs against a populist candidate supported by Russia, will be subject to the same kind of vile character assassination and fake news as Macron, Merkel and yes, Hillary. Just as many remain convinced that Obama was not born in the US, many are also convinced that Hillary was a choice between two evils, despite the disclosure of the Russian fake news. In my research, I simply did not find substantiation for that view.

Ontarians have that choice to make in June 2018. I want to vote liberal, but I am disillusioned with the current leadership. I seriously considered a Conservative vote until the Conservative party nominated Doug Ford in a controversial process. Doug Ford is the brother of former Toronto Mayor Rob Ford, who was so controversial that he was featured in American news and comedy shows. Doug Ford has a Trumpian leadership style and espouses similar values. His record as a former city councilor during his brother's administration belies his campaign promises. There are already allegations that a convicted fraudster was drumming up new memberships for the Progressive Conservative party nomination. Patrick Brown, the former leader of the PC party, was asked to step down just before the nomination, following allegations of sexual misconduct by two women. This is unlike the Republicans, who have refused to hold their leader accountable for his own behaviour, despite numerous complaints and evidence. Brown vehemently denies the claims and the story of one of the women has been revised while another person who claims to be a witness has contradicted some of the details provided by the accusers. If the allegations are not true, it is a travesty; if they are, Brown should not be the leader. Not believing women regarding sexual misconduct is dangerous.

I am not sure about the solution, but in the rare instances when the allegations are embellished or untrue, there does need to be some mechanism for due process to reduce the risk of condemning someone that is innocent. There may also be a need for consideration of the nature of the misconduct, the timing, and whether there has been a change in behaviour. Is our goal to change the culture or punish? All incidents should be taken seriously because they have a long-term psychological impact for the victims. In this new environment, it needs to be made clear that any unwanted touching is a violation. If an incident occurred thirty years ago, the misconduct did not involve a physical violation or the behaviour was not coerced or repeated when rejected, does that merit destroying someone's career? For example, the picture with Franken was inappropriate, and perhaps the nature of touching while taking pictures was as well. Has there been a change in behaviour? Is there regret that the behaviour caused discomfort for those women? Should it be judged alongside coercion such as that described in the Roy Moore case, the USA Gymnastics case, or the Cosby case? Excessive punishment may create resentment and backlash that undermines the cause.

I have a dilemma; I will vote but I will not vote for a Doug Ford. Sadly, he is leading in the polls.

In its 2018 Best Country Rankings, *US News* advised that "the Washington, D.C.-based Freedom House warned that democracy was 'in crisis' around the world, in no small part because of Trump's repeated attacks on the judiciary system and news media in the U.S., lack of seeking 'meaningful input' from relevant agencies and 'violations of basic ethical standards.'"[1691]

Perhaps the youth will be the salvation of democracy. Following yet another horrific school shooting in Parkland Florida, students have organized protests and rallies, calling for change in gun control. Their numbers at rallies and protests have been impressive and their speeches powerful, insightful and impassioned. Putting partisan politics aside, they are saying 'never again'.

In dealing with tyranny, H.L. Mencken warned that "[t]he trouble about fighting for human freedom is that you have to spend much of your life defending sons of b[#]tches: for oppressive laws are always aimed at them originally, and oppression must be stopped in the beginning if it is to be stopped at all. History demonstrates that the first casualty of hyper-partisan politics is often civil liberties."[1692]

If oppression must be stopped in the beginning, is it already too late? I remain hopeful that democracy will prevail, not only in the US, but also around the world.

Endnotes

1   Vocabulary.com Dictionary. n.d. *trump*. Accessed September 23, 2016. https://www.vocabulary.com/dictionary/trump.

2   Jay Asher. n.d. *Jay Asher > Quotes > Quotable Quote*. Accessed June 16, 2016. https://www.goodreads.com/quotes/164355-no-one-knows-for-certain-how-much-impact-they-have.

3   Ontario Ministry of Transportation. 2015. *Ontario Border Crossing*. Queen's Printer for Ontario. December 24. Accessed August 13, 2016. http://www.mto.gov.on.ca/english/ontario-511/ontario-border-crossings.shtml.

4   International Joint Commission. 2016. *Role of the IJC*. International Joint Commission. Accessed August 13, 2016. http://www.ijc.org/en_/Role_of_the_Commission.

5   The City of Windsor. 2016. *Illness Costs of Air Pollution*. Accessed August 13, 2016. http://www.citywindsor.ca/residents/environment/Environmental-Master-Plan/Goal-B-Create-Healthy-Communities/Pages/Illness-Costs-of-Air-Pollution.aspx.

6   Dave Battagello. 2014. *Windsor's Air Quality Better, but Still among Worst in Ontario, Report Says*. April 24. http://windsorstar.com/health/windsors-air-quality-better-but-still-among-worst-in-ontario-report-says.

7   The City of Windsor. 2016. *Illness Costs of Air Pollution*. Accessed August 13, 2016.

8   The Canadian Press. 2013. *NAFTA Turns 20: Mexico is Pact's Biggest Winner*. December 31. http://www.cbc.ca/news/canada/nafta-turns-20-mexico-is-pact-s-biggest-winner-1.2478480.

9   James McBride and Mohammed Aly Sergie. 2016. *NAFTA's Economic Impact*. July 26. http://www.cfr.org/trade/naftas-economic-impact/p15790.

10 Philippe Bergevin. 2008. *The Global Financial Crisis and Its Impact on Canada*. December. https://lop.parl.ca/content/lop/ResearchPublications/prb0834_05-e.htm.

11 Wikipedia Contributors. *Windsor, Ontario*. Wikipedia, The Free Encyclopedia. Accessed December 20, 2017. https://en.wikipedia.org/wiki/Windsor,_Ontario.

12 Statistics Canada. 2010. *Visible Minority Groups, 2006 Counts, for Canada, Provinces and Territories - 20% Sample Data*. October 6. http://www12.statcan.ca/census-recensement/2006/dp-pd/hlt/97-562/pages/page.cfm?Lang=E&Geo=PR&Code=01&Table=1&Data=Count&StartRec=1&Sort=11&Display=Page&CSDFilter=5000.

13 The Historica-Dominion Institute. n.d. *Black History Canada: Underground Railroad*. Accessed August 13, 2016. http://www.blackhistorycanada.ca/events.php?themeid=3&id=6.

14 Evan Morris. 2016. *Sheeny*. Accessed June 16, 2016. http://www.word-detective.com/2011/06/sheeny/.

15 A group of gangsters operating out of Detroit involved in bootlegging as well as other crimes, associated with Al Capone's gang.

16 "Black Day in July," written and sung by Canadian singer-songwriter Gordon Lightfoot about the riots in Detroit.

17 Ambrose Bierce. 2016. *Ambrose Bierce Quotes*. Accessed June 16, 2018. http://www.goodreads.com/quotes/1470-prejudice-is-a-vagrant-opinion-without-visible-means-of-support.

18 Alberto A. Martinez. 2015. *The Media Needs to Stop Telling this Lie about Donald Trump. I'm a Sanders Supporter — And Value Honesty*. December 21. http://www.salon.com/2015/12/21/the_media_needs_to_stop_telling_this_lie_about_donald_trump_im_a_sanders_supporter_and_value_honesty.

19 William Shakespeare. n.d. *William Shakespeare > Quotes > Quotable Quote*. Accessed June 16, 2016. https://www.goodreads.com/quotes/379204-all-that-glisters-is-not-gold-often-have-you-heard.

20 Think Progress. 2016. *Donald Trump's Son: My 'Billionaire' Dad Is Just a 'Blue Collar Guy.'* February 1. Accessed August 15, 2016. https://thinkprogress.org/donald-trumps-son-my-billionaire-dad-is-just-a-blue-collar-guy-f45aef100fd7#.ls7qme9x6.

21 Ibid.

22 Steve Reilly. 2016. *USA Today Exclusive: Hundreds Allege Donald Trump Doesn't Pay His Bills*. June 9. http://www.usatoday.com/story/news/politics/elections/2016/06/09/donald-trump-unpaid-bills-republican-president-laswuits/85297274/.

23 Bernard Condon. 2016. *The Star News World Donald Trump's Taj Mahal Failure Crushed Many of His Contractors*. June 29. https://www.thestar.com/news/world/2016/06/29/donald-trumps-taj-mahal-failure-crushed-many-of-his-contractors.html.

24 Ibid.

25 Drew Griffin et al. 2016. *Trump Maralago*. March 18. http://money.cnn.com/2016/03/18/news/economy/trump-maralago/.

26 Ibid.

27 Linda Qiu. 2016. *Yep, Donald Trump's Companies Have Declared Bankruptcy...More than Four*. June 21. http://www.politifact.com/truth-o-meter/statements/2016/jun/21/hillary-clinton/yep-donald-trumps-companies-have-declared-bankrupt/.

28 Ibid.

29 Nick Carey and Emily Stephenson. 2016. *Trump's Corporate Targets Face Tricky Task in Fending off His Attacks*. June 10. http://www.reuters.com/article/us-usa-election-trump-companies-iduskcn0yw1jz.

30 NPR Staff. 2016. *Fact Check and Full Transcript of the Final 2016 Presidential Debate*. October 19. http://www.npr.org/2016/10/19/498293478/fact-check-trump-and-clinton-s-final-presidential-debate.

31 Joseph Tanfani. 2016. *Trump Was Once So Involved in Trying to Block an Indian Casino that He Secretly Approved Attack Ads.* June 30. http://www.latimes.com/politics/la-na-pol-trump-anti-indian-campaign-20160630-snap-story.html.

32 Kathy Kiely. 2016. *The Making of Donald Trump, as Told by a Journalistic Nemesis.* August 6. http://www.commondreams.org/views/2016/08/06/making-donald-trump-told-journalistic-nemesis.

33 Ibid.

34 Ibid.

35 David Cay Johnston, Betsy McCaughey, interview by Michael Smerconish. 2016. *The Real Art of Trump's Deals.* August 27. http://transcripts.cnn.com/transcripts/1608/27/smer.01.html.

36 Nick Carey and Emily Stephenson. 2016. *Trump's Corporate Targets Face Tricky Task in Fending off His Attacks.* June 10.

37 Ibid.

38 NBC News . 2017. *Transcript: NBC News Commander-in-Chief Forum.* September 7. http://press.nbcnews.com/2016/09/07/transcript-nbc-news-commander-in-chief-forum/?cid=sm_tw.

39 Chris Cillizza. 2015. *The Dangerous Anger of Donald Trump.* November 13. https://www.washingtonpost.com/news/the-fix/wp/2015/11/13/the-remarkably-unappealling-anger-of-donald-trump/.

40 Jonathan Martin and Alan Rappeport. 2015. *Donald Trump Says John McCain Is No War Hero, Setting off Another Storm.* July 18. http://www.nytimes.com/2015/07/19/us/politics/trump-belittles-mccains-war-record.html.

41 Craig Whitlock. 2015. *Questions Linger about Trump's Draft Deferments During Vietnam War.* July 21. https://www.washingtonpost.com/world/national-security/questions-linger-about-trumps-draft-deferments-during-vietnam-war/2015/07/21/257677bc-2fdd-11e5-8353-1215475949f4_story.html.

42 Dan Lamothe. 2016. *It's Legal for Donald Trump to Accept a Purple Heart. How He Handled It Is Up for Debate.* August 3. https://www.washingtonpost.com/news/checkpoint/wp/2016/08/03/its-legal-for-donald-trump-to-accept-a-purple-heart-how-he-handled-it-is-up-for-debate/.

43 Steve Turnham. 2016. *Donald Trump to Father of Fallen Soldier: 'I've Made a Lot of Sacrifices'.* July 30. http://abcnews.go.com/Politics/donald-trump-father-fallen-soldier-ive-made-lot/story?id=41015051.

44 Brinley F. Bruton. 2016. *Gold Star Families Attack Trump over Comments about Ghazala Khan.* August 1. http://www.cnbc.com/2016/08/01/gold-star-families-attack-trump-over-comments-about-ghazala-khan.html.

45 CNN. 2016. *Trump Defends Tweet about Sexual Assault.* September 7. https://www.cnn.com/2016/09/08/politics/donald-trump-military-sexual-assault/index.html.

46 Ibid.

47 Donald J Trump. 2013 8:17 PM. *Twitter Post.* June 18. https://twitter.com/realdonaldtrump/status/347191326112112640.

48 Michele A. Berdy 2016. *Trump to Putin: What'd You Call Me?* March 25. https://themoscowtimes.com/articles/trump-to-putin-whatd-you-call-me-52252.

49 Jose Pagliery. 2016. *Donald Trump's Ties to Russia Explained.* July 31. http://money.cnn.com/2016/07/29/news/donald-trump-russia-ties/.

50 Kathy Kiely. 2016. *The Making of Donald Trump, as Told by a Journalistic Nemesis.* August 6. http://www.commondreams.org/views/2016/08/06/making-donald-trump-told-journalistic-nemesis.

51 Jose Pagliery. 2016. *Donald Trump's Ties to Russia Explained.* July 31.

52 Hazel Heyer. 2008. *Executive Talk: Donald Trump Jr. Bullish on Russia and Few Emerging Markets.* September 15. https://eturbonews.com/9788/executive-talk-donald-trump-jr-bullish-russia-and-few-emerging-ma.

53 Information sourced from *Wikipedia*, including the sources used in *Wikipedia*, are covered under the copyright terms of the Creative Commons Attribution Share-Alike license: https://creativecommons.org/licenses/by-sa/3.0/. This notice will serve for all succeeding references to *Wikipedia* and related sources.

54 Luke Harding. 2016. *How Trump's Campaign Chief Got a Strongman Elected President of Ukraine.* August 16. https://www.theguardian.com/us-news/2016/aug/16/donald-trump-campaign-paul-manafort-ukraine-yanukovich.

55 Wikipedia Contributors. n.d. *Viktor Yanukovych.* Accessed September 10, 2017. https://en.wikipedia.org/wiki/Viktor_Yanukovych.

56 Reuters. 2016. *Trump Refuses to Condemn Violence at His Rallies.* March 20. http://fortune.com/2016/03/20/trump-wont-condem-violence/.

57 Hank Berrien. 2016. *8 Times Donald Trump Showed He Hated Women.* March 24. http://www.dailywire.com/news/4391/8-times-donald-trump-showed-he-hated-women-hank-berrien.

58 David A. Graham. 2016. *The Lurking Menace of a Trump Rally.* March 10. http://www.theatlantic.com/politics/archive/2016/03/donald-trump-fayetteville/473169/.

59 Nick Corasaniti and Maggie Haberman. 2016. *Donald Trump Suggests 'Second Amendment People' Could Act against Hillary Clinton.* August 9. http://www.nytimes.com/2016/08/10/us/politics/donald-trump-hillary-clinton.html?_r=0.

60 Ashley Killough. 2016. *Trump Says He Would Like to 'Hit' DNC Speakers Who Disparaged Him.* July 29. http://www.cnn.com/2016/07/28/politics/donald-trump-dnc-response/.

61 BBC News. 2016. *US Election: 'I like Waterboarding a Lot', Says Donald Trump.* June 29. http://www.bbc.com/news/election-us-2016-36664752.

62 Louis Jacobson. 2016. Was Saddam Hussein Good at Killing Terrorists, as Donald Trump says? July 7. http://www.politifact.com/truth-o-meter/statements/2016/jul/07/donald-trump/was-saddam-hussein-good-killing-terrorists-donald-/.

63   Sean Sullivan and Jenna Johnson. 2016. *Trump: Clinton's Bodyguards Should 'Disarm Immediately' and 'See What Happens to Her.'* September 16. https://www.washingtonpost.com/news/post-politics/wp/2016/09/16/trump-clintons-bodyguards-should-disarm-immediately-and-see-what-happens-to-her/.

64   Daniel S. Levine 2017. *General Pershing Pig's Blood Myth: 5 Fast Facts You Need to Know.* August 17. http://heavy.com/news/2017/08/general-pershing-trump-bullets-dipped-in-pigs-blood-myth/.

65   Marie Brenner. 1990. *After the Gold Rush.* September. http://www.vanityfair.com/magazine/2015/07/donald-ivana-trump-divorce-prenup-marie-brenner.

66   Ibid.

67   Ibid.

68   Robin Lempel. 2016. *Donald Trump's Net Worth Extremely High? What Marla Maples and Ivana Trump Got as Financial Settlements after Their Divorces.* April 5. http://www.hollywoodtake.com/donald-trumps-net-worth-extremely-high-what-marla-maples-and-ivana-trump- got-financial-153321.

69   Ibid.

70   Carlos Lozada. 2015. *Donald Trump on Women, Sex, Marriage and Feminism.* August 5. https://www.washingtonpost.com/news/book-party/wp/2015/08/05/donald-trump-on-women-sex-marriage-and-feminism/?utm_term=.b027c280b922.

71   Tim Mak and Brandy Zadrozny. 2015. *Ex-wife: Donald Trump Made Me Feel 'Violated' during Sex.* July 27. http://www.thedailybeast.com/articles/2015/07/27/ex-wife-donald-trump-made-feel-violated-during-sex.html.

72   Nina Strochlic. 2015. *The Dumbest Stuff Donald Trump Has Ever Said.* June 30. http://www.thedailybeast.com/articles/2015/06/30/the-dumbest-stuff-donald-trump-has-ever-said.html.

73   Donald J. Trump. 2016 12:56 PM. *Twitter Post.* May 8. https://twitter.com/realdonaldjtunp/status/729399636134379520?lang=en.

74   MTV. 2006. *The Donald Thinks Angelina Jolie's a Dirty Whore.* October 10. http://www.mtv.com/news/2754132/the-donald-thinks-angelina-jolies-a-dirty-whore/.

75   Ryan Teague Beckwith. 2015. *Trump: Debate Moderator Had 'Blood Coming out of Her Wherever.'* August 7. http://time.com/3989652/donald-trump-megyn-kelly-blood-wherever/.

76   Team Marie Claire. 2016. *Donald Trump: The Man Behind the Mouth.* August 5. http://www.marieclaire.co.uk/blogs/550112/donald-trump-quotes.html.

77   Nick Gass. 2015. *The 15 Most Offensive Things That Have Come out of Trump's Mouth.* December 8. http://www.politico.eu/article/15-most-offensive-things-trump-campaign-feminism-migration-racism/.

78   Jordan Phelps. 2016. *Donald Trump in 1994: 'Putting a Wife to Work Is a Very Dangerous Thing.'* June 1. http://abcnews.go.com/Politics/donald-trump-1994-putting-wife-work-dangerous-thing/story?id=39537935.

79   Nina Bahadur. 2015. *18 Real Things Donald Trump Has Actually Said about Women.* August 19. http://www.huffingtonpost.com/entry/18-real-things-donald-trump-has-said-about-women_us_55d356a8e4b07addcb442023.

80   Kirsten Powers. 2016. *Trump Says He Hopes Ivanka Would Quit If She Got Harassed.* August 1. http://www.usatoday.com/story/opinion/2016/08/01/ailes-trump-sexual-harassment-fox-news-women-gretchen-kelly-greta-news-column/87915454/.

81   Nina Bahadur. 2015. *18 Real Things Donald Trump Has Actually Said about Women.* August 19.

82   Andy Bloxham 2011. *The World According to Donald Trump.* June 20. http://www.telegraph.co.uk/news/celebritynews/8586180/The-world-according-to-Donald-Trump.html.

83   Steve Benen. 2016. *Trump Backs Abortion Ban, Calls for 'Punishment' for Women.* March 30. http://www.msnbc.com/rachel-maddow-show/trump-backs-abortion-ban-calls-punishment-women.

84   Dennis Cook. 2006. *Trump Jokes about Dating His Daughter.* March 7. http://usatoday30.usatoday.com/life/people/2006-03-07-trump_x.htm.

85   Daniel Politi. 2016. *Trump Is OK with Calling Ivanka a "Piece of Ass" and Other Horrible Things He Told Howard Stern.* October 8. http://www.slate.com/blogs/the_slatest/2016/10/08/trump_to_howard_stern_you_can_call_ivanka_a_piece_of_ass.html.

86   Ibid.

87   Dean Obeidallah. 2016. *Trump Defends Roger Ailes: 'He Helped Those Women.'* July 24. http://www.thedailybeast.com/articles/2016/07/24/trump-s-indefensible-defense-of-roger-ailes-sexual-harassment.html.

88   Maggie Haberman and Ashley Parker. 2016. *Roger Ailes Is Advising Donald Trump ahead of Presidential Debates.* August 16. http://www.nytimes.com/2016/08/17/us/politics/donald-trump-roger-ailes.html?_r=0.

89   Alex Griswold. 2016. *'No Way' My Father Is Sexist, Because He Hired Me.* September 5. http://www.mediaite.com/tv/ivanka-trump-no-way-my-father-is-sexist-because-he-hired-me/.

90   Walter Ewing, Daniel E. Martínez and Rubén G. Rumbautf. 2015. *The Criminalization of Immigration in the United States.* July 13. https://www.americanimmigrationcouncil.org/research/criminalization-immigration-united-states.

91   Alan Gomez. 2015. *How Violent Are Undocumented Immigrants?* July 16. http://www.usatoday.com/story/news/nation/2015/07/16/voices-gomez-undocumented-immigrant-crime-san-francisco-shooting/30159479/.

92   Theodore Schleifer. 2026. *Trump Defends Criticism of Judge with Mexican Heritage.* June 5. http://www.cnn.com/2016/06/03/politics/donald-trump-tapper-lead/.

93   Ibid.

94   Ibid.

95   Justin Wm. Moyer. 2015. *Trump Says Fans Are 'Very Passionate' after Hearing One of Them Allegedly Assaulted Hispanic Man.* August 21. https://www.washingtonpost.com/news/morning-mix/wp/2015/08/21/trump-says-fans-are-very-passionate-after-hearing-one-of-them-allegedly-assaulted-hispanic-man/.

96   Nick Paumgarten. 2015. *The Death and Life of Atlantic City.* September 7. http://www.newyorker.com/magazine/2015/09/07/the-death-and-life-of-atlantic-city.

97   Congressional Record. 2016. *Donald Trump: Senate.* September 26, 114th Congress, 2nd Session, Issue: Vol. 162, No. 145. https://www.congress.gov/congressional-record/2016/9/26/senate-section/article/S6073-2.

98   Glenn Kessler. 2016. *Did Donald Trump Really Say Those Things?* July 25. https://www.washingtonpost.com/news/fact-checker/wp/2016/07/25/did-donald-trump-really-say-those-things/.

99   Douglas Feiden. 1996. *Trump Hit with Race Suit Blacks: Don Dealt Us out of Casino Jobs.* June 19. http://www.nydailynews.com/archives/money/trump-hit-race-suit-blacks-don-dealt-casino-jobs-article-1.726389.

100   Emily Crockett. 2016. *Trump Actually Pointed at a Supporter and Said "Look at My African American over Here.".* June 3. https://www.vox.com/2016/6/3/11856328/trump-look-at-my-african-american.

101   Ben Shapiro. 2016. *Disgusting: Trump Reverses Himself, Refuses to Disavow David Duke and KKK.* February 28. http://www.dailywire.com/news/3739/disgusting-trump-reverses-himself-refuses-disavow-ben-shapiro.

102   Ibid.

103   Ibid.

104   Amita Kelly. 2016. *Woman Asks Trump about Replacing TSA's 'Heebeejabis' with Veterans.* June 30. http://www.npr.org/2016/06/30/484229621/woman-asks-trump-about-replacing-tsas-heebejabis-with-veterans.

105   Ibid.

106   Sprinklr recently acquired Little Bird, which is a platform for conducting data analysis based on social media.

107   Little Bird. 2016. *62% of the People Trump Re-tweeted This Week Follow Multiple White Supremacist Accounts.* January 28. http://www.mintpressnews.com/213194-2/213194/.

108   Josh Harkinson. 2016. *Trump Selects a White Nationalist Leader as a Delegate in California.* July/August. http://www.motherjones.com/politics/2016/05/donald-trump-white-nationalist-afp-delegate-california/.

109   Ibid.

110   Ibid.

111   Ibid.

112   Aris Folley and Sylvia Cunningham. 2016. *Former 'Apprentice' Contestants Denounce Donald Trump's Candidacy.* April 15. http://www.nbcnews.com/news/nbcblk/former-apprentice-contestants-denounce-donald-trump-s-candidacy-n556306.

113   Ibid.

114   Ibid.

115   Ibid.

116   Ibid.

117   David Ferguson. 2016. *Black Georgia GOP Official Booted from Atlanta Trump Event with No Explanation.* June 26. http://www.rawstory.com/2016/06/black-georgia-gop-official-booted-from-atlanta-trump-event-with-no-explanation/.

118   David A. Graham. 2016. *The Many Scandals of Donald Trump: A Cheat Sheet.* September 7. http://www.theatlantic.com/politics/archive/2016/09/donald-trump-scandals/474726/.

119   Jon Greenberg. 2015. *Trump's Pants on Fire Tweet that Blacks Killed 81% of White Homicide Victims.* November 23. http://www.politifact.com/truth-o-meter/statements/2015/nov/23/donald-trump/trump-tweet-blacks-white-homicide-victims/.

120   Vice News. 2015. *Donald Trump Just Tweeted and Deleted a Picture Featuring Nazi SS Soldiers.* July 14. https://news.vice.com/article/donald-trump-just-tweeted-and-deleted-a-picture-featuring-nazi-ss-soldiers?utm_source=vicenewstwitter.

121   Jessica Chasmar. 2016. *Trump Spokeswoman Defends Tweet Calling Obama 'Head Negro in Charge.'* January 29. http://www.washingtontimes.com/news/2016/jan/29/katrina-pierson-donald-trump-spokeswoman-defends-t/.

122   Ibid.

123   Ibid.

124   Daniel White. 2016. *Nearly 20% of Trump Fans Think Freeing the Slaves Was a Bad Idea.* February 24. http://time.com/4236640/donald-trump-racist-supporters/.

125   Samantha Smith. 2016. *Trump Supporters Differ from Other GOP Voters on Foreign Policy, Immigration.* May 11. http://www.pewresearch.org/fact-tank/2016/05/11/trump-supporters-differ-from-other-gop-voters-on-foreign-policy-immigration-issues/.

126   Rmuse. 2016. *80 Percent of GOP Voters Say Trump's Racist Comments Are "Totally Fine."* June 12. http://www.politicususa.com/2016/06/12/80-percent-gop-voters-trumps-racist-comments-totally-fine.html.

127   Tessa Berenson. 2016. *Donald Trump Calls for 'Complete Shutdown' of Muslim Entry to U.S.* July 20. http://time.com/4139476/donald-trump-shutdown-muslim-immigration/.

128   Ibid.

129   Ibid.

130   Kim LaCapria. 2015. *Donald Trump Was Inaccurately Reported as Asserting that Muslims Should Wear ID Badges, a Claim That Drew Inevitable Comparisons to Adolf Hitler. But He Did Speak in Favor of a Muslim Registry.* November 19. http://www.snopes.com/donald-trump-muslims-id/.

131 Glenn Kessler. 2015. *Trump's Outrageous Claim that 'Thousands' of New Jersey Muslims Celebrated the 9/11 Attacks.* November 22. https://www.washingtonpost.com/news/fact-checker/wp/2015/11/22/donald-trumps-outrageous-claim-that-thousands-of-new-jersey-muslims-celebrated-the-911-attacks/.

132 Oliver Laughland. 2016. *Donald Trump and the Central Park Five.* February 17. https://www.theguardian.com/us-news/2016/feb/17/central-park-five-donald-trump-jogger-rape-case-new-york.

133 Noah Bierman. 2016. *Donald Trump Shakes Up Campaign by Hiring Executive from Conservative Breitbart News to Top Post.* August 17. http://www.latimes.com/politics/la-na-pol-trump-campaign-20160817-snap-story.html.

134 Jose A. DelReal. 2015. *Donald Trump Announces Presidential Bid.* June 16. https://www.washingtonpost.com/news/post-politics/wp/2015/06/16/donald-trump-to-announce-his-presidential-plans-today/.

135 Chase Peterson-Withorn. 2016. *Trump Says He's Filed New Financial Disclosure, Still Touting Questionable $10 Billion Fortune.* March 17. https://www.forbes.com/sites/chasewithorn/2016/05/17/trump-files-new-financial-disclosure-still-touting-questionable-10-billion-fortune/#1780063a7be0.

136 Jacob Koffler. 2015. *Donald Trump's 16 Biggest Business Failures and Successes.* August 7. http://time.com/3988970/donald-trump-business/.

137 David Segal. 2016. *What Donald Trump's Plaza Deal Reveals about His White House Bid.* January 16. http://www.nytimes.com/2016/01/17/business/what-donald-trumps-plaza-deal-reveals-about-his-white-house-bid.html?_r=0.

138 Linda Qiu. 2016. *Yep, Donald Trump's Companies Have Declared Bankruptcy...More than Four.* June 21.

139 Tara Clarke. 2015. *Donald Trump Bankruptcy: A Breakdown Ahead of the 2016 Elections.* July 7. http://moneymorning.com/2015/07/07/donald-trump-bankruptcy-a-breakdown-ahead-of-the-2016-elections/.

140 David Segal. 2016. *What Donald Trump's Plaza Deal Reveals about His White House Bid.* January 16.

141 Ibid.

142 Jacob Koffler. 2015. *Donald Trump's 16 Biggest Business Failures and Successes.* August 7.

143 Ibid.

144 Ibid.

145 Ibid.

146 Oliver Laughland. 2016. *Ex-Trump Workers Describe Egocentric Micromanager: 'Donald Loves Donald.'* March 14. https://www.theguardian.com/us-news/2016/mar/14/donald-trump-former-employee-interviews-ego-diversity.

147 Ibid.

148 Ibid.

149 Ibid.

150 Ibid.

151 Ibid.

152 Erkan. 2012. *10 Most Hilarious George Costanza Quotes.* May 8. Accessed October 9, 2017. http://www.themost10.com/hilarious-george-costanza-quotes.

153 Hillary Clinton and Mika Brzezinski, interview by Joe Scarborough. 2016. *Hillary Clinton on Pressure on High-Achieving Women.* MSNBC *Morning Joe.* February 26. https://www.youtube.com/watch?v=YkwyRhVclow.

154 Tim Murphy. 2015. *Here's the Sanders-Clinton Exchange on Gun Control Everyone Is Talking About.* October 14. http://www.motherjones.com/politics/2015/10/bernie-sanders-hillary-clinton-clash-over-guns-democratic-debate/.

155 Nik DeCosta-Klipa. 2016. *In Debate, Bernie Sanders Had No Specific Example of Wall Street Donations Affecting Hillary Clinton's Decisions.* April 14. https://www.boston.com/news/politics/2016/04/14/debate-bernie-sanders-no-example-donations-affecting-hillary-clintons.

156 Bernie Sanders. 2016. *Democrats Adopt Most Progressive Platform in Party History.* July 10. https://berniesanders.com/democrats-adopt-progressive-platform-party-history/.

157 Ibid.

158 Sarah Jones. 2016. *Fact Checkers Prove that 91% of the Things Donald Trump Says Are False.* August 16. http://www.politicususa.com/2016/03/31/ninety-one-percent-donald-trump-false.html.

159 Pew Research Center. 2017. *Hillary Clinton Favorability Timeline.* May 19. http://www.people-press.org/2015/05/19/hillary-clinton-approval-timeline/.

160 Truth or Fiction. n.d. *Hillary Clinton Ex-boss Says He Fired Her from Her Work on the Watergate Investigation for Being a "Liar" and "Unethical"-Truth! & Fiction!* Accessed November 1, 2017. https://www.truthorfiction.com/clinton-watergate/.

161 Matthew Dallek. 1996. *The Godless Constitution.* February 18. http://www.washingtonpost.com/wp-srv/style/longterm/books/reviews/matthewdallek.htm.

162 A US-government-owned asset management company run by Lewis William Seidman and charged with liquidating assets, primarily real-estate-related assets.

163 Wikipedia Contributors. n.d. *Whitewater Controversy.* Accessed August 22, 2016. https://en.wikipedia.org/w/index.php?title=Whitewater_controversy&oldid=782474574.

164 Wikipedia Contributors. n.d. *David Hale (Whitewater).* Accessed July 25, 2016. https://en.wikipedia.org/wiki/David_Hale_(Whitewater).

165 Ibid.

166 Ibid.

167 Michael Haddigan. 1996. *Tucker Sentenced to 4 Years' Probation.* August 20. https://www.washingtonpost.com/archive/politics/1996/08/20/tucker-sentenced-to-4-years-probation/0eeb9032-8afe-4caa-9cb5-1fb30bdfc6f7/?utm_term=.d71a191596c4.

168 Wikipedia Contributors. n.d. *Whitewater controversy.* Accessed August 22, 2016.

169 Ken Gormley. 2010. '*Clinton vs. Starr': A 'Definitive' Account.* February 16. http://www.npr.org/templates/story/story.php?storyId=123653000.

170 Wikipedia Contributors. n.d. *White House Travel Office Controversy.* Accessed August 12, 2016. https://en.wikipedia.org/wiki/White_House_travel_office_controversy.

171 Ibid.

172 Wikipedia Contributors. n.d. *Suicide of Vince Foster.* Accessed August 28, 2016. https://en.wikipedia.org/wiki/Suicide_of_Vince_Foster.

173 Russell Watson. 1994. *Vince Foster's Suicide: The Rumor Mill Churns.* March 20. http://www.newsweek.com/vince-fosters-suicide-rumor-mill-churns-185900.

174 Wikipedia Contributors. n.d. *Suicide of Vince Foster.* Accessed August 28, 2016.

175 Jose A. DelReal and Robert Costa. 2016. *Trump Escalates Attack on Bill Clinton.* May 23. https://www.washingtonpost.com/politics/trump-escalates-attack-on-bill-clinton/2016/05/23/ed109acc-2100-11e6-8690-f14ca9de2972_story.html?hpid=hp_rhp-top-table-main_trump-clinton-9pm%3Ahomepage%2Fstory&utm_term=.7cf925888072.

176 Wikipedia Contributors. n.d. *Impeachment of Bill Clinton.* Accessed November 2, 2017. https://en.wikipedia.org/wiki/Impeachment_of_Bill_Clinton.

177 Ibid.

178 Dan Rosenheck. 2003. *Larry Flynt Exposed.* October 2. http://www.thecrimson.com/article/2003/10/2/larry-flynt-exposed-it-sounds-like/.

179 Ibid.

180 Ibid.

181 Aaron Klein. 2016. *Bill Sex Accusers Back up Trump Remarks on Hillary the 'Enabler.'* May 7. http://www.breitbart.com/2016-presidential-race/2016/05/07/bills-sex-accusers-echo-trump-hillary-enabler/.

182 Wikipedia Contributors. n.d. *White House FBI Files Controversy.* Accessed August 13, 2016. https://en.wikipedia.org/wiki/White_House_FBI_files_controversy.

183 Ibid.

184 Ibid.

185 Ibid.

186 Betsy Combier. 2010. *Filegate Is Dismissed.* March 9. http://www.parentadvocates.org/nicecontent/dsp_printable.cfm?articleID=7716/nicecontent/dsp_printable.cfm?articleID=7716.

187 Wikipedia Contributors. n.d. *White House Travel Office Controversy.* Accessed August 12, 2016. https://en.wikipedia.org/wiki/White_House_travel_office_controversy.

188 Amy Chozick. 2016. *Kenneth Starr, Who Tried to Bury Bill Clinton, Now Only Praises Him.* May 24. https://www.bostonglobe.com/news/politics/2016/05/24/kenneth-starr-who-tried-bury-bill-clinton-now-praises-him/a0GN63PqIBCPvu0gfs951J/story.html.

189 Ibid.

190 Ibid.

191 Pete Mundo. 2016. *Baylor Bears: Ken Starr Steps Down as Baylor Chancellor.* June 1. https://www.heartlandcollegesports.com/index.php/2016/06/01/ken-starr-steps-down-as-baylor-chancellor.

192 Clayton Youngman. 2015. *Clinton: 7 Benghazi Probes So Far.* October 12. http://www.politifact.com/truth-o-meter/statements/2015/oct/12/hillary-clinton/clinton-there-have-been-7-benghazi-probes-so-far/.

193 Ibid.

194 Ibid.

195 Ibid.

196 Lis Power. 2015. *Fox News Finally Concedes Benghazi Committee Is Political after Republicans Admit to Partisan Nature of Investigation.* October 16. https://www.mediamatters.org/research/2015/10/16/fox-news-finally-concedes-benghazi-committee-is/206217.

197 Bill Adair and Lauren Carroll. 2016. *Checking Patricia Smith's Claims about Clinton and Benghazi.* July 18. http://www.politifact.com/truth-o-meter/article/2016/jul/18/checking-patricia-smiths-claims-about-clinton-and-/.

198 Wikipedia Contributors. n.d. *Hillary Clinton Email Controversy.* Accessed August 30, 2016. https://en.wikipedia.org/wiki/Hillary_Clinton_email_controversy.

199 Matt Zapotosky. 2016. *House Republicans Grill FBI Director Comey on Clinton Emails.* July 7. https://www.washingtonpost.com/world/national-security/fbi-director-set-to-appear-before-congressional-committee-to-answer-questions-on-clinton-investigation/2016/07/07/eb43ec7e-43c1-11e6-88d0-6adee48be8bc_story.html.

200 Annie Karni. 2016. *Clinton Caught in Email Hurricane.* July 7. http://www.politico.com/story/2016/07/hillary-clinton-email-fbi-testimony-225272.

201 Nick Gass. 2016. *15 Most Revealing Moments from Comey's Testimony on Clinton Emails.* July 7. http://www.politico.com/story/2016/07/james-comey-testimony-clinton-email-225224.

202 Eugene Kiely. 2016. *Partisan Spin on Clinton's Emails.* July 6. http://www.factcheck.org/2016/06/partisan-spin-on-clintons-emails.

203 Jason Easley. 2015. *Republican Colin Powell Deals a Death Blow to Hillary Clinton Email Scandal.* March 8. http://www.politicususa.com/2015/03/08/republican-colin-powell-deals-death-blow-hillary-clinton-email-scandal.html.

204 Media Matters Staff. 2016. *Concludes Past Secretaries of State "Definitively" Handled Classified Information on Private Email.* March 7. http://mediamatters.org/blog/2016/03/07/state-dept-concludes-past-secretaries-of-state/209044.

205 Amy Chozick. 2016. *Hillary Clinton Told F.B.I. Colin Powell Advised Her to Use Private Email.* August 18. http://www.nytimes.com/2016/08/19/us/politics/hillary-clinton-told-fbi-colin-powell-advised-her-to-use-private-email.html.

206 Ibid.

207 Ibid.

208 Ibid.

209 David E. Sanger. 2016. *Hillary Clinton's Email Was Probably Hacked, Experts Say.* July 6. http://www.nytimes.com/2016/07/07/us/hillary-clintons-email-was-probably-hacked-experts-say.html.

210 Jeffrey Fields, University of Southern California - Dornsife College of Letters, Arts and Sciences.

211 Jeffrey Fields. 2017. *Here's How Classified Information Got into Those Hillary Clinton Emails.* July 20. https://www.huffingtonpost.com/the-conversation-us/how-did-classified-inform_b_11074304.html.

212 A tent is designed to withstand eavesdropping, phone tapping, and computer hacking.

213 Chris Cillizza. 2016. *Hillary Clinton Just Gave Her Best Answer on the Email Controversy. By Far.* August 2. https://www.washingtonpost.com/news/the-fix/wp/2016/08/25/hillary-clinton-just-gave-her-best-answer-on-the-email-controversy-by-far/.

214 David A. Graham. 2016. *'Lock Her Up': How Hillary Hatred Is Unifying Republicans.* July 20. http://www.theatlantic.com/politics/archive/2016/07/lock-her-up-hillary-clinton/492173/.

215 Ibid.

216 AP. 2016. *House Republicans Want a New Hillary Clinton Investigation.* July 8. http://fortune.com/2016/07/08/house-republicans-new-clinton-investigation/.

217 Ibid.

218 Michael J. Morell. 2016. *I Ran the C.I.A. Now I'm Endorsing Hillary Clinton.* August 5. http://www.nytimes.com/2016/08/05/opinion/campaign-stops/i-ran-the-cia-now-im-endorsing-hillary-clinton.html.

219 Glenn Thrush. 2016. *Former CIA Chief Hayden: Clinton Better Prepared than 'Incoherent' Trump.* March 28. http://www.politico.com/story/2016/03/off-message-michael-hayden-hillary-clinton-2016-221276.

220 Alexa Corse. 2016. *All of the Top Republicans Voting for Hillary Clinton Instead of Donald Trump.* August 10. http://www.thedailybeast.com/articles/2016/08/09/all-of-the-top-republicans-voting-for-hillary-clinton-instead-of-donald-trump.html.

221 Ibid.

222 Hrafnkell Haraldsson. 2016. *Hillary Clinton Tops Trump's 88 with a List of 110 Generals and Admirals Backing Her.* September 9. http://www.politicususa.com/2016/09/09/hillary-clinton-tops-trumps-88-list-110-generals-admirals-backing.html.

223 Matt Zapotosky. 2016. *FBI Director: Clinton Email Case 'Was Not a Cliff-Hanger.'* September 7. https://www.washingtonpost.com/news/post-nation/wp/2016/09/07/fbi-director-clinton-email-case-was-not-a-cliff-hanger/?utm_term=.a5e9e4d3edbc.

224 Ibid.

225 Clinton Foundation. 2016. *Clinton Foundation.* August 31. https://www.clintonfoundation.org/.

226 Ibid.

227 AP. 2016. *Charity Watchdog Gives Perfect Rating to Clinton Foundation, but …* September 1. http://www.nj.com/politics/index.ssf/2016/09/clinton_foundation_gets_four_stars_from_charity_wa.html.

228 Emma Roller. 2016. *When Is a Scandal Really a Scandal?* August 30. http://www.nytimes.com/2016/08/30/opinion/campaign-stops/when-is-a-scandal-really-a-scandal.html.

229 Ibid.

230 Jessica Lussenhop. 2016. *Clinton Crime Bill: Why Is It So Controversial?* April 18. http://www.bbc.com/news/world-us-canada-36020717.

231 Ibid.

232 Ann Carson, E. 2014. *Prisoners in 2013.* September 30. https://www.bjs.gov/content/pub/pdf/p13.pdf.

233 Will Cabaniss. 2015. *Black Lives Matter Activist Says 'the Clintons' Passed Policy That Led to Mass Incarceration.* August 25. http://www.politifact.com/punditfact/statements/2015/aug/25/julius-jones/black-lives-matter-activist-says-clintons-passed-p/.

234 Jonathan Capehart. 2016. *Hillary Clinton on 'Superpredator' Remarks: 'I Shouldn't Have Used Those Words.'* February 25. https://www.washingtonpost.com/blogs/post-partisan/wp/2016/02/25/hillary-clinton-responds-to-activist-who-demanded-apology-for-superpredator-remarks/?utm_term=.d5f98260735e.

235 Jessica Lussenhop. 2016. *Clinton Crime Bill: Why Is It So Controversial?* April 18.

236 NAFTANow. 2012. *Frequently Asked Questions.* April 4. http://www.naftanow.org/faq_en.asp#faq-1.

237 Linda Qiu. 2016. *Donald Trump's Largely Accurate about Clinton's Past Support for NAFTA.* July 21. http://www.politifact.com/truth-o-meter/statements/2016/jul/21/donald-trump/donald-trumps-largely-accurate-about-clintons-past/.

238 Ibid.

239 Glenn Kessler. 2016. *Trump's False Claim that Clinton Only Recently Pledged to Renegotiate NAFTA.* August 8. https://www.washingtonpost.com/news/fact-checker/wp/2016/08/08/trumps-false-claim-that-clinton-only-recently-pledged-to-renegotiate-nafta/.

240 Soopermexican. 2016. *Huh? Donald Trump Is 'Branding' Hillary Clinton with a Really Weird Name!!* February 24. http://www.thepoliticalinsider.com/huge-announcement-will-help-ted-cruz-win-crucial-texas-primary/.

241 Bradford Richardson. 216. *Donald Trump Reveals New Nickname for Hillary Clinton — 'Crooked'.* April 17. http://www.washingtontimes.com/news/2016/apr/17/donald-trump-reveals-new-nickname-for-hillary-clin/.

242 Frank Camp. 2016. *Donald Trump Calls Hillary Clinton Something No Other Candidate Has Dared to Say.* February 9. https://ijr.com/2016/02/533244-donld-trump-calls-hillary-clinton-something-no-other-candidate-has-dared-to-say/.

243 Pamela Engel. 2016. *Donald Trump Is Trying out a New Nickname for Hillary Clinton.* May 20. http://www.businessinsider.com/donald-trump-heartless-hillary-clinton-guns-second-amendment-2016-5.

244 Soopermexican. 2016. *Huh? Donald Trump Is 'Branding' Hillary Clinton with a Really Weird Name!!* February 24.

245 Ali Vitali. 2016. *Trump: 'Hillary Clinton Is a Bigot.'* August 24. http://www.nbcnews.com/politics/2016-election/trump-hillary-clinton-bigot-n637476.

246 Ivan Levingston. 2016. *Trump Bashes Hillary Clinton's Foreign Policy, Calling Her a 'World-class Liar'.* June 22. http://www.cnbc.com/2016/06/22/trump-bashes-hillary-clintons-foreign-policy-calling-her-a-world-class-liar.html.

247 Chris Pleasance. 2016. *'Speaking of Mosquitoes, Hello Hillary!' Trump Swats Bug during Campaign Speech in Cincinnati before Likening It to Clinton.* July 7. http://www.dailymail.co.uk/news/article-3678310/Speaking-mosquitoes-hello-Hillary-Trump-swats-bug-campaign-speech-Cincinnati-likening-Clinton.html.

248 Zeke J. Miller. 2016. *Donald Trump Fires Back at Critics and Protesters in Chaotic Rally.* May 25. http://time.com/4347256/donald-trump-chaotic-rally.

249 Mary Pascaline. 2016. *Donald Trump Says 'Unstable' Hillary Clinton Unfit to Be President.* August 7. https://www.google.ca/webhp?sourceid=chrome-instant&ion=1&espv=2&ie=UTF-8#q=trump+calls+hillary+unfit.

250 AP. 2016. *Donald Trump Calls Hillary Clinton the Devil.* August 2. https://www.theguardian.com/us-news/video/2016/aug/02/donald-trump-calls-hillary-clinton-the-devil-video.

251 Jill Abramson. 2016. *This May Shock You: Hillary Clinton Is Fundamentally Honest.* March 28. https://www.theguardian.com/commentisfree/2016/mar/28/hillary-clinton-honest-transparency-jill-abramson.

252 Wikipedia Contributors. n.d. *Black Suffrage.* Accessed December 20, 2017. https://en.wikipedia.org/wiki/Black_suffrage.

253 Michelle Cottle. 2016. *The Era of 'the Bitch' Is Coming.* August 17. http://www.theatlantic.com/politics/archive/2016/08/the-era-of-the-bitch-is-coming/496154/.

254 Ibid.

255 Daniel Dale. 2016. *Will Sexism Hurt Hillary Clinton's Presidential Campaign?* June 8. https://www.thestar.com/news/world/2016/06/08/will-sexism-hurt-hillary-clintons-presidential-campaign.html.

256 Maarten Rikken. 2015. *Hillary Clinton and the Challenges of a Woman in the White House.* August 27. https://www.researchgate.net/blog/post/hillary-clinton-and-the-challenges-of-a-woman-in-the-white-house.

257 Michelle Cottle. 2016. *The Era of 'the Bitch' Is Coming.* August 17.

258 William Brangham, interview by Hari Sreenivaan. 2016. *Does Gender Bias Explain Why Hillary Clinton Has Fared So Poorly with White Male Voters?* July 28. http://www.pbs.org/newshour/bb/hillary-clinton-poorly-white-male-voters/.

259 Annie Linskey. 2015. *In Swing States, Clinton May Face Gender Bias.* September 9. https://www.bostonglobe.com/news/nation/2015/09/09/hillary-clinton-faces-challenges-unique-woman-running-for-office/Zkv99eyLTzAVzskuGn-vRPN/story.html.

260 Barbara Lee Family Foundation. 2010. *Turning Point: The Changing Landscape for Women Candidates.* Accessed November 19, 2016. http://www.barbaraleefoundation.org/research/turning-point-2010/.

261 Annie Linskey. 2015. *In Swing States, Clinton May Face Gender Bias.* September 9.

262 Michelle Cottle. 2016. *The Era of 'the Bitch' Is Coming.* August 17.

263 Ibid.

264 Ibid.

265 Amita Kelly. 2016. *Woman Asks Trump about Replacing TSA's 'Heebeejabis' with Veterans.* June 30.

266 Dodai. 2008. *Chris Matthews Has a Sexist History with Hillary Clinton.* January 15. http://jezebel.com/345237/chris-matthews-has-a-sexist-history-with-hillary-clinton.

267 Sandy Garossino. 2016. *What's Written in the Scars of Hillary Clinton.* August 1. http://www.nationalobserver.com/2016/08/01/analysis/whats-written-scars-hillary-clinton.

268 Carter Maness. 2016. *Harvard Study Confirms the Media Tore down Clinton, Built Up Trump and Sanders.* June 16. https://www.good.is/articles/hillary-clinton-negative-press.

269 Nicholas Confessore and Karen Yourish. 2016. *$2 Billion Worth of Free Media for Donald Trump.* March 15. http://www.nytimes.com/2016/03/16/upshot/measuring-donald-trumps-mammoth-advantage-in-free-media.html?_r=1.

270 Joseph Heller. 2016. *Joseph Heller > Quotes.* Accessed August 12, 2016. https://www.goodreads.com/author/quotes/3167.Joseph_Heller.

271 Politico. 2015. *What Is Hillary's Greatest Accomplishment?* September 17. http://www.politico.com/magazine/story/2015/09/carly-fiorina-debate-hillary-clintons-greatest-accomplishment-213157.

272 Marian Wright Edelman, the civil rights activist and prominent advocate for children.

273 Charles P. Pierce. 2015. *Why Hillary Clinton's Stint as a Civil-rights Secret Agent Matters Today*. December 28. http://www.esquire.com/news-politics/politics/news/a40772/hillary-clinton-undercover-civil-rights/.

274 Wikipedia Contributors. n.d. *Women's Rights Are Human Rights*. Accessed August 12, 2016. https://en.wikipedia.org/wiki/Women%27s_Rights_Are_Human_Rights.

275 Politico. 2015. *What Is Hillary's Greatest Accomplishment?* September 17. http://www.politico.com/magazine/story/2015/09/carly-fiorina-debate-hillary-clintons-greatest-accomplishment-213157.

276 Valentina Zarya. 2016. *This Equal Pay Champion Just Endorsed Hillary Clinton*. January 29. http://fortune.com/2016/01/29/lilly-ledbetter-clinton/.

277 Hillary Clinton. 2007. *S.804 - Count Every Vote Act of 2007*. March 7. https://www.congress.gov/bill/110th-congress/senate-bill/804.

278 Politico. 2015. *What Is Hillary's Greatest Accomplishment?* September 17.

279 Former senior strategist for Priorities USA Action, a super PAC in support of President Barack Obama.

280 Politico. 2015. *What Is Hillary's Greatest Accomplishment?* September 17.

281 Bradford Richardson. 2016. *Clinton Calls for New Sanctions on Iran*. January 16. http://thehill.com/policy/national-security/266173-clinton-calls-for-new-sanctions-on-iran.

282 Sandy Garossino. 2016. *What's Written in the Scars of Hillary Clinton*. August 1.

283 Tamara Keith. 2016. *Evolution or Expediency? Clinton's Changing Positions over a Long Career*. May 23. http://www.npr.org/2016/05/23/478973321/evolution-or-expediency-clintons-changing-positions-over-a-long-career.

284 Ibid.

285 Glenn Kessler. 2016. *Pence vs. Clinton on the Iraq War Vote 'Mistake.'* July 19. https://www.washingtonpost.com/news/fact-checker/wp/2016/07/19/pence-versus-clinton-on-the-iraq-war-vote-mistake/.

286 Voltaire. n.d. *Voltaire Argued that Religious Intolerance Was Against the Law of Nature and Was Worse than the "Right of the Tiger" (1763)*. Accessed October 9, 2017. http://oll.libertyfund.org/quote/90.

287 Meghan Murphy-Gill. 2017. *The Faith of Donald Trump*. January 19. http://www.uscatholic.org/articles/201701/faith-donald-trump-30910.

288 Ibid.

289 Sarah Eekhoff Zylstra. 2016. *Trump, Clinton, or Neither: How Evangelicals Are Expected to Vote*. May 5. http://www.christianitytoday.com/gleanings/2016/may/trump-clinton-neither-how-evangelical-expected-to-vote.html.

290 Emily McFarlan Miller n. 2016. *7 Conservative Christians Who Are Not Supporting Trump*. June 21. http://religionnews.com/2016/06/21/7-conservative-christians-who-are-not-supporting-trump/.

291 Ibid.

292 Cathy Lynn Grossman. 2016. *'I Will Protect Christians,' Donald Trump Tells Liberty University Students*. January 18. http://religionnews.com/2016/01/18/donald-trump-liberty-university-evangelicals/.

293 Deacon Keith Fournier. 2016. *Trump Is Right: Repeal the Johnson Amendment That Muzzles Pastors*. July 20. https://stream.org/trump-right-repeal-johnson-amendment-muzzles-pastors/.

294 Ibid.

295 Constitution Center. n.d. *Freedom of Religion, Speech, Press, Assembly and Petition*. Accessed September 19, 2016. http://constitutioncenter.org/interactive-constitution/amendments/amendment-i.

296 Lydia Saad. 2015. *Americans Choose "Pro-choice" for First Time in Seven Years*. May 29. http://www.gallup.com/poll/183434/americans-choose-pro-choice-first-time-seven-years.aspx.

297 Eugene Scott. 2015. *Church Says Donald Trump Is Not an 'Active Member.'* August 28. http://www.cnn.com/2015/08/28/politics/donald-trump-church-member/index.html.

298 Meghan Murphy-Gill. 2017. *The Faith of Donald Trump*. January 19.

299 Daniel Burke. 2016. *The Guilt-Free Gospel of Donald Trump*. October 24. http://www.cnn.com/2016/10/21/politics/trump-religion-gospel/index.html.

300 Allida Black et al. 2003. *Eleanor Roosevelt, John Kennedy and the Election of 1960: A Project of the Eleanor Roosevelt Papers*. https://www.gwu.edu/~erpapers/mep/displaydoc.cfm?docid=erps-acism.

301 Ken Dilanian. 2016. *Why Won't Obama Say Radical Islam*. June 13. http://www.nbcnews.com/storyline/orlando-nightclub-massacre/why-won-t-obama-say-radical-islam-n591196.

302 Wikipedia Contributors. n.d. *Christian Terrorism*. Accessed September 19, 2016. https://en.wikipedia.org/wiki/Christian_terrorism#Ku_Klux_Klan.

303 Wikipedia Contributors. n.d. *Murder of Michael Donald*. Accessed May 13, 2017. https://en.wikipedia.org/wiki/Michael_Donald.

304 Ibid.

305 Ibid.

306 Garikai Chengu. 2015. *The Ku Klux Klan: America's Long History of Accepting White Terrorist Organizations*. December 25. http://www.globalresearch.ca/the-ku-klux-klan-americas-long-history-of-accepting-white-terrorist-organizations/5497958.

307 Wikipedia Contributors. n.d. *David Koresh*. Accessed September 14, 2016. https://en.wikipedia.org/wiki/David_Koresh.

308 Mark Memmott. 2014. *'This Was a Hate Crime,' Police Say of Kansas City-area Killings*. April 14. http://www.npr.org/sections/thetwo-way/2014/04/14/302871181/suspect-in-killings-at-kansas-city-jewish-sites-linked-to-kkk.

309 T. Dugdale-Pointon 2007. *The Army of God.* August 17. http://www.historyofwar.org/articles/weapons_army_of_god.html.

310 Wikipedia Contributors. n.d. *Domestic Terrorism in the United States.* Accessed September 22, 2016. https://en.m.wikipedia.org/wiki/Domestic_terrorism_in_the_United_States#Terrorist_organizations.

311 T. Dugdale-Pointon 2007. *The Army of God.* August 17.

312 Marianne Goodland. 2015. *Most Colorado Republicans Are Silent after Planned Parenthood Shooting — But Not All.* December 1. http://www.coloradoindependent.com/156444/most-colorado-republicans-are-silent-after-planned-parenthood-shooting-but-not-all.

313 Click2Houston. 2016. *Grand Jury Takes No Action against Planned Parenthood; 2 Others Indicted.* January 26. http://www.click2houston.com/news/grand-jury-takes-no-action-against-planned-parenthood-gulf-coast-2-others-indicted.

314 Marianne Goodland. 2015. *Most Colorado Republicans Are Silent after Planned Parenthood Shooting — But Not All.* December 1.

315 Oyez. 2016. *"Roe v. Wade."* September 22. https://www.oyez.org/cases/1971/70-18.

316 Michael Lipka. 2016. *5 Facts about Abortion.* June 27. http://www.pewresearch.org/fact-tank/2016/06/27/5-facts-about-abortion/.

317 Marianne Goodland. 2015. *Most Colorado Republicans Are Silent after Planned Parenthood Shooting — But Not All.* December 1.

318 Ibid.

319 Wikipedia Contributors. n.d. *Islam by Country.* Accessed September 17, 2016. https://en.wikipedia.org/wiki/Islam_by_country.

320 Al Islam. n.d. *Why does the Quran say that Infidels Should be Killed?* Accessed September 19, 2016. https://www.alislam.org/egazette/updates/why-does-the-quran-say-that-infidels-should-be-killed/.

321 Stephen Smith. 2016. *Killing Non Believers.* September 2016. Accessed December 19, 2017. https://www.openbible.info/topics/killing_non_believers.

322 Fareed Zakaria. 2016. *Why They Hate Us.* May 23. http://www.cnn.com/2016/04/08/opinions/why-they-hate-us-zakaria/.

323 Robert Farley. 2016. *Trump's False Muslim Claim.* March 16. http://www.factcheck.org/2016/03/trumps-false-muslim-claim /.

324 Fareed Zakaria. 2016. *Why They Hate Us.* May 23.

325 Scott Atran. 2015. *Mindless Terrorists? The Truth about ISIS Is Much Worse.* November 15. https://www.theguardian.com/commentisfree/2015/nov/15/terrorists-isis.

326 CNN Wire. 2015. *Charleston Church Shooting Suspect, Dylann Storm Roof, Arrested in North Carolina.* June 18. http://fox59.com/2015/06/18/dylann-storm-roof-arrested-in-north-carolina-according-to-report/.

327 Lilly Workneh. 2014. *KKK Threatens 'Lethal Force' against Ferguson Protesters and Appears on TV to Explain Why.* November 14. http://www.huffingtonpost.ca/entry/kkk-threatens-lethal-force-protesters-ferguson_n_6155570.

328 Philip Bump. 2016. *Donald Trump Somehow Thinks Ferguson and Oakland Are Dangerous Like Iraq.* May 18. https://www.washingtonpost.com/news/the-fix/wp/2016/05/18/donald-trump-somehow-thinks-ferguson-and-oakland-are-dangerous-like-iraq/?utm_term=.4b6a778e7d60.

329 G. Dalia. 2015. *Meet the Nine Muslim Women Who Have Ruled Nations.* June 9. http://egyptianstreets.com/2015/06/09/meet-the-nine-muslim-women-who-have-ruled-nations/.

330 Islam 101. n.d. *Return Back to Peace.* Accessed December 23, 2017. http://returnbacktopeace.yolasite.com/islam-101.php.

331 Ministry of Attorney General. 2016. *Justice Laws Website.* September 8. http://laws-lois.justice.gc.ca/eng/acts/C-46/section-319.html.

332 Stop Racism and Hate Canada. 2016. *5. Legal Remedies - The Law in Canada.* September 20. http://antiracism.stopracism.ca/content/5-legal-remedies-law-canada.

333 National Post. 2016. *Calgary Neo-Nazi Who Beat a Bystander to Death Loses Bid for Reduction of 13-year Murder Sentence.* June 22. http://nationalpost.com/news/canada/calgary-neo-nazi-who-beat-a-bystander-to-death-loses-bid-for-reduction-of-13-year-murder-sentence.

334 Wikipedia Contributors. n.d. *Ernst Zündel.* Accessed November 16, 2016. https://en.wikipedia.org/wiki/Ernst_Z%C3%BCndel.

335 Stop Racism and Hate Canada. 2016. *5. Legal Remedies - The Law in Canada.* September 20.

336 Legal Information Institute. 2016. *18 U.S. Code: 249: Hate Crime Acts.* September 20. https://www.law.cornell.edu/uscode/text/18/249.

337 CBC. 2007. *Ernst Zundel Sentenced to 5 Years for Holocaust Denial.* February 15. http://www.cbc.ca/news/world/ernst-zundel-sentenced-to-5-years-for-holocaust-denial-1.659372.

338 Tim Hume. 2016. *British Lawmakers Debate Banning Donald Trump from UK for 'Hate Speech.'* January 18. http://www.cnn.com/2016/01/18/europe/uk-parliament-debates-trump-ban/.

339 Ibid.

340 Ibid.

341 Ibid.

342 U.S. Department of the Treasury. n.d. *History of 'In God We Trust.'* Accessed September 5, 2017. https://www.treasury.gov/about/education/Pages/in-god-we-trust.aspx.

343 Ibid.

344 Ibid.

345   David Boyajian. 2013. *The Myth of Turkish Secularism.* December 16. http://dissidentvoice.org/2013/12/the-myth-of-turkish-secularism/.

346   Fréderike Geerdink. 2016. *Stop Defending Turkey's 'Secularism' — It's Been a Lie All Along.* May 2. http://www.huffingtonpost.com/fraderike-geerdink-/turkey-secularism_b_9818250.html.

347   Harry Sterling. 2017. *Opinion: Erdogan Erodes Democracy in Turkey.* April 27. http://vancouversun.com/opinion/op-ed/opinion-erdogan-erodes-democracy-in-turkey.

348   Thanassis Cambanis. 2016. *Turkey's Model of Democracy.* August 4. https://www.bostonglobe.com/ideas/2016/08/04/thanassi-turkey/gjkxw1xoagd5jj776m8t6h/story.html.

349   The Holy Bible: King James Version. n.d. *John 7:53-8:11.* Accessed December 19, 2017. https://www.biblegateway.com/passage/?search=John%207:53-8:11.

350   Sarah Jones. 2017. *Even Republicans Are Getting Fed Up with Trump's Unqualified Judicial Nominees.* December 15. https://newrepublic.com/minutes/146309/even-republicans-getting-fed-trumps-unqualified-judicial-nominees.

351   Chris Massie, and Andrew Kaczynski. 2017. *Trump Judicial Nominee Said Transgender Children Are Part of 'Satan's Plan,' Defended 'Conversion Therapy.'* September 20. http://www.cnn.com/2017/09/20/politics/kfile-jeff-mateer-lgbt-remarks/index.html.

352   Paul Prather. 2016. *The Mystery of Christians' Support for Donald Trump Is Solved.* January 30. http://www.kentucky.com/living/religion/paul-prather/article57553638.html.

353   Ibid.

354   Ibid.

355   Steve Mount. n.d. *Jefferson's Wall of Separation Letter.* Accessed November 15, 2016. http://www.usconstitution.net/jeffwall.html.

356   Ibid.

357   Maya Angelou. n.d. *Maya Angelou Quotes.* Accessed October 9, 2017. https://www.brainyquote.com/quotes/quotes/m/mayaangelo148650.html.

358   Wikipedia Contributors. n.d. *Ugly American.* Accessed July 23, 2016. https://en.wikipedia.org/wiki/Ugly_American_(pejorative).

359   Katy Tur. 2016. *My Crazy Year with Trump.* August 10. http://www.marieclaire.com/politics/a21997/donald-trump-katy-tur/.

360   Ibid.

361   Mathew Ingram. 2016. *Could Donald Trump Actually Make Good on His Promise to 'Open Up' Libel Laws?* February 29. http://fortune.com/2016/02/29/trump-libel-law/.

362   Philip Bump. 2016. *Donald Trump's Threat to Sue Ted Cruz, Explained.* February 16. https://www.washingtonpost.com/news/the-fix/wp/2016/02/16/donald-trumps-threat-to-sue-ted-cruz-explained/.

363   Lucia Graves. 2016. *The Miss USA Hopeful Sued by Trump: 'There are Ways to Stand Your Ground.'* September 4. https://www.theguardian.com/us-news/2016/sep/04/sheena-monnin-donald-trump-miss-usa-lawsuit.

364   Paul Farhi. 2016. *What Really Gets under Trump's Skin? A Reporter Questioning His Net Worth.* March 8. https://www.washingtonpost.com/lifestyle/style/that-time-trump-sued-over-the-size-of-hiswallet/2016/03/08/785dee3e-e4c2-11e5-b0fd-073d5930a7b7_story.html.

365   David Goldman. 2015. *Donald Trump Wants to 'Close up' the Internet.* December 8. http://money.cnn.com/2015/12/08/technology/donald-trump-internet/index.html.

366   Ben Shapiro. 2015. *No, Donald Trump's Immigration Plan Isn't Unconstitutional.* December 8. http://www.dailywire.com/news/1685/no-donald-trumps-immigration-plan-isnt-ben-shapiro#.

367   Gregory Krieg. 2015. *Donald Trump: 'Strongly Consider' Shutting Mosques.* November 16. http://www.cnn.com/2015/11/16/politics/donald-trump-paris-attacks-close-mosques/.

368   Bryan A. Stevenson and John F. Stinneford. 2016. *The Eighth Amendment.* Accessed November 18, 2016. https://constitutioncenter.org/interactive-constitution/amendments/amendment-viii.

369   The Economist. 2016. *How a Trump Presidency Could Undermine the Rule of Law.* June 1. http://www.economist.com/blogs/democracyinamerica/2016/06/don-and-judge.

370   Corey Brettschneider. 2016. *Trump vs. the Constitution: A Guide.* August 4. http://www.politico.com/magazine/story/2016/08/2016-donald-trump-constitution-guide-unconstitutional-freedom-liberty-khan-214139.

371   Alex Emmons. 2016. *ACLU Gears Up to Fight Donald Trump's Long List of Unconstitutional Proposals.* July 14. https://theintercept.com/2016/07/14/aclu-gears-up-to-fight-donald-trumps-long-list-of-unconstitutional-proposals/.

372   ACLU. 2016. *The Trump Memos the ACLU's Constitutional Analysis of the Public.* https://action.aclu.org/sites/default/files/pages/trumpmemos.

373   Donald Trump. n.d. *Standing Up for Our Law Enforcement Community.* Accessed November 20, 2017. https://www.whitehouse.gov/law-enforcement-community.

374   Emily Flitter. 2016. *Trump Praises 'Stop-and-frisk' Police Tactic.* September 22. http://www.reuters.com/article/us-usa-election-trump-iduskcn11r2nz.

375   Stockman, Farah. 2016. *Donald Trump's Crime Policies Might Hit Minorities Harder, Experts Say.* September 22. http://www.nytimes.com/2016/09/23/us/politics/donald-trump-crime-terrorism-race.html.

376   Ibid.

377 Ehrenfreund, Max. 2016. *Donald Trump Claims New York's Stop-and-frisk Policy Reduced Crime. The Data Disagree.* September 22. https://www.washingtonpost.com/news/wonk/wp/2016/09/22/donald-trump-claims-new-yorks-stop-and-frisk-policy-reduced-crime-the-data-disagree/.

378 On the Issues. 2016. *Hillary Clinton on Crime.* August 18. http://www.ontheissues.org/2016/Hillary_Clinton_Crime.htm.

379 Hillary for America. 2016. *Criminal Justice Reform.* July 8. https://www.hillaryclinton.com/issues/criminal-justice-reform/.

380 Wikipedia Contributors. n.d. *List of American Police Officers Killed in the Line of Duty.* Accessed September 16, 2016. https://en.wikipedia.org/wiki/List_of_American_police_officers_killed_in_the_line_of_duty.

381 BBC. 2016. *US Police Shootings: How Many Die Each Year?* July 18. http://www.bbc.com/news/magazine-36826297.

382 Ibid.

383 Statista. 2016. *Countries with the Largest Number of Prisoners per 100,000 of the National Population, as of April 2016.* April 19. https://www.statista.com/statistics/262962/countries-with-the-most-prisoners-per-100-000-inhabitants/.

384 NAACP. n.d. *Criminal Justice Fact Sheet.* Accessed September 24, 2016. http://www.naacp.org/pages/criminal-justice-fact-sheet.

385 Mapping Police Violence. n.d. *Police Killed More than 100 Unarmed Black People in 2015.* http://mappingpoliceviolence.org/unarmed/.

386 Dana Farrington. 2016. *Ex-Reserve Deputy Who Confused Gun with Taser, Killing Suspect, Is Convicted.* April 28. http://www.npr.org/sections/thetwo-way/2016/04/28/476019878/ex-reserve-deputy-who-confused-gun-with-taser-killing-suspect-is-convicted.

387 Wills Robinson and Regina F. Graham. 2016. *White Female Cop Who Shot Dead Unarmed Black Man with Hands Up Is Charged with First Degree Manslaughter.* September 22. http://www.dailymail.co.uk/news/article-3802964/White-female-cop-shot-dead-unarmed-black-man-charged-degree-manslaughter.html.

388 Daniella Diaz. 2016. *North Carolina Congressman: Protesters 'Hate White People.'* September 23. http://www.cnn.com/2016/09/22/politics/robert-pittenger-north-carolina-charlotte-protests/.

389 Wikipedia Contributors. n.d. *Shooting of Walter Scott.* Accessed September 20, 2016. https://en.wikipedia.org/wiki/Shooting_of_Walter_Scott.

390 Jessica Wehrman and Michelle Everhart. 2016. *Trump Campaign County Chair Who Said 'No Racism until Obama Got Elected' Apologizes, Resigns.* September 22. http://www.dispatch.com/content/stories/local/2016/09/22/mahoning-county-donald-trump-campaign-chair-no_racism-before-obama.html.

391 Ralph Ellis. 2016. *Officer Charged with Manslaughter in Philando Castile Killing.* November 17. http://www.cnn.com/2016/11/16/us/officer-charged-philando-castile-killing/.

392 Jessica McBride. 2016. *Listen: Philando Castile Dispatch Audio/Police Scanner.* July 9. http://heavy.com/news/2016/07/philando-castile-armed-robbery-robber-suspect-stopped-police-dispatch-audio-scanner-traffic-reports-listen-jeronimo-yanez-broken-taillight-traffic-why-pulled-him-over-nose-record-criminal-history-arre/.

393 Media Matters Staff. 2016. *"Racial Persecution Really Isn't the Problem in Baltimore," It's "Personal Behavior."* April 28. http://mediamatters.org/video/2015/04/28/bill-oreilly-racial-persecution-really-isnt-the/203457.

394 Chauncey Devega. 2015. *White America's Racial Amnesia: The Sobering Truth about Our Country's "Race Riots."* May 1. http://www.salon.com/2015/05/01/white_americas_racial_amnesia_the_sobering_truth_about_our_countrys_race_riots_partner/.

395 Department of Justice Public Affairs. 2016. *Justice Department Announces Findings of Investigation into Baltimore Police Department.* August 10. https://www.justice.gov/opa/pr/justice-department-announces-findings-investigation-baltimore-police-department.

396 Emanuella Grinberg. 2016. *"Racial bias pervasive among Baltimore police, DOJ says."* February 18. https://www.cnn.com/2016/08/09/us/baltimore-justice-department-report/index.html.

397 Edwin Grimsley. 2013. *African American Wrongful Convictions Today.* March 29. http://www.innocenceproject.org/african-american-wrongful-convictions-today/.

398 Marti Hause and Ari Melber. 2016. *Jailed but Innocent: Record Number of People Exonerated in 2015.* February 3. http://www.nbcnews.com/news/us-news/jailed-innocent-record-number-people-exonerated-2015-n510196.

399 Bill Whittaker. 2015. *30 Years on Death Row.* October 11. http://www.cbsnews.com/news/30-years-on-death-row-exoneration-60-minutes/.

400 Ibid.

401 Ibid.

402 Ibid.

403 Anthony L. Fisher. 2016. *Glenn Ford Spent 30 Years on Death Row, Was Exonerated, Died, yet Is Still on Trial.* May 5. http://reason.com/blog/2016/05/05/glenn-ford-spent-30-years-on-death-row-w.

404 Wikipedia Contributors. n.d. *Central Park Jogger Case.* Accessed November 18, 2016. https://en.wikipedia.org/wiki/Central_Park_jogger_case.

405 Ibid.

406 Ibid.

407 Amy Davidson. 2014. *Donald Trump and the Central Park Five.* June 23. http://www.newyorker.com/news/amy-davidson/donald-trump-and-the-central-park-five.

408 Janell Ross. 2016. *Donald Trump's Doubling Down on the Central Park Five Reflects a Bigger Problem.* October 8. https://www.washingtonpost.com/news/the-fix/wp/2016/10/08/donald-trumps-doubling-down-on-the-central-park-five-reflects-a-bigger-problem/.

409 Ibid.

410 History. n.d. *Voting Rights Act.* Accessed September 24, 2016. http://www.history.com/topics/black-history/voting-rights-act.

411 Ibid.

412 Ibid.

413 Alana Wise and Doina Chiacu. 2016. *Republican Lawyers Take Issue with Trump's Allegations of Voter Fraud.* October 17. http://www.reuters.com/article/usa-election-idUSL1N1CN1R9.

414 Ibid.

415 The US is the only democracy that prevents felons from voting after they have served their sentences; this disproportionately affects minorities.

416 Voter caging is the practice of sending mass direct mailings to registered voters by non-forwardable mail, then compiling lists of voters, called "caging lists," from the returned mail in order to formally challenge their right to vote on that basis alone.

417 Greg Palast. 2016. *The GOP's Stealth War against Voters.* August 24. http://www.rollingstone.com/politics/features/the-gops-stealth-war-against-voters-w435890.

418 Ibid.

419 Michael Wines and Alan Blinder. 2016. *Federal Appeals Court Strikes Down North Carolina Voter ID Requirement.* July 29. http://www.nytimes.com/2016/07/30/us/federal-appeals-court-strikes-down-north-carolina-voter-id-provision.html.

420 Jay Michaelson. 2016. *North Carolina GOP Brags Racist Voter Suppression Is Working—And They're Right.* November 7. http://www.thedailybeast.com/articles/2016/11/07/north-carolina-s-racist-voter-suppression-is-working.html.

421 Taylor Link. 2016. *North Carolina Is Openly Celebrating Its Black Voter Suppression Efforts.* November 7. http://www.salon.com/2016/11/07/north-carolina-obama-coalition-crumbling-ncgop-celebrates-voting-suppression-efforts-in-a-press-release/.

422 Kyle Scott Clauss. 2016. *Did Bill Clinton, Mayor Walsh Break Massachusetts Voting Laws for Hillary?* March 1. http://www.bostonmagazine.com/news/blog/2016/03/01/bill-clinton-massachusetts-voting-laws/.

423 AP. 2006. *Lawmaker's Son Sentenced for Slashing Tires.* April 26. http://www.nbcnews.com/id/12498215/ns/politics/t/lawmakers-son-sentenced-slashing-tires/.

424 Van Jones, Boris Epshteyn, Paris Dennard, and Bob Beckel, interview by Don Lemon. 2016. *Donald Trump and Birthers* (September 9).

425 Jeremy Diamond. 2016. *Trump: Clinton Could Shoot Somebody and Not Be Arrested.* September 9. http://www.cnn.com/2016/09/09/politics/donald-trump-hillary-clinton-shoot-somebody/.

426 Abby Phillip and Jose A. DelReal. 2016. *Clinton Says She Regrets Labeling 'Half' of Trump Supporters 'Deplorable.'* September 10. https://www.washingtonpost.com/politics/republicans-jump-on-clintons-deplorables-remark/2016/09/10/91a3c148-775c-11e6-8149-b8d05321db62_story.html.

427 Tom Jensen. 2016. *Trump, Clinton Continue to Lead in SC.* February 16. http://www.publicpolicypolling.com/pdf/2015/PPP_Release_SC_21616.pdf.

428 Cate Martel. 2016. *Sheriff Thrills GOP: 'Blue Lives Matter.'* July 18. http://thehill.com/blogs/ballot-box/presidential-races/288258-sheriff-thrills-convention-blue-lives-matter.

429 Gabby Morrongiello. 2015. *Trump Slams Dems for 'Catering to' Black Lives Matter.* September 9. http://www.washington-examiner.com/trump-slams-dems-for-catering-to-black-lives-matter/article/2571641.

430 Alex Garofalo. 2016. *Who Are the 'Mothers of the Movement'? Families of Police Shooting Victims to Speak at Day 2 of DNC.* July 26. http://www.ibtimes.com/who-are-mothers-movement-families-police-shooting-victims-speak-day-2-dnc-2394960.

431 Eric Bradner and Eugene Scott. 2016. *'Mothers of the Movement' Makes Case for Hillary Clinton.* July 26. http://www.cnn.com/2016/07/26/politics/mothers-movement-dnc-hillary-clinton/.

432 Wikipedia Contributors. n.d. *New York City Draft Riots.* Accessed September 21, 2016. https://en.wikipedia.org/wiki/New_York_City_draft_riots.

433 Wikipedia Contributors. n.d. *Battle of Hayes Pond.* Accessed December 21, 2016. https://en.wikipedia.org/w/index.php?title=Battle_of_Hayes_Pond&oldid=756095876.

434 Johanna Markind. 2015. *Jews Are Still the Biggest Target of Religious Hate Crimes.* December 5. http://forward.com/news/325988/jews-are-still-the-biggest-target-of-hate-crimes/.

435 Martin Niemöller. 2016. *Martin Niemöller: "First They Came for the Socialists…"* July 2. https://www.ushmm.org/wlc/en/article.php?ModuleId=10007392.

436 Ibid.

437 This is the historically correct version preferred by the family.

438 Ismene Triant and Panos Valavanis. *Olympia and the Olympic Games* (Athens: Non Stop Printing L.T.D., 2008). 91.

439   Editors of Encyclopædia Britannica. 2010. *Mexico City 1968 Olympic Games.* July 28. https://www.britannica.com/event/Mexico-City-1968-Olympic-Games.

440   Erica Bulman. 2007. *Rights Group: 1.5 Million People Displaced by Preparations for 2008 Beijing Olympics.* June 5. http://usatoday30.usatoday.com/sports/olympics/2007-06-05-3431055449_x.htm.

441   Charles P. Pierce. 2016. *Death to the Olympics: Why the Games Should Have Been Moved from Rio.* August 3. http://www.si.com/olympics/2016/08/03/rio-olympics-problems-concerns-issues-controversy.

442   Maggie Maloney. 2016. *A Timeline of #LochteGate.* August 19. http://www.cosmopolitan.com/health-fitness/news/a63009/timeline-ryan-lochte-robbery-scandal/.

443   Ibid.

444   Steve Wyche. 2016. *Colin Kaepernick Explains Why He Sat during National Anthem.* August 27. http://www.nfl.com/news/story/0ap3000000691077/article/colin-kaepernick-explains-why-he-sat-during-national-anthem.

445   Scott Bixby. 2016. *Trump on Colin Kaepernick: 'He Should Find a Country That Works Better for Him.'* August 29. https://www.theguardian.com/sport/2016/aug/29/donald-trump-colin-kaepernick-national-anthem-protest.

446   ABC. 2016. *National Anthem Backlash Builds for 49ers QB Colin Kaepernick.* August 30. http://abcnews.go.com/GMA/video/national-anthem-backlash-builds-49ers-qb-colin-kaepernick-41737425.

447   I cannot find a citation for this information, but I believe that it was Samuel Jackson.

448   Breeanna Edwards. 2015. *NYC Taxi Driver Fined $25,000 for Refusing to Pick Up Black Family.* August 6. http://www.theroot.com/articles/news/2015/08/taxi_driver_fined_25_000_for_refusing_to_pick_up_black_family/.

449   Legal Information Institute. 2016. *West Virginia State Board of Education v. Barnette.* September 24. https://www.law.cornell.edu/supremecourt/text/319/624.

450   Frontline. 2005. *Holocaust Education in Germany: An Interview.* May 31. http://www.pbs.org/wgbh/pages/frontline/shows/germans/germans/education.html.

451   Answer Wiki. 2014. *The Holocaust: How Is World War II History Taught in Germany?* July 13. https://www.quora.com/The-Holocaust-How-is-World-War-II-history-taught-in-Germany.

452   Oprah Winfrey. 2011. *How a Gang of Skinheads Forever Changed the Course of the Oprah Winfrey Show.* May 13. http://www.oprah.com/oprahshow/how-a-gang-of-skin-heads-changed-oprah-show-history-video.

453   Ibid.

454   Bodhipaksa. n.d. *Holding onto Anger is Like Drinking Poison and Expecting the Other Person to Die.* Accessed November 18, 2016. http://fakebuddhaquotes.com/holding-onto-anger-is-like-drinking-poison/.

455   There are several versions of this quote attributed to various authors. The earliest version found is from 1930s book called *The Sermon on the Mount*, by Emmet Fox. Fox's book was widely used by AA and it is believed that over time the quotation was shortened and became more concise.

456   Jonathan Lockwood Huie. n.d. *Those Quotes and Sayings.* Accessed November 18, 2016. http://www.jonathanlockwoodhuie.com/quotes/those/.

457   Variation of Jonathan Lockwood Huie quote.

458   Bertrand Russell. n.d. *Bertrand Russell > Quotes > Quotable Quote.* Accessed October 9, 2017. https://www.goodreads.com/quotes/11234-fear-is-the-main-source-of-superstition-and-one-of.

459   Andrew Kaczynski and Nathan McDermott. 2016. *Donald Trump Said He Supported Invading Iraq.* February 18. https://www.buzzfeed.com/andrewkaczynski/in-2002-donald-trump-said-he-supported-invading-iraq-on-the?utm_term=.keo8q4L845#.alQwYe1wer.

460   Shane Goldmacher. 2016. *Donald Trump Calls Iraq 'Worst Decision' but Won't Repeat that Bush 'Lied.'* February 19. http://www.politico.com/blogs/south-carolina-primary-2016-live-updates-and-results/2016/02/2016-south-carolina-trump-george-w-bushs-iraq-219475.

461   Ibid.

462   Mollie Hemingway. 2016. *6 Problems with Media's Hysterical Reaction to Trump's ISIS Comments.* August 12. http://thefederalist.com/2016/08/12/6-problems-with-medias-hysterical-reaction-to-trumps-isis-comments/.

463   NBC News. 2017. *Transcript: NBC News Commander-in-Chief Forum.* September 7.

464   Glenn Kessler. 2016. *Pence vs. Clinton on the Iraq War Vote 'Mistake.'* July 19. https://www.washingtonpost.com/news/fact-checker/wp/2016/07/19/pence-versus-clinton-on-the-iraq-war-vote-mistake.

465   Ibid.

466   David Sherfinski. 2015. *Donald Trump Declines to Share His 'Foolproof' Plan for Winning against the Islamic State.* May 28. http://www.washingtontimes.com/news/2015/may/28/donald-trump-declines-share-his-foolproof-plan-win/.

467   The Hill Staff. 2016. *Transcript of Donald Trump's Speech on National Security in Philadelphia.* September 7. http://thehill.com/blogs/pundits-blog/campaign/294817-transcript-of-donald-trumps-speech-on-national-security-in.

468   Anup Shah. 2013. *World Military Spending.* June 30. http://www.globalissues.org/article/75/world-military-spending.

469   Fareed Zakaria, interview by Anderson Cooper. 2017. *Trump:" I'll Give the Generals 30 Days for a Plan to Fight ISIS."* (September 7).

470   Lt. Gen. Mark Hertling. interview by Anderson Cooper. 2016. *I'll Give Generals 30 Days for a Plan to Fight ISIS.*

471   Maria Cardona and Kayleigh McEnany, interview by Ashleigh Banfield. 2016. *Trump: US Should Have Taken Oil from Iraq* (September 9).

472   Louis Jacobson and Amy Sherman. 2016. *Donald Trump's Pants on Fire Claim that Barack Obama 'Founded' ISIS, Hillary Clinton Was 'Cofounder.'* August 11. http://www.politifact.com/truth-o-meter/statements/2016/aug/11/donald-trump/donald-trump-pants-fire-claim-obama-founded-isis-c/.

473   Rebecca Shabad. 2016. *Hillary Clinton Urges Americans to "Choose Resolve, Not Fear" after NY, NJ, MN Attacks.* September 19. http://www.cbsnews.com/news/hillary-clinton-urges-americans-to-choose-resolve-not-fear-after-ny-nj-mn-attacks/.

474   Lauren Carroll. 2016. *Donald Trump's Mostly False Claim that $400 Million Payment to Iran Was 'Ransom.'* August 24. http://www.politifact.com/truth-o-meter/statements/2016/aug/24/donald-trump/donald-trump-calls-400-million-payment-iran-ransom/.

475   Ibid.

476   Ibid.

477   President Barack Obama. 2015. *Statement by the President on the U.S. Government's Hostage Policy Review.* June 24. https://obamawhitehouse.archives.gov/the-press-office/2015/06/24/statement-president-us-governments-hostage-policy-review.

478   Sunny Freeman. 2016. *Canada's 'No' to Iraq War a Defining Moment for Prime Minister, Even 10 Years Later.* September 7. http://www.huffingtonpost.ca/2013/03/19/canada-iraq-war_n_2902305.html.

479   Michael J. Morell. 2016. *I Ran the C.I.A. Now I'm Endorsing Hillary Clinton.* August 5. http://www.nytimes.com/2016/08/05/opinion/campaign-stops/i-ran-the-cia-now-im-endorsing-hillary-clinton.html.

480   Eugene Scott. 2016. *Robert Gates: Trump 'beyond repair'.* September 17. http://www.cnn.com/2016/09/17/politics/robert-gates-donald-trump-hillary-clinton/.

481   David E. Sanger and Maggie Haberman. 2016. *50 G.O.P. Officials Warn Donald Trump Would Put Nation's Security 'at Risk.'* August 8. http://www.nytimes.com/2016/08/08/us/politics/national-security-gop-donald-trump.html?_r=0.

482   Kurt Eichenwald. 2014. *ISIS's Enemy List: 10 Reasons the Islamic State Is Doomed.* September 8. http://www.newsweek.com/2014/09/19/isiss-enemy-list-10-reasons-islamic-state-doomed-268953.html.

483   Evan Perez et al. 2016. *NY, NJ Bombings: Suspect Charged with Attempted Murder of Officers.* September 19. http://www.cnn.com/2016/09/19/us/new-york-explosion-investigation/.

484   AP. 2016. *Trump, Clinton Respond to New York City Explosion.* September 18. http://www.cnbc.com/2016/09/18/trump-clinton-respond-to-new-york-city-explosion.html.

485   Ibid.

486   Wikipedia Contributors. n.d. *Irv Rubin.* Accessed May 30, 2016. https://en.wikipedia.org/wiki/Irv_Rubin.

487   Ibid.

488   Ibid.

489   Bonnie Berkowitz and Denise Lu Lazaro Gamio. 2016. *The Math of Mass Shootings.* July 27. https://www.washingtonpost.com/graphics/national/mass-shootings-in-america/.

490   Paul Overberg et al. 2015. *Behind the Bloodshed.* April 16. http://www.gannett-cdn.com/GDContent/mass-killings/index.html#explore.

491   Ibid.

492   Doug Stanglin and Charles Ventura. 2016. *Gunman at Large after Killing 5 at Mall North of Seattle.* September 24. http://www.usatoday.com/story/news/nation-now/2016/09/24/seattle-shooting-cascade-mall-burlington/91009272/.

493   Pedro Oliveira Jr. 2014. *Anorexic, Unmedicated and Obsessed with a Murder-mad Cyber World: Adam Lanza's Mental Issues Went Untreated by Officials Who Allowed Sandy Hook Shooter's Mother to Overpower Them, Probe Finds.* November 21. http://www.dailymail.co.uk/news/article-2843674/New-report-details-schools-health-officials-repeatedly-appeased-Sandy-Hook-shooter-Adam-Lanza-s-mom-addressing-crippling-mental-health-issues.html.

494   Wikipedia Contributors. n.d. *List of School Shootings in the United States.* Accessed September 21, 2016. https://en.wikipedia.org/wiki/List_of_school_shootings_in_the_United_States.

495   Laura Gunderson. 2015. *Oregon Shooter: New Details Emerge about Chris Harper-Mercer.* October 2. http://www.oregonlive.com/pacific-northwest news/index.ssf/2015/10/new_details_emerge_on_umpqua_c.html.

496   Barack Obama. 2015. *Statement by the President on the Shootings at Umpqua Community College, Roseburg, Oregon.* October 1. https://www.whitehouse.gov/the-press-office/2015/10/01/statement-president-shootings-umpqua-community-college-roseburg-oregon.

497   Jennifer Mascia. 2016. *15 Statistics That Tell the Story of Gun Violence This Year.* September 22. https://www.thetrace.org/2015/12/gun-violence-stats-2015/.

498   Wikipedia Contributors. n.d. *List of Countries by Firearm-related Death Rate.* Accessed August 28, 2016. https://en.wikipedia.org/wiki/List_of_countries_by_firearm-related_death_rate.

499   Jessica Lussenhop and Ashley Gold. 2016. *Donald Trump: 30 Things the Republican Believes.* July 6. http://www.bbc.com/news/world-us-canada-34903577.

500   Linda Qiu. 2016. *Fact-checking the Second Presidential Debate.* October 9. http://www.politifact.com/truth-o-meter/article/2016/oct/09/fact-checks-second-presidential-debate/.

501   Hillary Clinton. 2016. *Gun Violence Prevention.* September 22. https://www.hillaryclinton.com/issues/gun-violence-prevention/.

502   Pew Research Center. 2015. *Continued Bipartisan Support for Expanded Background Checks on Gun Sales.* August 13. http://www.people-press.org/2015/08/13/continued-bipartisan-support-for-expanded-background-checks-on-gun-sales/.

503   Legal Information Institute. 2016. *18 U.S. Code: 249: Hate Crime Acts.* September 20. https://www.law.cornell.edu/uscode/text/18/249.

504   Shaunacy Ferro. 2016. *25 Unusual Foreign Travel Warnings for Visiting the U.S.* April 6. http://mentalfloss.com/article/68276/25-unusual-foreign-travel-warnings-visiting-us.

505   Ibid.

506   Jonathan Bachman. 2016. *Three Countries Urge Caution Traveling to U.S. Amid Protests, Violence.* July 10. http://www.reuters.com/article/us-usa-police-travel-iduskcn0zq0rm. Allida Black et al. 2003. *Eleanor Roosevelt, John Kennedy and the Election of 1960: A Project of the Eleanor Roosevelt Papers.* https://www.gwu.edu/~erpapers/mep/displaydoc.cfm?docid=erps-acism.

507   Ibid.

508   Ibid.

509   Caroline Halleman. 2016. *The U.S. Earns a Travel Warning from New Zealand, Germany and the U.K.* August 15. http://www.townandcountrymag.com/leisure/travel-guide/news/a7446/travel-warnings-against-united-states/.

510   Ashley Parker and Matthew Rosenberg. 2016. *Donald Trump Vows to Bolster Nation's Military Capacities.* September 7. http://www.nytimes.com/2016/09/08/us/politics/donald-trump-speech.html.

511   The Economist. 2016. *Scrimping on Sense.* August 13. http://www.economist.com/news/leaders/21704792-republican-nominees-ideas-economy-are-thoughtless-and-dangerous-scrimping-sense.

512   Brooks Jackson. 2016. *Obama's Numbers (January 2016 Update).* January 12. http://www.factcheck.org/2016/01/obamas-numbers-january-2016-update/.

513   The Economist. 2016. *Scrimping on Sense.* August 13.

514   Ibid.

515   Bernadette D. Proctor, Jessica L Semega and Melissa A. Kollar. 2016. *Income and Poverty Rates for the US: 2015.* September 13. http://www.census.gov/library/publications/2016/demo/p60-256.html.

516   BBC. 2016. *Trump v Clinton: Comparing Their Economic Plans.* September 16. http://www.bbc.com/news/business-37013670.

517   Josh Barro. 2015. *Trump Plan Is Tax Cut for the Rich, Even Hedge Fund.* September 28. http://www.nytimes.com/2015/09/29/upshot/trump-plan-is-tax-cut-for-the-rich-even-hedge-fund-managers.html.

518   BBC. 2016. *Trump v Clinton: Comparing Their Economic Plans.* September 16. http://www.bbc.com/news/business-37013670.

519   Ibid.

520   The Economist. 2016. *Scrimping on Sense.* August 13.

521   Ibid.

522   Ibid.

523   Ibid.

524   Anthony Cave. 2016. *Does the Economy Always Do Better under Democratic Presidents?* April 6. http://www.politifact.com/arizona/statements/2016/apr/06/hillary-clinton/does-economy-always-do-better-under-democratic-pre/.

525   Ibid.

526   Ibid.

527   Politics That Work. n.d. *About Politics That Work.* http://politicsthatwork.com/about.php.

528   Politics That Work. 2015. *Which Party Is Better for the Economy?* April 14. http://politicsthatwork.com/blog/which-party-is-better-for-the-economy.php.

529   Adam Smith was an 18th century philosopher renowned as the father of modern economics.

530   Briton Ryle. 2015. *Wages vs. Corporate Profits.* September 23. https://www.wealthdaily.com/articles/the-real-culprit/6276.

531   Chris Matthews. 2015. *The Myth of the 1% and the 99%.* March 2. http://fortune.com/2015/03/02/economic-inequality-myth-1-percent-wealth/.

532   Ibid.

533   Wikipedia Contributors. n.d. *General Motors Ignition Switch Recalls.* Accessed August 23, 2016. https://en.wikipedia.org/wiki/General_Motors_ignition_switch_recalls.

534   Ibid.

535   Forbes. 2016. *Warren Buffett.* September 5. http://www.forbes.com/profile/warren-buffett/#.

536   CBC. 2014. *H.J. Heinz Co. Leamington: 1909-2014.* June 26. http://www.cbc.ca/news/canada/windsor/h-j-heinz-co-leamington-1909-2014-1.2686019.

537   Jamie Sturgeon. 2014. *Buffett Keeps Word, Heinz Strikes 'Fair' Deal with Ont. Ketchup Workers.* January 16. http://globalnews.ca/news/1086996/buffett-keeps-word-heinz-strikes-fair-deal-with-ontario-ketchup-workers/.

538   CBC. 2014. *H.J. Heinz Co. Leamington: 1909-2014.* June 26.

539   Gerrit De Vynck. 2014. *How a Canadian Tomato Juice Law Helped Save Heinz's Plant in Leamington, Ont. from Closing.* March 5. http://business.financialpost.com/legal-post/how-a-canadian-tomato-juice-law-helped-save-heinzs-plant-in-leamington-ont-from-closing.

540   Melissa Stanger. 2015. *9 Billionaires Who Plan to Give Away the Majority of Their Fortunes.* October 15. http://www.businessinsider.com/billionaires-giving-away-their-money-2015-10/#warren-buffett-pledged-to-give-away-more-than-99-of-his-riches-and-has-already-donated-over-215-billion-4.

541   Chris Isidore. 2013. *Buffett Says He's Still Paying Lower Tax Rate than His Secretary.* March 4. http://money.cnn. com/2013/03/04/news/economy/buffett-secretary-taxes/.

542   G. William Domhoff. 2017. *Wealth, Income and Power.* April. http://www2.ucsc.edu/whorulesamerica/power/wealth.html.

543   Ibid.

544   Ibid.

545   Ibid.

546   Nadia Kounang. 2015. *Why Pharmaceuticals Are Cheaper Abroad.* September 28. http://www.cnn.com/2015/09/28/ health/us-pays-more-for-drugs/.

547   Ibid.

548   Wikipedia Contributors. n.d. *Prescription Drug Prices in the United States.* Accessed September 5, 2016. https://en.wikipedia. org/wiki/Prescription_drug_prices_in_the_United_States.

549   Ibid.

550   Ibid.

551   Ariana Eunjung Cha. 2015. *CEO Martin Shkreli: 4,000 Percent Drug Price Hike Is 'Altruistic,' Not Greedy.* September 22. https://www.washingtonpost.com/news/to-your-health/wp/2015/09/22/turing-ceo-martin-shkreli-explains- that-4000-percent-drug-price-hike-is-altruistic-not-greedy/?utm_term=.6063ebbb68c5.

552   Linda A. Johnson. 2016. *How EpiPen's Maker Raised Prices.* August 24. http://www.torontosun.com/2016/08/24/how- epipens-maker-raised-prices.

553   Julia La Roche. 2013. *Here's How Much 10 of the Richest People in the World Made per Minute in 2013.* December 19. http:// www.businessinsider.com/what-warren-buffett-makes-per-hour-2013-12.

554   Alice Gomstyn. 2010. *Walmart CEO Pay: More in an Hour than Workers Get All Year?* July 2. http://abcnews.go.com/ Business/walmart-ceo-pay-hour-workers-year/story?id=11067470.

555   Glenn Kessler. 2015. *Is the Estate Tax Killing Small Farms and Businesses?* April 14. https://www.washingtonpost.com/news/ fact-checker/wp/2015/04/14/the-facts-about-the-estate-tax-and-farmers/?utm_term=.a77d17e0bb57.

556   G. William Domhoff. 2017. *Wealth, Income and Power.* April.

557   Ibid.

558   Ibid.

559   Ibid.

560   G. William Domhoff. 2012. *An Investment Manager's View on the Top 1%.* January. http://www2.ucsc.edu/whorulesamerica/ power/investment_manager.html.

561   Ibid.

562   Ibid.

563   Ibid.

564   Ibid.

565   Jeremy Diamond. 2016. *Donald Trump in 2006: I 'Sort of Hope' Real Estate Market Tanks.* May 19. http://www.cnn. com/2016/05/19/politics/donald-trump-2006-hopes-real-estate-market-crashes/.

566   David Cay Johnston. 2011. *Beyond the 1 Percent.* October 25. http://blogs.reuters.com/david-cay-johnston/2011/10/25/ beyond-the-1-percent/.

567   Gordon Laxer. 2016. *If We're Renegotiating NAFTA, Let's Be Ready to Walk Away.* August 31. http://www.theglobeandmail. com/report-on-business/rob-commentary/if-were-renegotiating-nafta-lets-be-ready-to-walk-away/article31609876/.

568   Christine Murray. 2014. *Mexico Manufacturing Surge Hides Low-wage Drag on Economy.* June 2. http://www.reuters.com/ article/us-mexico-economy-analysis-iduskbn0ed20h20140602.

569   Ranking America. n.d. *The U.S. Ranks 11th in Working Hard.* Accessed February 26 2018. https://rankingamerica.wordpress. com/2013/07/18/the-u-s-ranks-11th-in-working-hard/.

570   Conner Forrest. 2015. *Chinese Factory Replaces 90% of Humans with Robots, Production Soars.* July 30. http://www.techrepublic. com/article/chinese-factory-replaces-90-of-humans-with-robots-production-soars/.

571   Maude Barlow. 2015. *NAFTA's ISDS: Why Canada Is One of the Most Sued Countries in the World.* October 23. http:// www.commondreams.org/views/2015/10/23/naftas-isds-why-canada-one-most-sued-countries-world.

572   Ibid.

573   Ibid.

574   Ibid.

575   US Government: Office of the United States Trade Representative. 2016. *Canada.* Accessed May 31, 2017. https://ustr. gov/countries-regions/americas/canada.

576   Ibid.

577   Gordon Laxer. 2016. *If We're Renegotiating NAFTA, Let's Be Ready to Walk Away.* August 31.

578   Ibid.

579   Ibid.

580   Ibid.

581   The Economist. 2016. *Scrimping on Sense.* August 13.

582   Ibid.

583 Olivier Compagne. n.d. *Anatomy of Peace.* Accessed February 8, 2017. https://sites.google.com/site/integralconflictresolution/conflic-resolution/the-anatomy-of-peace.

584 Ibid.

585 E. F. Schumacher. n.d. *E. F. Schumacher Quotes.* Accessed October 9, 2017. https://www.brainyquote.com/quotes/quotes/e/efschuma148840.html.

586 Wikipedia Contributors. n.d. *History of the United States Democratic Party.* Accessed November 14, 2016. https://en.wikipedia.org/wiki/History_of_the_United_States_Democratic_Party.

587 Ibid.

588 Ibid.

589 History. n.d. *Republican Party Founded.* Accessed November 22, 2016. http://www.history.com/this-day-in-history/republican-party-founded.

590 Civil War Trust. n.d. *A Brief Overview of the American Civil War.* Accessed November 22, 2016. http://www.civilwar.org/education/history/civil-war-overview/overview.html?referrer=https://www.google.ca/.

591 Ibid.

592 Wikipedia Contributors. n.d. *American Civil War.* Accessed November 22, 2016. https://en.wikipedia.org/wiki/American_Civil_War.

593 Paul D. Escott. 2014. *Racism and the Founding of the GOP: Abraham Lincoln, the Civil War and the Real History of the Republican Party.* September 13. http://www.salon.com/2014/09/13/racism_and_the_founding_of_the_gop_abraham_lincoln_the_civil_war_and_the_real_history_of_the_republican_party/.

594 Ibid.

595 Ibid.

596 Ibid.

597 Ibid.

598 Dinesh D'Souza. 2016. *Dinesh D'Souza: The Secret History of the Democratic Party.* July 22. http://www.foxnews.com/opinion/2016/07/22/dinesh-dsouza-secret-history-democratic-party.html.

599 Wikipedia Contributors. n.d. *Jim Crow Laws.* Accessed November 13, 2016. https://en.wikipedia.org/wiki/Jim_Crow_laws.

600 National Archives. n.d. *An Act of Courage, the Arrest Records of Rosa Parks.* Accessed November 23, 2016. https://www.archives.gov/education/lessons/rosa-parks.

601 National Archives. n.d. *The Civil Rights Act of 1964 and the Equal Employment Opportunity Commission.* Accessed November 23, 2016. https://www.archives.gov/education/lessons/civil-rights-act.

602 Natalie Wolchover. 2012. *Why Did the Democratic and Republican Parties Switch Platforms?* September 24. http://www.livescience.com/34241-democratic-republican-parties-switch-platforms.html.

603 Ibid.

604 Jon Ponder. 2007. *Scaife Funded 'Arkansas Project' to Destroy Clinton, Now Says He Was a 'Pretty Good' President.* February 19. http://www.pensitoreview.com/2007/02/19/scaife-recants-arkansas-project/.

605 Hanna Rosin. 2015. *Among the Hillary Haters.* March. http://www.theatlantic.com/magazine/archive/2015/03/among-the-hillary-haters/384976/.

606 Jon Ponder. 2007. *Scaife Funded 'Arkansas Project' to Destroy Clinton, Now Says He Was a 'Pretty Good' President.* February 19.

607 Hanna Rosin. 2015. *Among the Hillary Haters.* March.

608 Ibid.

609 Ibid.

610 Ibid.

611 Ibid.

612 Ibid.

613 Christopher Ruddy. 2016. *About.* http://www.mediamatters.org/about.

614 Sam Stein. 2014. *Robert Draper Book: GOP's Anti-Obama Campaign Started Night of Inauguration.* August 10. http://www.huffingtonpost.com/2012/04/25/robert-draper-anti-obama-campaign_n_1452899.html.

615 Ibid.

616 Mike Lillis. 2011. *Hoyer: Republicans Would See Country 'Fail' to Defeat Obama's Reelection Bid.* September 20. http://thehill.com/homenews/house/182637-hoyer-gop-would-see-country-fail-to-defeat-obama.

617 Ibid.

618 keepemhonest. 2012. *Newt Gingrich He and Paul Ryan Plotted to Sabotage the US Economy on January 20, 2012.* October 28. http://www.dailykos.com/story/2012/10/28/1151619/-video-gt-Newt-Gingrich-he-and-Paul-Ryan-plotted-to-sabotage-the-US-Economy-on-January-20-2009.

619 Ibid.

620 Democratic Whip Steny Hoyer. 2014. *Just the Facts: House Republicans' Record on Obstruction.* September 11. https://www.democraticwhip.gov/content/just-facts-house-republicans-record-obstruction.

621 keepemhonest. 2012. *Newt Gingrich He and Paul Ryan Plotted to Sabotage the US Economy on January 20, 2012.* October 28.

622 Dana Milbank. 2016. *Republicans' Mindless Obstruction Has Helped Create Something Far Worse.* March 11. https://www.washingtonpost.com/opinions/republicans-mindless-obstruction-has-helped-create-something-far-worse/2016/03/11/46ba9022-e723-11e5-b0fd-073d5930a7b7_story.html?utm_term=.b3b7d80bb04c.

623   Ibid.

624   Melanie Hicken. 2013. *Shutdown Took $24 Billion Bite out of Economy.* October 17. http://money.cnn.com/2013/10/16/news/economy/shutdown-economic-impact/.

625   Ian McCullough. 2013. *Why Did the U.S. Government Shut Down in October 2013?* October 3. http://www.forbes.com/sites/quora/2013/10/03/why-did-the-u-s-government-shut-down-in-october-2013/#54e0bca6527f.

626   Félix Pérez. 2016. *Congress Punts on Helping Flint, MI, Children, Families with Water Crisis.* September 30. http://education-votes.nea.org/2016/09/30/congress-punts-helping-flint-mi-children-families-water-crisis/.

627   Elizabeth A. Cobbs. 2015. *Why Boehner's Invite to Netanyahu Is Unconstitutional.* March 2. http://blogs.reuters.com/great-debate/2015/03/01/netanyahu-invite-is-a-symptom-of-boehners-grudge-match-against-the-u-s-constitution/.

628   E.J. Dionne Jr. 2015. *Kevin McCarthy's Truthful Gaffe on Benghazi.* September 30. https://www.washingtonpost.com/opinions/kevin-mccarthys-truthful-gaffe/2015/09/30/f12a9fac-67a8-11e5-8325-a42b5a459b1e_story.html?utm_term=.49cc8784b613.

629   Wikipedia Contributors. n.d. *Lewinsky Scandal.* Accessed August 31, 2016. https://en.wikipedia.org/wiki/Lewinsky_scandal.

630   Russ Baker. 1998. *Portrait of a Political "Pit Bull."* December 22. https://www.salon.com/1998/12/22/newsa950556369/.

631   Wikipedia Contributors. n.d. *Lewinsky Scandal.* Accessed August 31, 2016.

632   John Jacobs. 1999. *The Gingrich Affair: Hypocrisy and Betrayal.* November 22. http://www.sfgate.com/news/article/The-Gingrich-affair-Hypocrisy-and-betrayal-3057206.php,%20November%2022,%201999.

633   Katie Connolly. 2009. *Sex Scandals through the Years: Both Parties Even.* June 25. http://www.newsweek.com/sex-scandals-through-years-both-parties-even-212156.

634   Dan Rosenheck. 2003. *Larry Flynt Exposed.* October 2. http://www.thecrimson.com/article/2003/10/2/larry-flynt-exposed-it-sounds-like/.

635   Amy Moreno. 2016. *Hillary Gets Destroyed on Social Media in Response to Attacking Bernie Supporters with Trending Hashtag #Basementdwellers.* October 1. http://truthfeed.com/hillary-gets-destroyed-on-social-media-in-response-to-attacking-bernie-supporters-with-trending-hashtag-basementdwellers/26858/.

636   Ibid.

637   Cristiano Lima. 2016. *Clinton Gives Her Take on Sanders Supporters in Leaked Fundraising Recording.* September 30. http://www.politico.com/story/2016/09/hillary-clinton-bernie-sanders-supporters-audio-leak-228997.

638   Derek Hawkins. 2016. *No, You Can't Text Your Vote. But These Fake Ads Tell Clinton Supporters to Do Just That.* November 3. https://www.washingtonpost.com/news/morning-mix/wp/2016/11/03/no-you-cant-text-your-vote-but-these-ads-tell-clinton-supporters-to-do-just-that/.

639   Craig Silverman and Lawrence Alexander. 2016. *How Teens in the Balkans Are Duping Trump Supporters with Fake News.* November 3. https://www.buzzfeed.com/craigsilverman/how-macedonia-became-a-global-hub-for-pro-trump-misinfo?utm_term=.bhEXDYmkKX#.keVo6Yx2Ko.

640   Ibid.

641   Ibid.

642   Ibid.

643   Ibid.

644   Yochi Dreazen. 2016. *Facebook Is Full of Fake News Stories. On Election Day, Don't Fall for Them.* November 8. http://www.vox.com/presidential-election/2016/11/8/13557952/facebook-election-day-trump-clinton-fake-stories-lies-fox.

645   Brian Stelter. 2016. *Fake Story about Obamas, Hillary Clinton Ensnares Sean Hannity.* November 1. http://money.cnn.com/2016/11/01/media/sean-hannity-michelle-obama-hillary-clinton-fake-news/.

646   Ibid.

647   Ibid.

648   PolitiFact. n.d. *All False Statements Involving Donald Trump.* Accessed November 24, 2016. http://www.politifact.com/personalities/donald-trump/statements/byruling/false/?page=6.

649   PolitiFact. n.d. *All Pants on Fire! Statements Involving Donald Trump.* Accessed November 24, 2016. http://www.politifact.com/personalities/donald-trump/statements/byruling/pants-fire/?page=2.

650   Elise Foley. 2016. *Donald Trump Questions Hillary Clinton's 'Mental and Physical Stamina.'* August 15. http://www.huffingtonpost.com/entry/donald-trump-hillary-clinton-.

651   Denise Grady and Mark Landerler. 2013. *Clinton out of Hospital after Treatment for Clot.* January 2. http://www.nytimes.com/2013/01/03/us/politics/hillary-clinton-is-discharged-from-hospital-after-blood-clot.html.

652   Robert Powell. 2016. *Hillary Clinton Revealed to Possibly Have Serious Health Issues and Brain Damage.* August 8. http://regated.com/2016/08/hillary-clinton-revealed-serious-health-issues-possible-brain-damage/.

653   Jamie Wells. 2016. *Diagnosing Hillary Clinton's Medical Statement.* September 19. http://acsh.org/news/2016/09/19/diagnosing-hillary-clintons-medical-statement-10182.

654   PolitiFact. n.d. *All False Statements Involving Hillary Clinton.* Accessed November 24, 2016. http://www.politifact.com/personalities/hillary-clinton/statements/byruling/false/?page=2.

655   PolitiFact. n.d. *All Pants on Fire! Statements Involving Hillary Clinton.* Accessed November 24, 2016. http://www.politifact.com/personalities/hillary-clinton/statements/byruling/pants-fire/.

656   Mark Dent. 2016. *Sorry, Hillary: Trump Actually Has Made a Few Things in the USA.* August 1. http://www.politifact.com/pennsylvania/statements/2016/aug/01/hillary-clinton/hillary-clinton-went-overboard-calling-out-donald-/.

657   Louis Jacobson. 2015. *No Evidence for Hillary Clinton's Claim that ISIS Is Using Videos of Donald Trump as Recruiting Tool.* December 19. http://www.politifact.com/truth-o-meter/statements/2015/dec/19/hillary-clinton/fact-checking-hillary-clintons-claim-isis-using-vi/.

658   Lauren Carroll. 2016. *Clinton Twists Trump's Words on Rescuing the Auto Industry during Recession.* October 18. http://www.politifact.com/truth-o-meter/statements/2016/oct/18/hillary-clinton/clinton-twists-trumps-words-rescuing-auto-industry/.

659   Dan Evon. 2016. *Nope Francis.* July 24. http://www.snopes.com/pope-francis-donald-trump-endorsement/.

660   Baxter Dmitry. 2016. *Snopes Caught Lying For Hillary Again, Questions Raised.* August 20. http://yournewswire.com/snopes-caught-lying-for-hillary-again-questions-raised/.

661   Fort Liberty. n.d. *Web Sites Which Publish Fake News and Other Hoaxes.* Accessed November 25, 2016. http://www.fortliberty.org/hoax-sites.html.

662   Baxter Dmitry. 2016. *Snopes Caught Lying For Hillary Again*, Questions Raised. August 20.

663   Dan Roberts, Ben Jacobs and Alan Yuhas. 2016. *Debbie Wasserman Schultz to Resign as DNC Chair as Email Scandal Rocks Democrats.* July 25. https://www.theguardian.com/us-news/2016/jul/24/debbie-wasserman-schultz-resigns-dnc-chair-emails-sanders.

664   Dylan Byers. 2016. *Donna Brazile, the Acting Chairwoman of the Democratic National Committee, Resigned from Her Role as a CNN Contributor Earlier this Month.* October 31. http://money.cnn.com/2016/10/31/media/donna-brazile-cnn-resignation/index.html.

665   Michelle Ye Hee Lee. 2016. *Trump's Claim Tying Violence at His Rallies to the Clinton Campaign.* October 21. https://www.washingtonpost.com/news/fact-checker/wp/2016/10/21/trumps-claim-tying-violence-at-his-rallies-to-the-clinton-campaign/.

666   Steve Contorno. 2016. *Trump Says Clinton and Obama Paid People to Cause Violence at His Rallies.* October 20. http://www.politifact.com/truth-o-meter/article/2016/oct/20/trump-says-clinton-and-obama-caused-violence-his-r/.

667   Michelle Ye Hee Lee. 2016. *Trump's Claim Tying Violence at His Rallies to the Clinton Campaign.* October 21.

668   Ibid.

669   Ibid.

670   Clare Foran. 2016. *A $1 Million Fight against Hillary Clinton's Online Trolls.* May 31. http://www.theatlantic.com/politics/archive/2016/05/correct-the-record-online-trolls/484847/.

671   David Smith. 2016. *Wisconsin Rules GOP Gerrymandering Violates Democrats' Rights.* November 22. https://www.theguardian.com/us-news/2016/nov/21/wisconsin-gerrymandering-district-court-2016-election-decision.

672   Stephen Wolf. 2016. *No, Maryland Is Not the Most Gerrymandered State. There Is More to Gerrymandering than Ugly Shapes.* June 1. http://www.dailykos.com/story/2016/6/1/1532608/-No-Maryland-is-not-the-most-gerrymandered-state-There-is-more-to-gerrymandering-than-ugly-shapes.

673   Christopher Ingraham. 2014. *America's Most Gerrymandered Congressional Districts.* May 15. https://www.washingtonpost.com/news/wonk/wp/2014/05/15/americas-most-gerrymandered-congressional-districts/.

674   Sam Wang. 2012. *Gerrymanders, Part 1: Busting the Both-sides-do-it Myth.* December 30. http://election.princeton.edu/2012/12/30/gerrymanders-part-1-busting-the-both-sides-do-it-myth.

675   Ian Kershaw. n.d. *The Hitler Myth.* Accessed June 10, 2016. http://www.historytoday.com/ian-kershaw/hitler-myth.

676   Adelle Nazarian. 2016. *Teacher Suspended for Comparing Trump to Hitler.* November 15. http://www.breitbart.com/california/2016/11/15/hitler-teacher-suspended-for-comparing-trump/.

677   Adelle Nazarian. 2016. *Teacher Suspended for Comparing Trump to Hitler.* November 15.

678   Marie Brenner. 1990. *After the Gold Rush.* September. http://www.vanityfair.com/magazine/2015/07/donald-ivana-trump-divorce-prenup-marie-brenner.

679   Amanda Macias. 2015. *Donald Trump's Ex-wife Once Said Trump Kept a Book of Hitler's Speeches by His Bed.* September 1. http://www.businessinsider.com/donald-trumps-ex-wife-once-said-he-kept-a-book-of-hitlers-speeches-by-his-bed-2015-8.

680   Ian Kershaw. n.d. *The Hitler Myth.* Accessed June 10, 2016.

681   Ibid.

682   Jeremy Diamond. 2016. *Trump: I Could 'Shoot Somebody and I Wouldn't Lose Voters.* January 24. http://www.cnn.com/2016/01/23/politics/donald-trump-shoot-somebody-support/.

683   Ian Kershaw. n.d. *The Hitler Myth.* Accessed June 10, 2016.

684   Ibid.

685   Ibid.

686   Ibid.

687   Ibid.

688   Ibid.

689   Donald Trump. interview by Oprah Winfrey. 1998. "Donald Trump on the Role Genetics Play in Success." *The Oprah Winfrey Show.* Accessed November 23, 2016. https://www.youtube.com/watch?v=YclB7UDbnKQ.

690   Phil Han. 2010. *Donald Trump: I Have the Genes for Success.* February 11. http://www.cnn.com/2010/Showbiz/02/11/donald.trump.marriage.apprentice.

691   Chris Moody. 2015. *Donald Trump Tweets Photo of Nazi Uniforms.* July 16. http://www.cnn.com/2015/07/14/politics/trump-photo-nazi-uniforms/.

692   Katie Rogers. 2016. *Hillary Clinton's Campaign Calls Donald Trump's Star of David Tweet Anti-Semitic.* July 4. http://www.nytimes.com/2016/07/05/us/politics/hillary-clintons-campaign-calls-donald-trumps-star-of-david-tweet-anti-semitic.html.

693   Dean Obeidallah. 2015. *Donald Trump's Horrifying Words about Muslims.* November 21. http://www.cnn.com/2015/11/20/opinions/obeidallah-trump-anti-muslim/.

694   Aaron Blake. 2016. *Donald Trump Jr. Says Media Would Be 'Warming Up the Gas Chamber' If Trump Lied Like Clinton.* September 15. https://www.washingtonpost.com/news/the-fix/wp/2016/09/15/donald-trump-jr-says-media-would-be-warming-up-the-gas-chamber-if-trump-lied-like-clinton/.

695   Donald Trump. 2015. *Donald Trump on ISIS - "I Would Bomb the SHIT out of 'em!"* November 12. https://www.youtube.com/watch?v=aWejiXvd-P8.

696   Emma Graham-Harrison. 2016. *Russian Airstrikes in Syria Killed 2,000 Civilians in Six Months.* March 15. https://www.theguardian.com/world/2016/mar/15/russian-airstrikes-in-syria-killed-2000-civilians-in-six-months.

697   Lorraine Berry. 2016. *'A Lot of What He Believes, We Believe'— KKK Grand Imperial Wizard Endorses Trump.* April 20. http://www.rawstory.com/2016/04/a-lot-of-what-he-believes-we-believe-kkk-grand-imperial-wizard-endorses-trump/.

698   American Presidency Project (APP). n.d. *Franklin D. Roosevelt.* Accessed October 9, 2017. http://www.presidency.ucsb.edu/ws/?pid=15545.

699   Society of Professional Journalists. *SPJ Code of Ethics.* Accessed December 29, 2017. https://www.spj.org/ethicscode.asp.

700   American Press Institute. *The Elements of Journalism.* Accessed December 29, 2017. https://www.americanpressinstitute.org/journalism-essentials/what-is-journalism/elements-journalism/.

701   Constitution Center. n.d. *Freedom of Religion, Speech, Press, Assembly and Petition.* Accessed September 19, 2016.

702   Reporters Without Borders is an organization carrying out the mission to protect and defend journalists working both internationally and in the United States. The ranking is partly on a questionnaire sent to journalists, researchers, jurists and human rights activists around the world asking questions about pluralism, media independence, environment and self-censorship, legislative framework, transparency and infrastructure. More detail can be reviewed at https://en.wikipedia.org/wiki/Press_Freedom_Index.

703   Ibid.

704   Alison Bethel McKenzie. 2015. *Press Freedom Is Declining in the US.* May 3. http://america.aljazeera.com/opinions/2015/5/press-freedom-is-declining-in-the-us.html.

705   Travis J. Tritten. 2015. *NBC's Brian Williams Recants Iraq Story After Soldiers Protest.* February 4. http://www.stripes.com/news/us/nbc-s-brian-williams-recants-iraq-story-after-soldiers-protest-1.327792.

706   David Corn and Daniel Schulman. 2015. *Bill O'Reilly Has His Own Brian Williams Problem.* February 19. http://www.motherjones.com/politics/2015/02/bill-oreilly-brian-williams-falklands-war.

707   Benjamin Mullin. 2016. *The Intercept's Juan Thompson Fired for Fabrication.* February 2. http://www.poynter.org/2016/the-intercepts-juan-thompson-fired-for-fabrication/394707/.

708   Benjamin Mullin. 2016. *The Guardian Unpublishes 13 Stories after Investigation into Fabrication.* May 26. http://www.poynter.org/2016/the-guardian-unpublishes-13-stories-after-investigation-into-fabrication/413947/.

709   Plagiarism Today. 2012. *5 Famous Plagiarists: Where Are They Now?* August 21. https://www.plagiarismtoday.com/2012/08/21/5-famous-plagiarists-where-are-they-now/.

710   Conor Friedersdorf. 2016. *The Exaggerated Claims of Media Bias against Donald Trump.* August 16. http://www.theatlantic.com/politics/archive/2016/08/claims-of-media-bias-against-donald-trump-are-exaggerated/495977/.

711   Independent. 2016. *Donald Trump Gets Backing from Hezbollah over Claim Barack Obama Founded ISIS.* August 14. https://www.independent.co.uk/news/world/americas/us-elections/donald-trump-gets-backing-from-hezbollah-over-claim-barack-obama-founded-isis-a7189801.html.

712   Wikipedia Contributors. n.d. *Fox News Channel Controversies.* Accessed September 7, 2016. https://en.wikipedia.org/w/index.php?title=Fox_News_Channel_controversies&oldid=735122633.

713   Ibid.

714   Aaron Sharockman. 2015. *PunditFact Checks In on the Cable News Channels.* January 29. http://www.politifact.com/truth-o-meter/article/2015/jan/29/punditfact-checks-cable-news-channels/.

715   PolitiFact. n.d. *Hillary Clinton's File.* Accessed September 5, 2017. http://www.politifact.com/personalities/hillary-clinton/.

716   Ibid.

717   Brian Stelter and Dylan Byers. 2016. *Roger Ailes Has Resigned from Fox News amid Sexual Harassment Allegations -- An Ignoble End to His Legendary, Controversial Twenty-year Tenure Running the Country's Dominant Cable News Channel.* July 21. http://money.cnn.com/2016/07/21/media/roger-ailes-leaves-fox-news/.

718   James, Brendan. 2016. *Here's What Trump has said so Far about Sexual Harassment and Roger Ailes.* August 3. https://news.vice.com/article/donald-trump-sexual-harassment-roger-ailes-fox-news.

719   Mnar Muhawesh and MintPress News Desk Team. 2015. *'Pants on Fire': Analysis Shows 60% of Fox News 'Facts' Are Really Lies.* May 12. http://www.mintpressnews.com/pants-on-fire-analysis-shows-60-of-fox-news-facts-are-really-lies/205563.

720   John Oliver. 2014. *Miss America Pageant: Last Week Tonight with John Oliver (HBO).* September 21. https://www.youtube.com/watch?v=oDPCmmZifE8.

721   Stefano DellaVigna and Ethan Kaplan. 2006. *The Fox News Effect: Media Bias and Voting.* April. Accessed November 22, 2017. http://www.nber.org/papers/w12169.

722   Ibid.

723   Ibid.

724   Emily Steel and Michael S. Schmidt. 2017. *Bill O'Reilly Thrives at Fox News, Even as Harassment Settlements Add Up.* April 1. https://www.nytimes.com/2017/04/01/business/media/bill-oreilly-sexual-harassment-fox-news.html.

725   Dylan Byers. 2017. *Trump Defends Bill O'Reilly: 'I Don't Think Bill Did Anything Wrong.'* April 5. http://money.cnn.com/2017/04/05/media/donald-trump-defends-bill-oreilly/index.html.

726   Cleve R. Wootson Jr. 2017. *Bill O'Reilly's Ratings Are Soaring after the Sexual Harassment Allegations.* April 11. https://www.washingtonpost.com/news/arts-and-entertainment/wp/2017/04/09/bill-oreillys-ratings-are-actually-higher-than-they-were-since-the-sexual-harassment-allegations/?utm_term=.8a2762c8686e.

727   Joe Concha. 2017. *Report: O'Reilly to Get up to $25m in Fox Payout.* April 29. http://thehill.com/homenews/media/329766-report-oreilly-to-get-25m-in-fox-payout.

728   Wikipedia Contributors. n.d. *Jesse Watters.* Accessed September 20, 2017. https://en.wikipedia.org/wiki/Jesse_Watters.

729   AP. 2017. *Ted Koppel Calmly Tells Sean Hannity He's 'Bad for America.'* March 27. https://www.usatoday.com/story/news/politics/2017/03/27/ted-koppel-calmly-explains-sean-hannity-why-hes-bad-america/99680636/.

730   Wikipedia Contributors. n.d. *Information Overload.* Accessed August 11, 2016.

731   Paul Farhi. 2016. *CNN's Hiring of Corey Lewandowski Didn't Cause a Staff Revolt. in Fact, It Was the Opposite.* June 27. https://www.washingtonpost.com/lifestyle/cnns-hiring-of-corey-lewandowski-didnt-cause-a-staff-revolt-in-fact-it-was-the-opposite/2016/06/26/61ba30fe-3bcd-11e6-80bc-d06711fd2125_story.html.

732   Scott Horsley. 2016. *Fact Check: Hillary Clinton and Coal Jobs.* May 3. http://www.npr.org/2016/05/03/476485650/fact-check-hillary-clinton-and-coal-jobs.

733   Ibid.

734   Nick Fernandez. 2016. *The Associated Press Finally Deletes "Misleading" Tweet about the Clinton Foundation after Keeping It Posted for Two Weeks.* September 8. https://mediamatters.org/shows-and-publications/associated-press.

735   Ibid.

736   Jason Easley. 2016. *The Truth Comes out as CNN Admits They Are Going Easy on Donald Trump.* September 6. http://www.politicususa.com/2016/09/06/truth-cnn-admits-easy-donald-trump.html.

737   Jeffrey Gottfried et al. 2016. *Presidential Campaign – A News Event That's Hard to Miss.* 2016. http://www.journalism.org/2016/02/04/the-2016-presidential-campaign-a-news-event-thats-hard-to-miss/.

738   Rebecca Riffkin. 2015. *Americans' Trust in Media Remains at Historical Low.* September 28. http://www.gallup.com/poll/185927/americans-trust-media-remains-historical-low.aspx.

739   Chris Cillizza. 2015. *The Dangerous Anger of Donald Trump.* November 13.

740   Jackson Connor. 2015. *Rush Limbaugh Gives Himself a Pat on the Back for MSNBC's Ratings Troubles.* February 6. http://www.huffingtonpost.com/2015/02/06/rush-limbaugh-msnbc-ratings-troubles_n_6630306.html.

741   Amanda Prestigiacomo. 2016. *Want to Know Why the Media Love Trump? He Raises Ratings.* Daily Wire. March 10. https://www.dailywire.com/news/4035/want-know-why-media-love-trump-he-raises-ratings-amanda-prestigiacomo#exit-modal.

742   Author of *The Making of Donald Trump.*

743   Former Lieutenant Governor of New York, a Republican and staunch supporter of Donald Trump.

744   David Cay Johnston, Betsy McCaughey, interview by Michael Smerconish. 2016. *The Real Art of Trump's Deals.* August 27. http://transcripts.cnn.com/transcripts/1608/27/smer.01.html.

745   For more information on the Society of Professional Journalism, visit its website: https://www.spj.org/.

746   Brian Stelter, Jim Rutenberg and Alysin Camerota, interview by Chris Cuomo. 2016. *Why Do Campaigns Criticize Media When Pressed for Answers?* September 14. http://transcripts.cnn.com/transcripts/1609/14/nday.02.html.

747   Ibid.

748   Ibid.

749   Ibid.

750   Ibid.

751   Michael Kinsley. 2015. *Parsing the Plagiarism of Fareed Zakaria.* March. http://www.vanityfair.com/news/2015/02/michael-kinsley-fareed-zakaria-plagarism.

752   Dylan Byers. 2014. *The Wrongs of Fareed Zakaria.* September 16. http://www.politico.com/blogs/media/2014/09/the-wrongs-of-fareed-zakaria-195579.

753   Jason Easley. 2016. *The Truth Comes Out As CNN Admits They Are Going Easy On Donald Trump.* September 6. https://www.politicususa.com/2016/09/06/truth-cnn-admits-easy-donald-trump.html.

754   Craig Silverman. 2016. *This Analysis Shows How Fake Election News Stories Outperformed Real News on Facebook.* November 16. https://www.buzzfeed.com/craigsilverman/viral-fake-election-news-outperformed-real-news-on-facebook?utm_term=.kgr1lbglk#.xrmn5yv5b.

755   Ibid.

756   Jim Hoft. 2016. *Social Media Patterns Show Trump Is Looking at a Landslide Victory.* August 7. http://www.thegatewaypundit.com/2016/08/evidence-trump-landslide/.

757   The Burrard Street Journal. 2016. *Trump Claims America Should Never Have Given Canada Its Independence.* July 29. http://www.burrardstreetjournal.com/trump-canada-independence-was-mistake/.

758 Ben Yarberry. 2016. *Ashton Kutcher and His Organization Rescued over 6,000 Sex Trafficking Victims but He's Not Done Yet.* October 14. http://tribunist.com/news/ashton-kutcher-and-his-organization-rescued-over-6000-sex-trafficking-victims-but-he-has-not-done-yet/.

759 Nolan D. McCaskill. 2016. *'We Should Just Cancel the Election and Just Give It to Trump.'* October 27. http://www.politico.com/story/2016/10/donald-trump-election-cancel-230414.

760 J.E.B. Spredemann. n.d. *J.E.B. Spredemann > Quotes > Quotable Quote.* Accessed September 6, 2017. https://www.goodreads.com/quotes/839174-choices-made-whether-bad-or-good-follow-you-forever-and.

761 Morning Consult. 2016. *Clinton and Trump Are Historically Unpopular. Here's Why.* Accessed August 24, 2016. https://morningconsult.com/trump-clinton-unpopular/.

762 Politico. 2016. *Full Text: Donald Trump 2016 RNC Draft Speech Transcript.* July 21.

763 Marie Brenner. 1990. *After the Gold Rush.* September.

764 Adolf. Hitler. n.d. *Adolf Hitler > Quotes > Quotable Quote.* Accessed October 9, 2017. http://www.goodreads.com/quotes/553-if-you-tell-a-big-enough-lie-and-tell-it.

765 Angie Drobnic Holan and Linda Qiu. 2015. *Lie of the Year: The Campaign Misstatements of Donald Trump.* December 21. http://www.politifact.com/truth-o-meter/article/2015/dec/21/2015-lie-year-donald-trump-campaign-misstatements/.

766 Pulitzer Prize. 2009. *2009 Pulitzer Prizes.* http://www.pulitzer.org/prize-winners-by-year/2009.

767 PolitiFact. n.d. *Hillary Clinton's File.* Accessed September 5, 2017. http://www.politifact.com/personalities/hillary-clinton.

768 Hillary for America 2016. *Hillary Clinton, Tim Kaine Release Tax Returns While Donald Trump Defies Decades-Old Tradition of Disclosure.* https://www.hillaryclinton.com/page/tax-returns/.

769 Phil Mattingly. 2016. *Donald Trump's Tax Returns: Why Won't He Release Them?* September 7. http://edition.cnn.com/2016/09/07/politics/donald-trump-tax-audit-tax-returns/index.html.

770 Ford Vox. 2016. *Trump and Oz: A Match Made in TV Heaven.* September 18. http://www.cnn.com/2016/09/16/opinions/trump-clinton-health-war-vox-opinion/.

771 David A. Fahrenthold. 2016. *Trump Pays IRS a Penalty for His Foundation Violating Rules with Gift to Aid Florida Attorney General.* September 1. https://www.washingtonpost.com/news/post-politics/wp/2016/09/01/trump-pays-irs-a-penalty-for-his-foundation-violating-rules-with-gift-to-florida-attorney-general/?utm_term=.e5c3d1fe725b.

772 David A. Fahrenthold. 2016. *Trump Used $258,000 from His Charity to Settle Legal Problems.* September 20. https://www.washingtonpost.com/politics/trump-used-258000-from-his-charity-to-settle-legal-problems/2016/09/20/adc88f9c-7d11-11e6-ac8e-cf8e0dd91dc7_story.html.

773 Ibid.

774 David A. Fahrenthold. 2016. *Trump's Campaign Says He's Given 'Tens of Millions' to Charity, but Offers No Details and No Proof.* September 12. https://www.washingtonpost.com/news/post-politics/wp/2016/09/12/trumps-campaign-says-hes-given-tens-of-millions-to-charity-but-offers-no-details-and-no-proof/?utm_term=.1d004f16186d.

775 David A. Fahrenthold. 2012. *Trump Foundation Lacks the Certification Required for Charities That Solicit Money.* September 29. https://www.washingtonpost.com/politics/trump-foundation-lacks-the-certification-required-for-charities-that-solicit-money/2016/09/29/7dac6a68-8658-11e6-ac72-a29979381495_story.html.

776 Katie Reilly. 2016. *Trump Campaign Denies He Violated Embargo against Cuba.* September 29. http://fortune.com/2016/09/29/donald-trump-cuban-embargo-newsweek.

777 Jason Horowitz. 2016. *With Degree Debunked, Melania Trump Website Is Taken Down.* July 28. http://www.nytimes.com/2016/07/29/us/politics/melania-trump.html?_r=0.

778 Rebecca Savransky. 2016. *Trump Promises Press Conference on Melania's Immigration Story.* August 9. http://thehill.com/blogs/ballot-box/presidential-races/290935-trump-on-wifes-immigration-story-she-came-in-totally.

779 AP. 2016. *Melania Trump Releases Letter from Immigration Lawyer in Bid to Kill Rumours She Worked in U.S. Illegally.* September 15. http://nationalpost.com/news/world/melania-trump-releases-letter-from-immigration-lawyer-in-bid-to-kill-rumours-she-worked-in-u-s-illegally.

780 AP. 2016. *Melania Trump Was Paid for Modeling Jobs in US before Gaining Work Visa, Records Show.* November 5. https://www.theguardian.com/us-news/2016/nov/05/melania-trump-was-paid-modeling-before-work-visa-records-show.

781 Ibid.

782 AP. 2016. *Melania Trump Worked in the U.S. without Legal Permission.* November 5. http://fortune.com/2016/11/05/melania-trump-visa-immigration/.

783 Matea Gold. 2015. *Pro-Trump Super PAC Shutting Down amid Questions about Ties to Trump Campaign.* October 22. https://www.washingtonpost.com/news/post-politics/wp/2015/10/22/pro-trump-super-pac-shutting-down-amid-questions-about-ties-to-trump-campaign/.

784 Fredreka Schouten. 2016. *Hillary Clinton Will Push Constitutional Amendment to Overturn Citizens United.* July 18. http://www.usatoday.com/story/news/politics/onpolitics/2016/07/16/hillary-clinton-push-constitutional-amendment-overturn-citizens-united/87186452.

785 Ibid.

786 AP. 2016. *The Latest: Trump Taps Citizens United President as Deputy.* September 2.

787 Michael Hausam. 2015. *Donald Trump Keeps Saying His Campaign Is Self-funded. But That Is Just Not True.* November 11. http://ijr.com/2015/11/469588-donald-trump-keeps-saying-his-campaign-is-self-funded-but-that-is-just-not-true/.

788 Philip Bump. 2016. *Donald Trump's Threat to Sue Ted Cruz, Explained.* February 16.

789 Sam Stein. 2016. *Donald Trump Encourages Violence at Rallies.* March 10. http://www.huffingtonpost.com/entry/donald-trump-violence_us_56e1f16fe4b0b25c91815913.

790 Diane D. Blair, whose diaries were released to the University of Arkansas after her death in 2000.

791 Politico. 2016. *Full Transcript: Second 2016 Presidential Debate.* Politico. October 10, 2016. https://www.politico.com/story/2016/10/2016-presidential-debate-transcript-229519.

792 Tina Nguyen. 2016. *Donald Trump Says Accusers Are Too Ugly for Him to Have Groped.* October 14. https://www.vanityfair.com/news/2016/10/donald-trump-insults-accusers-ugly.

793 Jeremy Diamond and Eugene Scott. 2016. *Trump Says He'll Sue Sexual Misconduct Accusers.* October 22. http://www.cnn.com/2016/10/22/politics/trump-says-hell-sue-sexual-misconduct-accusers/index.html.

794 Eric Bradner. 2016. *Melania Trump: Donald Trump Was 'Egged on' into 'Boy Talk.'* October 18. http://www.cnn.com/2016/10/17/politics/melania-trump-interview/index.html.

795 Dan Balz. 2016. *How Everyone Looks Bad Because Bill Clinton Met with Loretta Lynch.* July 2. https://www.washingtonpost.com/politics/how-everyone-looks-bad-because-bill-clinton-met-with-loretta-lynch/2016/07/02/a7807adc-3ff4-11e6-a66f-aa6c1883b6b1_story.html.

796 Matt Zapotosky. 2016. *Attorney General Pledges to Accept FBI and Justice Findings in Clinton Email Probe.* July 1. https://www.washingtonpost.com/world/national-security/attorney-general-to-back-fbi-and-justice-findings-in-clinton-email-server-probe/2016/07/01/77ce6d8e-3f78-11e6-a66f-aa6c1883b6b1_story.html?tid=a_inl.

797 James Comey. 2016. *Statement by FBI Director James B. Comey on the Investigation of Secretary Hillary Clinton's Use of a Personal E-mail System.* July 5. https://www.fbi.gov/news/pressrel/press-releases/statement-by-fbi-director-james-b-comey-on-the-investigation-of-secretary-hillary-clinton2019s-use-of-a-personal-e-mail-system.

798 Matt Zapotosky. 2016. *House Republicans Grill FBI Director Comey on Clinton Emails.* July 7.

799 Elijah E. Cummings. 2016. *Cummings Releases Full Powell Email Advising Clinton on Personal Email Use.* September 7. https://medium.com/oversightdems/cummings-releases-full-powell-email-advising-clinton-on-personal-email-use-65904c1ccfa#.lkgp73p4c.

800 Josh Gerstein. 2016. *Advice to Clinton about Email Goes Public.* September 7. http://www.politico.com/story/2016/09/colin-powell-hillary-clinton-emails-227861.

801 Ibid.

802 Ibid.

803 Kenneth P. Vogel. 2016. *Inside the Clintons' Moroccan Money 'Mess.'* November 3. http://www.politico.com/story/2016/11/clinton-foundation-morocco-marrakech-230717.

804 Oliver Darcy. 2016. *Fact Check: Top Aide Did Not Say Hillary Clinton Hates 'Everyday Americans.'* October 11. http://www.businessinsider.com/wikileaks-email-hillary-clinton-everyday-americans-2016-10.

805 John Hawkins. 2016. *The 5 Biggest Revelations about Hillary Clinton from WikiLeaks.* October 29. http://townhall.com/columnists/johnhawkins/2016/10/29/the-5-biggest-revelations-about-hillary-clinton-from-wikileaks-n2238298.

806 Reuters. 2016. *18 Revelations from Wikileaks' Hacked Clinton Emails.* October 27. http://www.bbc.com/news/world-us-canada-37639370.

807 Yousef Saba. 2016. *Trump Went 'Too Far' at Catholic Roast.* October 24. http://www.politico.com/story/2016/10/clinton-trump-al-davis-catholic-dinner-reaction-230235.

808 Reuters. 2016. *18 Revelations from Wikileaks' Hacked Clinton Emails.* October 27.

809 Yousef Saba. 2016. *Trump Went 'Too Far' at Catholic Roast.* October 24.

810 Andy McDonald. 2016. *These Wikileaks Emails Prove Just What a Monster Hillary Clinton Is.* November 2. http://www.huffingtonpost.com/entry/these-wikileaks-emails-prove-just-what-a-monster-hillary-clinton-is_us_581a1ecce4b08f9841acad73.

811 Ibid.

812 Lauren Carroll. 2016. *Are the Clinton Wikileaks Emails Doctored, or Are They Authentic?* October 23. http://www.politifact.com/truth-o-meter/article/2016/oct/23/are-clinton-wikileaks-emails-doctored-or-are-they-/.

813 Emma Margolinfrank Thorp Vhallie Jackson. 2016. *Marco Rubio Warns Republicans: Don't Talk about Wikileaks.* October 19. http://www.nbcnews.com/card/marco-rubio-warns-republicans-dont-talk-about-wikileaks-n668746.

814 Ben Kamisar. 2016. *Trump Calls on Supporters to Monitor Polling Places for Fraud.* October 10. http://thehill.com/blogs/ballot-box/presidential-races/298856-trump-calls-on-supporters-to-monitor-polling-places-for.

815 Dan Levine and Mica Rosenberg. 2016. *Nevada Judge Rejects Trump Request for Order over Early Voting.* November 8. http://www.reuters.com/article/us-usa-election-lawsuit/nevada-judge-rejects-trump-request-for-order-over-early-voting-iduskbn1332d4?il=0.

816 Paulina Firozi. 2016. *Iowa GOP Voter Arrested for Alleged Voter Fraud: Report.* October 28. http://thehill.com/blogs/blog-briefing-room/news/303406-iowa-republican-voter-arrested-for-alleged-voter-fraud.

817 Joshua Green and Sasha Issenberg. 2016. *Inside the Trump Bunker, with Days to Go.* October 27. https://www.bloomberg.com/news/articles/2016-10-27/inside-the-trump-bunker-with-12-days-to-go.

818 Ibid.

819 NPR Staff. 2016. *Fact Check and Full Transcript of the Final 2016 Presidential Debate.* October 19. https://apps.npr.org/presidential-debate-factcheck-20161019/child.htmlhttps://apps.npr.org/presidential-debate-factcheck-20161019/child.html.

820   Julie Rovner. 2006. 'Partial-birth Abortion': Separating Fact from Spin. February 21. http://www.npr.org/2006/02/21/5168163/partial-birth-abortion-separating-fact-from-spin.

821   NPR Staff. 2016. Fact Check and Full Transcript of the Final 2016 Presidential Debate. October 19.

822   Linda Qiu and Amy Sherman. 2016. Trump: 'I've Been Proven Right' about Clinton Wanting Open Borders. October 12. http://www.politifact.com/truth-o-meter/statements/2016/oct/12/donald-trump/trump-ive-been-proven-right-about-clinton-wanting-/.

823   Louis Jacobson. 2016. Donald Trump Gets a Full Flop for Whether He's Had a Relationship to Vladimir Putin. August 1. http://www.politifact.com/truth-o-meter/statements/2016/aug/01/donald-trump/donald-trump-gets-full-flop-whether-hes-had-relati.

824   Ibid.

825   Ibid.

826   Ibid.

827   NPR Staff. 2016. Fact Check and Full Transcript of the Final 2016 Presidential Debate. October 19. https://apps.npr.org/presidential-debate-factcheck-20161019/child.htmlhttps://apps.npr.org/presidential-debate-factcheck-20161019/child.html.

828   Ibid.

829   Ibid.

830   Ibid.

831   Ibid.

832   Ibid.

833   Ibid.

834   Ibid.

835   Ibid.

836   Ibid.

837   Ibid.

838   Ibid.

839   Amber Phillips. 2016. The 5 House Seats That Could Signal a Democratic Majority in 2016. June 10. https://www.washingtonpost.com/news/the-fix/wp/2016/06/10/the-5-house-seats-that-could-signal-a-democratic-majority-in-2016/?utm_term=.a49f3a4bfc92.

840   Joshua Roberts. 2016. FBI Director Comey Released Letter in Fear of Leaks, Sources Say. November 3. http://www.newsweek.com/fbi-director-comey-released-letter-fear-leaks-516879.

841   Ali Vitali. 2016. Trump Claims Clinton Indictment Is Near. It's Not. November 3. http://www.nbcnews.com/card/trump-claims-clinton-indictment-near-its-not-n677596.

842   Ibid.

843   Wayne Barrett. 2016. Meet Donald Trump's Top FBI Fanboy. October 3. http://www.thedailybeast.com/articles/2016/11/03/meet-donald-trump-s-top-fbi-fanboy.html.

844   Gregory Korte. 2016. Obama Phones Trump, Offers White House Invitation. November 9. http://www.usatoday.com/story/news/politics/2016/11/09/obama-phones-trump-offer-congratulations-and-white-house-meeting/93534068/.

845   Alan Rappeport and Alexander Burns. 2016. Highlights of Hillary Clinton's Concession Speech and President Obama's Remarks. November 9. http://www.nytimes.com/2016/11/09/us/politics/donald-trump-won-now-what.html?_r=0.

846   Rick Riordan. n.d. The Lightning Thief Quotes. Accessed October 9, 2017. https://www.goodreads.com/work/quotes/3346751-the-lightning-thief.

847   Donald J. Trump. 2016 6:19 PM. Twitter Post. November 10. https://twitter.com/realdonaldtrump/status/796900183955095552?lang=en.

848   Donald J. Trump. 2016 3:14 AM. Twitter Post. November 11. https://twitter.com/realdonaldtrump/status/797034721075228672?lang=en.

849   Grant Smith and Daniel Trotta. 2017. U.S. Hate Crimes Up 20 Percent in 2016 Fueled by Election Campaign-Report. March 13. http://www.reuters.com/article/us-usa-crime-hate/u-s-hate-crimes-up-20-percent-in-2016-fueled-by-election-campaign-report-iduskbn16l0bo.

850   Donald J. Trump. 2017 11:00 AM. Twitter Post. January 15. https://twitter.com/realdonaldtrump/status/820707210565132288?lang=en.

851   Donald J. Trump. 2016 3:55 AM. Twitter Post. November 29. https://twitter.com/realdonaldtrump/status/803567993036754944?lang=en.

852   Donald J. Trump. 2016 3:20 AM. Twitter Post. November 30. https://twitter.com/realdonaldtrump/status/803921522784092160?lang=en.

853   Donald J. Trump. 2016 8:03 AM. Twitter Post. November 13. https://twitter.com/realdonaldtrump/status/797832229800050688?lang=en.

854   Max Fisher. 2016. What Is Donald Trump's Foreign Policy? November 11. https://www.nytimes.com/2016/11/12/world/what-is-donald-trumps-foreign-policy.html.

855   NY Times. 2016. Transcript: Donald Trump Expounds on His Foreign Policy Views. March 26. https://www.nytimes.com/2016/03/27/us/politics/donald-trump-transcript.html?_r=2.

856   Lauren Carroll. 2016. *Donald Trump Wrongly Tweets that He 'Never Said' More Countries Should Have Nuclear Weapons.* November 14. http://www.politifact.com/truth-o-meter/statements/2016/nov/14/donald-trump/donald-trump-wrongly-tweets-he-never-said-more-cou/.

857   Alex Koppelman and Brian Stelter. 2016. *Trump Uses Un-canceled Meeting with New York Times to Complain about the Times.* November 22. http://money.cnn.com/2016/11/22/media/trump-new-york-times-meeting.

858   Donald J. Trump. 2015 2:27 PM. *Twitter Post.* October 18. https://twitter.com/realdonaldtrump/status/655857881586 270208?lang=en.

859   Donald J. Trump. 2016 5:05 AM. *Twitter Post.* December 15. https://twitter.com/realdonaldtrump/status/8093839890 18497024?lang=en.

860   Rebecca Savransky. 2016. *Trump Attacks Vanity Fair: 'Way Down, Big Trouble, Dead.'* December 15. http://thehill.com/homenews/campaign/310516-trump-attacks-vanity-fair-way-down-big-trouble-dead.

861   Evan Perez et al. 2017. *Intel Chiefs Presented Trump with Claims of Russian Efforts to Compromise Him.* January 12. http://edition.cnn.com/2017/01/10/politics/donald-trump-intelligence-report-russia/index.html.

862   Donald J. Trump. 2017 5:19 PM. *Twitter Post.* January 10. https://twitter.com/realdonaldtrump/status/8189906554186 17856?lang=en.

863   Donald J. Trump. 2017 4:31 AM. *Twitter Post.* January 11. https://twitter.com/realdonaldtrump/status/819159806489 591809?lang=en.

864   Leinz Vales. 2017. *Anderson Cooper, Trump Adviser Clash over Russia Report.* January 11. http://www.cnn.com/2017/01/11/politics/anderson-cooper-kellyanne-conway-trump-intelligence-report-russia-cnntv/index.html.

865   Ibid.

866   Ibid.

867   Ibid.

868   Donald J. Trump. 2017 4:48 AM. *Twitter Post.* January 11. https://twitter.com/realdonaldtrump/status/819164172781 060096?lang=en.

869   Eugene Scott. 2017. *McCain: Dictators 'Get Started by Suppressing Free Press.'* February 20. http://www.cnn.com/2017/02/18/politics/john-mccain-donald-trump-dictators/index.html.

870   Donald J. Trump. 2016 5:34 AM. *Twitter Post.* November 15. https://twitter.com/realdonaldtrump/status/7985196004 13601792?lang=en.

871   Donald J. Trump. 2016 5:40 AM. *Twitter Post.* November 15. https://twitter.com/realdonaldtrump/status/7985210535 51140864?lang=en.

872   Gregory Krieg. 2016. *It's Official: Clinton Swamps Trump in Popular Vote.* December 22. http://edition.cnn.com/2016/12/21/politics/donald-trump-hillary-clinton-popular-vote-final-count.

873   Ibid.

874   Ibid.

875   Ibid.

876   NY Times. 2017. *Presidential Election Results: Donald J. Trump Wins.* January 4. http://www.nytimes.com/elections/results/president.

877   Theodore Schleifer. 2016. *Trump Stomps All over the Democrats' Blue Wall.* November 9. http://edition.cnn.com/2016/11/09/politics/donald-trump-hillary-clinton-blue-wall/.

878   NY Times. 2017. *Wisconsin Results.* February 10. https://www.nytimes.com/elections/results/wisconsin.

879   NY Times. 2017. *Michigan Results.* February 10. https://www.nytimes.com/elections/results/michigan.

880   NY Times. 2017. *Pennsylvania Results.* February 10. https://www.nytimes.com/elections/results/pennsylvania.

881   Donald J. Trump. 2016 12:30 PM. *Twitter Post.* November 27. https://twitter.com/realdonaldtrump/status/802972944 532209664?lang=en.

882   Issie Lapowsky. 2017. *Author of Trump's Favorite Voter Fraud Study Says Everyone's Wrong.* January 25. https://www.wired.com/2017/01/author-trumps-favorite-voter-fraud-study-says-everyones-wrong/.

883   John Walcott. 2016. *Russia Intervened to Help Trump Win Election: Intelligence Officials.* December 10. http://www.reuters.com/article/us-usa-election-cyber-russia-iduskbn13z05b *Officials.*

884   Ibid.

885   Donald J. Trump. 2016 4:31 PM. *Twitter Post.* November 27. https://twitter.com/realdonaldtrump/status/8030336425 45115140?lang=en.

886   Donald J. Trump. 2016 6:19 PM. *Twitter Post.* November 28. https://twitter.com/realdonaldtrump/status/8034232036 20245504?lang=en.

887   Donald J. Trump. 2016 5:21 AM. *Twitter Post.* December 12. https://twitter.com/realdonaldtrump/status/8083007069 14594816?lang=en.

888   Donald J. Trump. 2016 5:17 AM. *Twitter Post.* December 12. https://twitter.com/realdonaldtrump/status/8082998411 47248640?lang=en.

889   Andrew Osborn. 2016. *Russia Says It Was in Touch with Trump's Campaign during Election.* November 10. http://www.reuters.com/article/us-usa-election-russia-trump-iduskbn1351rj.

890   Toni Clarke and Dustin Volz. 2017. *Trump Acknowledges Russia Role in U.S. Election Hacking: Aide.* January 9. http://www.reuters.com/article/us-usa-russia-cyber-iduskbn14s0o6.

891　Aaron Blake. 2017. *The 11 Most Important Lines from the New Intelligence Report on Russia's Hacking.* January 6. https://www.washingtonpost.com/news/the-fix/wp/2017/01/06/the-most-important-lines-from-the-new-intelligence-report-on-russias-hacking/?utm_term=.eca440ea7b47.

892　Ibid.

893　Evan Perez and Daniella Diaz. 2017. *White House Announces Retaliation against Russia: Sanctions, Ejecting Diplomats.* January 3. http://edition.cnn.com/2016/12/29/politics/russia-sanctions-announced-by-white-house/.

894　Neil Macfarquhar. 2016. *Vladimir Putin Won't Expel U.S. Diplomats as Russian Foreign Minister Urged.* December 30. https://www.nytimes.com/2016/12/30/world/europe/russia-diplomats-us-hacking.html.

895　Donald J. Trump. 2016 11:41 AM. *Twitter Post.* December 30. https://twitter.com/realdonaldtrump/status/814919370711461890?lang=en.

896　Donald J. Trump. 2017 7:02 AM. *Twitter Post.* January 7. https://twitter.com/realdonaldtrump/status/817748207694467072?lang=en.

897　Donald J. Trump. 2017 7:10 AM. *Twitter Post.* January 7. https://twitter.com/realdonaldtrump/status/817750330196819968?lang=en

898　Donald J. Trump. 2017 7:21 AM. *Twitter Post.* January 7. https://twitter.com/realdonaldtrump/status/817753083707015168?lang=en.

899　This tweet spans three posts.

900　Matthew Nussbaum. 2016. *Indiana Official: Carrier Deal Is about Federal Contracts.* November 30. http://www.politico.com/story/2016/11/indiana-carrier-deal-federal-contracts-trump-232021.

901　Chris Isidore. 2016. *Carrier Union Boss: No Regrets about Calling Trump a Liar.* December 8. http://money.cnn.com/2016/12/08/news/companies/trump-carrier-union-boss/.

902　Ibid.

903　Ibid.

904　Ibid.

905　Nelson D. Schwartz. 2016. *Trump Saved Jobs at Carrier, but More Midwest Jobs Are in Jeopardy.* November 30. http://www.nytimes.com/2016/11/30/business/economy/trump-saved-jobs-at-carrier-but-more-midwest-jobs-are-in-jeopardy.html?_r=0.

906　Valentina Zarya. 2016. *Donald Trump Thinks He's the Reason You're Spending So Much Money.* December 27. http://fortune.com/2016/12/27/donald-trump-stock-market-holiday-spending/.

907　Jen Wieczner. 2016. *Donald Trump Bump Investors Have This Unlikely Stock to Thank for Dow Record.* December 9. http://fortune.com/2016/12/09/trump-stock-market-dow-close-goldman-sachs/.

908　Patrick Gillespie. 2016. *About That Trump Tweet: Confidence Has Climbed for Years.* December 28. http://money.cnn.com/2016/12/28/news/economy/consumer-confidence-trump.

909　Jennifer Wang. 2016. *Why Trump Won't Use a Blind Trust and What His Predecessors Did with Their Assets.* November 15. http://www.forbes.com/sites/jenniferwang/2016/11/15/why-trump-wont-use-a-blind-trust-and-what-his-predecessors-did-with-their-assets/#74514bf27915.

910　Donald J. Trump. 2016 6:14 PM. *Twitter Post.* November 21. https://twitter.com/realdonaldtrump/status/800885097775955974?lang=en.

911　Jennifer Wang. 2016. *Why Trump Won't Use a Blind Trust and What His Predecessors Did with Their Assets.* November 15.

912　Donald J. Trump. 2016 3:39 AM. *Twitter Post.* November 30. https://twitter.com/realdonaldtrump/status/803926488579973120?lang=en.

913　Donald J. Trump. 2016 3:44 AM. *Twitter Post.* November 30. https://twitter.com/realdonaldtrump/status/803927774784344064?lang=en.

914　Donald J. Trump. 2016 3:54 AM. *Twitter Post.* November 30. https://twitter.com/realdonaldtrump/status/803930240661811200?lang=en.

915　Donald J. Trump. 2016 3:59 AM. *Twitter Post.* November 30. https://twitter.com/realdonaldtrump/status/803931490514075648?lang=en.

916　Jeremy Venook. 2017. *Trump's Interests vs. America's, Expansion Edition.* January 27. http://www.theatlantic.com/business/archive/2017/01/donald-trump-conflicts-of-interests/508382/.

917　Donald J. Trump. 2016 5:34 AM. *Twitter Post.* November 19. https://twitter.com/realdonaldtrump/status/799969130237542400?lang=en.

918　Josh Gerstein. 2016. *Judge Delays Trump University Trial.* May 6. http://www.politico.com/story/2016/05/judge-sets-trump-university-trial-for-after-election-222917.

919　Brandy Zadrozny. 2016. *Eric Trump 'Charity' Spent $880K at Family-owned Golf Resorts.* September 3. http://www.thedailybeast.com/articles/2016/09/30/eric-trump-charity-spent-880k-at-family-owned-golf-resorts.html.

920　Daniella Diaz. 2016. *Trump Learns to Love Ryan: 'He's Like a Fine Wine.'* December 13. http://www.cnn.com/2016/12/13/politics/donald-trump-paul-ryan-wisconsin-thank-you-tour.

921　Ibid.

922　Chuck Todd, Sally Bronston and Matt Rivera. 2017. *Rep. John Lewis: 'I Don't See Trump as a Legitimate President.'* January 14. http://www.nbcnews.com/meet-the-press/john-lewis-trump-won-t-be-legitimate-president-n706676.

923 Donald J. Trump. 2017 4:50 AM. *Twitter Post.* January 14. https://twitter.com/realdonaldtrump/status/820251730407 473153?lang=en.

924 Donald J. Trump. 2017 5:07 AM. *Twitter Post.* January 14. https://twitter.com/realdonaldtrump/status/820255947956 383744?lang=en.

925 Linda Qiu. 2017. *Trump's Exaggerated Claim that John Lewis' District Is 'Falling Apart' and 'Crime Infested.'* January 15. http://www.politifact.com/truth-o-meter/statements/2017/jan/15/donald-trump/trumps-john-lewis-crime-invested-atlanta.

926 Ibid.

927 Kevin Slane. 2016. *New Hampshire Student Faced Death Threats After Donald Trump Insulted Her on Twitter.* December 9. https://www.boston.com/news/politics/2016/12/09/new-hampshire-student-faced-death-threats-after-donald-trump-insulted-her-on-twitter.

928 Global Editorial. 2016. *Stephen Bannon Is Not the Real Problem. Donald Trump Is.* November 17. http://www.theglobeandmail.com/opinion/editorials/stephen-bannon-is-not-the-real-problem-donald-trump-is/article32879856/.

929 Jeremy Bender. 2014. *Report: The US Military's Top Spy is Being Forced.* April 30. http://www.businessinsider.com/michael-t-flynn-fired-from-dia-2014-4.

930 Tim Weiner. 2017. *Commentary: Flynn Facts: A Threat to National Security.* February 13. https://www.reuters.com/article/us-flynn-national-security-commentary/commentary-flynn-facts-a-threat-to-national-security-iduskbn15s28e.

931 AP. 2017. *Michael Flynn, Fired Once by Obama, Now Resigns to Trump.* February 14. http://www.oregonlive.com/today/index.ssf/2017/02/michael_flynn_fired_once_by_a.html.

932 General Flynn. 2016 5:14 PM. *Twitter Post.* February 26. https://twitter.com/genflynn/status/703387702998278144?lang=en.

933 John Sexton. 2016. *Gen. Michael Flynn Compared Radical Islam to a Cancer 'Inside of the Islamic World.'* November 22. https://hotair.com/archives/2016/11/22/gen-michael-flynn-has-compared-radical-islam-to-cancer/.

934 Daniella Diaz. 2016. *53 Organizations to Trump: Dump Flynn as National Security Adviser.* December 6. http://edition.cnn.com/2016/12/05/politics/michael-flynn-donald-trump-national-security-adviser.

935 Ibid.

936 Jessie Hellmann. 2016. *New Yorker Profile: Flynn Broke 'Stupid' Rules during Army Career.* November 24. http://thehill.com/homenews/administration/307495-new-yorker-trumps-national-security-adviser-broke-stupid-rules-during.

937 Robert Sobel. 2016. *Gen. Michael Flynn Illegally Gave Classified Information to NATO, Report Explains.* November 24. http://us.blastingnews.com/news/2016/11/gen-michael-flynn-illegally-gave-classified-information-to-nato-report-explains-001283129.html.

938 Eugene Scott, Sara Murray and Jim Acosta. 2016. *Trump Picks South Carolina Gov. Nikki Haley to be US Ambassador to UN.* November 23. http://www.cnn.com/2016/11/23/politics/nikki-haley-picked-for-un-ambassador/index.html.

939 Ibid.

940 Ibid.

941 Jennifer William. 2017. *Nikki Haley, Trump's Pick for UN Ambassador, Doesn't Sound Anything Like Trump.* January 18. https://www.vox.com/world/2017/1/18/14311452/nikki-haley-senate-confirmation-hearing-un-ambassador.

942 Armin Rosen. 2016. *Here's How David Petraeus Got off with Only a Misdemeanor.* January 27. http://www.businessinsider.com/heres-how-david-petraeus-got-off-with-only-a-misdemeanor-2016-1.

943 Pamela Engel. 2016. *Petraeus Takes Center Stage amid Infighting about Trump Considering Romney for Secretary of State.* November 28. http://www.businessinsider.com/trump-petraeus-romney-secretary-of-state-2016-11.

944 Michael Tomasky. 2016. *Four Reasons Tapping Rex Tillerson as Secretary of State Is a Terrible Idea.* December 13. http://www.thedailybeast.com/articles/2016/12/13/four-reasons-tapping-rex-tillerson-as-secretary-of-state-is-a-terrible-idea.html.

945 Ibid.

946 Amber Phillips. 2017. *That Time the Senate Denied Jeff Sessions a Federal Judgeship over Accusations of Racism.* January 10. https://www.washingtonpost.com/news/the-fix/wp/2016/11/18/that-time-the-senate-denied-jeff-sessions-a-federal-judgeship-over-accusations-of-racism/?utm_term=.326834b14163.

947 Ibid.

948 Emily Bazelon. 2017. *The Voter Fraud Case Jeff Sessions Lost and Can't Escape.* January 9. https://www.nytimes.com/2017/01/09/magazine/the-voter-fraud-case-jeff-sessions-lost-and-cant-escape.html.

949 Amber Phillips. 2017. *That Time the Senate Denied Jeff Sessions a Federal Judgeship over Accusations of Racism.* January 10.

950 Ibid.

951 Donald J. Trump. 2016 5:39 AM. *Twitter Post.* November 20. https://twitter.com/realdonaldtrump/status/8003326398 44659201?lang=en.

952 Daniel S. Levine. 2016. *James Mattis on the Issues: 5 Fast Facts You Need to Know.* December 1. http://heavy.com/news/2016/12/general-james-mattis-issues-israel-defense-secretary-donald-trump-mad-dog-age-who-is-bio-views-isis-syria/.

953 Austin Wright and Jeremy Herb. 2017. *Mattis on the Issues.* January 12. http://www.politico.com/story/2017/01/mattis-on-the-issues-233522.

954 Eugene Scott. 2016. *Trump 'Surprised' by Mattis Waterboarding Comments.* November 24. http://edition.cnn.com/2016/11/23/politics/waterboarding-trump-mattis/.

955 Donald J. Trump. 2017 2:49 AM. *Twitter Post.* January 13. https://twitter.com/realdonaldtrump/status/819858926455 967744?lang=en.

956 David Smith. 2016. *Wisconsin Rules GOP Gerrymandering Violates Democrats' Rights.* November 22. https://www.theguardian. com/us-news/2016/nov/21/wisconsin-gerrymandering-district-court-2016-election-decision.

957 Nick Krieger. 2016. *2016 Election Results Show Effects of Gerrymandering in Michigan.* November 19. http://www.fixthemit-ten.com/blog/2016-election-results-show-effects-of-gerrymandering-in-michigan.

958 Ibid.

959 Donald J. Trump. 2016 6:22 PM. *Twitter Post.* November 21. https://twitter.com/realdonaldtrump/status/8008870877 80294656?lang=en.

960 Stephen Castle. 2016. *U.K. Rejects Donald Trump's Call for Nigel Farage to Be Made Ambassador.* November 22. https://www. nytimes.com/2016/11/22/world/europe/uk-donald-trump-nigel-farage.html.

961 Ibid.

962   Donald J Trump. 2017 5:11 AM. *Twitter Post.* January 17. https://twitter.com/realdonaldtrump/status/821344302651 555840?lang=en.

963 Jefferson, Thomas. n.d. *Jefferson's Draft.* Accessed October 9, 2017. https://jeffersonpapers.princeton.edu/selected-documents/jefferson%E2%80%99s-draft.

964 Donald J. Trump. 2016 5:59 PM. *Twitter Post.* December 22. https://twitter.com/realdonaldtrump/status/8121155017 91006720?lang=en.

965 Matt Wilstein. 2016. *Trump's Inauguration Nightmare: All the Musicians Who Have Turned Down Invites.* December 22. http:// www.thedailybeast.com/articles/2016/12/22/trump-s-inauguration-nightmare-all-the-musicians-who-have-turned-down-invites.

966 Jessica McBride. 2017. *Robert Jeffress: 5 Fast Facts You Need to Know.* January 19. http://heavy.com/news/2017/01/robert-jeffress-donald-trump-inauguration-pastor-inaugural-service-gays-muslims-islam-video-bio-catholics-mormons/.

967 Ibid.

968 Ibid.

969 Ibid.

970 Donald Trump. 2017. *President Trump's Inaugural Address, Annotated.* January 20. http://www.npr.org/2017/01/20/510629447/watch-live-president-trumps-inauguration-ceremony.

971 Ibid.

972 Ibid.

973 Philip Elliott. 2017. *These Ohio Voters Made Trump President. They're Still with Him.* July 25. http://time.com/4873955/donald-trump-youngstown-ohio-support/.

974 Donald Trump. 2017. *President Trump's Inaugural Address, Annotated.* January 20.

975 Globe Staff. 2017. *As the Women's March on Washington Goes Global, Here Are the Highlights.* January 22. http://www. theglobeandmail.com/news/world/womens-march-on-washington-goesglobal/article33696482.

976 Ryan Browne. 2017. *Ex-CIA Chief Brennan Bashes Trump over Speech during CIA Visit.* January 22. http://www.cnn. com/2017/01/21/politics/trump-to-cia-i-am-so-behind-you/index.html.

977 Jon Greenberg. 2017. *Trump Wrongly Blames Press for Feud with Intel Community.* January 22. http://www.politifact.com/truth-o-meter/statements/2017/jan/22/donald-trump/trump-wrongly-blames-press-feud-intel-community.

978 Matt Ford. 2017. *Trump's Press Secretary Falsely Claims: 'Largest Audience Ever to Witness an Inauguration, Period.'* January 21. https://www.theatlantic.com/politics/archive/2017/01/inauguration-crowd-size/514058/.

979 Ibid.

980 Donald J. Trump. 2012 8:45 PM. *Twitter Post.* November 6. https://twitter.com/realdonaldtrump/status/26603855650 4494082?lang=en.

981 Donald J. Trump. 2012 8:33 PM. *Twitter Post.* November 6. https://twitter.com/realdonaldtrump/status/26603550916 2303492?lang=en.

982 Donald J. Trump. 2012 8:39 PM. *Twitter Post.* November 6. https://twitter.com/realdonaldtrump/status/26603714362 8038144?lang=en.

983 Donald J. Trump. 2012 8:30 PM. *Twitter Post.* November 6. https://twitter.com/realdonaldtrump/status/26603495787 5544064?lang=en.

984 Rachel Weiner. 2011. *Virginia GOPer Writes Racist Anti-Obama Column.* May 25. http://www.huffingtonpost. com/2008/10/05/virginia-goper-writes-rac_n_132014.html.

985 Tony Pugh and McClatchy. 2009. *There's No Denying Obama's Race Plays a Role in Protests.* September 20. http://www. truth-out.org/archive/item/86139:theres-no-denying-obamas-race-plays-a-role-in-protests.

986 Ibid.

987 Justin Trudeau. 2016. *Statement by the Prime Minister of Canada on the Result of the US Presidential Election.* November 9. https://pm.gc.ca/eng/news/2016/11/09/statement-prime-minister-canada-result-us-presidential-election.

988 Joanna Walters. 2017. *Stories of Those Who Were Detained This Weekend.* January 31. https://www.theguardian.com/us-news/2017/jan/31/people-detained-airports-trump-travel-ban.

989 Nina Golgowski. 2017. *5-year-old Has Heart-wrenching Reunion with Mom after Airport Detention.* January 29. http://www. huffingtonpost.com.mx/entry/detained-child-reunited_us_588e48d6e4b0b065cbbcb559.

990 Sara Elizabeth Williams, Amman Ensor and Josie Ensor. 2017. '*I Regret Helping the Americans Now' Says Iraqi Refugee Banned from US.* January 30. http://www.telegraph.co.uk/news/2017/01/30/regret-helping-americans-now-says-iraqi-refugee-banned-us/.

991 Eliza Mackintosh. 2017. *Trump Ban Is Boon for ISIS Recruitment, Former Jihadists and Experts Say.* January 31. http://edition.cnn.com/2017/01/30/politics/trump-ban-boosts-isis-recruitment/.

992 Juan Cole. 2017. *Trump's Muslim Ban Hurts US Troops and Helps Islamist Extremists.* January 30. https://www.thenation.com/article/trumps-muslim-ban-hurts-us-troops-and-helps-islamist-extremists/.

993 Rowena Mason. 2017. *Theresa May 'Does Not Agree' with Donald Trump's Immigration Ban.* January 29. https://www.theguardian.com/politics/2017/jan/28/may-under-pressure-to-condemn-trumps-immigration-ban.

994 Lynne O'Donnell. 2017. *Trump Ban Inspires Wide Anger, Some Applause across World.* January 29. http://abcnews.go.com/International/wireStory/european-leaders-oppose-trump-travel-ban-applauds-45122487.

995 AP. 2017. *Petition Calling on UK to Cancel Donald Trump State Visit Reaches 500,000 Signatures.* January 29. https://globalnews.ca/news/3212492/petition-uk-cancel-state-visit-trump/.

996 Shehab Khan. 2017. *Angela Merkel 'Explains' to Donald Trump the Obligations of Geneva Refugee Convention after His Immigration Ban.* January 30. http://www.independent.co.uk/news/world/europe/anglea-merkel-explains-donald-trump-geneva-refugee-convention-obligations-muslim-immigration-ban-us-a7552506.html.

997 AP. 2017. *Widespread Anger, Opposition from World Leaders at Trump Travel Ban.* January 29. http://www.macleans.ca/politics/widespread-anger-opposition-from-world-leaders-at-trump-travel-ban/.

998 Justin Trudeau. 2017 12:20 PM. *Twitter Post.* January 28. https://twitter.com/justintrudeau/status/825438460265762816?lang=en.

999 J. Weston Phippen. 2017. *The CEOs Revolting against Trump's Travel Ban.* January 30. https://www.theatlantic.com/news/archive/2017/01/companies-against-trumps-ban/515028.

1000 Ibid.

1001 Madeline Farber. 2017. *Here Are the Republicans Who Have Criticized President Trump's Immigration Ban.* January 30. http://fortune.com/2017/01/29/donald-trump-immigration-ban-republicans/.

1002 Ibid.

1003 Claire Groden. 2015. *Dick Cheney Slams Donald Trump's Proposed Ban on Muslim Admissions.* December 8. http://fortune.com/2015/12/08/dick-cheney-slams-donald-trumps-proposed-ban-on-muslim-admissions/.

1004 Phil Torres. 2017. *Donald Trump's "Muslim Ban" Is Already Backfiring — And Its Consequences Will Only Get Worse.* January 30. http://www.salon.com/2017/01/30/donald-trumps-muslim-ban-is-already-backfiring-and-its-consequences-will-only-get-worse/.

1005 911 Memorial & Museum. n.d. *Facts about 911.* Accessed January 29, 2017. https://www.911memorial.org/faq-about-911.

1006 Daniel Burke. 2017. *Trump Says US Will Prioritize Christian Refugees.* January 28. http://edition.cnn.com/2017/01/27/politics/trump-christian-refugees.

1007 Ibid.

1008 Rebecca Savransky. 2017. *Giuliani: Trump Asked Me How to Do a Muslim Ban 'Legally.'* January 29. http://thehill.com/homenews/administration/316726-giuliani-trump-asked-me-how-to-do-a-muslim-ban-legally.

1009 Mike Pence. 2015 7:30 AM. *Twitter Post.* December 8. https://twitter.com/govpencein/status/674249808610066433?lang=en.

1010 Maxwell Tani. 2017. *Trump Used the Most Controversial Phrase inside His Administration during His Major Address to the UN.* September 19. http://www.businessinsider.com/trump-mcmaster-radical-islamic-terrorism-2017-9.

1011 The History Place. 2016. *Ronald Reagan Tear Down this Wall.* Accessed January 29, 2017. http://www.historyplace.com/speeches/reagan-tear-down.htm.

1012 Pamela Engel. 2016. *Ronald Reagan's Son Says 'the Whole Family' Is Insulted by Trump Comparisons.* June 7. http://www.businessinsider.com/ronald-reagan-son-donald-trump-2016-6.

1013 Evan Perez and Jeremy Diamond. 2017. *Trump Fires Acting AG After She Declines to Defend Travel Ban.* January 31. http://edition.cnn.com/2017/01/30/politics/donald-trump-immigration-order-department-of-justice/.

1014 Matthew Weaver, Claire Phipps and Amber Jamieson. 2017. *Donald Trump Rounds on Democrats as UN Refugee Agency Warns on Travel Ban – As It Happened.* January 31. https://www.theguardian.com/us-news/live/2017/jan/30/trump-travel-ban-executive-order-world-protests-live.

1015 Michael D. Shear et al. 2017. *Trump Fires Acting Attorney General Who Defied Him.* January 30. https://www.nytimes.com/2017/01/30/us/politics/trump-immigration-ban-memo.html.

1016 Evan Perez and Jeremy Diamond. 2017. *Trump Fires Acting AG After She Declines to Defend Travel Ban.* January 31.

1017 Noah Feldman. 2017. *In Yates versus Trump, the Constitution Won.* January 31. https://www.bloomberg.com/view/articles/2017-01-31/in-yates-vs-trump-the-constitution-won.

1018 Bryan Logan. 2017. *Video Shows Jeff Sessions Asking Sally Yates If She Would Say No to the President If He Asked for Something 'Improper.'* January 30. http://www.businessinsider.com/sally-yates-jeff-sessions-video-2015-confirmation-hearing-2017-1.

1019 Ibid.

1020 Andrew Couts. 2017. *Federal Court Halts Trump's Immigration Ban.* January 28. http://www.dailydot.com/layer8/federal-judge-trump-muslim-ban-immigration-ban/.

1021   Shannon Dooling. 2017. *Boston Federal Court Puts Hold on Trump's Travel, Refugee Ban*. January 29. http://www.wbur. org/news/2017/01/29/boston-ruling-trump-executive-order.

1022   Jeffrey Gettleman. 2017. *State Dept. Dissent Cable on Trump's Ban Draws 1,000 Signatures*. January 31. http://www. msn.com/en-us/news/politics/state-dept-dissent-cable-on-trump%E2%80%99s-ban-draws-1000-signatures/ar-aamt9bv?li=bbnb7kz.

1023   Ibid.

1024   Nahal Toosi. 2017. *White House Slap at Dissenting Diplomats Sparks Fear of Reprisal*. January 30. http://www.politico. com/story/2017/01/trump-immigration-ban-state-department-dissent-channel-memo-234364.

1025   Lou Colagiovanni. 2017. *Conway Just Called for Any Journalist Who Criticizes Trump to Be Fired*. January 30. http:// occupydemocrats.com/2017/01/30/conway-just-called-journalist-criticizes-trump-fired/.

1026   CBC. 2017. *Only 1 Suspect in Deadly Quebec Mosque Shooting, Police Say*. January 30. http://www.cbc.ca/news/canada/montreal/quebec-city-mosque-gun-shots-1.3957686.

1027   Justin Trudeau. 2017. *Statement by the Prime Minister of Canada on the Fatal Shooting in the City of Québec*. January 29. http://pm.gc.ca/eng/news/2017/01/29/statement-prime-minister-canada-fatal-shooting-city-quebec.

1028   Joanna Smith. 2017. *PMO Slams Fox News for Inaccurate Tweet about Quebec Shooting Suspect*. January 31. https://www.thestar. com/news/canada/2017/01/31/pmo-slams-fox-news-for-inaccurate-tweet-about-quebec-shooting-suspect.html.

1029   Ibid.

1030   Ibid.

1031   Daniel Dale. 2017. *The White House Cited the Quebec Mosque Attack to Justify Trump's Policies*. January 30. https://www.thestar. com/news/world/2017/01/30/the-white-house-just-cited-the-quebec-mosque-attack-to-justify-trumps-policies.html.

1032   Ibid.

1033   Les Perreaux et al. 2017. *The Quebec City Mosque Attack: What We Know So Far*. February 1. http://www.theglobeandmail. com/news/national/quebec-city-mosque-shooting-what-we-know-so-far/article33826078.

1034   Ibid.

1035   Lawrence Hurley and Steve Holland. 2017. *Trump Picks Conservative Judge Gorsuch for U.S. Supreme Court*. January 31. http://www.reuters.com/article/us-usa-court-trump-iduskbn15f1ow.

1036   Eric Pianin. 2015. *$478B Infrastructure Bill Blocked by Senate GOP*. March 25. http://www.thefiscaltimes. com/2015/03/25/478B-Infrastructure-Bill-Blocked-Senate-GOP.

1037   Jason Easley. 2015. *Senate Republicans Block a Bill That Would Create 1 Million New Jobs for Young People*. July 16. http:// www.politicususa.com/2015/07/16/senate-republicans-block-bill-create-1-million-jobs-young-people.html.

1038   David Wright. 2016. *Lock Her Up? Maybe Not So Much, Giuliani and Christie Say*. November 10. http://www.cnn. com/2016/11/10/politics/giuliani-christie-interviews-clinton-prosecutor/index.html.

1039   Alan Rappeport and Alexander Burns. 2016. *Highlights of Hillary Clinton's Concession Speech and President Obama's Remarks*. November 9. http://www.nytimes.com/2016/11/09/us/politics/donald-trump-won-now-what.html?_r=0.

1040   Karen Marie Moning. n.d. *Karen Marie Moning > Quotes > Quotable Quote*. Accessed October 9, 2017. https://www. goodreads.com/quotes/217304-words-can-be-twisted-into-any-shape-promises-can-be.

1041   Donald Trump. 2016. *Donald Trump's Contract*. November 23. https://assets.donaldjtrump.com/_landings/contract/o-tru-102316-contractv02.pdf.

1042   Steve Kopack and John W. Schoen. 2017. *Here's a Progress Report on Trump's First 100 Days*. April 12. http://www.cnbc. com/2017/04/11/heres-a-progress-report-on-trumps-first-100-days.html.

1043   Donald Trump. 2016. *Donald Trump's Contract*. November 23. https://assets.donaldjtrump.com/_landings/contract/o-tru-102316-contractv02.pdf.

1044   Ibid.

1045   Ibid.

1046   Rose Troup Buchanan. 2015. *The Six Nations Where It Is Still Illegal to Have an Abortion*. May 6. http://www.independent. co.uk/life-style/health-and-families/international-abortion-laws-the-six-nations-where-it-is-still-illegal-to-have-an-abortion-10229567.html.

1047   Rose Troup Buchanan. 2015. *Amnesty International Claim Treatment of 10-year-old Girl Raped by Her Stepfather but Denied*. April 30. http://www.independent.co.uk/news/world/americas/amnesty-international-claim-treatment-of-10-year-old-girl-raped-by-her-stepfather-but-denied-10216264.html.

1048   NCSL. 2016. *State Policies on Sex Education in Schools*. February 16. http://www.ncsl.org/research/health/state-policies-on-sex-education-in-schools.aspx.

1049   Nikki Tucker. 2012. *U.S. Teen Pregnancy Rate Is Three Times Higher than Other Developed Nations*. August 20. http://www. medicaldaily.com/us-teen-pregnancy-rate-three-times-higher-other-developed-nations-242060.

1050   Lisa B. Haddad and Nawal M. Nour. 2009. *Unsafe Abortion: Unnecessary Maternal Mortality*. Rev Obstet Gynecol, 2(2): 122–126, Spring 2009. https://www.ncbi.nlm.nih.gov/pmc/articles/pmc2709326.

1051   Ibid.

1052   Steve Kopack and John W. Schoen. 2017. *Here's a Progress Report on Trump's First 100 Days*. April 12.

1053   Ibid.

1054   Donald Trump. 2016. *Donald Trump's Contract*. November 23.

1055   *NPR Staff. 2016. Fact Check and Full Transcript of the Final 2016 Presidential Debate*. October 19.

1056   Brooks Jackson. 2017. *What President Trump Inherits.* January 20. http://www.factcheck.org/2017/01/what-president-trump-inherits/.

1057   Donald Trump. 2016. *Donald Trump's Contract.* November 23.

1058   Jane C. Timm. 2017. *Fact Checking Donald Trump's Job Creation Claims.* March 15. http://www.nbcnews.com/politics/donald-trump/fact-check-how-many-jobs-has-trump-created-n730236.

1059   *NPR Staff.* 2016. *Fact Check and Full Transcript of the Final 2016 Presidential Debate.* October 19.

1060   Ibid.

1061   Ian Thibodeau. 2017. *Ford's Mich. Assembly, Flat Rock Face Temporary Idling.* September 19. http://www.detroitnews.com/story/business/autos/ford/2017/09/19/ford-north-america-shutdowns/105795002/.

1062   Ibid.

1063   Ibid.

1064   Jane C. Timm. 2017. *Fact Checking Donald Trump's Job Creation Claims.* March 15.

1065   Wikipedia Contributors. n.d. *First 100 Days of Donald Trump's Presidency.* Accessed October 9, 2017. https://en.wikipedia.org/wiki/First_100_days_of_Donald_Trump%27s_presidency.

1066   Wikipedia Contributors. n.d. *List of Executive Actions by Donald Trump.* Accessed October 28, 2017. https://en.wikipedia.org/wiki/List_of_executive_actions_by_Donald_Trump#cite_note-130.

1067   Paul Hunter. 2017. *'We Don't Blame You': Wisconsin Farmers on Trump's Blast at Canada's Dairy Industry.* April 22. http://www.cbc.ca/news/world/dairy-farmers-wisconsin-trump-1.4081391.

1068   Judi Bottoni. 2017. *NAFTA, Dairy and Softwood: What's Going on with Trump? A Guide to the Trade File.* April 28. http://www.theglobeandmail.com/news/politics/nafta-dairy-softwood-what-do-trump-and-canada-want/article33715250/.

1069   Dr. Mercola. 2013. *The Subsidized Crop That Drives Our Fast-food Nation.* September 7. https://articles.mercola.com/sites/articles/archive/2013/09/07/king-corn-documentary.aspx.

1070   Ibid.

1071   Ibid.

1072   Caitlin Dewey. 2017. *How Nafta May Have Made Canada Fat.* July 11. https://www.thestar.com/news/canada/2017/07/11/how-nafta-may-have-made-canada-fat.html.

1073   Stats Canada. 2015. *Adult Obesity Prevalence in Canada and the United States.* November 27. https://www.statcan.gc.ca/pub/82-625-x/2011001/article/11411-eng.htm.

1074   Steven Chase and Peter Kennedy. 2009. *U.S. Expected to Seek Timber Auctions.* March 20. http://www.theglobeandmail.com/report-on-business/us-expected-to-seek-timber-auctions/article25291863/.

1075   Judi Bottoni. 2017. *NAFTA, Dairy and Softwood: What's Going on with Trump? A Guide to the Trade File.* April 28.

1076   Charles Wallace. 2017. *Trump's First Target for Trade Penalties Is Canadian Lumber.* April 25. https://www.forbes.com/sites/charleswallace1/2017/04/25/trumps-first-target-for-trade-penalties-is-canadian-lumber/#7902e019713f.

1077   Wikipedia Contributors. n.d. *List of Executive Actions by Donald Trump.* Accessed October 28, 2017.

1078   Matt Egan. 2017. *Trump's Energy Plan isn't a Game-changer.* April 27. http://money.cnn.com/2017/04/27/investing/trump-oil-coal-energy-plan/index.html.

1079   Matt Egan. 2017. *Why Trump's Coal Promises are Doomed.* CNN. April 25. http://money.cnn.com/2017/04/25/investing/coal-trump-jobs-promise/index.html.

1080   Wikipedia Contributors. n.d. *List of Executive Actions by Donald Trump.* Accessed October 28, 2017.

1081   Dan Merica. 2017. *Trump to Sign Agriculture Executive Order Tuesday.* April 24. http://www.cnn.com/2017/04/24/politics/trump-agriculture-executive-order/index.html.

1082   Ibid.

1083   Wikipedia Contributors. n.d. *List of Executive Actions by Donald Trump.* Accessed October 28, 2017.

1084   Kate Taylor. 2016. *Fast-food CEO Says He's Investing in Machines Because the Government Is Making It Difficult to Afford Employees.* March 16. http://www.businessinsider.com/carls-jr-wants-open-automated-location-2016-3.

1085   Wikipedia Contributors. n.d. *List of Executive Actions by Donald Trump.* Accessed October 28, 2017.

1086   Nelson D. Schwartz. 2017. *Economy Needs Workers, but Drug Tests Take a Toll.* July 24. https://www.nytimes.com/2017/07/24/business/economy/drug-test-labor-hiring.html?mcubz=1&_r=0.

1087   Oliver Roeder. 2015. *Releasing Drug Offenders Won't End Mass Incarceration.* July 17. https://fivethirtyeight.com/features/releasing-drug-offenders-wont-end-mass-incarceration.

1088   Ibid.

1089   Wikipedia Contributors. n.d. *List of Executive Actions by Donald Trump.* Accessed October 28, 2017.

1090   Bob Sullivan. 2017. *Trump's Mortgage Fee Cut Reversal: What It Really Means for House-Hunters.* January 24. http://www.foxbusiness.com/features/2017/01/24/trumps-mortgage-fee-cut-reversal-what-it-really-means-for-house-hunters.html.

1091   Wikipedia Contributors. n.d. *List of Executive Actions by Donald Trump.* Accessed October 28, 2017.

1092   Ibid.

1093   Ibid.

1094   Josh Gerstein. 2017. Trump White House Grants Waivers of Ethics Rules. Politico. May 31. https://www.politico.com/story/2017/05/31/trump-white-house-waivers-ethics-239011.

1095   Wikipedia Contributors. n.d. *List of Executive Actions by Donald Trump.* Accessed October 28, 2017.

1096   Tal Kopan. 2017. *Judge Blocks Part of Trump's Sanctuary Cities Executive Order.* April 26. http://www.cnn.com/2017/04/25/
        politics/sanctuary-cities-injunction/index.html Kopan, Tal. 2017. *Judge Blocks Part of Trump's Sanctuary Cities Executive
        Order.* April 26. http://www.cnn.com/2017/04/25/politics/sanctuary-cities-injunction/index.html.

1097   Wikipedia Contributors. n.d. *List of Executive Actions by Donald Trump.* Accessed October 28, 2017.

1098   Wikipedia Contributors. n.d. *Mexico City Policy.* Accessed September 6, 2017. https://en.wikipedia.org/wiki/Mexico_
        City_policy.

1099   Larry Ladutke. 2014. *What Happens When Abortion Is Banned.* September 25. http://blog.amnestyusa.org/americas/
        what-happens-when-abortion-is-banned/.

1100   Ibid.

1101   Wikipedia Contributors. n.d. *List of Executive Actions by Donald Trump.* Accessed October 28, 2017.

1102   The Star. 2016. *Here's The Full Transcript of Donald Trump's Victory Speech.* November 9.

1103   Brian Ross et al. 2017. *ABC 20/20 Life and Death at the Border.* July 30. http://abcnews.go.com/2020/deepdive/
        video-border-officers-actions-lead-tragedy-48912222.

1104   Zack Beauchamp. 2017. *Trump's Bizarre, Dangerous Calls with the Leaders of Mexico and Australia, Explained.* February
        2. http://www.vox.com/world/2017/2/2/14483560/trump-mexico-australia-calls.

1105   Stephen Collinson. 2017. *Trump Stands by Wiretapping Claim during Merkel Visit.* March 18. http://www.cnn.
        com/2017/03/17/politics/donald-trump-angela-merkel/index.html.

1106   Brian Bennett. 2017. *Citing No Evidence, Trump Accuses Obama of Tapping His Phones during the Election.* March 4. http://
        www.latimes.com/politics/la-pol-updates-everything-president-trump-accuses-obama-of-wiretapping-1488648248-ht-
        mlstory.html.

1107   Ben Westcott, Dan Merica and Jim Sciutto. 2017. *White House: No Apology to British Government over Spying Claims.*
        March 18. http://www.cnn.com/2017/03/17/politics/gchq-trump-wiretap-denial/index.html.

1108   United Nations. 2016. *Security Council Strengthens Sanctions on Democratic Republic of Korea, Unanimously Adopting Resolution
        2321 (2016).* November 30. https://www.un.org/press/en/2016/sc12603.doc.htm.

1109   Brenda Goh and Michael Martina. 2017. *Chinese State Media Cheer Xi-Trump Meeting, Say Confrontation Not Inevitable.*
        April 8. http://www.reuters.com/article/us-usa-china-media-iduskbn17a06y.

1110   Phil Stewart. 2017. *As Trump Warned North Korea, His 'Armada' Was Headed Toward Australia.* April 18. https://www.
        reuters.com/article/us-northkorea-usa-carrier/as-trump-warned-north-korea-his-armada-was-headed-toward-australia-
        iduskbn17l03j.

1111   Peter Cahill. 2017. *VP Mike Pence Warns North Korea: 'We Will Defeat Any Attack'.* April 19. https://www.nbcnews.com/
        news/world/vp-mike-pence-warns-north-korea-we-will-defeat-any-n748161.

1112   Junko Ogura and Susannah Cullinane. 2017. *North Korea Threatens to Sink US Aircraft Carrier.* April 24. http://www.cnn.
        com/2017/04/23/politics/uss-carl-vinson-japan-us-drills/.

1113   Jeremy Diamond. 2016. *'We Can't Continue to Allow China to Rape Our Country.'* May 2. http://www.cnn.com/2016/05/01/
        politics/donald-trump-china-rape/index.html.

1114   Amanda Erickson. 2017. *Trump Thought China Could Get North Korea to Comply. It's Not That Easy.* April 13. https://
        www.washingtonpost.com/news/worldviews/wp/2017/04/13/trump-thought-china-could-get-n-korea-to-comply-
        its-not-that-easy/?utm_term=.74bf7fb56210.

1115   Michael Wilner. 2017. *Trump Warns Israel: Stop Announcing New Settlements.* February 2. http://www.jpost.com/Israel-
        News/Politics-And-Diplomacy/Trump-warns-Israel-Stop-announcing-new-settlements-480446.

1116   Lauren Gambino. 2017. *Trump Congratulates Erdoğan after Turkey Vote Grants Sweeping Powers.* April 18. https://www.
        theguardian.com/us-news/2017/apr/17/donald-trump-erdogan-turkey-referendum-congratulations.

1117   Ibid.

1118   Ashley Dejean. 2017. *Donald Trump Has a Conflict of Interest in Turkey. Just Ask Donald Trump.* April 18. http://www.
        motherjones.com/politics/2017/04/trump-turkey-erdogan-conflict-interest.

1119   Abby Phillip and Mike DeBonis. 2017. *Tillerson, Haley Issue Differing Statements on Future of Assad in Syria.* April 9. https://
        www.washingtonpost.com/news/post-politics/wp/2017/04/09/tillerson-haley-issue-differing-statements-on-future-
        of-assad-in-syria/?utm_term=.6831ad82d04a.

1120   Ibid.

1121   Martin Chulov and Kareem Shaheen. 2017. *Syria Chemical Weapons Attack Toll Rises to 70 as Russian Narrative Is Dismissed.*
        April 5. https://www.theguardian.com/world/2017/apr/04/syria-chemical-attack-idlib-province.

1122   Ibid.

1123   Adam K. Raymond. 2017. *Trump Gleefully Recalls the 'Beautiful Chocolate Cake' He Ate While Bombing Syria.* April 12. http://
        nymag.com/daily/intelligencer/2017/04/trump-ate-beautiful-chocolate-cake-while-bombing-syria.html.

1124   Barbara Lee, interview by Brooke Baldwin. 2017. "Strike Against Syria." *CNN Newsroom With Brooke Baldwin.* April
        7. https://archive.org/details/CNNW_20170407_180000_CNN_Newsroom_With_Brooke_Baldwin.

1125   Hisham Melhem. 2017. *How Obama's Syrian Chemical Weapons Deal Fell Apart.* April 10. https://www.theatlantic.com/
        international/archive/2017/04/how-obamas-chemical-weapons-deal-fell-apart/522549.

1126   Donald J. Trump. 2013 11:14 AM. *Twitter Post.* August 29. https://twitter.com/realdonaldtrump/status/37314663718
        4401408?lang=en.

1127 David M. Tafuri. 2017. *Why Trump's Attack on Syria Is Legal.* April 1. http://www.politico.eu/article/syria-war-chemical-attack-why-donald-trump-attack-is-legal-assad-putin/.

1128 Nicole Gaouette and Richard Roth. 2017. *UN Ambassador Haley Hits Russia Hard on Ukraine.* February 3. http://www.cnn.com/2017/02/02/politics/haley-russia-un/.

1129 AP. 2017. *U.S. Ambassador to the UN: No Question Russia Meddled in Election.* April 2. http://news.nationalpost.com/news/world/u-s-ambassador-to-the-un-no-question-russia-meddled-in-election.

1130 Max Greenwood. 2017. *Haley Rips into Russia as Security Council Weighs Resolution on Syrian Chemical Attack.* April 5. http://thehill.com/policy/international/327407-trumps-un-envoy-rips-into-russia-over-syria-chemical-weapons-attack.

1131 Ibid.

1132 Julian Borger and Alec Luhn. 2017. *Donald Trump Says US Relations with Russia 'May Be at All-time Low.'* April 13. https://www.theguardian.com/us-news/2017/apr/12/us-russia-relations-tillerson-moscow-press-conference.

1133 BBC. 2015. *France: Marine Le Pen Goes on Trial over Muslim Remarks.* October 20. http://www.bbc.com/news/world-europe-34580169.

1134 Harriet Alexander. 2017. *Donald Trump Wades into French Election with Apparent Endorsement of Marine Le Pen after Paris Attack.* April 21. http://www.telegraph.co.uk/news/2017/04/21/donald-trump-wades-french-election-apparent-endorsement-marine/.

1135 Marshall Cohen. 2017. *What We Know about the Trump Campaign, His Administration and Russia.* March 22. http://www.cnn.com/2017/02/16/politics/trump-russia-timeline/.

1136 Spencer Ackerman. 2017. *Devin Nunes Steps aside from House Intelligence Committee's Russia Inquiry.* April 6. https://www.theguardian.com/world/2017/apr/06/devin-nunes-leaves-house-intelligence-committee-russia-inquiry-ethics-inquiry.

1137 Keysha Whitaker. 2017. *Your Russian Connection: Is There Any There, There?* March 21. https://www.newyorker.com/humor/daily-shouts/your-russian-connection-is-there-any-there-there.

1138 Alex Seitz-Wald. 2011. *10 Things Conservatives Don't Want You to Know about Ronald Reagan.* February 5. https://thinkprogress.org/10-things-conservatives-dont-want-you-to-know-about-ronald-reagan-7a87723a4f68#.utz3sxhs2.

1139 Ibid.

1140 Fred Kaplan. 2004. *Reagan's Osama Connection.* June 10. http://www.slate.com/articles/news_and_politics/war_stories/2004/06/reagans_osama_connection.html.

1141 Chauncey Devega. 2015. *White America's Racial Amnesia: The Sobering Truth about Our Country's "Race Riots."* May 1.

1142 History. n.d. *Did Marie-Antoinette Really Say "Let Them Eat Cake"?* Accessed October 4, 2016. http://www.history.com/news/ask-history/did-marie-antoinette-really-say-let-them-eat-cake.

1143 Wikipedia Contributors. n.d. Let them eat cake. Accessed September 14, 2016. https://en.wikipedia.org/wiki/Let_them_eat_cake.

1144 History. n.d. *Did Marie-Antoinette Really Say "Let Them Eat Cake"?* Accessed October 4, 2016.

1145 Daniel Castillo. 2003. *German Economy in the 1920s.* December. Accessed November 27, 2016. http://www.history.ucsb.edu/faculty/marcuse/classes/33d/projects/1920s/Econ20s.htm.

1146 Ibid.

1147 Ibid.

1148 Erik Moshe. 2016. *Ben Bernanke Says "Hitler Was the Guy Who Got Economics Right in the 1930s."* February 21. http://historynewsnetwork.org/article/161968.

1149 Virginia Postrel. 2004. *Consequences of 1960's Riots Come into View.* December 30. http://www.nytimes.com/2004/12/30/business/the-consequences-of-the-1960s-race-riots-come-into-view.html?_r=0&mtrref=undefined&gwh=07436e71b29f5825edfe11c5db45587d&gwt=pay.

1150 Wikipedia Contributors. n.d. *Kerner Commission.* Accessed July 17, 2016. https://en.wikipedia.org/wiki/Kerner_Commission.

1151 Ibid.

1152 Ibid.

1153 Ibid.

1154 Brendan James. 2015. *Rand Paul: Baltimore Violence Is about 'Lack of Fathers' and Morals.* April 28. http://talkingpointsmemo.com/livewire/rand-paul-freddie-gray-baltimore-morals.

1155 Anatole France. n.d. *Anatole France > Quotes > Quotable Quote.* Accessed September 6, 2017. https://www.goodreads.com/quotes/361132-the-law-in-its-majestic-equality-forbids-rich-and-poor.

1156 Charles Bagli. 2016. *How Donald Trump Bankrupted His Atlantic City Casinos, but Still Earned Millions.* June 11. http://www.nytimes.com/2016/06/12/nyregion/donald-trump-atlantic-city.html.

1157 Guardian Staff. 2016. *Oklahoma Shaken by Strong Earthquake Causing 'Significant' Damage.* November 7. https://www.theguardian.com/world/2016/nov/07/strong-earthquake-central-oklahoma-damage.

1158 Office of the Secretary of Energy & Environment. n.d. *Earthquakes in Oklahoma.* Accessed November 24, 2016. https://earthquakes.ok.gov/faqs/.

1159 Caitlin Keating. 2016. *How Sick Are the Kids in Flint? Inside the Shocking Health Effects of the Devastating Water Crisis.* January 28. http://people.com/human-interest/flint-water-crisis-inside-the-shocking-health-effects/.

1160 Zygmunt Bauman. n.d. *Zygmunt Bauman Quotes.* Accessed October 9, 2017. https://www.brainyquote.com/quotes/quotes/z/zygmuntbau536850.html.

1161   Encyclopedia of the New American Nation. n.d. *Exceptionalism - The Leader of the Free World*. Accessed December 17, 2016. http://www.americanforeignrelations.com/E-N/Exceptionalism-The-leader-of-the-free-world.html.

1162   Ibid.

1163   Ibid.

1164   Andy Nulman. 2013. *Canada's Dopey Reputation Needs to Change*. June 30. http://www.huffingtonpost.ca/andy-nulman/canada-day-2013_b_3522955.html.

1165   Bill Mann. 2013. *Americans Are Clueless about Canada -- And Other Countries, Too*. July 24. http://www.huffingtonpost.ca/bill-mann/canadians-vs-americans_b_3645097.html.

1166   Ibid.

1167   Ibid.

1168   Jesse Byrnes. 2016. *Blog Briefing Room: Canada's Prime Minister to Americans: Pay More Attention to the World*. March 4. http://thehill.com/blogs/blog-briefing-room/news/271780-canadian-president-americans-should-be-more-aware-of-global.

1169   Central Intelligence Agency. 2016. *Country Comparisons: World Population*. July. https://www.cia.gov/library/publications/the-world-factbook/rankorder/2119rank.html html.

1170   Pierre Trudeau. n.d. *Quotes by Prime Ministers - Pierre Trudeau*. Accessed October 9, 2017. http://canadachannel.ca/canadianbirthdays/index.php/Quotes_by_Prime_Ministers_-_Pierre_Trudeau.

1171   Statistics Canada. 2016. *International Perspective*. October 7. https://www.statcan.gc.ca/pub/11-402-x/2012000/chap/geo/geo01-eng.htm.

1172   James Erwin. 2014. *4 Times the U.S. Invaded Canada*. December 5. http://mentalfloss.com/article/60380/4-times-us-invaded-canada.

1173   James Marsh and Pierre Berton. n.d. *War of 1812 Overview*. Accessed November 21, 2016. http://www.eighteentwelve.ca/?q=eng/Topic/2.

1174   Mollie Dunsmuir. 1992. *Referendums: The Canadian Experience*. January. http://publications.gc.ca/Collection-r/lopbdp/bp/bp271-e.htm.

1175   Natasha Henry. 2013. *Slavery in Canada? I Never Learned That!* October 23. http://activehistory.ca/2013/10/slavery-in-canada-i-never-learned-that/.

1176   A&E. 2016. *This Day in History: Slavery Abolished in America*. Accessed December 20, 2017. http://www.history.com/this-day-in-history/slavery-abolished-in-america.

1177   Pierre Trudeau. 1971. *Trudeau and Cultural Diversity*. October 9. Accessed December 20, 2017. https://www.edu.gov.mb.ca/k12/cur/socstud/foundation_gr9/blms/9-1-4g.pdf.

1178   The Conference Board of Canada. 2012. *Income Per Capita*. http://www.conferenceboard.ca/hcp/details/economy/income-per-capita.aspx.

1179   G. William Domhoff. 2012. *An Investment Manager's View on the Top 1%*. January.

1180   The Conference Board of Canada. 2012. *Health*. February. http://www.conferenceboard.ca/hcp/details/health.aspx.

1181   OECD. 2012. *OECD Health Statistics 2014: How Does Canada Compare?* http://www.oecd.org/els/health-systems/Briefing-Note-Canada-2014.pdf.

1182   Peter G. Peterson Foundation. 2016. *United States Per Capita Healthcare Spending Is More Than Twice the Average of Other Developed Countries*. October 17. http://www.pgpf.org/chart-archive/0006_health-care-oecd.

1183   Ranking America. n.d. *The U.S. Ranks 24th in Literacy*. Accessed May 29, 2017. https://rankingamerica.wordpress.com/2013/06/11/the-u-s-ranks-9th-in-retirement-security/.

1184   Ranking America. n.d. *The U.S. Ranks 9th in Retirement Security*. Accessed May 29, 2017. https://rankingamerica.wordpress.com/2013/06/11/the-u-s-ranks-9th-in-retirement-security/.

1185   Ryan Maloney. 2016. *Donald Trump Presidency a Very Concerning Notion for Canadians: Poll*. August 10. http://www.huffingtonpost.ca/2016/08/10/donald-trump-canada-poll-white-house_n_11432840.html.

1186   Ibid.

1187   Peter Layton. 2017. *The 2 Percent NATO Benchmark Is a Red Herring*. February 16. http://nationalinterest.org/blog/the-buzz/the-2-percent-nato-benchmark-red-herring-19472.

1188   Steve Peoples. 2016. *Trump Vows to Significantly Boost Military Spending ahead of Security Forum*. September 7. https://www.thestar.com/news/world/2016/09/07/trump-vows-to-significantly-boost-military-spending-ahead-of-security-forum.html.

1189   Ryan Browne. 2017. *NATO Members to Increase Defense Spending*. June 29. http://www.cnn.com/2017/06/29/politics/nato-members-increase-defense-spending/index.html.

1190   Justin McCurry. 2016. *Trump Says US May Not Automatically Defend NATO Allies under Attack*. July 21. https://www.theguardian.com/world/2016/jul/21/donald-trump-america-automatically-nato-allies-under-attack.

1191   Matt Lundy. 2016. *How a Trump Presidency Would Affect Canada's Economy*. August 23. http://www.theglobeandmail.com/report-on-business/economy/how-a-trump-presidency-would-impact-canadas-economy/article31115880/.

1192   The US Census Bureau. 2013. *Top Trading Partners - December 2013*. December. https://www.census.gov/foreign-trade/statistics/highlights/top/top1312yr.html.

1193   US Government: Office of the United States Trade Representative. 2016. *Canada*. Accessed May 31, 2017.

1194   AP. 2016. *Canada Sets Record for New Vehicle Sales in 2015*. January 5. http://www.cbc.ca/news/canada/windsor/canada-sets-record-for-new-vehicle-sales-in-2015-1.3390498.

1195   CBC. 2013. *Iran Hostage 'Canadian Caper' 1979 Rescue No Secret to Some*. August 20. http://www.cbc.ca/news/canada/montreal/iran-hostage-canadian-caper-1979-rescue-no-secret-to-some-1.1357927.

1196   Adam Randel. 2016. *Survivor Says Gander Was Therapeutic Experience*. September 11. http://www.thetelegram.com/news/local/2016/9/11/9-11-survivor-says-gander-was-therapeuti-4637992.html.

1197   CBC. 2005. *Canadians Donate over $1 Million for Hurricane Katrina Relief*. September 3. http://www.cbc.ca/news/canada/canadians-donate-over-1-million-for-hurricane-katrina-relief-1.540263.

1198   Mark LoProto. 2017. *Declarations of War after Pearl Harbor*. June 27. https://visitpearlharbor.org/declarations-war-pearl-harbor.

1199   Newsmax. 2013. *Trump: 'China Wouldn't Exist Without Us.'* April 10. http://www.newsmax.com/Newsfront/trump-china-north-korea/2013/04/10/id/498766.

1200   Jennifer Williams. 2016. *Trump May Have Just Thrown Decades of US-China Relations into Disarray*. December 5. http://www.vox.com/world/2016/12/2/13824092/trump-phone-call-president-taiwan-china.

1201   Ibid.

1202   Ting Shi et al. 2016. *China Warns Trump against Using Taiwan for Leverage on Trade*. December 12. https://www.bloomberg.com/politics/articles/2016-12-12/chinese-media-warn-trump-against-using-taiwan-as-bargaining-chip.

1203   Pedro Nicolaci da Costa. 2017. *Trump Has a Shocking Conflict of Interest with China*. February 17. http://www.businessinsider.com/trumps-conflict-of-interest-with-china-2017-2.

1204   Nafeesa Syeed, Nick Wadhams and David Tweed. 2016. *Pentagon Says China to Return Drone; Trump Says They Can Keep It*. December 17. https://www.bloomberg.com/politics/articles/2016-12-18/pentagon-says-china-to-return-drone-trump-says-they-can-keep-it.

1205   Ibid.

1206   Ibid.

1207   Ting Shi, Nick Wadhams and David Tweed. 2016. *As Trump Tweets, China Quietly Weighs Options to Retaliate*. December 18. https://www.bloomberg.com/news/articles/2016-12-18/as-trump-tweets-china-quietly-considers-options-to-retaliate.

1208   Donald J. Trump. 2017 3:05 PM. *Twitter Post*. January 2. https://twitter.com/realdonaldtrump/status/816057920223846400?lang=en.

1209   Donald J. Trump. 2017 3:47 PM. *Twitter Post*. January 2. https://twitter.com/realdonaldtrump/status/816068355555815424?lang=en.

1210   Nic Robertson. 2017. *Why Gadhafi's Downfall Scares the Life out of Kim Jong Un*. August 10. http://www.cnn.com/2017/08/10/opinions/kim-john-un-gaddafi-robertson-opinion/index.html.

1211   BBC. 2016. *TPP: What Is It and Why Does It Matter?* November 22. http://www.bbc.com/news/business-32498715.

1212   Cathleen Cimino-Isaacs. 2016. *Labor Standards in the TPP* .41-63. March. https://piie.com/system/files/documents/piieb16-4.pdf.

1213   Adrian Morrow. 2017. *Trump Withdraws from TPP, but Offers Canada Hope on NAFTA*. January 23. https://beta.theglobeandmail.com/news/world/us-politics/trump-executive-order-tpp/article33701019/?ref=http://www.theglobeandmail.com&.

1214   John Brinkley. 2017. *Trump Hands China a Gift in Dumping Trans-Pacific Partnership*. January 24. https://www.forbes.com/sites/johnbrinkley/2017/01/24/trump-dumps-trans-pacific-partnership-sad/#2a4f4b6775dc.

1215   Ibid.

1216   Ibid.

1217   Ibid.

1218   Donald J. Trump. 2016 5:37 AM. *Twitter Post*. December 22. https://twitter.com/realdonaldtrump/status/811928543366148096?lang=en.

1219   Donald J. Trump. 2016 8:50 AM. *Twitter Post*. December 22. https://twitter.com/realdonaldtrump/status/811977223326625792?lang=en.

1220   Mark Katkov. 2016. *Trump's Pick for Ambassador to Israel: 'End the 2-state Narrative.'* December 16. http://www.npr.org/sections/thetwo-way/2016/12/16/505805411/trumps-pick-for-ambassador-to-israel-end-the-2-state-narrative.

1221   Ibid.

1222   Aaron David Miller. 2016. *Don't Move the Embassy to Jerusalem; the Downsides Are Too Great*. December 27. http://www.nytimes.com/roomfordebate/2016/12/27/should-the-us-embassy-be-moved-from-tel-aviv-to-jerusalem/dont-move-the-embassy-to-jerusalem-the-downsides-are-too-great.

1223   Ibid.

1224   Rebecca Kheel. 2016. *Israel Will Share 'Evidence' of Obama-UN Collusion with Trump, Ambassador Says*. December 26. http://thehill.com/policy/defense/311836-israel-will-share-evidence-of-obama-un-collusion-with-trump-ambassador-says.

1225   Rebecca Kaplan et al. 2015. *5 Things to Know about Netanyahu's Speech to Congress*. March 3. http://www.cbsnews.com/news/five-things-netanyahu-speech/.

1226   Tim Daiss. 2016. *Trump Pledges to Rip Up Iran Deal; Israelis Say Not So Fast*. November 22. http://www.forbes.com/sites/timdaiss/2016/11/22/trumps-iran-deal-rhetoric-israelis-say-not-so-fast/#383271061c6b.

1227   Ibid.

1228   Ibid.

1229   Laura Hughes. 2016. *Iran Nuclear Deal 'Vital,' Warns Theresa May After Donald Trump Vows to Scrap it.* December 7. http://www.telegraph.co.uk/news/2016/12/07/iran-nuclear-deal-vital-warns-theresa-may-donald-trump-vows/.

1230   Seyed Hossein Mousavian. 2016. *Who Benefits Most from a Sabotaged Iran Nuclear Deal.* September 7. http://www.huffingtonpost.com/seyed-hossein-mousavian/sabotaged-iran-nuclear-deal_b_11897718.html.

1231   Elise Labott and Eugene Scott. 2016. *Graham: Defund UN after Israeli Settlement Vote.* December 25. http://www.cnn.com/2016/12/24/politics/lindsey-graham-united-nations/index.html.

1232   Tracy Wilkinson. 2016. *Trump's Plans to Scuttle or Amend the Iran Nuclear Deal Remain a Work in Progress.* November 10. http://www.latimes.com/nation/la-fg-trump-iran-nuclear-deal-20161111-story.html.

1233   Peter Baker and Julie Hirschfeld Davis. 2016. *U.S. Finalizes Deal to Give Israel $38 Billion in Military Aid.* September 13. http://www.nytimes.com/2016/09/14/world/middleeast/israel-benjamin-netanyahu-military-aid.html.

1234   Emma Green. 2016. *Why Does the United States Give So Much Money to Israel?* September 15. http://www.theatlantic.com/international/archive/2016/09/united-states-israel-memorandum-of-understanding-military-aid/500192/.

1235   Carol Morello and Ruth Eglash. 2016. *Netanyahu Blasts U.N., Obama over West Bank Settlements Resolution.* December 24. https://www.washingtonpost.com/world/netanyahu-calls-un-resolution-on-settlements-shameful/2016/12/23/2d45fbac-c94c-11e6-bf4b-2c064d32a4bf_story.html?utm_term=.ca436d1ef0ab.

1236   UN Security Council. n.d. *Current Members.* Accessed December 31, 2016. http://www.un.org/en/sc/members/.

1237   Nir Hasson. 2014. *Despite It All, Most Israelis Still Support the Two-state Solution.* July 7. http://www.haaretz.com/peace/1.601996.

1238   Tom LoBianco. 2015. *Trump 'Postpones' Israel Trip after Netanyahu Criticism.* December 10. http://www.cnn.com/2015/12/10/politics/donald-trump-postpones-israel-trip/.

1239   Carolyn Kenney and John Norris. 2017. *Trump's Conflicts of Interest in Israel.* June 14. https://www.americanprogress.org/issues/security/news/2017/06/14/433942/trumps-conflicts-interest.

1240   Ibid.

1241   Chris Flynn. 2016. *The 15 Worst Atrocities Committed by Fidel Castro.* December 7. http://www.therichest.com/shocking/the-15-worst-atrocities-committed-by-fidel-castro/.

1242   President Barack Obama. 2017. *Charting a New Course on Cuba.* January 2. https://obamawhitehouse.archives.gov/node/352651.

1243   Jeremy Berke. 2016. *Obama on Fidel Castro's Death: 'History Will Record and Judge the Enormous Impact of this Singular Figure.'* November 26. http://www.businessinsider.com/obama-fidel-castro-death-dead-2016-11.

1244   Jeremy Berke. 2016. *Trump: 'Fidel Castro is Dead!'* November 26. http://www.businessinsider.com/trump-fidel-castro-dead-death-2016-11.

1245   John Geddes. 2016. *On Castro's Death, a Look at Fidel and Pierre—and Justin.* November 26. http://www.macleans.ca/politics/ottawa/on-castros-death-a-look-at-fidel-and-pierre-and-justin.

1246   Ibid.

1247   Donald J. Trump. 2016 6:02 AM. *Twitter Post.* 28 November. https://twitter.com/realdonaldtrump/status/803237535178772481?lang=en.

1248   Adam Taylor. 2013. *7 Remarkable Stories of Vladimir Putin Being One of the World's Most Brutal Thugs.* June 17. http://www.businessinsider.com/7-stories-of-putins-thuggish-behaviour-2013-6.

1249   Ibid.

1250   Ibid.

1251   Reporters Without Borders. 2016. *2016 World Freedom of the Press Index.* Accessed June 3, 2016. https://rsf.org/en/ranking?#.

1252   Linda Qiu. 2016. *Does Vladimir Putin Kill Journalists?* January 4. http://www.politifact.com/punditfact/article/2016/jan/04/does-vladimir-putin-kill-journalists/.

1253   Ibid.

1254   Ibid.

1255   Adam Taylor. 2013. *7 Remarkable Stories of Vladimir Putin Being One of the World's Most Brutal Thugs.* June 17.

1256   Wikipedia Contributors. n.d. *Mikhail Khodorkovsky.* Accessed September 6, 2017. https://en.*wikipedia*.org/wiki/Mikhail_Khodorkovsky.

1257   Adam Taylor. 2013. *7 Remarkable Stories of Vladimir Putin Being One of the World's Most Brutal Thugs.* June 17.

1258   Donald Lambro. 2016. *Trump Ignores 'Buddy' Putin's Atrocities.* September 30. http://townhall.com/columnists/donald-lambro/2016/09/30/trump-ignores-buddy-putins-atrocities-n2225476.

1259   Ibid.

1260   Ibid.

1261   John Bacon. 2016. *After Trump Chat, Putin's Airstrikes Pound Syria.* November 15. http://www.usatoday.com/story/news/world/2016/11/15/after-trump-chat-putins-airstrikes-pound-syria/93876876/.

1262   Max J. Rosenthal. 2016. *Russia Has Killed Almost 10,000 Syrians in the Past Year, Says a New Report.* September 30. http://www.motherjones.com/politics/2016/09/russia-has-killed-almost-10000-syrians-year-says-new-report.

1263   Laura Smith-Spark. 2016. *Kerry Urges Russia, Syria to Seek Ceasefire in Aleppo.* December 10. http://www.cnn.com/2016/12/10/middleeast/syria-aleppo-conflict/.

1264   Angela Dewan, and Onur Cakir. 2016. *Turkey and Russia Agree on Draft Syria Ceasefire, Report Says.* December 28. http://www.cnn.com/2016/12/28/middleeast/syria-ceasefire-russia-turkey.

1265   Evan Perez and Steve Almasy. 2016. *Vermont Utility Finds Alleged Russian Malware on Computer.* December 31. http://www.cnn.com/2016/12/30/us/grizzly-steppe-malware-burlington-electric/.

1266   Adam Taylor. 2013. *7 Remarkable Stories of Vladimir Putin Being One of the World's Most Brutal Thugs.* June 17.

1267   Josh Rogin. 2016. *Russia Is Harassing U.S. Diplomats All over Europe.* June 27. https://www.washingtonpost.com/opinions/global-opinions/russia-is-harassing-us-diplomats-all-over-europe/2016/06/26/968d1a5a-3bdf-11e6-84e8-1580c7db5275_story.html?utm_term=.a5d8a72ae20b.

1268   Jeff Nesbit. 2016. *Donald Trump's Many, Many, Many, Many Ties to Russia.* August 15. http://time.com/4433880/donald-trump-ties-to-russia/.

1269   Ibid.

1270   Stephanie Akin. 2016. *Donald Trump and the Russian Connection.* December 28. http://www.rollcall.com/news/politics/donald-trump-russia-vladimir-putin.

1271   Ibid.

1272   Ibid.

1273   David Jackson. 2016. *Secretary of State Nominee Rex Tillerson's Ties to Russia Worry GOP, Too.* December 13. http://www.usatoday.com/story/news/politics/elections/2016/2016/12/13/donald-trump-rex-tillerson-secretary-of-state/95365434/.

1274   Darren Samuelsohn. 2016. *Stone 'Happy to Cooperate' with FBI on WikiLeaks, Russian Hacking Probes.* October 14. http://www.politico.com/story/2016/10/roger-stone-fbi-wikileaks-russia-229821.

1275   Eric Hananoki. 2016. *Trump Ally Roger Stone Falls for Fake WikiLeaks Email.* November 2. http://www.mediamatters.org/blog/2016/11/02/trump-ally-roger-stone-falls-fake-wikileaks-email/214246.

1276   Jeff Nesbit. 2016. *Donald Trump's Many, Many, Many, Many Ties to Russia.* August 15.

1277   Ibid.

1278   Ibid.

1279   Andrew Osborn. 2016. *Russia Says It Was in Touch with Trump's Campaign during Election.* November 10.

1280   David Jackson. 2016. *Secretary of State Nominee Rex Tillerson's Ties to Russia Worry GOP, Too.* December 13.

1281   John Bacon. 2016. *After Trump Chat, Putin's Airstrikes Pound Syria.* November 15.

1282   Christopher Miller. 2015. *No, We Can't Just 'Bomb the Hell out of ISIS,' Donald Trump.* November 18. http://mashable.com/2015/11/18/why-we-cant-bomb-the-hell-out-of-isis-trump/#IzpLxpPW7Gq5.

1283   Laura Smith-Spark. 2016. *Kerry Urges Russia, Syria to Seek Ceasefire in Aleppo.* December 10.

1284   Antonio José Vielma. 2016. *Obama Says Russia Is a Smaller, Weaker Country than the US.* December 16. http://www.cnbc.com/2016/12/16/obama-says-russians-cant-change-us-or-weaken-us.html.

1285   Donald J. Trump. 2016 1:41 PM. *Twitter Post.* December 26. https://twitter.com/realdonaldtrump/status/813500123053490176?lang=en.

1286   Tim Stelloh. 2017. *Donald Trump Promises Post-Brexit Britain a 'Fair' Trade Deal.* January 15. http://www.nbcnews.com/storyline/brexit-referendum/donald-trump-promises-post-brexit-britain-fair-trade-deal-n707176.

1287   Zeke J. Miller. 2015. *Donald Trump Called Germany's Angela Merkel 'The Greatest' Last Year.* August 15. http://time.com/4453084/donald-trump-angela-merkel-germany-immigration/.

1288   Napoleon Bonaparte. n.d. *Napoleon Bonaparte (1769-1821) Quotes.* Accessed October 31, 2017. http://www.world-diplomacy.org/Quotes/NapoleonBonapartequotes.html.

1289   Steve Holland and Jeff Mason. 2017. *Trump Fires FBI Director Comey, Setting off U.S. Political Storm.* May 10. http://www.reuters.com/article/us-usa-trump-comey-iduskbn1852mv.

1290   Ibid.

1291   Donald J. Trump. 2017 8:26 AM. *Twitter Post.* May 12. https://twitter.com/realDonaldTrump/status/863007411132649473.

1292   Chris D'Angelo. 2017. *Trump Says He Considered FBI's Russia Probe before Firing Comey.* May 11. http://www.huffingtonpost.com/entry/trump-comey-firing-nbc-us_us_5914df83e4b0fe039b337700.

1293   Aaron Blake. 2017. *Why Trump Should Be Very Afraid of James Comey's Memos.* May 17. https://www.washingtonpost.com/news/the-fix/wp/2017/05/16/president-trump-should-be-very-afraid-of-james-comeys-memos/?utm_term=.0532e8beaad0.

1294   Michael S. Schmidt. 2017. *Comey Memo Says Trump Asked Him to End Flynn Investigation.* May 16. https://www.nytimes.com/2017/05/16/us/politics/james-comey-trump-flynn-russia-investigation.html.

1295   Ibid.

1296   Natasha Bertrand. 2017. *Report: Comey Acted on Clinton Email Probe Based on Russian Intel That He Knew Was Fake.* May 26. http://www.businessinsider.com/james-comey-russian-intelligence-fake-cnn-hillary-email-2017-5/.

1297   Nate Silver. 2016. *How Much Did Comey Hurt Clinton's Chances?* November 6. https://fivethirtyeight.com/features/how-much-did-comey-hurt-clintons-chances/.

1298   Donald J. Trump. 2017 4:52 AM. *Twitter Post.* May 18. https://twitter.com/realdonaldtrump/status/865173176854204416?lang=en.

1299   Greg Miller and Greg Jaffe. 2017. *Trump Revealed Highly Classified Information to Russian Foreign Minister and Ambassador.* May 15. https://www.washingtonpost.com/world/national-security/

trump-revealed-highly-classified-information-to-russian-foreign-minister-and-ambassador/2017/05/15/530c172a-3960-11e7-9e48-c4f199710b69_story.html?utm_term=.fe69d71038d5.

1300   Heather Stewart, Robert Booth and Vikram Dodd. 2017. *Theresa May to Tackle Donald Trump over Manchester Bombing Evidence.* May 24. https://www.theguardian.com/uk-news/2017/may/24/theresa-may-to-tackle-donald-trump-over-manchester-bombing-evidence.

1301   Yaron Steinbuch. 2017. *Trump Just Shoved a NATO Leader out of His Way.* May 25. http://nypost.com/2017/05/25/trump-just-shoved-a-nato-leader-out-of-his-way/.

1302   Jonathan Lemire and Julie Pace. 2017. *Trump Scolds NATO Leaders for Not Paying Up, Vows Crackdown on Manchester Leaks.* May 25. https://www.thestar.com/news/world/2017/05/25/trump-meets-european-leaders-as-uk-cuts-off-intel-sharing-over-leaks.html.

1303   Ibid.

1304   Ryan Browne. 2017. *NATO Members to Increase Defense Spending.* June 29. http://www.cnn.com/2017/06/29/politics/nato-members-increase-defense-spending/index.html.

1305   Ibid.

1306   Ibid.

1307   Ibid.

1308   Ibid.

1309   BBC. 2017. *G7 Talks: Trump Isolated over Paris Climate Change.* May 28. http://www.bbc.com/news/world-europe-40069636.

1310   Robert Fife. 2017. *Trudeau, Other G7 Leaders Fail to Persuade Trump to Endorse Climate-change Accord.* May 27. https://www.theglobeandmail.com/news/politics/trudeau-and-trump-talk-nafta-global-security-at-g7/article35138355/.

1311   Jon Henley. 2017. *Angela Merkel: EU Cannot Completely Rely on US and Britain Any More.* May 28. https://www.theguardian.com/world/2017/may/28/merkel-says-eu-cannot-completely-rely-on-us-and-britain-any-more-g7-talks.

1312   Reed Abelson. 2016. *Donald Trump Says He May Keep Parts of Obama Health Care Act.* November 11. https://www.nytimes.com/2016/11/12/business/insurers-unprepared-for-obamacare-repeal.html?mcubz=1.

1313   Haeyoun Park, Alicia Parlapiano and Margot Sanger-Katz. 2017. *The Three Plans to Repeal Obamacare.* July 28. https://www.nytimes.com/interactive/2017/07/25/us/which-health-bill-will-the-senate-vote-on.html?_r=1.

1314   Madeline Conway. 2017. *Trump: 'Nobody Knew that Health Care Could Be So Complicated.'* February 27. http://www.politico.com/story/2017/02/trump-nobody-knew-that-health-care-could-be-so-complicated-235436.

1315   Robert Pear. 2017. *Senate Rejects Slimmed-down Obamacare Repeal as McCain Votes No.* July 27. https://www.nytimes.com/2017/07/27/us/politics/obamacare-partial-repeal-senate-republicans-revolt.html?mcubz=1&_r=0.

1316   Ibid.

1317   Ibid.

1318   Josh Dawsey and Paul Demko. 2017. *Trump Will Scrap Critical Obamacare Subsidies.* October 13. http://www.politico.com/story/2017/10/12/trump-obamacare-subsidy-243736.

1319   Jessie Hellmann. 2017. *Majority of Voters Want Obamacare Fix, Not Repeal.* March 5. http://thehill.com/policy/healthcare/322504-poll-majority-of-voters-want-to-fix-obamacare-instead-of-repealing-it.

1320   Dan Mangan. 2017. *American Medical Association Opposes Obamacare Repeal Bill, Citing Coverage Losses by Millions of Americans.* September 19. https://www.cnbc.com/2017/09/19/groups-line-up-to-oppose-gop-obamacare-repeal-bill-as-deadline-looms.html.

1321   Thomas Kaplan and Robert Pear. 2017. *Health Bill Would Add 24 Million Uninsured but Save $337 Billion, Report Says.* March 13. https://www.nytimes.com/2017/03/13/us/politics/affordable-care-act-health-congressional-budget-office.html?_r=0.

1322   Ibid.

1323   Advisory Board. 2017. *Where the States Stand on Medicaid Expansion.* May 19. https://www.advisory.com/daily-briefing/resources/primers/medicaidmap.

1324   Dan Mangan. 2016. *Obamacare's Medicaid Expansion Leading to Health Insurance Boom in Some.* July 20. https://www.cnbc.com/2016/07/20/obamacares-medicaid-expansion-leading-to-health-insurance-boom-in-some-states.html.

1325   Nina Martin and Renee Montagne Propublica. 2017. *U.S. Has the Worst Rate of Maternal Deaths in the Developed World.* May 12. http://www.npr.org/2017/05/12/528098789/u-s-has-the-worst-rate-of-maternal-deaths-in-the-developed-world.

1326   Bob Bryan. 2017. *A Group of Democratic and Republican Governors Just Released a Plan to Fix Obamacare.* August 31. http://www.businessinsider.com/kasich-hickenlooper-plan-obamacare-health-care-2017-8.

1327   Sonam Sheth and Skye Gould. 2017. *Who's Running the Government? Trump Has Yet to Fill 85% of Key Executive Branch Positions.* April 22. http://www.businessinsider.com/whos-running-the-government-trump-unfilled-executive-branch-positions-2017-4.

1328   Chas Danner. 2017. *Reports: Frustrated and Isolated Trump Considering Staff Shakeup at Demoralized White House.* May 14. http://nymag.com/daily/intelligencer/2017/05/trump-considering-staff-shakeup-at-demoralized-white-house.html.

1329   Len De Groot, Chris Keller and Jon Schleuss. 2017. *The Most Notable Firings and Resignations in the Trump White House.* July 28. http://www.latimes.com/projects/la-na-pol-trump-firings-resignations/.

1330   Nicholas Fandos. 2017. *Government Ethics Chief Resigns, Casting Uncertainty over Agency.* July 6. https://www.nytimes.com/2017/07/06/us/politics/walter-shaub-office-of-government-ethics-resign.html?mcubz=1&_r=0.

1331 Peter Overby and Marilyn Geewax. 2017. *Ethics Office Director Walter Shaub Resigns, Saying Rules Need to Be Tougher.* July 6. http://www.npr.org/2017/07/06/535781749/ethics-office-director-walter-shaub-resigns-saying-rules-need-to-be-tougher.

1332 Ibid.

1333 Nicholas Fandos. 2017. *Government Ethics Chief Resigns, Casting Uncertainty over Agency.* July 6

1334 Julia Horowitz and Cristina Alesci. 2017. *Outgoing Ethics Chief Urges Trump to Stop Visiting His Properties.* July 17. http://money.cnn.com/2017/07/17/news/walter-shaub-oge-interview/index.html.

1335 Jeremy Diamond, Jeff Zeleny, Dana Bash and Kaitlan Collins. 2017. *Sean Spicer, White House press secretary, resigns.* July 21. http://www.cnn.com/2017/07/21/politics/sean-spicer-resigns-anthony-scaramucci/index.html.

1336 Ibid.

1337 Ryan Lizza. 2017. *Anthony Scaramucci Called Me to Unload about White House Leakers, Reince Priebus and Steve Bannon.* July 27. http://www.newyorker.com/news/ryan-lizza/anthony-scaramucci-called-me-to-unload-about-white-house-leakers-reince-priebus-and-steve-bannon.

1338 Tom Phillips. 2017. *North Korea Missile Test Shows It Could Reach New York, Say Experts.* July 29. https://www.theguardian.com/world/2017/jul/28/north-korea-fires-missile-japan-reports-say.

1339 Jeffrey Lewis is the director of the East Asia nonproliferation program at the Middlebury Center of International Studies at Monterey in California and a columnist for *Foreign Policy.*

1340 Jeffrey Lewis. 2017. *Let's Face It: North Korean Nuclear Weapons Can Hit the U.S.* August 3. https://www.nytimes.com/2017/08/03/opinion/north-korea-nukes.html?_r=0.

1341 Susan Heavey and Jack Kim. 2017. *Message from North Korean Missile over Japan 'Loud and Clear': Trump.* August 28. https://www.reuters.com/article/us-northkorea-missiles-iduskcn1b8283.

1342 Ibid.

1343 Ibid.

1344 Richard Gonzales. 2017. *U.N. Security Council Approves New North Korea Sanctions.* September 11. http://www.npr.org/sections/thetwo-way/2017/09/11/550301634/u-n-security-council-approves-new-north-korea-sanctions.

1345 Steve Holland and Jeff Mason. 2017. *If Threatened, U.S. Will 'Totally Destroy' North Korea, Trump Vows.* September 19. http://www.reuters.com/article/us-un-assembly-trump/if-threatened-u-s-will-totally-destroy-north-korea-trump-vows-iduskcn1bu0b3.

1346 Scott A. Snyder. 2017. *Kim Jong Un's Direct Response to Trump's Threatening UN Speech.* September 27. https://www.cfr.org/blog/kim-jong-uns-direct-response-trumps-threatening-un-speech.

1347 David E. Sanger. 2017. *U.S. in Direct Communication with North Korea, Says Tillerson.* September 30. https://www.nytimes.com/2017/09/30/world/asia/us-north-korea-tillerson.html.

1348 Ibid.

1349 The Guardian. 2017. *'Don't Be Too Nice': Trump Seems to Back Rougher Policing in Immigration Speech.* July 28. https://www.theguardian.com/us-news/2017/jul/28/donald-trump-police-long-island-speech.

1350 Brian Rosenthal. 2017. *Police Criticize Trump for Urging Officers Not to Be 'Too Nice' with Suspects.* July 29. https://www.nytimes.com/2017/07/29/nyregion/trump-police-too-nice.html?mcubz=1.

1351 Joan Biskupic. 2017. *Why Joe Arpaio Was Found Guilty.* August 24. http://www.cnn.com/2017/08/24/politics/why-joe-arpaio-was-found-guilty/index.html.

1352 Kevin Liptak, Daniella Diaz and Sophie Tatum. 2017. *Trump Pardons Former Sheriff Joe Arpaio.* August 27. http://www.cnn.com/2017/08/25/politics/sheriff-joe-arpaio-donald-trump-pardon/index.html.

1353 Brian Bennett. 2017. *Trump to Support 'Merit-Based' Immigration System That Would Cut Number of U.S. Migrants in Half.* August 2. https://www.thestar.com/news/world/2017/08/02/trump-to-support-merit-based-immigration-system-that-would-cut-number-of-us-migrants-in-half.html.

1354 Ibid.

1355 Alexander Panetta. 2017. *Canada's Immigration Policy Inspired Donald Trump's New Plan: White House.* August 2. http://globalnews.ca/news/3643835/trump-immigration-canada/.

1356 Ibid.

1357 Ibid.

1358 Ibid.

1359 Library of Congress. n.d. *Points-Based Immigration Systems: Canada.* Accessed September 6, 2017. https://www.loc.gov/law/help/points-based-immigration/canada.php.

1360 Matt Zapotosky. 2017. *Grandparents, Other Extended Relatives Exempt from Trump Travel Ban, Federal Judge Rules.* July 14. https://www.washingtonpost.com/world/national-security/grandparents-other-extended-relatives-exempt-from-trump-travel-ban-federal-judge-rules/2017/07/14/ce67aa72-6888-11e7-8eb5-cbccc2e7bfbf_story.html?utm_term=.fd97187ed08b.

1361 Nolan D. McCaskill. 2017. *Trump Says He Will Treat Dreamers 'with Heart.'* February 16. http://www.politico.com/story/2017/02/trump-press-conference-dreamers-heart-235103.

1362 Dara Lind. 2017. *9 Facts That Explain DACA, the Immigration Program Trump Is Threatening to End.* September 5. https://www.vox.com/policy-and-politics/2017/8/31/16226934/daca-trump-dreamers-immigration.

1363 Stephen Collinson. 2017. *Trump's DACA Decision Triggers Anguish, Political Firestorm.* September 5. http://www.cnn.com/2017/09/05/politics/trump-daca-politics/index.html.

1364 Amy Minsky. 2017. *Would-be Refugees Fleeing Donald Trump Policy May Not Fare Better in Canada.* August 3. http://globalnews.ca/news/3646272/refugees-canada-haiti-donald-trump/.

1365 Candice Malcolm. 2017. *Canada, in Fact, Removed Special Status for Haitians Long before the U.S.* August 9. http://www.torontosun.com/2017/08/09/canada-in-fact-removed-special-status-for-haitians-long-before-the-us.

1366 Ibid.

1367 Ibid.

1368 Ibid.

1369 Ibid

1370 Lucia Mutikani. 2017. *Strong U.S. Jobs Report Bolsters Case for Further Fed Tightening.* August 4. https://www.reuters.com/article/us-usa-economy/strong-u-s-jobs-report-bolsters-case-for-further-fed-tightening-iduskbn1ak09w.

1371 Eugene Kiely. 2017. *Scott Pruitt and Coal Jobs.* June 5. http://www.factcheck.org/2017/06/scott-pruitt-coal-jobs.

1372 Ibid.

1373 Ibid.

1374 Dominic Rushe. 2017. *Top US Coal Boss Robert Murray: Trump 'Can't Bring Mining Jobs Back.'* March 27. https://www.theguardian.com/environment/2017/mar/27/us-coal-industry-clean-power-plan-donald-trump.

1375 Ibid.

1376 Ibid.

1377 Ibid.

1378 Ibid.

1379 Kimberly Amadeo. 2017. *What Is the GDP Growth Rate?* June 12. https://www.thebalance.com/what-is-the-gdp-growth-rate-3306016.

1380 Kenneth Rapoza. 2017. *World Bank: Trump GDP Growth Will Be Worse Than Obama's.* June 6. https://www.forbes.com/sites/kenrapoza/2017/06/06/world-bank-trump-gdp-growth-will-be-worse-than-obamas/#5ca75f572776.

1381 Maggie Astor, Christina Caron and Daniel Victor. 2017. *A Guide to the Charlottesville Aftermath.* August 13. https://www.nytimes.com/2017/08/13/us/charlottesville-virginia-overview.html?mcubz=1.

1382 Jonah Engel Bromwich and Alan Blinder. 2017. *What We Know about James Alex Fields, Driver Charged in Charlottesville Killing.* August 13. https://www.nytimes.com/2017/08/13/us/james-alex-fields-charlottesville-driver-.html.

1383 Maggie Astor, Christina Caron and Daniel Victor. 2017. *A Guide to the Charlottesville Aftermath.* August 13

1384 Matt Pearce. 2017. *Who Was Responsible for the Violence in Charlottesville? Here's What Witnesses Say.* August 15. http://www.latimes.com/nation/la-na-charlottesville-witnesses-20170815-story.html.

1385 Ibid.

1386 Frances Robles. 2017. *As White Nationalist in Charlottesville Fired, Police 'Never Moved.'* August 25. https://www.nytimes.com/2017/08/25/us/charlottesville-protest-police.html?mcubz=1.

1387 Maggie Astor, Christina Caron and Daniel Victor. 2017. *A Guide to the Charlottesville Aftermath.* August 13.

1388 Ibid.

1389 Yair Rosenberg. 2017. *'Jews Will Not Replace Us': Why White Supremacists Go After Jews.* August 14. https://www.washingtonpost.com/news/acts-of-faith/wp/2017/08/14/jews-will-not-replace-us-why-white-supremacists-go-after-jews/?utm_term=.7b50e02b7653.

1390 Ray Sanchez. 2017. *Who Are White Nationalists and What Do They Want?* August 13. http://www.cnn.com/2017/08/13/us/white-nationalism-explainer-trnd/index.html.

1391 Ibid.

1392 Jena McGregor and Damian Paletta. 2017. *Trump's Business Advisory Councils Disband as CEOs Abandon President over Charlottesville Views.* August 16. https://www.washingtonpost.com/news/on-leadership/wp/2017/08/16/after-wave-of-ceo-departures-trump-ends-business-and-manufacturing-councils/?utm_term=.c90ce54d35b1.

1393 W.J. Hennigan. 2017. *U.S. Military Leaders Condemn Racism Following Trump's Comments on Charlottesville Violence.* August 16. http://www.latimes.com/politics/washington/la-na-essential-washington-updates-u-s-military-leaders-condemn-racism-1502898652-htmlstory.html.

1394 Sarah Pulliam Bailey. 2017. *Megachurch Pastor Resigns from Trump's Evangelical Council.* August 18. https://www.washingtonpost.com/news/acts-of-faith/wp/2017/08/18/megachurch-pastor-resigns-from-trumps-evangelical-council/?utm_term=.0b59a080001a.

1395 Ibid.

1396 Daniel Levintova and Hannah Schulman. 2017. *The Flynn Scandal Explodes: What This Means and How It Happened.* May 18. http://www.motherjones.com/politics/2017/05/michael-flynn-scandal-timeline-trump.

1397 Ibid.

1398 Ibid.

1399 Ellen Nakashima, Adam Entous and Greg Miller. 2017. *Russian Ambassador Told Moscow that Kushner Wanted Secret Communications Channel with Kremlin.* May 26. https://www.washingtonpost.com/world/national-security/russian-ambassador-told-moscow-that-kushner-wanted-secret-communications-channel-with-kremlin/2017/05/26/520a14b4-422d-11e7-9869-bac8b446820a_story.html?tid=sm_tw&utm_term=.9120a88637aa.

1400 Darren Samuelsohn. 2017. *Blumenthal: '99 Percent Sure' of Russia Indictments.* September 26. http://www.politico.com/story/2017/09/26/indictments-michael-flynn-paul-manafort-richard-blumenthal-says-243158.

1401 Ibid.

1402 Yamiche Alcindor. 2017. *Paul Manafort Expects to Be Indicted, Longtime Trump Adviser Says.* September 26. https://www.nytimes.com/2017/09/26/us/politics/roger-stone-testimony-paul-manafort.html?mcubz=0&_r=0.

1403 Robert Valencia. 2017. *Will Trump Be Impeached? Here's What We Know about Robert Mueller's Russia Probe So Far.* October 10. http://www.newsweek.com/will-trump-be-impeached-heres-what-we-know-about-robert-muellers-russia-probe-687356.

1404 Rosalind S. Helderman and Tom Hamburger. 2017. *Eighth Person in Trump Tower Meeting Is Identified.* July 18. https://www.washingtonpost.com/politics/eighth-person-in-trump-tower-meeting-is-identified/2017/07/18/e971234a-6bce-11e7-9c15-177740635e83_story.html?hpid=hp_hp-top-table-low_8thman-1225pm%3Ahomepage%2Fstory&utm_term=.23550c5cde52.

1405 Ibid.

1406 Robert Valencia. 2017. *Will Trump Be Impeached? Here's What We Know about Robert Mueller's Russia Probe So Far.* October 10.

1407 Harry Cockburn. 2017. *Former Facebook Employees Regret Working for Company as Russia Election Probe Continues: 'What Have I Done?'* October 19. http://www.independent.co.uk/news/world/americas/us-politics/facebook-russia-adverts-us-election-probe-former-employees-regret-working-company-donald-trump-a8008921.html.

1408 Ibid.

1409 Eva Matsa and Kristine Lu. 2016. *10 Facts about the Changing Digital News Landscape.* September 14. http://www.pewresearch.org/fact-tank/2016/09/14/facts-about-the-changing-digital-news-landscape/.

1410 Manu Raju, Dylan Byers and Dana Bash. 2017. *Exclusive: Russian-linked Facebook Ads Targeted Michigan and Wisconsin.* October 4. http://www.cnn.com/2017/10/03/politics/russian-facebook-ads-michigan-wisconsin/index.html.

1411 John Solomon. 2017. *Senate Judiciary Opens Probe into Obama-era Russian Nuclear Bribery Case.* October 17. http://thehill.com/policy/national-security/355957-senate-judiciary-opens-probe-into-obama-era-russian-nuclear-bribery.

1412 Evan Perez. 2017. *White House Lawyers Research Impeachment.* May 19. http://www.cnn.com/2017/05/19/politics/donald-trump-white-house-lawyers-research-impeachment.

1413 Ibid.

1414 Rebecca Harrington. 2017. *Trump Reportedly Didn't Know about the Loophole in the 25th Amendment That Lets 14 People Remove a Sitting President from Office.* October 11. http://www.businessinsider.com/25th-amendment-how-can-you-remove-president-from-office-2017-3.

1415 Gabriel Sherman. 2017. *"I Hate Everyone in the White House!": Trump Seethes as Advisers Fear the President Is "Unraveling."* October 11. https://www.vanityfair.com/news/2017/10/donald-trump-is-unraveling-white-house-advisers/amp.

1416 Dana Milbank. 2016. *Trump Supporters Are Talking about Civil War. Could a Loss Provide the Spark?* October 18. https://www.washingtonpost.com/opinions/trump-supporters-are-talking-about-civil-war-could-a-loss-provide-the-spark/2016/10/18/f5ce081a-9573-11e6-bb29-bf2701dbe0a3_story.html?utm_term=.b8ca246fb215.

1417 Ibid.

1418 Greg Miller, Reuben Fischer-Baum and Julie Vitkovskaya. 2017. *'This Deal Will Make Me Look Terrible': Full Transcripts of Trump's Calls with Mexico and Australia.* August 3. https://www.washingtonpost.com/graphics/2017/politics/australia-mexico-transcripts/?utm_term=.de16ed068745.

1419 Ibid.

1420 Ibid.

1421 Ibid.

1422 Ibid.

1423 Charlie Savage and Eileen Sullivan. 2017. *Leak Investigations Triple under Trump, Sessions Says.* August 4. https://www.nytimes.com/2017/08/04/us/politics/jeff-sessions-trump-leaks-attorney-general.html?mcubz=1&_r=0.

1424 Ibid.

1425 David Nakamura and Abby Phillip. 2017. *Trump Announces New Strategy for Afghanistan That Calls for a Troop Increase.* August 21. https://www.washingtonpost.com/politics/trump-expected-to-announce-small-troop-increase-in-afghanistan-in-prime-time-address/2017/08/21/eb3a513e-868a-11e7-a94f-3139abce39f5_story.html?utm_term=.569682e45047.

1426 Ibid.

1427 Ibid.

1428 Joshua Keating. 2017. *Kim Jong-un Is Calling Trump's Bluff.* August 29. http://www.slate.com/blogs/the_slatest/2017/08/29/kim_jong_un_is_calling_trump_s_bluff.html.

1429 Oliver Milman. 2017. *US Federal Department Is Censoring Use of Term 'Climate Change,'* August 7. https://www.theguardian.com/environment/2017/aug/07/usda-climate-change-language-censorship-emails.

1430 Jacqueline Howard. 2017. *Where Climate Change Is Threatening the Health of Americans.* April 13. http://www.cnn.com/2017/04/13/health/climate-change-health-risks-us-map-explainer/index.html.

1431 Ibid.

1432 Ibid.

1433 Ibid.

1434 Union of Concerned Scientists. n.d. *Each Country's Share of CO2 Emissions*. Accessed August 23, 2017. http://www.ucsusa.org/global_warming/science_and_impacts/science/each-countrys-share-of-co2.html#.we4bbmhszde.

1435 Coral Davenport et al. 2017. *What Is the Clean Power Plan and How Can Trump Repeal It?* October 10. https://www.nytimes.com/2017/10/10/climate/epa-clean-power-plan.html.

1436 Ibid.

1437 Donald J. Trump. 2014 3:48 PM. *Twitter Post*. January 25. https://twitter.com/realDonaldTrump/status/427226424987385856.

1438 Mark Abadi. 2017. *Trump Did a 180 on Harvey and Irma after He Was Asked about Climate Change*. September 24. http://www.businessinsider.com/trump-response-to-hurricane-harvey-and-irma-climate-change-2017-9.

1439 Ibid.

1440 Ibid.

1441 CNN Library. 2017. *2017 Atlantic Hurricane Season Fast Facts*. October 26. http://www.cnn.com/2017/05/15/us/2017-atlantic-hurricane-season-fast-facts/index.html.

1442 Ibid.

1443 Ibid.

1444 Ryan Struyk. 2017. *Trump's Approval Again Reaches 40% after Positive Reaction to Hurricane Response*. September 22. http://www.cnn.com/2017/09/21/politics/trump-approval-40-percent-hurricanes-north-korea/index.html.

1445 Aaron Blake. 2017. *Trump's Puerto Rico Poll Numbers Are Worse than Bush's after Katrina*. October 12. https://www.washingtonpost.com/news/the-fix/wp/2017/10/12/puerto-rico-is-officially-a-problem-for-trump-his-numbers-are-worse-than-bushs-post-katrina/?utm_term=.154168ee73bf.

1446 Eliza Relman. 2017. *Trump on Puerto Rican Crisis: 'This Is an Island Surrounded by Water, Big Water, Ocean Water.'* September 29. http://www.businessinsider.com/trump-puerto-rico-hurricane-maria-island-water-2017-9.

1447 Ron Nixon and Matt Stevens. 2017. *Harvey, Irma, Maria: Trump Administration's Response Compared*. September 27. https://www.nytimes.com/2017/09/27/us/politics/trump-puerto-rico-aid.html.

1448 Daniella Diaz. 2017. *Trump Authorizes Waiver to Loosen Shipping Regulations for Puerto Rico*. September 28. http://www.cnn.com/2017/09/28/politics/puerto-rico-governor-white-house-jones-act-waiver/index.html.

1449 Ron Nixon and Matt Stevens. 2017. *Harvey, Irma, Maria: Trump Administration's Response Compared*. September 27.

1450 Ibid.

1451 Brian Naylor and Scott Horsley. 2017. *Trump's Texas Visit Highlights Federal Response Effort*. August 29. http://www.npr.org/2017/08/29/546861395/trump-texas-visit-highlights-federal-response-effort.

1452 Ibid.

1453 Jack Holmes. 2017. *President Trump Embarrassed You Again Today*. October 23. http://www.esquire.com/news-politics/a12772874/trump-puerto-rico-ruin-budget/.

1454 Eric Levenson. 2017. *3 storms, 3 responses: Comparing Harvey, Irma and Maria*. September 27. http://www.cnn.com/2017/09/26/us/response-harvey-irma-maria/index.html.

1455 Ibid.

1456 Ron Nixon and Matt Stevens. 2017. *Harvey, Irma, Maria: Trump Administration's Response Compared*. September 27.

1457 Ibid.

1458 Ibid.

1459 AP. 2017. *Trump Says Puerto Rico in Trouble after Hurricane, Suffering from 'Broken Infrastructure' and 'Massive Debt.'* September 26. https://www.cnbc.com/2017/09/25/trump-says-puerto-rico-in-trouble-after-hurricane-debt-must-be-dealt-with.html.

1460 Jeremy Diamond. 2017. *Trump Administration Projects Confidence amid Puerto Rico Crisis*. September 28. http://www.cnn.com/2017/09/28/politics/elaine-duke-puerto-rico-response/index.html.

1461 Kathryn Watson. 2017. *In Puerto Rico, Paul Ryan Says Government Is Committed "for the Long Haul."* October 13. https://www.cbsnews.com/news/paul-ryan-in-puerto-rico-says-federal-government-is-in-for-the-long-haul/.

1462 Ibid.

1463 Donald J. Trump. 2017 4:07 AM. *Twitter Post*. October 12. https://twitter.com/realdonaldtrump/status/918432809282342912.

1464 Alex Sundby. 2017. *Puerto Rico Mayor Pleads for Help after Hurricane Maria: "People are Dying."* September 26. https://www.cbsnews.com/news/puerto-rico-mayor-help-hurricane-maria-people-are-dying/.

1465 NASA. 2017. *Fires and Snow in the Pacific Northwest*. September 29. https://www.nasa.gov/image-feature/goddard/2017/fires-and-snow-in-the-pacific-northwest.

1466 AP. 2017. *'Getting the Upper Hand' against Deadly Wildfires*. October 15. https://www.cnbc.com/2017/10/15/california-wildfires-death-toll-reaches-40-fires-now-100-miles-wide.html.

1467 NBC News. n.d. *Las Vegas Shooting*. Accessed October 23, 2017. https://www.nbcnews.com/storyline/las-vegas-shooting.

1468 Brandon Carter. 2017. *Bill O'Reilly: Las Vegas Shooting 'the Price of Freedom.'* October 2. http://thehill.com/homenews/media/353503-bill-oreilly-las-vegas-shooting-the-price-of-freedom.

1469 Jeff Mason. 2017. *In Meeting with Military, Trump Talks of 'Calm before the Storm.'* October 5. http://www.reuters.com/article/us-usa-trump-military/in-meeting-with-military-trump-talks-of-calm-before-the-storm-iduskbn1cb03c.

1470 Ibid.

1471   Adolf Hitler. n.d. *Adolf Hitler > Quotes > Quotable Quote.* Accessed October 9, 2017. https://www.goodreads.com/quotes/74363-the-receptivity-of-the-masses-is-very-limited-their-intelligence.

1472   Janyce McGregor. 2017. *Kevin O'Leary Makes Late Entry into Conservative Leadership Race.* January 18. http://www.cbc.ca/news/politics/oleary-conservative-leadership-race-1.3940596.

1473   Alex Boutilier. 2017. *Kevin O'Leary Says His Past Comments Were Good Television, Not Policy.* January 18. https://www.thestar.com/news/canada/2017/01/18/kevin-oleary-announces-run-for-conservative-leadership.html.

1474   Kirk LaPointe. 2011. *Review from the Office of the Ombudsman | English Services.* November 18. http://www.ombudsman.cbc.radio-canada.ca/en/complaint-reviews/2011/unions/.

1475   Christopher Matthews. 2014. *Shark Tank Star Thinks Poverty Is "Fantastic News."* January 22. http://business.time.com/2014/01/22/kevin-oleary-says-3-5-billion-living-in-poverty-is-fantastic/.

1476   Ibid.

1477   David Beers. 2017. *The Political Pearls of Kevin O'Leary.* January 18. https://thetyee.ca/Opinion/2017/01/18/Political-Pearls-Kevin-OLeary.

1478   Julie Pace. 2017. *Trump Says Presidency Involves More 'Human Responsibility' Than Business.* April 24. http://globalnews.ca/news/3398433/trump-100-days-interview/.

1479   Arlene Dickinson. 2017. *Arlene Dickinson on Kevin O'Leary's Entry into Conservative Leadership Race.* January 18. http://www.cbc.ca/news/canada/calgary/kevin-o-leary-conservative-run-arlene-dickinson-opinion-1.3942349.

1480   Ibid.

1481   US History. n.d. *The Declaration of Independence.* Accessed August 30, 2016. http://www.ushistory.org/declaration/document/.

1482   Geoffrey Stone and Eugene Volokh. n.d. *Common Interpretation: Freedom of the Press.* Accessed August 18, 2016. https://constitutioncenter.org/interactive-constitution/amendments/amendment-i/the-freedom-of-speech-and-of-the-press-clause/interp/33.

1483   Liberty State Park, Liberty Science Center. n.d. *Statue of Liberty National Monument.* Accessed August 30, 2017. http://www.libertystatepark.com/emma.htm.

1484   Dorothy Law Nolte. 2017. *Children Learn What They Live.* October 23. https://www.rootsofaction.com/children-learn-what-they-live-lessons-from-dorothy-law-nolte.

1485   National Association of Adult Survivors of Child Abuse. n.d. *Resources Statistics of Child Abuse.* Accessed September 5, 2016. http://www.naasca.org/2012-Resources/010812-StaisticsOfChildAbuse.htm.

1486   DW Made for Minds. 2017. *UNICEF: 20 Percent of Children in Developed Countries Living in Poverty.* June 15. http://www.dw.com/en/unicef-20-percent-of-children-in-developed-countries-living-in-poverty/a-39259716.

1487   NVEE. n.d. *Statistics.* Accessed September 5, 2016. http://www.nveee.org/statistics/.

1488   Kelly Wallace and Sandee LaMotte. 2016. *The Collateral Damage after Students' 'Build a Wall' Chant Goes Viral.* December 28. http://www.cnn.com/2016/12/28/health/build-a-wall-viral-video-collateral-damage-middle-school/index.html.

1489   Albert Samaha, Hayes Mike and Talal Ansari. 2017. *Kids Are Quoting Trump to Bully Their Classmates and Teachers Don't Know What to Do about It.* June 6. https://www.buzzfeed.com/albertsamaha/kids-are-quoting-trump-to-bully-their-classmates?utm_term=.ifZJ0nq2Y#.pa2gpbkPo.

1490   Rachel Siegel. 2017. *8-year-old Biracial Boy Was Hanged from Rope by N.H. Teenagers Because of His Race, Family Says.* September 13. https://www.washingtonpost.com/news/morning-mix/wp/2017/09/13/8-year-old-boy-was-hung-from-rope-by-n-h-teenagers-because-of-his-race-family-says/?utm_term=.82cb45d0e3aa.

1491   Louis Nelson and Rebecca Morin. 2017. *Melania Trump Condemns Bullying at U.N. Luncheon.* September 20. http://www.politico.com/story/2017/09/20/melania-trump-un-lunch-bullying-242920.

1492   Jodi Kantor and Megan Twohey. 2017. *Harvey Weinstein Paid Off Sexual Harassment Accusers for Decades.* October 5. https://www.nytimes.com/2017/10/05/us/harvey-weinstein-harassment-allegations.html?_r=0.

1493   Brian Lowry. 2017. *Harvey Weinstein: Nine Days of Accusations and Collateral Damage.* October 14. http://money.cnn.com/2017/10/13/media/harvey-weinstein-recap/index.html.

1494   Sophie Tatum. 2017. *Democrats Pressured to Return Donations from Harvey Weinstein.* October 5. http://www.cnn.com/2017/10/05/politics/harvey-weinstein-donations/index.html.

1495   Eli Watkins and Dan Merica. 2017. *As Democrats Denounce Weinstein, Clintons and Obama Stay Mum.* October 10. http://www.cnn.com/2017/10/09/politics/clinton-obama-weinstein/index.html.

1496   Jessica Garrison and Kendall Taggart. 2017. *Trump Given a Subpoena for All Documents Relating to Assault Allegations.* October 15. https://www.buzzfeed.com/jessicagarrison/subpoena-orders-trump-to-turn-over-documents-from-assault?utm_term=.qdvxJKVYl#.fj78moAqr.

1497   Ibid.

1498   Perry Stein. 2017. *Trump's Lewd 'Access Hollywood' Tape Is Playing on Repeat for 12 Hours on the Mall.* October 6. https://www.washingtonpost.com/local/the-trump-access-hollywood-tape-is-playing-on-repeat-for-12-hours-on-the-mall/2017/10/06/c19a4d52-aaa2-11e7-92d1-58c702d2d975_story.html?utm_term=.f620a8cd852f.

1499   Allan Smith. 2016. *Trump Apologizes After Shocking Audio Emerges of Lewd 2005 Comments about Women.* October 6. https://www.businessinsider.com.au/trump-leaked-recording-women-audio-billy-bush-2016-10.

1500   Nick Gass. 2015. *Donald Trump Was for the Clintons Before He Was against Them.* December 29. http://www.politico.com/story/2015/12/donald-trump-hillary-bill-clinton-relationship-217191.

1501 Stephanie Mencimer. 2016. *How Paula Jones Paved the Way for Donald Trump to Be Repeatedly Dragged into Court as President.* November 15. http://www.motherjones.com/politics/2016/11/president-trump-can-thank-paula-jones-his-legal-troubles.

1502 Alanna Vagianos. 2017. *Gretchen Carlson on Harvey Weinstein Allegations: 'This Is the Watershed Moment.'* October 17. http://www.huffingtonpost.ca/entry/gretchen-carlson-on-harvey-weinstein-allegations-this-is-the-watershed-moment_us_59e6090fe4b02a215b334316.

1503 Ryan Struyk. 2017. *6 in 10 People Who Approve of Trump Say They'll Never, Ever, Ever Stop Approving.* August 17. http://www.cnn.com/2017/08/17/politics/trump-approvers-never-stop-approving-poll/index.html.

1504 Steve Wyche. 2016. *Colin Kaepernick Explains Why He Sat during National Anthem.* August 27.

1505 Michael Dixon. 2017. *Colin Kaepernick's Latest Round of Donations Includes $25k to Veteran's Group.* February 9. https://sportsnaut.com/2017/02/colin-kaepernick-donations-includes-25k-veterans/.

1506 Sophie Tatum. 2017. *Trump: NFL Owners Should Fire Players Who Protest the National Anthem.* September 23. http://www.cnn.com/2017/09/22/politics/donald-trump-alabama-nfl/index.html.

1507 USA Today. 2017. *Trump: NFL Should 'Fire or Suspend' Players Who Kneel during Anthem.* September 24. https://www.usatoday.com/story/sports/nfl/2017/09/24/trump-nfl-should-fire-suspend-players-who-kneel-during-anthem/697680001/.

1508 Tyler Lauletta. 2017. *The NFL Is Getting Hammered After Another Game Was Played in a Half-Empty Stadium.* September 22. http://www.businessinsider.com/nfl-attendance-down-2017-9.

1509 NFL News. 2017. *NFL: No Mandate for Players to Stand During National Anthem.* October 11. http://www.nfl.com/news/story/0ap3000000860129/article/nfl-no-mandate-for-players-to-stand-during-national-anthem

1510 Donald J. Trump. 2017 4:06 AM. *Twitter Post.* October 18. https://twitter.com/realdonaldtrump/status/920606910109356032.

1511 David Moshman. 2012. *Compulsory Patriotism: Requiring the Pledge of Allegiance.* January 16. http://www.huffingtonpost.com/david-moshman/pledge-of-allegiance_b_1098584.html.

1512 Ibid.

1513 Donald J. Trump. 2017 6:55 AM. *Twitter Post.* October 11. https://twitter.com/realdonaldtrump/status/918112884630093825.

1514 Matthew Yglesias. 2017. *Trump Threatens to Cancel NBC's Broadcast License over Critical Reporting.* October 11. https://www.vox.com/2017/10/11/16458362/trump-nbc-tweet.

1515 Ibid.

1516 BBC. 2017. *Donald Trump: A List of Potential Conflicts of Interest.* April 18. http://www.bbc.com/news/world-us-canada-38069298.

1517 Ibid.

1518 Ibid.

1519 Ibid.

1520 Ibid.

1521 Ibid.

1522 Ibid.

1523 Ibid.

1524 Ed Mazza. 2017. *Report: Secret Service Booted to the Sidewalk after Trump Tower Rent Dispute.* August 3. http://www.huffingtonpost.ca/entry/secret-service-trump-tower-dispute_us_5983a08ce4b041356ebee1b8.

1525 Ibid.

1526 Jeff Ostrowski. 2017. *Despite Rich Value of Trump National Golf Club in Jupiter, Trump Loses Tax Appeals.* July 18. http://realtime.blog.palmbeachpost.com/2017/07/18/despite-rich-value-of-trump-national-golf-club-in-jupiter-trump-has-lost-value-appeals-three-years-in-a-row-realdonaldtrump/.

1527 Jeremy Diamond. 2017. *Donating to Trump? Campaign Is Spending $1 of Every $10 on Legal Fees.* October 17. http://www.cnn.com/2017/10/17/politics/donald-trump-campaign-legal-fees/index.html?sr=twCNN101717donald-trump-campaign-legal-fees0100PMStory.

1528 Ibid.

1529 Jennifer Hansler. 2017. *Almost a Dozen Trump Nominees Have Withdrawn from Consideration for Administration.* October 17. http://www.cnn.com/2017/10/17/politics/tom-marino-trump-nomination-withdrawals/index.html?sr=twCNN101717tom-marino-trump-nomination-withdrawals0144PMStory.

1530 Eugene Kiely. 2016. *Trump's Employee Exaggeration in Jersey.* May 25. http://www.factcheck.org/2016/05/trumps-employee-exaggeration-in-jersey/.

1531 Forbes. 2017. *What's Donald Trump Really Worth?* September. Accessed October 23, 2017. https://www.forbes.com/donald-trump/#4dd3b4792899.

1532 InsideGov. n.d. *2017 United States Budget Estimate.* Accessed October 24, 2017. http://federal-budget.insidegov.com/l/120/2017-Estimate.

1533 Juliet Eilperin and Sean Sullivan. 2017. *Trump Appears to Back Further Away from Bipartisan Health-care.* October 18. https://www.washingtonpost.com/powerpost/trump-appears-to-back-further-away-from-bipartisan-health-care-push/2017/10/18/d08c4b0c-b40d-11e7-a908-a3470754bbb9_story.html?utm_term=.8e22cbb98df2.

1534 CBS. 2017. *U.S. Soldiers Killed in Niger Were Caught by Surprise, Official Says.* October 18. https://www.cbsnews.com/news/green-berets-killed-in-niger-were-caught-by-surprise-u-s-official-says/.

1535 Philip Rucker and Dan Lamothe. 2017. *'Somebody Screwed Up Here': Why Did Trump Take 12 Days to Address the Deaths of Four Soldiers and Why Did He Attack Obama?* October 18. https://www.thestar.com/news/world/2017/10/18/somebody-screwed-up-here-why-did-trump-take-12-days-to-address-the-deaths-of-four-soldiers-and-why-did-he-attack-obama.html.

1536 Alana Abramson. 2017. *President Trump Just Spoke about Everything from Puerto Rico to Robert Mueller.* October 16. http://time.com/4984507/donald-trump-mitch-mcconnell-rose-garden-press-conference.

1537 Ibid.

1538 Ibid.

1539 Dan Merica. 2017. *Trump: Ask Kelly Whether Obama Called After His Son Was Killed in Action.* October 18. http://www.cnn.com/2017/10/17/politics/president-donald-trump-john-kelly-obama-phone-call/index.html.

1540 Rebecca Savransky. 2017. *Kelly Caught off Guard when Trump Mentioned Obama Didn't Call After His Son Died: Report.* October 19. http://thehill.com/homenews/administration/356191-kelly-didnt-expect-trump-to-bring-up-publicly-that-obama-didnt-call.

1541 Amy Davidson Sorkin. 2017. *Donald Trump's Unseemly Condolence-call Bragging Game.* October 18. https://www.newyorker.com/news/amy-davidson-sorkin/donald-trumps-unseemly-condolence-call-bragging-game.

1542 CNN. 2017. *Trump's Alleged Insensitive Comments Regarding Killed U.S. Soldier Ignite Firestorm; White House Press Briefing.* October 18. http://transcripts.cnn.com/transcripts/1710/18/cnr.07.html.

1543 Ibid.

1544 Manuela Tobias. 2017. *Donald Trump's Misleading Comments on Obama's Calls to Fallen Soldiers' Families.* October 17. http://www.politifact.com/truth-o-meter/article/2017/oct/17/donald-trump-obamas-calls-fallen-soldiers-families.

1545 Ibid.

1546 Bryan Logan. 2017. *Trump Reportedly Tells the Widow of a US Soldier Killed in Action, 'He Knew What He Signed Up For.'* October 17. http://www.businessinsider.com/trump-he-knew-what-he-signed-up-for-ladavid-johnson-niger-attack-2017-10.

1547 Mark Landler and Yamiche Alcindor. 2017. *Trump's Condolence Call to Soldier's Widow Ignites an Imbroglio.* October 18. https://www.nytimes.com/2017/10/18/us/politics/trump-widow-johnson-call.html?_r=1.

1548 Ibid.

1549 Ibid.

1550 CNN. 2017. *Trump's Alleged Insensitive Comments Regarding Killed U.S. Soldier Ignite Firestorm; White House Press Briefing.* October 18. http://transcripts.cnn.com/TRANSCRIPTS/1710/18/cnr.07.html.

1551 Ibid.

1552 NY Times. 2017. *Full Transcript and Video: Kelly Defends Trump's Handling of Soldier's Death and Call to Widow.* October 19. https://www.nytimes.com/2017/10/19/us/politics/statement-kelly-gold-star.html?_r=0.

1553 General John Kelly. 2017. *Press Briefing by Press Secretary Sarah Sanders and Chief of Staff General John Kelly. The White House: Office of the Press Secretary.* October 19. https://www.whitehouse.gov/the-press-office/2017/10/19/press-briefing-press-secretary-sarah-sanders-and-chief-staff-general.

1554 Ibid.

1555 Ibid.

1556 Yamiche Alcindor. 2017. *Rep. Frederica Wilson on Trump: 'That Is Not What You Say to a Grieving Widow'.* October 18. https://www.nytimes.com/2017/10/18/us/politics/congresswoman-wilson-trump-niger-call-widow.html.

1557 Maxwell Tani. 2017. *John Kelly Makes Rare Appearance at White House Briefing to Say He Doesn't 'Think He's Getting Fired Today' and Is Not 'Frustrated' with His Job.* October 12. http://www.businessinsider.com/john-kelly-fired-quitting-frustrated-2017-10.

1558 Jeff Mason. 2017. *White House Chief of Staff Not Quitting, Says Job Is Not to Control Trump.* October 12. https://www.reuters.com/article/us-usa-trump-kelly/white-house-chief-of-staff-not-quitting-says-job-is-not-to-control-trump-idUSKBN1CH2P6.

1559 Ibid.

1560 General John Kelly. 2017. *Press Briefing by Press Secretary Sarah Sanders and Chief of Staff General John Kelly. The White House: Office of the Press Secretary.* October 19.

1561 Larry Barszewski. 2017. *Frederica Wilson 2015 Video Shows John Kelly Got It Wrong.* October 28. http://www.sun-sentinel.com/local/broward/fl-reg-wilson-kelly-tape-of-speech-20171020-story.html?dfdfdfd.

1562 Ibid.

1563 Ibid.

1564 Frederica S. Wilson. n.d. *Congresswoman Frederica S. Wilson Stands by Account of President Trump's Condolence Call to the Widow of Sgt. La David Johnson.* Accessed October 24, 2017. https://wilson.house.gov/media-center/press-releases/congresswoman-frederica-s-wilson-stands-by-account-of-president-trump-s.

1565 Kevin Liptak and Miranda Green. 2017. *Price out as HHS Secretary after Private Plane Scandal.* September 29. http://www.cnn.com/2017/09/29/politics/tom-price-resigns/index.html.

1566   Alana Abramson. 2017. '*We Love This Job.*' *Jeff Sessions Says He Won't Resign Despite Trump Criticism*. July 20. http://time. com/4866280/jeff-sessions-donald-trump-resign-recuse.

1567   Barbara Starr. 2017. *US Launches Investigation into Deadly Niger Ambush and Confusion That Followed*. October 17. http:// edition.cnn.com/2017/10/17/politics/us-niger-military-investigation-confusion/index.html.

1568   Mallory Shelbourne. 2017. *Dem Lawmaker: Deaths of Soldiers in Niger Is Trump's Benghazi*. October 18. http://thehill. com/homenews/house/356114-dem-lawmaker-deaths-of-soldiers-in-niger-is-trumps-benghazi.

1569   Todd Beamon. 2017. *Fla. Legislator Rips Trump for Comment to Soldier's Widow*. October 17. http://www.newsmax.com/ Newsfront/gold-star-phone-call-frederica-wilson-green-beret/2017/10/17/id/820399.

1570   Barbara Starr. 2017. *US Launches Investigation into Deadly Niger Ambush and Confusion That Followed*. October 17.

1571   Lauren Gambino and David Smith. 2015. *House Benghazi Report Faults Military Response, Not Clinton, for Deaths*. June 28. https://www.theguardian.com/us-news/2016/jun/28/house-benghazi-report-clinton-attack-military.

1572   Matt Apuzzo and Maggie Haberman. 2017. *At Least 6 White House Advisers Used Private Email Accounts*. September 25. https://www.nytimes.com/2017/09/25/us/politics/private-email-trump-kushner-bannon.html.

1573   Ibid.

1574   Josh Dawsey and Andrea Peterson. 2017. *White House Launches Probe of Private Email Accounts*. September 28. http:// www.politico.com/story/2017/09/28/white-house-launches-probe-private-email-accounts-243281.

1575   ABC the View. 2017. *Julianne Moore ("Wonderstruck," "Suburbicon"); Patti LuPone (Broadway's "War Paint")*. October 19. http://abc.go.com/shows/the-view/episode-guide.

1576   Ibid.

1577   World Nuclear News. 2017. *EU Committed to Iran Nuclear Deal*. October 16. http://www.world-nuclear-news.org/ NP-EU-committed-to-Iran-nuclear-deal-1610177.html.

1578   Ibid.

1579   Ibid.

1580   James Conca. 2017. *The Iran Nuclear Deal Without the United States*. October 17. https://www.forbes.com/sites/james-conca/2017/10/17/the-iran-nuclear-deal-without-the-united-states/#144e89ec3c94.

1581   Ibid.

1582   World Nuclear News. 2017. *EU Committed to Iran Nuclear Deal*. October 16.

1583   Ibid.

1584   Ibid.

1585   James Conca. 2017. *The Iran Nuclear Deal Without the United States*. October 17.

1586   Ibid.

1587   Ibid.

1588   Ibid.

1589   Ibid.

1590   Ibid.

1591   Mythili Sampathkumar. 2017. *North Korea Says It Is Not Interested in Diplomacy Until It Has Missile Capable of Hitting America*. October 16. http://www.independent.co.uk/news/world/americas/us-politics/north-korea-trump-us-latest-news-diplomacy-not-interested-missile-hit-america-a8003846.html.

1592   Choe Sang-Hun. 2017. *North Korean Hackers Stole U.S.-South Korean Military Plans, Lawmaker Says*. October 10. https:// www.nytimes.com/2017/10/10/world/asia/north-korea-hack-war-plans.html.

1593   Arwa Damon, Ghazi Balkiz and Laura Smith-Spark. 2017. *Raqqa: US-Backed Forces Declare 'Total Liberation' of ISIS Stronghold*. October 20. http://www.cnn.com/2017/10/20/middleeast/raqqa-syria-isis-total-liberation/index.html.

1594   Zachary Cohen and Dan Merica. 2017. *Trump Takes Credit for ISIS 'Giving Up.'* October 17. http://www.cnn. com/2017/10/17/politics/trump-isis-raqqa/index.html.

1595   Ibid.

1596   Isabel Coles and Ali Nabhan. 2017. *Kurds Protesting in Iraq Turn Their Anger against U.S.* October 20. https://www.wsj. com/articles/kurds-protesting-in-iraq-turn-their-anger-against-u-s-1508524008.

1597   Tim Lister. 2015. *ISIS Atrocity in Libya Demonstrates Its Growing Reach in North Africa*. February 17. http://www.cnn. com/2015/02/16/africa/isis-libya-north-africa/index.html.

1598   James Conca. 2017. *The Iran Nuclear Deal Without the United States*. October 17

1599   Jonathan Martin and Mark Landler. 2017. *Bob Corker Says Trump's Recklessness Threatens 'World War III.'* October 8. https:// www.nytimes.com/2017/10/08/us/politics/trump-corker.html?smprod=nytcore-iphone&smid=nytcore-iphone-share.

1600   Ibid.

1601   Ibid.

1602   Jennifer Agiesta. 2017. *CNN Poll: Trump Approval Steady, but More Say He's Leading in the Wrong Direction*. October 17. http://www.cnn.com/2017/10/17/politics/cnn-poll-trump-approval-steady/index.html.

1603   Ryan Struyk. 2017. *6 in 10 People Who Approve of Trump Say They'll Never, Ever, Ever Stop Approving*. August 17.

1604   Dana Bash. 2017. *Steve Bannon Is Looking for Retribution after Alabama Win. And He's Recruiting*. September 28. http:// www.cnn.com/2017/09/28/politics/steve-bannon-retribution-recruiting/index.html.

1605   Mary Kay Linge. 2017. *Bannon Declares War on GOP Establishment*. October 14. http://nypost.com/2017/10/14/ bannon-warns-gop-incumbents-nobody-can-run-and-hide.

1606   Dana Bash. 2017. *Steve Bannon Is Looking for Retribution after Alabama Win. And He's Recruiting.* September 28.

1607   Mary Kay Linge. 2017. *Bannon Declares War on GOP Establishment.* October 14.

1608   Reihan Salam. 2017. *Steve Bannon's Enemy Isn't the Republican Party.* October 12. http://www.slate.com/articles/news_and_politics/politics/2017/10/steve_bannon_s_enemy_isn_t_the_gop_it_s_donald_trump.html.

1609   Terence Burlij and Jennifer Agiesta. 2017. *CNN Poll: Opinion of the Republican Party Falls to All-time Low.* September 25. http://www.cnn.com/2017/09/24/politics/cnn-poll-republican-party-approval/index.html.

1610   Mayra Cuevas. 2017. *Undocumented Husband of Indiana Trump Supporter Deported to Mexico.* April 6. http://www.cnn.com/2017/04/05/us/undocumented-husband-deported/.

1611   Maria Sacchetti. 2017. *ICE Immigration Arrests of Noncriminals Double under Trump.* April 16. https://www.washingtonpost.com/local/immigration-arrests-of-noncriminals-double-under-trump/2017/04/16/98a2f1e2-2096-11e7-be2a-3a1fb24d4671_story.html?utm_term=.75d90c81f488.

1612   Jeff Gammage. 2017. *Adopted Years ago, Thousands Learn They're Not U.S. Citizens.* April 4. http://www.philly.com/philly/news/Adopted-from-Vietnam-as-a-baby---but-told-shes-not-an-American-citizen.html.

1613   The Globe and Mail. 2016. '*Not Flawless': Five Speechwriters Rate Obama's Historic Address to Canada.* June 30. http://www.theglobeandmail.com/news/politics/not-flawless-five-speechwriters-rate-obamas-historic-address-to-canada/article30702288.

1614   Ibid.

1615   Ibid.

1616   Jesse Mechanic. 2017. *Our Criminal Justice System Is Broken and Jeff Sessions Has No Interest in Fixing It.* April 12. http://www.huffingtonpost.com/entry/our-criminal-justice-system-is-broken-and-jeff-sessions_us_58ee52f0e4b0a3bddb60a61e.

1617   Desmond Tutu. n.d. *Desmond Tutu.* Accessed August 30, 2017. https://www.goodreads.com/quotes/132838-differences-are-not-intended-to-separate-to-alienate-we-are.

1618   Philip Elliott. 2017. *These Ohio Voters Made Trump President. They're Still with Him.* July 25.

1619   Robert Ferris. 2017. *Why Voters Might be Choosing Dominant, Authoritarian Leaders around the World.* June 12. https://www.cnbc.com/2017/06/12/why-voters-might-be-choosing-dominant-authoritarian-leaders-around-the-world.html.

1620   Ibid.

1621   Ibid.

1622   Laura Hankin. 2017. *3 Ways the GOP's Tax Plan Could Hurt Families If It Becomes Law.* Accessed January 4, 2018. https://www.romper.com/p/3-ways-the-gops-tax-plan-could-hurt-families-if-it-becomes-law-6772656.

1623   Sam Fleming and Lauren Leatherby. 2017. *US Richest 1% to Gain Most from Republican Tax Plan, Report Says.* November 8. https://www.ft.com/content/0de96cb6-c4ce-11e7-a1d2-6786f39ef675.

1624   Drew Harwell and Jonathan O'Connell. 2017. *The Many Ways President Trump Would Benefit from the GOP's Tax Plan.* November 10. https://www.washingtonpost.com/business/economy/the-many-ways-president-trump-would-benefit-from-the-gops-tax-plan/2017/11/10/d82c8116-c4ba-11e7-aae0-cb18a8c29c65_story.html?utm_term=.9f4aca2bf57c.

1625   PBS. 2017. *Who Benefits from the New GOP Tax Plan?* December 16. https://www.pbs.org/newshour/show/who-benefits-from-the-new-gop-tax-plan#transcript.

1626   Bob Bryan. 2017. *The Government Scorekeeper Says the GOP Tax Bill Would Fall Short of Republicans' Promises.* November 30. http://www.businessinsider.com/trump-tax-plan-senate-bill-jct-dynamic-scoring-analysis-2017-11.

1627   Andrew Van Dam. 2017. *The Essential Tradeoff in the Republican Tax Bill, in One Chart.* December 16. https://www.washingtonpost.com/news/wonk/wp/2017/12/16/the-essential-tradeoff-in-the-republican-tax-bill-in-one-chart/?utm_term=.f50d522b39ba.

1628   Annie Lowrey. 2017. *The 7 Myths of the GOP Tax Bill.* December 1. https://www.theatlantic.com/business/archive/2017/12/the-7-myths-of-the-gop-tax-bill/547322/.

1629   Ibid.

1630   Matthew Yglesias. 2017. *Watch CEOs Admit They Won't Actually Invest More If Tax Reform Passes.* November 15. https://www.vox.com/policy-and-politics/2017/11/15/16653698/ceos-investment-tax-reform.

1631   Kimberly Clausing and Edward Kleinbard. 2017. *Trump's Economists Say a Corporate Tax Cut Will Raise Wages by $4,000. It Doesn't Add Up.* October 20. https://www.vox.com/the-big-idea/2017/10/20/16506256/cea-report-corporate-taxes-wages-boost-job-growth.

1632   Ibid.

1633   Mike Stone. 2017. *CEOs Suggest Trump Tax Cut May Lift Investors More than Jobs.* October 26. https://www.reuters.com/article/us-usa-tax-companies/ceos-suggest-trump-tax-cut-may-lift-investors-more-than-jobs-iduskbn1cv38q.

1634   Danielle Paquette. 2018. *U.S. Added 148,000 Jobs in December, in Lagging Finish to Year of Strong Growth.* January 5. https://www.washingtonpost.com/news/wonk/wp/2018/01/05/u-s-added-200000-jobs-in-december-capping-year-of-strong-growth-economists-predict/?utm_term=.188f7d7cd49f.

1635   Randi Druzin. 2018. Canada's Social Fabric Bares Raw Threads. January 26. https://www.usnews.com/news/best-countries/articles/2018-01-26/canada-confronts-growing-tensions-between-its-ethnic-communities.

1636   Adam Lusher. 2016. *What Actually Happens at the World's Most Secretive Gathering of Global Elites, and Who Is Attending.* June 7. http://www.independent.co.uk/news/world/bilderberg-group-meeting-what-is-it-and-who-is-attending-global-elites-a7069561.html.

1637   Ibid.

1638 Ibid.

1639 Catherine E. Shoichet and Euan McKirdy. 2016. *Brazil's Senate Ousts Dilma Rousseff in Impeachment Vote.* September 1. http://www.cnn.com/2016/08/31/americas/brazil-rousseff-impeachment-vote/.

1640 BBC. 2012. *Ai Weiwei: China's Dissident Artist.* July 20. http://www.bbc.com/news/world-asia-pacific-12997324.

1641 Eli Watkins and Kevin Liptak. 2017. *All 5 Living Former Presidents Launch Appeal for Help for Harvey Victims.* September 8. http://www.cnn.com/2017/09/07/politics/george-hw-bush-former-presidents-harvey/index.html.

1642 Ibid.

1643 Samantha Cooney. 2017. *Here Are All the Public Figures Who've Been Accused of Sexual Misconduct after Harvey Weinstein.* December 15. http://time.com/5015204/harvey-weinstein-scandal/.

1644 Ibid.

1645 Elisabeth Ponsot. 2017. *These Nine Women Have Accused Roy Moore of Sexual Misconduct.* December 7. https://qz.com/1147348/these-nine-women-have-accused-roy-moore-of-sexual-misconduct/.

1646 Benjamin Goggin. 2017. *Twice-fired State Supreme Court Justice Wins Alabama Primary — Here's What You Need to Know.* September 26. https://digg.com/2017/alabama-primary-senate.

1647 Ibid.

1648 Michael Martin. 2017. *Roy Moore: Getting Rid of Constitutional Amendments after 10th Would 'Eliminate Many Problems.'* December 11. https://www.metro.us/news/politics/roy-moore-constitutional-amendments.

1649 Ibid.

1650 Whoopie Goldberg, Joy Behar, Sonny Hostin, Sarah Haines, and Meghan McCain. 2017. *Day of Hot Topics.* November 30. http://abc.go.com/shows/the-view/episode-guide/2017-11/30-thursday-november-30-2017.

1651 Henry Grabar, 2018. *150,000 American Students Have Experienced a School Shooting.* February 15. https://slate.com/news-and-politics/2018/02/150-000-american-students-have-experienced-a-school-shooting.html.

1652 Greg Gutfeld. 2017. *Gutfeld: Obama Compares Trump to Hitler.* December 7. http://www.foxnews.com/transcript/2017/12/07/gutfeld-obama-compares-trump-to-hitler.html.

1653 Ibid.

1654 Jake Tapper, Amanda Carpenter, Marc Lotter, Nina Turner, and Bakari Sellers. 2017. *Obama Invokes Nazi Germany in Warning about Today's Politics.* December 10. http://transcripts.cnn.com/transcripts/1712/10/sotu.01.html.

1655 Global Affairs Canada. 2018. *Minister Champagne Welcomes Progress on the Comprehensive and Progressive Trans-Pacific Partnership.* January 23. https://www.canada.ca/en/global-affairs/news/2017/11/minister_champagnewelcomesprogressonthecomprehensiveandprogressi.html.

1656 Elaine Glusac. 2017. *International Tourism to the U.S. Declined in Early 2017.* September 19. https://www.nytimes.com/2017/09/19/travel/tourism-united-states-international-decline.html.

1657 Rebecca Savransky . 2018. *Tourism Down in Us since Trump Took Office.* January 24. http://thehill.com/policy/transportation/370437-tourism-down-in-us-since-trump-took-office.

1658 Donald J. Trump. 2018 4:49 PM. *Twitter Post.* January 2. https://twitter.com/realdonaldtrump/status/948355557022420992.

1659 Shehab Al-Makahleh. 2017. *Putin in Ankara to Forge Alliance of Russia, Turkey and Iran.* September 26. http://english.alarabiya.net/en/views/news/middle-east/2017/09/26/Putin-in-Ankara-to-forge-alliance-of-Russia-Turkey-and-Iran.html.

1660 Tom Batchelor. 2017. *Austria's Conservatives Strike Deal with Far-Right Party Founded by Ex-Nazis to Form Coalition Government.* December 15. http://www.independent.co.uk/news/world/europe/austria-government-far-right-nazis-party-deal-latest-a8113626.html.

1661 Anthony Mills. 2016. *Austria's Far-right Seals Pact with Russia.* December 20. https://euobserver.com/beyond-brussels/136356.

1662 Paul Hockenos. 2018. *Germany Has a Far-Right Enemy Within.* March 27. https://www.cnn.com/2018/03/27/opinions/afd-german-enemy-within-intl/index.html.

1663 Kim Hjelmgaard. 2017. *There Is Meddling in Germany's Election — Not by Russia, but by U.S. Right Wing.* September 20. https://www.usatoday.com/story/news/world/2017/09/20/meddling-germany-election-not-by-u-s-right-wing/676142001/.

1664 Rated by *Media Bias/FactCheck* as having a right to center bias with high factual reporting.

1665 Maria Snegovaya. 2017. *Russian Propaganda in Germany: More Effective than You Think.* October 17. https://www.the-american-interest.com/2017/10/17/russian-propaganda-germany-effective-think/.

1666 Kim Hjelmgaard. 2017. *There Is Meddling in Germany's Election — Not by Russia, but by U.S. Right Wing.* September 20.

1667 Ibid.

1668 Ibid.

1669 Ibid.

1670 Ibid.

1671 AP. 2017. *Russian Trolls Used Social Media to Fuel NFL National Anthem Debate, Senator Says.* September 28. http://www.foxnews.com/politics/2017/09/28/russian-trolls-used-social-media-to-fuel-nfl-national-anthem-debate-senator-says.html.

1672 Aaron Sorkin. 2014. *The Newsroom Script Episode 1 Quotes.* Accessed October 9, 2017. https://www.goodreads.com/work/quotes/23633463-the-newsroom-script-episode-1.

1673 Ranking America. n.d. *Health Care.* Accessed October 9, 2017. https://rankingamerica.wordpress.com/?s=health+care+.

1674　World Factbook. n.d. *Country Comparison: Distribution of Family Income - Gini Index.* Accessed October 9, 2017. https://www.cia.gov/library/publications/the-world-factbook/rankorder/2172rank.html.

1675　United Nations Office on Drugs and Crime. n.d. *Global Study on Homicide.* Accessed October 9, 2017. http://www.unodc.org/gsh/en/data.html.

1676　Ibid.

1677　Ranking America. n.d. *The U.S. Ranks 43rd in Homicide Rates.* Accessed October 9, 2017. https://rankingamerica.wordpress.com/tag/crime/.

1678　World Prison Brief. n.d. *Highest to Lowest - Prison Population Total.* Accessed October 9, 2017. http://www.prisonstudies.org/highest-to-lowest/prison-population-total?field_region_taxonomy_tid=All.

1679　Ranking America. n.d. *The U.S. Ranks 64th in Human Security.* Accessed America 9, 2017. https://rankingamerica.wordpress.com/category/health-and-welfare/page/19/.

1680　David A. Hastings. 2009. *From Human Development to Human Security: A Prototype Human Security Index.* October. http://www.unescap.org/sites/default/files/wp-09-03_0.pdf.

1681　Leyland Cecco. 2016. *Canada Takes Second Spot Globally on Social-progress Ranking.* June 29. https://beta.theglobeandmail.com/news/social-progress-index-canada-isalright/article30647376/?ref=http://www.theglobeandmail.com&.

1682　Ranking America. n.d. *The U.S. Ranks 17th in Happiness.* Accessed October 9, 2017. https://rankingamerica.wordpress.com/?s=happiness.

1683　John McCain. 2018. Statement by SASC Chairman John McCain on President Trump Congratulating Vladimir Putin. March 20. https://www.mccain.senate.gov/public/index.cfm/2018/3/statement-by-sasc-chairman-john-mccain-on-president-trump-congratulating-vladimir-putin.

1684　Catharine Tunney and Joe Lofaro. 2018. *Sen. Lynn Beyak Kicked Out of Conservative Caucus* after Refusing to *Remove 'Racist' Comments Online.* January 5. http://www.cbc.ca/news/politics/lynn-beyak-kicked-out-conservative-caucus-1.4474130.

1685　BBC. 2018. *Clinton Foundation Investigated by Justice Department.* January 5. http://www.bbc.com/news/world-us-canada-42579732.

1686　Aaron Couch. 2011. *Martin Luther King Day: 10 Memorable MLK Quotes.* The Christian Science Monitor. January 17. https://www.csmonitor.com/USA/2011/0117/Martin-Luther-King-Day-10-memorable-MLK-quotes/Let-no-man-pull-you-low.

1687　US News. 2018. United States. Accessed January 25, 2018. https://www.usnews.com/news/best-countries/united-states.

1688　US News. 2018. Best Countries Overall. Accessed January 25, 2018. https://www.usnews.com/news/best-countries/rankings-index.

1689　Julie Ray. 2018. *World's Approval of U.S. Leadership Drops to New Low.* January 18. http://news.gallup.com/poll/225761/world-approval-leadership-drops-new-low.aspx.

1690　US News. 2018. America Slips in the Eyes of the World. Accessed: January 25, 2018. https://www.usnews.com/news/best-countries/articles/us-news-unveils-best-countries-rankings.

1691　Ibid.

1692　Alan Dershowitz. 2017. *Dershowitz: Mueller's Special Counsel Appointment Begs the Question -- Are Our Civil Liberties Now at Risk?* May 20. http://www.foxnews.com/opinion/2017/05/20/dershowitz-muellers-special-counsel-appointment-begs-question-are-our-civil-liberties-now-at-risk.html.

Bibliography

911 Memorial & Museum. n.d. *Facts about 911*. Accessed January 29, 2017. https://www.911memorial.org/faq-about-911.

A&E. 2016. *This Day in History: Slavery Abolished in America*. Accessed December 20, 2017. http://www.history.com/this-day-in-history/slavery-abolished-in-america.

Abadi, Mark. 2017. *Trump Did a 180 on Harvey and Irma after He Was Asked about Climate Change*. September 24. http://www.businessinsider.com/trump-response-to-hurricane-harvey-and-irma-climate-change-2017-9.

ABC. 2016. *National Anthem Backlash Builds for 49ers QB Colin Kaepernick*. August 30. http://abcnews.go.com/GMA/video/national-anthem-backlash-builds-49ers-qb-colin-kaepernick-41737425.

ABC The View. 2017. *Julianne Moore ("Wonderstruck," "Suburbicon"); Patti LuPone (Broadway's "War Paint")*. October 19. http://abc.go.com/shows/the-view/episode-guide October 19.

Abelson, Reed. 2016. *Donald Trump Says He May Keep Parts of Obama Health Care Act*. November 11. https://www.nytimes.com/2016/11/12/business/insurers-unprepared-for-obamacare-repeal.html?mcubz=1.

Abramson, Alana. 2017. *President Trump Just Spoke about Everything from Puerto Rico to Robert Mueller*. October 16. http://time.com/4984507/donald-trump-mitch-mcconnell-rose-garden-press-conference/.

—. 2017. *'We Love This Job.' Jeff Sessions Says He Won't Resign Despite Trump Criticism*. July 20. http://time.com/4866280/jeff-sessions-donald-trump-resign-recuse/.

Abramson, Jill. 2016. *This May Shock You: Hillary Clinton Is Fundamentally Honest*. March 28. https://www.theguardian.com/commentisfree/2016/mar/28/hillary-clinton-honest-transparency-jill-abramson.

Ackerman, Spencer. 2017. *Devin Nunes Steps aside from House Intelligence Committee's Russia Inquiry*. April 6. https://www.theguardian.com/world/2017/apr/06/devin-nunes-leaves-house-intelligence-committee-russia-inquiry-ethics-inquiry.

ACLU. 2016. *The Trump Memos: The ACLU's Constitutional Analysis of the Public*. https://www.aclu.org/report/trump-memos.

Adair, Bill, and Lauren Carroll. 2016. *Checking Patricia Smith's Claims about Clinton and Benghazi*. July 18. http://www.politifact.com/truth-o-meter/article/2016/jul/18/checking-patricia-smiths-claims-about-clinton-and-/.

Advisory Board. 2017. *Where the States Stand on Medicaid Expansion*. May 19. https://www.advisory.com/daily-briefing/resources/primers/medicaidmap.

Agiesta, Jennifer. 2017. *CNN Poll: Trump Approval Steady, but More Say He's Leading in the Wrong Direction*. October 17. http://www.cnn.com/2017/10/17/politics/cnn-poll-trump-approval-steady/index.html.

Akin, Stephanie. 2016. *Donald Trump and the Russian Connection*. December 28. http://www.rollcall.com/news/politics/donald-trump-russia-vladimir-putin.

Alcindor, Yamiche. 2017. *Paul Manafort Expects to Be Indicted, Longtime Trump Adviser Says*. September 26. https://www.nytimes.com/2017/09/26/us/politics/roger-stone-testimony-paul-manafort.html?mcubz=0&_r=0.

—. 2017. *Rep. Frederica Wilson on Trump: 'That Is Not What You Say to a Grieving Widow'*. October 18. https://www.nytimes.com/2017/10/18/us/politics/congresswoman-wilson-trump-niger-call-widow.html.

Alexander, Harriet. 2017. *Donald Trump Wades into French Election with Apparent Endorsement of Marine Le Pen after Paris Attack*. April 21. http://www.telegraph.co.uk/news/2017/04/21/donald-trump-wades-french-election-apparent-endorsement-marine/.

AlIsalm. n.d. *Why Does the Quran Say that Infidels Should Be Killed?* Accessed September 19, 2016. https://www.alislam.org/egazette/updates/why-does-the-quran-say-that-infidels-should-be-killed/.

Al-Makahleh, Shehab. 2017. *Putin in Ankara to Forge Alliance of Russia, Turkey and Iran*. September 26. http://english.alarabiya.net/en/views/news/middle-east/2017/09/26/Putin-in-Ankara-to-forge-alliance-of-Russia-Turkey-and-Iran.html.

Amadeo, Kimberly. 2017. *What Is the GDP Growth Rate?* June 12. https://www.thebalance.com/what-is-the-gdp-growth-rate-3306016.

American Presidency Project (APP). n.d. *Franklin D. Roosevelt.* Accessed October 9, 2017. http://www.presidency.ucsb.edu/ws/?pid=15545.

American Press Institute. *The Elements of Journalism.* Accessed December 29, 2017. https://www.americanpressinstitute.org/journalism-essentials/what-is-journalism/elements-journalism/.

Angelou, Maya. n.d. *Maya Angelou Quotes.* Accessed October 9, 2017. https://www.brainyquote.com/quotes/quotes/m/mayaangelo148650.html.

Answer Wiki. 2014. *The Holocaust: How Is World War II History Taught in Germany?* July 13. https://www.quora.com/The-Holocaust-How-is-World-War-II-history-taught-in-Germany.

AP. 2016. *Canada Sets Record for New Vehicle Sales in 2015.* January 5. http://www.cbc.ca/news/canada/windsor/canada-sets-record-for-new-vehicle-sales-in-2015-1.3390498.

—. 2016. *Charity Watchdog Gives Perfect Rating to Clinton Foundation, but….* September 1. http://www.nj.com/politics/index.ssf/2016/09/clinton_foundation_gets_four_stars_from_charity_wa.html.

—. 2016. *Donald Trump Calls Hillary Clinton the Devil.* August 2. https://www.theguardian.com/us-news/video/2016/aug/02/donald-trump-calls-hillary-clinton-the-devil-video.

—. 2017. *'Getting the Upper Hand' against Deadly Wildfires.* October 15. https://www.cnbc.com/2017/10/15/california-wildfires-death-toll-reaches-40-fires-now-100-miles-wide.html.

—. 2016. *House Republicans Want a New Hillary Clinton Investigation.* July 8. http://fortune.com/2016/07/08/house-republicans-new-clinton-investigation/.

—. 2006. *Lawmaker's Son Sentenced for Slashing Tires.* April 26. http://www.nbcnews.com/id/12498215/ns/politics/t/lawmakers-son-sentenced-slashing-tires/.

—. 2016. *Melania Trump Releases Letter from Immigration Lawyer in Bid to Kill Rumours She Worked in U.S. Illegally.* September 15. http://nationalpost.com/news/world/melania-trump-releases-letter-from-immigration-lawyer-in-bid-to-kill-rumours-she-worked-in-u-s-illegally.

—. 2016. *Melania Trump Was Paid for Modeling Jobs in US before Gaining Work Visa, Records Show.* November 5. https://www.theguardian.com/us-news/2016/nov/05/melania-trump-was-paid-modeling-before-work-visa-records-show.

—. 2016. *Melania Trump Worked in the U.S. without Legal Permission.* November 5. http://fortune.com/2016/11/05/melania-trump-visa-immigration/.

—. 2017. *Michael Flynn, Fired Once by Obama, Now Resigns to Trump.* February 14. http://www.oregonlive.com/today/index.ssf/2017/02/michael_flynn_fired_once_by_a.html.

—. 2017. *Petition Calling on UK to Cancel Donald Trump State Visit Reaches 500,000 Signatures.* January 29. https://globalnews.ca/news/3212492/petition-uk-cancel-state-visit-trump/.

—. 2017. *Russian Trolls Used Social Media to Fuel NFL National Anthem Debate, Senator Says.* September 28. http://www.foxnews.com/politics/2017/09/28/russian-trolls-used-social-media-to-fuel-nfl-national-anthem-debate-senator-says.html.

—. 2017. *Ted Koppel Calmly Tells Sean Hannity He's 'Bad for America.'* March 27. https://www.usatoday.com/story/news/politics/2017/03/27/ted-koppel-calmly-explains-sean-hannity-why-hes-bad-for-america/99680636/.

—. 2016. *The Latest: Trump Taps Citizens United President as Deputy.* September 2. http://www.providencejournal.com/news/20160901/latest-trump-taps-citizens-united-president-as-deputy.

—. 2017. *Trump Says Puerto Rico in Trouble after Hurricane, Suffering from 'Broken Infrastructure' and 'Massive Debt.'* September 26. https://www.cnbc.com/2017/09/25/trump-says-puerto-rico-in-trouble-after-hurricane-debt-must-be-dealt-with.html.

—. 2016. *Trump, Clinton Respond to New York City Explosion.* September 18. http://www.cnbc.com/2016/09/18/trump-clinton-respond-to-new-york-city-explosion.html.

—. 2017. *U.S. Ambassador to the UN: No Question Russia Meddled in Election.* April 2. http://news.nationalpost.com/news/world/u-s-ambassador-to-the-un-no-question-russia-meddled-in-election.

—. 2017. *Widespread Anger, Opposition from World Leaders at Trump Travel Ban.* January 29. http://www.macleans.ca/politics/widespread-anger-opposition-from-world-leaders-at-trump-travel-ban/.

Apuzzo, Matt, and Maggie Haberman. 2017. *At Least 6 White House Advisers Used Private Email Accounts.* September 25. https://www.nytimes.com/2017/09/25/us/politics/private-email-trump-kushner-bannon.html.

Asher, Jay. n.d. *Jay Asher > Quotes > Quotable Quote.* Accessed June 16, 2016. https://www.goodreads.com/quotes/164355-no-one-knows-for-certain-how-much-impact-they-have.

Astor, Maggie, Christina Caron, and Daniel Victor. 2017. *A Guide to the Charlottesville Aftermath.* August 13. https://www.nytimes.com/2017/08/13/us/charlottesville-virginia-overview.html?mcubz=1.

Atran, Scott. 2015. *Mindless Terrorists? The Truth about Isis Is Much Worse.* November 15. https://www.theguardian.com/commentisfree/2015/nov/15/terrorists-isis.

Bachman, Jonathan. 2016. *Three Countries Urge Caution Traveling to U.S. Amid Protests, Violence.* July 10. http://www.reuters.com/article/us-usa-police-travel-idUSKCN0ZQ0RM.

Bacon, John. 2016. *After Trump Chat, Putin's Airstrikes Pound Syria.* November 15. http://www.usatoday.com/story/news/world/2016/11/15/after-trump-chat-putins-airstrikes-pound-syria/93876876/.

Bagli, Charles. 2016. *How Donald Trump Bankrupted His Atlantic City Casinos, but Still Earned Millions.* June 11. http://www.nytimes.com/2016/06/12/nyregion/donald-trump-atlantic-city.html.

Bahadur, Nina. 2015. *18 Real Things Donald Trump Has Actually Said about Women.* August 19. http://www.huffingtonpost.com/entry/18-real-things-donald-trump-has-said-about-women_us_55d356a8e4b07addcb442023.

Bailey, Sarah Pulliam. 2017. *Megachurch Pastor Resigns from Trump's Evangelical Council.* August 18. https://www.washingtonpost.com/news/acts-of-faith/wp/2017/08/18/megachurch-pastor-resigns-from-trumps-evangelical-council/?utm_term=.0b59a080001a.

Baker, Peter, and Julie Hirschfeld Davis. 2016. *U.S. Finalizes Deal to Give Israel $38 Billion in Military Aid.* September 13. http://www.nytimes.com/2016/09/14/world/middleeast/israel-benjamin-netanyahu-military-aid.html.

Baker, Russ. 1998. *Portrait of a Political "Pit Bull."* December 22. https://www.salon.com/1998/12/22/newsa950556369/.

Balz, Dan. 2016. *How Everyone Looks Bad Because Bill Clinton Met with Loretta Lynch.* July 2. https://www.washingtonpost.com/politics/how-everyone-looks-bad-because-bill-clinton-met-with-loretta-lynch/2016/07/02/a7807adc-3ff4-11e6-a66f-aa6c1883b6b1_story.html.

Barbara Lee Family Foundation. 2011. *Turning Point: The Changing Landscape for Women Candidates.* Cambridge: Barbara Lee Family Foundation. http://www.barbaraleefoundation.org/research/turning-point-2010/.

Barlow, Maude. 2015. *NAFTA's ISDS: Why Canada Is One of the Most Sued Countries in the World.* October 23. http://www.commondreams.org/views/2015/10/23/naftas-isds-why-canada-one-most-sued-countries-world.

Barrett, Wayne. 2016. *Meet Donald Trump's Top FBI Fanboy.* October 3. http://www.thedailybeast.com/articles/2016/11/03/meet-donald-trump-s-top-fbi-fanboy.html.

Barro, Josh. 2015. *Trump Plan Is Tax Cut for the Rich, Even Hedge Fund.* September 28. http://www.nytimes.com/2015/09/29/upshot/trump-plan-is-tax-cut-for-the-rich-even-hedge-fund-managers.html.

Barszewski, Larry. 2017. *Frederica Wilson 2015 Video Shows John Kelly Got It Wrong.* October 28. http://www.sun-sentinel.com/local/broward/fl-reg-wilson-kelly-tape-of-speech-20171020-story.html?dfdfdfd.

Bash, Dana. 2017. *Steve Bannon Is Looking for Retribution after Alabama Win. And He's Recruiting.* September 28. http://www.cnn.com/2017/09/28/politics/steve-bannon-retribution-recruiting/index.html.

Batchelor, Tom. 2017. *Austria's Conservatives Strike Deal with Far-Right Party Founded by Ex-Nazis to Form Coalition Government.* December 15. http://www.independent.co.uk/news/world/europe/austria-government-far-right-nazis-party-deal-latest-a8113626.html.

Battagello, Dave. 2014. *Windsor's Air Quality Better, but Still among Worst in Ontario, Report Says.* April 24. http://windsorstar.com/health/windsors-air-quality-better-but-still-among-worst-in-ontario-report-says.

Bauman, Zygmunt. n.d. *Zygmunt Bauman Quotes.* Accessed October 9, 2017. https://www.brainyquote.com/quotes/quotes/z/zygmuntbau536850.html.

Bazelon, Emily. 2017. *The Voter Fraud Case Jeff Sessions Lost and Can't Escape.* January 9. https://www.nytimes.com/2017/01/09/magazine/the-voter-fraud-case-jeff-sessions-lost-and-cant-escape.html.

BBC. 2012. *Ai Weiwei: China's Dissident Artist.* July 20. http://www.bbc.com/news/world-asia-pacific-12997324.

—. 2018. *Clinton Foundation Investigated by Justice Department.* January 5. http://www.bbc.com/news/world-us-canada-42579732.

—. 2017. *Donald Trump: A List of Potential Conflicts of Interest.* April 18. http://www.bbc.com/news/world-us-canada-38069298.

—. 2015. *France: Marine Le Pen Goes on Trial over Muslim Remarks.* October 20. http://www.bbc.com/news/world-europe-34580169.

—. 2017. *G7 Talks: Trump Isolated over Paris Climate Change.* May 28. http://www.bbc.com/news/world-europe-40069636.

—. 2016. *'I Like Waterboarding a Lot,' Says Donald Trump.* June 29. http://www.bbc.com/news/election-us-2016-36664752.

—. 2016. *TPP: What Is It and Why Does It Matter?* November 22. http://www.bbc.com/news/business-32498715.

—. 2016. *Trump v Clinton: Comparing Their Economic Plans.* September 16. http://www.bbc.com/news/business-37013670.

—. 2016. *US Police Shootings: How Many Die Each Year?* July 18. http://www.bbc.com/news/magazine-36826297.

Beamon, Todd. 2016. *Fla. Legislator Rips Trump for Comment to Soldier's Widow.* http://www.newsmax.com/Newsfront/gold-star-phone-call-frederica-wilson-green-beret/2017/10/17/id/820399.

Beauchamp, Zack. 2017. *Trump's Bizarre, Dangerous Calls with the Leaders of Mexico and Australia, Explained.* February 2. http://www.vox.com/world/2017/2/2/14483560/trump-mexico-australia-calls.

Beckwith, Ryan Teague. 2015. *Trump: Debate Moderator Had 'Blood Coming out of Her Wherever.'* August 7. http://time.com/3989652/donald-trump-megyn-kelly-blood-wherever/.

Beers, David. 2017. *The Political Pearls of Kevin O'Leary.* January 18. https://thetyee.ca/Opinion/2017/01/18/Political-Pearls-Kevin-OLeary/.

Bender, Jeremy. 2014. *Report: The US Military's Top Spy is Being Forced.* April 30. http://www.businessinsider.com/michael-t-flynn-fired-from-dia-2014-4.

Benen, Steve. 2016. *Trump Backs Abortion Ban, Calls for 'Punishment' for Women.* March 30. http://www.msnbc.com/rachel-maddow-show/trump-backs-abortion-ban-calls-punishment-women.

Bennett, Brian. 2017. *Citing No Evidence, Trump Accuses Obama of Tapping His Phones during the Election.* March 4. http://www.latimes.com/politics/la-pol-updates-everything-president-trump-accuses-obama-of-wiretapping-1488648248-htmlstory.html.

—. 2017. *Trump to Support 'Merit-Based' Immigration System That Would Cut Number of U.S. Migrants in Half.* August 2. https://www.thestar.com/news/world/2017/08/02/trump-to-support-merit-based-immigration-system-that-would-cut-number-of-us-migrants-in-half.html.

Berdy, Michele A. 2016. *Trump to Putin: What'd You Call Me?* March 25. https://themoscowtimes.com/articles/trump-to-putin-whatd-you-call-me-52252.

Berenson, Tessa. 2016. *Donald Trump Calls for 'Complete Shutdown' of Muslim Entry to U.S.* July 20. http://time.com/4139476/donald-trump-shutdown-muslim-immigration/.

Bergevin, Philippe. 2008. *The Global Financial Crisis and Its Impact on Canada.* December. https://lop.parl.ca/content/lop/ResearchPublications/prb0834_05-e.htm.

Berke, Jeremy. 2016. *Obama on Fidel Castro's Death: 'History Will Record and Judge the Enormous Impact of this Singular Figure.'* November 26. http://www.businessinsider.com/obama-fidel-castro-death-dead-2016-11.

—. 2016. *Trump: 'Fidel Castro is Dead!'* November 26. http://www.businessinsider.com/trump-fidel-castro-dead-death-2016-11.

Berkowitz, Bonnie, and Denise Lu Lazaro Gamio. 2016. *The Math of Mass Shootings.* July 27. https://www.washingtonpost.com/graphics/national/mass-shootings-in-america/.

Berrien, Hank. 2016. *8 Times Donald Trump Showed He Hated Women.* March 24. http://www.dailywire.com/news/4391/8-times-donald-trump-showed-he-hated-women-hank-berrien.

Berry, Lorraine. 2016. *'A Lot of What He Believes, We Believe' — KKK Grand Imperial Wizard Endorses Trump.* April 20. http://www.rawstory.com/2016/04/a-lot-of-what-he-believes-we-believe-kkk-grand-imperial-wizard-endorses-trump/.

Bertrand, Natasha. 2017. *Report: Comey Acted on Clinton Email Probe Based on Russian Intel That He Knew Was Fake.* May 26. http://www.businessinsider.com/james-comey-russian-intelligence-fake-cnn-hillary-email-2017-5.

Bierce, Ambrose. 2016. *Ambrose Bierce Quotes.* Accessed June 16, 2017. http://www.goodreads.com/quotes/1470-prejudice-is-a-vagrant-opinion-without-visible-means-of-support.

Bierman, Noah. 2016. *Donald Trump Shakes Up Campaign by Hiring Executive from Conservative Breitbart News to Top Post.* August 17. http://www.latimes.com/politics/la-na-pol-trump-campaign-20160817-snap-story.html.

Biskupic, Joan. 2017. *Why Joe Arpaio Was Found Guilty.* August 24. http://www.cnn.com/2017/08/24/politics/why-joe-arpaio-was-found-guilty/index.html.

Bixby, Scott. 2016. *Trump on Colin Kaepernick: 'He Should Find a Country That Works Better for Him.' Wouldn't Lose Voters* August 29. https://www.theguardian.com/sport/2016/aug/29/donald-trump-colin-kaepernick-national-anthem-protest.

Black, Allida, June Hopkins, John Sears, Christopher Alhambra, Mary Jo Binker, Christopher Brick, John S. Emrich, Eugenia Gusev, Kristen E. Gwinn, and Bryan D. Peery. 2003. *Eleanor Roosevelt, John Kennedy, and the Election of 1960: A Project of the Eleanor Roosevelt Papers.* https://www.gwu.edu/~erpapers/mep/displaydoc.cfm?docid=erps-acism.

Blake, Aaron. 2016. *Donald Trump Jr. Says Media Would Be 'Warming Up the Gas Chamber' If Trump Lied Like Clinton.* September 15. https://www.washingtonpost.com/news/the-fix/wp/2016/09/15/donald-trump-jr-says-media-would-be-warming-up-the-gas-chamber-if-trump-lied-like-clinton/.

—. 2017. *The 11 Most Important Lines from the New Intelligence Report on Russia's Hacking.* January 6. https://www.washingtonpost.com/news/the-fix/wp/2017/01/06/the-most-important-lines-from-the-new-intelligence-report-on-russias-hacking/?utm_term=.eca440ea7b47.

—. 2017. *Trump's Puerto Rico Poll Numbers Are Worse than Bush's after Katrina.* October 12. https://www.washingtonpost.com/news/the-fix/wp/2017/10/12/puerto-rico-is-officially-a-problem-for-trump-his-numbers-are-worse-than-bushs-post-katrina/?utm_term=.154168ee73bf.

—. 2017. *Why Trump Should Be Very Afraid of James Comey's Memos.* May 17. https://www.washingtonpost.com/news/the-fix/wp/2017/05/16/president-trump-should-be-very-afraid-of-james-comeys-memos/?utm_term=.0532e8beaad0.

Bloxham, Andy. 2011. *The World According to Donald Trump.* June 20. http://www.telegraph.co.uk/news/celebritynews/8586180/The-world-according-to-Donald-Trump.html.

Bodhipaksa. n.d. *Holding onto Anger is Like Drinking Poison and Expecting the Other Person to Die.* Accessed November 18, 2016. http://fakebuddhaquotes.com/holding-onto-anger-is-like-drinking-poison/.

Bonaparte, Napoleon. n.d. *Napoleon Bonaparte (1769-1821) Quotes.* Accessed October 31, 2017. http://www.worlddiplomacy.org/Quotes/NapoleonBonapartequotes.html.

Borger, Julian, and Alec Luhn. 2017. *Donald Trump Says US Relations with Russia 'May Be at All-time Low.'* April 13. https://www.theguardian.com/us-news/2017/apr/12/us-russia-relations-tillerson-moscow-press-conference.

Bottoni, Judi. 2017. *NAFTA, Dairy and Softwood: What's Going on with Trump? A Guide to the Trade File.* April 28. http://www.theglobeandmail.com/news/politics/nafta-dairy-softwood-what-do-trump-and-canada-want/article33715250/.

Boutilier, Alex. 2017. *Kevin O'Leary Says His Past Comments Were Good Television, Not Policy.* January 18. https://www.thestar.com/news/canada/2017/01/18/kevin-oleary-announces-run-for-conservative-leadership.html.

Boyajian, David. 2013. *The Myth of Turkish Secularism.* December 16. http://dissidentvoice.org/2013/12/the-myth-of-turkish-secularism/.

Bradner, Eric. 2016. *Melania Trump: Donald Trump Was 'Egged on' into 'Boy Talk.'* October 18. http://www.cnn.com/2016/10/17/politics/melania-trump-interview/index.html.

Bradner, Eric, and Eugene Scott. 2016. *'Mothers of the Movement' Makes Case for Hillary Clinton.* July 26. http://www.cnn.com/2016/07/26/politics/mothers-movement-dnc-hillary-clinton/.

Brangham, William, interview by Hari Sreenivaan. 2016. *Does Gender Bias Explain Why Hillary Clinton Has Fared So Poorly with White Male Voters?* PBS. July 28. http://www.pbs.org/newshour/bb/hillary-clinton-poorly-white-male-voters/.

Brenner, Marie. 1990. *After the Gold Rush.* September. http://www.vanityfair.com/magazine/2015/07/donald-ivana-trump-divorce-prenup-marie-brenner.

Brettschneider, Corey. 2016. *Trump vs. the Constitution: A Guide.* August 4. http://www.politico.com/magazine/story/2016/08/2016-donald-trump-constitution-guide-unconstitutional-freedom-liberty-khan-214139.

Brinkley, John. 2017. *Trump Hands China a Gift in Dumping Trans-Pacific Partnership.* January 24. https://www.forbes.com/sites/johnbrinkley/2017/01/24/trump-dumps-trans-pacific-partnership-sad/#2a4f4b6775dc.

Bromwich, Jonah Engel, and Alan Blinder. 2017. *What We Know about James Alex Fields, Driver Charged in Charlottesville Killing.* August 13. https://www.nytimes.com/2017/08/13/us/james-alex-fields-charlottesville-driver-.html

Browne, Ryan. 2017. *Ex-CIA Chief Brennan Bashes Trump over Speech during CIA Visit.* January 22. http://www.cnn.com/2017/01/21/politics/trump-to-cia-i-am-so-behind-you/index.html.

—. 2017. *NATO Members to Increase Defense Spending.* June 29. http://www.cnn.com/2017/06/29/politics/nato-members-increase-defense-spending/index.html.

Bruton, F. Brinley. 2016. *Gold Star Families Attack Trump over Comments about Ghazala Khan.* August 1. http://www.cnbc.com/2016/08/01/gold-star-families-attack-trump-over-comments-about-ghazala-khan.html.

Bryan, Bob. 2017. *A Group of Democratic and Republican Governors Just Released a Plan to Fix Obamacare.* August 31. http://www.businessinsider.com/kasich-hickenlooper-plan-obamacare-health-care-2017-8.

—. 2017. *The Government Scorekeeper Says the GOP Tax Bill Would Fall Short of Republicans' Promises.* November 30. http://www.businessinsider.com/trump-tax-plan-senate-bill-jct-dynamic-scoring-analysis-2017-11.

Buchanan, Rose Troup. 2015. *Amnesty International Claim Treatment of 10-year-old Girl Raped by Her Stepfather but Denied.* April 30. http://www.independent.co.uk/news/world/americas/amnesty-international-claim-treatment-of-10-year-old-girl-raped-by-her-stepfather-but-denied-10216264.html.

—. 2015. *The Six Nations Where It Is Still Illegal to Have an Abortion.* May 6. http://www.independent.co.uk/life-style/health-and-families/international-abortion-laws-the-six-nations-where-it-is-still-illegal-to-have-an-abortion-10229567.html.

Bulman, Erica. 2007. *Rights Group: 1.5 Million People Displaced by Preparations for 2008 Beijing Olympics.* June 5. http://usatoday30.usatoday.com/sports/olympics/2007-06-05-3431055449_x.htm.

Bump, Philip. 2016. *Donald Trump Somehow Thinks Ferguson and Oakland Are Dangerous Like Iraq.* May 18. https://www.washingtonpost.com/news/the-fix/wp/2016/05/18/donald-trump-somehow-thinks-ferguson-and-oakland-are-dangerous-like-iraq/?utm_term=.4b6a778e7d60.

—. 2016. *Donald Trump's Threat to Sue Ted Cruz, Explained.* February 16. https://www.washingtonpost.com/news/the-fix/wp/2016/02/16/donald-trumps-threat-to-sue-ted-cruz-explained/.

Burke, Daniel. 2016. *The Guilt-Free Gospel of Donald Trump.* October 24. http://www.cnn.com/2016/10/21/politics/trump-religion-gospel/index.html.

—. 2017. *Trump Says US Will Prioritize Christian Refugees.* January 28. http://edition.cnn.com/2017/01/27/politics/trump-christian-refugees/.

Burlij, Terence, and Jennifer Agiesta. 2017. *CNN Poll: Opinion of the Republican Party Falls to All-time Low.* September 25. http://www.cnn.com/2017/09/24/politics/cnn-poll-republican-party-approval/index.html.

Byers, Dylan. 2016. *Donna Brazile, the Acting Chairwoman of the Democratic National Committee, Resigned from Her Role as a CNN Contributor Earlier this Month.* October 31. http://money.cnn.com/2016/10/31/media/donna-brazile-cnn-resignation/index.html.

—. 2017. *Trump Defends Bill O'Reilly: 'I Don't Think Bill Did Anything Wrong.'* April 5. http://money.cnn.com/2017/04/05/media/donald-trump-defends-bill-oreilly/index.html.

—. 2014. *The Wrongs of Fareed Zakaria.* September 16. http://www.politico.com/blogs/media/2014/09/the-wrongs-of-fareed-zakaria-195579.

Byrnes, Jesse. 2016. *Blog Briefing Room: Canada's Prime Minister to Americans: Pay More Attention to the World.* March 4. http://thehill.com/blogs/blog-briefing-room/news/271780-canadian-president-americans-should-be-more-aware-of-global.

Cabaniss, Will. 2015. *Black Lives Matter Activist Says 'the Clintons' Passed Policy That Led to Mass Incarceration.* August 25. http://www.politifact.com/punditfact/statements/2015/aug/25/julius-jones/black-lives-matter-activist-says-clintons-passed-p/.

Cahill, Peter. 2017. *VP Mike Pence Warns North Korea: 'We Will Defeat Any Attack'.* April 19. https://www.nbcnews.com/news/world/vp-mike-pence-warns-north-korea-we-will-defeat-any-n748161.

Cambanis, Thanassis. 2016. *Turkey's Model of Democracy.* August 4. https://www.bostonglobe.com/ideas/2016/08/04/thanassi-turkey/gjkXW1XOagD5jJ776M8t6H/story.html.

Camp, Frank. 2016. *Donald Trump Calls Hillary Clinton Something No Other Candidate Has Dared to Say.* February 9. http://ijr.com/2016/02/533244-donld-trump-calls-hillary-clinton-something-no-other-candidate-has-dared-to-say/.

Stop Racism and Hate Canada. 2016. *5. Legal Remedies - The Law in Canada.* September 20. http://antiracism.stopracism.ca/content/5-legal-remedies-law-canada.

Capehart, Jonathan. 2016. *Hillary Clinton on 'Superpredator' Remarks: 'I Shouldn't Have Used Those Words.'* February 25. https://www.washingtonpost.com/blogs/post-partisan/wp/2016/02/25/hillary-clinton-responds-to-activist-who-demanded-apology-for-superpredator-remarks/?utm_term=.d5f98260735e.

Cardona, Maria, and Kayleigh McEnany, interview by Ashleigh Banfield. 2016. *Trump: US Should Have Taken Oil from Iraq* (September 9).

Carey, Nick, and Emily Stephenson. 2016. *Trump's Corporate Targets Face Tricky Task in Fending off His Attacks.* June 10. http://www.reuters.com/article/us-usa-election-trump-companies-idUSKCN0YW1JZ.

Carroll, Lauren. 2016. *Are the Clinton Wikileaks Emails Doctored, or Are They Authentic?* October 23. http://www.politifact.com/truth-o-meter/article/2016/oct/23/are-clinton-wikileaks-emails-doctored-or-are-they-/.

—. 2016. *Clinton Twists Trump's Words on Rescuing the Auto Industry during Recession.* October 18. http://www.politifact.com/truth-o-meter/statements/2016/oct/18/hillary-clinton/clinton-twists-trumps-words-rescuing-auto-industry/.

—. 2016. *Donald Trump Wrongly Tweets that He 'Never Said' More Countries Should Have Nuclear Weapons.* November 14. http://www.politifact.com/truth-o-meter/statements/2016/nov/14/donald-trump/donald-trump-wrongly-tweets-he-never-said-more-cou/.

—. 2016. *Donald Trump's Mostly False Claim that $400 Million Payment to Iran Was 'Ransom.'* August 24. http://www.politifact.com/truth-o-meter/statements/2016/aug/24/donald-trump/donald-trump-calls-400-million-payment-iran-ransom/.

Carson, E. Ann. 2014. *Prisoners in 2013.* September 30. https://www.bjs.gov/content/pub/pdf/p13.pdf.

Carter, Brandon. 2017. *Bill O'Reilly: Las Vegas Shooting 'the Price of Freedom.'* October 2. http://thehill.com/homenews/media/353503-bill-oreilly-las-vegas-shooting-the-price-of-freedom.

Castillo, Daniel. 2003. *German Economy in the 1920s.* December. Accessed November 27, 2016. http://www.history.ucsb.edu/faculty/marcuse/classes/33d/projects/1920s/Econ20s.htm.

Castle, Stephen. 2016. *U.K. Rejects Donald Trump's Call for Nigel Farage to Be Made Ambassador.* November 22. https://www.nytimes.com/2016/11/22/world/europe/uk-donald-trump-nigel-farage.html.

Cave, Anthony. 2016. *Does the Economy Always Do Better under Democratic Presidents?* April 6. http://www.politifact.com/arizona/statements/2016/apr/06/hillary-clinton/does-economy-always-do-better-under-democratic-pre/.

CBC. 2005. *Canadians Donate over $1 Million for Hurricane Katrina Relief.* September 3. http://www.cbc.ca/news/canada/canadians-donate-over-1-million-for-hurricane-katrina-relief-1.540263.

—. 2007. *Ernst Zundel Sentenced to 5 Years for Holocaust Denial.* February 15. http://www.cbc.ca/news/world/ernst-zundel-sentenced-to-5-years-for-holocaust-denial-1.659372.

—. 2014. *H.J. Heinz Co. Leamington: 1909-2014.* June 26. http://www.cbc.ca/news/canada/windsor/h-j-heinz-co-leamington-1909-2014-1.2686019.

—. 2013. *Iran Hostage 'Canadian Caper' 1979 Rescue No Secret to Some.* August 20. http://www.cbc.ca/news/canada/montreal/iran-hostage-canadian-caper-1979-rescue-no-secret-to-some-1.1357927.

—. 2017. *Only 1 Suspect in Deadly Quebec Mosque Shooting, Police Say.* January 30. http://www.cbc.ca/news/canada/montreal/quebec-city-mosque-gun-shots-1.3957686.

CBS. 2017. *U.S. Soldiers Killed in Niger Were Caught by Surprise, Official Says.* October 18. https://www.cbsnews.com/news/green-berets-killed-in-niger-were-caught-by-surprise-u-s-official-says/.

Cecco, Leyland. 2016. *Canada Takes Second Spot Globally on Social-progress Ranking.* June 29. https://beta.theglobeandmail.com/news/social-progress-index-canada-isalright/article30647376/?ref=http://www.theglobeandmail.com&.

Central Intelligence Agency. 2016. *Country Comparisons: World Population.* July. https://www.cia.gov/library/publications/the-world-factbook/rankorder/2119rank.html.

Cha, Ariana Eunjung. 2015. *CEO Martin Shkreli: 4,000 Percent Drug Price Hike Is 'Altruistic,' Not Greedy.* September 22. https://www.washingtonpost.com/news/to-your-health/wp/2015/09/22/turing-ceo-martin-shkreli-explains-that-4000-percent-drug-price-hike-is-altruistic-not-greedy/?utm_term=.6063ebbb68c5.

Chase, Steven, and Peter Kennedy. 2009. *U.S. Expected to Seek Timber Auctions.* March 20. http://www.theglobeandmail.com/report-on-business/us-expected-to-seek-timber-auctions/article25291863/.

Chasmar, Jessica. 2016. *Trump Spokeswoman Defends Tweet Calling Obama 'Head Negro in Charge.'* January 29. http://www.washingtontimes.com/news/2016/jan/29/katrina-pierson-donald-trump-spokeswoman-defends-t/.

Chengu, Garikai. 2015. *The Ku Klux Klan: America's Long History of Accepting White Terrorist Organizations.* December 25. http://www.globalresearch.ca/the-ku-klux-klan-americas-long-history-of-accepting-white-terrorist-organizations/5497958.

Choe Sang-Hun. 2017. *North Korean Hackers Stole U.S.-South Korean Military Plans, Lawmaker Says.* October 10. https://www.nytimes.com/2017/10/10/world/asia/north-korea-hack-war-plans.html.

Chozick, Amy. 2016. *Hillary Clinton Told F.B.I. Colin Powell Advised Her to Use Private Email.* August 18. http://www.nytimes.com/2016/08/19/us/politics/hillary-clinton-told-fbi-colin-powell-advised-her-to-use-private-email.html.

—. 2016. *Kenneth Starr, Who Tried to Bury Bill Clinton, Now Only Praises Him.* May 24. https://www.bostonglobe.com/news/politics/2016/05/24/kenneth-starr-who-tried-bury-bill-clinton-now-praises-him/a0GN63PqIBCPvu0gfs951J/story.html.

Chulov, Martin, and Kareem Shaheen. 2017. *Syria Chemical Weapons Attack Toll Rises to 70 as Russian Narrative Is Dismissed.* April 5. https://www.theguardian.com/world/2017/apr/04/syria-chemical-attack-idlib-province.

Cillizza, Chris. 2015. *The Dangerous Anger of Donald Trump.* November 13. https://www.washingtonpost.com/news/the-fix/wp/2015/11/13/the-remarkably-unappealling-anger-of-donald-trump/?utm_term=.23ddc49b96a4.

—. 2016. *Hillary Clinton Just Gave Her Best Answer on the Email Controversy. By Far.* August 2. https://www.washingtonpost.com/news/the-fix/wp/2016/08/25/hillary-clinton-just-gave-her-best-answer-on-the-email-controversy-by-far/.

Cimino-Isaacs, Cathleen. 2016. *Labor Standards in the TPP*, 41-63. March. https://piie.com/publications/chapters_preview/7137/15iie7137.pdf .

Civil War Trust. n.d. *A Brief Overview of the American Civil War.* Accessed November 22, 2016. http://www.civilwar.org/education/history/civil-war-overview/overview.html?referrer=https://www.google.ca/.

Clarke, Tara. 2015. *Donald Trump Bankruptcy: A Breakdown Ahead of the 2016 Elections.* July 7. http://moneymorning.com/2015/07/07/donald-trump-bankruptcy-a-breakdown-ahead-of-the-2016-elections/.

Clarke, Toni, and Dustin Volz. 2017. *Trump Acknowledges Russia Role in U.S. Election Hacking: Aide.* January 9. http://www.reuters.com/article/us-usa-russia-cyber-idUSKBN14S0O6.

Clausing, Kimberly, and Edward Kleinbard. 2017. *Trump's Economists Say a Corporate Tax Cut Will Raise Wages by $4,000. It Doesn't Add Up.* October 20. https://www.vox.com/the-big-idea/2017/10/20/16506256/cea-report-corporate-taxes-wages-boost-job-growth.

Clauss, Kyle Scott. 2016. *Did Bill Clinton, Mayor Walsh Break Massachusetts Voting Laws for Hillary?* March 1. http://www.bostonmagazine.com/news/blog/2016/03/01/bill-clinton-massachusetts-voting-laws/.

Click2Houston. 2016. *Grand Jury Takes No Action against Planned Parenthood; 2 Others Indicted.* January 26. http://www.click2houston.com/news/grand-jury-takes-no-action-against-planned-parenthood-gulf-coast-2-others-indicted.

Clinton Foundation. 2016. *Clinton Foundation.* August 31. https://www.clintonfoundation.org/our-work.

Clinton, Hillary. 2016. *Gun Violence Prevention*. September 22. https://www.hillaryclinton.com/issues/gun-violence-prevention/.

—. 2007. *S.804 - Count Every Vote Act of 2007*. March 7. https://www.congress.gov/bill/110th-congress/senate-bill/804.

Clinton, Hillary, and Mika Brzezinski, interview by Joe Scarborough. 2016. *Hillary Clinton on Pressure on High-Achieving Women*. MSNBC *Morning Joe*. February 26. https://www.youtube.com/watch?v=YkwyRhVclow.

CNN. 2016. *Trump Defends Tweet about Sexual Assault*. September 7. http://transcripts.cnn.com/Transcripts/1609/07/acd.01.html.

—. 2017. *Trump's Alleged Insensitive Comments Regarding Killed U.S. Soldier Ignite Firestorm; White House Press Briefing*. October 18. http://transcripts.cnn.com/TRANSCRIPTS/1710/18/cnr.07.html.

CNN Library. 2017. *2017 Atlantic Hurricane Season Fast Facts*. October 26. http://www.cnn.com/2017/05/15/us/2017-atlantic-hurricane-season-fast-facts/index.html.

CNN Wire. 2015. *Charleston Church Shooting Suspect, Dylann Storm Roof, Arrested in North Carolina*. June 18. http://fox59.com/2015/06/18/dylann-storm-roof-arrested-in-north-carolina-according-to-report/.

Cobbs, Elizabeth A. 2015. *Why Boehner's Invite to Netanyahu Is Unconstitutional*. March 2. http://blogs.reuters.com/great-debate/2015/03/01/netanyahu-invite-is-a-symptom-of-boehners-grudge-match-against-the-u-s-constitution/.

Cockburn, Harry. 2017. *Former Facebook Employees Regret Working for Company as Russia Election Probe Continues: 'What Have I Done?'* October 19. http://www.independent.co.uk/news/world/americas/us-politics/facebook-russia-adverts-us-election-probe-former-employees-regret-working-company-donald-trump-a8008921.html.

Cohen, Marshall. 2017. *What We Know about the Trump Campaign, His Administration and Russia*. March 22. http://www.cnn.com/2017/02/16/politics/trump-russia-timeline/.

Cohen, Zachary, and Dan Merica. 2017. *Trump Takes Credit for ISIS 'Giving Up.'* October 17. http://www.cnn.com/2017/10/17/politics/trump-isis-raqqa/index.html.

Colagiovanni, Lou. 2017. *Conway Just Called for Any Journalist Who Criticizes Trump to Be Fired*. January 30. http://occupydemocrats.com/2017/01/30/conway-just-called-journalist-criticizes-trump-fired/.

Cole, Juan. 2017. *Trump's Muslim Ban Hurts US Troops and Helps Islamist Extremists*. January 30. https://www.thenation.com/article/trumps-muslim-ban-hurts-us-troops-and-helps-islamist-extremists/.

Coles, Isabel, and Ali Nabhan. 2017. *Kurds Protesting in Iraq Turn Their Anger against U.S.* October 20. https://www.wsj.com/articles/kurds-protesting-in-iraq-turn-their-anger-against-u-s-1508524008.

Collinson, Stephen. 2017. *Trump Stands by Wiretapping Claim during Merkel Visit*. March 18. http://www.cnn.com/2017/03/17/politics/donald-trump-angela-merkel/index.html.

—. 2017. *Trump's DACA Decision Triggers Anguish, Political Firestorm*. September 5. http://www.cnn.com/2017/09/05/politics/trump-daca-politics/index.html.

Combier, Betsy. 2010. *Filegate Is Dismissed*. March 9. http://www.parentadvocates.org/nicecontent/dsp_printable.cfm?articleID=7716/nicecontent/dsp_printable.cfm?articleID=7716.

Comey, James. 2016. *Statement by FBI Director James B. Comey on the Investigation of Secretary Hillary Clinton's Use of a Personal E-mail System*. July 5. https://www.fbi.gov/news/pressrel/press-releases/statement-by-fbi-director-james-b-comey-on-the-investigation-of-secretary-hillary-clinton2019s-use-of-a-personal-e-mail-system.

Compagne, Olivier. n.d. *Anatomy of Peace*. Accessed February 8, 2017. https://sites.google.com/site/integralconflictresolution/conflic-resolution/the-anatomy-of-peace.

Conca, James. 2017. *The Iran Nuclear Deal Without the United States*. October 17. https://www.forbes.com/sites/jamesconca/2017/10/17/the-iran-nuclear-deal-without-the-united-states/#144e89ec3c94.

Concha, Joe. 2017. *Report: O'Reilly to Get up to $25m in Fox Payout*. April 29. http://thehill.com/homenews/media/329766-report-oreilly-to-get-25m-in-fox-payout.

Condon, Bernard. 2016. *The Star News World Donald Trump's Taj Mahal Failure Crushed Many of His Contractors*. June 29. https://www.thestar.com/news/world/2016/06/29/donald-trumps-taj-mahal-failure-crushed-many-of-his-contractors.html.

Confessore, Nicholas, and Karen Yourish. 2016. *$2 Billion Worth of Free Media for Donald Trump.* March 15. http://www.nytimes.com/2016/03/16/upshot/measuring-donald-trumps-mammoth-advantage-in-free-media.html?_r=1.

Congressional Record. 2016. *Donald Trump: Senate.* September 26, 114th Congress, 2nd Session, Issue: Vol. 162, No. 145. https://www.congress.gov/congressional-record/2016/9/26/senate-section/article/S6073-2.

Connolly, Katie. 2009. *Sex Scandals through the Years: Both Parties Even.* June 25. http://www.newsweek.com/sex-scandals-through-years-both-parties-even-212156.

Connor, Jackson. 2015. *Rush Limbaugh Gives Himself a Pat on the Back for MSNBC's Ratings Troubles.* February 6. http://www.huffingtonpost.com/2015/02/06/rush-limbaugh-msnbc-ratings-troubles_n_6630306.html.

Constitution Center. n.d. *Freedom of Religion, Speech, Press, Assembly and Petition.* Accessed September 19, 2016. http://constitutioncenter.org/interactive-constitution/amendments/amendment-i.

Contorno, Steve. 2016. *Trump Says Clinton and Obama Paid People to Cause Violence at His Rallies.* October 30. http://www.politifact.com/truth-o-meter/article/2016/oct/20/trump-says-clinton-and-obama-caused-violence-his-r/.

Conway, Madeline. 2017. *Trump: 'Nobody Knew that Health Care Could Be So Complicated.'* February 27. http://www.politico.com/story/2017/02/trump-nobody-knew-that-health-care-could-be-so-complicated-235436.

Cook, Dennis. 2006. *Trump Jokes about Dating His Daughter.* March 7. http://usatoday30.usatoday.com/life/people/2006-03-07-trump_x.htm.

Cooney, Samantha. 2017. *Here Are All the Public Figures Who've Been Accused of Sexual Misconduct after Harvey Weinstein.* December 15. http://time.com/5015204/harvey-weinstein-scandal/.

Corasaniti, Nick, and Maggie Haberman. 2016. *Donald Trump Suggests 'Second Amendment People' Could Act against Hillary Clinton.* August 9. http://www.nytimes.com/2016/08/10/us/politics/donald-trump-hillary-clinton.html?_r=0.

Corn, David, and Daniel Schulman. 2015. *Bill O'Reilly Has His Own Brian Williams Problem.* February 19. http://www.motherjones.com/politics/2015/02/bill-oreilly-brian-williams-falklands-war.

Corse, Alexa. 2016. *All of the Top Republicans Voting for Hillary Clinton Instead of Donald Trump.* August 10. http://www.thedailybeast.com/articles/2016/08/09/all-of-the-top-republicans-voting-for-hillary-clinton-instead-of-donald-trump.html.

Cottle, Michelle. 2016. *The Era of 'the Bitch' Is Coming.* August 17. http://www.theatlantic.com/politics/archive/2016/08/the-era-of-the-bitch-is-coming/496154/.

Couch, Aaron. 2011. Martin Luther King Day: 10 Memorable MLK Quotes. The Christian Science Monitor. January 17. https://www.csmonitor.com/USA/2011/0117/Martin-Luther-King-Day-10-memorable-MLK-quotes/Let-no-man-pull-you-low.

Couts, Andrew. 2017. *Federal Court Halts Trump's Immigration Ban.* January 28. http://www.dailydot.com/layer8/federal-judge-trump-muslim-ban-immigration-ban/.

Crockett, Emily. 2016. *Trump Actually Pointed at a Supporter and Said "Look at My African American over Here".* June 3. https://www.vox.com/2016/6/3/11856328/trump-look-at-my-african-american.Cummings.

Cuevas, Mayra. 2017. *Undocumented Husband of Indiana Trump Supporter Deported to Mexico.* April 6. http://www.cnn.com/2017/04/05/us/undocumented-husband-deported/.

Cummings, Elijah E. 2016. *Cummings Releases Full Powell Email Advising Clinton on Personal Email Use.* September 7. https://medium.com/oversightdems/cummings-releases-full-powell-email-advising-clinton-on-personal-email-use-65904c1ccfa#.lkgp73p4c.

D'Angelo, Chris. 2017. *Trump Says He Considered FBI's Russia Probe before Firing Comey.* May 11. http://www.huffingtonpost.com/entry/trump-comey-firing-nbc-us_us_5914df83e4b0fe039b337700.

da Costa, Pedro Nicolaci. 2017. *Trump Has a Shocking Conflict of Interest with China.* February 17. http://www.businessinsider.com/trumps-conflict-of-interest-with-china-2017-2.

Daiss, Tim. 2016. *Trump Pledges to Rip Up Iran Deal; Israelis Say Not So Fast.* November 22. http://www.forbes.com/sites/timdaiss/2016/11/22/trumps-iran-deal-rhetoric-israelis-say-not-so-fast/#383271061c6b.

Dale, Daniel. 2017. *The White House Cited the Quebec Mosque Attack to Justify Trump's Policies.* January 30. https://www.thestar.com/news/world/2017/01/30/the-white-house-just-cited-the-quebec-mosque-attack-to-justify-trumps-policies.html.

—. 2016. *Will Sexism Hurt Hillary Clinton's Presidential Campaign?* June 8. https://www.thestar.com/news/world/2016/06/08/will-sexism-hurt-hillary-clintons-presidential-campaign.html.

Dalia, G. 2015. *Meet the Nine Muslim Women Who Have Ruled Nations.* June 9. http://egyptianstreets.com/2015/06/09/meet-the-nine-muslim-women-who-have-ruled-nations/.

Dallek, Matthew. 1996. *The Godless Constitution.* February 18. http://www.washingtonpost.com/wp-srv/style/longterm/books/reviews/matthewdallek.htm.

Damon, Arwa, Ghazi Balkiz, and Laura Smith-Spark. 2017. *Raqqa: US-Backed Forces Declare 'Total Liberation' of ISIS Stronghold.* October 20. http://www.cnn.com/2017/10/20/middleeast/raqqa-syria-isis-total-liberation/index.html.

Danner, Chas. 2017. *Reports: Frustrated and Isolated Trump Considering Staff Shakeup at Demoralized White House.* May 14. http://nymag.com/daily/intelligencer/2017/05/trump-considering-staff-shakeup-at-demoralized-white-house.html.

Darcy, Oliver. 2016. *Fact Check: Top Aide Did Not Say Hillary Clinton Hates 'Everyday Americans.'* October 11. http://www.businessinsider.com/wikileaks-email-hillary-clinton-everyday-americans-2016-10.

Davenport, Coral, Jonathan Ellis, Lisa Friedman, Brad Plumer, and Tatiana Schlossberg. 2017. *What Is the Clean Power Plan, and How Can Trump Repeal It?* October 10. https://www.nytimes.com/2017/10/10/climate/epa-clean-power-plan.html.

Davidson, Amy. 2014. *Donald Trump and the Central Park Five.* June 23. http://www.newyorker.com/news/amy-davidson/donald-trump-and-the-central-park-five.

Dawsey, Josh, and Andrea Peterson. 2017. *White House Launches Probe of Private Email Accounts.* September 28. http://www.politico.com/story/2017/09/28/white-house-launches-probe-private-email-accounts-243281.

Dawsey, Josh, and Paul Demko. 2017. *Trump Will Scrap Critical Obamacare Subsidies.* October 13. http://www.politico.com/story/2017/10/12/trump-obamacare-subsidy-243736.

De Groot, Len, Chris Keller, and Jon Schleuss. 2017. *The Most Notable Firings and Resignations in the Trump White House.* July 28. http://www.latimes.com/projects/la-na-pol-trump-firings-resignations/.

DeCosta-Klipa, Nik. 2016. *In Debate, Bernie Sanders Had No Specific Example of Wall Street Donations Affecting Hillary Clinton's Decisions.* April 14. https://www.boston.com/news/politics/2016/04/14/debate-bernie-sanders-no-example-donations-affecting-hillary-clintons.

Dejean, Ashley. 2017. *Donald Trump Has a Conflict of Interest in Turkey. Just Ask Donald Trump.* April 18. http://www.motherjones.com/politics/2017/04/trump-turkey-erdogan-conflict-interest.

DelReal, Jose A. 2015. *Donald Trump Announces Presidential Bid.* June 16. https://www.washingtonpost.com/news/post-politics/wp/2015/06/16/donald-trump-to-announce-his-presidential-plans-today/.

DelReal, Jose A., and Robert Costa. 2016. *Trump Escalates Attack on Bill Clinton.* May 23. https://www.washingtonpost.com/politics/trump-escalates-attack-on-bill-clinton/2016/05/23/ed109acc-2100-11e6-8690-f14ca9de2972_story.html?hpid=hp_rhp-top-table-main_trump-clinton-9pm%3Ahomepage%2Fstory&utm_term=.7cf925888072.

Dent, Mark. 2016. *Sorry, Hillary: Trump Actually Has Made a Few Things in the USA.* August 1. http://www.politifact.com/pennsylvania/statements/2016/aug/01/hillary-clinton/hillary-clinton-went-overboard-calling-out-donald-/.

Department of Justice Public Affairs. 2016. *Justice Department Announces Findings of Investigation into Baltimore Police Department.* August 10. https://www.justice.gov/opa/pr/justice-department-announces-findings-investigation-baltimore-police-department.

Dershowitz, Alan. 2017. *Dershowitz: Mueller's Special Counsel Appointment Begs the Question -- Are Our Civil Liberties Now at Risk?* May 20. http://www.foxnews.com/opinion/2017/05/20/dershowitz-muellers-special-counsel-appointment-begs-question-are-our-civil-liberties-now-at-risk.html.

Devega, Chauncey. 2015. *White America's Racial Amnesia: The Sobering Truth about Our Country's "Race Riots."* May 1. http://www.salon.com/2015/05/01/white_americas_racial_amnesia_the_sobering_truth_about_our_countrys_race_riots_partner/.

Dewan, Angela, and Onur Cakir. 2016. *Turkey and Russia Agree on Draft Syria Ceasefire, Report Says.* December 28. http://www.cnn.com/2016/12/28/middleeast/syria-ceasefire-russia-turkey/.

Dewey, Caitlin. 2017. *How Nafta May Have Made Canada Fat.* July 11. https://www.thestar.com/news/canada/2017/07/11/how-nafta-may-have-made-canada-fat.html.

Diamond, Jeremy. 2016. *Donald Trump in 2006: I 'Sort of Hope' Real Estate Market Tanks.* May 19. http://www.cnn.com/2016/05/19/politics/donald-trump-2006-hopes-real-estate-market-crashes/.

—. 2017. *Donating to Trump? Campaign Is Spending $1 of Every $10 on Legal Fees.* October 17. http://www.cnn.com/2017/10/17/politics/donald-trump-campaign-legal-fees/index.html?sr=twCNN101717donald-trump-campaign-legal-fees0100PMStory.

—. 2017. *Trump Administration Projects Confidence amid Puerto Rico Crisis.* September 28. http://www.cnn.com/2017/09/28/politics/elaine-duke-puerto-rico-response/index.html.

—. 2016. *Trump: Clinton Could Shoot Somebody and Not Be Arrested.* September 9. http://www.cnn.com/2016/09/09/politics/donald-trump-hillary-clinton-shoot-somebody/.

—. 2016. *Trump: I Could 'Shoot Somebody and I Wouldn't Lose Voters.*' January 24. http://www.cnn.com/2016/01/23/politics/donald-trump-shoot-somebody-support/.

—. 2016. *'We Can't Continue to Allow China to Rape Our Country.*' May 2. http://www.cnn.com/2016/05/01/politics/donald-trump-china-rape/index.html.

Diamond, Jeremy, and Eugene Scott. 2016. *Trump Says He'll Sue Sexual Misconduct Accusers.* October 22. http://www.cnn.com/2016/10/22/politics/trump-says-hell-sue-sexual-misconduct-accusers/index.html.

Diamond, Jeremy, and Jeff Zeleny, Dana Bash and Kaitlan Collins. 2017. *Sean Spicer, White House press secretary, resigns.* July 21. http://www.cnn.com/2017/07/21/politics/sean-spicer-resigns-anthony-scaramucci/index.html.

Diaz, Daniella. 2016. *53 Organizations to Trump: Dump Flynn as National Security Adviser.* December 6. http://edition.cnn.com/2016/12/05/politics/michael-flynn-donald-trump-national-security-adviser/.

—. 2016. *North Carolina Congressman: Protesters 'Hate White People.'* September 23. http://www.cnn.com/2016/09/22/politics/robert-pittenger-north-carolina-charlotte-protests/.

—. 2017. *Trump Authorizes Waiver to Loosen Shipping Regulations for Puerto Rico.* September 28. http://www.cnn.com/2017/09/28/politics/puerto-rico-governor-white-house-jones-act-waiver/index.html.

—. 2016. *Trump Learns to Love Ryan: 'He's Like a Fine Wine.'* December 13. http://www.cnn.com/2016/12/13/politics/donald-trump-paul-ryan-wisconsin-thank-you-tour/.

Dickinson, Arlene. 2017. *Arlene Dickinson on Kevin O'Leary's Entry into Conservative Leadership Race.* January 18. http://www.cbc.ca/news/canada/calgary/kevin-o-leary-conservative-run-arlene-dickinson-opinion-1.3942349.

Dilanian, Ken. 2016. *Why Won't Obama Say Radical Islam.* June 13. http://www.nbcnews.com/storyline/orlando-nightclub-massacre/why-won-t-obama-say-radical-islam-n591196.

Dmitry, Baxter. 2016. *Snopes Caught Lying For Hillary Again, Questions Raised.* August 20. http://yournewswire.com/snopes-caught-lying-for-hillary-again-questions-raised/.

Dionne, Jr., E.J. 2015. *Kevin McCarthy's Truthful Gaffe on Benghazi.* September 30. https://www.washingtonpost.com/opinions/kevin-mccarthys-truthful-gaffe/2015/09/30/f12a9fac-67a8-11e5-8325-a42b5a459b1e_story.html?utm_term=.49cc8784b613.

Dixon, Michael. 2017. *Colin Kaepernick's Latest Round of Donations Includes $25k to Veteran's Group.* February 9. https://sportsnaut.com/2017/02/colin-kaepernick-donations-includes-25k-veterans/.

Dodai. 2008. *Chris Matthews Has a Sexist History with Hillary Clinton.* January 15. http://jezebel.com/345237/chris-matthews-has-a-sexist-history-with-hillary-clinton.

Domhoff, G. William. 2012. *An Investment Manager's View on the Top 1%.* January. http://www2.ucsc.edu/whorulesamerica/power/investment_manager.html.

—. 2017. *Wealth, Income, and Power.* April. http://www2.ucsc.edu/whorulesamerica/power/wealth.html.

Dooling, Shannon. 2017. *Boston Federal Court Puts Hold on Trump's Travel, Refugee Ban.* January 29. http://www.wbur.org/news/2017/01/29/boston-ruling-trump-executive-order.

Dreazen, Yochi. 2016. *Facebook Is Full of Fake News Stories. On Election Day, Don't Fall for Them.* November 8. http://www.vox.com/presidential-election/2016/11/8/13557952/facebook-election-day-trump-clinton-fake-stories-lies-fox.

Druzin, Randi. 2018. Canada's Social Fabric Bares Raw Threads. January 26. https://www.usnews.com/news/best-countries/articles/2018-01-26/canada-confronts-growing-tensions-between-its-ethnic-communities.

D'Souza, Dinesh. 2016. *Dinesh D'Souza: The Secret History of the Democratic Party.* July 22. http://www.foxnews.com/opinion/2016/07/22/dinesh-dsouza-secret-history-democratic-party.html.

Dugdale-Pointon, T. 2007. *The Army of God.* August 17. http://www.historyofwar.org/articles/weapons_army_of_god.html.

Dunsmuir, Mollie. 1992. *Referendums: The Canadian Experience.* January. http://publications.gc.ca/Collection-R/LoPBdP/BP/bp271-e.htm.

DW Made for Minds. 2017. *Unicef: 20 Percent of Children in Developed Countries Living in Poverty.* June 15. http://www.dw.com/en/unicef-20-percent-of-children-in-developed-countries-living-in-poverty/a-39259716.

Easley, Jason. 2016. *CNN Shows Their Anti-Clinton Bias by Going All in for Trump with Corey Lewandowski Hire.* June 23. http://www.politicususa.com/2016/06/23/cnn-shows-anti-clinton-bias-trump-corey-lewandowsi-hire.html.

—. 2015. *Republican Colin Powell Deals a Death Blow to Hillary Clinton Email Scandal.* March 8. http://www.politicususa.com/2015/03/08/republican-colin-powell-deals-death-blow-hillary-clinton-email-scandal.html.

—. 2015. *Senate Republicans Block a Bill That Would Create 1 Million New Jobs for Young People.* July 16. http://www.politicususa.com/2015/07/16/senate-republicans-block-bill-create-1-million-jobs-young-people.html.

—. 2016. *The Truth Comes out as CNN Admits They Are Going Easy on Donald Trump.* September 6. http://www.politicususa.com/2016/09/06/truth-cnn-admits-easy-donald-trump.html.

Editors of Encyclopædia Britannica. 2010. *Mexico City 1968 Olympic Games.* July 28. https://www.britannica.com/event/Mexico-City-1968-Olympic-Games.

Edwards, Breeanna. 2015. *NYC Taxi Driver Fined $25,000 for Refusing to Pick Up Black Family.* August 6. http://www.theroot.com/articles/news/2015/08/taxi_driver_fined_25_000_for_refusing_to_pick_up_black_family/.

Egan, Matt. 2017. *Trump's Energy Plan isn't a Game-changer.* April 27. http://money.cnn.com/2017/04/27/investing/trump-oil-coal-energy-plan/index.html.

—. 2017. *Why Trump's Coal Promises Are Doomed.* April 25. http://money.cnn.com/2017/04/25/investing/coal-trump-jobs-promise/index.html.

Ehrenfreund, Max. 2016. *Donald Trump Claims New York's Stop-and-frisk Policy Reduced Crime. The Data Disagree.* September 22. https://www.washingtonpost.com/news/wonk/wp/2016/09/22/donald-trump-claims-new-yorks-stop-and-frisk-policy-reduced-crime-the-data-disagree/.

Eichenwald, Kurt. 2014. *ISIS's Enemy List: 10 Reasons the Islamic State Is Doomed.* September 8. http://www.newsweek.com/2014/09/19/isiss-enemy-list-10-reasons-islamic-state-doomed-268953.html.

Eilperin, Juliet, and Sean Sullivan. 2017. *Trump Appears to Back Further Away from Bipartisan Health-care.* October 18. https://www.washingtonpost.com/powerpost/trump-appears-to-back-further-away-from-bipartisan-health-care-push/2017/10/18/d08c4b0c-b40d-11e7-a908-a3470754bbb9_story.html?utm_term=.8e22cbb98df2.

Elliott, Philip. 2017. *These Ohio Voters Made Trump President. They're Still with Him.* July 25. http://time.com/4873955/donald-trump-youngstown-ohio-support/.

Ellis, Ralph. 2016. *Officer Charged with Manslaughter in Philando Castile Killing.* November 17. http://www.cnn.com/2016/11/16/us/officer-charged-philando-castile-killing/.

Emmons, Alex. 2016. *ACLU Gears Up to Fight Donald Trump's Long List of Unconstitutional Proposals.* July 14. https://theintercept.com/2016/07/14/aclu-gears-up-to-fight-donald-trumps-long-list-of-unconstitutional-proposals/.

Encyclopedia of the New American Nation. n.d. *Exceptionalism - The Leader of the Free World*. Accessed December 17, 2016. http://www.americanforeignrelations.com/E-N/Exceptionalism-The-leader-of-the-free-world.html.

Engel, Pamela. 2016. *Donald Trump Is Trying out a New Nickname for Hillary Clinton*. May 20. http://www.businessinsider.com/donald-trump-heartless-hillary-clinton-guns-second-amendment-2016-5.

—. 2016. *Petraeus Takes Center Stage amid Infighting about Trump Considering Romney for Secretary of State*. November 28. http://www.businessinsider.com/trump-petraeus-romney-secretary-of-state-2016-11.

—. 2016. *Ronald Reagan's Son Says 'the Whole Family' Is Insulted by Trump Comparisons*. June 7. http://www.businessinsider.com/ronald-reagan-son-donald-trump-2016-6.

Erickson, Amanda. 2017. *Trump Thought China Could Get North Korea to Comply. It's Not That Easy*. April 13. https://www.washingtonpost.com/news/worldviews/wp/2017/04/13/trump-thought-china-could-get-n-korea-to-comply-its-not-that-easy/?utm_term=.74bf7fb56210.

Erkan. 2012. *10 Most Hilarious George Costanza Quotes*. May 8. Accessed October 9, 2017. http://www.themost10.com/hilarious-george-costanza-quotes.

Erwin, James. 2014. *4 Times the U.S. Invaded Canada*. December 5. http://mentalfloss.com/article/60380/4-times-us-invaded-canada.

Escott, Paul D. 2014. *Racism and the Founding of the GOP: Abraham Lincoln, the Civil War and the Real History of the Republican Party*. September 13. http://www.salon.com/2014/09/13/racism_and_the_founding_of_the_gop_abraham_lincoln_the_civil_war_and_the_real_history_of_the_republican_party/.

Evon, Dan. 2016. *Nope Francis*. July 24. http://www.snopes.com/pope-francis-donald-trump-endorsement/.

Ewing, Walter, Daniel E. Martínez, and Rubén G. Rumbautf. 2015. *The Criminalization of Immigration in the United States*. July 13. https://www.americanimmigrationcouncil.org/research/criminalization-immigration-united-states.

Fahrenthold, David A. 2012. *Trump Foundation Lacks the Certification Required for Charities That Solicit Money*. September 29. https://www.washingtonpost.com/politics/trump-foundation-lacks-the-certification-required-for-charities-that-solicit-money/2016/09/29/7dac6a68-8658-11e6-ac72-a29979381495_story.html.

—. 2016. *Trump Pays IRS a Penalty for His Foundation Violating Rules with Gift to Aid Florida Attorney General*. September 1. https://www.washingtonpost.com/news/post-politics/wp/2016/09/01/trump-pays-irs-a-penalty-for-his-foundation-violating-rules-with-gift-to-florida-attorney-general/?utm_term=.e5c3d-1fe725b.

—. 2016. *Trump Used $258,000 from His Charity to Settle Legal Problems*. September 20. https://www.washingtonpost.com/politics/trump-used-258000-from-his-charity-to-settle-legal-problems/2016/09/20/adc88f9c-7d11-11e6-ac8e-cf8e0dd91dc7_story.html.

—. 2016. *Trump's Campaign Says He's Given 'Tens of Millions' to Charity, but Offers No Details and No Proof*. September 12. https://www.washingtonpost.com/news/post-politics/wp/2016/09/12/trumps-campaign-says-hes-given-tens-of-millions-to-charity-but-offers-no-details-and-no-proof/?utm_term=.1d004f16186d.

Fandos, Nicholas. 2017. *Government Ethics Chief Resigns, Casting Uncertainty over Agency*. July 6. https://www.nytimes.com/2017/07/06/us/politics/walter-shaub-office-of-government-ethics-resign.html?mcubz=1&_r=0.

Farber, Madeline. 2017. *Here Are the Republicans Who Have Criticized President Trump's Immigration Ban*. January 30. http://fortune.com/2017/01/29/donald-trump-immigration-ban-republicans/.

Farhi, Paul. 2016. *CNN's Hiring of Corey Lewandowski Didn't Cause a Staff Revolt. in Fact, It Was the Opposite*. June 27. https://www.washingtonpost.com/lifestyle/cnns-hiring-of-corey-lewandowski-didnt-cause-a-staff-revolt-in-fact-it-was-the-opposite/2016/06/26/61ba30fe-3bcd-11e6-80bc-d06711fd2125_story.html?utm_term=.7d01c5cc8f8b.

—. 2016. *What Really Gets under Trump's Skin? A Reporter Questioning His Net Worth*. March 8. https://www.washingtonpost.com/lifestyle/style/that-time-trump-sued-over-the-size-of-hiswallet/2016/03/08/785dee3e-e4c2-11e5-b0fd-073d5930a7b7_story.html.

Farley, Robert. 2016. *Trump's False Muslim Claim*. March 16. http://www.factcheck.org/2016/03/trumps-false-muslim-claim/.

Farrington, Dana. 2016. *Ex-Reserve Deputy Who Confused Gun with Taser, Killing Suspect, Is Convicted.* April 28. http://www.npr.org/sections/thetwo-way/2016/04/28/476019878/ex-reserve-deputy-who-confused-gun-with-taser-killing-suspect-is-convicted.

Feiden, Douglas. 1996. *Trump Hit with Race Suit Blacks: Don Dealt Us out of Casino Jobs.* June 19. http://www.nydailynews.com/archives/money/trump-hit-race-suit-blacks-don-dealt-casino-jobs-article-1.726389.

Feldman, Noah. 2017. *In Yates versus Trump, the Constitution Won.* January 31. https://www.bloomberg.com/view/articles/2017-01-31/in-yates-vs-trump-the-constitution-won.

Ferguson, David. 2016. *Black Georgia GOP Official Booted from Atlanta Trump Event with No Explanation.* June 26. http://www.rawstory.com/2016/06/black-georgia-gop-official-booted-from-atlanta-trump-event-with-no-explanation/.

Fernandez, Nick. 2016. *The Associated Press Finally Deletes "Misleading" Tweet about the Clinton Foundation after Keeping It Posted for Two Weeks.* September 8. https://mediamatters.org/shows-and-publications/associated-press.

Ferris, Robert. 2017. *Why Voters Might Be Choosing Dominant, Authoritarian Leaders around the World.* June 12. https://www.cnbc.com/2017/06/12/why-voters-might-be-choosing-dominant-authoritarian-leaders-around-the-world.html.

Ferro, Shaunacy. 2016. *25 Unusual Foreign Travel Warnings for Visiting the U.S.* April 6. http://mentalfloss.com/article/68276/25-unusual-foreign-travel-warnings-visiting-us.

Fields, Jeffrey. 2017. *Here's How Classified Information Got into Those Hillary Clinton Emails.* July 20. https://www.huffingtonpost.com/the-conversation-us/how-did-classified-inform_b_11074304.html.

Fife, Robert. 2017. *Trudeau, Other G7 Leaders Fail to Persuade Trump to Endorse Climate- change Accord.* May 27. https://www.theglobeandmail.com/news/politics/trudeau-and-trump-talk-nafta-global-security-at-g7/article35138355/.

Firozi, Paulina. 2016. *Iowa GOP Voter Arrested for Alleged Voter Fraud: Report.* October 28. http://thehill.com/blogs/blog-briefing-room/news/303406-iowa-republican-voter-arrested-for-alleged-voter-fraud.

Fisher, Anthony L. 2016. *Glenn Ford Spent 30 Years on Death Row, Was Exonerated, Died, yet Is Still on Trial.* May 5. http://reason.com/blog/2016/05/05/glenn-ford-spent-30-years-on-death-row-w.

Fisher, Max. 2016. *What Is Donald Trump's Foreign Policy?* November 11. https://www.nytimes.com/2016/11/12/world/what-is-donald-trumps-foreign-policy.html.

Fleming, Sam, and Lauren Leatherby. 2017. *US Richest 1% to Gain Most from Republican Tax Plan, Report Says.* November 8. https://www.ft.com/content/0de96cb6-c4ce-11e7-a1d2-6786f39ef675.

Flitter, Emily. 2016. *Trump Praises 'Stop-and-frisk' Police Tactic.* September 22. http://www.reuters.com/article/us-usa-election-trump-idUSKCN11R2NZ.

Flynn, Chris. 2016. *The 15 Worst Atrocities Committed by Fidel Castro.* December 7. http://www.therichest.com/shocking/the-15-worst-atrocities-committed-by-fidel-castro/.

Flynn, General. 2016 5:14 PM. *Twitter Post.* February 26. https://twitter.com/genflynn/status/703387702998278144?lang=en.

Foley, Elise. 2016. *Donald Trump Questions Hillary Clinton's 'Mental and Physical Stamina.'* August 15. http://www.huffingtonpost.com/entry/donald-trump-hillary-clinton-health_us_57b221dbe4b007c36e4fc559.

Folley, Aris, and Sylvia Cunningham. 2016. *Former 'Apprentice' Contestants Denounce Donald Trump's Candidacy.* April 15. http://www.nbcnews.com/news/nbcblk/former-apprentice-contestants-denounce-donald-trump-s-candidacy-n556306

Foran, Clare. 2016. *A $1 Million Fight against Hillary Clinton's Online Trolls.* May 31. http://www.theatlantic.com/politics/archive/2016/05/correct-the-record-online-trolls/484847/.

Forbes. 2016. *Warren Buffett.* September 5. http://www.forbes.com/profile/warren-buffett/#.

—. 2017. *What's Donald Trump Really Worth?* September. Accessed October 23, 2017. https://www.forbes.com/donald-trump/#4dd3b4792899.

Ford, Matt. 2017. *Trump's Press Secretary Falsely Claims: 'Largest Audience Ever to Witness an Inauguration, Period.'* January 21. https://www.theatlantic.com/politics/archive/2017/01/inauguration-crowd-size/514058/.

Forrest, Conner. 2015. *Chinese Factory Replaces 90% of Humans with Robots, Production Soars.* July 30. http://www.techrepublic.com/article/chinese-factory-replaces-90-of-humans-with-robots-production-soars/.

Fort Liberty. n.d. *Web Sites Which Publish Fake News and Other Hoaxes.* Accessed November 25, 2016. http://www.fortliberty.org/hoax-sites.html.

Fournier, Deacon Keith. 2016. *Trump Is Right: Repeal the Johnson Amendment That Muzzles Pastors.* July 20. https://stream.org/trump-right-repeal-johnson-amendment-muzzles-pastors/.

France, Anatole. n.d. *Anatole France > Quotes > Quotable Quote.* Accessed September 6, 2017. https://www.goodreads.com/quotes/361132-the-law-in-its-majestic-equality-forbids-rich-and-poor.

Freeman, Sunny. 2016. *Canada's 'No' to Iraq War a Defining Moment for Prime Minister, Even 10 Years Later.* September 7. http://www.huffingtonpost.ca/2013/03/19/canada-iraq-war_n_2902305.html.

Friedersdorf, Conor. 2016. *The Exaggerated Claims of Media Bias against Donald Trump.* August 16. http://www.theatlantic.com/politics/archive/2016/08/claims-of-media-bias-against-donald-trump-are-exaggerated/495977/.

Frontline. 2005. *Holocaust Education in Germany: An Interview.* May 31. http://www.pbs.org/wgbh/pages/frontline/shows/germans/germans/education.html.

Gambino, Lauren. 2017. *Trump Congratulates Erdoğan after Turkey Vote Grants Sweeping Powers.* April 18. https://www.theguardian.com/us-news/2017/apr/17/donald-trump-erdogan-turkey-referendum-congratulations.

Gambino, Lauren, and David Smith. 2015. *House Benghazi Report Faults Military Response, Not Clinton, for Deaths.* June 28. https://www.theguardian.com/us-news/2016/jun/28/house-benghazi-report-clinton-attack-military.

Gammage, Jeff. 2017. *Adopted Years ago, Thousands Learn They're Not U.S. Citizens.* April 4. http://www.philly.com/philly/news/Adopted-from-Vietnam-as-a-baby---but-told-shes-not-an-American-citizen.html.

Gaouette, Nicole, and Richard Roth. 2017. *UN Ambassador Haley Hits Russia Hard on Ukraine.* February 3. http://www.cnn.com/2017/02/02/politics/haley-russia-un/.

Garofalo, Alex. 2016. *Who Are the 'Mothers of the Movement'? Families of Police Shooting Victims to Speak at Day 2 of DNC.* July 26. http://www.ibtimes.com/who-are-mothers-movement-families-police-shooting-victims-speak-day-2-dnc-2394960.

Garossino, Sandy. 2016. *What's Written in the Scars of Hillary Clinton.* August 1. http://www.nationalobserver.com/2016/08/01/analysis/whats-written-scars-hillary-clinton.

Garrison, Jessica, and Kendall Taggart. 2017. *Trump Given a Subpoena for All Documents Relating to Assault Allegations.* October 15. https://www.buzzfeed.com/jessicagarrison/subpoena-orders-trump-to-turn-over-documents-from-assault?utm_term=.qdvxJKVYl#.fj78moAqr.

Gass, Nick. 2015. *The 15 Most Offensive Things That Have Come out of Trump's Mouth.* December 8. http://www.politico.eu/article/15-most-offensive-things-trump-campaign-feminism-migration-racism/.

—. 2016. *15 Most Revealing Moments from Comey's Testimony on Clinton Emails.* July 7. http://www.politico.com/story/2016/07/james-comey-testimony-clinton-email-225224.

—. 2015. *Donald Trump Was for the Clintons Before He Was against Them.* December 29. http://www.politico.com/story/2015/12/donald-trump-hillary-bill-clinton-relationship-217191.

Geddes, John. 2016. *On Castro's Death, a Look at Fidel and Pierre—and Justin.* November 26. http://www.macleans.ca/politics/ottawa/on-castros-death-a-look-at-fidel-and-pierre-and-justin/.

Geerdink, Fréderike. 2016. *Stop Defending Turkey's 'Secularism'— It's Been a Lie All Along.* May 2. http://www.huffingtonpost.com/fraderike-geerdink-/turkey-secularism_b_9818250.html.

Gerstein, Josh. 2016. *Advice to Clinton about Email Goes Public.* September 7. http://www.politico.com/story/2016/09/colin-powell-hillary-clinton-emails-227861.

—. 2016. *Judge Delays Trump University Trial.* May 6. http://www.politico.com/story/2016/05/judge-sets-trump-university-trial-for-after-election-222917.

—. 2017. *Trump White House Grants Waivers of Ethics Rules.* Politico. May 31. https://www.politico.com/story/2017/05/31/trump-white-house-waivers-ethics-239011.

Gettleman, Jeffrey. 2017. *State Dept. Dissent Cable on Trump's Ban Draws 1,000 Signatures.* January 31. http://www.msn.com/en-us/news/politics/state-dept-dissent-cable-on-trump%E2%80%99s-ban-draws-1000-signatures/ar-AAmt9bV?li=BBnb7Kz.

Gillespie, Patrick. 2016. *About That Trump Tweet: Confidence Has Climbed for Years.* December 28. http://money.cnn.com/2016/12/28/news/economy/consumer-confidence-trump/.

Global Affairs Canada. 2018. Minister Champagne Welcomes Progress on the Comprehensive and Progressive Trans-Pacific Partnership. January 23. https://www.canada.ca/en/global-affairs/news/2017/11/minister_champagnewelcomesprogressonthecomprehensiveandprogressi.html.

Global Editorial. 2016. *Stephen Bannon Is Not the Real Problem. Donald Trump Is.* November 17. http://www.theglobeandmail.com/opinion/editorials/stephen-bannon-is-not-the-real-problem-donald-trump-is/article32879856/.

Globe Staff. 2017. *As the Women's March on Washington Goes Global, Here Are the Highlights.* January 22. http://www.theglobeandmail.com/news/world/womens-march-on-washington-goesglobal/article33696482/.

Glusac, Elaine. 2017. International Tourism to the U.S. Declined in Early 2017. September 19. https://www.nytimes.com/2017/09/19/travel/tourism-united-states-international-decline.html.

Goggin, Benjamin. 2017. *Twice-fired State Supreme Court Justice Wins Alabama Primary — Here's What You Need to Know.* September 26. https://digg.com/2017/alabama-primary-senate.

Goh, Brenda, and Michael Martina. 2017. *Chinese State Media Cheer Xi-Trump Meeting, Say Confrontation Not Inevitable.* April 8. http://www.reuters.com/article/us-usa-china-media-iduskbn17a06y.

Gold, Matea. 2015. *Pro-Trump Super PAC Shutting Down amid Questions about Ties to Trump Campaign.* October 22. https://www.washingtonpost.com/news/post-politics/wp/2015/10/22/pro-trump-super-pac-shutting-down-amid-questions-about-ties-to-trump-campaign/.

Goldberg, Whoopie, Joy Behar, Sonny Hostin, Sarah Haines, and Meghan McCain. 2017. *Day of Hot Topics.* November 30. http://abc.go.com/shows/the-view/episode-guide/2017-11/30-thursday-november-30-2017.

Goldmacher, Shane. 2016. *Donald Trump Calls Iraq 'Worst Decision' but Won't Repeat that Bush 'Lied.'* February 19. http://www.politico.com/blogs/south-carolina-primary-2016-live-updates-and-results/2016/02/2016-south-carolina-trump-george-w-bushs-iraq-219475.

Goldman , David . 2015. *Donald Trump Wants to 'Close up' the Internet.* December 8. http://money.cnn.com/2015/12/08/technology/donald-trump-internet/index.html.

Golgowski, Nina. 2017. *5-year-old Has Heart-wrenching Reunion with Mom after Airport Detention.* January 29. http://www.huffingtonpost.com.mx/entry/detained-child-reunited_us_588e48d6e4b0b065cbbcb559.

Gomez, Alan. 2015. *How Violent Are Undocumented Immigrants?* July 16. http://www.usatoday.com/story/news/nation/2015/07/16/voices-gomez-undocumented-immigrant-crime-san-francisco-shooting/30159479/.

Gomstyn, Alice. 2010. *Walmart CEO Pay: More in an Hour than Workers Get All Year?* July 2. http://abcnews.go.com/Business/walmart-ceo-pay-hour-workers-year/story?id=11067470.

Gonzales, Richard. 2017. *U.N. Security Council Approves New North Korea Sanctions.* September 11. http://www.npr.org/sections/thetwo-way/2017/09/11/550301634/u-n-security-council-approves-new-north-korea-sanctions.

Goodland, Marianne. 2015. *Most Colorado Republicans Are Silent after Planned Parenthood Shooting — But Not All.* December 1. http://www.coloradoindependent.com/156444/most-colorado-republicans-are-silent-after-planned-parenthood-shooting-but-not-all.

Gormley, Ken. 2010. *'Clinton vs. Starr': A 'Definitive' Account.* February 16. http://www.npr.org/templates/story/story.php?storyId=123653000.

Gottfried, Jeffrey, Michael Barthel, Elisa Shearer, and Amy Mitchell. 2016. *Presidential Campaign – A News Event That's Hard to Miss.* 2016. http://www.journalism.org/2016/02/04/the-2016-presidential-campaign-a-news-event-thats-hard-to-miss/.

Government of Canada. 2015. *Canadarm.* April 23. http://www.asc-csa.gc.ca/eng/canadarm/.

Grabar, Henry. 2018. 150,000 American Students Have Experienced a School Shooting. February 15. https://slate.com/news-and-politics/2018/02/150-000-american-students-have-experienced-a-school-shooting.html.

Grady, Denise, and Mark Landerler. 2013. *Clinton out of Hospital after Treatment for Clot.* January 2. http://www.nytimes.com/2013/01/03/us/politics/hillary-clinton-is-discharged-from-hospital-after-blood-clot.html.

Graham, David A. 2016. *'Lock Her Up': How Hillary Hatred Is Unifying Republicans.* July 20. http://www.theatlantic.com/politics/archive/2016/07/lock-her-up-hillary-clinton/492173/.

—. 2016. *The Lurking Menace of a Trump Rally.* March 10. http://www.theatlantic.com/politics/archive/2016/03/donald-trump-fayetteville/473169/.

—. 2016. *The Many Scandals of Donald Trump: A Cheat Sheet.* September 7. http://www.theatlantic.com/politics/archive/2016/09/donald-trump-scandals/474726/.

Graham-Harrison, Emma. 2016. *Russian Airstrikes in Syria Killed 2,000 Civilians in Six Months.* March 15. https://www.theguardian.com/world/2016/mar/15/russian-airstrikes-in-syria-killed-2000-civilians-in-six-months.

Graves, Lucia. 2016. *The Miss USA Hopeful Sued by Trump: 'There Are Ways to Stand Your Ground.'* September 4. https://www.theguardian.com/us-news/2016/sep/04/sheena-monnin-donald-trump-miss-usa-lawsuit.

Green, Amanda. 2013. *19 Things You Might Not Know Were Invented in Canada.* July 1. http://mentalfloss.com/article/51467/19-things-you-might-not-know-were-invented-canada.

Green, Emma. 2016. *Why Does the United States Give So Much Money to Israel?* September 15. http://www.theatlantic.com/international/archive/2016/09/united-states-israel-memorandum-of-understanding-military-aid/500192/.

Green, Joshua, and Sasha Issenberg. 2016. *Inside the Trump Bunker, with Days to Go.* October 27. https://www.bloomberg.com/news/articles/2016-10-27/inside-the-trump-bunker-with-12-days-to-go.

Greenberg, Jon. 2017. *Trump Wrongly Blames Press for Feud with Intel Community.* January 22. http://www.politifact.com/truth-o-meter/statements/2017/jan/22/donald-trump/trump-wrongly-blames-press-feud-intel-community/.

—. 2015. *Trump's Pants on Fire Tweet that Blacks Killed 81% of White Homicide Victims.* November 23. http://www.politifact.com/truth-o-meter/statements/2015/nov/23/donald-trump/trump-tweet-blacks-white-homicide-victims/.

Greenwood, Max. 2017. *Haley Rips into Russia as Security Council Weighs Resolution on Syrian Chemical Attack.* April 5. http://thehill.com/policy/international/327407-trumps-un-envoy-rips-into-russia-over-syria-chemical-weapons-attack.

Griffin, Drew, Scott Bronstein, Curt Devine, and Adam Mintzer. 2016. *Trump Maralago.* March 18. http://money.cnn.com/2016/03/18/news/economy/trump-maralago/.

Grimsley, Edwin. 2013. *African American Wrongful Convictions Today.* March 29. http://www.innocenceproject.org/african-american-wrongful-convictions-today/.

Grinberg, Emanuella. 2016. *Racial Bias Pervasive among Baltimore Police, DOJ Says.* August 10. http://www.cnn.com/2016/08/09/us/baltimore-justice-department-report/.

Griswold, Alex. 2016. *'No Way' My Father Is Sexist, Because He Hired Me.* September 5. http://www.mediaite.com/tv/ivanka-trump-no-way-my-father-is-sexist-because-he-hired-me/.

Groden, Claire. 2015. *Dick Cheney Slams Donald Trump's Proposed Ban on Muslim Admissions.* December 8. http://fortune.com/2015/12/08/dick-cheney-slams-donald-trumps-proposed-ban-on-muslim-admissions/.

Grossman, Cathy Lynn. 2016. *'I Will Protect Christians,' Donald Trump Tells Liberty University Students.* January 18. http://religionnews.com/2016/01/18/donald-trump-liberty-university-evangelicals/.

Guardian Staff. 2016. *Oklahoma Shaken by Strong Earthquake Causing 'Significant' Damage.* November 7. https://www.theguardian.com/world/2016/nov/07/strong-earthquake-central-oklahoma-damage.

Gunderson, Laura. 2015. *Oregon Shooter: New Details Emerge about Chris Harper-Mercer.* October 2. http://www.oregonlive.com/pacific-northwest-news/index.ssf/2015/10/new_details_emerge_on_umpqua_c.html.

Gutfeld, Greg. 2017. *Gutfeld: Obama Compares Trump to Hitler.* December 7. http://www.foxnews.com/transcript/2017/12/07/gutfeld-obama-compares-trump-to-hitler.html.

Haberman, Maggie, and Ashley Parker. 2016. *Roger Ailes Is Advising Donald Trump ahead of Presidential Debates.* August 16. http://www.nytimes.com/2016/08/17/us/politics/donald-trump-roger-ailes.html?_r=0.

Haddad, Lisa B, and Nawal M Nour. 2009. *Unsafe Abortion: Unnecessary Maternal Mortality.* Rev Obstet Gynecol, 2(2): 122–126, Spring. https://www.ncbi.nlm.nih.gov/pmc/articles/PMC2709326/.

Haddigan, Michael. 1996. *Tucker Sentenced to 4 Years' Probation.* August 20. https://www.washingtonpost.com/archive/politics/1996/08/20/tucker-sentenced-to-4-years-probation/0eeb9032-8afe-4caa-9cb5-1fb30bdfc6f7/?utm_term=.d71a191596c4.

Hankin, Laura. 2017. *3 Ways the GOP's Tax Plan Could Hurt Families If It Becomes Law.* Accessed January 4, 2018. https://www.romper.com/p/3-ways-the-gops-tax-plan-could-hurt-families-if-it-becomes-law-6772656.

Halleman, Caroline. 2016. *The U.S. Earns a Travel Warning from New Zealand, Germany, and the U.K.* August 15. http://www.townandcountrymag.com/leisure/travel-guide/news/a7446/travel-warnings-against-united-states/.

Han, Phil. 2010. *Donald Trump: I Have the Genes for Success.* February 11. http://www.cnn.com/2010/Showbiz/02/11/donald.trump.marriage.apprentice.

Hananoki, Eric. 2016. *Trump Ally Roger Stone Falls for Fake WikiLeaks Email.* November 2. http://www.mediamatters.org/blog/2016/11/02/trump-ally-roger-stone-falls-fake-wikileaks-email/214246.

Hansler, Jennifer. 2017. *Almost a Dozen Trump Nominees Have Withdrawn from Consideration for Administration.* October 17. http://www.cnn.com/2017/10/17/politics/tom-marino-trump-nomination-withdrawals/index.html?sr=twCNN101717tom-marino-trump-nomination-withdrawals0144PMStory.

Haraldsson, Hrafnkell. 2016. *Hillary Clinton Tops Trump's 88 with a List of 110 Generals and Admirals Backing Her.* September 9. http://www.politicususa.com/2016/09/09/hillary-clinton-tops-trumps-88-list-110-generals-admirals-backing.html.

Harding, Luke. 2016. *How Trump's Campaign Chief Got a Strongman Elected President of Ukraine.* August 16. https://www.theguardian.com/us-news/2016/aug/16/donald-trump-campaign-paul-manafort-ukraine-yanukovich.

Harkinson, Josh. 2016. *Trump Selects a White Nationalist Leader as a Delegate in California.* July/August. http://www.motherjones.com/politics/2016/05/donald-trump-white-nationalist-afp-delegate-california/.

Harrington, Rebecca. 2017. *Trump Reportedly Didn't Know about the Loophole in the 25th Amendment That Lets 14 People Remove a Sitting President from Office.* October 11. http://www.businessinsider.com/25th-amendment-how-can-you-remove-president-from-office-2017-3.

Harwell, Drew, and Jonathan O'Connell. 2017. *The Many Ways President Trump Would Benefit from the GOP's Tax Plan.* November 10. https://www.washingtonpost.com/business/economy/the-many-ways-president-trump-would-benefit-from-the-gops-tax-plan/2017/11/10/d82c8116-c4ba-11e7-aae0-cb18a8c29c65_story.html?utm_term=.9f4aca2bf57c.

Hasson, Nir. 2014. *Despite It All, Most Israelis Still Support the Two-state Solution.* July 7. http://www.haaretz.com/peace/1.601996.

Hastings, David A. 2009. *From Human Development to Human Security: A Prototype Human Security Index.* October. http://www.unescap.org/sites/default/files/wp-09-03_0.pdf.

Hausam, Michael. 2015. *Donald Trump Keeps Saying His Campaign Is Self-funded. But That Is Just Not True.* November 11. http://ijr.com/2015/11/469588-donald-trump-keeps-saying-his-campaign-is-self-funded-but-that-is-just-not-true/.

Hause, Marti, and Ari Melber. 2016. *Jailed but Innocent: Record Number of People Exonerated in 2015.* February 3. http://www.nbcnews.com/news/us-news/jailed-innocent-record-number-people-exonerated-2015-n510196.

Hawkins, Derek. 2016. *No, You Can't Text Your Vote. But These Fake Ads Tell Clinton Supporters to Do Just That.* November 3. https://www.washingtonpost.com/news/morning-mix/wp/2016/11/03/no-you-cant-text-your-vote-but-these-ads-tell-clinton-supporters-to-do-just-that/.

Hawkins, John. 2016. *The 5 Biggest Revelations about Hillary Clinton from WikiLeaks.* October 29. http://townhall.com/columnists/johnhawkins/2016/10/29/the-5-biggest-revelations-about-hillary-clinton-from-wikileaks-n2238298.

Heavey, Susan, and Jack Kim. 2017. *Message from North Korean Missile over Japan 'Loud and Clear': Trump.* August 28. https://www.reuters.com/article/us-northkorea-missiles-idUSKCN1B8283.

Helderman, Rosalind S., and Tom Hamburger. 2017. *Eighth Person in Trump Tower Meeting Is Identified.* July 18. https://www.washingtonpost.com/politics/eighth-person-in-trump-tower-meeting-is-identified/2017/07/18/e971234a-6bce-11e7-9c15-177740635e83_story.html?hpid=hp_hp-top-table-low_8thman-1225pm%3Ahomepage%2Fstory&utm_term=.23550c5cde52.

Heller, Joseph. n.d. *Joseph Heller > Quotes.* Accessed August 12, 2016. https://www.goodreads.com/author/quotes/3167.Joseph_Heller.

Hellmann, Jessie. 2017. *Majority of Voters Want Obamacare Fix, Not Repeal.* March 5. http://thehill.com/policy/healthcare/322504-poll-majority-of-voters-want-to-fix-obamacare-instead-of-repealing-it.

—. 2016. *New Yorker Profile: Flynn Broke 'Stupid' Rules during Army Career.* November 24. http://thehill.com/homenews/administration/307495-new-yorker-trumps-national-security-adviser-broke-stupid-rules-during.

Hemingway, Mollie. 2016. *6 Problems with Media's Hysterical Reaction to Trump's ISIS Comments.* August 12. http://thefederalist.com/2016/08/12/6-problems-with-medias-hysterical-reaction-to-trumps-isis-comments/.

Henley, Jon. 2017. *Angela Merkel: EU Cannot Completely Rely on US and Britain Any More.* May 28. https://www.theguardian.com/world/2017/may/28/merkel-says-eu-cannot-completely-rely-on-us-and-britain-any-more-g7-talks.

Hennigan, W.J. 2017. *U.S. Military Leaders Condemn Racism Following Trump's Comments on Charlottesville Violence.* August 16. http://www.latimes.com/politics/washington/la-na-essential-washington-updates-u-s-military-leaders-condemn-racism-1502898652-htmlstory.html.

Henry, Natasha. 2013. *Slavery in Canada? I Never Learned That!* October 23. http://activehistory.ca/2013/10/slavery-in-canada-i-never-learned-that/.

Hertling, Lt. Gen. Mark, interview by Anderson Cooper. 2016. *I'll Give Generals 30 Days for a Plan to Fight ISIS* (September 7).

Heyer, Hazel. 2008. *Executive Talk: Donald Trump Jr. Bullish on Russia and Few Emerging Markets.* September 15. https://eturbonews.com/9788/executive-talk-donald-trump-jr-bullish-russia-and-few-emerging-ma.

Hicken, Melanie. 2013. *Shutdown Took $24 Billion Bite out of Economy.* October 17. http://money.cnn.com/2013/10/16/news/economy/shutdown-economic-impact/.

Hillary for America. 2016. *Criminal Justice Reform.* July 8. https://www.hillaryclinton.com/issues/criminal-justice-reform/.

—. 2016. *Hillary Clinton, Tim Kaine Release Tax Returns While Donald Trump Defies Decades-Old Tradition of Disclosure.* https://www.hillaryclinton.com/page/tax-returns/.

History.com. n.d. *Did Marie-Antoinette Really Say "Let Them Eat Cake"?* Accessed October 4, 2016. http://www.history.com/news/ask-history/did-marie-antoinette-really-say-let-them-eat-cake.

—. n.d. *Republican Party Founded.* Accessed November 22, 2016. http://www.history.com/this-day-in-history/republican-party-founded.

—. n.d. *Voting Rights Act.* Accessed September 24, 2016. http://www.history.com/topics/black-history/voting-rights-act.

Hitler, Adolf. n.d. *Adolf Hitler > Quotes > Quotable Quote.* Accessed October 9, 2017. http://www.goodreads.com/quotes/553-if-you-tell-a-big-enough-lie-and-tell-it.

—. n.d. *Adolf Hitler > Quotes > Quotable Quote.* Accessed October 9, 2017. https://www.goodreads.com/quotes/74363-the-receptivity-of-the-masses-is-very-limited-their-intelligence.

Hjelmgaard, Kim. 2017. *There Is Meddling in Germany's Election — Not by Russia, but by U.S. Right Wing.* September 20. https://www.usatoday.com/story/news/world/2017/09/20/meddling-germany-election-not-russia-but-u-s-right-wing/676142001/.

Hockenos, Paul . 2018. *Germany Has a Far-Right Enemy Within.* March 27. https://www.cnn.com/2018/03/27/opinions/afd-german-enemy-within-intl/index.html.

Hoft, Jim. 2016. *Social Media Patterns Show Trump Is Looking at a Landslide Victory.* August 7. http://www.thegatewaypundit.com/2016/08/evidence-trump-landslide/.

Holan, Angie Drobnic and Linda Qiu. 2015. *Lie of the Year: The Campaign Misstatements of Donald Trump.* December 21. http://www.politifact.com/truth-o-meter/article/2015/dec/21/2015-lie-year-donald-trump-campaign-misstatements/.

Holland, Steve, and Jeff Mason. 2017. *If Threatened, U.S. Will 'Totally Destroy' North Korea, Trump Vows.* September 19. http://www.reuters.com/article/us-un-assembly-trump/if-threatened-u-s-will-totally-destroy-north-korea-trump-vows-iduskcn1bu0b3.

—. 2017. *Trump Fires FBI Director Comey, Setting off U.S. Political Storm.* May 10. http://www.reuters.com/article/us-usa-trump-comey-iduskbn1852mv.

Holmes, Jack. 2017. *President Trump Embarrassed You Again Today.* October 23. http://www.esquire.com/news-politics/a12772874/trump-puerto-rico-ruin-budget/.

The Holy Bible: King James Version. n.d. John 7:53-8:11. Accessed December 19, 2017. https://www.biblegateway.com/passage/?search=John%207:53-8:11.

Horowitz, Jason. 2016. *With Degree Debunked, Melania Trump Website Is Taken Down.* July 28. http://www.nytimes.com/2016/07/29/us/politics/melania-trump.html?_r=0.

Horowitz, Julia, and Cristina Alesci. 2017. *Outgoing Ethics Chief Urges Trump to Stop Visiting His Properties.* July 17. http://money.cnn.com/2017/07/17/news/walter-shaub-oge-interview/index.html.

Horsley, Scott. 2016. *Fact Check: Hillary Clinton and Coal Jobs.* May 3. http://www.npr.org/2016/05/03/476485650/fact-check-hillary-clinton-and-coal-jobs.

Howard, Jacqueline. 2017. *Where Climate Change Is Threatening the Health of Americans.* April 13. http://www.cnn.com/2017/04/13/health/climate-change-health-risks-us-map-explainer/index.html.

Howe, Caleb. 2016. *Lyin' Don: Trump Just Totally Made Up the Story that He Talked to Marco Rubio Recently.* May 7. http://www.redstate.com/absentee/2016/05/07/lyin-don-trump-just-totally-made-story-talked-marco-rubio-recently/.

Hoyer, Steny. 2014. *Just the Facts: House Republicans' Record on Obstruction.* September 11. https://www.democraticwhip.gov/content/just-facts-house-republicans-record-obstruction.

Hughes, Laura. 2016. *Iran Nuclear Deal 'Vital,' Warns Theresa May After Donald Trump Vows to Scrap it.* December 7. http://www.telegraph.co.uk/news/2016/12/07/iran-nuclear-deal-vital-warns-theresa-may-donald-trump-vows/.

Huie, Jonathan Lockwood. n.d. *Those Quotes and Sayings.* Accessed November 18, 2016. http://www.jonathan-lockwoodhuie.com/quotes/those/.

Hume, Tim. 2016. *British Lawmakers Debate Banning Donald Trump from UK for 'Hate Speech.'* January 18. http://www.cnn.com/2016/01/18/europe/uk-parliament-debates-trump-ban/.

Hunter, Paul. 2017. *'We Don't Blame You': Wisconsin Farmers on Trump's Blast at Canada's Dairy Industry.* April 22. http://www.cbc.ca/news/world/dairy-farmers-wisconsin-trump-1.4081391.

Hurley, Lawrence, and Steve Holland. 2017. *Trump Picks Conservative Judge Gorsuch for U.S. Supreme Court.* January 31. http://www.reuters.com/article/us-usa-court-trump-iduskbn15f1ow.

Independent. 2016. *Donald Trump Gets Backing from Hezbollah over Claim Barack Obama Founded Isis.* August 14. https://www.independent.co.uk/news/world/americas/us-elections/donald-trump-gets-backing-from-hezbollah-over-claim-barack-obama-founded-isis-a7189801.html.

Ingraham, Christopher. 2014. *America's Most Gerrymandered Congressional Districts.* May 15. https://www.washingtonpost.com/news/wonk/wp/2014/05/15/americas-most-gerrymandered-congressional-districts/.

Ingram, Mathew. 2016. *Could Donald Trump Actually Make Good on His Promise to 'Open Up' Libel Laws?* February 29. http://fortune.com/2016/02/29/trump-libel-law/.

InsideGov. n.d. *2017 United States Budget Estimate.* Accessed October 24, 2017. http://federal-budget.insidegov.com/l/120/2017-Estimate.

International Joint Commission. 2016. *Role of the IJC.* International Joint Commission. Accessed August 13, 2016. http://www.ijc.org/en_/Role_of_the_Commission.

Isidore, Chris. 2013. *Buffett Says He's Still Paying Lower Tax Rate than His Secretary.* March 4. http://money.cnn.com/2013/03/04/news/economy/buffett-secretary-taxes/.

—. 2016. *Carrier Union Boss: No Regrets about Calling Trump a Liar.* December 8. http://money.cnn.com/2016/12/08/news/companies/trump-carrier-union-boss/.

Islam 101. n.d. *Return Back to Peace.* Accessed December 23, 2017. http://returnbacktopeace.yolasite.com/islam-101.php.

Jackson, Brooks. 2016. *Obama's Numbers (January 2016 Update).* January 12. http://www.factcheck.org/2016/01/obamas-numbers-january-2016-update/.

—. 2017. *What President Trump Inherits.* January 20. http://www.factcheck.org/2017/01/what-president-trump-inherits/.

Jackson, David. 2016. *Secretary of State Nominee Rex Tillerson's Ties to Russia Worry GOP, Too.* December 13. http://www.usatoday.com/story/news/politics/elections/2016/2016/12/13/donald-trump-rex-tillerson-secretary-of-state/95365434/.

Jackson, Emma Margolinfrank Thorp Vhallie. 2016. *Marco Rubio Warns Republicans: Don't Talk about Wikileaks.* October 19. http://www.nbcnews.com/card/marco-rubio-warns-republicans-dont-talk-about-wikileaks-n668746.

Jacobs, John. 1999. *The Gingrich Affair: Hypocrisy and Betrayal.* November 22. http://www.sfgate.com/news/article/The-Gingrich-affair-Hypocrisy-and-betrayal-3057206.php,%20November%2022,%201999.

Jacobson, Louis, and Amy Sherman. 2016. *Donald Trump's Pants on Fire Claim that Barack Obama 'Founded' ISIS, Hillary Clinton Was 'Cofounder.'* August 11. http://www.politifact.com/truth-o-meter/statements/2016/aug/11/donald-trump/donald-trump-pants-fire-claim-obama-founded-isis-c/.

Jacobson, Louis. 2016. *Donald Trump Gets a Full Flop for Whether He's Had a Relationship to Vladimir Putin.* August 1. http://www.politifact.com/truth-o-meter/statements/2016/aug/01/donald-trump/donald-trump-gets-full-flop-whether-hes-had-relati/.

—. 2015. *No Evidence for Hillary Clinton's Claim that ISIS Is Using Videos of Donald Trump as Recruiting Tool.* December 19. http://www.politifact.com/truth-o-meter/statements/2015/dec/19/hillary-clinton/fact-checking-hillary-clintons-claim-isis-using-vi/.

—. 2016. *Was Saddam Hussein Good at Killing Terrorists, as Donald Trump says?* July 7. http://www.politifact.com/truth-o-meter/statements/2016/jul/07/donald-trump/was-saddam-hussein-good-killing-terrorists-donald-/.

James, Brendan. 2016. *Here's What Trump Has Said So Far about Sexual Harassment and Roger Ailes.* August 3. https://news.vice.com/article/donald-trump-sexual-harassment-roger-ailes-fox-news.

—. 2015. *Rand Paul: Baltimore Violence Is about 'Lack of Fathers' and Morals.* April 28. http://talkingpointsmemo.com/livewire/rand-paul-freddie-gray-baltimore-morals.

Jefferson, Thomas. n.d. *Jefferson's Draft.* Accessed October 9, 2017. https://jeffersonpapers.princeton.edu/selected-documents/jefferson%E2%80%99s-draft.

Mason, Jeff, and Steve Holland. 2017. *White House Chief of Staff Not Quitting, Says Job Is Not to Control Trump.* October 12. https://www.reuters.com/article/us-usa-trump-kelly/white-house-chief-of-staff-not-quitting-says-job-is-not-to-control-trump-idUSKBN1CH2P6.

Jensen, Tom. 2016. *Trump, Clinton Continue to Lead in SC.* February 16. http://www.publicpolicypolling.com/pdf/2015/PPP_Release_SC_21616.pdf.

Johnson, Linda A. 2016. *How EpiPen's Maker Raised Prices.* August 24. http://www.torontosun.com/2016/08/24/how-epipens-maker-raised-prices.

Johnston, David Cay, Betsy McCaughey, interview by Michael Smerconish. 2016. *The Real Art of Trump's Deals.* August 27. http://transcripts.cnn.com/Transcripts/1608/27/smer.01.html.

Johnston, David Cay. 2011. *Beyond the 1 Percent.* October 25. http://blogs.reuters.com/david-cay-johnston/2011/10/25/beyond-the-1-percent/.

Jones, Sarah. 2017. *Even Republicans Are Getting Fed Up with Trump's Unqualified Judicial Nominees.* December 15. https://newrepublic.com/minutes/146309/even-republicans-getting-fed-trumps-unqualified-judicial-nominees.

—. 2016. *Fact Checkers Prove that 91% of the Things Donald Trump Says Are False.* August 16. http://www.politicususa.com/2016/03/31/ninety-one-percent-donald-trump-false.html.

Jones, Van, Boris Epshteyn, Paris Dennard, and Bob Beckel, interview by Don Lemon. 2016. *Donald Trump and Birthers* (September 9).

Kaczynski, Andrew, and Nathan McDermott. 2016. *Donald Trump Said He Supported Invading Iraq.* February 18. https://www.buzzfeed.com/andrewkaczynski/in-2002-donald-trump-said-he-supported-invading-iraq-on-the?utm_term=.keo8q4L845#.alQwYe1wer.

Kamisar, Ben. 2016. *Trump Calls on Supporters to Monitor Polling Places for Fraud.* October 10. http://thehill.com/blogs/ballot-box/presidential-races/298856-trump-calls-on-supporters-to-monitor-polling-places-for.

Kantor, Jodi, and Megan Twohey. 2017. *Harvey Weinstein Paid off Sexual Harassment Accusers for Decades.* October 5. https://www.nytimes.com/2017/10/05/us/harvey-weinstein-harassment-allegations.html?_r=0.

Kaplan, Fred. 2004. *Reagan's Osama Connection*. June 10. http://www.slate.com/articles/news_and_politics/war_stories/2004/06/reagans_osama_connection.html.

Kaplan, Rebecca, Jake Miller, Alicia Amling, John Nolen, and Steven Portnoy. 2015. *5 Things to Know about Netanyahu's Speech to Congress*. March 3. http://www.cbsnews.com/news/five-things-netanyahu-speech-congress/.

Kaplan, Thomas, and Robert Pear. 2017. *Health Bill Would Add 24 Million Uninsured but Save $337 Billion, Report Says*. March 13. https://www.nytimes.com/2017/03/13/us/politics/affordable-care-act-health-congressional-budget-office.html?_r=0.

Karni, Annie. 2016. *Clinton Caught in Email Hurricane*. July 7. http://www.politico.com/story/2016/07/hillary-clinton-email-fbi-testimony-225272.

Katkov, Mark. 2016. *Trump's Pick for Ambassador to Israel: 'End the 2-state Narrative.'* December 16. http://www.npr.org/sections/thetwo-way/2016/12/16/505805411/trumps-pick-for-ambassador-to-israel-end-the-2-state-narrative.

Keating, Caitlin. 2016. *How Sick Are the Kids in Flint? Inside the Shocking Health Effects of the Devastating Water Crisis*. January 28. http://people.com/human-interest/flint-water-crisis-inside-the-shocking-health-effects/.

Keating, Joshua. 2017. *Kim Jong-un Is Calling Trump's Bluff*. August 29. http://www.slate.com/blogs/the_slatest/2017/08/29/kim_jong_un_is_calling_trump_s_bluff.html.

keepemhonest. 2012. *Newt Gingrich He and Paul Ryan Plotted to Sabotage the US Economy on January 20, 2009*. October 28. http://www.dailykos.com/story/2012/10/28/1151619/-VIDEO-gt-Newt-Gingrich-he-and-Paul-Ryan-plotted-to-sabotage-the-US-Economy-on-January-20-2009.

Keith, Tamara. 2016. *Evolution or Expediency? Clinton's Changing Positions over a Long Career*. May 23. http://www.npr.org/2016/05/23/478973321/evolution-or-expediency-clintons-changing-positions-over-a-long-career.

Kelly, Amita. 2016. *Woman Asks Trump about Replacing TSA's 'Heebeejabis' with Veterans*. June 30. http://www.npr.org/2016/06/30/484229621/woman-asks-trump-about-replacing-tsas-heebejabis-with-veterans.

Kelly, General John. 2017. *Press Briefing by Press Secretary Sarah Sanders and Chief of Staff General John Kelly*. The White House: Office of the Press Secretary. October 19. https://www.whitehouse.gov/the-press-office/2017/10/19/press-briefing-press-secretary-sarah-sanders-and-chief-staff-general.

Kenney, Carolyn, and John Norris. 2017. *Trump's Conflicts of Interest in Israel*. June 14. https://www.american-progress.org/issues/security/news/2017/06/14/433942/trumps-conflicts-interest-.

Kershaw, Ian. n.d. *The Hitler Myth*. Accessed June 10, 2016. http://www.historytoday.com/ian-kershaw/hitler-myth.

Kessler, Glenn. 2016. *Did Donald Trump Really Say Those Things?* July 25. https://www.washingtonpost.com/news/fact-checker/wp/2016/07/25/did-donald-trump-really-say-those-things/.

—. 2015. *Is the Estate Tax Killing Small Farms and Businesses?* April 14. https://www.washingtonpost.com/news/fact-checker/wp/2015/04/14/the-facts-about-the-estate-tax-and-farmers/?utm_term=.a77d17e0bb57.

—. 2016. *Pence vs. Clinton on the Iraq War Vote 'Mistake.'* July 19. https://www.washingtonpost.com/news/fact-checker/wp/2016/07/19/pence-versus-clinton-on-the-iraq-war-vote-mistake/.

—. 2016. *Trump's False Claim that Clinton Only Recently Pledged to Renegotiate NAFTA*. August 8. https://www.washingtonpost.com/news/fact-checker/wp/2016/08/08/trumps-false-claim-that-clinton-only-recently-pledged-to-renegotiate-nafta/.

—. 2015. *Trump's Outrageous Claim that 'Thousands' of New Jersey Muslims Celebrated the 9/11 Attacks*. November 22. https://www.washingtonpost.com/news/fact-checker/wp/2015/11/22/donald-trumps-outrageous-claim-that-thousands-of-new-jersey-muslims-celebrated-the-911-attacks/.

Khan, Shehab. 2017. *Angela Merkel 'Explains' to Donald Trump the Obligations of Geneva Refugee Convention after His Immigration Ban*. January 30. http://www.independent.co.uk/news/world/europe/anglea-merkel-explains-donald-trump-geneva-refugee-convention-obligations-muslim-immigration-ban-us-a7552506.html.

Kheel, Rebecca. 2016. *Israel Will Share 'Evidence' of Obama-UN Collusion with Trump, Ambassador Says*. December 26. http://thehill.com/policy/defense/311836-israel-will-share-evidence-of-obama-un-collusion-with-trump-ambassador-says.

Kiely, Eugene. 2016. *Partisan Spin on Clinton's Emails.* July 6. http://www.factcheck.org/2016/06/partisan-spin-on-clintons-emails/.

—. 2017. *Scott Pruitt and Coal Jobs.* June 5. http://www.factcheck.org/2017/06/scott-pruitt-coal-jobs/.

—. 2016. *Trump's Employee Exaggeration in Jersey.* May 25. http://www.factcheck.org/2016/05/trumps-employee-exaggeration-in-jersey/.

Kiely, Kathy. 2016. *The Making of Donald Trump, as Told by a Journalistic Nemesis.* August 6. http://www.commondreams.org/views/2016/08/06/making-donald-trump-told-journalistic-nemesis.

Killough, Ashley. 2016. *Trump Says He Would Like to 'Hit' DNC Speakers Who Disparaged Him.* July 29. http://www.cnn.com/2016/07/28/politics/donald-trump-dnc-response/.

Kinsley, Michael. 2015. *Parsing the Plagiarism of Fareed Zakaria.* March. http://www.vanityfair.com/news/2015/02/michael-kinsley-fareed-zakaria-plagarism.

Klein, Aaron. 2016. *Bill Sex Accusers Back up Trump Remarks on Hillary the 'Enabler.'* May 7. http://www.breitbart.com/2016-presidential-race/2016/05/07/bills-sex-accusers-echo-trump-hillary-enabler/.

Koffler, Jacob. 2015. *Donald Trump's 16 Biggest Business Failures and Successes.* August 7. http://time.com/3988970/donald-trump-business/.

Kopack, Steve, and John W. Schoen. 2017. *Here's a Progress Report on Trump's First 100 Days.* April 12. http://www.cnbc.com/2017/04/11/heres-a-progress-report-on-trumps-first-100-days.html.

Kopan, Tal. 2017. *Judge Blocks Part of Trump's Sanctuary Cities Executive Order.* April 26. http://www.cnn.com/2017/04/25/politics/sanctuary-cities-injunction/index.html.

Koppelman, Alex, and Brian Stelter. 2016. *Trump Uses Un-canceled Meeting with New York Times to Complain about the Times.* November 22. http://money.cnn.com/2016/11/22/media/trump-new-york-times-meeting/.

Korte, Gregory. 2016. *Obama Phones Trump, Offers White House Invitation.* November 9. http://www.usatoday.com/story/news/politics/2016/11/09/obama-phones-trump-offer-congratulations-and-white-house-meeting/93534068/.

Kounang, Nadia. 2015. *Why Pharmaceuticals Are Cheaper Abroad.* September 28. http://www.cnn.com/2015/09/28/health/us-pays-more-for-drugs/.

Krieg, Gregory. 2015. *Donald Trump: 'Strongly Consider' Shutting Mosques.* November 16. http://www.cnn.com/2015/11/16/politics/donald-trump-paris-attacks-close-mosques/.

—. 2016. *It's Official: Clinton Swamps Trump in Popular Vote.* December 22. http://edition.cnn.com/2016/12/21/politics/donald-trump-hillary-clinton-popular-vote-final-count/.

Krieger, Nick. 2016. *2016 Election Results Show Effects of Gerrymandering in Michigan.* November 19. http://www.fixthemitten.com/blog/2016-election-results-show-effects-of-gerrymandering-in-michigan/.

Labott, Elise, and Eugene Scott. 2016. *Graham: Defund UN after Israeli Settlement Vote.* December 25. http://www.cnn.com/2016/12/24/politics/lindsey-graham-united-nations/index.html.

LaCapria, Kim. 2015. *Donald Trump Was Inaccurately Reported as Asserting that Muslims Should Wear ID Badges, a Claim That Drew Inevitable Comparisons to Adolf Hitler. But He Did Speak in Favor of a Muslim Registry.* November 19. http://www.snopes.com/donald-trump-muslims-id/.

Ladutke, Larry. 2014. *What Happens When Abortion Is Banned.* September 25. http://blog.amnestyusa.org/americas/what-happens-when-abortion-is-banned/.

Lambro, Donald. 2016. *Trump Ignores 'Buddy' Putin's Atrocities.* September 30. http://townhall.com/columnists/donaldlambro/2016/09/30/trump-ignores-buddy-putins-atrocities-n2225476.

Lamothe, Dan. 2016. *It's Legal for Donald Trump to Accept a Purple Heart. How He Handled It Is Up for Debate.* August 3. https://www.washingtonpost.com/news/checkpoint/wp/2016/08/03/its-legal-for-donald-trump-to-accept-a-purple-heart-how-he-handled-it-is-up-for-debate/.

Landler, Mark, and Yamiche Alcindor. 2017. *Trump's Condolence Call to Soldier's Widow Ignites an Imbroglio.* October 18. https://www.nytimes.com/2017/10/18/us/politics/trump-widow-johnson-call.html?_r=1.

LaPointe, Kirk. 2011. *Review from the Office of the Ombudsman | English Services.* November 18. http://www.ombudsman.cbc.radio-canada.ca/en/complaint-reviews/2011/unions/.

Lapowsky, Issie. 2017. *Author of Trump's Favorite Voter Fraud Study Says Everyone's Wrong.* January 25. https://www.wired.com/2017/01/author-trumps-favorite-voter-fraud-study-says-everyones-wrong/.

Laughland, Oliver. 2016. *Donald Trump and the Central Park Five.* February 17. https://www.theguardian.com/us-news/2016/feb/17/central-park-five-donald-trump-jogger-rape-case-new-york.

—. 2016. *Ex-Trump Workers Describe Egocentric Micromanager: 'Donald Loves Donald.'* March 14. https://www.theguardian.com/us-news/2016/mar/14/donald-trump-former-employee-interviews-ego-diversity.

Lauletta, Tyler. 2017. *The NFL Is Getting Hammered After Another Game Was Played in a Half-Empty Stadium.* September 22. http://www.businessinsider.com/nfl-attendance-down-2017-9.

Laxer, Gordon. 2016. *If We're Renegotiating NAFTA, Let's Be Ready to Walk Away.* August 31. http://www.theglobeandmail.com/report-on-business/rob-commentary/if-were-renegotiating-nafta-lets-be-ready-to-walk-away/article31609876/.

Layton, Peter. 2017. *The 2 Percent NATO Benchmark Is a Red Herring.* February 16. http://nationalinterest.org/blog/the-buzz/the-2-percent-nato-benchmark-red-herring-19472.

Lee, Barbara, interview by Brooke Baldwin. 2017. "Strike against Syria." *CNN Newsroom With Brooke Baldwin.* (April 7). https://archive.org/details/CNNW_20170407_180000_CNN_Newsroom_With_Brooke_Baldwin.

Lee, Michelle Ye Hee. 2016. *Trump's Claim Tying Violence at His Rallies to the Clinton Campaign.* October 21. https://www.washingtonpost.com/news/fact-checker/wp/2016/10/21/trumps-claim-tying-violence-at-his-rallies-to-the-clinton-campaign/.

Legal Information Institute. 2016. *18 U.S. Code § 249 - Hate Crime Acts.* September 20. https://www.law.cornell.edu/uscode/text/18/249.

—. 2016. *West Virginia State Board of Education v. Barnette.* September 24. https://www.law.cornell.edu/supremecourt/text/319/624.

Lemire, Jonathan, and Julie Pace. 2017. *Trump Scolds NATO Leaders for Not Paying Up, Vows Crackdown on Manchester Leaks.* May 25. https://www.thestar.com/news/world/2017/05/25/trump-meets-european-leaders-as-uk-cuts-off-intel-sharing-over-leaks.html.

Lempel, Robin. 2016. *Donald Trump's Net Worth Extremely High? What Marla Maples and Ivana Trump Got as Financial Settlements after Their Divorces.* April 5. http://www.hollywoodtake.com/donald-trumps-net-worth-extremely-high-what-marla-maples-and-ivana-trump-got-financial-153321.

Levenson, Eric. 2017. *3 Storms, 3 Responses: Comparing Harvey, Irma and Maria.* September 27. http://www.cnn.com/2017/09/26/us/response-harvey-irma-maria/index.html.

Levine, Dan, and Mica Rosenberg. 2016. *Nevada Judge Rejects Trump Request for Order over Early Voting.* November 8. http://www.reuters.com/article/us-usa-election-lawsuit/nevada-judge-rejects-trump-request-for-order-over-early-voting-iduskbn1332d4?il=0.

Levine, Daniel S. 2017. *General Pershing Pig's Blood Myth: 5 Fast Facts You Need to Know.* August 17. http://heavy.com/news/2017/08/general-pershing-trump-bullets-dipped-in-pigs-blood-myth/.

—. 2016. *James Mattis on the Issues: 5 Fast Facts You Need to Know.* December 1. http://heavy.com/news/2016/12/general-james-mattis-issues-israel-defense-secretary-donald-trump-mad-dog-age-who-is-bio-views-isis-syria/.

Levingston, Ivan. 2016. *Trump Bashes Hillary Clinton's Foreign Policy, Calling Her a 'World-class Liar'.* June 22. http://www.cnbc.com/2016/06/22/trump-bashes-hillary-clintons-foreign-policy-calling-her-a-world-class-liar.html.

Levintova, Daniel, and Hannah Schulman. 2017. *The Flynn Scandal Explodes: What this Means and How It Happened.* May 18. http://www.motherjones.com/politics/2017/05/michael-flynn-scandal-timeline-trump.

Lewis, Jeffrey. 2017. *Let's Face It: North Korean Nuclear Weapons Can Hit the U.S.* August 3. https://www.nytimes.com/2017/08/03/opinion/north-korea-nukes.html?_r=0.

Liberty State Park, Liberty Science Center. n.d. *Statue of Liberty National Monument.* Accessed August 30, 2017. http://www.libertystatepark.com/emma.htm.

Library of Congress. n.d. *Points-Based Immigration Systems: Canada.* Accessed September 6, 2017. https://www.loc.gov/law/help/points-based-immigration/canada.php.

Lillis, Mike. 2011. *Hoyer: Republicans Would See Country 'Fail' to Defeat Obama's Reelection Bid.* September 20. http://thehill.com/homenews/house/182637-hoyer-gop-would-see-country-fail-to-defeat-obama.

Lima, Cristiano. 2016. *Clinton Gives Her Take on Sanders Supporters in Leaked Fundraising Recording.* September 30. http://www.politico.com/story/2016/09/hillary-clinton-bernie-sanders-supporters-audio-leak-228997.

Lind, Dara. 2017. *9 Facts That Explain DACA, the Immigration Program Trump Is Threatening to End.* September 5. https://www.vox.com/policy-and-politics/2017/8/31/16226934/daca-trump-dreamers-immigration.

Linge, Mary Kay. 2017. *Bannon Declares War on GOP Establishment.* October 14. http://nypost.com/2017/10/14/bannon-warns-gop-incumbents-nobody-can-run-and-hide/.

Link, Taylor. 2016. *North Carolina Is Openly Celebrating Its Black Voter Suppression Efforts.* November 7. http://www.salon.com/2016/11/07/north-carolina-obama-coalition-crumbling-ncgop-celebrates-voting-suppression-efforts-in-a-press-release/.

Linskey, Annie. 2015. *In Swing States, Clinton May Face Gender Bias.* September 9. https://www.bostonglobe.com/news/nation/2015/09/09/hillary-clinton-faces-challenges-unique-woman-running-for-office/Zkv99eyLTzAVzskuGnvRPN/story.html.

Lipka, Michael. 2016. *5 Facts about Abortion.* June 27. http://www.pewresearch.org/fact-tank/2016/06/27/5-facts-about-abortion/.

Liptak, Kevin, and Miranda Green. 2017. *Price out as HHS Secretary after Private Plane Scandal.* September 29. http://www.cnn.com/2017/09/29/politics/tom-price-resigns/index.html.

Liptak, Kevin, Daniella Diaz, and Sophie Tatum. 2017. *Trump Pardons Former Sheriff Joe Arpaio.* August 27. http://www.cnn.com/2017/08/25/politics/sheriff-joe-arpaio-donald-trump-pardon/index.html.

Lister, Tim. 2015. *ISIS Atrocity in Libya Demonstrates Its Growing Reach in North Africa.* February 17. http://www.cnn.com/2015/02/16/africa/isis-libya-north-africa/index.html.

Little Bird. 2016. *62% of the People Trump Re-tweeted This Week Follow Multiple White Supremacist Accounts.* January 28. http://www.mintpressnews.com/213194-2/213194/.

Lizza, Ryan. 2017. *Anthony Scaramucci Called Me to Unload about White House Leakers, Reince Priebus, and Steve Bannon.* July 27. http://www.newyorker.com/news/ryan-lizza/anthony-scaramucci-called-me-to-unload-about-white-house-leakers-reince-priebus-and-steve-bannon.

LoBianco, Tom. 2015. *Trump 'Postpones' Israel Trip after Netanyahu Criticism.* December 10. http://www.cnn.com/2015/12/10/politics/donald-trump-postpones-israel-trip/.

Logan, Bryan. 2017. *Trump Reportedly Tells the Widow of a US Soldier Killed in Action, 'He Knew What He Signed Up For.'* October 17. http://www.businessinsider.com/trump-he-knew-what-he-signed-up-for-ladavid-johnson-niger-attack-2017-10.

—. 2017. *Video Shows Jeff Sessions Asking Sally Yates If She Would Say No to the President If He Asked for Something 'Improper.'* January 30. http://www.businessinsider.com/sally-yates-jeff-sessions-video-2015-confirmation-hearing-2017-1.

LoProto, Mark. 2017. *Declarations of War after Pearl Harbor.* June 27. https://visitpearlharbor.org/declarations-war-pearl-harbor/.

Lowrey, Annie. 2017. *The 7 Myths of the GOP Tax Bill.* December 1. www.theatlantic.com/business/archive/2017/12/the-7-myths-of-the-gop-tax-bill/547322/.

Lowry, Brian. 2017. *Harvey Weinstein: Nine Days of Accusations and Collateral Damage.* October 14. http://money.cnn.com/2017/10/13/media/harvey-weinstein-recap/index.html.

Lozada, Carlos. 2015. *Donald Trump on Women, Sex, Marriage and Feminism.* August 5. https://www.washingtonpost.com/news/book-party/wp/2015/08/05/donald-trump-on-women-sex-marriage-and-feminism/?utm_term=.b027c280b922.

Lundy, Matt. 2016. *How a Trump Presidency Would Affect Canada's Economy.* August 23. http://www.theglobeandmail.com/report-on-business/economy/how-a-trump-presidency-would-impact-canadas-economy/article31115880/.

Lusher, Adam. 2016. *What Actually Happens at the World's Most Secretive Gathering of Global Elites, and Who Is Attending.* June 7. http://www.independent.co.uk/news/world/bilderberg-group-meeting-what-is-it-and-who-is-attending-global-elites-a7069561.html.

Lussenhop, Jessica. 2016. *Clinton Crime Bill: Why Is It So Controversial?* April 18. http://www.bbc.com/news/world-us-canada-36020717.

Lussenhop, Jessica, and Ashley Gold. 2016. *Donald Trump: 30 Things the Republican Believes.* July 6. http://www. bbc.com/news/world-us-canada-34903577.

Macfarquhar, Neil. 2016. *Vladimir Putin Won't Expel U.S. Diplomats as Russian Foreign Minister Urged.* December 30. https://www.nytimes.com/2016/12/30/world/europe/russia-diplomats-us-hacking.html.

Macias, Amanda. 2015. *Donald Trump's Ex-wife Once Said Trump Kept a Book of Hitler's Speeches by His Bed.* September 1. http://www.businessinsider.com/donald-trumps-ex-wife-once-said-he-kept-a-book-of-hitlers-speeches-by-his-bed-2015-8.

Mackintosh, Eliza. 2017. *Trump Ban Is Boon for ISIS Recruitment, Former Jihadists and Experts Say.* January 31. http://edition.cnn.com/2017/01/30/politics/trump-ban-boosts-isis-recruitment/.

Mak, Tim, and Brandy Zadrozny. 2015. *Ex-wife: Donald Trump Made Me Feel 'Violated' during Sex.* July 27. http://www.thedailybeast.com/articles/2015/07/27/ex-wife-donald-trump-made-feel-violated-during-sex.html.

Malcolm, Candice. 2017. *Canada, in Fact, Removed Special Status for Haitians Long before the U.S.* August 9. http://www.torontosun.com/2017/08/09/canada-in-fact-removed-special-status-for-haitians-long-before-the-us.

Maloney, Maggie. 2016. *A Timeline of #LochteGate.* August 19. http://www.cosmopolitan.com/health-fitness/news/a63009/timeline-ryan-lochte-robbery-scandal/.

Maloney, Ryan. 2016. *Donald Trump Presidency a Very Concerning Notion for Canadians: Poll.* August 10. http://www.huffingtonpost.ca/2016/08/10/donald-trump-canada-poll-white-house_n_11432840.html.

Maness, Carter. 2016. *Harvard Study Confirms the Media Tore down Clinton, Built Up Trump and Sanders.* June 16. https://www.good.is/articles/hillary-clinton-negative-press.

Mangan, Dan. 2017. *American Medical Association Opposes Obamacare Repeal Bill, Citing Coverage Losses by Millions of Americans.* September 19. https://www.cnbc.com/2017/09/19/groups-line-up-to-oppose-gop-obamacare-repeal-bill-as-deadline-looms.html.

—. 2016. *Obamacare's Medicaid Expansion Leading to Health Insurance Boom in Some.* July 20. https://www.cnbc.com/2016/07/20/obamacares-medicaid-expansion-leading-to-health-insurance-boom-in-some-states.html.

Mann, Bill. 2013. *Americans Are Clueless about Canada -- And Other Countries, Too.* July 24. http://www.huffingtonpost.ca/bill-mann/canadians-vs-americans_b_3645097.html.

Mapping Police Violence. n.d. *Police Killed More than 100 Unarmed Black People in 2015.* http://mappingpoliceviolence.org/unarmed/.

Markind, Johanna. 2015. *Jews Are Still the Biggest Target of Religious Hate Crimes.* December 5. http://forward.com/news/325988/jews-are-still-the-biggest-target-of-hate-crimes/.

Marsh, James, and Pierre Berton. n.d. *War of 1812 Overview.* Accessed November 21, 2016. http://www.eighteentwelve.ca/?q=eng/Topic/2.

Martel, Cate. 2016. *Sheriff Thrills GOP: 'Blue Lives Matter.'* July 18. http://thehill.com/blogs/ballot-box/presidential-races/288258-sheriff-thrills-convention-blue-lives-matter.

Martin, Jonathan, and Alan Rappeport. 2015. *Donald Trump Says John McCain Is No War Hero, Setting off Another Storm.* July 18. http://www.nytimes.com/2015/07/19/us/politics/trump-belittles-mccains-war-record.html.

Martin, Jonathan, and Mark Landler. 2017. *Bob Corker Says Trump's Recklessness Threatens 'World War III.'* October 8. https://www.nytimes.com/2017/10/08/us/politics/trump-corker.html?smprod=nytcore-iphone&smid=nytcore-iphone-share.

Martin, Michael. 2017. *Roy Moore: Getting Rid of Constitutional Amendments after 10th Would 'Eliminate Many Problems.'* December 11. https://www.metro.us/news/politics/roy-moore-constitutional-amendments.

Martin, Nina, and Renee Montagne Propublica. 2017. *U.S. Has the Worst Rate of Maternal Deaths in the Developed World.* May 12. http://www.npr.org/2017/05/12/528098789/u-s-has-the-worst-rate-of-maternal-deaths-in-the-developed-world.

Martinez, Alberto A. 2015. *The Media Needs to Stop Telling this Lie about Donald Trump. I'm a Sanders Supporter — And Value Honesty.* December 21. http://www.salon.com/2015/12/21/the_media_needs_to_stop_telling_this_lie_about_donald_trump_im_a_sanders_supporter_and_value_honesty/.

Mascia, Jennifer. 2016. *15 Statistics That Tell the Story of Gun Violence This Year.* September 22. https://www.thetrace.org/2015/12/gun-violence-stats-2015/.

Mason, Jeff. 2017. *In Meeting with Military, Trump Talks of 'Calm before the Storm.'* October 5. http://www.reuters. com/article/us-usa-trump-military/in-meeting-with-military-trump-talks-of-calm-before-the-storm-iduskbn1cb03c.

Mason, Rowena. 2017. *Theresa May 'Does Not Agree' with Donald Trump's Immigration Ban.* January 29. https:// www.theguardian.com/politics/2017/jan/28/may-under-pressure-to-condemn-trumps-immigration-ban.

Massie, Chris, and Andrew Kaczynski. 2017. *Trump Judicial Nominee Said Transgender Children Are Part of 'Satan's Plan,' Defended 'Conversion Therapy.'* September 20. http://www.cnn.com/2017/09/20/politics/kfile-jeff-mateer-lgbt-remarks/index.html.

Matsa, Katerina Eva, and Kristine Lu. 2016. *10 Facts about the Changing Digital News Landscape.* September 14. http://www.pewresearch.org/fact-tank/2016/09/14/facts-about-the-changing-digital-news-landscape/.

Matthews, Chris. 2015. *The Myth of the 1% and the 99%.* March 2. http://fortune.com/2015/03/02/economic-inequality-myth-1-percent-wealth/.

Matthews, Christopher. 2014. *Shark Tank Star Thinks Poverty Is "Fantastic News."* January 22. http://business. time.com/2014/01/22/kevin-oleary-says-3-5-billion-living-in-poverty-is-fantastic/.

Mattingly, Phil. 2016. Donald Trump's Tax Returns: Why Won't He Release Them? September 7. http:// edition.cnn.com/2016/09/07/politics/donald-trump-tax-audit-tax-returns/index.html.

Mazza, Ed. 2017. *Report: Secret Service Booted to the Sidewalk after Trump Tower Rent Dispute.* August 3. http:// www.huffingtonpost.ca/entry/secret-service-trump-tower-dispute_us_5983a08ce4b041356ebee1b8.

McBride, James, and Mohammed Aly Sergie. 2016. *NAFTA's Economic Impact.* July 26. http://www.cfr.org/trade/naftas-economic-impact/p15790.

McBride, Jessica. 2016. *Listen: Philando Castile Dispatch Audio/Police Scanner.* July 9. http://heavy.com/news/2016/07/philando-castile-armed-robbery-robber-suspect-stopped-police-dispatch-audio-scanner-traffic-reports-listen-jeronimo-yanez-broken-taillight-traffic-why-pulled-him-over-nose-record-criminal-history-arre/.

——. 2017. *Robert Jeffress: 5 Fast Facts You Need to Know.* January 19. http://heavy.com/news/2017/01/robert-jeffress-donald-trump-inauguration-pastor-inaugural-service-gays-muslims-islam-video-bio-catholics-mormons/.

McCain, John. 2018. *Statement by SASC Chairman John McCain on President Trump Congratulating Vladimir Putin.* March 20. https://www.mccain.senate.gov/public/index.cfm/2018/3/statement-by-sasc-chairman-john-mccain-on-president-trump-congratulating-vladimir-putin.

McCaskill, Nolan D. 2017. *Trump Says He Will Treat Dreamers 'with Heart.'* February 16. http://www.politico. com/story/2017/02/trump-press-conference-dreamers-heart-235103.

——. 2016. *'We Should Just Cancel the Election and Just Give It to Trump.'* October 27. http://www.politico.com/story/2016/10/donald-trump-election-cancel-230414.

McClatchy, Tony Pugh. 2009. *There's No Denying Obama's Race Plays a Role in Protests.* September 20. http://www.truth-out.org/archive/item/86139:theres-no-denying-obamas-race-plays-a-role-in-protests.

McCullough, Ian. 2013. *Why Did the U.S. Government Shut Down in October 2013?* October 3. http://www.forbes.com/sites/quora/2013/10/03/why-did-the-u-s-government-shut-down-in-october-2013/#54e0bca6527f.

McCurry, Justin. 2016. *Trump Says US May Not Automatically Defend NATO Allies under Attack.* July 21. https://www.theguardian.com/world/2016/jul/21/donald-trump-america-automatically-nato-allies-under-attack.

McDonald, Andy. 2016. *These Wikileaks Emails Prove Just What a Monster Hillary Clinton Is.* November 2. http://www.huffingtonpost.com/entry/these-wikileaks-emails-prove-just-what-a-monster-hillary-clinton-is_us_581a1ecce4b08f9841acad73.

McGregor, Janyce. 2017. *Kevin O'Leary Makes Late Entry into Conservative Leadership Race.* January 18. http://www.cbc.ca/news/politics/oleary-conservative-leadership-race-1.3940596.

McGregor, Jena, and Damian Paletta. 2017. *Trump's Business Advisory Councils Disband as CEOs Abandon President over Charlottesville Views.* August 16. https://www.washingtonpost.com/news/on-leadership/wp/2017/08/16/after-wave-of-ceo-departures-trump-ends-business-and-manufacturing-councils/?utm_term=.c90ce54d35b1.

McKenzie, Alison Bethel. 2015. *Press Freedom Is Declining in the US.* May 3. http://america.aljazeera.com/opinions/2015/5/press-freedom-is-declining-in-the-us.html.

Mechanic, Jesse. 2017. *Our Criminal Justice System Is Broken, and Jeff Sessions Has No Interest in Fixing It.* April 12. http://www.huffingtonpost.com/entry/our-criminal-justice-system-is-broken-and-jeff-sessions_us_58ee52f0e4b0a3bddb60a61e.

Media Matters Staff. 2016. *Concludes Past Secretaries of State "Definitively" Handled Classified Information on Private Email.* March 7. http://mediamatters.org/blog/2016/03/07/state-dept-concludes-past-secretaries-of-state/209044.

—. 2016. *"Racial Persecution Really Isn't the Problem in Baltimore," It's "Personal Behavior."* April 28. http://mediamatters.org/video/2015/04/28/bill-oreilly-racial-persecution-really-isnt-the/203457.

Melhem, Hisham. 2017. *How Obama's Syrian Chemical Weapons Deal Fell Apart.* April 10. https://www.theatlantic.com/international/archive/2017/04/how-obamas-chemical-weapons-deal-fell-apart/522549/.

Memmott, Mark. 2014. *'This Was a Hate Crime,' Police Say of Kansas City-area Killings.* April 14. http://www.npr.org/sections/thetwo-way/2014/04/14/302871181/suspect-in-killings-at-kansas-city-jewish-sites-linked-to-kkk.

Mencimer, Stephanie. 2016. *How Paula Jones Paved the Way for Donald Trump to Be Repeatedly Dragged into Court as President.* November 15. http://www.motherjones.com/politics/2016/11/president-trump-can-thank-paula-jones-his-legal-troubles.

Mercola, Dr. 2013. *The Subsidized Crop That Drives Our Fast-food Nation.* September 7. https://articles.mercola.com/sites/articles/archive/2013/09/07/king-corn-documentary.aspx.

Merica, Dan. 2017. *Trump to Sign Agriculture Executive Order Tuesday.* April 24. http://www.cnn.com/2017/04/24/politics/trump-agriculture-executive-order/index.html.

—. 2017. *Trump: Ask Kelly Whether Obama Called After His Son Was Killed in Action.* October 18. http://www.cnn.com/2017/10/17/politics/president-donald-trump-john-kelly-obama-phone-call/index.html.

Michaelson, Jay. 2016. *North Carolina GOP Brags Racist Voter Suppression Is Working—And They're Right.* November 7. http://www.thedailybeast.com/articles/2016/11/07/north-carolina-s-racist-voter-suppression-is-working.html.

Milbank, Dana. 2016. *Republicans' Mindless Obstruction Has Helped Create Something Far Worse.* March 11. https://www.washingtonpost.com/opinions/republicans-mindless-obstruction-has-helped-create-something-far-worse/2016/03/11/46ba9022-e723-11e5-b0fd-073d5930a7b7_story.html?utm_term=.b3b7d80bb04c.

—. 2016. *Trump Supporters Are Talking about Civil War. Could a Loss Provide the Spark?* October 18. https://www.washingtonpost.com/opinions/trump-supporters-are-talking-about-civil-war-could-a-loss-provide-the-spark/2016/10/18/f5ce081a-9573-11e6-bb29-bf2701dbe0a3_story.html?utm_term=.b8ca246fb215.

Miller, Aaron David. 2016. *Don't Move the Embassy to Jerusalem; the Downsides Are Too Great.* December 27. http://www.nytimes.com/roomfordebate/2016/12/27/should-the-us-embassy-be-moved-from-tel-aviv-to-jerusalem/dont-move-the-embassy-to-jerusalem-the-downsides-are-too-great.

Miller, Christopher. 2015. *No, We Can't Just 'Bomb the Hell out of ISIS,' Donald Trump.* November 18. http://mashable.com/2015/11/18/why-we-cant-bomb-the-hell-out-of-isis-trump/#IzpLxpPW7Gq5.

Miller, Emily McFarlan. 2016. *7 Conservative Christians Who Are Not Supporting Trump.* June 21. http://religionnews.com/2016/06/21/7-conservative-christians-who-are-not-supporting-trump/.

Miller, Greg, and Greg Jaffe. 2017. *Trump Revealed Highly Classified Information to Russian Foreign Minister and Ambassador.* May 15. https://www.washingtonpost.com/world/national-security/trump-revealed-highly-classified-information-to-russian-foreign-minister-and-ambassador/2017/05/15/530c172a-3960-11e7-9e48-c4f199710b69_story.html?utm_term=.fe69d71038d5.

Miller, Greg, Reuben Fischer-Baum, and Julie Vitkovskaya. 2017. *'This Deal Will Make Me Look Terrible': Full Transcripts of Trump's Calls with Mexico and Australia.* August 3. https://www.washingtonpost.com/graphics/2017/politics/australia-mexico-transcripts/?utm_term=.de16ed068745.

Miller, Zeke J. 2016. *Donald Trump Called Germany's Angela Merkel 'The Greatest' Last Year.* August 15. http://time.com/4453084/donald-trump-angela-merkel-germany-immigration/.

—. 2016. *Donald Trump Fires Back at Critics and Protesters in Chaotic Rally.* May 25. http://time.com/4347256/donald-trump-chaotic-rally/.

Mills, Anthony. 2016. *Austria's Far-right Seals Pact with Russia.* December 20. https://euobserver.com/beyond-brussels/136356.

Milman, Oliver. 2017. *US Federal Department Is Censoring Use of Term 'Climate Change,'* August 7. https://www.theguardian.com/environment/2017/aug/07/usda-climate-change-language-censorship-emails.

Ministry of Attorney General. 2016. *Justice Laws Website.* September 8. http://laws-lois.justice.gc.ca/eng/acts/C-46/section-319.html.

Minsky, Amy. 2017. *Would-be Refugees Fleeing Donald Trump Policy May Not Fare Better in Canada.* August 3. http://globalnews.ca/news/3646272/refugees-canada-haiti-donald-trump/.

Moning, Karen Marie. n.d. *Karen Marie Moning > Quotes > Quotable Quote.* Accessed October 9, 2017. https://www.goodreads.com/quotes/217304-words-can-be-twisted-into-any-shape-promises-can-be.

Moody, Chris. 2015. *Donald Trump Tweets Photo of Nazi Uniforms.* July 16. http://www.cnn.com/2015/07/14/politics/trump-photo-nazi-uniforms/.

Morell, Michael J. 2016. *I Ran the C.I.A. Now I'm Endorsing Hillary Clinton.* August 5. http://www.nytimes.com/2016/08/05/opinion/campaign-stops/i-ran-the-cia-now-im-endorsing-hillary-clinton.html.

Morello, Carol, and Ruth Eglash. 2016. *Netanyahu Blasts U.N., Obama over West Bank Settlements Resolution.* December 24. https://www.washingtonpost.com/world/netanyahu-calls-un-resolution-on-settlements-shameful/2016/12/23/2d45fbac-c94c-11e6-bf4b-2c064d32a4bf_story.html?utm_term=.ca436d1ef0ab.

Moreno, Amy. 2016. *Hillary Gets Destroyed on Social Media in Response to Attacking Bernie Supporters with Trending Hashtag #Basementdwellers.* October 1. http://truthfeed.com/hillary-gets-destroyed-on-social-media-in-response-to-attacking-bernie-supporters-with-trending-hashtag-basementdwellers/26858/.

Morning Consult. 2016. *Clinton and Trump Are Historically Unpopular. Here's Why.* Accessed August 24, 2016. https://morningconsult.com/trump-clinton-unpopular/.

Morris, Evan. 2016. *Sheeny.* Accessed June 16, 2016. http://www.word-detective.com/2011/06/sheeny/.

Morrongiello, Gabby. 2015. *Trump Slams Dems for 'Catering to' Black Lives Matter.* September 9. http://www.washingtonexaminer.com/trump-slams-dems-for-catering-to-black-lives-matter/article/2571641.

Morrow, Adrian. 2017. *Trump Withdraws from TPP, but Offers Canada Hope on NAFTA.* January 23. https://beta.theglobeandmail.com/news/world/us-politics/trump-executive-order-tpp/article33701019/?ref=http://www.theglobeandmail.com&.

Moshe, Erik. 2016. *Ben Bernanke Says "Hitler Was the Guy Who Got Economics Right in the 1930s."* February 21. http://historynewsnetwork.org/article/161968.

Moshman, David. 2012. *Compulsory Patriotism: Requiring the Pledge of Allegiance.* January 16. http://www.huffingtonpost.com/david-moshman/pledge-of-allegiance_b_1098584.html.

Mount, Steve. n.d. *Jefferson's Wall of Separation Letter.* Accessed November 15, 2016. http://www.usconstitution.net/jeffwall.html.

Mousavian, Seyed Hossein. 2016. *Who Benefits Most from a Sabotaged Iran Nuclear Deal.* September 7. http://www.huffingtonpost.com/seyed-hossein-mousavian/sabotaged-iran-nuclear-deal_b_11897718.html.

Moyer, Justin Wm. 2015. *Trump Says Fans Are 'Very Passionate' after Hearing One of Them Allegedly Assaulted Hispanic Man.* August 21. https://www.washingtonpost.com/news/morning-mix/wp/2015/08/21/trump-says-fans-are-very-passionate-after-hearing-one-of-them-allegedly-assaulted-hispanic-man/.

MTV. 2006. *The Donald Thinks Angelina Jolie's a Dirty Whore.* October 10. http://www.mtv.com/news/2754132/the-donald-thinks-angelina-jolies-a-dirty-whore/.

Muhawesh, Mnar, and MintPress News Desk Team. 2015. *'Pants on Fire': Analysis Shows 60% of Fox News 'Facts' Are Really Lies.* May 12. http://www.mintpressnews.com/pants-on-fire-analysis-shows-60-of-fox-news-facts-are-really-lies/205563/.

Mullin, Benjamin. 2016. *The Guardian Unpublishes 13 Stories after Investigation into Fabrication.* May 26. http://www.poynter.org/2016/the-guardian-unpublishes-13-stories-after-investigation-into-fabrication/413947/.

—. 2016. *The Intercept's Juan Thompson Fired for Fabrication.* February 2. http://www.poynter.org/2016/the-intercepts-juan-thompson-fired-for-fabrication/394707/.

Mundo, Pete. 2016. *Baylor Bears: Ken Starr Steps Down as Baylor Chancellor.* June 1. https://www.heartlandcollegesports.com/index.php/2016/06/01/ken-starr-steps-down-as-baylor-chancellor/.

Murphy, Tim. 2015. *Here's the Sanders-Clinton Exchange on Gun Control Everyone Is Talking About.* October 14. http://www.motherjones.com/politics/2015/10/bernie-sanders-hillary-clinton-clash-over-guns-democratic-debate/.

Murphy-Gill, Meghan. 2017. *The Faith of Donald Trump.* January 19. http://www.uscatholic.org/articles/201701/faith-donald-trump-30910.

Murray, Christine. 2014. *Mexico Manufacturing Surge Hides Low-wage Drag on Economy.* June 2. http://www.reuters.com/article/us-mexico-economy-analysis-idUSKBN0ED20H20140602.

Mutikani, Lucia. 2017. *Strong U.S. Jobs Report Bolsters Case for Further Fed Tightening.* August 4. https://www.reuters.com/article/us-usa-economy/strong-u-s-jobs-report-bolsters-case-for-further-fed-tightening-idUSKBN1AK09W.

NAACP. n.d. *Criminal Justice Fact Sheet.* Accessed September 24, 2016. http://www.naacp.org/pages/criminal-justice-fact-sheet.

NAFTANow. 2012. *Frequently Asked Questions.* April 4. http://www.naftanow.org/faq_en.asp#faq-1.

Nakamura, David, and Abby Phillip. 2017. *Trump Announces New Strategy for Afghanistan That Calls for a Troop Increase.* August 21. https://www.washingtonpost.com/politics/trump-expected-to-announce-small-troop-increase-in-afghanistan-in-prime-time-address/2017/08/21/eb3a513e-868a-11e7-a94f-3139abce39f5_story.html?utm_term=.569682e45047.

Nakashima, Ellen, Adam Entous, and Greg Miller. 2017. *Russian Ambassador Told Moscow that Kushner Wanted Secret Communications Channel with Kremlin.* May 26. https://www.washingtonpost.com/world/national-security/russian-ambassador-told-moscow-that-kushner-wanted-secret-communications-channel-with-kremlin/2017/05/26/520a14b4-422d-11e7-9869-bac8b446820a_story.html?tid=sm_tw&utm_term=.9120a88637aa.

NASA. 2017. *Fires and Snow in the Pacific Northwest.* September 29. https://www.nasa.gov/image-feature/goddard/2017/fires-and-snow-in-the-pacific-northwest.

National Archives. n.d. *An Act of Courage, the Arrest Records of Rosa Parks.* Accessed November 23, 2016. https://www.archives.gov/education/lessons/rosa-parks.

—. n.d. *The Civil Rights Act of 1964 and the Equal Employment Opportunity Commission.* Accessed November 23, 2016. https://www.archives.gov/education/lessons/civil-rights-act.

National Association of Adult Survivors of Child Abuse. n.d. *Resources Statistics of Child Abuse.* Accessed September 5, 2016. http://www.naasca.org/2012-Resources/010812-StaisticsOfChildAbuse.htm.

National Post. 2016. *Calgary Neo-Nazi Who Beat a Bystander to Death Loses Bid for Reduction of 13-year Murder Sentence.* National Post. June 22. http://nationalpost.com/news/canada/calgary-neo-nazi-who-beat-a-bystander-to-death-loses-bid-for-reduction-of-13-year-murder-sentence.

Naylor, Brian, and Scott Horsley. 2017. *Trump's Texas Visit Highlights Federal Response Effort.* August 29. http://www.npr.org/2017/08/29/546861395/trump-texas-visit-highlights-federal-response-effort.

Nazarian, Adelle. 2016. *Teacher Suspended for Comparing Trump to Hitler.* November 15. http://www.breitbart.com/california/2016/11/15/hitler-teacher-suspended-for-comparing-trump/.

NBC News. n.d. *Las Vegas Shooting.* Accessed October 23, 2017. https://www.nbcnews.com/storyline/las-vegas-shooting.

—. 2017. *Transcript: NBC News Commander-In-Chief Forum.* September 7. http://press.nbcnews.com/2016/09/07/transcript-nbc-news-commander-in-chief-forum/?cid=sm_tw.

NCSL. 2016. *State Policies on Sex Education in Schools.* February 16. http://www.ncsl.org/research/health/state-policies-on-sex-education-in-schools.aspx.

Nelson, Louis, and Rebecca Morin. 2017. *Melania Trump Condemns Bullying at U.N. Luncheon.* September 20. http://www.politico.com/story/2017/09/20/melania-trump-un-lunch-bullying-242920.

Nesbit, Jeff. 2016. *Donald Trump's Many, Many, Many, Many Ties to Russia.* August 15. http://time.com/4433880/donald-trump-ties-to-russia/.

Newsmax. 2013. *Trump: 'China Wouldn't Exist Without Us.'* April 10. http://www.newsmax.com/Newsfront/trump-china-north-korea/2013/04/10/id/498766/.

NFL News. 2017. *NFL: No Mandate for Players to Stand during National Anthem.* October 11. http://www.nfl.com/news/story/0ap3000000860129/article/nfl-no-mandate-for-players-to-stand-during-national-anthem.

Nguyen, Tina. 2016. *Donald Trump Says Accusers Are Too Ugly for Him to Have Groped.* October 14. https://www.vanityfair.com/news/2016/10/donald-trump-insults-accusers-ugly.

Niemöller, Martin. 2016. *Martin Niemöller: "First They Came for the Socialists…"* July 2. https://www.ushmm.org/wlc/en/article.php?ModuleId=10007392.

Nixon, Ron, and Matt Stevens. 2017. *Harvey, Irma, Maria: Trump Administration's Response Compared.* September 27. https://www.nytimes.com/2017/09/27/us/politics/trump-puerto-rico-aid.html.

Nolte, Dorothy Law. 2017. *Children Learn What They Live.* October 23. https://www.rootsofaction.com/children-learn-what-they-live-lessons-from-dorothy-law-nolte/.

NPR Staff. 2016. *Fact Check and Full Transcript of the Final 2016 Presidential Debate.* October 19. http://www.npr.org/2016/10/19/498293478/fact-check-trump-and-clinton-s-final-presidential-debate.

Nulman, Andy. 2013. *Canada's Dopey Reputation Needs to Change.* June 30. http://www.huffingtonpost.ca/andy-nulman/canada-day-2013_b_3522955.html.

Nussbaum, Matthew. 2016. *Indiana Official: Carrier Deal Is about Federal Contracts.* November 30. http://www.politico.com/story/2016/11/indiana-carrier-deal-federal-contracts-trump-232021.

NVEE. n.d. *Statistics.* Accessed September 5, 2016. http://www.nveee.org/statistics/.

NY Times. 2017. *Full Transcript and Video: Kelly Defends Trump's Handling of Soldier's Death and Call to Widow.* October 19. https://www.nytimes.com/2017/10/19/us/politics/statement-kelly-gold-star.html?_r=0.

—. 2017. *Michigan Results.* February 10. https://www.nytimes.com/elections/results/michigan.

—. 2017. *Pennsylvania Results.* February 10. https://www.nytimes.com/elections/results/pennsylvania.

—. 2017. *Presidential Election Results: Donald J. Trump Wins.* January 4. http://www.nytimes.com/elections/results/president.

—. 2016. *Transcript: Donald Trump Expounds on His Foreign Policy Views.* March 26. https://www.nytimes.com/2016/03/27/us/politics/donald-trump-transcript.html?_r=2.

—. 2017. *Wisconsin Results.* February 10. https://www.nytimes.com/elections/results/wisconsin.

Obama, Barack. 2015. *Statement by the President on the Shootings at Umpqua Community College, Roseburg, Oregon.* October 1. https://www.whitehouse.gov/the-press-office/2015/10/01/statement-president-shootings-umpqua-community-college-roseburg-oregon.

Obama, President Barack. 2017. *Charting a New Course on Cuba.* January 2. https://obamawhitehouse.archives.gov/node/352651.

—. 2015. *Statement by the President on the U.S. Government's Hostage Policy Review.* June 24. https://obamawhitehouse.archives.gov/the-press-office/2015/06/24/statement-president-us-governments-hostage-policy-review.

Obeidallah, Dean. 2015. *Donald Trump's Horrifying Words about Muslims.* November 21. http://www.cnn.com/2015/11/20/opinions/obeidallah-trump-anti-muslim/.

—. 2016. *Trump Defends Roger Ailes: 'He Helped Those Women.'* July 24. http://www.thedailybeast.com/articles/2016/07/24/trump-s-indefensible-defense-of-roger-ailes-sexual-harassment.html.

O'Donnell, Lynne. 2017. *Trump Ban Inspires Wide Anger, Some Applause across World.* January 29. http://abcnews.go.com/International/wireStory/european-leaders-oppose-trump-travel-ban-applauds-45122487.

OECD. 2012. *OECD Health Statistics 2014: How Does Canada Compare?* http://www.oecd.org/els/health-systems/Briefing-Note-Canada-2014.pdf.

Office of the Secretary of Energy & Environment. n.d. *Earthquakes in Oklahoma.* Accessed November 24, 2016. https://earthquakes.ok.gov/faqs/.

Ogura, Junko, and Susannah Cullinane. 2017. *North Korea Threatens to Sink US Aircraft Carrier.* April 24. http://www.cnn.com/2017/04/23/politics/uss-carl-vinson-japan-us-drills/.

Oliveira Jr., Pedro. 2014. *Anorexic, Unmedicated and Obsessed with a Murder-mad Cyber World: Adam Lanza's Mental Issues Went Untreated by Officials Who Allowed Sandy Hook Shooter's Mother to Overpower Them, Probe Finds.* November 21. http://www.dailymail.co.uk/news/article-2843674/New-report-details-schools-health-officials-repeatedly-appeased-Sandy-Hook-shooter-Adam-Lanza-s-mom-addressing-crippling-mental-health-issues.html.

Oliver, John. 2014. *Miss America Pageant: Last Week Tonight with John Oliver (HBO).* September 21. https://www.youtube.com/watch?v=oDPCmmZifE8.

On the Issues. 2016. *Hillary Clinton on Crime.* August 18. http://www.ontheissues.org/2016/Hillary_Clinton_Crime.htm.

Ontario Ministry of Transportation. 2015. *Ontario Border Crossing.* Queen's Printer for Ontario. December 24. Accessed August 13, 2016. http://www.mto.gov.on.ca/english/ontario-511/ontario-border-crossings.shtml.

Osborn, Andrew. 2016. *Russia Says It Was in Touch with Trump's Campaign during Election.* November 10. http://www.reuters.com/article/us-usa-election-russia-trump-idUSKBN1351RJ.

Ostrowski, Jeff. 2017. *Despite Rich Value of Trump National Golf Club in Jupiter, Trump Loses Tax Appeals.* July 18. http://realtime.blog.palmbeachpost.com/2017/07/18/despite-rich-value-of-trump-national-golf-club-in-jupiter-trump-has-lost-value-appeals-three-years-in-a-row-realdonaldtrump/.

Overberg, Paul, Jodi Upton, Meghan Hoyer, Mark Hannan, Barbie Hansen, and Erin Durkin. 2015. *Behind the Bloodshed.* April 16. http://www.gannett-cdn.com/GDContent/mass-killings/index.html#explore.

Overby, Peter, and Marilyn Geewax. 2017. *Ethics Office Director Walter Shaub Resigns, Saying Rules Need to Be Tougher.* July 6. http://www.npr.org/2017/07/06/535781749/ethics-office-director-walter-shaub-resigns-saying-rules-need-to-be-tougher.

Oyez. 2016. *"Roe v. Wade."* September 22. https://www.oyez.org/cases/1971/70-18.

Pace, Julie. 2017. *Trump Says Presidency Involves More 'Human Responsibility' Than Business.* April 24. http://globalnews.ca/news/3398433/trump-100-days-interview/.

Pagliery, Jose. 2016. *Donald Trump's Ties to Russia Explained.* July 31. http://money.cnn.com/2016/07/29/news/donald-trump-russia-ties/.

Palast, Greg. 2016. *The GOP's Stealth War against Voters.* August 24. http://www.rollingstone.com/politics/features/the-gops-stealth-war-against-voters-w435890.

Panetta, Alexander. 2017. *Canada's Immigration Policy Inspired Donald Trump's New Plan: White House.* August 2. http://globalnews.ca/news/3643835/trump-immigration-canada/.

Paquette, Danielle. 2018. *U.S. Added 148,000 Jobs in December, in Lagging Finish to Year of Strong Growth.* January 5. https://www.washingtonpost.com/news/wonk/wp/2018/01/05/u-s-added-200000-jobs-in-december-capping-year-of-strong-growth-economists-predict/?utm_term=.188f7d7cd49f.

Park, Haeyoun, Alicia Parlapiano, and Margot Sanger-Katz. 2017. *The Three Plans to Repeal Obamacare.* July 28. https://www.nytimes.com/interactive/2017/07/25/us/which-health-bill-will-the-senate-vote-on.html?_r=1.

Parker, Ashley, and Matthew Rosenberg. 2016. *Donald Trump Vows to Bolster Nation's Military Capacities.* September 7. http://www.nytimes.com/2016/09/08/us/politics/donald-trump-speech.html.

Pascaline, Mary. 2016. *Donald Trump Says 'Unstable' Hillary Clinton Unfit to Be President.* August 7. https://www.google.ca/webhp?sourceid=chrome-instant&ion=1&espv=2&ie=UTF-8#q=trump+calls+hillary+unfit.

Paumgarten, Nick. 2015. *The Death and Life of Atlantic City.* September 7. http://www.newyorker.com/magazine/2015/09/07/the-death-and-life-of-atlantic-city.

PBS. 2017. *Who Benefits from the New GOP Tax Plan?* December 16. https://www.pbs.org/newshour/show/who-benefits-from-the-new-gop-tax-plan#transcript.

Pear, Robert. 2017. *Senate Rejects Slimmed-down Obamacare Repeal as McCain Votes No.* July 27. https://www.nytimes.com/2017/07/27/us/politics/obamacare-partial-repeal-senate-republicans-revolt.html?mcubz=1&_r=0.

Pearce, Matt. 2017. *Who Was Responsible for the Violence in Charlottesville? Here's What Witnesses Say.* August 15. http://www.latimes.com/nation/la-na-charlottesville-witnesses-20170815-story.html.

Pence, Mike. 2015 7:30 AM. *Twitter Post.* December 8. https://twitter.com/govpencein/status/674249808610066433?lang=en.

Peoples, Steve. 2016. *Trump Vows to Significantly Boost Military Spending ahead of Security Forum.* September 7. https://www.thestar.com/news/world/2016/09/07/trump-vows-to-significantly-boost-military-spending-ahead-of-security-forum.html.

Perez, Evan. 2017. *White House Lawyers Research Impeachment.* May 19. http://www.cnn.com/2017/05/19/politics/donald-trump-white-house-lawyers-research-impeachment/.

Perez, Evan, and Daniella Diaz. 2017. *White House Announces Retaliation against Russia: Sanctions, Ejecting Diplomats.* January 3. http://edition.cnn.com/2016/12/29/politics/russia-sanctions-announced-by-white-house/.

Perez, Evan, and Jeremy Diamond. 2017. *Trump Fires Acting AG After She Declines to Defend Travel Ban.* January 31. http://edition.cnn.com/2017/01/30/politics/donald-trump-immigration-order-department-of-justice/.

Perez, Evan, and Steve Almasy. 2016. *Vermont Utility Finds Alleged Russian Malware on Computer.* December 31. http://www.cnn.com/2016/12/30/us/grizzly-steppe-malware-burlington-electric/.

Perez, Evan, Jim Sciutto, Jake Tapper, and Carl Bernstein. 2017. *Intel Chiefs Presented Trump with Claims of Russian Efforts to Compromise Him.* January 12. http://edition.cnn.com/2017/01/10/politics/donald-trump-intelligence-report-russia/index.html.

Perez, Evan, Shimon Prokupecz, Emanuella Grinberg, and Holly Yan. 2016. *NY, NJ Bombings: Suspect Charged with Attempted Murder of Officers.* September 19. http://www.cnn.com/2016/09/19/us/new-york-explosion-investigation/.

Pérez, Félix. 2016. *Congress Punts on Helping Flint, MI, Children, Families with Water Crisis.* September 30. http://educationvotes.nea.org/2016/09/30/congress-punts-helping-flint-mi-children-families-water-crisis/.

Perreaux, Les, Nicolas Van Praet, Verity Stevenson, Tu Thanh Ha, Ingrid Peritz, Sean Gordon, André Picard, Rhéal Séguin, Daniel Leblanc, Colin Freeze, Laura Stone, Marty Klinkenberg, and Sunny Dhillon. 2017. *The Quebec City Mosque Attack: What We Know So Far.* February 1. http://www.theglobeandmail.com/news/national/quebec-city-mosque-shooting-what-we-know-so-far/article33826078/.

Peter G. Peterson Foundation. 2016. *United States Per Capita Healthcare Spending Is More Than Twice the Average of Other Developed Countries.* October 17. http://www.pgpf.org/chart-archive/0006_health-care-oecd.

Peterson-Withorn, Chase. 2016. *Trump Says He's Filed New Financial Disclosure, Still Touting Questionable $10 Billion Fortune.* March 17. https://www.forbes.com/sites/chasewithorn/2016/05/17/trump-files-new-financial-disclosure-still-touting-questionable-10-billion-fortune/#1780063a7be0.

Pew Research Center. 2015. *Continued Bipartisan Support for Expanded Background Checks on Gun Sales.* August 13. http://www.people-press.org/2015/08/13/continued-bipartisan-support-for-expanded-background-checks-on-gun-sales/.

—. 2017. *Hillary Clinton Favorability Timeline.* May 19. http://www.people-press.org/2015/05/19/hillary-clinton-approval-timeline/.

Phelps, Jordan. 2016. *Donald Trump in 1994: 'Putting a Wife to Work Is a Very Dangerous Thing.'* June 1. http://abcnews.go.com/Politics/donald-trump-1994-putting-wife-work-dangerous-thing/story?id=39537935.

Phillip, Abby, and Jose A. DelReal. 2016. *Clinton Says She Regrets Labeling 'Half' of Trump Supporters 'Deplorable.'* September 10. https://www.washingtonpost.com/politics/republicans-jump-on-clintons-deplorables-remark/2016/09/10/91a3c148-775c-11e6-8149-b8d05321db62_story.html.

Phillip, Abby, and Mike DeBonis. 2017. *Tillerson, Haley Issue Differing Statements on Future of Assad in Syria.* April 9. https://www.washingtonpost.com/news/post-politics/wp/2017/04/09/tillerson-haley-issue-differing-statements-on-future-of-assad-in-syria/?utm_term=.6831ad82d04a.

Phillips, Amber. 2016. *The 5 House Seats That Could Signal a Democratic Majority in 2016.* June 10. https://www.washingtonpost.com/news/the-fix/wp/2016/06/10/the-5-house-seats-that-could-signal-a-democratic-majority-in-2016/?utm_term=.a49f3a4bfc92.

—. 2017. *That Time the Senate Denied Jeff Sessions a Federal Judgeship over Accusations of Racism.* January 10. https://www.washingtonpost.com/news/the-fix/wp/2016/11/18/that-time-the-senate-denied-jeff-sessions-a-federal-judgeship-over-accusations-of-racism/?utm_term=.326834b14163.

Phillips, Tom. 2017. *North Korea Missile Test Shows It Could Reach New York, Say Experts.* July 29. https://www.theguardian.com/world/2017/jul/28/north-korea-fires-missile-japan-reports-say.

Phippen, J. Weston. 2017. *The CEOs Revolting against Trump's Travel Ban.* January 30. https://www.theatlantic.com/news/archive/2017/01/companies-against-trumps-ban/515028/.

Pianin, Eric. 2015. *$478B Infrastructure Bill Blocked by Senate GOP.* March 25. http://www.thefiscaltimes.com/2015/03/25/478B-Infrastructure-Bill-Blocked-Senate-GOP.

Pierce, Charles P. *Death to the Olympics: Why the Games Should Have Been Moved from Rio.* August 3. http://www.si.com/olympics/2016/08/03/rio-olympics-problems-concerns-issues-controversy.

—. 2015. *Why Hillary Clinton's Stint as a Civil-rights Secret Agent Matters Today.* December 28. http://www.esquire.com/news-politics/politics/news/a40772/hillary-clinton-undercover-civil-rights/.

Plagiarism Today. 2012. *5 Famous Plagiarists: Where Are They Now?* August 21. https://www.plagiarismtoday. com/2012/08/21/5-famous-plagiarists-where-are-they-now/.

Pleasance, Chris. 2016. '*Speaking of Mosquitoes, Hello Hillary!' Trump Swats Bug during Campaign Speech in Cincinnati before Likening It to Clinton.* July 7. http://www.dailymail.co.uk/news/article-3678310/Speaking-mosquitoes-hello-Hillary-Trump-swats-bug-campaign-speech-Cincinnati-likening-Clinton.html.

Politi, Daniel. 2016. *Trump Is OK with Calling Ivanka a "Piece of Ass" and Other Horrible Things He Told Howard Stern.* October 8. http://www.slate.com/blogs/the_slatest/2016/10/08/trump_to_howard_stern_you_can_call_ivanka_a_piece_of_ass.html.

Politico. 2016. *Full Text: Donald Trump 2016 RNC Draft Speech Transcript.* July 21. http://www.politico.com/story/2016/07/full-transcript-donald-trump-nomination-acceptance-speech-at-rnc-225974.

—. 2016. *Full Transcript: Second 2016 Presidential Debate.* October 10. https://www.politico.com/story/2016/10/2016-presidential-debate-transcript-229519.

—. 2015. *What Is Hillary's Greatest Accomplishment?* September 17. http://www.politico.com/magazine/story/2015/09/carly-fiorina-debate-hillary-clintons-greatest-accomplishment-213157.

Politics That Work. n.d. *About Politics That Work.* http://politicsthatwork.com/about.php.

Politics That Work. 2015. *Which Party Is Better for the Economy?* April 14. http://politicsthatwork.com/blog/which-party-is-better-for-the-economy.php.

Politifact. n.d. *All False Statements Involving Donald Trump.* Accessed November 24, 2016. http://www.politifact.com/personalities/donald-trump/statements/byruling/false/?page=6.

—. n.d. *All False Statements Involving Hillary Clinton.* Accessed November 24, 2016. http://www.politifact.com/personalities/hillary-clinton/statements/byruling/false/?page=2.

—. n.d. *All Pants on Fire! Statements Involving Donald Trump.* Accessed November 24, 2016. http://www.politifact.com/personalities/donald-trump/statements/byruling/pants-fire/?page=2.

—. n.d. *All Pants on Fire! Statements Involving Hillary Clinton.* Accessed November 24, 2016. http://www.politifact.com/personalities/hillary-clinton/statements/byruling/pants-fire/.

—. 2016. *All Statements Involving Donald Trump.* Accessed November 24, 2016. http://www.politifact.com/personalities/donald-trump/statements/.

—. n.d. *Hillary Clinton's File.* Accessed September 5, 2017. http://www.politifact.com/personalities/hillary-clinton/.

Ponder, Jon. 2007. *Scaife Funded 'Arkansas Project' to Destroy Clinton, Now Says He Was a 'Pretty Good' President.* February 19. http://www.pensitoreview.com/2007/02/19/scaife-recants-arkansas-project/.

Ponsot, Elisabeth. 2017. *These Nine Women Have Accused Roy Moore of Sexual Misconduct.* December 7. https://qz.com/1147348/these-nine-women-have-accused-roy-moore-of-sexual-misconduct/.

Postrel, Virginia. 2004. *Consequences of 1960's Riots Come into View.* December 30. http://www.nytimes.com/2004/12/30/business/the-consequences-of-the-1960s-race-riots-come-into-view.html?_r=0&mtrref=undefined&gwh=07436E71B29F5825EDFE11C5DB45587D&gwt=pay.

Powell, Robert. 2016. *Hillary Clinton Revealed to Possibly Have Serious Health Issues and Brain Damage.* August 8. http://regated.com/2016/08/hillary-clinton-revealed-serious-health-issues-possible-brain-damage/.

Power, Lis. 2015. *Fox News Finally Concedes Benghazi Committee Is Political after Republicans Admit to Partisan Nature of Investigation.* October 16. https://www.mediamatters.org/research/2015/10/16/fox-news-finally-concedes-benghazi-committee-is/206217.

Powers, Kirsten. 2016. *Trump Says He Hopes Ivanka Would Quit If She Got Harassed.* August 1. http://www.usatoday.com/story/opinion/2016/08/01/ailes-trump-sexual-harassment-fox-news-women-gretchen-kelly-greta-news-column/87915454/.

Prather, Paul. 2016. *The Mystery of Christians' Support for Donald Trump Is Solved.* January 30. http://www.kentucky.com/living/religion/paul-prather/article57553638.html.

Prestigiacomo, Amanda. 2016. *Want to Know Why the Media Love Trump? He Raises Ratings.* Daily Wire. March 10. https://www.dailywire.com/news/4035/want-know-why-media-love-trump-he-raises-ratings-amanda-prestigiacomo#exit-modal.

Price, Greg. 2017. *Hurricane Harvey Latest: Alerts, Pictures and Updates on Texas and Louisiana Storm.* August 25. http://www.newsweek.com/harvey-hurricane-updates-live-655302.

Proctor, Bernadette D., Jessica L Semega, and Melissa A. Kollar. 2016. *Income and Poverty Rates for the US: 2015.* September 13. http://www.census.gov/library/publications/2016/demo/p60-256.html.

Pulitzer Prize. 2009. *2009 Pulitzer Prizes.* http://www.pulitzer.org/prize-winners-by-year/2009.

Qiu, Linda, and Amy Sherman. 2016. *Trump: 'I've Been Proven Right' about Clinton Wanting Open Borders.* October 12. http://www.politifact.com/truth-o-meter/statements/2016/oct/12/donald-trump/trump-ive-been-proven-right-about-clinton-wanting-/.

Qiu, Linda. 2016. *Does Vladimir Putin Kill Journalists?* January 4. http://www.politifact.com/punditfact/article/2016/jan/04/does-vladimir-putin-kill-journalists/.

—. 2016. *Donald Trump's Largely Accurate about Clinton's Past Support for NAFTA.* July 21. http://www.politifact.com/truth-o-meter/statements/2016/jul/21/donald-trump/donald-trumps-largely-accurate-about-clintons-past/.

—. 2016. *Fact-checking the Second Presidential Debate.* October 9. http://www.politifact.com/truth-o-meter/article/2016/oct/09/fact-checks-second-presidential-debate/.

—. 2017. *Trump's Exaggerated Claim that John Lewis' District Is 'Falling Apart' and 'Crime Infested.'* January 15. http://www.politifact.com/truth-o-meter/statements/2017/jan/15/donald-trump/trumps-john-lewis-crime-invested-atlanta/.

—. 2016. *Yep, Donald Trump's Companies Have Declared Bankruptcy...More than Four.* June 21. http://www.politifact.com/truth-o-meter/statements/2016/jun/21/hillary-clinton/yep-donald-trumps-companies-have-declared-bankrupt/.

Raju, Manu, Dylan Byers, and Dana Bash. 2017. *Exclusive: Russian-linked Facebook Ads Targeted Michigan and Wisconsin.* October 4. http://www.cnn.com/2017/10/03/politics/russian-facebook-ads-michigan-wisconsin/index.html.

Randel, Adam. 2016. *Survivor Says Gander Was Therapeutic Experience.* September 11. http://www.thetelegram.com/news/local/2016/9/11/9-11-survivor-says-gander-was-therapeuti-4637992.html.

Ranking America. n.d. *The U.S. Ranks 11th in Working Hard.* Accessed February 26 2018. https://rankingamerica.wordpress.com/2013/07/18/the-u-s-ranks-11th-in-working-hard/.

—. n.d. *Health Care.* Accessed October 9, 2017. https://rankingamerica.wordpress.com/?s=health+care+.

—. n.d. *The U.S. Ranks 17th in Happiness.* Accessed October 9, 2017. https://rankingamerica.wordpress.com/?s=happiness.

—. n.d. *The U.S. Ranks 24th in Literacy.* Accessed May 29, 2017. https://rankingamerica.wordpress.com/2013/06/11/the-u-s-ranks-9th-in-retirement-security/.

—. n.d. *The U.S. Ranks 43rd in Homicide Rates.* Accessed October 9, 2017. https://rankingamerica.wordpress.com/tag/crime/.

—. n.d. *The U.S. Ranks 64th in Human Security.* Accessed May 29, 2017. https://rankingamerica.wordpress.com/category/health-and-welfare/page/19/.

—. n.d. *The U.S. Ranks 9th in Retirement Security.* Accessed May 29, 2017. https://rankingamerica.wordpress.com/2013/06/11/the-u-s-ranks-9th-in-retirement-security/.

Rapoza, Kenneth. 2017. *World Bank: Trump GDP Growth Will Be Worse Than Obama's.* June 6. https://www.forbes.com/sites/kenrapoza/2017/06/06/world-bank-trump-gdp-growth-will-be-worse-than-obamas/#5ca75f572776.

Rappeport, Alan, and Alexander Burns. 2016. *Highlights of Hillary Clinton's Concession Speech and President Obama's Remarks.* November 9. http://www.nytimes.com/2016/11/09/us/politics/donald-trump-won-now-what.html?_r=0.

Ray, Julie. 2018. World's Approval of U.S. Leadership Drops to New Low. January 18. http://news.gallup.com/poll/225761/world-approval-leadership-drops-new-low.aspx.

Raymond, Adam K. 2017. *Trump Gleefully Recalls the 'Beautiful Chocolate Cake' He Ate While Bombing Syria.* April 12. http://nymag.com/daily/intelligencer/2017/04/trump-ate-beautiful-chocolate-cake-while-bombing-syria.html.

Reilly, Katie. 2016. *Trump Campaign Denies He Violated Embargo against Cuba.* September 29. http://fortune.com/2016/09/29/donald-trump-cuban-embargo-newsweek/.

Reilly, Steve. 2016. *USA Today Exclusive: Hundreds Allege Donald Trump Doesn't Pay His Bills.* June 9. http://www.usatoday.com/story/news/politics/elections/2016/06/09/donald-trump-unpaid-bills-republican-president-laswuits/85297274/.

Relman, Eliza. 2017. *Trump on Puerto Rican Crisis: 'This Is an Island Surrounded by Water, Big Water, Ocean Water.'* September 29. http://www.businessinsider.com/trump-puerto-rico-hurricane-maria-island-water-2017-9.

Reporters Without Borders. 2016. *2016 World Freedom of the Press Index.* Accessed June 3, 2016. https://rsf.org/en/ranking?#.

—. n.d. *First Amendment under Increasing Attack.* Accessed December 13, 2017. https://rsf.org/en/united-states.

Reuters. 2016. *18 Revelations from Wikileaks' Hacked Clinton Emails.* October 27. http://www.bbc.com/news/world-us-canada-37639370.

—. 2016. *Trump Refuses to Condemn Violence at His Rallies.* March 20. http://fortune.com/2016/03/20/trump-wont-condem-violence/.

Richardson, Bradford. 2016. *Clinton Calls for New Sanctions on Iran.* January 16. http://thehill.com/policy/national-security/266173-clinton-calls-for-new-sanctions-on-iran.

—. 2016. *Donald Trump Reveals New Nickname for Hillary Clinton — 'Crooked'.* April 17. http://www.washingtontontimes.com/news/2016/apr/17/donald-trump-reveals-new-nickname-for-hillary-clin/.

Riffkin, Rebecca. 2015. *Americans' Trust in Media Remains at Historical Low.* September 28. http://www.gallup.com/poll/185927/americans-trust-media-remains-historical-low.aspx.

Rikken, Maarten. 2015. *Hillary Clinton and the Challenges of a Woman in the White House.* August 27. https://www.researchgate.net/blog/post/hillary-clinton-and-the-challenges-of-a-woman-in-the-white-house.

Riordan, Rick. n.d. *The Lightning Thief Quotes.* Accessed October 9, 2017. https://www.goodreads.com/work/quotes/3346751-the-lightning-thief.

Rmuse. 2016. *80 Percent of GOP Voters Say Trump's Racist Comments Are "Totally Fine."* June 12. http://www.politicususa.com/2016/06/12/80-percent-gop-voters-trumps-racist-comments-totally-fine.html.

Roberts, Dan, Ben Jacobs, and Alan Yuhas. 2016. *Debbie Wasserman Schultz to Resign as DNC Chair as Email Scandal Rocks Democrats.* July 25. https://www.theguardian.com/us-news/2016/jul/24/debbie-wasserman-schultz-resigns-dnc-chair-emails-sanders.

Roberts, Joshua. 2016. *FBI Director Comey Released Letter in Fear of Leaks, Sources Say.* November 3. http://www.newsweek.com/fbi-director-comey-released-letter-fear-leaks-516879.

Robertson, Nic. 2017. *Why Gadhafi's Downfall Scares the Life out of Kim Jong Un.* August 10. http://www.cnn.com/2017/08/10/opinions/kim-john-un-gaddafi-robertson-opinion/index.html.

Robinson, Wills, and Regina F. Graham. 2016. *White Female Cop Who Shot Dead Unarmed Black Man with His Hands Up Is Charged with First Degree Manslaughter.* September 22. http://www.dailymail.co.uk/news/article-3802964/White-female-cop-shot-dead-unarmed-black-man-charged-degree-manslaughter.html.

Robles, Frances. 2017. *As White Nationalist in Charlottesville Fired, Police 'Never Moved.'* August 25. https://www.nytimes.com/2017/08/25/us/charlottesville-protest-police.html?mcubz=1.

Roche, Julia La. 2013. *Here's How Much 10 of the Richest People in the World Made per Minute in 2013.* December 19. http://www.businessinsider.com/what-warren-buffett-makes-per-hour-2013-12.

Roeder, Oliver. 2015. *Releasing Drug Offenders Won't End Mass Incarceration.* July 17. https://fivethirtyeight.com/features/releasing-drug-offenders-wont-end-mass-incarceration.

Rogers, Katie. 2016. *Hillary Clinton's Campaign Calls Donald Trump's Star of David Tweet Anti-Semitic.* July 4. http://www.nytimes.com/2016/07/05/us/politics/hillary-clintons-campaign-calls-donald-trumps-star-of-david-tweet-anti-semitic.html.

Rogin, Josh. 2016. *Russia Is Harassing U.S. Diplomats All over Europe.* June 27. https://www.washingtonpost.com/opinions/global-opinions/russia-is-harassing-us-diplomats-all-over-europe/2016/06/26/968d1a5a-3bdf-11e6-84e8-1580c7db5275_story.html?utm_term=.a5d8a72ae20b.

Roller, Emma. 2016. *When Is a Scandal Really a Scandal?* August 30. http://www.nytimes.com/2016/08/30/opinion/campaign-stops/when-is-a-scandal-really-a-scandal.html.

Rosen, Armin. 2016. *Here's How David Petraeus Got off with Only a Misdemeanor.* January 27. http://www.businessinsider.com/heres-how-david-petraeus-got-off-with-only-a-misdemeanor-2016-1.

Rosenberg, Yair. 2017. *'Jews Will Not Replace Us': Why White Supremacists Go After Jews.* August 14. https://www.washingtonpost.com/news/acts-of-faith/wp/2017/08/14/jews-will-not-replace-us-why-white-supremacists-go-after-jews/?utm_term=.7b50e02b7653.

Rosenheck, Dan. 2003. *Larry Flynt Exposed.* October 2. http://www.thecrimson.com/article/2003/10/2/larry-flynt-exposed-it-sounds-like/.

Rosenthal, Brian. 2017. *Police Criticize Trump for Urging Officers Not to Be 'Too Nice' with Suspects.* July 29. https://www.nytimes.com/2017/07/29/nyregion/trump-police-too-nice.html?mcubz=1.

Rosenthal, Max J. 2016. *Russia Has Killed Almost 10,000 Syrians in the Past Year, Says a New Report.* September 30. http://www.motherjones.com/politics/2016/09/russia-has-killed-almost-10000-syrians-year-says-new-report.

Rosin, Hanna. 2015. *Among the Hillary Haters.* March. http://www.theatlantic.com/magazine/archive/2015/03/among-the-hillary-haters/384976/.

Ross, Brian, Brian Epstein, John Carlos Frey, and Pete Madden. 2017. *ABC 20/20 Life and Death at the Border.* July 30. http://abcnews.go.com/2020/deepdive/video-border-officers-actions-lead-tragedy-48912222.

Ross, Janell. 2016. *Donald Trump's Doubling Down on the Central Park Five Reflects a Bigger Problem.* October 8. https://www.washingtonpost.com/news/the-fix/wp/2016/10/08/donald-trumps-doubling-down-on-the-central-park-five-reflects-a-bigger-problem/.

Rovner, Julie. 2006. *'Partial-birth Abortion': Separating Fact from Spin.* February 21. http://www.npr.org/2006/02/21/5168163/partial-birth-abortion-separating-fact-from-spin.

Rucker, Philip, and Dan Lamothe. 2017. *'Somebody Screwed Up Here': Why Did Trump Take 12 Days to Address the Deaths of Four Soldiers, and Why Did He Attack Obama?* October 18. https://www.thestar.com/news/world/2017/10/18/somebody-screwed-up-here-why-did-trump-take-12-days-to-address-the-deaths-of-four-soldiers-and-why-did-he-attack-obama.html.

Ruddy, Christopher. 2016. *About.* http://www.mediamatters.org/about.

Rushe, Dominic. 2017. *Top US Coal Boss Robert Murray: Trump 'Can't Bring Mining Jobs Back.'* March 27. https://www.theguardian.com/environment/2017/mar/27/us-coal-industry-clean-power-plan-donald-trump.

Russell, Bertrand. n.d. *Bertrand Russell > Quotes > Quotable Quote.* Accessed October 9, 2017. https://www.goodreads.com/quotes/11234-fear-is-the-main-source-of-superstition-and-one-of.

Ryle, Briton. 2015. *Wages vs. Corporate Profits.* September 23. https://www.wealthdaily.com/articles/the-real-culprit/6276.

Saad, Lydia. 2015. *Americans Choose "Pro-choice" for First Time in Seven Years.* May 29. http://www.gallup.com/poll/183434/americans-choose-pro-choice-first-time-seven-years.aspx.

Saba, Yousef. 2016. *Trump Went 'Too Far' at Catholic Roast.* October 24. http://www.politico.com/story/2016/10/clinton-trump-al-davis-catholic-dinner-reaction-230235.

Sacchetti, Maria. 2017. *ICE Immigration Arrests of Noncriminals Double under Trump.* April 16. https://www.washingtonpost.com/local/immigration-arrests-of-noncriminals-double-under-trump/2017/04/16/98a2f1e2-2096-11e7-be2a-3a1fb24d4671_story.html?utm_term=.75d90c81f488.

Salam, Reihan. 2017. *Steve Bannon's Enemy Isn't the Republican Party.* October 12. http://www.slate.com/articles/news_and_politics/politics/2017/10/steve_bannon_s_enemy_isn_t_the_gop_it_s_donald_trump.html.

Samaha, Albert, Hayes Mike, and Talal Ansari. 2017. *Kids Are Quoting Trump to Bully Their Classmates and Teachers Don't Know What to Do about It.* June 6. https://www.buzzfeed.com/albertsamaha/kids-are-quoting-trump-to-bully-their-classmates?utm_term=.ifZJ0nq2Y#.pa2gpbkPo.

Sampathkumar, Mythili. 2017. *North Korea Says It Is Not Interested in Diplomacy Until It Has Missile Capable of Hitting America.* October 16. http://www.independent.co.uk/news/world/americas/us-politics/north-korea-trump-us-latest-news-diplomacy-not-interested-missile-hit-america-a8003846.html.

Samuelsohn, Darren. 2017. *Blumenthal: '99 Percent Sure' of Russia Indictments.* September 26. http://www.politico.com/story/2017/09/26/indictments-michael-flynn-paul-manafort-richard-blumenthal-says-243158.

—. 2016. *Stone 'Happy to Cooperate' with FBI on WikiLeaks, Russian Hacking Probes.* October 14. http://www.politico.com/story/2016/10/roger-stone-fbi-wikileaks-russia-229821.

Sanchez, Ray. 2017. *Who Are White Nationalists and What Do They Want?* August 13. http://www.cnn.com/2017/08/13/us/white-nationalism-explainer-trnd/index.html.

Sanders, Bernie. 2016. *Democrats Adopt Most Progressive Platform in Party History.* July 10. https://berniesanders.com/democrats-adopt-progressive-platform-party-history/.

Sanger, David E. 2016. *Hillary Clinton's Email Was Probably Hacked, Experts Say.* July 6. http://www.nytimes.com/2016/07/07/us/hillary-clintons-email-was-probably-hacked-experts-say.html.

—. 2017. *U.S. in Direct Communication with North Korea, Says Tillerson.* September 30. https://www.nytimes.com/2017/09/30/world/asia/us-north-korea-tillerson.html.

Sanger, David E., and Maggie Haberman. 2016. *50 G.O.P. Officials Warn Donald Trump Would Put Nation's Security 'at Risk.'* August 8. http://www.nytimes.com/2016/08/09/us/politics/national-security-gop-donald-trump.html?_r=0.

Savage, Charlie, and Eileen Sullivan. 2017. *Leak Investigations Triple under Trump, Sessions Says.* August 4. https://www.nytimes.com/2017/08/04/us/politics/jeff-sessions-trump-leaks-attorney-general.html?mcubz=1&_r=0.

Savransky, Rebecca. 2017. *Giuliani: Trump Asked Me How to Do a Muslim Ban 'Legally.'* January 29. http://thehill.com/homenews/administration/316726-giuliani-trump-asked-me-how-to-do-a-muslim-ban-legally.

—. 2017. *Kelly Caught off Guard when Trump Mentioned Obama Didn't Call After His Son Died: Report.* October 19. http://thehill.com/homenews/administration/356191-kelly-didnt-expect-trump-to-bring-up-publicly-that-obama-didnt-call.

—. 2018. *Tourism Down in Us since Trump Took Office.* January 24. http://thehill.com/policy/transportation/370437-tourism-down-in-us-since-trump-took-office

—. 2016. *Trump Attacks Vanity Fair: 'Way Down, Big Trouble, Dead.'* December 15. http://thehill.com/homenews/campaign/310516-trump-attacks-vanity-fair-way-down-big-trouble-dead.

—. 2016. *Trump Promises Press Conference on Melania's Immigration Story.* August 9. http://thehill.com/blogs/ballot-box/presidential-races/290935-trump-on-wifes-immigration-story-she-came-in-totally.

Schleifer, Theodore. 2026. *Trump Defends Criticism of Judge with Mexican Heritage.* June 5. http://www.cnn.com/2016/06/03/politics/donald-trump-tapper-lead/.

—. 2016. *Trump Stomps All over the Democrats' Blue Wall.* November 9. http://edition.cnn.com/2016/11/09/politics/donald-trump-hillary-clinton-blue-wall/.

Schmidt, Michael S. 2017. *Comey Memo Says Trump Asked Him to End Flynn Investigation.* May 16. https://www.nytimes.com/2017/05/16/us/politics/james-comey-trump-flynn-russia-investigation.html.

Schouten, Fredreka. 2016. *Hillary Clinton Will Push Constitutional Amendment to Overturn Citizens United.* July 18. http://www.usatoday.com/story/news/politics/onpolitics/2016/07/16/hillary-clinton-push-constitutional-amendment-overturn-citizens-united/87186452/.

Schumacher, E. F. n.d. *E. F. Schumacher Quotes.* Accessed October 9, 2017. https://www.brainyquote.com/quotes/quotes/e/efschuma148840.html.

Schwartz, Nelson D. 2017. *Economy Needs Workers, but Drug Tests Take a Toll.* July 24. https://www.nytimes.com/2017/07/24/business/economy/drug-test-labor-hiring.html?mcubz=1&_r=0.

—. 2016. *Trump Saved Jobs at Carrier, but More Midwest Jobs Are in Jeopardy.* November 30. http://www.nytimes.com/2016/11/30/business/economy/trump-saved-jobs-at-carrier-but-more-midwest-jobs-are-in-jeopardy.html?_r=0.

Scott, Eugene. 2015. *Church Says Donald Trump Is Not an 'Active Member.'* August 28. http://www.cnn.com/2015/08/28/politics/donald-trump-church-member/index.html.

—. 2017. *McCain: Dictators 'Get Started by Suppressing Free Press.'* February 20. http://www.cnn.com/2017/02/18/politics/john-mccain-donald-trump-dictators/index.html.

—. 2016. *Robert Gates: Trump 'beyond repair'.* September 17. http://www.cnn.com/2016/09/17/politics/robert-gates-donald-trump-hillary-clinton/.

—. 2016. *Trump 'Surprised' by Mattis Waterboarding Comments.* November 24. http://edition.cnn.com/2016/11/23/politics/waterboarding-trump-mattis/.

Scott, Eugene, Sara Murray, and Jim Acosta. 2016. *Trump Picks South Carolina Gov. Nikki Haley to be US Ambassador to UN.* November 23. http://www.cnn.com/2016/11/23/politics/nikki-haley-picked-for-un-ambassador/index.html.

Segal, David. 2016. *What Donald Trump's Plaza Deal Reveals about His White House Bid.* January 16. http://www.nytimes.com/2016/01/17/business/what-donald-trumps-plaza-deal-reveals-about-his-white-house-bid.html?_r=0.

Seitz-Wald, Alex. 2011. *10 Things Conservatives Don't Want You to Know about Ronald Reagan.* February 5. https://thinkprogress.org/10-things-conservatives-dont-want-you-to-know-about-ronald-reagan-7a87723a4f68#.utz3sxhs2.

Sexton, John. 2016. *Gen. Michael Flynn Compared Radical Islam to a Cancer 'Inside of the Islamic World.'* November 22. https://hotair.com/archives/2016/11/22/gen-michael-flynn-has-compared-radical-islam-to-cancer/.

Shabad, Rebecca. 2016. *Hillary Clinton Urges Americans to "Choose Resolve, Not Fear" after NY, NJ, MN Attacks.* September 19. http://www.cbsnews.com/news/hillary-clinton-urges-americans-to-choose-resolve-not-fear-after-ny-nj-mn-attacks/.

Shah, Anup. 2013. *World Military Spending.* June 30. http://www.globalissues.org/article/75/world-military-spending.

Shakespeare, William. n.d. *William Shakespeare > Quotes > Quotable Quote.* Accessed June 16, 2016. https://www.goodreads.com/quotes/379204-all-that-glisters-is-not-gold-often-have-you-heard.

Shapiro, Ben. 2016. *Disgusting: Trump Reverses Himself, Refuses to Disavow David Duke and KKK.* February 28. http://www.dailywire.com/news/3739/disgusting-trump-reverses-himself-refuses-disavow-ben-shapiro.

—. 2015. *No, Donald Trump's Immigration Plan Isn't Unconstitutional.* December 8. http://www.dailywire.com/news/1685/no-donald-trumps-immigration-plan-isnt-ben-shapiro#.

Sharockman, Aaron. 2015. *PunditFact Checks In on the Cable News Channels.* January 29. http://www.politifact.com/truth-o-meter/article/2015/jan/29/punditfact-checks-cable-news-channels/.

Shear, Michael D., Mark Landler, Matt Apuzzo, and Eric Lichtblau. 2017. *Trump Fires Acting Attorney General Who Defied Him.* January 30. https://www.nytimes.com/2017/01/30/us/politics/trump-immigration-ban-memo.html.

Shelbourne, Mallory. 2017. *Dem Lawmaker: Deaths of Soldiers in Niger Is Trump's Benghazi.* October 18. http://thehill.com/homenews/house/356114-dem-lawmaker-deaths-of-soldiers-in-niger-is-trumps-benghazi.

Sherfinski, David. 2015. *Donald Trump Declines to Share His 'Foolproof' Plan for Winning against the Islamic State.* May 28. http://www.washingtontimes.com/news/2015/may/28/donald-trump-declines-share-his-foolproof-plan-win/.

Sherman, Gabriel. 2017. *"I Hate Everyone in the White House!": Trump Seethes as Advisers Fear the President Is "Unraveling."* October 11. https://www.vanityfair.com/news/2017/10/donald-trump-is-unraveling-white-house-advisers/amp.

Sheth, Sonam. 2016. *A Timeline of Rex Tillerson's Relationship with Russian President Vladimir Putin.* December 13. http://www.businessinsider.com/trump-rex-tillerson-vladimir-putin-russia-exxon-2016-12.

Sheth, Sonam, and Skye Gould. 2017. *Who's Running the Government? Trump Has Yet to Fill 85% of Key Executive Branch Positions.* April 22. http://www.businessinsider.com/whos-running-the-government-trump-unfilled-executive-branch-positions-2017-4.

Shi, Ting, David Tweed, Debra Mao, Adela Lin, Tom Schoenberg, Nick Wadhams, and Kevin Hamlin. 2016. *China Warns Trump against Using Taiwan for Leverage on Trade.* December 12. https://www.bloomberg.com/politics/articles/2016-12-12/chinese-media-warn-trump-against-using-taiwan-as-bargaining-chip.

Shi, Ting, Nick Wadhams, and David Tweed. 2016. *As Trump Tweets, China Quietly Weighs Options to Retaliate.* December 18. https://www.bloomberg.com/news/articles/2016-12-18/as-trump-tweets-china-quietly-considers-options-to-retaliate.

Shoichet, Catherine E., and Euan McKirdy. 2016. *Brazil's Senate Ousts Dilma Rousseff in Impeachment Vote.* September 1. http://www.cnn.com/2016/08/31/americas/brazil-rousseff-impeachment-vote/.

Siegel, Rachel. 2017. *8-year-old Biracial Boy Was Hanged from Rope by N.H. Teenagers Because of His Race, Family Says.* September 13. https://www.washingtonpost.com/news/morning-mix/wp/2017/09/13/8-year-old-boy-was-hung-from-rope-by-n-h-teenagers-because-of-his-race-family-says/?utm_term=.82cb45d0e3aa.

Silver, Nate. 2016. *How Much Did Comey Hurt Clinton's Chances?* November 6. https://fivethirtyeight.com/features/how-much-did-comey-hurt-clintons-chances/.

Silverman, Craig. 2016. *This Analysis Shows How Fake Election News Stories Outperformed Real News on Facebook.* November 16. https://www.buzzfeed.com/craigsilverman/viral-fake-election-news-outperformed-real-news-on-facebook?utm_term=.kgr1LbGLK#.xrmN5Yv5B.

Silverman, Craig, and Lawrence Alexander. 2016. *How Teens in the Balkans Are Duping Trump Supporters with Fake News.* November 3. https://www.buzzfeed.com/craigsilverman/how-macedonia-became-a-global-hub-for-pro-trump-misinfo?utm_term=.bhEXDYmkKX#.keVo6Yx2Ko.

Slane, Kevin. 2016. *New Hampshire Student Faced Death Threats After Donald Trump Insulted Her on Twitter.* December 9. https://www.boston.com/news/politics/2016/12/09/new-hampshire-student-faced-death-threats-after-donald-trump-insulted-her-on-twitter.

Smith, Allan. 2016. *Trump Apologizes After Shocking Audio Emerges of Lewd 2005 Comments about Women.* October 6. https://www.businessinsider.com.au/trump-leaked-recording-women-audio-billy-bush-2016-10.

Smith, David. 2016. *Wisconsin Rules GOP Gerrymandering Violates Democrats' Rights.* November 22. https://www.theguardian.com/us-news/2016/nov/21/wisconsin-gerrymandering-district-court-2016-election-decision.

Smith, Diane. 2016. *GOP Quickly Unifies around Trump; Clinton Still Has Modest Lead.* May 10. http://www.publicpolicypolling.com/main/2016/05/gop-quickly-unifies-around-trump-clinton-still-has-modest-lead.html#more.

Smith, Grant, and Daniel Trotta. 2017. *U.S. Hate Crimes Up 20 Percent in 2016 Fueled by Election Campaign-Report.* March 13. http://www.reuters.com/article/us-usa-crime-hate/u-s-hate-crimes-up-20-percent-in-2016-fueled-by-election-campaign-report-idUSKBN16L0BO.

Smith, Joanna. 2017. *PMO Slams Fox News for Inaccurate Tweet about Quebec Shooting Suspect.* January 31. https://www.thestar.com/news/canada/2017/01/31/pmo-slams-fox-news-for-inaccurate-tweet-about-quebec-shooting-suspect.html.

Smith, Samantha. 2016. *Trump Supporters Differ from Other GOP Voters on Foreign Policy, Immigration.* May 11. http://www.pewresearch.org/fact-tank/2016/05/11/trump-supporters-differ-from-other-gop-voters-on-foreign-policy-immigration-issues/.

Smith, Stephen. 2016. *Killing Non Believers.* September 2016. Accessed December 19, 2017. https://www.openbible.info/topics/killing_non_believers.

Smith-Spark, Laura. 2016. *Kerry Urges Russia, Syria to Seek Ceasefire in Aleppo.* December 10. http://www.cnn.com/2016/12/10/middleeast/syria-aleppo-conflict/.

Snegovaya, Maria. 2017. *Russian Propaganda in Germany: More Effective than You Think.* October 17. https://www.the-american-interest.com/2017/10/17/russian-propaganda-germany-effective-think/.

Snyder, Scott A. 2017. *Kim Jong Un's Direct Response to Trump's Threatening UN Speech.* September 27. https://www.cfr.org/blog/kim-jong-uns-direct-response-trumps-threatening-un-speech.

Sobel, Robert. 2016. *Gen. Michael Flynn Illegally Gave Classified Information to NATO, Report Explains.* November 24. http://us.blastingnews.com/news/2016/11/gen-michael-flynn-illegally-gave-classified-information-to-nato-report-explains-001283129.html.

Society of Professional Journalists. *SPJ Code of Ethics.* Accessed December 29, 2017. https://www.spj.org/ethicscode.asp.

Solomon, John. 2017. *Senate Judiciary Opens Probe into Obama-era Russian Nuclear Bribery Case.* October 17. http://thehill.com/policy/national-security/355957-senate-judiciary-opens-probe-into-obama-era-russian-nuclear-bribery.

Soopermexican. 2016. *Huh? Donald Trump Is 'Branding' Hillary Clinton with a Really Weird Name!!* February 24. http://www.thepoliticalinsider.com/huge-announcement-will-help-ted-cruz-win-crucial-texas-primary/.

Sorkin, Aaron. 2014. *The Newsroom Script Episode 1 Quotes.* Accessed October 9, 2017. https://www.goodreads.com/work/quotes/23633463-the-newsroom-script-episode-1.

Sorkin, Amy Davidson. 2017. *Donald Trump's Unseemly Condolence-call Bragging Game.* October 18. https://www.newyorker.com/news/amy-davidson-sorkin/donald-trumps-unseemly-condolence-call-bragging-game.

Spredemann, J.E.B. n.d. *J.E.B. Spredemann > Quotes > Quotable Quote.* Accessed September 6, 2017. https://www.goodreads.com/quotes/839174-choices-made-whether-bad-or-good-follow-you-forever-and.

Stanger, Melissa. 2015. *9 Billionaires Who Plan to Give Away the Majority of Their Fortunes.* October 15. http://www.businessinsider.com/billionaires-giving-away-their-money-2015-10/#warren-buffett-pledged-to-give-away-more-than-99-of-his-riches-and-has-already-donated-over-215-billion-4.

Stanglin, Doug, and Charles Ventura. 2016. *Gunman at Large after Killing 5 at Mall North of Seattle.* September 24. http://www.usatoday.com/story/news/nation-now/2016/09/24/seattle-shooting-cascade-mall-burlington/91009272/.

Starr, Barbara. 2017. *US Launches Investigation into Deadly Niger Ambush and Confusion That Followed.* October 17. http://edition.cnn.com/2017/10/17/politics/us-niger-military-investigation-confusion/index.html.

Statista. 2016. *Countries with the Largest Number of Prisoners per 100,000 of the National Population, as of April 2016.* April 19. https://www.statista.com/statistics/262962/countries-with-the-most-prisoners-per-100-000-inhabitants/.

Statistics Canada. 2015. *Adult Obesity Prevalence in Canada and the United States.* November 27. https://www.statcan.gc.ca/pub/82-625-x/2011001/article/11411-eng.htm.

—. 2016. *International Perspective.* October 7. https://www.statcan.gc.ca/pub/11-402-x/2012000/chap/geo/geo01-eng.htm.

—. 2010. *Visible Minority Groups, 2006 Counts, for Canada, Provinces and Territories - 20% Sample Data.* October 6. http://www12.statcan.ca/census-recensement/2006/dp-pd/hlt/97-562/pages/page.cfm?Lang=E&Geo=PR&Code=01&Table=1&Data=Count&StartRec=1&Sort=11&Display=Page&CSDFilter=5000.

Steel, Emily, and Michael S. Schmidt. 2017. *Bill O'Reilly Thrives at Fox News, Even as Harassment Settlements Add Up.* April 1. https://www.nytimes.com/2017/04/01/business/media/bill-oreilly-sexual-harassment-fox-news.html.

Stein, Perry. 2017. *Trump's Lewd 'Access Hollywood' Tape Is Playing on Repeat for 12 Hours on the Mall.* October 6. https://www.washingtonpost.com/local/the-trump-access-hollywood-tape-is-playing-on-repeat-for-12-hours-on-the-mall/2017/10/06/c19a4d52-aaa2-11e7-92d1-58c702d2d975_story.html?utm_term=.f620a8cd852f.

Stein, Sam. 2016. *Donald Trump Encourages Violence at Rallies.* March 10. http://www.huffingtonpost.com/entry/donald-trump-violence_us_56e1f16fe4b0b25c91815913.

—. 2014. *Robert Draper Book: GOP's Anti-Obama Campaign Started Night of Inauguration.* August 10. http://www.huffingtonpost.com/2012/04/25/robert-draper-anti-obama-campaign_n_1452899.html.

Steinbuch, Yaron. 2017. *Trump Just Shoved a NATO Leader out of His Way.* May 25. http://nypost.com/2017/05/25/trump-just-shoved-a-nato-leader-out-of-his-way/.

Stelloh, Tim. 2017. *Donald Trump Promises Post-Brexit Britain a 'Fair' Trade Deal.* January 15. http://www.nbcnews.com/storyline/brexit-referendum/donald-trump-promises-post-brexit-britain-fair-trade-deal-n707176.

Stelter, Brian. 2016. *Fake Story about Obamas, Hillary Clinton Ensnares Sean Hannity.* November 1. http://money.cnn.com/2016/11/01/media/sean-hannity-michelle-obama-hillary-clinton-fake-news/.

Stelter, Brian, and Dylan Byers. 2016. *Roger Ailes Has Resigned from Fox News amid Sexual Harassment Allegations -- An Ignoble End to His Legendary, Controversial Twenty-year Tenure Running the Country's Dominant Cable News Channel.* July 21. http://money.cnn.com/2016/07/21/media/roger-ailes-leaves-fox-news/.

Stelter, Brian, Jim Rutenberg, and Alysin Camerota, interview by Chris Cuomo. 2016. *Why Do Campaigns Criticize Media When Pressed for Answers?* (September 14). http://transcripts.cnn.com/transcripts/1609/14/nday.02.html.

Sterling, Harry. 2017. *Opinion: Erdogan Erodes Democracy in Turkey.* April 27. http://vancouversun.com/opinion/op-ed/opinion-erdogan-erodes-democracy-in-turkey.

Stevenson, Bryan A., and John F. Stinneford. 2016. *The Eighth Amendment.* Accessed November 18, 2016. https://constitutioncenter.org/interactive-constitution/amendments/amendment-viii.

Stewart, Heather, Robert Booth, and Vikram Dodd. 2017. *Theresa May to Tackle Donald Trump over Manchester Bombing Evidence.* May 24. https://www.theguardian.com/uk-news/2017/may/24/theresa-may-to-tackle-donald-trump-over-manchester-bombing-evidence.

Stewart, Phil. 2017. *As Trump Warned North Korea, His 'Armada' Was Headed Toward Australia*. April 18. https://www.reuters.com/article/us-northkorea-usa-carrier/as-trump-warned-north-korea-his-armada-was-headed-toward-australia-idUSKBN17L03J.

Stockman, Farah. 2016. *Donald Trump's Crime Policies Might Hit Minorities Harder, Experts Say*. September 22. http://www.nytimes.com/2016/09/23/us/politics/donald-trump-crime-terrorism-race.html. Stone, Geoffrey, and Eugene Volokh. n.d. *Common Interpretation: Freedom of the Press*. Accessed August 18, 2016. https://constitutioncenter.org/interactive-constitution/amendments/amendment-i/the-freedom-of-speech-and-of-the-press-clause/interp/33.

Stone, Mike. 2017. *CEOs Suggest Trump Tax Cut May Lift Investors More than Jobs*. October 26. https://www.reuters.com/article/us-usa-tax-companies/ceos-suggest-trump-tax-cut-may-lift-investors-more-than-jobs-iduskbn1cv38q.

Strochlic, Nina. 2015. *The Dumbest Stuff Donald Trump Has Ever Said*. June 30. http://www.thedailybeast.com/articles/2015/06/30/the-dumbest-stuff-donald-trump-has-ever-said.html.

Struyk, Ryan. 2017. *6 in 10 People Who Approve of Trump Say They'll Never, Ever, Ever Stop Approving*. August 17. http://www.cnn.com/2017/08/17/politics/trump-approvers-never-stop-approving-poll/index.html.

—. 2017. *Trump's Approval Again Reaches 40% after Positive Reaction to Hurricane Response*. September 22. http://www.cnn.com/2017/09/21/politics/trump-approval-40-percent-hurricanes-north-korea/index.html.

Sturgeon, Jamie. 2014. *Buffett Keeps Word, Heinz Strikes 'Fair' Deal with Ont. Ketchup Workers*. January 16. http://globalnews.ca/news/1086996/buffett-keeps-word-heinz-strikes-fair-deal-with-ontario-ketchup-workers/.

Sullivan, Bob. 2017. *Trump's Mortgage Fee Cut Reversal: What It Really Means for House-Hunters*. January 24. http://www.foxbusiness.com/features/2017/01/24/trumps-mortgage-fee-cut-reversal-what-it-really-means-for-house-hunters.html.

Sullivan, Sean, and Jenna Johnson. 2016. *Trump: Clinton's Bodyguards Should 'Disarm Immediately' and 'See What Happens to Her.'* September 16. https://www.washingtonpost.com/news/post-politics/wp/2016/09/16/trump-clintons-bodyguards-should-disarm-immediately-and-see-what-happens-to-her/.

Sundby, Alex. 2017. *Puerto Rico Mayor Pleads for Help after Hurricane Maria: "People are Dying."* September 26. https://www.cbsnews.com/news/puerto-rico-mayor-help-hurricane-maria-people-are-dying/.

Syeed, Nafeesa, Nick Wadhams, and David Tweed. 2016. *Pentagon Says China to Return Drone; Trump Says They Can Keep It*. December 17. https://www.bloomberg.com/politics/articles/2016-12-18/pentagon-says-china-to-return-drone-trump-says-they-can-keep-it.

Tafuri, David M. 2017. *Why Trump's Attack on Syria Is Legal*. April 1. http://www.politico.eu/article/syria-war-chemical-attack-why-donald-trump-attack-is-legal-assad-putin/.

Tanfani, Joseph. 2016. *Trump Was Once So Involved in Trying to Block an Indian Casino that He Secretly Approved Attack Ads*. June 30. http://www.latimes.com/politics/la-na-pol-trump-anti-indian-campaign-20160630-snap-story.html.

Tani, Maxwell. 2017. *John Kelly Makes Rare Appearance at White House Briefing to Say He Doesn't 'Think He's Getting Fired Today' and Is Not 'Frustrated' with His Job*. October 12. http://www.businessinsider.com/john-kelly-fired-quitting-frustrated-2017-10.

—. 2017. *Trump Used the Most Controversial Phrase inside His Administration during His Major Address to the UN*. September 19. http://www.businessinsider.com/trump-mcmaster-radical-islamic-terrorism-2017-9.

Tapper, Jake, Amanda Carpenter, Marc Lotter, Nina Turner, and Bakari Sellers. 2017. *Obama Invokes Nazi Germany in Warning about Today's Politics*. December 10. http://transcripts.cnn.com/transcripts/1712/10/sotu.01.html.

Tatum, Sophie. 2017. *Democrats Pressured to Return Donations from Harvey Weinstein*. October 5. http://www.cnn.com/2017/10/05/politics/harvey-weinstein-donations/index.html.

—. 2017. *Trump: NFL Owners Should Fire Players Who Protest the National Anthem*. September 23. http://www.cnn.com/2017/09/22/politics/donald-trump-alabama-nfl/index.html.

Taylor, Adam. 2013. *7 Remarkable Stories of Vladimir Putin Being One of the World's Most Brutal Thugs*. June 17. http://www.businessinsider.com/7-stories-of-putins-thuggish-behaviour-2013-6.

Taylor, Kate. 2016. *Fast-food CEO Says He's Investing in Machines Because the Government Is Making It Difficult to Afford Employees*. March 16. http://www.businessinsider.com/carls-jr-wants-open-automated-location-2016-3.

Team Marie Claire. 2016. *Donald Trump: The Man Behind the Mouth.* August 5. http://www.marieclaire.co.uk/blogs/550112/donald-trump-quotes.html.

The Burrard Street Journal. 2016. *Trump Claims America Should Never Have Given Canada Its Independence.* July 29. http://www.burrardstreetjournal.com/trump-canada-independence-was-mistake/.

The Canadian Press. 2013. *Mexico Is Pact's Biggest Winner.* December 31. http://www.cbc.ca/news/canada/nafta-turns-20-mexico-is-pact-s-biggest-winner-1.2478480.

The City of Windsor. 2016. *Illness Costs of Air Pollution.* Accessed August 13, 2016. http://www.citywindsor.ca/residents/environment/Environmental-Master-Plan/Goal-B-Create-Healthy-Communities/Pages/Illness-Costs-of-Air-Pollution.aspx.

The Conference Board of Canada. 2012. *Health.* February. http://www.conferenceboard.ca/hcp/details/health.aspx.

—. 2012. *Income Per Capita.* http://www.conferenceboard.ca/hcp/details/economy/income-per-capita.aspx.

The Economist. 2016. *How a Trump Presidency Could Undermine the Rule of Law.* June 1. http://www.economist.com/blogs/democracyinamerica/2016/06/don-and-judge.

—. 2016. *Scrimping on Sense.* August 13. http://www.economist.com/news/leaders/21704792-republican-nominees-ideas-economy-are-thoughtless-and-dangerous-scrimping-sense.

The Globe & Mail. 2016. '*Not Flawless': Five Speechwriters Rate Obama's Historic Address to Canada.* June 30. http://www.theglobeandmail.com/news/politics/not-flawless-five-speechwriters-rate-obamas-historic-address-to-canada/article30702288/.

The Guardian. 2017. '*Don't Be Too Nice': Trump Seems to Back Rougher Policing in Immigration Speech.* July 28. https://www.theguardian.com/us-news/2017/jul/28/donald-trump-police-long-island-speech.

The Hill Staff. 2016. *Transcript of Donald Trump's Speech on National Security in Philadelphia.* September 7. http://thehill.com/blogs/pundits-blog/campaign/294817-transcript-of-donald-trumps-speech-on-national-security-in.

The Historica-Dominion Institute. n.d. *Black History Canada: Underground Railroad.* Accessed August 13, 2016. http://www.blackhistorycanada.ca/events.php?themeid=3&id=6.

The History Place. 2016. *Ronald Reagan: "Tear Down This Wall."* Accessed January 29, 2017. http://www.historyplace.com/speeches/reagan-tear-down.htm.

The Holy Bible: King James Version. n.d. *John 7:53-8:11.* Accessed December 19, 2017. https://www.biblegateway.com/passage/?search=John%207:53-8:11.

—. n.d. *John 1:9-11.* Accessed December 19, 2017. https://www.biblegateway.com/passage/?search=2%20John%201:9-11&version=KJV.

The Star. 2016. *Here's the Full Transcript of Donald Trump's Victory Speech.* November 9. https://www.thestar.com/news/world/uselection/2016/11/09/heres-the-full-transcript-of-donald-trumps-victory-speech.html.

The US Census Bureau. 2013. *Top Trading Partners - December 2013.* December. https://www.census.gov/foreign-trade/statistics/highlights/top/top1312yr.html.

Thibodeau, Ian. 2017. *Ford's Mich. Assembly, Flat Rock Face Temporary Idling.* September 19. http://www.detroitnews.com/story/business/autos/ford/2017/09/19/ford-north-america-shutdowns/105795002/.

Think Progress. 2016. *Donald Trump's Son: My 'Billionaire' Dad Is Just a 'Blue Collar Guy.'* February 1. Accessed August 15, 2016. https://thinkprogress.org/donald-trumps-son-my-billionaire-dad-is-just-a-blue-collar-guy-f45aef100fd7#.ls7qme9x6.

Thrush, Glenn. 2016. *Former CIA Chief Hayden: Clinton Better Prepared than 'Incoherent' Trump.* March 28. http://www.politico.com/story/2016/03/off-message-michael-hayden-hillary-clinton-2016-221276.

Timm, Jane C. 2017. *Fact Checking Donald Trump's Job Creation Claims.* March 15. http://www.nbcnews.com/politics/donald-trump/fact-check-how-many-jobs-has-trump-created-n730236.

Tobias, Manuela. 2017. *Donald Trump's Misleading Comments on Obama's Calls to Fallen Soldiers' Families.* October 17. http://www.politifact.com/truth-o-meter/article/2017/oct/17/donald-trump-obamas-calls-fallen-soldiers-families/.

Todd, Chuck, Sally Bronston, and Matt Rivera. 2017. *Rep. John Lewis: 'I Don't See Trump as a Legitimate President.'* January 14. http://www.nbcnews.com/meet-the-press/john-lewis-trump-won-t-be-legitimate-president-n706676.

Tomasky, Michael. 2016. *Four Reasons Tapping Rex Tillerson as Secretary of State Is a Terrible Idea.* December 13. http://www.thedailybeast.com/articles/2016/12/13/four-reasons-tapping-rex-tillerson-as-secretary-of-state-is-a-terrible-idea.html.

Toosi, Nahal. 2017. *White House Slap at Dissenting Diplomats Sparks Fear of Reprisal.* January 30. http://www.politico.com/story/2017/01/trump-immigration-ban-state-department-diseent-channel-memo-234364.

Torres, Phil. 2017. *Donald Trump's "Muslim Ban" Is Already Backfiring — And Its Consequences Will Only Get Worse.* January 30. http://www.salon.com/2017/01/30/donald-trumps-muslim-ban-is-already-backfiring-and-its-consequences-will-only-get-worse/.

Triant, Ismene, and Panos Valavanis. 2008. *Olympia and the Olympic Games.* Athens: Non Stop Printing L.T.D. 91.

Tritten, Travis J. 2015. *NBC's Brian Williams Recants Iraq Story After Soldiers Protest.* February 4. http://www.stripes.com/news/us/nbc-s-brian-williams-recants-iraq-story-after-soldiers-protest-1.327792.

Trudeau, Justin. 2017. *Statement by the Prime Minister of Canada on the Fatal Shooting in the City of Québec.* January 29. http://pm.gc.ca/eng/news/2017/01/29/statement-prime-minister-canada-fatal-shooting-city-quebec.

—. 2016. *Statement by the Prime Minister of Canada on the Result of the US Presidential Election.* November 9. https://pm.gc.ca/eng/news/2016/11/09/statement-prime-minister-canada-result-us-presidential-election.

—. 2017 12:20 PM. *Twitter Post.* January 28. https://twitter.com/justintrudeau/status/825438460265762816?lang=en.

Trudeau, Pierre. n.d. *Quotes by Prime Ministers - Pierre Trudeau.* Accessed October 9, 2017. http://canadachannel.ca/canadianbirthdays/index.php/Quotes_by_Prime_Ministers_-_Pierre_Trudeau.

—. 1971. *Trudeau and Cultural Diversity.* October 9. Accessed December 20, 2017. https://www.edu.gov.mb.ca/k12/cur/socstud/foundation_gr9/blms/9-1-4g.pdf.

Trump, Donald. 2015. *Donald Trump on ISIS - "I Would Bomb the SHIT out of 'em!"* November 12. https://www.youtube.com/watch?v=aWejiXvd-P8.

—. 2016. *Donald Trump's Contract.* November 23. https://assets.donaldjtrump.com/_landings/contract/O-TRU-102316-Contractv02.pdf.

—. 2017. *President Trump's Inaugural Address, Annotated.* January 20. http://www.npr.org/2017/01/20/510629447/watch-live-president-trumps-inauguration-ceremony.

—. n.d. *Standing Up for Our Law Enforcement Community.* Accessed November 20, 2017. https://www.whitehouse.gov/law-enforcement-community.

Trump, Donald, interview by Oprah Winfrey. 1998. "Donald Trump on the Role Genetics Play in Success." *The Oprah Winfrey Show.* Accessed November 23, 2016. https://www.youtube.com/watch?v=YclB7UDbnKQ.

Trump, Donald J. 2012 8:30 PM. *Twitter Post.* November 6. https://twitter.com/realdonaldtrump/status/266034957875544064?lang=en.

—. 2012 8:33 PM. *Twitter Post.* November 6. https://twitter.com/realdonaldtrump/status/266035509162303492?lang=en.

—. 2012 8:39 PM. *Twitter Post.* November 6. https://twitter.com/realdonaldtrump/status/266037143628038144?lang=en.

—. 2012 8:45 PM. *Twitter Post.* November 6. https://twitter.com/realdonaldtrump/status/266038556504494082?lang=en.

—. 2013 8:17 PM. *Twitter Post.* June 18. https://twitter.com/realdonaldtrump/status/347191326112112640.

—. 2013 11:14 AM. *Twitter Post.* August 29. https://twitter.com/realdonaldtrump/status/373146637184401408?lang=en.

—. 2014 3:48PM. *Twitter Post.* January 25. https://twitter.com/realDonaldTrump/status/427226424987385856.

—. 2015 2:27 PM. *Twitter Post.* October 18. https://twitter.com/realdonaldtrump/status/655857881586270208?lang=en.

— 2016 12:56 PM. *Twitter Post.* May 8. https://twitter.com/realdonaldjtunp/status/729399636134379520?lang=en.

—. 2016 6:19 PM. *Twitter Post.* November 10. https://twitter.com/realdonaldtrump/status/796900183955095 552?lang=en.

—. 2016 3:14 AM. *Twitter Post.* November 11. https://twitter.com/realdonaldtrump/status/797034721075228 672?lang=en.

—. 2016 8:03 AM. *Twitter Post.* November 13. https://twitter.com/realdonaldtrump/status/797832229800050 688?lang=en.

—. 2016 5:34 AM. *Twitter Post.* November 15. https://twitter.com/realdonaldtrump/status/798519600413601 792?lang=en.

—. 2016 5:40 AM. *Twitter Post.* November 15. https://twitter.com/realdonaldtrump/status/798521053551140 864?lang=en.

—. 2016 5:34 AM. *Twitter Post.* November 19. https://twitter.com/realdonaldtrump/status/799969130237542 400?lang=en.

—. 2016 5:39 AM. *Twitter Post.* November 20. https://twitter.com/realdonaldtrump/status/800332639844659 201?lang=en.

—. 2016 6:14 PM. *Twitter Post.* November 21. https://twitter.com/realdonaldtrump/status/800885097775955 974?lang=en.

—. 2016 6:22 PM. *Twitter Post.* November 21. https://twitter.com/realdonaldtrump/status/800887087780294 656?lang=en.

—. 2016 12:30 PM. *Twitter Post.* November 27. https://twitter.com/realdonaldtrump/status/80297294453220 9664?lang=en.

—. 2016 4:31 PM. *Twitter Post.* November 27. https://twitter.com/realdonaldtrump/status/803033642545115 140?lang=en.

—. 2016 6:02 AM. *Twitter Post.* 28 November. https://twitter.com/realdonaldtrump/status/803237535178772 481?lang=en.

—. 2016 6:19 PM. *Twitter Post.* November 28. https://twitter.com/realdonaldtrump/status/803423203620245 504?lang=en.

—. 2016 3:55 AM. *Twitter Post.* November 29. https://twitter.com/realdonaldtrump/status/803567993036754 944?lang=en.

—. 2016 3:20 AM. *Twitter Post.* November 30. https://twitter.com/realdonaldtrump/status/803921522784092 160?lang=en.

—. 2016 3:39 AM. *Twitter Post.* November 30. https://twitter.com/realdonaldtrump/status/803926488579973 120?lang=en.

—. 2016 3:44 AM. *Twitter Post.* November 30. https://twitter.com/realdonaldtrump/status/803927774784344 064?lang=en.

—. 2016 3:54 AM. *Twitter Post.* November 30. https://twitter.com/realdonaldtrump/status/803930240661811 200?lang=en.

—. 2016 3:59 AM. *Twitter Post.* November 30. https://twitter.com/realdonaldtrump/status/803931490514075 648?lang=en.

—. 2016 5:17 AM. *Twitter Post.* December 12. https://twitter.com/realdonaldtrump/status/808299841147248 640?lang=en.

—. 2016 5:21 AM. *Twitter Post.* December 12. https://twitter.com/realdonaldtrump/status/808300706914594 816?lang=en.

—. 2016 5:05 AM. *Twitter Post.* December 15. https://twitter.com/realdonaldtrump/status/809383989018497 024?lang=en.

—. 2016 5:37 AM. *Twitter Post.* December 22. https://twitter.com/realdonaldtrump/status/811928543366148 096?lang=en.

—. 2016 8:50 AM. *Twitter Post.* December 22. https://twitter.com/realdonaldtrump/status/811977223326625 792?lang=en.

—. 2016 5:59 PM. *Twitter Post.* December 22. https://twitter.com/realdonaldtrump/status/812115501791006 720?lang=en.

—. 2016 3:58 AM. *Twitter Post*. December 23. https://twitter.com/realdonaldtrump/status/812266152684650 496?lang=en.

—. 2016 1:41 PM. *Twitter Post*. December 26. https://twitter.com/realdonaldtrump/status/813500123053490 176?lang=en.

—. 2016 11:41 AM. *Twitter Post*. December 30. https://twitter.com/realdonaldtrump/status/81491937071146 1890?lang=en.

—. 2017 3:05 PM. *Twitter Post*. January 2. https://twitter.com/realdonaldtrump/status/816057920223846400? lang=en.

—. 2017 3:47 PM. *Twitter Post*. January 2. https://twitter.com/realdonaldtrump/status/816068355555815424? lang=en.

—. 2017 7:02 AM. *Twitter Post*. January 7. https://twitter.com/realdonaldtrump/status/817748207694467072? lang=en.

—. 2017 7:10 AM. *Twitter Post*. January 7. https://twitter.com/realdonaldtrump/status/817750330196819968? lang=en.

—. 2017 7:21 AM. *Twitter Post*. January 7. https://twitter.com/realdonaldtrump/status/817753083707015168? lang=en.

—. 2017 5:19 PM. *Twitter Post*. January 10. https://twitter.com/realdonaldtrump/status/818990655418617856 ?lang=en.

—. 2017 4:31 AM. *Twitter Post*. January 11. https://twitter.com/realdonaldtrump/status/81915980648959180 9?lang=en.

—. 2017 4:48 AM. *Twitter Post*. January 11. https://twitter.com/realdonaldtrump/status/81916417278106009 6?lang=en.

—. 2017 2:49 AM. *Twitter Post*. January 13. https://twitter.com/realdonaldtrump/status/81985892645596774 4?lang=en.

—. 2017 4:50 AM. *Twitter Post*. January 14. https://twitter.com/realdonaldtrump/status/82025173040747315 3?lang=en.

—. 2017 5:07 AM. *Twitter Post*. January 14. https://twitter.com/realdonaldtrump/status/82025594795638374 4?lang=en.

—. 2017 11:00 AM. *Twitter Post*. January 15. https://twitter.com/realdonaldtrump/status/82070721056513228 8?lang=en.

—. 2017 5:11 AM. *Twitter Post*. January 17. https://twitter.com/realdonaldtrump/status/82134430265155584 0?lang=en.

—. 2017 8:26 AM. *Twitter Post*. May 12. https://twitter.com/realDonaldTrump/status/863007411132649473.

—. 2017 4:52 AM. *Twitter Post*. May 18. https://twitter.com/realdonaldtrump/status/865173176854204416?la ng=en.

—. 2017 6:55 AM. *Twitter Post*. October 11. https://twitter.com/realdonaldtrump/ status/918112884630093825.

—. 2017 4:07 AM. *Twitter Post*. October 12. https://twitter.com/realdonaldtrump/ status/918432809282342912.

—. 2017 4:06 AM. *Twitter Post*. October 18. https://twitter.com/realdonaldtrump/ status/920606910109356032.

—. 2018 4:49 PM. *Twitter Post*. January 2. https://twitter.com/realdonaldtrump/status/948355557022420992.

Truth or Fiction. n.d. *Hillary Clinton Ex-boss Says He Fired Her from Her Work on the Watergate Investigation for Being a "Liar" and "Unethical"-Truth! & Fiction!* Accessed November 1, 2017. https://www.truthorfiction. com/clinton-watergate/.

Tucker, Nikki. 2012. *U.S. Teen Pregnancy Rate Is Three Times Higher than Other Developed Nations.* August 20. http://www.medicaldaily.com/us-teen-pregnancy-rate-three-times-higher-other-developed-na- tions-242060.

Tunney, Catharine, and Joe Lofaro. 2018. *Sen. Lynn Beyak Kicked Out of Conservative Caucus after Refusing to Remove 'Racist' Comments Online.* January 5. http://www.cbc.ca/news/politics/lynn-beyak-kicked-out- conservative-caucus-1.4474130.

Tur, Katy. 2016. *My Crazy Year with Trump*. August 10. http://www.marieclaire.com/politics/a21997/donald-trump-katy-tur/.

Turnham, Steve. 2016. *Donald Trump to Father of Fallen Soldier: 'I've Made a Lot of Sacrifices'*. July 30. http://abcnews.go.com/Politics/donald-trump-father-fallen-soldier-ive-made-lot/story?id=41015051.

Tutu, Desmond. n.d. *Desmond Tutu*. Accessed August 30, 2017. https://www.goodreads.com/quotes/132838-differences-are-not-intended-to-separate-to-alienate-we-are.

U.S. Department of the Treasury. n.d. *History of 'in God We Trust.'* Accessed September 5, 2017. https://www.treasury.gov/about/education/Pages/in-god-we-trust.aspx.

UN Security Council. n.d. *Current Members*. Accessed December 31, 2016. http://www.un.org/en/sc/members/.

Union of Concerned Scientists. n.d. *Each Country's Share of CO2 Emissions*. Accessed August 23, 2017. http://www.ucsusa.org/global_warming/science_and_impacts/science/each-countrys-share-of-co2.html#.We4bbmhSzDe.

United Nations Office on Drugs and Crime. n.d. *Global Study on Homicide*. Accessed October 9, 2017. http://www.unodc.org/gsh/en/data.html.

United Nations. 2016. *Security Council Strengthens Sanctions on Democratic Republic of Korea, Unanimously Adopting Resolution 2321 (2016)*. November 30. https://www.un.org/press/en/2016/sc12603.doc.htm.

US Government: Office of the United States Trade Representative. 2016. *Canada*. Accessed May 31, 2017. https://ustr.gov/countries-regions/americas/canada.

US News. 2018. America Slips in the Eyes of the World. Accessed: January 25, 2018. https://www.usnews.com/news/best-countries/articles/us-news-unveils-best-countries-rankings.

—. 2018. Best Countries Overall. Accessed January 25, 2018. https://www.usnews.com/news/best-countries/rankings-index.

—. 2018. United States. Accessed January 25, 2018.] https://www.usnews.com/news/best-countries/united-states.

USA Today. 2017. *Trump: NFL Should 'Fire or Suspend' Players Who Kneel during Anthem*. September 24. https://www.usatoday.com/story/sports/nfl/2017/09/24/trump-nfl-should-fire-suspend-players-who-kneel-during-anthem/697680001/.

UShistory.org. n.d. *The Declaration of Independence*. Accessed August 30, 2016. http://www.ushistory.org/declaration/document/.

Vagianos, Alanna. 2017. *Gretchen Carlson on Harvey Weinstein Allegations: 'This Is the Watershed Moment.'* October 17. http://www.huffingtonpost.ca/entry/gretchen-carlson-on-harvey-weinstein-allegations-this-is-the-watershed-moment_us_59e6090fe4b02a215b334316.

Valencia, Robert. 2017. *Will Trump Be Impeached? Here's What We Know about Robert Mueller's Russia Probe So Far*. October 10. http://www.newsweek.com/will-trump-be-impeached-heres-what-we-know-about-robert-muellers-russia-probe-687356.

Vales, Leinz. 2017. *Anderson Cooper, Trump Adviser Clash over Russia Report*. January 11. http://www.cnn.com/2017/01/11/politics/anderson-cooper-kellyanne-conway-trump-intelligence-report-russia-cnntv/index.html.

Van Dam, Andrew. 2017. *The Essential Tradeoff in the Republican Tax Bill, in One Chart*. December 16. https://www.washingtonpost.com/news/wonk/wp/2017/12/16/the-essential-tradeoff-in-the-republican-tax-bill-in-one-chart/?utm_term=.f50d522b39ba.

Venook, Jeremy. 2017. *Trump's Interests vs. America's, Expansion Edition*. January 27. http://www.theatlantic.com/business/archive/2017/01/donald-trump-conflicts-of-interests/508382/.

Vice News. 2015. *Donald Trump Just Tweeted and Deleted a Picture Featuring Nazi SS Soldiers*. July 14. https://news.vice.com/article/donald-trump-just-tweeted-and-deleted-a-picture-featuring-nazi-ss-soldiers?utm_source=vicenewstwitter.

Vielma, Antonio José. 2016. *Obama Says Russia Is a Smaller, Weaker Country than the US*. December 16. http://www.cnbc.com/2016/12/16/obama-says-russians-cant-change-us-or-weaken-us.html.

Vigna, Stefano Della, and Ethan Kaplan. 2006. The Fox News Effect: Media Bias and Voting. April. Accessed November 22, 2017. http://www.nber.org/papers/w12169.pdf.

Vitali, Ali. 2016. *Trump Claims Clinton Indictment Is Near. It's Not.* November 3. http://www.nbcnews.com/card/trump-claims-clinton-indictment-near-its-not-n677596.

—. 2016. *Trump: 'Hillary Clinton Is a Bigot.'* August 24. http://www.nbcnews.com/politics/2016-election/trump-hillary-clinton-bigot-n637476.

Vocabulary.com Dictionary. n.d. *trump.* Accessed September 23, 2016. https://www.vocabulary.com/dictionary/trump.

Vogel, Kenneth P. 2016. *Inside the Clintons' Moroccan Money 'Mess.'* November 3. http://www.politico.com/story/2016/11/clinton-foundation-morocco-marrakech-230717.

Voltaire. n.d. *Voltaire Argued that Religious Intolerance Was against the Law of Nature and Was Worse than the "Right of the Tiger."* Accessed October 9, 2017. http://oll.libertyfund.org/quote/90.

Vox, Ford. 2016. *Trump and Oz: A Match Made in TV Heaven.* September 18. http://www.cnn.com/2016/09/16/opinions/trump-clinton-health-war-vox-opinion/.

Vynck, Gerrit De. 2014. *How a Canadian Tomato Juice Law Helped Save Heinz's Plant in Leamington, Ont. from Closing.* March 5. http://business.financialpost.com/legal-post/how-a-canadian-tomato-juice-law-helped-save-heinzs-plant-in-leamington-ont-from-closing.

Walcott, John. 2016. *Russia Intervened to Help Trump Win Election: Intelligence Officials.* December 10. http://www.reuters.com/article/us-usa-election-cyber-russia-idUSKBN13Z05B.

Wallace, Charles. 2017. *Trump's First Target for Trade Penalties Is Canadian Lumber.* April 25. https://www.forbes.com/sites/charleswallace1/2017/04/25/trumps-first-target-for-trade-penalties-is-canadian-lumber/#7902e019713f.

Wallace, Kelly, and Sandee LaMotte. 2016. *The Collateral Damage after Students' 'Build a Wall' Chant Goes Viral.* December 28. http://www.cnn.com/2016/12/28/health/build-a-wall-viral-video-collateral-damage-middle-school/index.html.

Walters, Joanna. 2017. *Stories of Those Who Were Detained This Weekend.* January 31. https://www.theguardian.com/us-news/2017/jan/31/people-detained-airports-trump-travel-ban.

Wang, Jennifer. 2016. *Why Trump Won't Use a Blind Trust and What His Predecessors Did with Their Assets.* November 15. http://www.forbes.com/sites/jenniferwang/2016/11/15/why-trump-wont-use-a-blind-trust-and-what-his-predecessors-did-with-their-assets/#74514bf27915.

Wang, Sam. 2012. *Gerrymanders, Part 1: Busting the Both-sides-do-it Myth.* December 30. http://election.princeton.edu/2012/12/30/gerrymanders-part-1-busting-the-both-sides-do-it-myth/.

Watkins, Eli, and Dan Merica. 2017. *As Democrats Denounce Weinstein, Clintons and Obama Stay Mum.* October 10. http://www.cnn.com/2017/10/09/politics/clinton-obama-weinstein/index.html.

Watkins, Eli, and Kevin Liptak. 2017. *All 5 Living Former Presidents Launch Appeal for Help for Harvey Victims.* September 8. http://www.cnn.com/2017/09/07/politics/george-hw-bush-former-presidents-harvey/index.html.

Watson, Kathryn. 2017. *In Puerto Rico, Paul Ryan Says Government Is Committed "for the Long Haul."* October 13. https://www.cbsnews.com/news/paul-ryan-in-puerto-rico-says-federal-government-is-in-for-the-long-haul/.

Watson, Russell. 1994. *Vince Foster's Suicide: The Rumor Mill Churns.* March 20. http://www.newsweek.com/vince-fosters-suicide-rumor-mill-churns-185900.

Weaver, Matthew, Claire Phipps, and Amber Jamieson. 2017. *Donald Trump Rounds on Democrats as UN Refugee Agency Warns on Travel Ban – As It Happened.* January 31. https://www.theguardian.com/us-news/live/2017/jan/30/trump-travel-ban-executive-order-world-protests-live.

Wehrman, Jessica, and Michelle Everhart. 2016. *Trump Campaign County Chair Who Said 'No Racism until Obama Got Elected' Apologizes, Resigns.* September 22. http://www.dispatch.com/content/stories/local/2016/09/22/mahoning-county-donald-trump-campaign-chair-no_racism-before-obama.html.

Weiner, Rachel. 2011. *Virginia GOPer Writes Racist Anti-Obama Column.* May 25. http://www.huffingtonpost.com/2008/10/05/virginia-goper-writes-rac_n_132014.html.

Weiner, Tim. 2017. *Commentary: Flynn Facts: A Threat to National Security.* February 13. https://www.reuters.com/article/us-flynn-national-security-commentary/commentary-flynn-facts-a-threat-to-national-security-idUSKBN15S28E.

Wells, Jamie. 2016. *Diagnosing Hillary Clinton's Medical Statement.* September 19. http://acsh.org/news/2016/09/19/diagnosing-hillary-clintons-medical-statement-10182.

Westcott, Ben, Dan Merica, and Jim Sciutto. 2017. *White House: No Apology to British Government over Spying Claims.* March 18. http://www.cnn.com/2017/03/17/politics/gchq-trump-wiretap-denial/index.html.

Whitaker, Keysha. 2017. *Your Russian Connection: Is There Any There, There?* March 21. https://www.newyorker.com/humor/daily-shouts/your-russian-connection-is-there-any-there-there.

White, Daniel. 2016. *Nearly 20% of Trump Fans Think Freeing the Slaves Was a Bad Idea.* February 24. http://time.com/4236640/donald-trump-racist-supporters/.

Whitlock, Craig. 2015. *Questions Linger about Trump's Draft Deferments During Vietnam War.* July 21. https://www.washingtonpost.com/world/national-security/questions-linger-about-trumps-draft-deferments-during-vietnam-war/2015/07/21/257677bc-2fdd-11e5-8353-1215475949f4_story.html.

Whittaker, Bill. 2015. *30 Years on Death Row.* October 11. http://www.cbsnews.com/news/30-years-on-death-row-exoneration-60-minutes/.

Wieczner, Jen. 2016. *Donald Trump Bump Investors Have This Unlikely Stock to Thank for Dow Record.* December 9. http://fortune.com/2016/12/09/trump-stock-market-dow-close-goldman-sachs/.

Wikipedia Contributors. n.d. *American Civil War.* Accessed November 22, 2016. https://en.wikipedia.org/wiki/American_Civil_War.

—. n.d. *Battle of Hayes Pond.* Accessed December 21, 2016. https://en.wikipedia.org/w/index.php?title=Battle_of_Hayes_Pond&oldid=756095876.

—. n.d. *Black Suffrage.* Accessed December 20, 2017. https://en.wikipedia.org/wiki/Black_suffrage.

—. n.d. *Central Park Jogger Case.* Accessed November 18, 2016. https://en.wikipedia.org/wiki/Central_Park_jogger_case.

—. n.d. *Christian Terrorism.* Accessed September 19, 2016. https://en.wikipedia.org/wiki/Christian_terrorism#Ku_Klux_Klan.

—. n.d. *David Hale (Whitewater).* Accessed July 25, 2016. https://en.wikipedia.org/wiki/David_Hale_(Whitewater).

—. n.d. *David Koresh.* Accessed September 14, 2016. https://en.wikipedia.org/wiki/David_Koresh.

—. n.d. *Domestic Terrorism in the United States.* Accessed September 22, 2016. https://en.m.wikipedia.org/wiki/Domestic_terrorism_in_the_United_States#Terrorist_organizations.

—. n.d. *Ernst Zündel.* Accessed November 16, 2016. https://en.wikipedia.org/wiki/Ernst_Z%C3%BCndel.

—. n.d. *First 100 Days of Donald Trump's Presidency.* Accessed October 9, 2017. https://en.wikipedia.org/wiki/First_100_days_of_Donald_Trump%27s_presidency.

—. n.d. *Fox News Channel Controversies.* Accessed September 7, 2016. https://en.wikipedia.org/w/index.php?title=Fox_News_Channel_controversies&oldid=735122633.

—. n.d. *General Motors Ignition Switch Recalls.* Accessed August 23, 2016. https://en.wikipedia.org/wiki/General_Motors_ignition_switch_recalls.

—. n.d. *Hillary Clinton Email Controversy.* Accessed August 30, 2016. https://en.wikipedia.org/wiki/Hillary_Clinton_email_controversy.

—. n.d. *History of the United States Democratic Party.* Accessed November 14, 2016. https://en.wikipedia.org/wiki/History_of_the_United_States_Democratic_Party.

—. n.d. *Impeachment of Bill Clinton.* Accessed November 2, 2017. https://en.wikipedia.org/wiki/Impeachment_of_Bill_Clinton.

—. n.d. *Information Overload.* Accessed August 11, 2016. https://en.wikipedia.org/w/index.php?title=Information_overload&oldid=734073680.

—. n.d. *Irv Rubin.* Accessed May 30, 2016. https://en.wikipedia.org/wiki/Irv_Rubin.

—. n.d. *Islam by Country.* Accessed September 17, 2016. https://en.wikipedia.org/wiki/Islam_by_country.

—. n.d. *Jesse Watters.* Accessed September 20, 2017. https://en.wikipedia.org/wiki/Jesse_Watters.

—. n.d. *Jim Crow Laws.* Accessed November 13, 2016. https://en.wikipedia.org/wiki/Jim_Crow_laws.

—. n.d. *Kerner Commission.* Accessed July 17, 2016. https://en.wikipedia.org/wiki/Kerner_Commission.

—. n.d. Let them eat cake. Accessed September 14, 2016. https://en.wikipedia.org/wiki/Let_them_eat_cake.

—. n.d. *Lewinsky Scandal*. Accessed August 31, 2016. https://en.wikipedia.org/wiki/Lewinsky_scandal.

—. n.d. *List of American Police Officers Killed in the Line of Duty*. Accessed September 16, 2016. https://en.wikipedia.org/wiki/List_of_American_police_officers_killed_in_the_line_of_duty.

—. n.d. *List of Countries by Firearm-related Death Rate*. Accessed August 28, 2016. https://en.wikipedia.org/wiki/List_of_countries_by_firearm-related_death_rate.

—. n.d. *List of Executive Actions by Donald Trump*. Accessed October 28, 2017. https://en.wikipedia.org/wiki/List_of_executive_actions_by_Donald_Trump#cite_note-130.

—. n.d. *List of School Shootings in the United States*. Accessed September 21, 2016. https://en.wikipedia.org/wiki/List_of_school_shootings_in_the_United_States.

—. n.d. *Mexico City Policy*. Accessed September 6, 2017. https://en.wikipedia.org/wiki/Mexico_City_policy.

—. 2017. *Mikhail Khodorkovsky*. September 6. https://en.wikipedia.org/wiki/Mikhail_Khodorkovsky.

—. n.d. *Murder of Michael Donald*. Accessed May 13, 2017. https://en.wikipedia.org/wiki/Michael_Donald.

—. n.d. *New York City Draft Riots*. Accessed September 21, 2016. https://en.wikipedia.org/wiki/New_York_City_draft_riots.

—. 2017. *Nicolás Maduro*. September 5. https://en.wikipedia.org/wiki/Nicol%C3%A1s_Maduro.

—. n.d. *Prescription Drug Prices in the United States*. Accessed September 5, 2016. https://en.wikipedia.org/wiki/Prescription_drug_prices_in_the_United_States.

—. n.d. *Shooting of Walter Scott*. Accessed September 20, 2016. https://en.wikipedia.org/wiki/Shooting_of_Walter_Scott.

—. n.d. *Suicide of Vince Foster*. Accessed August 28, 2016. https://en.wikipedia.org/wiki/Suicide_of_Vince_Foster.

—. n.d. *Ugly American*. Accessed July 23, 2016. https://en.wikipedia.org/wiki/Ugly_American_(pejorative).

—. n.d. *Viktor Yanukovych*. Accessed September 10, 2017. https://en.wikipedia.org/wiki/Viktor_Yanukovych.

—. n.d. *White House FBI Files Controversy*. Accessed August 13, 2016. https://en.wikipedia.org/wiki/White_House_FBI_files_controversy.

—. n.d. *White House Travel Office Controversy*. Accessed August 12, 2016. https://en.wikipedia.org/wiki/White_House_travel_office_controversy.

—. n.d. *Whitewater Controversy*. Accessed August 22, 2016. https://en.wikipedia.org/w/index.php?title=Whitewater_controversy&oldid=782474574.

—. n.d. Windsor, Ontario. Accessed December 20 20, 2017. https://en.wikipedia.org/wiki/Windsor,_Ontario.

—. n.d. *Women's Rights Are Human Rights*. Accessed August 12, 2016. https://en.wikipedia.org/wiki/Women%27s_Rights_Are_Human_Rights.

Wilkinson, Tracy. 2016. *Trump's Plans to Scuttle or Amend the Iran Nuclear Deal Remain a Work in Progress*. November 10. http://www.latimes.com/nation/la-fg-trump-iran-nuclear-deal-20161111-story.html.

William, Jennifer. 2017. *Nikki Haley, Trump's Pick for UN Ambassador, Doesn't Sound Anything Like Trump*. January 18. https://www.vox.com/world/2017/1/18/14311452/nikki-haley-senate-confirmation-hearing-un-ambassador.

Williams, Jennifer. 2016. *Trump May Have Just Thrown Decades of US-China Relations into Disarray*. December 5. http://www.vox.com/world/2016/12/2/13824092/trump-phone-call-president-taiwan-china.

Williams, Sara Elizabeth, Amman Ensor, and Josie Ensor. 2017. *'I Regret Helping the Americans Now' Says Iraqi Refugee Banned from US*. January 30. http://www.telegraph.co.uk/news/2017/01/30/regret-helping-americans-now-says-iraqi-refugee-banned-us/.

Wilner, Michael. 2017. *Trump Warns Israel: Stop Announcing New Settlements*. February 2. http://www.jpost.com/Israel-News/Politics-And-Diplomacy/Trump-warns-Israel-Stop-announcing-new-settlements-480446.

Wilson, Frederica S. n.d. *Congresswoman Frederica S. Wilson Stands by Account of President Trump's Condolence Call to the Widow of Sgt. La David Johnson*. Accessed October 24, 2017. https://wilson.house.gov/media-center/press-releases/congresswoman-frederica-s-wilson-stands-by-account-of-president-trump-s.

Wilstein, Matt. 2016. *Trump's Inauguration Nightmare: All the Musicians Who Have Turned Down Invites*. December 22. http://www.thedailybeast.com/articles/2016/12/22/trump-s-inauguration-nightmare-all-the-musicians-who-have-turned-down-invites.

Wines, Michael, and Alan Blinder. 2016. *Federal Appeals Court Strikes Down North Carolina Voter ID Requirement.* July 29. http://www.nytimes.com/2016/07/30/us/federal-appeals-court-strikes-down-north-carolina-voter-id-provision.html.

Winfrey, Oprah. 2011. *How a Gang of Skinheads Forever Changed the Course of the Oprah Winfrey Show.* May 13. http://www.oprah.com/oprahshow/how-a-gang-of-skin-heads-changed-oprah-show-history-video.

Wise, Alana, and Doina Chiacu. 2016. *Republican Lawyers Take Issue with Trump's Allegations of Voter Fraud.* October 17. http://www.reuters.com/article/usa-election-idUSL1N1CN1R9.

Wolchover, Natalie. 2012. *Why Did the Democratic and Republican Parties Switch Platforms?* September 24. http://www.livescience.com/34241-democratic-republican-parties-switch-platforms.html.

Wolf, Stephen. 2016. *No, Maryland Is Not the Most Gerrymandered State. There Is More to Gerrymandering than Ugly Shapes.* June 1. http://www.dailykos.com/story/2016/6/1/1532608/-No-Maryland-is-not-the-most-gerrymandered-state-There-is-more-to-gerrymandering-than-ugly-shapes.

Wootson Jr., Cleve R. 2017. *Bill O'Reilly's Ratings Are Soaring after the Sexual Harassment Allegations.* April 11. https://www.washingtonpost.com/news/arts-and-entertainment/wp/2017/04/09/bill-oreillys-ratings-are-actually-higher-than-they-were-since-the-sexual-harassment-allegations/?utm_term=.8a2762c8686e.

Workneh, Lilly. 2014. *KKK Threatens 'Lethal Force' against Ferguson Protesters and Appears on TV to Explain Why.* November 14. http://www.huffingtonpost.ca/entry/kkk-threatens-lethal-force-protesters-ferguson_n_6155570.

World Factbook. n.d. *Country Comparison: Distribution of Family Income - Gini Index.* Accessed October 9, 2017. https://www.cia.gov/library/publications/the-world-factbook/rankorder/2172rank.html.

World Nuclear News. 2017. *EU Committed to Iran Nuclear Deal.* October 16. http://www.world-nuclear-news.org/NP-EU-committed-to-Iran-nuclear-deal-1610177.html.

World Prison Brief. n.d. *Highest to Lowest - Prison Population Total.* Accessed October 9, 2017. http://www.prisonstudies.org/highest-to-lowest/prison-population-total?field_region_taxonomy_tid=All.

Wright, Austin, and Jeremy Herb. 2017. *Mattis on the Issues.* January 12. http://www.politico.com/story/2017/01/mattis-on-the-issues-233522.

Wright, David. 2016. *Lock Her Up? Maybe Not So Much, Giuliani and Christie Say.* November 10. http://www.cnn.com/2016/11/10/politics/giuliani-christie-interviews-clinton-prosecutor/index.html.

Wyche, Steve. 2016. *Colin Kaepernick Explains Why He Sat during National Anthem.* August 27. http://www.nfl.com/news/story/0ap3000000691077/article/colin-kaepernick-explains-why-he-sat-during-national-anthem.

Yarberry, Ben. 2016. *Ashton Kutcher and His Organization Rescued over 6,000 Sex Trafficking Victims but He's Not Done Yet.* October 14. http://tribunist.com/news/ashton-kutcher-and-his-organization-rescued-over-6000-sex-trafficking-victims-but-he-has-not-done-yet/.

Yglesias, Matthew. 2017. *Trump Threatens to Cancel NBC's Broadcast License over Critical Reporting.* October 11. https://www.vox.com/2017/10/11/16458362/trump-nbc-tweet.

—. 2017. *Watch CEOs Admit They Won't Actually Invest More If Tax Reform Passes.* November 15. https://www.vox.com/policy-and-politics/2017/11/15/16653698/ceos-investment-tax-reform.

Youngman, Clayton. 2015. *Clinton: 7 Benghazi Probes So Far.* October 12. http://www.politifact.com/truth-o-meter/statements/2015/oct/12/hillary-clinton/clinton-there-have-been-7-benghazi-probes-so-far/.

Zadrozny, Brandy. 2016. *Eric Trump 'Charity' Spent $880K at Family-owned Golf Resorts.* September 3. http://www.thedailybeast.com/articles/2016/09/30/eric-trump-charity-spent-880k-at-family-owned-golf-resorts.html.

Zakaria, Fareed, interview by Anderson Cooper. 2017. *Trump:" I'll Give the Generals 30 Days for a Plan to Fight ISIS."* (September 7).

—. 2016. *Why They Hate Us.* May 23. http://www.cnn.com/2016/04/08/opinions/why-they-hate-us-zakaria/.

Zapotosky, Matt. 2016. *Attorney General Pledges to Accept FBI and Justice Findings in Clinton Email Probe.* July 1. https://www.washingtonpost.com/world/national-security/attorney-general-to-back-fbi-and-justice-findings-in-clinton-email-server-probe/2016/07/01/77ce6d8e-3f78-11e6-a66f-aa6c1883b6b1_story.html?tid=a_inl.

——. 2016. *FBI Director: Clinton Email Case 'Was Not a Cliff-Hanger.'* September 7. https://www.washingtonpost. com/news/post-nation/wp/2016/09/07/fbi-director-clinton-email-case-was-not-a-cliff-hanger/?utm_ term=.a5e9e4d3edbc.

——. 2017. *Grandparents, Other Extended Relatives Exempt from Trump Travel Ban, Federal Judge Rules.* July 14. https://www.washingtonpost.com/world/national-security/grandparents-other-extended-relatives-exempt-from-trump-travel-ban-federal-judge-rules/2017/07/14/ce67aa72-6888-11e7-8eb5-cbccc2e7bfbf_ story.html?utm_term=.fd97187ed08b.

——. 2016. *House Republicans Grill FBI Director Comey on Clinton Emails.* July 7. https://www.washingtonpost. com/world/national-security/fbi-director-set-to-appear-before-congressional-committee-to-answer-questions-on-clinton-investigation/2016/07/07/eb43ec7e-43c1-11e6-88d0-6adee48be8bc_story.html.

Zarya, Valentina. 2016. *Donald Trump Thinks He's the Reason You're Spending So Much Money.* December 27. http://fortune.com/2016/12/27/donald-trump-stock-market-holiday-spending/.

——. 2016. *This Equal Pay Champion Just Endorsed Hillary Clinton.* January 29. http://fortune.com/2016/01/29/ lilly-ledbetter-clinton/.

Zylstra, Sarah Eekhoff. 2016. *Trump, Clinton, or Neither: How Evangelicals Are Expected to Vote.* May 5. http:// www.christianitytoday.com/gleanings/2016/may/trump-clinton-neither-how-evangelical-expected-to-vote.html.

CPSIA information can be obtained
at www.ICGtesting.com
Printed in the USA
LVHW03s0553170818
586990LV00001B/1/P